Modern Portfolio Management

Modern Portfolio Management

Moving Beyond Modern Portfolio Theory

TODD E. PETZEL

WILEY

Published by John Wiley & Sons, Inc., Hoboken, New Jersey.
Published simultaneously in Canada.

For general information on our other products and services or for technical support, please contact our Customer Care Department within the United States at (800) 762-2974, outside the United States at (317) 572-3993, or fax (317) 572-4002.

Wiley publishes in a variety of print and electronic formats and by print-on-demand. Some material included with standard print versions of this book may not be included in e-books or in print-on-demand. If this book refers to media such as a CD or DVD that is not included in the version you purchased, you may download this material at http://booksupport.wiley.com. For more information about Wiley products, visit www.wiley.com.

Library of Congress Cataloging-in-Publication Data is Available:

ISBN 9781119818502 (hardback)
ISBN 9781119818205 (ePDF)
ISBN 9781119818199 (ePub)

Cover Design: Wiley
Cover Image: ©MR.Cole_Photographer/Getty Image

SKY10093531_121124

To Kate, Sarah, Rebecca, and all the grandchildren who give support and joy in countless ways.

Contents

CHAPTER 6
Tactics for Enhancing Returns

Preface

This book arose from a frustration over how the broad investment industry and specific funds and products are sold to the public. Having mostly been on the receiving end of these sales pitches for over 25 years, too often they are wrapped in a scientific mystique. People who are collectively responsible for trillions of dollars of assets are regularly told that they may not grasp the minutia, and they should trust those assets to fund managers who rigorously apply the science of finance to create superior risk-adjusted returns. While our understanding of finance is today far better than it was 50 years ago, it is far from complete and it never will be. Investing is a human endeavor, and because humans react to events and change behaviors, it will never be as orderly as the experiments in a high school physics lab. Managers pretending otherwise are guilty of hubris or deception. Unfortunately, many targets of these pitches are ill equipped to evaluate them carefully. The goal here is to provide the tools needed to better even the playing field.

Knowledge of a subject comes at different levels. At the most basic level one simply memorizes a formula, say for the Sharpe Ratio, and can parrot it back. The next level of understanding allows one to apply those learned principles to different situations to help analyze new problems. Level three allows one to teach others using everything on the first steps to bring new students along. The final level is when one does original research to move the knowledge frontier out. This book breaks little new research ground, but hopefully will help the interested reader to improve their understanding of portfolio construction to at least level two of the knowledge ladder. If it is successful it is because many people over many years have helped me better understand this fascinating and ever evolving process.

Acknowledgments are never complete as the people who contributed directly or indirectly are too many to count. This book is the product of more than 30 years of studying and participating in markets. Finding a single, good investment idea is not easy. Building effective portfolios is even harder. The challenge in producing this book was to distill all of that so that some of the many lessons learned could be passed on. Colleagues at Commonfund, Azimuth Partners, and Offit Capital expanded my understanding. Thirty years of market events etched lesson after lesson into my memory. A decade of teaching the course "Endowment Institute" with Bill Spitz and Andre Perold not only expanded my understanding of the topic but also honed the communication of that knowledge. These two colleagues and friends will see their fingerprints on many parts of this book.

Every major project has easy stretches and sticking points. As this manuscript was coming together, the sticking points were the many graphs and charts throughout. In the summer of 2019, Offit Capital was blessed with three interns: Jesse Rosenblatt, Jared Rosenbaum, and Brandon Rosenbaum, who came ready to do anything that was asked of them. This trio downloaded data, created figures, and updated charts for weeks on end. They took a book that was at the five-yard line, and like a great offensive line, made it easy to go in for the score. They did this with curiosity about the subject, enthusiasm, and good cheer. They deserve credit and great thanks.

Nobody can be effective in the investment world living on an island. The world changes too fast for that. Great partners and colleagues challenge you regularly and welcome your challenges. Ned, Dan, and Morris Offit invited me to join Offit Capital at its inception, and fourteen years later we, with our other partners and colleagues, still engage continuously in the process of trying to improve the investment experience of our clients. The Offits appropriately strive to build a great and lasting business, but they also understand that is achieved by putting client results first. This ethos runs deep and anyone who has met Morris Offit over his 80-plus years knows this is at his core. I am grateful and privileged to call these gentlemen my partners and friends. They created the world that allowed this book to be written.

One person that deserves particular mention is Peter Bernstein. He had nothing to do directly with the production of the book, but he had everything to do with its content. Peter was the ultimate scholar and skeptic when it came to investing. His descriptions of the market were never promotional. He sought the truth, which often placed him in the position of saying the emperor had no clothes. His communications were crisp and he rarely equivocated. He set the standard for a generation of investment professionals. There is nothing in this book where I did not ask myself how Peter could have made it better. There is no doubt this effort fell short, but aiming at his standards improved it.

Family members always sacrifice, mostly silently, while these projects incubate. Blessedly my daughters, Sarah and Rebecca, are far enough along on their own paths that they did not feel the impact of this task too severely. They were, however, a strong motivation to see it through, and hopefully they will take from this that no project is too ambitious to consider or too big to make real. The final acknowledgement goes to my wife, Kate, who no doubt wondered what I must be thinking, spending hours sitting in front of the computer with no apparent end in sight. Her unwavering support and encouragement made it so much easier to get back at the effort when the simplest course would have been a strategic retreat. Thank you all.

CHAPTER 1

Introduction

There are countless books that try to explain how to manage portfolios of stocks, bonds, real assets, and virtually every other investment opportunity. An obvious question is, "Why does anyone need another one now?" In the past 15 years there has been a gut-wrenching liquidity crisis and stock market crash followed by one of the least loved bull markets in history. Then a booming economy and market was laid low by the COVID-19 pandemic. As people stumble through this minefield, it seems at a basic level either that previous books do not have the right prescriptions or that few investors have learned enough from them.

There are two distinct reasons a new discussion is timely. First, the investment world has shifted dramatically toward more analytically based approaches over the past 40 years, but these models are either defective or were applied incorrectly, leading to the great financial crisis. The second reason regards significant institutional change in the investment world. The old approach had a broker assemble securities into a portfolio. Profits from the old way of managing portfolios have shrunk dramatically because of negotiated commission and other basic competitive forces. To replace those profits, firms have turned to financial engineers to construct customized structured products and more exotic, "scientifically grounded" investment funds for their sales forces. These products appear straightforward on the surface but can have hidden risks and costs that can meaningfully erode investment performance. Today's investor simply must acquire a basic knowledge of how securities, derivatives, and other investment vehicles work before they can make informed portfolio decisions.

Some believe that before the 1970s investing was something of a folk art, full of quaint habits that produced inferior performance. As modern portfolio theory (MPT) developed, the "science" of investing was refined. Investments could be systematically evaluated in terms of risk and combined to produce "optimized" portfolios. By the time the twenty-first century arrived, portfolio management had become highly dependent upon, and some would say dominated by, quantitative methods and financial engineers. The fact that many markets around the world almost melted down in 2008 and early 2009, destroying years of wealth creation and catching legions of quants off guard, suggests that currently accepted portfolio management practice has some serious flaws.

More than a dozen years after the financial crisis, many of the old, bad habits of selling financial products based on their promised analytical superiority have crept back into everyday use. Sadly, few of the deficiencies have been repaired. The structure and precision of our portfolio modeling have been grossly oversold to investors.

Models rely on expected returns, risks, and correlations that are estimated from thousands of data points. Before the widespread use of computers, these calculations took days and weeks to complete. Early finance pioneers like Bill Sharpe and Harry Markowitz would spend considerable time gathering data and carefully thinking about the construction of a problem before rolling up their sleeves and actually cranking out their complicated estimates. Today, finance professionals routinely download data sets in seconds and complete countless calculations in the blink of an eye. Unfortunately, one of the downsides of this is that the cost of poorly specified models to the researcher is almost nil. To the investor, however, the costs have been massive.

Too many people believe that investing can be reduced to a science. Today, portfolio models are based on data sets too large to have been collected or analyzed just a few years ago. Statistics teaches that as the number of observations in the sample grows, greater confidence can be placed on the model, but many of the basic foundations of statistics are not present when dealing with market information. New data are piled upon old, and the models are reestimated. Few critically ask whether the unstated assumptions behind the statistical models truly apply to the markets being studied.

Economics in general and finance in particular are not physical sciences. They are behavioral disciplines, and the difference is profound. A chemist can try to duplicate a complicated physical reaction hundreds of times, each time carefully observing the outcomes. The more tightly the experimental environment can be controlled, the closer the outcomes should cluster. When the data do not fit the model being tested, it is likely due to some error in the model specification. That is how science advances. When the data fail to match the predictions of the model, the scientist rethinks the interaction of the variables, sometimes rearranging them or sometimes discovering that new variables need to be introduced.

In contrast, consider the economist. They may have a collection of thousands of market prices or returns to examine, but unlike the chemist's data set, these observations came from real life and not from any experiments. Each day may bring a new set of market data; however, it was not produced by a controlled experiment, *nor can the researcher ever control the environment*. Today, economists are being asked to model the impact of exploding federal deficits on interest rates, inflation, and real economic growth. How large and lasting will the impact of COVID-19 be on incomes and wealth? While these are important thought exercises, there is nothing in the history of the United States that provides data on which to build a precise model with these conditions. An examination of other nations that have experienced huge national debt may be suggestive, but none of these countries have had the same population, technology base, or government structures, to name just three of innumerable variables that cannot be controlled. Economic models are simply suggestions about what might happen, and the range of actual outcomes can and does vary widely.

When financial engineers travel the modeling path, the problems are similar. Despite attempts to account for all the factors that play a role, no database drawn from market data can possibly have the statistical rigor of a set of physical science experiments. Not only do the histories fail to reflect all the possible outcomes, but there is also the basic problem of markets: people who invest react to their environments, and the environments, in turn, change because of these actions. An example will show the difference.

Suppose you walk into a casino and notice that everyone around the roulette wheel has bet on 13 black. This could mean one of two things: either the crowd has figured out that the wheel is defective or rigged and 13 black has a higher-than-average chance of happening, or it is a superstitious bunch with a common bias. If the wheel is fair, there is a 1 in 38 chance of the spinning ball landing in 13 black. It does not matter how many people bet on that number in any turn of the wheel; the probability stays the same.

Markets are different.

If large numbers of market participants try to buy Chinese stocks, gold, bitcoin, mortgage securities, or any other traded good, the market price will change. And as seen in the near financial meltdowns in the second half of 2008 and March 2020, when those traders suddenly turn to sell, prices can change in ways that seemingly defy the probabilities. *Whenever enough other participants join an investor in the same trade, the price of the trade changes, and the probability of any given subsequent outcome shifts, sometimes in completely unanticipated ways.*

The world has too often seen the response to such seismic shifts. The quantitative fund manager, who has frequently just lost a great deal of other people's money, proclaims complete shock that these virtually impossible events occurred. Then they race back to the computer with the new data in hand to try to fix the flaws in the model. At the most basic level, however, it is not the model that is broken; It is the entire premise behind it.

This is not to suggest that quantitative methods do not have a place in portfolio management. However, the pendulum may have swung too far, resulting in inflated expectations for their benefits. Moderation and skepticism, which are very useful tools for investors, have often been pushed aside. When a manager is on a winning streak and gathering investors, it is often hard to ask what can go wrong or to question whether an approach that worked with $100 million under management is likely to work with $20 billion or more. Investors want to believe that a successful manager's historical record is a product of skill and not luck and that skill is as reliable as identifying the true odds on the roulette wheel. This is rarely the case.

The complexity of quantitative approaches to trading and portfolio construction only adds to this mystique for some. If the lay investor cannot comprehend the trading model, it must be profound. But the frequent market disasters that can be linked to these quants, almost always losing great sums of other people's money, should suggest otherwise. A theoretical chemist might be able to recite incomprehensible formulas about how egg protein reacts to heat, but that does not mean they make an edible omelet.

It is time for the pendulum to swing back toward the art of investing to find an appropriate balance. Throughout this book, models will be questioned. Are all the variables considered? Are the estimated models drawn from a broad enough experience? Does the game change if many are looking at the world in a similar way? *What can go wrong outside the model?* That is why this book is subtitled Moving Beyond Modern Portfolio Theory. It is foolish to completely reject the quantitative advances of the past 50 years. It is equally foolish to believe that pushing further down the same quantitative path today can totally solve the problems in portfolio management.

This book suggests a middle ground. It starts with a quantitative foundation, but there is no promise of completeness or any easy solutions. Nothing will be optimized. To suggest there is a single best approach is total hubris. The living, breathing organizations we call markets will continue to evolve and react to the steps and mis-steps of their participants. Investors must embrace this uncertainty and incorporate dynamism into their approach to succeed.

There are four main sections in this book. The first is designed to explain modern portfolio theory in a way that is accessible to most readers. Chapter 2 focuses on the key question of setting objectives. If you do not know where you are going, how do you expect to get there? Chapter 3 digs into the key concepts and may be a somewhat challenging discussion for those who are bit removed from their time in the class-room; the principles are important all the same. So many fund managers and brokers use and misuse these concepts in their sales pitches that the only way any investor evens the playing field is to have at least a basic knowledge of this material.

Chapter 4 returns to shallower analytical waters, where we shall stay. Here the building blocks of portfolio construction are described and the process of asset allo-cation developed.

The second section is devoted to the steps of building portfolios. The many practi-cal challenges to executing any asset allocation are presented in Chapter 5. Chapter 6 sorts out suggestions regularly presented to investors to earn an enhanced return. Spoiler alert: most are not worth trying.

It has been more than a decade since the financial crisis, but the memories of those events still shape our investment thinking. Chapters 7 and 8 dig deeper into the topics of tail risk, bubbles, and crashes. The third section consists of three chapters (Chapter 9–11) that can be viewed as reference material to be drawn on as needed. The goal is to give you informative descriptions of the vast array of investment vehi-cles regularly included in modern portfolios. Traditional securities, derivatives, and a wide array of structures and packages are explained and compared.

The final section covers four chapters (Chapter 12–15) that are both practical and philosophical in nature. What is the nature of decision-making around invest-ments? How are investments regulated, and how does that affect your decisions? How is the investment world likely to evolve, and what does that mean for us? And finally, what are the major lessons we can take from throughout this book? It was not easy to keep the list to 10, but if the reader wants a handy reminder of things to keep top of mind, Chapter 15 is the one to bookmark.

As we create this foundation, we will regularly challenge many parts of accepted wisdom. An aggressive marketer might assert that their book is all any investor needs. This is never true. Most people will not build their portfolios without help. This book will prepare you to ask the right questions of investment managers, bro-kers, or advisors and then to appreciate their answers. When finished, you should have a framework to grow capital through time, avoid major pitfalls, and be able to adapt to worlds not yet seen or even imagined.

The Foundation of a Modern Portfolio

CHAPTER 2

Setting Goals and Objectives

It is quite remarkable to see how often individuals or committees pursue investments before they have firmly established their objectives. They may have gotten what seemed like a good idea at a cocktail party. They may have heard from a friendly rival that their alma mater's endowment grew faster last year than their own. They may have simply been overwhelmed by all the investment advice available 24 hours a day in our media-rich world.

This book starts with the hope that all of those sources of confusion can be blocked out for a while. The two most important questions to ask before anything else are, "What do you want to try to achieve with your investments?" and "How much risk are you willing to take?" We shall learn that neither of these questions can be answered with certainty, but without an honest effort to address them, everything one does in investing devolves to emotion and luck.

The already wealthy, multigenerational family may have very different goals than the newly married couple who were the first people in their families to go to college. Both of these are likely different than a perpetual college endowment, a liquidating foundation, or a pension plan. The starting point of any portfolio discussion has to be:

- Where am I now?
- Where would I like to be at different points in the future?
- What happens if it doesn't work?

After the wealth destruction of 2008 and early 2009, too many individuals and groups were scrambling in damage control. They may have carefully thought about the first two questions before setting up their portfolios, but the third was often missing. The new generation that has begun investing after the crisis has no real concept of how bad things can feel in a severe market.

Beginning with the first question, one's starting point is not only the current level of assets but also any anticipated flows. Consider a 30-something couple who are both Lehman Brothers mid-level executives in the spring of 2007. Everything about their foreseeable earnings stream was dependent upon Lehman. The largest part of their assets was likely split between a house (with a mortgage) and Lehman Brothers stock. Earnings at Lehman were strong. The stock price was high. The home was appreciating at a good enough clip to take out a second mortgage to remodel the kitchens and bathrooms. Life was good.

Looking at that same couple 18 months later, a different picture emerges. Lehman is bankrupt. Its stock is worthless. If lucky, the young executives have found other positions on Wall Street, but future income projections are probably reduced. The value of their home has already tumbled and is about to enter a period of meaningful decline with few opportunities to sell it for more than they owe on their mortgages.

While the above story is stylized, anyone in the New York metropolitan area in 2008/2009 knows too many real examples from financial professionals who previously worked at Lehman, Bear Stearns, or any of a myriad of failed hedge funds. The 10% of the labor force generally unemployed in America at the end of 2009 had stories with many similarities. So, what happened?

In the case of the Lehman couple in 2007, the problem can be seen as a classic failure to diversify. Not only were the couple's resources concentrated, they were in assets that were highly correlated to their earnings power. This is often viewed as a good thing from the employer's perspective. It keeps the employees focused and motivated to do the right thing for shareholders. But there is a major disconnect in this logic when applied to major corporations with thousands of employees.

It is virtually impossible for a single employee to materially improve a corporation's bottom line (Michael Milken at Drexel Burnham in the 1980s might be an exception). It is however possible for a single person to destroy that same bottom line (e.g. Milken later in the Drexel story, Nick Leason at Barings, and others throughout history). It is undoubtedly good to encourage all employees to work hard and enhance share prices. But, should anyone expect employees to concentrate their wealth to a point where the acts of a handful of people at a firm could destroy their family's future?

The importance of the above parable may seem limited to the reader anxious to dive right into the portfolio construction process, but it holds several guiding principles:

- Never assume good performance is going to persist. Always ask what can go wrong and prepare for it.
- Correlations are important across more than just portfolio assets. If one's regular income is completely linked to one's current portfolio, the outcomes are likely to be binomial, either very good or very bad.
- Most people understand that correlations can shift around dramatically through time. Experience shows, however, that in bad times correlations almost always increase, magnifying the impact of any shock.
- Creating a sleep-well-at-night pool of assets against extremely negative outcomes allows one to maintain the most important elements of one's lifestyle or business plan at the primary cost of missing out on higher returns when that safety is not needed. Everyone can choose how big a cushion provides peace of mind, but ignoring the possibility of a severe downturn does not make the risk go away.

2.1 SETTING THE OBJECTIVES

Objectives across investors can vary widely. Examples of how four distinct types of investors might set their objectives will demonstrate the general principles that can be applied in virtually any circumstance. In turn, we shall discuss:

- The high-net-worth family looking to provide for the future of several generations.
- The young family looking to grow wealth to provide education and retirement resources.

- The perpetual endowment or foundation.
- The insurance company or pension fund with reasonably well-defined future liabilities.

2.1.1 The High-net-worth Family

A familiar story in America is the entrepreneur who spends many years building a successful business. He or she may have experienced lean years in the beginning, but probably enjoyed a strong income stream as the business grew. As welcome as that income was, the real wealth of the family was building within the business. At some point there is a realization that the entrepreneur is mortal, and that the future of the business must be planned for without the founder. Some transitions pass the business to other family hands. Others may experience a liquidity event like an initial public offering (IPO) that opens the firm to outsiders. Some founders simply sell their businesses and move on completely. The effect on the entrepreneur of such a transition is to transform locked-up, embedded wealth into more liquid assets that need to be managed in a completely different way than the original enterprise.

While the bulk of the wealth was tied up in the business, there were not many decisions to be made. The entrepreneur was completely married to the illiquid investments. Diversification was not an option. The business either succeeded or it did not. There may be cash flow questions to be managed along the way in these stories, but there is little in the way of portfolio management to consider.

Everything changes with the liquidity event. Suddenly decisions need to be made and multiple objectives considered:

- How much safe money do we need to maintain our desired lifestyle?
- How much of our wealth do we want to leave to the next generations? What are the most efficient ways to do that?
- Are there charitable causes that we want to support? How much and over what period of time?

The first question can be answered reasonably precisely, *as long as the cost of living remains stable.* If inflation or deflation enters the picture unexpectedly, the most carefully estimated goals might be woefully in error. Truly safe money is insulated from these forces, which means putting those assets into short-duration, highest-quality funds like T-bills (Treasury bills) and top rated municipal bonds. If unexpected inflation appears, nominal interest rates rise, as will the yield on the short-duration portfolio.

Note that the answer to the first question is not expressed as a percentage of overall wealth. This is a strict dollar calculation and has nothing to do with whether the stock market is rising, falling, or holding steady. Once this calculation is made, then one can turn to the "growth" part of the portfolio.

The second two questions on the list defining the major goals are the kinds of issues, along with an investor's fundamental tolerance for risk, that shape the investments in the growth portfolio. Chapter 4 discusses investment choices, the trade-offs between liquid and illiquid securities, and other practical considerations in setting one's asset allocation targets that are relevant to the goals.

2.1.2 The Young Family

The biggest difference between the couple just starting out and the high-net-worth family mentioned above is the form of their wealth. Assuming that they do not have inherited assets, the young couple's wealth is primarily in the form of *human capital*, or simply their capacity to generate earnings through time. Fundamentally, smarter and more educated people tend, on average, to have more human capital, but other skills are important as well. Leadership, emotional maturity, entrepreneurial talent, and ability in the arts or athletics are all forms of human capital that have the potential to be translated into an income stream and ultimately financial wealth.

The young family's objectives should start with the same discussion of sleep-well-at-night money. Protecting against a calamity trumps every other wealth-building idea. While it is hard to lose human capital, it is not impossible. Specific job skills become obsolete, young athletes are injured, and start-up businesses commonly fail. Setting aside enough to protect against those unexpected events can make the difference between a lifestyle well below one's desires and expectations, and one that can bounce back from setbacks to ultimately reach one's goals.

Those goals likely include children and their educational needs, a certain target lifestyle along the way, and ultimately retirement at a similar standard of living. The growth portfolio for the young family should reflect those goals, their risk appetite, and the fact that distant goals allow additional latitude when it comes to shorter term market volatility.

2.1.3 The Endowment or Foundation

In many cases an endowment or foundation starts with the goal of living forever. A secondary goal is often to provide "intergenerational equality," where today's students or grant recipients receive roughly the same benefits as those coming after them. While some foundations are built to be self-liquidating after a specific mission is achieved, many more envision their good deeds going on through time.

One might think that the perpetual orientation of these pools eliminates the need to have sleep-well-at-night funds. One of the many lessons of 2008 was that even carefully constructed perpetual asset pools could hit crises of such magnitude that the mission of the organization is permanently impaired. Trustees of these organizations need to confront these risks and set aside safe money as well. If one's immediate programs are eliminated because of a market crash, today's endowment beneficiaries feel a disproportionate impact of the crisis. Sleep-well-at-night funds are as important for trustees and organizations as they are for individuals.

The other challenge in setting the goals of an endowment or foundation is the less defined nature of future needs. Often trustees are hard pressed to articulate the goals of the investment program. Growing the endowment in real terms after spending and expenses, at some ill-defined rate, is often the stated goal. A common unstated objective is growing faster than one's archrival. The lack of a well-defined liability stream and precise growth targets has led many institutions to poorly designed and riskier investment portfolios than they needed to reach their objectives.

One sometimes hears the argument that the perpetual nature of endowments and foundations allows them to set loftier growth goals and achieve those goals by investing more in illiquid assets. On the surface this makes some sense, but every rule has its limitations. Too many endowments and foundations entering 2007 under-appreciated the risk attendant with illiquid investments. As the recovery from the financial crisis reaches 10 years there are signs that some of those hard-learned lessons may already be fading.

2.1.4 The Insurance Company or Pension Plan

The biggest advantage insurance companies and pension plans have over individuals and endowments or foundations is the more defined nature of their liabilities. One can estimate with high precision how many people are likely to retire each year and how long they will subsequently receive benefits. These actuarial assumptions stake out fairly clear goals that can be a meaningful advantage in planning investment portfolios.

Unfortunately this advantage is sometimes squandered. At the peak of the bull market in late 1999, many pension plans were meaningfully overfunded because of the rapid appreciation of the plans' equity holdings in the previous decade. Some could have liquidated every stock they owned, purchased Treasury bonds, and been secure in meeting all their future liabilities with virtually no market risk.

Few did. Instead of keeping sight of their liability goals, they became enamored with the idea of peer comparisons. How did your pension plan stack up to all the other corporate or public sector peers? Which CIO was just featured on the cover of *Institutional Investor?* Investment goals silently shifted from meeting the needs of future beneficiaries, to racing against other funds. The first decade of the twenty-first century showed the folly of that behavior.

Today the problem facing these plans is completely different. Major central banks pursue zero interest rate policies to support lagging economies suffering from echoes of the Great Financial Crisis and the COVID 19 pandemic. With such low rates, plan sponsors struggle to come up with any asset allocation that has both a comfortable level of risk and an ability to reach target returns. The environment matters when setting portfolio allocations. Just because a firm or individual has particular needs is no reason to believe the market will always provide a means to achieve them.

2.2 SLEEP-WELL-AT-NIGHT MONEY

If an individual or an organization has not asked the following question, it should become one's highest priority:

> *How much money do you need to allow you to maintain your lifestyle or business plan for an extended period in the absence of current income or investment gains?*

If one sets aside this amount, which we shall call sleep-well-at-night money, there are funds available to see you through unemployment, business disruptions, and severe market downturns. The most important feature of these reserves is that they need to be ultimately safe and available under all circumstances.

Determining the answer to the critical question depends greatly on one's degree of risk tolerance. Does an individual need six months' expenses? Twelve months'?

Three years'? What about an endowment or a not-for-profit organization? Individual circumstances matter. Diving into this puzzle will be done in Chapter 4.

A young person employed in a high-demand sector may believe that there are few possible disruptions that could befall him or her. Barring the proverbial event of being run over by a bus, income should be reliable and current obligations covered. But while the probability of a disaster may be small, the impact of such an event could be devastating and should be taken into account.

Any organization, whether for-profit or not-for-profit, should go through a similar exercise. Events from 2008 and 2009 show vividly that assuming ready access to liquidity through credit channels is a serious mistake. Sleep-well-at-night money does not depend on the kindness or abilities of bankers at a time of crisis.

How long a period of crisis should the sleep-well-at-night money target? This depends on the individual's or the organization's ability to adjust spending or revenues. One not-for-profit might conservatively want to have a year's worth of expenses set aside on the belief that if disaster strikes a year would be long enough to change programs or develop new sources of revenues. Another organization might think six months' reserves are more than adequate.

Individuals will want to assess which current expenditures are mandatory and which are more discretionary. Adjustments to lifestyle or programs are rarely pleasant, but much can be done if the runway is long enough.

The key discussion involves asking the hardest questions about what can go wrong. Even small probability events happen sometimes, and modeling what they might mean allows one to plan against the worst contingencies. Setting aside reserves that allow one to get through the worst of times is the true definition of sleep-well-at-night money.

It may seem obvious that these reserves should be invested in as close to risk-free funds as possible, but this common-sense notion is often violated. Not-for-profit organizations should hold these assets in short-duration sovereign debt of the country where their liabilities reside. This largely eliminates interest rate risk, currency risk, and inflation risk, as short-term interest rates typically adjust quickly to changes in inflation. Taxpayers will follow a similar strategy, but adjusted for their effective tax rates. The goal is to squeeze as many market risks as possible out of these portfolios. A side benefit is that these highest-quality assets tend to be in great demand during crisis periods. You want to own enough of them before the crisis happens.

Such investment standards are incredibly rigid and lead to the lowest rates of return of all the choices. As such, people have historically tried to cheat by relaxing one or more of the criteria. Auction rate securities, structured notes, and collateralized deposit obligations (CDOs) were all advertised as highly secure ways to earn extra returns on one's cash. Each was too clever in different ways, and when investors discovered their flaws, all fell dramatically in price and liquidity. *"Almost safe" is a far cry from safe. Any time one receives a higher return than the risk-free rate, there must be one or more incremental risks attached.* There is a good chance that the extra risks can stay hidden for months or even years, but they will eventually surface and are likely to destroy the notion of sleeping well at night.

The investor must reconcile the fundamental difference between genuine minimum risk investing for one's reserves and appropriate risk in the long-term growth portfolio. The lines between the two tend to blur when times are good and risk appears slight. As individuals or organizations age there may be many valid reasons for changing the size of the sleep-well-at-night liquidity reserve, but there will be few good reasons to compromise on its investment guidelines.

2.3 LONG-TERM GROWTH PORTFOLIOS

If you begin with $5 and your goal is to have $1 million by the end of the year, the best growth portfolio you might be able to create is a lottery ticket. Such a portfolio is almost certain to fail, but there are no other imaginable portfolios that have *any* probability of success. The point is that goals and portfolios have to be consistent. One just might have to lower one's sights if a realistic portfolio cannot be constructed.

Start with a reasonable set of goals. Once you set up your safe assets, the rest of the portfolio should focus on growth. But not all paths to growth are created equal. Chapter 4 goes into detail on how to combine different investments to shape both risk and return, but how does one gain confidence that any set of investments will achieve one's goals? There are three fundamental rules that no investor should forget:

- Compound interest is one of the greatest forces in investing. Small differences in return, if they can be maintained through time, produce massive differences in ultimate outcomes.
- Additional returns should never be expected without the assumption of additional risk. Risks translate into volatility in the value of one's portfolio. How each individual reacts to that volatility is highly subjective.
- If an investment loses 100%, no amount of future return can help you. Zero principal, compounded at any rate of return, is still zero.

2.3.1 The Power of Compounding

Allowing today's investment returns to build upon previous profits, or *compound*, increases wealth exponentially through time. Compound interest is the force that separates superior long-term performance from mediocre results, and mediocre returns from losing ground.

The power of compounding surprises most people who haven't thought carefully about the concept. As a case study, consider Investor A, who was evaluating his portfolio in 2010. He had invested $1 million with an active large-cap US stock manager at the start of 1985. Twenty-five years later, which included three major stock market drawdowns, his account stood at $8 million and he concluded the manager had done a solid job increasing his wealth eightfold.

But how well had the manager really done? From the start of 1985 to the end of 2009, the S&P 500 had an average total return (price appreciation plus dividends) of over 10.6% annually. Investor A's $1 million dollars invested in an index fund and left untouched so returns could compound for that 25 years would have grown to more than $12.4 million!

There is a simple rule of thumb to demonstrate the power of compound interest that is called "The Rule of 72."[1] If an investment earns X% through time, compounded each year, it will take 72/X years to double one's money. That is, a 2% rate of return will double one's capital roughly every 36 years. A 7.2% rate of return will do the trick in a decade. The 10.6% rate earned by the S&P 500 from 1985 through 2009 doubled an investor's money, on average, every 6.8 years.

The most powerful part of the calculation is the doubling. $1 million in 1985 became $2 million by the third quarter of 1991. That $2 million was $4 million in 1998, and $8 million by 2005. If the calculation date had not been the start of 2010, but only a little more than two years later, *and the average rate of return had not changed,* the investment would have doubled again to $16 million.

Small differences in average rates of return can mean massive differences in end values. Figure 2.1 shows the growth of a dollar over 25 years at different rates of growth. In the first example above, Investor A's manager seriously underperformed the index, creating a third less wealth over the period. But the manager's average rate of return for the 25 years was less than 2% per year behind the index. Because of compounding, even minor slippage can be costly through time.

In *Get Rich Slowly*, a wonderful book with a title sure to discourage enthusiastic and impatient investors, Bill Spitz describes the many dimensions of this important principle.[2] Small differences in return mean a lot, which translates not only into seeking the right portfolio mix but also on shaving away every cost that cannot be justified by incremental return. Time is just as important.

In a dramatic example of how important both time and return are, the *Chicago Tribune* reported in March 2010 on a $7 million gift to Lake Forest College by Grace Groner, who made her donation when she died at age 100.[3] The incredible part of the story is that the gift started in 1935 when Ms. Groner purchased three $60 shares of specially issued stock in Abbott Labs. Ms. Groner never sold any shares, even after many stock splits, and dutifully reinvested any dividends she received. Over the 75 years her $180 investment grew to $7 million, a seemingly near impossible achievement. In fact, if one calculates the average compound rate of return for the investment, it turns out to be just over 15% per year.

---

[1]The Rule of 72 is not a modern invention. An early reference to the rule is in the *Summa de Arithmetica* (Venice, 1494. Fol. 181, n. 44) of Luca Pacioli (1445–1514). He presents the rule in a discussion regarding the estimation of the doubling time of an investment, but does not derive or explain the rule, and it is thus assumed that the rule predates Pacioli by some time. *"A voler sapere ogni quantita a tanto per 100 l'anno, in quanti anni sara tornata doppia tra utile e capitale, tieni per regola 72, a mente, il quale sempre partirai per l'interesse, e quello che ne viene, in tanti anni sara raddoppiato. Esempio: Quando l'interesse e a 6 per 100 l'anno, dico che si parta 72 per 6; ne vien 12, e in 12 anni sara raddoppiato il capitale. (emphasis added)."* Roughly translated: *"In wanting to know for any percentage, in how many years the capital will be doubled, you bring to mind the* **rule of 72***, which you always divide by the interest, and the result is in how many years it will be doubled. Example: When the interest is 6 percent per year, I say that one divides 72 by 6; obtaining 12, and in 12 years the capital will be doubled."*

[2]Spitz, W. (1992). *Get Rich Slowly: Building Your Financial Future Through Common Sense.* John Wiley and Sons.

[3]Keilman, J. (2010). Amazing Grace: Lake Forest Secret Millionaire Donates Fortune to College. *Chicago Tribune.* (4 March).

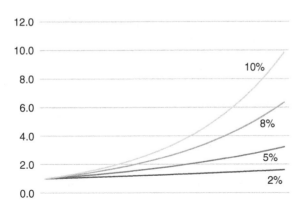

FIGURE 2.1 25-Year Compound Growth of $1 for Different Interest Rates

Now 15% per year is a fine rate of return, but just a few percent higher than the stock market in general did over that period. An equally important push came from the passage of time. At 15%, Ms. Groner's investment doubled on average every 4.8 years (72/15 = 4.8). *Over 75 years this meant that the investment doubled 15 times!* Each dollar grew by a factor of two raised to the 15th power, which is 32,768 times. Clearly, the surest way to turn $180 into $7 million is to start when you are 25, earn a good rate of return, and live to be 100.

Like most principles, the guiding light of compound returns can be pushed too far. The trend among endowments in the first part of the twenty-first century was to devote large proportions of their portfolios to illiquid partnership investments. There was a basic belief that the expected incremental return would allow their funds to grow a little faster, and given the perpetual nature of the endowment, sacrificing short-term liquidity for additional compounding would be an attractive strategy. The liquidity-driven crisis of 2008 and early 2009 showed that there are risks beyond market volatility that can threaten one's capital and enterprise.

The *Tribune* story also noted that Ms. Groner led a modest existence despite her considerable wealth, apparently never placing herself in a position where a downturn would threaten her lifestyle. Staying power is what counts in the world of compounding. *One must be able to maintain one's portfolio throughout any market cycle to achieve the ultimate investment goals.*

2.3.2   Incremental Expected Return = Greater Risk

The most fundamental truth in investing is that to get higher rates of expected return one must assume higher risk. If this were not true every risk-averse investor would opt for the higher yielding, lower risk choice and improve both the expected return and the risk profile of their portfolios. While this appears on the surface to be straightforward, there are in fact several subtle dimensions that are easily missed.

The first is that at any given point in time current projected yield is not a perfect indicator of risk. There is no better example of this than highly rated structured securities based on mortgages widely sold in 2006 and early 2007. These structures certainly offered a higher yield than Treasury notes and bonds of comparable maturity, but they offered nothing close to the return necessary to adequately compensate investors for the inherent risks.

History suggests that current rates of return reflect the market's *perception* of risk. Bonds with large spreads to treasuries are perceived to be riskier than those with small spreads. On average the market does a decent job of getting these relationships correct, but there are times when either errors in judgment or other factors move market prices and forecast returns away from reasonable reflections of true risk. Quiet market periods tend to lull investors into a sense of security that leads to underpricing of risk. Similarly at times of market stress, interest rate spreads and option volatilities extend well beyond historical norms and may overstate future risk.

In theory, even if the price of overall market risk is too high or too low, there should be a consistent relationship across investment alternatives. Unfortunately, even this is not always the case. Periodic enthusiasm for a specific investment (e.g. railroad bonds in the late nineteenth century, silver in 1979–1980, or Dutch tulip bulbs in 1637) can produce distorted prices and risk patterns. While the market usually is a reasonable guide to the relative riskiness of investments, it is ultimately the investor's obligation to determine whether today's expected returns are adequate compensation for the full array of risks actually present, but perhaps lurking.

The second complication comes from how any particular investment contributes to risk in a portfolio. Before there were advances in the theory of portfolio construction (discussed in more detail in Chapter 3), each investment was examined individually. Is the bond yield steady and reliably paid? How much does the stock price vary day-to-day or month-to-month? Most investors still think of risk in this way. The missing dimension is how any investment varies in return *relative to all the other investments in the portfolio.*

A simple example of this effect can be seen with car theft insurance. Each month that one's car is not stolen, there is a 100% loss of premium. Only if a theft occurs while the policy is in place is there ever a payoff, but that payoff is many times the size of the monthly "investment."

In fact, if one compared the payoff pattern of auto theft insurance to that of a lottery ticket, they would look remarkably similar. Both, on a stand-alone basis, are highly risky. But car theft insurance is not bought on a stand-alone basis, but in conjunction with the ownership of a car. The "portfolio" in this case is the car and the insurance, which has a lower risk profile than either the car or the policy taken separately.

The same thinking should be applied to traditional investment portfolios. A specific investment may be risky on a stand-alone basis, but could be much less of a problem within the portfolio. Investors should not expect to get paid much of an extra return for risk that can be diversified away.

The final complication is that risk comes from many directions. Market price volatility is simply the most obvious one of many risks. There are other risks, including liquidity risk, for which one should reasonably demand a higher expected return before investing. These risks too may be mispriced at any point in time, but every effort should be made to incorporate them into any valuation.

As will be discussed in Chapters 5.4 and 5.5, there are a myriad of operational and fraud risks that impact investors all too often. In theory, one should be compensated for taking on these risks, but in practice no fund manager ever offers a higher rate of return while warning investors they have shoddy business practices. Risks of this nature are not correlated in an advantageous way with any other investments. Diversification is vital here simply to contain any possible loss; there is no other portfolio advantage to pooling operational and fraud risk.

2.3.3   Losing 100% Is "Game Over"

The obvious sometimes needs emphatic restating. Investors focusing on the power of compound returns sometimes reach for incremental return without realizing that they are meaningfully increasing the chance of losing all of their investment. One of the most fundamental rules of investing is to strive for enough true diversification, which will likely include an appropriate allocation to sleep-well-at-night money, so that a 100% loss of portfolio is as nearly eliminated as possible. A portfolio's average rate of return over a long string of time periods is relevant only if none of those period's return is –100%. Once the investment corpus is lost, nothing after that matters. Zero compounded at any rate of return is still zero.

The reader may believe that this is an academic discussion without practical importance. After all, if one owns a diversified portfolio of stocks, a few might fail, but the market, as a whole, still exists. Such an attitude can lead to trouble. After the 1929 stock market crash, too much leverage produced many complete wipeouts for individual stock investors.

While the United States has been blessed by a stock market that has operated continuously for over 200 years, there are few other countries that can say that. Wars, revolutions, and hyperinflations have each destroyed entire asset markets. The investor that says, "Such things can't happen to me," should instead say, "I suspect a complete wipeout is a small-probability event, but if it happens, how will I cope?"

It is not just extreme political events or irresponsible borrowing by individuals that can cause a complete loss. Fraud and fund leverage are very real considerations as well. Too many Bernie Madoff victims had all their eggs in one basket. Investors in Long Term Capital Management (LTCM) in 1998 and many other hedge funds in 2007 and 2008 also suffered almost complete losses when seemingly reasonable trades became toxic because they were highly levered and then lost more per trade than the fund managers or investors had ever experienced before.

2.4   BETA AND THE POWER OF THE MARKET

Less experienced investors tend to want to jump to specific investment ideas right away when thinking about their portfolios. The Internet retailer, the property in Florida, or the cult status hedge fund manager all make for great cocktail party conversation. They do not, however, really help address the portfolio construction problem. Collections of individually selected investment ideas, even ones that are better than average, do not typically make a strong portfolio. After one decides on the right amount of sleep-well-at-night money and sets one's long-term growth goals, the next step is to sketch out the amount of money to be invested in each asset class. Bonds, stocks, real assets, and alternative investments are the broad categories available to virtually any investor. In Chapter 4 we shall go through the process of establishing a policy portfolio.

If there were no expected rate of return to investing, there would be no point in taking on any risk. Having said that, how does one estimate what any particular investment is likely to earn over time? Before the rise of modern portfolio theory and the collection of massive data sets of investment returns, there were few complete answers to that question. In the first half of the twentieth century, the common wisdom was that cautious investors only dealt in bonds. Stocks, whose prices could fluctuate widely on the basis of rumor, inside information and manipulation, were only to be traded by people seeking a speculative thrill. Nothing from the experience of the Roaring 20s and the subsequent Great Depression helped dispel such impressions.

After Harry Markowitz's and Bill Sharpe's pioneering efforts to model the behavior of a portfolio of stocks, the world recognized that each type of investment was driven by multiple factors.[4] For example, any particular stock's daily price would be affected by the following three influences:

- Particular information about the company (e.g. new customer contracts, a new patent awarded, the size of the CEO's pay package or his recent Tweets).
- Information about the sector (e.g. trade tariffs affecting the industry).
- Forces at work on the stock market as a whole, which is everything else not included in the first two points.

Notice that at any point in time all the factors working on individual companies or sectors aggregate up to contribute to the movement of the market as a whole, but they are not the whole story. If the Administration publicly announced a plan to double the capital gains tax, there is an excellent chance the stock market would take a dive even in the absence of any company or sector news.

Concentrating primarily on returns from individual stocks and bonds runs the risk of attributing too much to the skill, or lack thereof, of the security analyst. Anyone who bought a specific stock for their retirement account on 13 October 1987 got a rude shock when the entire market tumbled 8.9% in the next three days, only to fall another 22.6% on Black Monday, 19 October. That did not make them a bad stock analyst. The fortunes of the company whose stock was purchased had probably not changed materially in less than a week. This was a case where the vast majority of stock price change resulted from market-wide forces including a large dose of panic.

Beta is the extent to which any stock price moves with the market as a whole. This term is often misused in the investment lexicon, being sometimes confused with correlation.[5] It is always a term used in comparisons such as "The stock's beta with respect to large-cap US stocks taken as a whole is 1.2." One can calculate the beta of any security with respect to any other single security or group of securities, but some comparisons make no sense. Claiming that a US tech company's 10-year bond has a beta of 0.4 with respect to an index of Chinese stocks may be accurately calculated from the simple statistics between the two series, but one would be hard pressed to explain why there should be any connection. More importantly, blindly relying on such calculated betas can lead to serious errors in judgment.

Figure 2.2, shows the path of three hypothetical investments, demonstrating the concept of beta.

[4]Markowitz, H. (1952). Portfolio Selection. *Journal of Finance.*
Sharpe, W.F. (1964). Capital Asset Prices. *Journal of Finance.*
[5]Correlation and its importance in portfolio construction are discussed in Chapter 5.3.2.

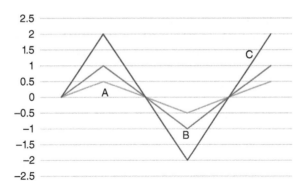

FIGURE 2.2 Visualizing Beta

Choosing among the three investments A, B, and C clearly involves different risks. Investment A (light gray line) fluctuates between +0.5 and −0.5, Investment B (medium gray) between +1 and −1, and Investment C (dark gray) between +2 and −2. If one assumes that the relationships across the investments can be expected to persist through time, what is the beta of each investment?

The right answer is to first ask another question, "The beta with respect to what?" If Investment B is the benchmark asset, A moves in every period exactly half that of B, so A's beta with respect to B is 0.5. Similarly since C moves twice as much as B every period, it has a beta of 2 with respect to B. The beta of B with respect to itself is always equal to 1, by definition.

If the beta calculation was performed relative to A, Investment B would have a beta of 2 with respect to A, and C's beta would be 4. Beta always captures the ratio of movements between two investment options and the choice of the reference investment is entirely arbitrary. When an investment manager states that his portfolio of stocks has a beta of 0.95, one needs to determine to what that beta refers.

Notice that in the stylized example in Figure 2.2 all three investments move in lock step. That is, they are perfectly correlated. Changing the proportions of A, B, and C in a portfolio will alter the total risk, but only because of the different underlying volatilities. There is no directional benefit from having a portfolio. If one investment makes money, they all do, and conversely. This is the first of many demonstrations in this book that high positive correlation is the enemy of the portfolio investor.

All three of the investments in Figure 2.2 are perfectly correlated to each other. Correlation tells the investor nothing about the size of an investment's calculated beta. It is generally true, however, that investments that are highly correlated produce more reliable beta estimates than those that are not.

If one expects an economy to grow through time, and there is an active stock market to support that growth, it is perfectly reasonable to expect that owning a broad portfolio of stocks should also produce a positive return. Hiring an active portfolio manager to help build one's wealth will generate returns from a combination of market forces and manager skill. Beta helps to distinguish between the two.

Ms. Groner's simple holdings from Section 2.3.1 can be examined through this lens. Over 75 years the Abbott stock's total return averaged about 15% while a proxy for US stocks averaged 10.8%. One might try to argue that Ms. Groner was a particularly gifted stock analyst in her ability to foresee Abbott's superior performance.

The fact that Ms. Groner was a secretary at Abbott for 43 years suggests, however, that her motivation for holding those particular shares did not depend on her analysis or foresight. It seems that a better explanation for the outperformance is that Abbott's stock had a beta with respect to the entire market that was 1.36 (=15/11). *Anyone* holding Abbott stock over that same 75-year period would have performed as well.

The first principle conclusion is that if one invests in growth assets, active management is not necessary to make a positive return. Beta creates its own force in the portfolio. Controlling and shaping various betas and the risks that come with them is, however, an active job to improve the odds that one's entire portfolio will meet one's target objectives.

Companies typically raise capital either by borrowing money or by issuing equity. The two sources of capital are not equal in the eyes of the law. Bondholders agree to lend capital in exchange for a promise that the capital will be repaid at some point in the future. Interest may be paid either in regular intervals or in a lump sum at the maturity of the bond. Bondholders have priority claim on the assets of the firm and in that sense are said to be *higher in the capital structure* than equity owners.

Stocks, being junior to bonds in the capital structure of a corporation, should tend to be riskier and also offer higher long-term returns. The bondholder is promised an interest payment and an ultimate return of capital. The equity owner waits to see if the bondholder gets paid and then benefits from the remaining profits.

Jeremy Siegel in his popular book, *Stocks for the Long Run*, which first appeared in 1994 in the middle of a raging bull market, argues that the long-run return to a broadly diversified portfolio of stocks should, on average, outpace a collection of high-quality bonds by several hundred basis points a year.[6] Given the power of compounding, such an advantage translates into huge differences through time.

Figure 2.3 shows the growth paths for Treasury bills, high-quality corporate bonds and large-cap domestic stocks for the 90 years since 1928. The chart is shown in logarithmic scale so that the massive compounding over that period doesn't distort the chart and the basic message. There is no question that over this history, stocks were a superior investment, and Siegel argues that investors should generally expect that to be the case.

There is an important caveat that should be included in the Siegel conclusions. While the history presented includes a mountain of data, it still remains just one history. The fact that the United States has managed to have a continuously trading stock market all during a period of relatively free capitalism and growing GDP does not guarantee that the next 200 years will be as kind. This is a common error in the study of financial markets. If the data shows that an event *has not* happened, it is too frequently inferred that it *cannot* happen. Siegel understands this idea well but far too many casual readers of his valuable book miss this point entirely.

The importance of this distinction can be shown by analogy. A lifelong resident of Manhattan who walks to work every day has obviously avoided death from pedestrian accidents. Does this imply that the pedestrian no longer has to watch for traffic? Obviously not, and the more savvy pedestrian recalls vividly the close calls over the years and makes special allowances for those potential events. Why should our

---

[6]Siegel, J.J. (1994). *Stocks for the Long Run*, McGraw Hill.

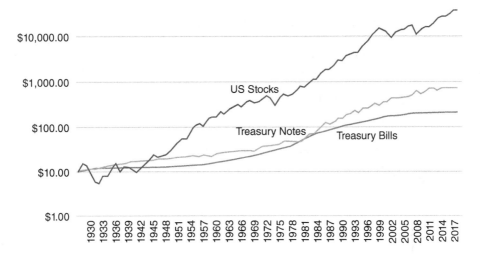

FIGURE 2.3 Hypothetical Growth of a $10 Investment in US stocks, Treasury Notes, and Treasury Bills from 1928 through 2018

approach to investing be different? Just because the market has not gone to zero in the United States does not mean it could not at some point in the future. It pays to focus on the traffic that can kill investments as the investment journey progresses.

The reader might respond that the analogy is flawed because people do die in pedestrian accidents in Manhattan, and one can and should learn from those tragic tales. An individual walking across Manhattan is always faced with specific risks that cannot be diversified away. Investors have more options. By investing in "the market," people can achieve a higher degree of certainty. Some individuals may lose all their wealth through poor investment decisions and fraud, but such risks are avoidable with enough diversification.

If one could produce a cross section of data across all the world's stock markets that show no instances of complete failure, the rejoinder might have more merit. However, in the history of equity investing, finding stock markets like the United States that have an unbroken streak of activity is actually quite hard. Revolutions, hyperinflations, wars, and a myriad of other factors can and do cause equity markets to go essentially to zero. Pretending that disasters cannot happen is hubris or wishful thinking and not risk management.

2.5   DO ALTERNATIVE INVESTMENTS HAVE AN IDENTIFIABLE BETA?

One can easily calculate the beta of stocks or bonds in one's portfolio, but what about alternative investments like hedge funds or private equity partnerships? As the range of investments within alternative investments has no bounds, it is tricky to make assumptions about any investment's beta.

One of the clearest examples of this comes from the history of the hedge fund Amaranth. Amaranth was formed in September 2000 and was advertised as a multistrategy hedge fund, which meant that it would try to profit from a variety of strategies that had different sources of returns. While the approaches included relative value trading that the founders were known for, there was never a promise that the fund would avoid directional trades.

The fund's early success was impressive. Despite a terrible bear market in stocks, it earned 4.2% (partial year returns), 21.7%, and 11.3% in 2000, 2001, and 2002, respectively. In that first period there were only five losing months. The next three years continued the string, with net returns of 16.9%, 9.4%, and 18.0% with only 8 losing months, the largest of which was –2.2%. By the end of 2005, Amaranth was hailed as one of the most successful hedge funds ever, showing an ability to make steady returns in both bull and bear markets. With such a track record, many less sophisticated investors flocked in. Investors with more understanding of finance wanted first to get a better understanding of the sources of the return.

Amaranth was not the most transparent of funds. Investors were not given detailed return attribution statistics, but the fund's investment letters spoke qualitatively about the types of trades that had been profitable. Statistically adept investors took the matter into their own hands to explore the issue further.

If one compares a fund's monthly performance to the monthly returns for another asset group, there are statistical tools to estimate the beta of the fund with respect to that asset. Typically the calculations are made against stocks, Treasury bonds, and some measure of credit. In the case of Amaranth, such tests suggested that there was *no* reliable beta between the fund and stocks, bonds or credit. *Everything the fund earned appeared to be independent of the direction of the underlying markets! Everything seemed to be what is called pure alpha.*

A manager that can produce regular returns that are uncorrelated to everything else in the market is the equivalent to the Holy Grail in the investment world. Adding that manager to any portfolio should improve its risk characteristics. For many institutional and individual investors, the combination of the strong, steady returns and the near-zero correlations was all that was necessary to make a major commitment to Amaranth.

Other investors remained cautious. If the beta to stocks and bonds was essentially zero, what was the source of the return? Could it be possible that every manager's trading decision was correct? There were suggestions in Amaranth's investor letters that a significant part of 2005's returns were earned on energy trades in the natural gas market. A closer statistical examination of Amaranth's track record revealed a significant beta to energy prices. Amaranth had become much less a multi-strategy, relative-value hedge fund and much more a macro fund with large commodity bets. The fact that they had not experienced any large losses in their six-year history was no guarantee against future disappointments.

By the summer of 2006 strong returns and large new commitments by investors, including a large number of funds-of-funds, had grown Amaranth's assets under management (AUM) to over $9 billion. Many investors arrived just in time for the fireworks. In August and September the natural gas market realized that there would likely be ample supplies to carry through the North American winter. The Hurricane Katrina-induced disruptions to supply from the previous year were in the distant past. Amaranth had mammoth spread trades that were betting on short supplies, and the positions were rapidly losing money. Additional margin was called for to cover the losses on the leveraged positions, and Amaranth was forced to liquidate their natural gas book.

A trade that had made the fund $1 billion in 2005 lost over $6 billion in a matter of days a year later. Amaranth's posted losses for September were more than 60% of the fund's AUM. Investors were horrified to learn there had been that much risk in the portfolio. Enough LPs demanded the return of their remaining assets that Amaranth liquidated what was left of the fund.

The primary lesson of Amaranth is that it is extraordinarily rare to have no beta to any major market risk. As will be discussed in detail in Chapter 5, statistical measures based on monthly returns can be completely misleading. Unless one has enough position transparency to identify the risks before they occur, well-considered allocations are almost impossible.

Almost all alternative investments have a beta to something. Identifying that beta is one of the most important challenges investors face. There is nothing in the broad definition of alternative investments that constrains managers in terms of the type or magnitude of the beta they assume. Investors who make a percentage allocation to hedge funds have really said nothing about how their ultimate portfolio will behave. In each case the investment needs to be analyzed and then assessed as to whether the process justifies the high active management fees and limited liquidity that typically come with these investments. Investors need to be particularly cautious about manager claims that their returns are largely independent of market forces.

2.6 LIQUIDITY OF THE PORTFOLIO AND ACCESS TO THE CREDIT MARKETS

A major trend in investments over the past 30 years has been the increasing use of illiquid investments in both individual and institutional portfolios. The theory is basic enough. If an investor has a long-term horizon and can accept the risks of tying money up for a period of years, he or she should be rewarded with a higher expected return. This greater reward can get compounded for a long period and produce dramatically higher end results.

The higher return should arise from a natural reluctance to part with liquidity. At the extreme, investors seek out short-dated Treasury securities because they are both safe and liquid. Giving money to a stock manager at a mutual fund has more risks, but if market conditions change or the manager doesn't meet expectations, the manager can be terminated on any business day. Long-dated private partnerships are very different. An investor enters a legal commitment to provide capital, the return of which is almost entirely at the discretion of the general partner. If there were not a significant expected premium to the risk-free rate, why would anyone invest?

Liquidity is not a discrete concept, either liquid or illiquid, but instead runs along a scale. Short-dated Treasuries are perhaps the most liquid investment option that (usually) pays more than cash (but don't expect this in Germany or Japan in 2021!). Marketable bonds, stocks and mutual funds that trade daily and settle in two to three days are highly liquid.

Hedge funds have varying degrees of liquidity. Some allow access to funds monthly; others quarterly, and still others have annual liquidity or worse. Usually there are notice periods that need to be observed before redemptions can be made. Initial investment lockups of a year or more are also not unusual. This places hedge funds into an intermediate category of being neither liquid nor completely illiquid.

The credit crisis of 2008 revealed another dimension to hedge fund illiquidity. In most partnership agreements there are well-defined terms covering when LPs can ask for the return of their funds. In addition to these clauses, there are often general terms that allow the GP to deviate from the specific rules if, in the GP's sole discretion, there is a concern that meeting the redemption requests would cause damage to either liquidating or remaining LPs. As credit markets seized up after the Lehman bankruptcy, many hedge fund managers invoked these rules to limit or completely curtail redemptions. Limited partners were surprised and outraged to learn that the stated fund terms were not being honored. One lesson from 2008 is that LPs have considerably less control over hedge fund liquidity than they previously believed. More than a decade after the crisis there are still funds sitting at brand name hedge funds that have not been returned to LPs that asked for all of their money.

Truly illiquid assets include multiyear partnerships, real estate holdings, control positions in stocks or distressed debt, or investments in private companies. While, by definition, virtually anything can be sold at a given time, the bids one might receive for these illiquid assets in a "fire sale" may be so far below the intrinsic value to make selling the assets completely onerous.

Should an investor limit the amount allocated to less liquid or illiquid assets? Intuitively the answer is yes, but defining those limits is not an easy task. A great deal has to do with the size of the investment pool and the needs placed upon it. A young person setting aside retirement funds may be in the best position to "invest and forget" in illiquid partnerships. Perpetual endowments and pension funds should also be able tie up funds for a prolonged period, but once again, the stressed markets of 2008 and early 2009 showed that portfolios can be turned upside down when too many types of assets cannot be traded.

Some investors tried to use access to the credit markets as a way to justify outsized commitments to illiquid equity securities. The theory was that if distributions from private investments fell for any reason, it would always be possible to borrow cash to cover immediate needs as a temporary substitute. The borrowing would be repaid when the market cycle turned more favorable.

Such a plan might work for idiosyncratic disruptions to the investment programs, or with typical cyclical downturns, but it failed profoundly after the bankruptcy of Lehman. Every market seized up. Private partnerships stopped virtually all distributions and both the publicly traded equity and credit markets went into freefall. More critically, stressed banks tried to cut existing lines of credit to their customers. Any investor who had simply assumed that the credit markets would be there on demand found historically wide spreads and very few willing suppliers of fresh capital.

There is ultimately no substitute for true liquidity. Asset allocations should recognize this and if errors are going to be made, it should be in favor of too much liquidity and not too little.

2.7   NOT-FOR-PROFIT ORGANIZATIONS AND SPENDING RULES

Setting investment objectives should be closely tied to one's needs and risk tolerances. Individuals typically do this heuristically and not by any mechanical rule. Over the past 30 years or so, a trend among not-for-profit organizations has emerged away from such basics and toward more formula-driven approaches. During the strong bull markets of the 1980s and 1990s, analytical drivers of both spending and investment began to gain wide acceptance. Problems with these approaches appeared after the tech bubble burst and the financial crisis.

Many endowments and permanent foundations suffered mightily from the market turmoil that began in the second half of 2007. Healing after varied depending on the fundamental soundness of the institution. The COVID-19 pandemic created a different set of challenges and boards and professional staff have scrambled to protect their organizations' mission-critical activities. Today institutions are examining everything about their process in order to avoid a repeat of those crisis years. While most of the focus has been on the investment portfolio and the market, at least part of the attention has been on the spending policy. When a mechanical spending policy begins to dominate setting investment policies, it is perhaps time that it be rethought and possibly scrapped.

Private foundations have certain legal restrictions on how much they are required to spend every year. Failure to meet these requirements can jeopardize a foundation's legal and tax status. Academic institutions have many more degrees of freedom. Despite these legal differences, spending policies and their relationship to endowment investment policy have evolved in similar ways. There is today a great dependence on formulas to achieve "consistency" of spending, but there are vulnerabilities to such approaches.

Less than 50 years ago the standard spending policy of a not-for-profit organization was annually to spend the income generated by the endowment. The philosophy was that by only spending coupons and dividends (current income), the corpus of the endowment might fluctuate with the market, but it would never be invaded.

The 1970s and a rapid rise in inflation uncovered many problems with this approach. As institutions tried to maximize their payouts, they tilted portfolios toward bonds and away from stocks that paid little or no dividends. Even if the capital value of the endowment stayed intact in nominal terms (and with rising interest rates, many times it did not), the real purchasing power of the endowment steadily diminished. Another approach was needed.

The concept of spending a target percentage of the total value of the endowment began to gain wide acceptance in the 1980s and is nearly universally used today. The chief advantage of this type of spending rule is that the portfolio can be constructed with a total return focus that largely ignores whether the return comes from interest, dividends, or capital appreciation. Since taxes are not an issue for these investors, all sources of return are equally valuable.

Spending a fixed percentage of a 31 December or 30 June asset value each year is the simplest kind of total return rule, but one that is subject to considerable market volatility. Institutions try to smooth out those effects by employing a multi-quarter moving average, often extending three or more years, which minimizes the short-term market fluctuations and provides a more reliable stream of contributions.

Simulation studies based on historical investment returns suggest what rates of spending might be sustainable. An endowment that has a spending rate of zero should be expected to grow through time. This raises the question, however, who is ever going to benefit from the endowment? At the other end of the spectrum, a spending rate of 15% a year will likely exhaust the endowment at some date not that far into the future. An accepted rule of thumb is that spending rates in the range of 4–5% are probably sustainable because, on average, they likely will not deplete the corpus. Such a spending rate will also not likely generate endowment growth in real terms, which would favor future generations of beneficiaries versus today's program participants.

From the target spending rate, the investment goals are then developed. Just because an institution wants to spend 5% of its endowment annually does not mean that 5% should be the target return. The target return goal should be spending, plus inflation, plus the expenses of running the endowment. If the actual return matches the target, the real purchasing power of the endowment should, on average, be maintained through time.

The above description summarizes the most widely held views on spending today, and there is probably little risk to trustees in following such a policy. But the question should be raised, is there a better practice?

The market events of the last 20 years, including the pandemic and the tumultuous period of 2008 and early 2009, point to a number of defects in the current spending practice. They can be summarized as follows:

- Illiquid investments may earn more on average, but they are imperfect substitutes for liquid investments when it comes to meeting current spending needs.
- Percentage-spending rules mean that investment results dictate budget policy at institutions. An optimal spending rule should be based on budgetary goals first, with a secondary objective being the sustainability of the endowment.

2.7.1 Illiquid Investments

The biggest flaw in current spending rules is in the treatment of illiquid investments. With spending rules and portfolio models stressing total return, many not-for-profits embraced expanded allocations to private partnerships or direct investments in real estate or commodities. *It was always assumed that the capital markets would be readily available to convert endowment assets into spendable cash when the budget called for it.*

FAS 157 rules have effectively mandated that endowments mark their portfolios to market and be able to justify these values. Naturally, spending rule calculations are based on these marks. In bull markets, this has produced rising endowment values and accelerating spending, even if the assets are not readily available to fund that spending.

The severe downturn in 2008 and early 2009 showed the error of this approach. Prior to the market decline, spending calculations could be based on rising marks, and not realized gains, from illiquid partnerships. As markets tumbled in the crisis, illiquid investments were probably not marked down as rapidly as the rest of the portfolio. Despite horrible reported losses, the calculated value of many endowments heavily committed to illiquid investments was probably still overstated.

Total return spending rules were then applied to these questionable marks and a contribution from the endowment was calculated. Unfortunately, in many cases marketable securities had to be sold at fire sale prices to meet the budgeted allocations. In other instances, institutions chose to borrow for their operating expenses as their marketable portfolios were either inadequate to meet spending needs or the sale of marketable securities would have completely and unacceptably skewed the remaining endowment portfolio.

In hindsight, there were two mistakes made. Spending rules could have been modified to identify returns to illiquid investments only when they were realized.

The second error was that as investment committees made increasingly larger commitments to illiquid investments in a quest for higher total returns, they did so too willingly. Chasing the advantage that even small differences in returns make when compounded over years, they accepted too little in terms of projected returns in exchange for the liquidity they gave up.

2.7.2 Investments Should Not Determine Budgets

In a logical world, the first step of a not-for-profit should be establishing program priorities and then deciding on budgets that can achieve those goals. With a percentage-spending rule, this world is turned somewhat upside down. Each year the financial officer runs a calculation based on past endowment values and announces that a certain amount is available for spending. The Board then works with the remaining revenue items to make all the pieces fit.

For institutions that derive only a small percentage of their operating budgets from their endowments, market fluctuations rarely interfere with mission critical plans. But many institutions receive a third or more of their annual budgets from their endowments, and here severe market downturns unavoidably translate into meaningful program changes. Foundations that have no independent sources of income are totally dependent upon the market.

Nobody complained about this state of the world during the bull markets of the 1980s and 1990s when percentage-spending rules became prevalent. Endowments grew faster than historical investment returns would have predicted, contributions from the endowments grew apace, and the money was spent. Some programs grew because money was available, not because they were critical to the organization's mission, or, more importantly, sustainable financially. The market declines in 2000, 2002, 2008, and early 2009, showed that a percentage-spending rule is a blade that cuts both ways.

2.7.3 An Alternative Approach to Spending Policy

Imagine an alternative approach: an institution constructs its operating budget and plans out several years. All sources of revenue are identified and the difference between spending and revenue is scheduled to come from the endowment. Each year both the expense and income items are adjusted for inflation and the contribution from endowment only changes to reflect the differential. In theory, the dollar endowment contribution should grow roughly in line with the budget and no faster.

Through time the results of this process will produce an endowment that is either sustainable or not. The Board should stress in its original budgeting process a sufficient balance between expected revenues and expenses so that the necessary contribution from the endowment will not deplete the corpus.

During prolonged bull markets like the 1990s, endowments can be expected to grow faster than forecast. This, in turn, allows the Board to occasionally reassess the level of programs at the institution. Can the institution move to a higher level in a sustained fashion? In every case the discussion flows from the institution's programs to the endowment and not the other way around.

In contrast, after a major market decline, the contribution from the endowment would be held roughly constant in dollar terms to support the existing budget. Only after several years of down markets would the Board need to confront long-term program changes, which hopefully could be phased in as part of the regular budget process rather than implemented in an emergency.

The institution's Finance and Investment Committees should aim at clear dollar targets and not average growth rates. To be successful in all stress situations, the organization might want to hold a minimum dollar amount equal to one to two years planned endowment contribution that is invested in highly secure, liquid assets. Even not-for-profits need sleep-well-at-night money. These low-risk investments may appear to be a drag on total portfolio return, but they will insure against having to sell assets at highly depressed prices or having the institution face a crisis of illiquidity. If the process has integrity, the sustainability of the endowment contribution will be demonstrated in *all* markets.

The combination of generally rising markets and percentage-based spending rules has allowed some boards to become more passive in the last three decades. Investment returns were generous, and programs grew without enough consideration for the market risks that they carried with them. The sudden downturn in endowments in 2008 and early 2009 forced many not-for-profits to triage their activities, dramatically cutting those that were considered lower priorities. Such discussions are always difficult. It is far better to have a budget in place that shows more resilience in the face of a crisis. A modification of today's common spending policy methodology can facilitate that.

The most important difference between the suggested approach and the common spending rules of today is that the discussion always begins on the program side of the organization. Trustees, by definition, must be more engaged. By not automatically directing investment windfalls into the budget, institutions can create extra protection against market declines. They can also construct investment programs that are consistent with the priorities of the organization and are not simply designed to earn "more," often at the expense of a margin of investment safety and liquidity.

Spending one's current income is a poor spending rule that has justifiably been rejected by most not-for-profits. Perhaps it is time to evolve again away from mechanical rules that leave the mission of the organization too much at the mercy of market fluctuations.

2.7.4　Spending Rules and the Pandemic

Investing is all about uncertainty. While there were many experts to claim after the fact that the world should have prepared better for the COVID-19 pandemic, the reality is that one cannot build an investment program around the theoretical possibility of events that have never happened. When these Black Swan events do occur, the successful investor has had in place a general risk profile that allows them to cover their immediate needs and take advantage of emerging opportunities. The shocks, however, do not just hit the investment portfolio. Budgets can be severely disrupted, and this is where the interplay between the investment and operating functions are so important. It may be time to retreat temporarily from any spending regimen.

Education is a prime example of the challenges from the pandemic. From pre-K through graduate school we have always been told that small class sizes and intimate interaction with teachers is a key determinant of quality. While the virus remains a serious health threat, parents, teachers, and administrators are all struggling with finding the right balance between that highly personal experience and the safety of all concerned. Universities opened for in-person instruction in the fall of 2020, only to sometimes see an outbreak of the virus, forcing a retreat. There are no easy answers.

Adapting to the new reality comes with costs. With high unemployment, can families afford tuitions without large subsidies? How much new spending is required to reconfigure learning space into safer, socially distant plans? What other costs accelerate as regular private testing for the virus becomes the norm along with extra-thorough cleaning? The uncertainty around budgets on both the cost and revenue side explodes.

Trustees need to be fluid in their thinking while considering both immediate needs and longer term goals during these crisis events. Flexibility around any spending rule may be one of the first areas of adjustment.

For institutions that aspire to a permanent endowment, a bedrock principle is intergenerational equality. Having a low spend rate today may see the endowment grow, but this means future generations of students or foundation grant participants will see benefits denied today's recipients. Overspending does the reverse. In most circumstances, the ideal is to be as fair across time as possible. If there are grand plans to upgrade the experience, they are usually addressed through fundraising.

Then there are events like the pandemic. Operating deficits can rapidly appear at schools. The needs of the community served by a foundation can explode. Trustees are faced with choices about how deeply to reach into the piggy bank and for how long. These decisions are all made in a highly uncertain environment.

A rigid adherence to a spending rule may preserve the long-term corpus of the endowment but will likely push all the economic impact of the pandemic onto the current generation of a school's students and faculty and a foundation's grant recipients. Since everyone expects the impact of events like the pandemic to be temporary, the action that appears on the surface to be fiscally responsible likely assures intergenerational inequality.

There are always at least a few who criticize the idea of funding extra spending in a crisis, calling it a pillaging of the endowment. They say the right solution is to cut the fat out of bloated budgets to meet immediate needs and preserve the long-term growth of the endowment. There is little doubt economizing can be done at most organizations. But to suggest that extraordinary needs can be met solely by budget cuts does a disservice to the vast majority of trustees and administrators who plan their budgets and use their resources carefully.

Only the most narrow-minded investment committee members would advocate for such a strict approach. Thankfully, most people who serve on not-for-profit boards do not primarily measure success by the size of the endowment. They keep front of mind the broader mission of the organization and at times of crisis the typical response is, "This is why we have an endowment!"

The pandemic unambiguously negatively impacted the current generation. By increasing spending from the endowment beyond normal levels, part of that pain is mitigated. In one sense this draws on resources normally expected to be available to future generations. This is not the most desirable form of intergenerational equality, but it may be necessary to maintain the mission of the organization.

Life runs in cycles and there is an important prescription from this discussion for happier times as well. When the world seems to be a nurturing place, with investment returns stringing together years of above-average returns and operating budgets are not strained, it is important not to expect that good fortune to persist indefinitely. Too many institutions did exactly that in the 1990s, mechanically and happily following a spending rule that created windfalls to the operating budget. Trustees should think about under spending the formula in great times in order to provide for the inevitable rainy days like what we are experiencing now.

It is the rare and fortunate organization that got through the pandemic period without considering extra demands on their endowment. For some not-for-profits the challenges from the COVID-19 crisis were existential in nature. Either the necessary steps were taken to preserve the mission, or there would be no future generations to worry about. As difficult as these times can be, it is important to remember that the worst will pass, allowing for a return to normal endowment draws. When the good times inevitably reappear, memories of such trying times should rein in any extreme optimism. There will be other rainy days for which a long-term perspective is essential.

CHAPTER 3

The Pillars of Portfolio Theory and Their Limitations

Harry Markowitz in 1952 published "Portfolio Selection," one of the most influential articles in the history of finance and investing.[1] For the first time there was analytical rigor behind two intuitive concepts: 1) nothing ventured, nothing gained, and 2) don't put all your eggs into one basket. As important as this work turned out to be, it was not immediately embraced broadly by the academic community, and it would be many more years before its concepts would be used by real investors.[2] Still, Markowitz's article can be thought of as kicking off a vibrant 25-year period of finance research during which all the major pillars of modern portfolio theory were established.

Markowitz demonstrated that as long as all assets in a portfolio were not perfectly correlated, there would be benefits from diversification. He went on to identify the most "efficient" portfolios from the limitless combinations available to investors which could be seen as providing the best-expected return for any given level of risk, or similarly, the lowest risk for any given target return.

"Portfolio Selection" was primarily concerned with how groups of investments behaved. By the early 1960s, Bill Sharpe, Jack Treynor, and John Lintner had developed models to explain how the expected return of a particular investment could be thought of as a combination of the risk-free rate and a risk premium.[3] This opened the door to more analytical approaches to stock and bond valuations and most of the quantitative trading models employed today.

While the early years of this revolution were marked by great theoretical strides, very little of this work immediately found its way to Wall Street. It wasn't until the 1970s that the analytical approach began making serious inroads with the traditional investment community. When financial futures and options markets were developed in that decade, they were major beneficiaries of the new theories.

---

[1]Markowitz, H. (1952). Portfolio Selection. *Journal of Finance.*

[2]Peter Bernstein's *Capital Ideas,* John Wiley & Sons, 2005, is a wonderful book detailing the intellectual progression of modern portfolio theory. Anyone seeking a better idea of how the theories evolved and then came to shape Wall Street can find no better reference.

[3]Sharpe, W.F. (1964). Capital Asset Prices. *Journal of Finance.* Lintner, J. (1965). The Valuation of Risk Assets and the Selection of Risky Investments in Stock Portfolio and Capital Budgets. *Review of Economics and Statistics.* Treynor, J.L. (1961). Toward a Theory of Market Value for Risky Assets. Unpublished paper, Arthur D. Little.

Unlike the stock market, there was little tradition that needed to be overcome in these new markets.

Events have moved much more rapidly since. Old-fashioned approaches to portfolio management have been swept away. Today's investors can be easily overwhelmed by all the analytical firepower on display by Wall Street's financial engineers. Few of these rocket scientists were born when Markowitz's seminal paper first appeared, but they are all well versed in the basics of modern portfolio theory. Unfortunately, many of them treat actual markets as if they were linear accelerators designed to carry out their theoretical experiments and not the living, breathing entities that they are.

There is almost no chance that individual or institutional investors will be on equal footing with these financial engineers. At the micro level, this makes it hard for investors to evaluate the worth of different fund approaches. Everything looks so complicated and impressive. At a macro level, it leaves everyone susceptible to harm when one of the analytically driven trends in the markets gains too big of a following and blows up. To combat these problems, investors need to have enough knowledge of the theory to make informed judgments on specific investments and perhaps to get out of the way of the worst disasters before they happen.

Gaining this knowledge is the goal of this chapter. In the next sections you will find an overview of the key elements of modern portfolio theory as it is widely followed today. Along the way, care will be taken to highlight the limitations of the theory. Nothing in this section will be news to the people who developed these ideas. They know that markets are not frictionless and that not every investor has access to the same information at the same time. These limitations are not a reason to abandon the advances from the theory but instead to be cautious about blindly accepting the broadest conclusions.

Understanding the basics of the theory and its limitations will allow you to make better judgments about investment funds and approaches to portfolio construction. Financial engineers often want to test their theories with your money. If they get it right, you make some returns and they are rewarded handsomely. But when they are wrong, you bear the full burden of the loss. This asymmetry is reason enough to become more informed about the theories behind investing.

3.1 RISK PREMIUMS ACROSS ASSETS

The starting point for the basic analysis is, "Is this security cheap?" This one question has kept legions of academics and practitioners busy long before the pioneers of modern portfolio theory broke the ice. Sharpe, Treynor, and Lintner did most of the heavy lifting to get the answer onto a solid analytical foundation with the development of what is called the Capital Asset Pricing Model (CAPM). Scholars have been adding to the basics ever since.

The basic proposition is that the expected return of any asset is equal to the risk-free rate plus a risk premium that is a function of that asset's relationship to the market.

$$E\left(R_i\right) = R_f + \text{risk premium} \tag{3.1}$$

There won't be a need for many equations in this section, but this one sets the table for much of what follows where R_i is the risky asset that we are analyzing, and $E(R_i)$ is the designation of its expected return. R_f is the symbol for the risk-free rate. The meat of the problem comes from figuring out what goes into the undefined risk premium term.

Sharpe's CAPM had only one factor determining the risk premium, and that was the risk of the overall market.

$$E\left(R_i\right) = R_f + \beta_i\left[E\left(R_M\right) - R_f\right]$$ (3.2)

$E(R_M) - R_f$ is the excess return the market is expected to make beyond the risk-free rate. β_i is the infamous *beta* that investment people toss about. The beta of a stock is how sensitive it is relative to the overall market. If a stock generally moves 2% whenever the market moves 1%, it has a beta of 2. Quiet, more conservative companies, like regulated utilities, often have a beta that is less than 1. Higher flying growth companies have betas that are often greater than 1.

The higher the beta, the more volatility a stock will have relative to the always available option of owning an index fund that captures the entire market. Since investors generally prefer less volatility, they require a higher expected return to hold the riskier assets. This is all equation 3.2 says.

Once a security's beta is established, it provides a clear guide to what that security should be priced at relative to the market overall. Any time the actual price is at odds with what it should be; there is an arbitrage opportunity that traders who are knowledgeable can exploit.

The assumptions behind CAPM are strict. They include:

- Investors make investment choices based on expected returns and the variance of those returns.
- Investors are rational and risk averse.
- There is a risk-free asset in the market and anyone can borrow or lend at that rate.
- Capital markets are competitive with no costs to transact.

Most readers will raise issues with all of the assumptions, but that is not a justification for tossing out all of the implications of CAPM. Academics use restrictive assumptions so their mathematical models can have tidy solutions. However, the ultimate test of a model is not whether it is theoretically elegant (though you might be surprised how important that is among academic economists these days), but whether its predictions conform to what is observed in the market. By that measure, there is plenty of justification for CAPM to still be around after almost 50 years.

The way CAPM is tested is through a technique called linear regression. Historical returns for a security are plotted against the returns of the broad market and then a line is fitted to the data that best explains the relationship. Figure 3.1 shows how this works in practice.

If the CAPM theory were perfect, all the data points would fall precisely on the estimated line, but equation (3.2) is only a theoretical construct. When trying to apply it to actual prices in the market, it usually fits the data pretty well, but rarely perfectly. These "errors" in the model, shown in the chart as data points off the line, could be due to random events or noise, or they could be a result of basic model is not being

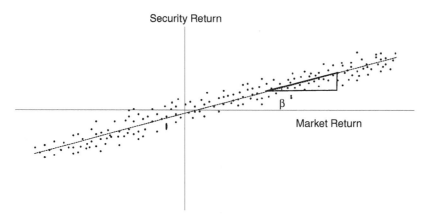

Security Return

β

Market Return

FIGURE 3.1 Estimating Market β from Returns Data

correctly specified. It is this latter possibility that has kept academic researchers and financial engineers busy in the decades since CAPM appeared.

If you try to trade stocks based on the predictions of CAPM, the "errors" can be quite costly. This has led researchers to try to improve the basic, single-factor CAPM model. The natural way to seek improvements is to try to determine whether the "errors" are purely random or due to other systematic factors that can also be included in the model.

This has led to "multifactor" models of security pricing. Some multifactor models are considered *Macroeconomic Factor Models*, which use variables like interest rates, inflation, GDP growth, and the like to try to explain stock price returns. *Fundamental Factor Models* stick a little closer to the stock market. They look at whether company and industry attributes like cap size, price-to-earning (P/E) ratios, or price-to-book (P/B) ratios are effective in explaining movements in a stock's price.

There is no agreed-upon list defining strictly which factors should be used in the model. A theoretical case can be made to include all kinds of variables, but usually the deciding factor is empirical effectiveness. Does the inclusion of a factor improve the fit of the regression? Does it lessen the average error in predicting how a stock's price will move?

There is a large and active industry that provides factor models to investors of all stripes. Most of this industry can be traced back to Barr Rosenberg, a finance professor at the University of California, Berkeley in the 1970s. His 1974 paper greatly extended the number of fundamental factors that could be used to explain equity prices, and was the foundation for his consulting company that came to be known as BARRA.[4] *BARRA Factors* is a common term in the trade that has come to mean the most important fundamental variables used to explain variation in stock prices.

The ultimate quest is to separate two kinds of risks:

- Systematic risk
- Idiosyncratic or firm-specific risk

---

[4]Rosenberg, B. (1974). Extra Market Components of Covariance in Security Returns. *Journal of Finance and Quantitative Analysis* (March), pp. 263–274. Today, BARRA is part of MSCI, which supplies analytical services to portfolio managers globally.

Systematic Risk is due to movements in the market or some other common factor. Every stock in a portfolio has a greater or lesser amount of this risk, which cannot be diversified away. Firm-specific risk (e.g. the company's CEO comes down with a serious illness, an important union goes on strike against only that company, or a company's clinical trials fail) is much more difficult to estimate before the fact. But this risk has the benefit of being diversifiable.

Consider the extreme case of someone holding all of his or her wealth in one stock. This produces exposures to all of the market, or systematic risk along with a maximum dose of idiosyncratic, firm-specific risk. Intuitively it might seem that by adding another unique stock to the portfolio that the problem should get worse. After all, there is another new set of idiosyncratic things to worry about. This, however, is not true. Because odd-ball events happen to companies at different times, and not all idiosyncratic events are negative, adding the second, third, and fourth companies to a portfolio can have big payoffs in reducing overall idiosyncratic risk. Figure 3.2 shows how as portfolio names are added, idiosyncratic risk falls until you own the market and only systematic risk is left.

The more one can add securities that have their own unique forms of risk, the better the risk profile of the entire portfolio. The challenge is to not overestimate the amount of idiosyncratic risk any asset has. That might give the investor a mistaken impression that diversification would be a bigger help in lowering risk than it really is.

Sharpe's early work suggested that the only relevant common factor was the movement of the overall stock market. As more fundamental factors were determined for different stocks, it became clear that there were more common factors to contend with. Holding a portfolio of 20 pharmaceutical company stocks would not offer nearly the diversification benefits of a 20-stock portfolio drawn randomly from all the industries in the market.

The two most important factors for most stocks are the market as a whole and the company's industry. However, systematic risks do not stop there. Style factors like growth, value, momentum, capitalization, quality, and numerous accounting factors have all been used to try to ferret out as many of the systematic components as possible.

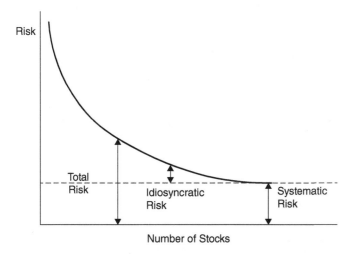

FIGURE 3.2　Systematic and Idiosyncratic Portfolio Risk

This is where the footing begins to get slippery. The *theory* behind the factor models is unassailable. Everyone should be aware of any factor concentration that appears in a portfolio because that translates to an undiversifiable risk. The *practice* of employing factor models is almost entirely an exercise of looking backward in data and identifying statistically significant relationships.

The tests are rarely developed in the same way physical scientists set up their experiments, with controls that can be replicated many times. We might like to believe that if we have enough market data we have the equivalent of many experiments, but this is not the case. Each observation is a market outcome that was produced at a unique moment in time. *There is no opportunity to control anything an experimental scientist would like to control.* This means that if a statistical relationship is identified in the data, it should be annotated with a warning, "*This result is likely to hold true only in conditions identical to the history that produced the data.*"

The social scientist always faces these kinds of problems. Experiments that social scientists construct to avoid these problems rarely can hold constant important elements of the actual environment. When they do their tests using real data, they cannot have adequate control to have genuinely repeatable trials. This is a basic conflict, with which everybody working in the social sciences struggles.

To see the practical challenges of this kind of empirical analysis, consider the case of two gold mining stocks, Goldcorp (now Newmont Goldcorp) and Kinross. Figure 3.3 shows the time series of the two companies' stock prices from 2006 through 2008. While there is some independent movement along the way, most of the difference can best be thought of as wiggles around a common factor. It would

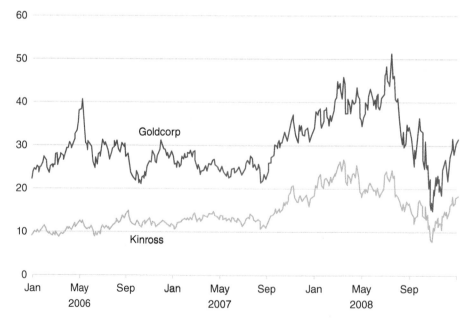

FIGURE 3.3 GoldCorp vs Kinross 2006–2008
Source: Bloomberg

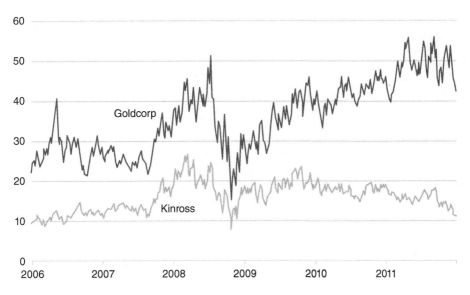

FIGURE 3.4 GG vs KGC 2006–2011
Source: Bloomberg

appear that owning both of these companies would not provide much diversification versus owning just one.

Figure 3.4 extends the time series an additional three years and the story suddenly changes. Both stocks seem to be impacted with the change in the price of gold, but their paths are quite different. Goldcorp follows a general upward trend, while Kinross is flat to slightly downward over the period. Now it appears there is meaningful idiosyncratic risk.

Fundamental stock analysts like Figure 3.4 much more than the shorter time series. They can disagree forever about what it means. Has the market suddenly come to realize the hidden value in Goldcorp? Is Kinross an inferior producer or is it simply underappreciated? The point here is not to decide what points of view are correct on these stocks, but only to show that stock-specific risk can seemingly appear or disappear in the data. There is no definitive answer.

This is not the only challenge. Suppose a researcher discovers that a certain group of stocks in one industry shows a strong negative relationship to another group of stocks in another industry. This is a valuable finding. By owning both groups in a portfolio, temporary ups and downs in the overall market can be reduced compared to owning either group on its own. Now suppose the researcher publishes a paper on the findings and simultaneously offers an analytical service to maximize the efficiency of client portfolios. Money pours into the strategy, buying both groups of stocks.

Over time as more and more people seek to exploit the apparent negative correlation, a perfectly logical thing happens. The flows into and out of (because people sometimes sell stocks too!) both groups of stocks trend together. The once-strong negative correlation turns into a positive one. People acting on it have changed the fundamental factor analysis that pointed to the benefits of owning both groups. As *Exchange-Traded Funds (ETFs)* have become a major feature of the investment landscape, these trades of groups of stocks are more common.

This kind of phenomenon is rarely discussed in academic literature. Worse, it is too often ignored by portfolio managers trying to fine-tune their trading models. Throughout the book we will note examples of market disruptions and horrible investment surprises caused by the belief that markets operate independently of the people trading them.

3.2 THE "FREE LUNCH" OF DIVERSIFICATION

Every investor before Markowitz understood intuitively that diversification had its benefits. Avoiding concentrated bets, which carried with them at least a small chance of a complete loss, was considered prudent on the surface. Portfolio theory provided the chance to move beyond feel and intuition as a guide to how much diversification would be beneficial.

Researchers trying to formalize models of security prices that were assumed in Markowitz's portfolio developed the factor analysis work described in the previous section. Markowitz simply asserted that stocks, or other investments, are risky in different ways, and then showed that portfolios work better than undiversified investments in providing return per unit of risk.

While portfolio theory works for collections containing as many investments as you wish to consider, the key principles can be most easily seen with portfolios containing only two assets. The simplest combination to consider is shown in Figure 3.5, which depicts all the possible combinations between the risk-free asset R and the risky asset A.

It is important for the reader to get comfortable with the framework for this figure. The horizontal axis measures risk and the vertical axis captures return. Asset R is by definition risk-free. Since it has zero risk, it is positioned on the vertical axis at a level equal to R_f, the risk-free rate of return. Asset A is the risky asset. It falls on

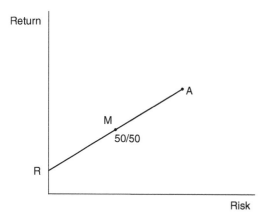

FIGURE 3.5 Portfolios of One Risk-free and One Risky Asset

the chart at a position to the right (higher risk) and above (higher expected return) than R. How much higher risk and expected return Asset A has is not important at this stage of the discussion. The line connecting the two Assets represents all the possible combinations. M is the midpoint of the line and represents a 50/50 mix of the two assets.

This is a simple and special case of a portfolio. If the risk-free rate is 4% and the expected return on Asset A is 10%, it should be obvious that the range of expected returns will fall between 4% and 10% for any portfolio containing any amount of both assets.[5] It will equal the weighted average of the returns of each asset, where the weights are the proportion in each investment. For a 50/50 mix, the expected return is 7%. No matter how many assets are in a portfolio, the portfolio expected return is always the weighted average of the individual expected returns.

Risk is generally different, but in this special case it works similarly. Suppose you started owning Asset A as your only investment. Since Asset R is completely risk free, adding any of it to the mix must dilute the overall risk of the portfolio proportionately. Putting 50 cents in each of Asset A and R has half the risk of putting a dollar into Asset A alone. This boring result depends entirely on the risk-free nature of Asset R. Things get more interesting when the portfolio has two risky assets.

Figure 3.6 shows what happens with two risky assets. Asset B has a higher risk and higher expected return than Asset A. If the two assets are perfectly correlated ($\rho = 1$ in the figure), then their returns must be determined by the same

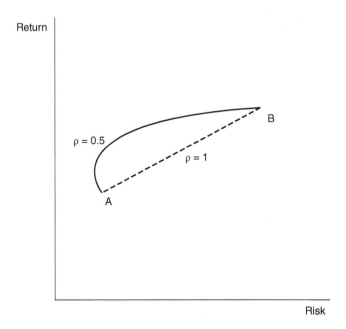

FIGURE 3.6 Portfolios of Two Risky Assets

---

[5]As will be seen later in the chapter, this is not precisely true for a world where one can use leverage in the portfolio. For this first example we are assuming the holdings of each asset fall between 0% and 100% and their sum equals 100%, i.e. no leverage.

fundamental factors.[6] Another way of saying this is that neither investment choice has any idiosyncratic risk relative to the other. This is exactly what you do not want in a portfolio, since it is impossible to diversify away any of this risk. The risk-return profile of any portfolio containing A and B will once again be a weighted average of the individual investments.

Correlation is a measure of how closely two assets move together. As was first shown in Figure 2.2, correlation only pertains to direction, not the size of the move. Think of a parent walking hand in hand with a toddler. The little one may take many more steps to cover the same distance but if the parent's grip is firm, the direction the two take will be identical. The straight dashed line between A and B in Figure 3.6 corresponds to a lock tight grip between the two assets.

Now, suppose the toddler is put on a tether instead of holding hands. The parent and child now will generally move in the same direction but there will be times when they diverge at least slightly. This is a metaphor for positive correlation, though it isn't a perfect correlation. In the figure, the solid line gives the risk-return of all the portfolio combinations from all in Asset A to all in Asset B when the correlation is picked arbitrarily to be 0.5. Because the assets are not completely linked, there will be times when losses in one investment will be offset by gains in the other. This is a net benefit on the risk front. If one wants to visualize no correlation, take the toddler off the tether.

The principles behind the chart may be more evident in a simple numerical example suggested by Tables 3.1 and 3.2. Start with the two risky Assets A and B, each of which can only earn one of three equally likely outcomes in any period you own them.

Asset B looks on average to be just Asset A levered up by two, which it would be if they were perfectly correlated. But this does not have to be the case. We'll see how important correlation is in the tables below.

TABLE 3.1 Simple Outcomes from Two Assets

Outcome	(1)	(2)	(3)
Asset A	−1	1	3
Asset B	−2	2	6

---

[6]Correlation gives a measure of how well two variables are linked directionally and is measured between −1 (perfectly inversely correlated) to +1 (perfectly positively correlated). Variables with no connectivity on average should have a zero correlation. Correlation never implies which variable is causing the other to move. Implying causality is one of the major abuses of correlation statistics in finance.

The first step in the analysis is to know the expected returns and standard deviations for each of the individual asset choices.[7]

TABLE 3.2 Expected Returns and Standard Deviations from Two Assets

	Expected return	Standard deviation
Asset A	1	2
Asset B	2	4

Now consider the most naive portfolio that places 50 cents in each of the two assets. In each period any of the three outcomes can happen, so there are nine possible combinations $(0.5 * a_1 + 0.5 * b_1, 0.5 * a_1 + 0.5 * b_2, \ldots, 0.5 * a_3 + 0.5 * b_3)$.

Table 3.3 shows what each of the nine portfolio payoffs would be for the 50/50 combination of Assets A and B. It then goes further, assuming that the two assets are completely uncorrelated. This implies that the $a_1 b_1$ outcome is as likely as $a_3 b_2$, or any other of the nine cells in the table. Taking the average of all nine cells, since all are equally likely, gives an expected return of 1.5, which is the same result of the averaging of the expected returns for the two assets.

TABLE 3.3 Payoff from a 50/50 Combination of Two Assets Correlation $= 0$

			$\rho = 0$		
			B		
			(b_1)	(b_2)	(b_3)
			-2	2	6
	(a_1)	-1	-1.5	0.5	2.5
A	(a_2)	1	-0.5	1.5	3.5
	(a_3)	3	0.5	2.5	4.5

expected return $= 1.5$
standard deviation $= 1.94$

---

[7]The expected return of a portfolio is the weighted average of the possible outcomes for all the assets where the weights are the probabilities of the outcomes. The formula is $E(R) = \sum_{i=1}^{N}(R_i \cdot P_{Ri})$, where R_i are the outcomes and PR_i are the probabilities associated with them. Standard deviation measures how much these outcomes deviate from the expected return. It is given by $\sqrt{(1/N)\sum_{i=1}^{N}(R_i - E(R))^2}$. Note that because the formula squares the variation above or below the expected value, positive or negation differences contribute equally to standard deviation.

The standard deviation of the 50/50 portfolio is 1.94. This is meaningfully below 3, the simple average of the two standard deviations. When A is gets a bad outcome, B is at its middle or best result which helps balance out some of the extremes when both A and B are up or down together.

The matrix can also be useful to show the impact of correlation. At one extreme there is perfect positive correlation. That is, whenever A is having its best result, B is also on the top of its game. It is also true that the middle outcomes and the worst outcome also *always* come together.

TABLE 3.4   Payoff from a 50/50 Combination of Two Assets Correlation = 1

			$\rho = 1$		
			B		
			(b_1)	(b_2)	(b_3)
			−2	2	6
	(a_1)	−1	**−1.5**	0.5	2.5
A	(a_2)	1	−0.5	**1.5**	3.5
	(a_3)	3	0.5	2.5	**4.5**
			expected return = 1.5		
			standard deviation = 3.0		

In this case only the cells in bold can happen, and each is equally likely. The other cells from the previous example by definition cannot happen and have a probability of zero. The expected return is still 1.5, but now the standard deviation has gone up to 3, which is the 50/50 weighted average of the two choices. There are no gains from diversification. This is a point along the dashed line in Figure 3.6.

Now consider the opposite case, where the best outcomes in A *always* appear with the worst results in B, and vice versa. This would be a correlation of −1 is in Table 3.5.

TABLE 3.5   Payoff from a 50/50 Combination of Two Assets Correlation = −1

			TWO ASSET PAYOFFS		
			$\rho = -1$		
			B		
			(b_1)	(b_2)	(b_3)
			−2	2	6
	(a_1)	−1	−1.5	0.5	**2.5**
A	(a_2)	1	−0.5	**1.5**	3.5
	(a_3)	3	**0.5**	2.5	4.5
			expected return = 1.5		
			standard deviation = 1.0		

Here again, the example is rigged so that only the diagonal elements in bold can occur. Every other cell has a zero probability. The expected return is still 1.5, but now the standard deviation has dropped to 1.0. In this example it is impossible to have a losing outcome in the portfolio even though each asset taken independently has a 1/3 chance of posting a loss. This is the "free lunch" of diversification!

This example can be driven even harder. Suppose instead of a 50/50 allocation between the perfectly negatively correlated Assets A and B, we put 2/3 in A and 1/3 in B. Table 3.6 shows what those payoffs would look like.

TABLE 3.6   Payoff from a 66.6/33.3 Combination of Two Assets Correlation $= -1$

			$\rho = -1$		
			B		
			(b1)	(b2)	(b3)
			-2	2	6
	(a1)	-1	-1.33	0	**1.33**
A	(a2)	1	0	**1.33**	2.67
	(a3)	3	**1.33**	2.67	4
			expected return $= 1.33$		
			standard deviation $= \mathbf{0}$		

With the correlation of -1, once again the best outcomes of A must match the worst of B, etc., leading to the bold cells above as the only possible portfolio outcomes. The expected return has fallen a bit to 1.33, which should be expected as we have put more weight in the less risky asset. But the standard deviation has fallen completely to zero! No matter what random state of the world occurs, our portfolio will make the expected return of 1.33.

This is powerful stuff, and explains investors' desire to find negatively correlated assets. It leaves open the question, however, "Is the zero variance portfolio better than the 50/50 portfolio?"

For some investors the answer would be an unambiguous "yes." But what about the investors for whom the 1.33 assured return falls short of their goal. A pension plan that is obliged to pay out 1.4 every period might hope for the idea of zero risk, but that portfolio is a recipe for certain failure measured against their needs.

The correct answer is that there is no single "right" portfolio that you can discern from this analysis. Each of the portfolio combinations is efficient in that you can't get any higher expected return without adding risk, but it is up to each investor to come up with how much risk they are willing to assume for each target return.

Figure 3.7 shows what the various portfolios comprised of two assets look like, depending on the correlation between them. With a small positive correlation there is some diversification benefit, which increases as the correlation drops. As shown in Figure 3.7, there is real power if the correlation is negative. In the extreme case, it is possible to create a riskless portfolio with the right combination of risky assets if those investments are perfectly negatively correlated.

The biggest challenge that most people struggle with intuitively is to start thinking of the risk of an asset only in terms of how that asset affects the portfolio. Stand-alone risk does not matter. To see how hard a concept this is, start with the zero risk portfolio. You have $2 invested in the low-risk Asset A for every $1 in high-risk Asset B. If you take $1 away from the riskier Asset B and place it in A, *total portfolio risk increases!* As you continuously take money from B and add to A, portfolio risk will continue to grow until you reach point A. (100% allocated to Asset A) in Figure 3.7.

This happens is that whatever absolute risk reduction comes from the extra allocation to the lower risk asset is not enough to offset the lost diversification benefits from eliminating some of the negatively correlated Asset B. It should also be clear from Figure 3.7 that any increase in Asset A above the level that produces the risk-free portfolio not only increases risk but also lowers expected return. These outcomes are obviously inferior to other portfolio combinations available and will be avoided by the rational investor.

The two-asset portfolio case demonstrates most of the key elements of Markowitz portfolio theory, but it is useful to push a little further. Real world portfolios contain many assets, and building a strong multi-asset intuition is both important and challenging. Figure 3.8 starts with the same two-asset risk-return surface that we have developed to this point. Asset A and Asset B are not perfectly correlated either positively or negatively, so there is some diversification benefit, but risk cannot be eliminated. Point C in the chart is the minimum risk portfolio.

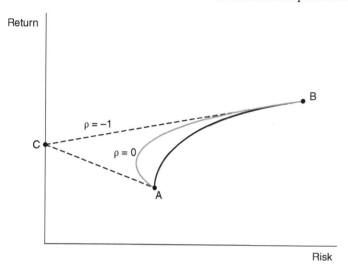

FIGURE 3.7   The Impact of Correlation on the Two-asset Portfolios

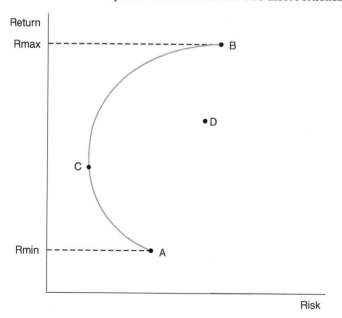

FIGURE 3.8   Adding a Third Asset to the Two-Asset Portfolio

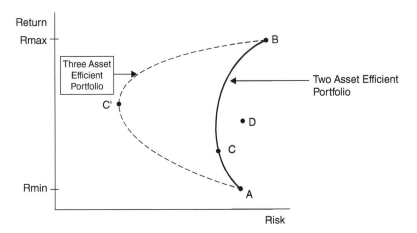

FIGURE 3.9 The Three-Asset Efficient Portfolio

Introduce a third asset, called D. Individually it falls between A and B on the risk spectrum. Assume it is not perfectly correlated with either of the other assets. From its position in Figure 3.8 versus the two-asset efficient frontier, it would appear that it is inferior to any of the portfolios made up of A and B.

This is where most people's intuition starts to fail. Just because Asset D falls below the efficient portfolio frontier made up of A and B does not mean it cannot make a contribution. It all depends on the correlation of Asset D with the two assets already in the mix. The only thing that is obvious is that nobody should put all of their assets into D, since they can get the same expected return at a much lower risk level, or a higher expected return at the same risk.

Figure 3.9 shows how the addition of some amount of D can lower the risk for every portfolio expected return. The minimum variance portfolio moves from C to C'. It is not possible to tell what the proportions of the three assets A, B, and D are from the chart. Because Asset D had an expected return between those of A and B, the range of expected returns does not change. The worst expected return is still from a portfolio that is 100% invested in A, while the highest expected return is from a portfolio that is 100% in B. No amount of D mixed into an unleveraged portfolio can change those limits.

To actually get the recipe at any point along the frontier between C' and B requires getting into the algebra behind the chart, and is not an important exercise for this discussion. All that is important to remember is that because Asset D is not perfectly correlated with either Asset A or Asset B some investment in this third asset will lower the risk for every level of expected return.

Of course the world is not limited to three assets. There is no bound conceptually to how many assets can be added to the portfolio model. In the early days of this research, the biggest constraint to looking for a solution was on computational capacity. Every time an asset was added to the mix, not only would a new expected return and standard deviation have to be estimated, but there would also be additional correlations between the new asset and every other asset. For a 20-asset portfolio, this translates into 190 unique correlations. For a 200-asset portfolio, the number soars to 19,900![8]

---

[8]The covariance between A and B is the same as the covariance between B and A, so order does not matter. If there are n assets, there are (n)(n−1)/2 distinct pairs of the assets for which covariances need to be estimated.

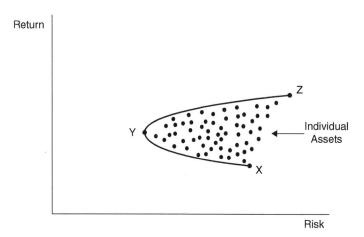

FIGURE 3.10 The Multi-asset Efficient Portfolio Frontier

But today, with high-speed computers, the calculations can be made and when they are the picture looks like Figure 3.10. In this picture, point X is the minimum return portfolio (consisting of 100% of the minimum return asset) and point Z marks the highest expected return achievable without leverage (owning 100% of the highest return asset). Point Y represents the lowest-risk portfolio mix and the span between Y and Z is the *efficient frontier*.

Having confidence that all of the inputs to the calculation are accurately estimated is almost certainly a bigger challenge than actually doing all the math required to find a solution to the efficient frontier. Today's impressive computer firepower allows even the largest portfolios to be analyzed. That does not mean, however, that the results are enlightening or dependable. Chapter 4.4 discusses in some detail the practical problems of this approach.

Even if we have some confidence in the estimation of the portfolio frontier, that information does not tell us where we are likely to be among all the possible portfolios. For that we need the concept of the *capital market line*.

We start with the concept from Figure 3.11 that when we combine one risk-free and one risky asset, all of the combinations create a straight-line trade-off between return and risk. Assuming we always can put some assets to work to earn the risk-free return, we can augment the last chart by drawing a line from the risk-free return to the highest point of tangency on the frontier. We mark this point O to designate the optimal risky portfolio.

R_f represents 100% invested in the risk-free rate and O is 100% in the optimal risky portfolio. All of the points along the line between R_f and O are available to the investor by adjusting the shares in the two choices. Note that Y is no longer the minimum risk portfolio. By having some money invested in R_f and some in O, Y' can be achieved, which gives the same expected return as Y, but at a lower risk.

If the investor can borrow at the risk-free rate, the gray line in Figure 3.11 extends beyond point O. This is the basic concept of leverage. The investor borrows at R_f and then uses the proceeds to buy more of the optimal portfolio. As long as borrowing is allowed, the gray line in its entirety represents the effective opportunity set for investors.

Where any particular investor will end up on the gray line depends on what their target return is and how tolerant they are with risk. The economic modeling behind

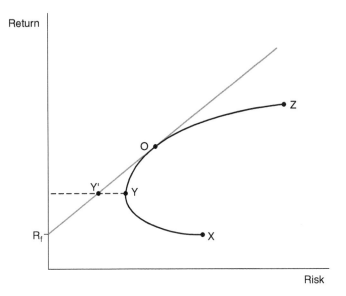

FIGURE 3.11 The Capital Market Line

this decision relies on *utility theory*, which has, perhaps, even less empirical grounding than the exercise of finding the efficient investment frontier. All that is important for this discussion is that risk-averse investors typically won't want leverage and therefore will find themselves someplace between R_f and O.

This single concept that an optimal portfolio exists and can be identified is the foundation for much of the *model portfolio* work expounded by many brokers and consultants today. These firms build what they argue is the best portfolio available and then tell clients to simply dial up and down the capital markets line depending on how much risk they want to take.

The arrogance behind this approach is profound. Not only is there great confidence that the optimal portfolio, O, can be identified, there is the often unstated assumption that the only relevant investment choices are marketable securities. It disregards other assets the investor may already have, as neither non-marketable assets nor human capital are parts of the theory.

Brokers and consultants often hide behind the theory in order to solve two of their problems. First, it is quite complicated to build up appropriate portfolios that take into account the unique characteristics of each investor's permanent endowment and risk tolerances. Rather than adjust the target portfolio for things like personal real estate, tax rates, and the type and quantity of education, it is easier to assume those particular features away and assert there is a single best portfolio.

The second problem that is avoided by the optimal portfolio approach is one of compliance. No broker or investor can be accused of treating one client preferentially over another if everyone gets the same advice. While this is a safe outcome for the firm giving the advice, it is not one that should give the investor confidence that they are getting the right answer for them.

Figure 3.12 gives our first introduction to one of the most popular metrics in investments, the Sharpe Ratio. Bill Sharpe knew that if an investment earned, say, 12% over a period it might appear after the fact to have been a good idea. Looking in

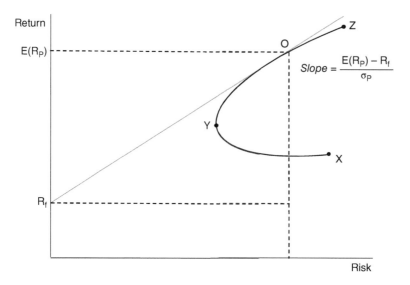

FIGURE 3.12 The Geometry of the Sharpe Ratio

a rear view mirror, however, is not the way to evaluate a portfolio investment. Sharpe emphasized the importance of looking at return per unit of risk, rather than on return alone. He knew that if the 12% return was earned in a manner that could be expected to be highly risky, it should not automatically be considered a good investment.

The slope of the capital market line in Figure 3.12 is the difference between the expected return on the optimal portfolio and the risk-free rate divided by the standard deviation of the optimal portfolio. This is the "excess" return per unit of risk, which is the way different investment returns should be compared.

The tangent to the portfolio frontier at point O is the steepest capital market line possible. If the risk portfolio chosen is closer to either point Y or point Z, the capital market line has a lower slope, which is the same as saying it has a lower Sharpe Ratio. This is why managers selling their products focus so much on high Sharpe Ratios when they appear over a reasonable marking period. It gives the impression that their investment vehicle is close to the efficient frontier.

Investors face the same kind of statistical problems with estimated Sharpe Ratios that they do with estimated optimal portfolios. These are also discussed in detail in Chapter 5, but the key message is there is great uncertainty around each of these statistics. In the final analysis it is hard to tell the difference across managers with any kind of confidence using this or any other similar measure.

The bigger problem is that the objective is always to build a portfolio, and not a simple collection of investments. A single investment that has a high Sharpe Ratio may not be all that useful in a portfolio if it is highly correlated with many other investments. Everyone pitching the case for any investment idea will focus on his or her most attractive statistical characteristics. It is up to the investor to do the evaluation in a portfolio context.

Finally, consider the impact of a declining risk-free rate of return. Figure 3.13 shows that as the risk-free rate falls from R_{f1} to R_{f2} the optimal portfolio shifts toward the minimum risk portfolio. Since the point of tangency is to the left and lower than

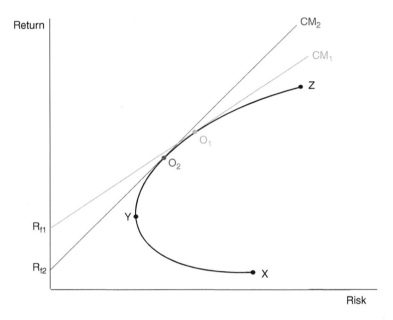

FIGURE 3.13   The Impact of a Lower Risk-Free Rate

the original optimal portfolio, there are no unlevered portfolios on the capital markets line that are as attractive as the original outcome before the risk-free rate fell.

Immediately after the credit and market crisis of 2008, the US Federal Reserve embarked upon a policy of near-zero interest rates to support the banking sector and the economy. This was quickly followed by the central banks in Europe and Japan. If you believe that the fundamental investment opportunity set did not change materially because of this policy, what is depicted in Figure 3.13 is what investors faced. With every possible unleveraged portfolio, the expected return fell with the capital markets line.

If your investment return objectives were not met with the new opportunity set, the only choice would be to add leverage. The good news here is that at low interest rates, that added leverage is cheap. The capital market line is steeper, indicating that as the risk-free rate goes down, the Sharpe ratio increases. Investors willing to take on leverage are actually made better off by the policy, assuming everything other than the risk-free rate has stayed the same.

That is a big assumption. We have seen that most investments are thought of as having an expected return equal to the risk-free rate plus a risk premium. If the risk premium does not change when the Fed changes policies, then the expected returns across a wide range of assets will fall. As this happens, the efficient frontier will simply shift down as well. Unfortunately we cannot magically increase Sharpe Ratios by having the Fed cut interest rates. The most likely impact of a cut in the risk-free rate is a comparable drop in all portfolio expected returns.

The challenges do not end there. Belief in the darker gray line in Figure 3.13 has probably caused more market disruptions than any other part of modern portfolio theory. Portfolio managers, particularly in the hedge fund space, discover trades that they believe have extraordinarily high Sharpe Ratios. Unfortunately these trades usually also have tiny expected absolute returns. The solution is to apply leverage and move smartly up the darker gray line to returns that are well above that available to the unlevered portfolio.

This kind of behavior was behind the portfolios of the Granite Fund (dissolved 1994), Long Term Capital Management (dissolved 1998), Amaranth (dissolved 2006) and billions in credit and convertible arbitrage funds that all failed in 2008. There was a common denominator in every instance. Each put on trades that would be completely unattractive without leverage. However, the portfolio managers in each case convinced themselves that they could apply, sometimes considerable amounts of leverage, exploit the high Sharpe Ratio, and reap outsized returns.

If one trader follows such a path with a small amount of capital, it might possibly work. But when multiple traders all follow the same model, applying billions of dollars of capital to the trade, it translates into a high probability of tail risk and perhaps even systemic failure. Manager risk models to date have been exceedingly weak in identifying whether a trade is crowded or not, and whether expectations formed from traveling out on the darker gray line will come suddenly apart. It is your job as an investor to look past the model, to be skeptical, and to keep your capital out of harm's way from behavior by the herd.

3.3   YOU SHOULD "OWN THE MARKET"

The concept of the efficient frontier of portfolios developed by Markowitz naturally led to the question, "What does the optimum portfolio look like?" While it was possible to try to identify it analytically by looking at the statistics behind thousands of potential investments, the greater challenge lay in finding the theoretically right answer.

Bill Sharpe demonstrated with CAPM that the optimal portfolio in equilibrium was the *market portfolio*.[9] That is, the most risk efficient portfolio consists of all assets available to investors in proportion to their capitalization. Everyone should "own the market."

This is so far from most people's intuition that a few words should be devoted to what Sharpe did and did not say. Most importantly, he was speaking of the risky part of the portfolio. He did not say that everyone had the same risk tolerance. People who are extremely risk averse will meet their concerns by combining more of the riskless asset with the risky market portfolio. That still, however, leaves the question as to how the market is everyone's best risk portfolio.

This result falls out directly from the model's assumptions, which include:

- Every investor thinks in Markowitz *mean-variance* terms.
- All investors have the same investment horizon.
- All investors have the same information about expected returns and correlations.
- Markets are frictionless – you can hold any asset without transaction costs.

---

[9]Sharpe, W.F. (1964). Capital Asset Prices. *Journal of Finance.* Fama, E.F. (1970). Efficient Capital Markets: A Review of Theory and Empirical Work. *Journal of Finance* (May), pp. 383–417.

Because all risky assets have to be held by *somebody*, and *everybody* is making decisions the same way with the same information, it follows directly that everyone will own the market as their risky portfolio.

Given the unrealistic nature of the assumptions, it is tempting to immediately throw out the main conclusion, but this would be a mistake. The power of the CAPM comes not from the accuracy of the assumptions but from the predictions of the model. On that score it has largely stood the test of time.

The key word in this discussion is "largely." As we have seen, the single factor model has been replaced by a multi-factor approach, and the factors have been actively refined as investigators and investors seek more predictive power. These refinements have not, however, kept some in the investment community from continuing to promote the most extreme conclusions of Sharpe for their own benefit. To be appropriately thoughtful about your own portfolio construction, you need to be alert to where the theory can break down.

Shortly after Sharpe's seminal paper, the index mutual fund industry appeared on the scene. At first these funds were too radical for most investors accustomed to active managers building portfolios stock by stock. But the index fund creators relied on Sharpe and the theoretical superiority of owning the market to promote their cause. They were greatly aided in this effort by the generally mediocre performance and high fees of much of the active fund management industry. Beating most of the managers much of the time gave added credence to indexers and the theory.

Almost immediately nagging questions appeared. While it may be desirable to own the market, is it practical? Isn't everything tradable at one time or another? Just because something is not listed on an exchange, does that mean it should not be in the market basket portfolio? Compromises to the theory came quickly in practice.

Funds based on the S&P 500 were the early leaders in reflecting the U.S. stock market. Even though that index fails to include small and mid-cap stocks, its breadth combined with low-cost execution made it a good proxy candidate. Today S&P 500 Index funds continue to hold a dominant position among US index funds, though the field has gotten considerably more populated over time.

Chapter 5.2 discusses the challenges to indexing in greater detail. For now, it is most important to remember that "owning the market" should be interpreted as endorsing the concept of owning a widely diversified group of risk assets within the practical limits of executing such a strategy. Deviating from this base case depends on your ability to identify risk-reward opportunities in the market that others have missed. This leads directly to the question, "Are markets efficient?"

3.4 THE EFFICIENT MARKET IN ITS MANY FORMS: RATIONAL EXPECTATIONS

A University of Chicago economist and a friend were engaged in an animated conversation as they walked toward campus. A bit ahead of them was a $50 bill on the sidewalk. The economist did not break stride or pause in the conversation as they passed by. When the friend finally interrupted and asked why they had not stopped to pick up the money, the economist replied that it could not have possibly been there. If there had been $50 on the sidewalk, someone would have picked it up already.

This apocryphal story is sometimes used by people to deride the efficient markets hypothesis, which has received some of its most articulate support from the economics and business school faculties at the University of Chicago. There is quite a bit more to the theory than the story indicates, though too many people seem to base their entire understanding of the topic on this joke. The theory helps us understand how market prices evolve through time, and whether some trading systems can be exploited by investors.

Across the academic community, many economists have made significant contributions to the debate. But it is perhaps the Nobel Prize–winning Chicago economist Eugene Fama who crystallized the discussion in his 1970 survey article.[10] Fama laid out the various forms of market efficiency that could be present, and then evaluated the considerable empirical work that was being amassed to either prove or disprove that markets were efficient.

The topic is of interest to economists primarily because if markets are efficient, prices will reflect all relevant information concerning supply and demand. This in turn allows consumption and resource allocation decisions to be made without waste. If prices are inefficient by being too low, consumers will overindulge relative to what is best for society. Similarly, if they are too high, entrepreneurs will wastefully devote new resources to increase the supply of the product. Efficient markets produce "just right" prices and asset allocations.

Investors probably couldn't care less about the ideal of economic efficiency. They want to know if they can make money by allocating their capital in one place versus another. The efficient markets hypothesis is problematic for investors. The more efficient a market is, the harder it is for any investor to establish an edge over other investors. Since investors have been around forever, and did not become extinct when the efficient markets hypothesis was developed and generally defended, the truth probably lies between the extremes of "markets are always inefficient and exploitable" and "that $50 bill did not exist."

There are three forms of market efficiency typically discussed:

- Strong-form efficiency
- Semi strong-form efficiency
- Weak-form efficiency

As the labels suggest, there are a range of compromises included in the theory in an attempt to accommodate the realities of the marketplace. The ultimate question about efficiency always involves whether market prices fully reflect all the relevant information. These terms are most often applied to stock market prices, though they apply to any traded market. For the purposes of this discussion, however, the examples will come from the stock market where the reader likely has a good background and intuition.

Fama noted three conditions that if met would be sufficient to produce capital market efficiency:

1. There are no transaction costs in trading securities (i.e. bending down to pick up the money is effortless).

---

[10]Fama, E.F. (1970). Efficient Capital Markets: A Review of Theory and Empirical Work. *Journal of Finance* (May), pp. 383–417.

2. All relevant information is freely available to all market participants (everyone sees the $50 at the same time).

3. Everyone agrees on what that information means ("Pick up the money!").

Once again we have a theoretical world that stands in pretty stark contrast to what we know exists in the real world. But Fama and the other academics in the debate clearly acknowledge that while these three factors would be sufficient, they are not necessary for markets to generally behave as if they were efficient. Sooner or later (probably sooner), the $50 gets picked up.[11]

Strong-form efficiency in stock prices implies that today's price fully reflects *all* of the relevant fundamental information about the company. Note that the adjective "public" was not placed before the noun "information" in the previous sentence above. The strong-form version of efficient markets sets a high bar. All relevant information, whether it is public or closely held by company insiders, needs to be reflected in the stock price.

Some would say that insider-trading laws were created to keep markets from ever being strong-form efficient. If nobody cared about fairness between public investors and insiders, then there would be no reason to have such laws, and whenever a company's fortunes changed, an insider would likely jump to buy or sell shares and the stock price would adjust. Depending on what country you trade in today, insider-trading rules are more or less present and enforced.

Semi-strong-form efficiency says that today's stock price fully reflects all of the publicly available information. This includes the past history of prices as well as fundamental data like sales, profit margins, and balance sheets for not only the firm in question but also all its competitors. When one considers the amount of effort that thousands of fundamental stock market analysts devote to the practice of collecting information and then running models on it, it is probably safe to conclude that semi strong-form efficiency, if it exists, is the result of a lot of effort.

Weak-form efficiency is perhaps the most relevant concept to the average investor. Markets are weak-form efficient if there is no information in the past history of prices that can be used to predict future prices. On the surface, this would seem to rule out profits from chart following, moving average models, or statistical arbitrage. But there have been active traders using all of these tools for years. How can this reality be reconciled with any notion of weak-form efficiency?

Fama's 1970 summary of the empirical studies generally supported the notion that markets could be considered largely efficient on a weak-form and semi-strong-form basis. Researchers in the next 40 years would uncover what appeared to be violations of efficiency, but finding such cases that persisted was indeed rare. This makes sense in that if an anomaly or trading pattern can be identified, the act of exploiting it will eventually reverse the pattern.

The biggest assault on market efficiency came from Fama working with Ken French. In their famous 1992 paper, they identified what they believed were

---

[11]Another famous Chicagoan, but not an economist, Studs Terkel, periodically threw a pocketful of change on the sidewalk to let others find and pick up. He knew the expense to him was slight, and he imagined the value of the pleasant surprise to those finding the change would be greater. Terkel implicitly counted on the efficient markets hypothesis to work.

important violations of CAPM.[12] Specifically, they identified company size and price-to-book as two variables that strongly influenced stock returns. Once these two variables were controlled for, calculated stock betas no longer correlated positively with return. Fama-French created a cottage industry of academics trying to confirm or deny the major implications.

As interesting as the past 20 years academic effort is to the finance community, it is a bit harder to swallow for the average investor. Most of the debate has centered on the quality of the data and the tests, which, of course, change from period to period. There are some true believers in Fama-French among the fund community. They have created quantitatively oriented funds that pick stocks using screens across non-CAPM factors. The fact that these managers sometimes outperform their benchmarks is not proof of the model. Random results could produce similar records.

Fama-French-oriented managers and their intellectual cousins have not routinely beaten either pure passive or fundamentally active models. Even if Fama-French is right, this could be expected. If small-cap or low book-to-value stocks were always expected to earn an outsized return *independent of their beta,* money would flow into those areas eliminating the edge. The challenging part to investors being sold trading programs is that there is always enough noise around investment returns that periodically the results will be strong and the story will sound quite persuasive. A few thousand students graduate with their master of business administration (MBA) each year from business schools around the world. Almost all of them have read Fama-French and some of them understand it. The chance that a handful of them have found the uniquely profitable factor combination that always beats the market is remote indeed.

In general, empirical research on real markets suggests that traders operate in generally efficient markets and the process by which they form expectations is rational. Some behaviorists have challenged this notion of rational expectations, but extraordinary trading results based on the idea that markets are not rational have also been hard to find.

The competitive pressures of investing make quantitative-based investment trading particularly fragile. Models may produce profits for a while and then suddenly stop working. It should not be surprising when someone thinks they have a good recipe, others have found it too. In a good way, their collective action nudges out any inefficiency they market might have discovered. In the extreme, if enough traders pile onto the bandwagon, they might distort the market, eventually creating exploitable opportunities from the other side. This latter pattern is of interest to behavioral finance experts, and is discussed later in this chapter.

The efficient markets hypothesis may not work perfectly in every environment, but it is a far smarter bet to assume that markets are largely efficient rather than that there are systematic inefficiencies ripe for exploitation. Put another way, there may be an occasional $50 bill on the sidewalk to be picked up, but it is probably a poor strategy to spend all day strolling the sidewalks looking for it.

---

[12]Fama, E.F. and French, K.R. (1992). The Cross Section of Expected Stock Returns. *Journal of Finance* 47, pp. 427–66.

3.5   THE MODIGLIANI-MILLER PROPOSITIONS

Franco Modigliani and Merton Miller turned the world of corporate finance on its head with a series of articles that shaped their famous proposition that the value of a company was independent of whether the firm was financed with debt or stock issuance.[13] Generations of finance students and corporate executives who had labored trying to decide whether it was better for their companies to issue new debt or equity were suddenly told it did not matter. This was radical stuff.

The major implication of the M&M propositions, as they have been called for years, is that a firm cannot change its total value by altering its capital structure. Issuing debt to buy back stock, or issuing stock to retire debt cannot increase the value of the firm. That value is solely determined by the expected future profitability of the business. The market, in equilibrium, will ensure that the financing options available to the firm are priced in such a way to keep that profit stream the same.

If M&M is literally true, investors should not penalize companies that pile on debt versus maintaining a more conservative balance sheet. Given the periodic credit binges that have happened in the United States since the 1980s, which have been universally followed by a big upswing in bankruptcies, it seems hard to accept the notion that the amount of debt on a company's balance sheet does not matter.

The M&M propositions are like all of the theories discussed in this chapter. They are built upon a number of assumptions that have to be questioned. Two that stand out are that the credit markets are always available if refinancing is needed, and that management only borrows to make wealth-increasing investments.

There were many credit-worthy enterprises in the second half of 2008 that saw their access to reasonable credit cutoff as the markets seized up. Companies with inadequate cash on the balance sheets and maturing debt had three unattractive options: 1) refinance at historically wide credit spreads; 2) issue new, very expensive equity in an unreceptive market; or 3) default. It is not surprising that in such an uncertain environment, the stock prices of these companies tumbled precipitously.

It is also perhaps not a coincidence that the companies that borrowed most lavishly in the years leading up to the crisis were also among the most vulnerable when trouble hit. One of the biggest problems with easy credit is that it tempts some managements to borrow simply because it is cheap and to spend the money on projects of questionable worth. Not all executives are created equal in terms of their vision or their ability to execute. Cheap credit encourages both the worthy and the unworthy.

Given that there are unreliable cycles in credit and management skills vary, some investors shy away from firms that have significant debt on their balance sheets even if they seem to have little difficulty acquiring financing at the moment. These companies may look as attractive as any other on an M&M basis, but they have little margin for error should in the credit markets stumble. One need not reject M&M at a theoretical level to prefer the risk profile of low-debt companies over highly leveraged ones.

---

[13]Miller, M. and Modigliani, F. (1961). Dividend Policy, Growth and the Value of Shares. *Journal of Business*. (October). Modigliani, F. and Miller, M. (1958). The Cost of Capital, Corporation Finance, and the Theory of Investment. *American Economic Review*. (June).

Another troublesome assumption M&M is that taxes do not matter. In the United States, corporate interest paid on debt is currently fully deductible, whereas dividends are not. This suggests that if companies are distributing income through dividend paying stock, they could enhance their value by using that income to pay interest on new debt used to buy back that stock. M&M can be reasonably modified for these kinds of differences in tax treatment. When the model is adjusted for differences in taxes, the prices of stocks and bonds adjust to the point where there is no longer an advantage of shifting toward debt.

Perhaps the most significant contribution of M&M to the investment side of finance came from their use of "no arbitrage" conditions to prove their basic proposition. This was a radical innovation in the way people thought about securities. Simply put, M&M noted that if there was an advantage to financing with bonds over stocks, or vice versa, a profitable risk-free arbitrage would be created.

This simple technique opened the doors to the analysis of all kinds of securities. It formed the backbone for the Black-Scholes option pricing model and a whole host of applications that followed. More importantly, it gave structure to the trading activity known as arbitrage. Dealers who made markets intuitively or on the basis of rules of thumb, lost out to traders armed with the no-arbitrage analytical framework. Modern finance radically and permanently changed the way markets work.

3.6   ARBITRAGE PRICING THEORY

Pricing securities so that there are no arbitrage opportunities is a completely basic concept. At the simplest level it cannot be called a theory in the same way as CAPM or M&M. But it has been enhanced to account for multiple risk factors and has become such a dominant practice in the way securities are analyzed, that it must be considered one of the dominant pillars of modern portfolio theory.

The basic idea of arbitrage is best demonstrated with an example. Suppose the spot exchange rate between the US dollar (USD) and the Brazilian real (BRL) is 3.0 real to each dollar. In addition to spot transactions in foreign exchange, there are also many reasons why importers, exporters, and traders are interested in forward exchange rates. Assume the market thinks the real is fairly valued relative to the dollar, and the one-year forward rate is also 3.0.

If spot and forward foreign exchange were all that people traded, the rates would be determined by what the market expected. But there are other relevant markets, and this is where the no-arbitrage rule comes in.

Let the risk-free dollar interest rate for one year be 0% and the same term rate in Brazil be 10%. We can see this kind of disparity because of different macroeconomic conditions. The United States could be in a high unemployment, low inflation environment where the Federal Reserve wants to promote recovery. Brazil could be fearful of accelerating inflation, so their central bank could try to set rates high in an attempt to get in front of the problem.

At first blush, there may be no obvious connection between macroeconomic policies and spot and forward exchange rates, but the arbitrageur sees the matter differently. They say, why not borrow $1 million today at 0% interest, convert to 3.0 million Brazilian real, and then immediately put those real to work at 10%? These will grow to 3.3 million BRL, which the spot rate says should be worth $1.1 million in a year. This sounds good on the surface, but there is still risk. What happens if the forward rate was wrong and the Brazilian real tumbles against the dollar over the year, so that the net proceeds are less than $1 million? One more step eliminates this risk.

After investing the converted BRL, the arbitrageur sells the 3.3 million BRL forward at the 3.0 rate and locks in $1.1 million. This is a classic currency hedge, and in this example it is also a money machine. If one can do such a trade with a million dollars, why not trade with $1 billion or 10 billion? The no-arbitrage conditions of asset pricing say something is amiss in the example.

What is wrong is the relationship between the spot and forward currency rates. If arbitrageurs saw the original prices and started buying BRL in the spot market and selling it forward the two values would diverge no matter what the world thought of the prospects for trade and inflation in Brazil and the United States. The difference between the spot and forward rates would have to reflect the interest rate differentials between the two countries so that no arbitrage opportunities remained.

To keep the arithmetic simple, let the spot exchange rate stay at 3.0. This means that the forward rate would have to be 3.3 BRL to the dollar. The trader attempting to do the previous three-legged transaction (borrow dollars, convert to spot BRL, hedge the currency risk) would find that the projected quantity of dollars would equal exactly the $1 million they started with and what they would earn investing dollars at home. There would be no gain from arbitrage.

Notice how the no-arbitrage constraints can lead to some counterintuitive market outcomes. In the example, the United States is struggling with its economy, while Brazil is growing with inflation. One might think the forward rate for BRL should predict a strengthening currency, but instead it seems to imply the market expects a 10% devaluation. This is just the first of many examples we shall see where the no-arbitrage rule dominates any fundamental assessment of security values.

You may complain that the example is unrealistic because nobody but the US government gets to borrow at the risk-free rate, so the transaction cannot take place. In truth, if one has good enough collateral, almost anyone can borrow very near the risk-free rate. Even if there is a small credit risk premium charged there is a pretty good arbitrage available in the first example. The equilibrium spot-forward rate relationship will ultimately reflect the relevant interest rate differential and not a market forecast of how the forward rate will evolve.

The example is about as straightforward as you can find. Could the basic arbitrage principles be applied to more complicated investment programs? Stephen Ross developed *Arbitrage Pricing Theory* (APT) for portfolios of equities as an alternative to CAPM.[14] Ross suggested that an asset's expected return was based on a variety of risk factors compared with CAPM that relied on market risk alone. While Ross did not specify what these risk factors were, he demonstrated that you could theoretically construct a package of assets that behaved the same as another target asset. If the price of the package and the target asset were not the same, an arbitrage opportunity would be available to exploit.

Ross's work opened the door to portfolio managers studying collections of assets to look for common risk elements, and then buying those that appeared to be priced too cheaply and selling short the overpriced set. This was the intellectual foundation

---

[14]Ross, S.A. (1976). The Arbitrage Theory of Capital Asset Pricing. *Journal of Economic Theory* (December), pp. 343–362.

for much of the market neutral equity hedge fund industry. The BARRA risk factors discussed earlier are an example of the kind of tool set used to set up such trading programs.

Here again the assumptions matter. The APT approach assumes that any asset can be bought or sold short with no transaction costs. It also assumes that the risk factors can be identified and relied on to be predictive. These are both questionable in the real world.

Transaction costs and impediments to selling short drive most would-be arbitrageurs crazy. Just when you think you have discovered a trade that provides a great arbitrage return, you discover that you either can't do the trade at all because of some limitation on shorting, or that the transaction's costs eat up any target profit.

These two *trading frictions* that exist in the real world should not cause anyone to reject APT completely. Instead, you should understand that APT keeps prices aligned to within the bands defined by the trading costs. This is an important distinction. Suppose it costs $2 per ounce to ship gold between New York and London, fully insured. This is an obvious cost to arbitrage. If you saw the price in New York at $1,500/oz. and at $1,501/oz. in London, you would see New York as a better place to buy, but there would be no arbitrage possibility to force the two prices together. If the prices were $1,499 and $1,502, however, it would pay to buy gold in New York, physically ship it to London, and sell it at a guaranteed $1 profit.

The same principle applies to collections of stocks or other assets. Even if one has complete confidence in the risk factor analysis that makes two assets equivalent, the transaction costs involved in arbitrage will allow their prices to vary somewhat independently as long as they stay within the boundaries of the trading costs. Market participants watch these *arbitrage bands* carefully. If the two asset prices fall outside the arbitrage bands then a profitable arbitrage opportunity exists.

Many trading strategies being marketed to investors are referred to as arbitrage but very actually are. The strict definition of arbitrage includes only trades like buying gold in New York and selling it in London at a price difference greater than the cost of transportation. This kind of activity can force the prices of the two markets to come together, or at least get close enough so that no further arbitrage is profitable.

If I buy gold in New York at $1,500 and then take a short position in London at $1,501, I may try to label this arbitrage, but it is in fact just *spread trading*. I can take comfort that the prices should not move too much farther apart, but there is nothing I am doing that can force the prices together unless my trading is very large. In that case everything is fine until I go to buy the gold in London to cover my short position and the price gets bid right back higher.

Managers who call themselves arbitrageurs are mostly people who are using the principles of APT to identify overpriced and underpriced securities. They take what they believe are offsetting long and short positions and then wait for the prices to move back toward the theoretically right levels. If they have done their job correctly, they do not care about any systematic risk because it has all been hedged away.

The potential slippage in these models is profound. You need to have confidence in the risk factors and your ability to pair them off to create neutrality. There cannot be high transaction costs that eat into potential gains. Finally, and most importantly, you have to be a small part of any market you are trading. If the market becomes crowded with similar quantitative traders applying their theory with leverage, the table is set for a severe reversal. Since this is not true arbitrage that can force a trading gain, there is a meaningful risk that the spread trades can be blown apart before they get a chance to show a profit.

This was the basic problem of the afore mentioned Granite Fund in 1994 and Long Term Capital Management in 1998. Both funds believed they had identified "arbitrage" opportunities and established heavily leveraged spread trades to exploit them. You can debate whether these funds failed because they incorrectly specified their models or whether a sudden change in liquidity forced them out of what should have been winning positions. All that matters is that real-world deviations from the restrictive assumptions of APT cost investors hundreds of millions of dollars as these funds imploded.

Another arbitrage area that has shown a tendency toward periodic meltdowns has been dynamic option replication strategies. Fischer Black and Myron Scholes developed their famous options pricing model completely around arbitrage principles.[15] They never tried to say whether a stock's price or an option's premium was too high or too low in a fundamental sense. Instead, their formula determined what the *fair value* of a call was relative to the price of a stock. Fairness in this instance is the same as saying no arbitrage profits exist.

Unlike the simple gold arbitrage example, options arbitrage is a trickier business. Call options with strike prices well above the current stock price are said to be *out-of-the-money* and they can be expected to move relatively little whenever the stock price changes. At the other end of the spectrum are call options that are so far *in-the-money* that they behave almost identically to the underlying stock. The Black-Scholes model suggests how much any given strike price and maturity call option will move when the underlying stock price changes.

The key factor is the *hedge ratio*, or the number of offsetting shares you have to own to offset a given short call option position. If the options are struck *at-the-money*, the hedge ratio will be approximately 2:1. That is, if you write call options on 100 shares of stock, you can be hedged against small price movements by owning 50 shares.

If this ratio stayed constant, hedging would be a snap. Unfortunately as the price of the stock increases, so does the number of shares you need to own to keep fully hedged. Similarly, as the stock price declines you need to sell shares to maintain the proper hedge ratio.

The Black-Scholes model assumes this can be done *at no cost* (the favorite magic wand assumption!), but it also assumes this can be done *continuously*. This means there are no jumps in price in either the stock or the option. The last vital assumption in Black-Scholes is that the underlying *volatility* of the stock remains constant over the life of the option.

These assumptions are violated all of the time in the real world. Just when you think you have locked in an arbitrage profit by selling some overvalued calls and buying just the right number of relatively undervalued shares, the company announces a fraud by the chief financial officer (CFO) and the stock falls by 50% without a trade. You have hit the trifecta of assumption violations: 1) you probably face a massive bid/ask spread to trade the stock or the options; 2) volatility has spiked off the charts;

---

[15]Black, F. and Scholes, M. (1973). The Pricing of Options and Corporate Liabilities. *Journal of Political Economy*, p. 81 (May–June).

and 3) the actual price change was a gap of 50% rather than a series of infinitesimal small changes where you could trade along the way.

Options-based arbitrage strategies are among the most fragile in the trading world. Traders who placed too much faith in the power of their models are no longer with us to tell their stories. Successful professional options market makers have developed variations on these no-arbitrage models along with rigorous risk-management programs to help them through inevitable rough periods.

There was nothing like that in place in the mid-1980s when *portfolio insurance* came into vogue. LOR, a firm created by Hayne Leland, John O'Brien, and Mark Rubinstein started with the facts that many people had equity exposure over which they were worried, and that buying puts on that exposure for the desired period of coverage was not always available.[16] The solution they came up with was a synthetic option replication program they called portfolio insurance.

They noted that one could mimic the payoff pattern of a put option by going short the market in an amount guided by the hedge ratio calculated from the option-pricing model they employed. This had the advantage of avoiding any up-front payment of an option premium. They also chose to execute their strategy efficiently using stock index futures, which came into being in the last quarter of 1982.

LOR leaned on the implied APT features of the market in two ways. Their first reliance was on their belief that arbitrage forces could hold in line the stock market, real options, and their dynamic trading program to replicate those options. By executing their strategy with S&P 500 Index futures positions, they were also counting on arbitrageurs to hold together the values of those futures and the market as a whole. Neither assumption held in practice.

Through the first years of the bull market after 1982, portfolio insurance was billed as a way to get the benefits of owning puts without the up-front premium expense. Of course, there was a fee paid to LOR to manage these diverse trading algorithms. Some investors were emboldened to take bigger overall equity positions than they would have normally, with the understanding that they were not really adding to risk since their portfolios were insured.

But this was not insurance in any traditional sense. There was no pool of assets set aside against an actuarial risk of loss. There was only a model that said once the stock market started falling, an increasing number of futures contracts would be sold short until the downside risk of the portfolio was eventually covered.

LOR was widely successful in their marketing. By 1987 it is estimated that LOR had around $60 billion in their portfolio insurance programs. Since the concept behind the LOR product was not copyrighted, it attracted many imitators, which raised the assets covered by tens of billions of dollars more.

When the stock market began to crack in the United States on Friday, October 16, 1987, LOR's portfolio insurance programs and all of its imitators started selling S&P 500 futures at the Chicago Mercantile Exchange (CME). This added selling

---

[16]Leyland and Rubinstein were finance professors at University of California, Berkeley and O'Brien was a senior employee at A.G. Becker. O'Brien grasped the practical significance of some of the pioneering work being done particularly by Rubinstein and developed the main concept. When A.G. Becker rejected the idea of offering portfolio insurance to its clients, LOR was begun with Leyland and Rubinstein providing the academic backbone and O'Brien the marketing and organizational strength.

pressure to an already soft market. Arbitrageurs trading between the CME futures market and the cash market at the New York Stock Exchange bought the depressed futures and then sold cash stocks. This is exactly how arbitrage transmits information from one market to another.

By the close of the market on Friday afternoon, the S&P 500 was off by almost 10%, which made October 16, 1987 one of the largest losing single trading days in history. But there was worse to come. When Hong Kong, Tokyo, and Sydney all opened Monday morning October 19, they all sold off dramatically. As markets across Europe opened, this rush to sell equities continued around the globe. At the Monday opening bell in New York and Chicago, there were massive imbalances to sell both stocks and futures.

All of the assumptions behind portfolio insurance had been violated. Volatility spiked, prices gapped down, and transaction costs exploded. More puzzling to the founders of LOR and other portfolio insurers was the wedge that emerged between stock index futures and the apparent value of the underlying stocks. Everything collapsed in price, but futures fell well below the values expected from the arbitrage models. What happened?

One of the basic tenets of arbitrage models is that there will always be an unlimited supply of rational people with access to capital whose only job is to make sure relative prices do not get stupid. On 19 October 1987 either those people were on holiday or the world had changed to the point where it was not easy to identify obvious arbitrage profits.

Behavioral finance, discussed in the next section, often relies on people's irrationality to explain apparent violations of efficient markets. But the events of October 1987 were something different. There had been billions of dollars of arbitrage capital working between the equity cash and futures markets for years. This capital typically does not go on vacation. The people driving that capital did not become irrational overnight.

Instead, what likely happened was that rational people with capital realized that some of their previously held assumptions could not be true. Long-standing, reputable firms or clearinghouses might fail, scarce and expensive credit could become even more scarce and expensive, and governments could step in to change the rules of the game. The fact that none of the worst of these fears came to pass in the crash of 1987 does not mean that it was irrational to consider them at the time.

The exact same type of process that built portfolio insurance was followed by the financial engineers who developed leveraged interest rate swaps that blew up in 1994, heavily leveraged interest rate market neutral strategies (1998), convertible bond arbitrage (2005 and again in 2008), structured products like CLOs and CDOs (2007/2008), and CDS (2008).

Arbitrageurs are an essential element to any well-functioning market, but they can become the tail that wags the dog. Hedge funds buying up convertible bonds for arbitrage trades early in the twenty-first century drove the price of these bonds to such levels that traditional investors no longer found them attractive for their portfolios. When a combination of shifting credit conditions and hedge fund redemptions caused these funds to try to liquidate, prices had to gap down dramatically before the traditional buyers became interested.

As modern finance has evolved over the past 40 years, this seems to be the most frequently repeated mistake by adherents to modern portfolio theory. Pursuers of highly quantitative strategies seem to believe that they will be protected by an infinite supply of rational capital blessed with perfect foresight. Those possessing such resources will use the powers of arbitrage to keep markets tied together and volatility low. The extreme market events that have occurred regularly since 1987 don't seem to have changed the minds of the true believers. A new supply of quantitative "edges" appears regularly.

Investors need to tiptoe through these fields carefully. Anytime a quantitative product relying heavily on arbitrage principles and readily available capital starts to attract large sums of money, warning sirens should sound. When this happens there is a good chance that the pricing of the assets has been taken away from those who have a fundamental supply or demand interest. Distortions are created that are hard to ease out of. Many times the corrections come with a spike in volatility.

Some would argue that these problems are due to errors in constructing the models in a generally rational world. Others counter that many irrational elements in the investment process keep the traditional models from ever being able to operate well. This is where the discussion of behavioral economics and finance comes in.

3.7 BEHAVIORAL FINANCE CONTRIBUTIONS

As mainstream finance advanced from Markowitz and Sharpe, most of the academic effort was devoted to testing the proposed models and to offering modest modifications to the basic theme. Alongside this stream was a smaller group of economists, often joined by psychologists, who worked to challenge the basic assumptions on which modern portfolio theory was based. These pioneers developed what is now known as *behavioral finance*.

To see the contrast between the two approaches, consider the following stylized example. Figure 3.14 shows a classic scatter diagram of data points plotting the

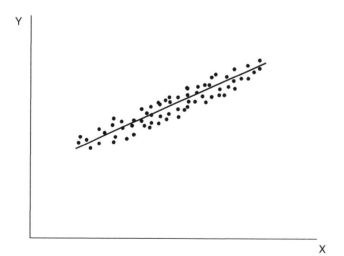

FIGURE 3.14 A Linear Model with a Very Good Fit

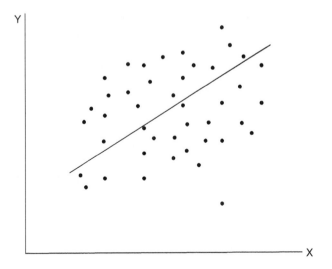

FIGURE 3.15   A Linear Model with a Less Good Fit

expected return of a stock (Y) against its market beta (X). One of the basic predictions of CAPM is that higher beta stocks should be associated with higher rates of return. In addition to the data points, the regression line estimated from the data is also shown. The fit would be considered quite good in this example. The regression line explains most of the variation in the individual observations.

Note that while almost all of the data points fall very close to the line, the relationship is not perfect. In such situations, one likely reason for the model not being 100% precise is measurement errors. If the data collection process was more accurate, there would be even less deviation away from the predictions of the regression line. Economists who propose models love this kind of result as it provides strong statistical support for their hypothesis.

Unfortunately, they almost never get this outcome. Instead, a more common result is something like that shown in Figure 3.15. There still may be a statistically significant regression line that can be found, but many points fall away from their predicted values. Some of these deviations may be large enough that they seem to offer an arbitrage opportunity.

The traditional finance economist may attempt to explain the deviation by identifying missing variables, which means modifying the market model being debated. This is precisely what kept the profession busy for 40 years after Markowitz and Sharpe. Markets do not wait for the research results, but instead keep providing new data, which makes the challenge of finding a definitive answer even more daunting. At the end of the process, any model will end up explaining as much of the data as it can and the rest will be considered noise.

Behaviorists attack the problem somewhat differently. They do not treat deviations from the rational-market model as noise, but instead the result of sometimes-irrational human decision makers. They attack the basic premises of utility maximization and efficient markets, trying to explain market events in a psychological context.

This is not a new discussion. John Stuart Mill's famous thesis, *Utilitarianism*, published in 1863, was an early exposition describing economic man as a rational decision-maker. It is filled with responses to critics of rationality that sound completely familiar today.[17] Traditional economists say that people make informed, rational decisions. Behaviorists say that regular observations of irrational behavior refute this and therefore the very foundations of modern portfolio theory should be challenged.

Pioneers in the area include Richard Thaler, Amos Tversky, and Daniel Kahneman, a psychologist by training.[18] Kahneman was awarded the Nobel Prize in economics six years after Tversky's death, with the Nobel Committee citing several of their joint works. Thaler was awarded his Nobel Prize in 2017. Using a variety of experimental techniques, these researchers sought to show that not only are people irrational in their decision-making, they are *predictably* irrational. That is, there are some mistakes that we can count on people making on a regular basis. For example, people worry about losses more than they value equal-sized gains. They value assets more once they own them than they did before. They anchor onto beliefs and hold them despite evidence that they should change, and, much like their opinion of their driving abilities, they are typically overconfident about their abilities to invest.

One of the challenges of reconciling traditional and behavioral approaches to finance is the fact that the two approaches almost never use the same data. Traditional research pours over market prices looking for the best explanatory models. The data never fit the model perfectly, and it is not possible to go back and "interview" the outliers to try to discern why they behaved at variance with the model. Behaviorists, by contrast, have relied heavily on experiments that attempt to see how people would act in different market situations. If the answers suggest a pattern of behavior that deviates from rationality, this may help explain why the real world fails to fit the neat MPT models.

An example will demonstrate the approach. Suppose the researcher wants to test the basic thesis that to accept more risk, there has to be the potential for a greater return. Markowitz, Sharpe, and all of their descendants take this as a given, but the theory is subject to testing. The reader can be the subject. The behaviorist sets up an experiment where you are asked whether you would prefer a certain payment of $50,000, or the chance to play in a game where there is a 50% chance of winning $100,000 and a 50% chance of winning nothing. Actuarially this is a fair game, since if you were to go through this process an infinite number of times you should expect to earn the same thing from either choice.

But this was not the offer. You don't get to repeatedly play this game. You have one choice. And given that one choice is uncertain and the other has no risk, you should be expected to say that you would prefer the certain $50,000. Did you?

You might have said that you would still like to play the 50/50 game in such experiments. Are you being irrational, or have the researchers simply found in you one of a few people who aren't desperate for $50,000 and that like to gamble? To test

---

[17]Mill, J.S. (1863). *Utilitarianism (1 ed.)*. Parker, Son & Bourn: London.

[18]Among the many contributions of the three authors dating back into the 1970s, the following papers are considered among the most influential.

Thaler, R. (1980). Toward a Positive Theory of Consumer Choice. *Journal of Economic Behavior and Organization,* 1, pp. 39–60.

Tversky, A. and Kahneman, D. (1991). Loss Aversion in Riskless Choice: A Reference-Dependent Model. *Quarterly Journal of Economics,* 106, pp. 1039–1061.

the concept further, the researchers change the questions. The certain outcome becomes $500,000 and the 50/50 bet has payoffs of zero and $1 million dollars. Then the researchers explore the opposite direction and make the choices between 50 cents and a zero/one dollar bet. Did your answers change?

Then the researcher explores the loss side of the experiment. Here you are told to choose between a certain loss of $40,000 and a game in which you have a 75% chance of losing $50,000 and a 25% chance of losing $30,000. This game has an expected value of −$45,000, and yet significant numbers of people pick the probability game in the experiments.[19]

Daniel Kahneman, Richard Thaler, and Amos Tverskey focused their research probing the ways that people shape their decisions involving risk. They discovered that the answers given in these experiments often indicated logical inconsistencies, and rarely did the responses look like anything predicted by mean-variance optimization. They wondered if market participants cannot decide consistently among risky options, then how can the traditional finance models be accurate?

It would seem that if most people behave irrationally it would be impossible to have an efficient market. But do people behave in the real world the way they are predicted to behave from their experimental responses? It is a major challenge for behavioral researchers to create experiments that are realistic. In the stylized example above, the researcher might have the budget to run experiments choosing between $1 certain outcomes and 50/50 games paying nothing or $2, but there are no tests involving sums 10,000 times larger. If the subject is deemed irrational in the choice of $1 payoffs, does that indicate a true behavioral bias, or a perfectly rational reaction to a game where the payoff is not large enough to cause the subject to think too hard about their choices?

The loss side of the experiment sheet is even trickier. In the example where the subject is offered a certain loss of $40,000, or a 75/25 chance of losing $50,000 or $30,000, the sensible subject says, "I'd rather not play at all, thank-you." When told that is not an option, they make a choice reflective of what they think they would do. It is not moral to actually extract wealth from experimental subjects, so loss experiments must stay on a rather abstract plane.

But markets do not do that. If you make stupid choices, the market makes you pay. Presumably, unless you derive a great deal of happiness from losing money, you either learn from your mistakes or you find another activity. The ultimate challenge for the behaviorists is to try to design effective experiments that can capture the iterative process of learning from our mistakes.

In the past decade, researchers have tried to accomplish that with their choice of tests. John List has shown that some of the irrational parts of the endowment effect disappear as one's market experience grows. His tests were based on trades in actual markets that would have occurred independent of the academic study being undertaken.[20]

---

[19]The expected value of any such game is the weighted average of the outcomes, where the weights equal the probability of the event. In this case the game is equal to $(0.75)(-50,000) + (0.25)(-30,000)$, which is $-45,000$.

[20]List, J. (2003). Does Market Experience Eliminate Market Anomalies? *The Quarterly Journal of Economics*, 118, pp. 41–71.

For readers who are much more interested in how to improve their investments versus the question of whether their markets are theoretically efficient or not, most of the academic discussion is a bit remote. It is certainly possible for markets to be largely efficient and for people to make mistakes in their investment choices. They can even make repeated mistakes. Brokers call these people sheep. The existence of behavioral biases may or may not make it easier to make money or avoid one's own mistakes.

As the finance profession continues to study and debate, investors need to get on with their lives. The remaining section of this chapter discusses briefly the major behavioral biases that investors can demonstrate. Human psychology is a complicated mix of emotions and analysis, so it is not possible to pinpoint exact cause-and-effect relationships. Instead, these biases are listed to suggest potential errors to be avoided as well as offer up suggestions on how to exploit the weaknesses of others. We shall see that unwavering attachment to modern portfolio theory is actually a behavioral bias that has led many otherwise smart investors astray.

3.7.1 Loss Aversion

Logic tells investors that they should cut their losses quickly, but let their winners run. In fact, studies have shown that many people do just the reverse. Why? People in general seem to dislike losses much more than they like similarly sized gains. This is known as *loss aversion*. By holding onto losing positions, the investor has only a paper loss and not a realized one. While the act of seeing losses on paper is painful, actually closing the position and realizing the loss is worse. People avoid such sales, hoping that the market will reverse and allow them to at least get even before covering. The net effect is that bad positions often become worse.

The opposite side is that realizing a profit on a stock that has advanced is pleasurable, so the investor seeks to do that as often as possible. Since a $2 gain is not twice as pleasurable as a $1 gain for most people, harvesting winners tends to be more frequent but with smaller amounts than covering losses.

A related behavior when it comes to losses is *inertia*. Because people focus more on what they might lose from an action like selling a stock at a loss ("I'll be just sick if I sell it now and it rebounds!") than on what they could earn from a better allocation of those assets, they sit tight and hope for the best.

These behaviors show up in the management of individual stocks and bonds that might be in the portfolio, but also in the assessment of external managers. Suppose a manager has been put into the portfolio to exploit a perceived specific opportunity or risk. But then the market does not play out according to plan and the investor is looking at a meaningful loss. They may not want to admit that they were wrong in their judgment, which is what implicitly seems to be happening if the manager is terminated and the loss realized.

Instead, the investor hopes for the best and while they are waiting they rationalize that since this manager lost money while other parts of the portfolio were profiting, the manager acted as an overall "hedge" and reduced volatility. There is not much time spent probing the questions about why you want to limit upside volatility, or whether this manager should be expected to act as an equally effective hedge if those previously successful parts of the portfolio fall.

3.7.2   The Endowment Effect

How much is something worth to you? The utility maximizer's basic answer is that an object's worth is directly related to how much happiness it provides to that individual. But it is more complicated than that. One needs to compare the happiness that a dollar spent on one item brings relative to spending that dollar on some other source of happiness. It is a highly personalized evaluation. This explains why some people own 100 pairs of shoes and no fishing gear while others with the same income have every manner of fishing lure and three pairs of shoes.

The utility maximizer understands that people have widely different desires and abilities to act on those desires, but they generally believe that people know their own minds. This is where the behaviorists differ. Through their experiments, they have shown that people value the same object very differently depending on whether they already own it. This has been called the *endowment effect*.

One example of the endowment effect was discovered when researchers asked college students how much they would pay to get coveted tickets to an important basketball game against a traditional rival, or sell those tickets if they already had one. These were Duke students and not Cal Tech ones, so there is significant excess demand for the scarce commodity of tickets against North Carolina. Duke tries to solve this allocation problem by making students queue up. They line up not for the actual tickets, but merely for the right to be selected in a later lottery.

Zvi Carmon and Dan Ariely understood that this arrangement provided the background for an experiment.[21] All the students that queued up for the right to win a ticket had invested about the same time for their chance. After the lottery, winners and losers were publicly posted. Carmon and Ariely asked the losers how much they would pay to get one of the tickets. They asked the winners how much they would need to part with theirs.

Not surprisingly, the offering prices were above the bids. The surprise was how much higher the selling prices were. The potential buyers said they would pay $170 to see the game. The sellers would not sell that right for less than $2,400. The market oriented observer sees a wide bid-ask spread. The behaviorist sees someone who does not really know what the ticket is worth to him since its apparent value changed so dramatically by the outcome of the lottery.

The experiment tested the hypothesis that actually owning an asset would change its perceived value. In the case of basketball tickets all of the students were equal before the experiment. It was only after the lottery that the students radically changed their view of what the ticket was worth. One could argue that this is an artificial environment in that the winning students received a grant that the losers never would have had access to. But why should such a grant make such a large difference in the valuation placed on the tickets? Whether we view this as an accurate reflection of individual human behavior, it does draw out an important distinction between people who own a particular asset and people who do not.

The application to the financial markets is direct. People own stocks in their portfolios but there are many more stocks that they do not own. It is certainly possible that individual investors become married to their picks. Once the stock is in a

---

[21]Carmon, Z. and Ariely, D. (2000). Focusing on the Forgone: How Value Can Appear So Different to Buyers and Sellers. *Journal of Consumer Research*.

portfolio we may believe there is a value beyond what the market sees. Nothing in ownership, per se, should make this true. But the endowment effect could lead us to hold stocks, or any other asset, in ways where there is an emotional attachment beyond the intrinsic value.

The endowment effect also has implications for our perception of values of assets like houses, paintings, or other collectibles. Once we acquire one of these objects, which are special in terms of their unique attributes, our sense of what the true value is can often be shaped by our emotions. This partially explains wide bid ask spreads in these markets, and perhaps helps explain why negotiations on these assets can become highly emotional and personal. Once emotion comes into play, it is very difficult to compare objective market forces. This often leads to the reliance on previous values as the foundation for current worth. These previous values make an impression on our decision-making process. This process is known as *anchoring*.

3.7.3 Anchoring

When there is not a lot of readily available market information about what an object is worth, people tend to anchor around values. These anchors can sometimes be highly arbitrary. Researchers have shown that the mere suggestion of someone's Social Security number can actually influence their perceived value of a good or service. These experiments demonstrate that people can draw information from a wide variety of irrelevant sources. When anchoring is a major problem, people can put values on assets that bear little relationship to the market fundamentals.

For the investor, anchoring combined with the endowment effect can lead to holding losing positions for a long time. The sequence goes like this: 1) acquire an asset at a given market price, 2) watch the market fall, 3) believe that the asset in your portfolio must be worth at least what you paid for it, and 4) stubbornly hold on to the asset in the face of market evidence that it is worth considerably less.

Behavioral researchers have demonstrated that anchoring is not permanent, but that it can fade. This is encouraging in that it suggests that people can incorporate new information into their valuation process. It does, however, take time. And while any anchoring behavior is dominating, inefficient decisions are made.

Anchoring also distorts a person's expectations. If the risk-free rate of return has generally averaged 3% over decades, then it is very difficult for people to cope with an interest rate policy that sets interest rates near zero. No matter what the Federal Reserve sets as the risk-free rate, some people will believe that certain strategies and investments should earn a double-digit rate of return even though that implies an unrealistic risk premium. Unfortunately, there are times in the investment cycle when you have to content yourself with not making a lot of return because it is simply not there to be earned.

Anchoring can sometimes help policy makers. The early days of any upturn in inflation are almost always greeted warmly. People see their wages going up and don't immediately connect that good event with the bad news that everything costs more. There is an illusion of increased wealth, which is precisely what policy makers are looking for with easy monetary policies. People, however, soon connect the dots, and history has shown that this form of anchoring fades as well, much to the chagrin of the optimistic policy makers.

Anchoring is a behavioral phenomenon that can easily be fixed if there is a consistent set of market data conveying the truth. But that market data needs to be unambiguous, easily available, and consistently reinforcing of the truth. If the market data varies, people tend to attach higher weight to that data that reinforces their previously held and anchored views. The other major challenge with the anchoring phenomenon is when many people in the group share the same anchor and biases. This produces herding behavior among the investment crowd, an issue that has been discussed at length for as long as there have been commentators on the markets.

3.7.4 Herding Behavior

Cautionary tales about herding behavior among investors significantly predate the identification of behavioral finance as a discipline. Every historical bubble since Dutch tulip bulbs in the seventeenth century and South Sea Island investments a hundred years later have been explained as manias that swept a crowd.[22] Why people behave in a herding fashion is what fascinates almost everyone but especially the behavioral finance crowd.

It all begins with the fact that we, like the vast majority of our primate cousins, tend to live in communities. It was perhaps easier to hunt in packs or to be able to divide responsibilities among a larger number of beings that caused groups of humans to survive better than individuals. With communities comes the development of social norms of behavior, and it seems that what we call herding behavior in investing has deep roots in basic social norms.

Most individuals have a fundamental need to be accepted as part of a group. There are, of course, exceptions, but when we say someone is a "Lone Wolf" or is said to "march to the beat of a different drummer," there is more than a touch of suspicion conveyed by the choice of descriptions. To be out of step with the group invites ridicule and scorn, which is just as meaningful among your investment choices as with your choice of cocktail party companions.

Herding behavior can manifest in a number of ways in the investment process. Most obvious are investment bubbles that continue to grow in the face of strong evidence that the prices cannot be supported by fundamentals. "Farm land does not fall in price," "That tech company is worth twice what I paid for it," and "There's no need for a down payment for this mortgage" are all phrases that large groups of people had come to believe before markets abruptly reversed.

Reinhart and Rogoff, in their book, *This Time is Different: Eight Centuries of Financial Folly*, document the rhyming nature of past credit investment bubbles.[23] If theirs had been the first careful history of the phenomenon, we might be able to say that our human frailties had finally been exposed to us and we could move on. Unfortunately, this is just the most recent (and one of the more statistically complete) cautionary tales that never seem to fully educate the fallible human population. One can predict with confidence that there will be future writers on the same subject,

---

[22]Kindleberger, C.P. (1989). *Manias, Panics and Crashes: A History of Financial Crises.* Basic Books: New York. Reinhart, C.M. and Rogoff, K.S. (2009). *This Time Is Different: Eight Centuries of Financial Folly.* Princeton University Press: Princeton, NJ.

[23]op. cit.

using Reinhart and Rogoff as a background reference, to explain the most recent herd induced bubble phenomenon.

The most hopeful element in this history is that we tend to learn specific lessons. There has been only one tulip bulb mania in 500 years. Wild speculation in Louisiana land by eighteenth-century Europeans was not repeated. Unfortunately, there are too many rhyming elements across market bubbles to suggest that humans are learning any great general lessons. Being part of a pack, riding a market wave, still has a lot of short-term appeal.

We tend to give too much credence to the "smart people" who have the best recent returns and want to join into their trend. This is what creates market bubbles. Silver was in short supply in 1978 when the price started moving from $8 to $10 an ounce. But from $10 to $45 over the next 18 months there was only a steady stream of people who came to believe a story of permanent inadequate supply. They joined the herd in stages, propelling the market higher long past the point where the fundamental story held true.

Don't be too quick to pooh-pooh any market commentator who suggests the current market emperor has no clothes. But also don't be too courageous in bucking the trend. In the case of the Hunt Brothers silver bubble in 1979–1980, many thoughtful analysts noted that it was costing miners only $12 or so to produce large new supplies of silver. Contrarians who started shorting at that level had huge losses to contend with as the bull market forged ahead.

A more recent example of the same phenomenon can be found in the credit markets in the years leading up to the 2008 crisis. Careful lenders looked at credit spreads in 2005 as too tight to compensate for the credit risks. Spreads got tighter in 2006 and early in 2007. The herd was riding along on excess liquidity and heavy applications of leverage believing in analytical models that suggested the risk could be easily diversified away. Managers like John Paulson placed large bets against the herd being right forever. Some investors profitably joined up with that side of the market, but many more stayed with the pack on the wrong side until the crisis. After the blowout occurred, and the best trades were in the past, the pack decided they needed to check out the new superstars.

This is perhaps the most relevant aspect of herding behavior for investors. Blaise Pascal said, "You always admire what you really don't understand." People do understand that they are not savvy about markets. They know investing is highly competitive, and they are not likely to succeed on their own. They therefore seek out the best and the brightest managers in order to tag along with their anticipated success.

Nowhere is this better seen than at the annual meetings of fund managers who have just completed a high return year. The mood is like a 1960s love-in. Everyone thanks the manager for having assembled the best investment team and portfolio imaginable. The manager acknowledges that there were of course a few stumbles and things could have been better, but that in general the returns were "satisfactory." Investors congratulate one another for having the wisdom for being part of such a successful crowd. The fact that the vast majority of the investors have no clue how the returns were generated or what risks were taken to get them bothers almost nobody. All that matters is that for the last marking period, the manager put a lot of points on the board.

Such events tend to be great advertisements to attract new investors. History is full of examples of managers that string together a few great years and then attract so much capital that it becomes impossible to continue the strong historical track record. When asked along the way whether the new assets will impede returns, there are replies talking about "better opportunities coming from more resources" and "deep and liquid markets." It is almost as hard for the manager to ignore the cries from the herd to take their money as it is for the herd to resist the story.

Such tales can change, and have changed, quickly. Previously brilliant managers apparently become stupid overnight. The adoring crowd becomes an unruly mob at the next annual meeting, often with many late entry members who had not been part of the previous happier parties. Losing trades are examined with a scrutiny never previously applied to the winners. "How did you not see the coming collapse in the housing market?" "I pay you large fees to avoid the mistakes I could make myself."

There are managers who try to exploit general herding behavior. These *momentum* managers spend little time looking at fundamentals of supply and demand. Instead they look at past patterns of prices to identify trends that they believe are signals of future herd behavior. As we have discussed in the section of this chapter on efficient markets, such activity is easily carried out by anyone with a computer and access to historical data. The successful momentum manager will be one who stays objectively apart from any emotion attached to a trend and has the discipline to exit any trade once it shows signs of reversing.

Herding behavior also occurs among those who are most likely to deny ever acting as a pack. The true believers of modern portfolio theory have time and again developed models to exploit perceived inefficiencies in markets. Believing that their models are true reflections of the world, they apply capital in such amounts that they create reality rather than reflect it. This has been a phenomenon of the last 30 years. Portfolio insurance, LTCM-style relative value trades, convertible bond arbitrage, and CDOs and CLOs are all examples of basically sound analytical strategies that were carried to the point of market collapse.

One might argue that this is a different type of problem from the herd behavior behind the tech stock bubble of the 1990s or the more recent mortgage crisis since there is no human emotion in modern portfolio theory. It may be a different kind of emotion, but it is an emotion nonetheless. A group of people believes they are smarter than the markets. They believe that they have discovered the true answer to the investing puzzle. While they are making money they are just as confident and smug as any amateur investor bragging at a cocktail party about the value of their condo in Florida or their most recent Bitcoin or FAANG stock purchase.

Overconfident quantitative managers along with the herd of investors they attract seem to have played a major role in all of the major market disruptions since the 1980s. There were plenty of contributors to the credit crisis of 2007–2008, but models consistently saying there was little risk in the system were vital in reinforcing the delusion that the situation was different this time. This may be the hardest herding problem to avoid since the behavior appears to be grounded in science and not emotion.

Understanding herding behavior among investors cannot pinpoint winning trades, but it can help avoid situations where risk is building with little fanfare. Whenever thoughtful comments about extreme markets are brushed aside with a chorus of voices, there's a good chance that the herd has taken over. Whether it is an overvalued stock or market, or a manager that is gathering new assets apparently without limitation, avoiding those moments that produce sudden and great reversals can define long-term success as an investor.

3.7.5 Behavioral Elements to Portfolio Construction

Mean-variance optimization is the antithesis of behavioral finance. There are no emotions or biases involved, only statistics that if ignored lead to suboptimal decisions. The fact that most investors do not follow any analytical optimization is a source of encouragement to the followers of modern portfolio theory. They point to emotional investors as an opportunity base from which to create superior returns. If one follows the right path, versus being distracted by emotions, higher returns are available at every level of expected risk.

The irony in this thinking is that it runs counter to one of the basic efficient market tenets. If the vast majority of investors invest without total reliance on an analytical model, and they have done so for generations, is it not likely that it is this approach that maximizes utility for those investors? This is the method that has stood the test of time, even after 50 years of modern portfolio theory.

Investment advisors and behavioral finance professionals who have studied portfolio construction have often turned to rules of thumb in an attempt to meet both the analytical and emotional elements of the problem. Hersh Shefrin summarizes much of the behavioral literature as it pertains to portfolio construction.[24] He describes an "emotional time line" consisting of hope and fear that dominates most investment thought. People have basic needs that they fear won't be met. They have aspirations that they hope to reach.

Shefrin uses the analogy of the subsistence farmer to describe the process. Falling short of one's basic needs has disastrous consequences, so the farmer's first priority is planting and attending to a quantity of subsistence crops to ensure success. Only after that target is reached are cash crops, which are the path to aspirational goals, pursued. Investors, he believes, typically act similarly.

This leads to a "pyramid" approach to portfolio construction. On the bottom are the basic sources of capital security like cash and Treasury bills. This forms the base of the pyramid and acts as a foundation for riskier investments above it. Bonds come next and then stocks, real estate, commodities, and even lottery tickets. Figure 3.16 is a generalized pyramid typical of illustrations in many how-to investment guides.

The intuition behind why the pyramid approach meets the emotional desires of investors is direct. Basic needs are met first and then risk is added to the degree needed to reach for aspirations. While the intuition is sound, such simple rules of thumb can lead to other not very useful conclusions. For example, the pyramid seems to suggest that the safest assets should form a thick, meaningful base of the allocation. For a high earning individual who has no difficulty exceeding all necessities, this may be exactly upside down. Cash and Treasuries may be held only to provide instant liquidity for an opportunistic purchase of speculative assets.

There have been efforts over the years to systematize rules of thumb so that investors can have the benefit of analytical rigor while meeting emotional needs. Mutual fund companies offer "lifestyle" funds that try to capture the profiles of investors with different ages and risk profiles. Bill Sharpe founded a software platform in 1996 called Financial Engines with similar goals that has the added appeal of being designed by someone with a Nobel Prize (herding behavior returns).

---

[24]Shefrin, H. (2002). *Beyond Greed and Fear*. Oxford University Press: New York.

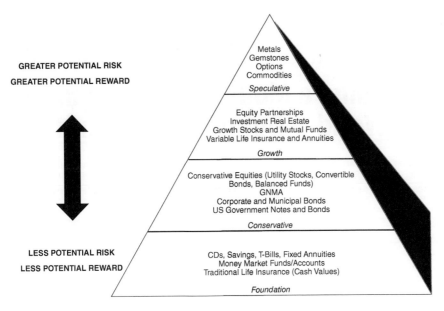

FIGURE 3.16   A Pyramid Approach to Portfolio Construction

Rules of thumb are often very basic, like one should hold a greater percentage of bonds as one grows older. Such rules should be taken with varying size grains of salt. Unless the factors used to determine any rule match your circumstances and risk profile exactly, there is a good chance that an exception to every suggested rule can be found that will be an improvement to your portfolio.

It would be nice if portfolio construction could be reduced to a formula. It wouldn't matter whether the formula was based on the rigors of modern portfolio theory or on a set of behavioral rules. If such a formula existed, all of our investment decisions could be set with confidence that our goals would be met efficiently. There would be the added benefit of knowing we were all part of a very thoughtful crowd.

Unfortunately, portfolio construction done well is a highly individualistic activity. By necessity it requires a customized solution based on the needs, aspirations, and risk tolerance of the investor. These factors are all considered, not in an academic vacuum of historical data, but in the current market environment. The next chapter begins outlining this process. That is all any book can do. Everyone can follow the process, but the individual paths will almost certainly produce different answers. If someone writes that they have the one true recipe for success, you can almost be sure that it is the wrong recipe for you.

CHAPTER **4**

Building a Modern Portfolio in the Real World – Defining Your Strategy

4.1 THE "SLEEP-WELL-AT-NIGHT" ASSETS

4.1.1 Defining How Much Is Enough

Popular investment theory suggests that long-term investors should shun cash and other low yielding assets in favor of investments that have greater growth potential. Leaning on modern portfolio theory (MPT), these safe assets are typically "dominated" by stocks, bonds, and other assets that can be combined into a diversified portfolio. Apparently, cash, Treasury bills, and other ultrasafe assets simply do not offer enough return for their risk advantages.

In Chapter 2 it was asserted that the starting point for any portfolio discussion should be determining how many safe assets, generally shunned by MPT, were needed to let you sleep well at night. The difference between this view and the classic MPT approach often defined the division between those investors who weathered the financial crisis and those who got turned upside down. Believing in the power of diversification and building portfolios largely based on mean-variance optimization, many individuals and institutions invested with little regard to liquidity or the potential for extreme risk. The basic lesson is still of paramount importance today in setting the right course, even after the decade-long bull market run after the crisis.

The right size for the cushion is completely subjective, but every individual and institution should probe their own circumstances and risk tolerance to reach their own best answer. We shall begin this chapter with a deeper dive into the factors one should consider in this analysis. Consider the following as possible causes of "prolonged market stress":

- Risk markets like stocks and corporate bonds see declines of 25% or more.
- Liquidity for normally actively traded securities slows to a trickle.
- Major financial institutions fail without government rescue for large investors.
- Illiquid assets, including real estate, have virtually no bids.
- You lose major sources of income.

Before 2008, many Americans would have only considered the list above an academic possibility. That year proved that just because an event had not yet occurred in one's lifetime doesn't mean it could not happen. As extreme as actual events turned out to be, they could have been a great deal worse if the Treasury and the Federal Reserve had not taken decisive action as the crisis was accelerating.

The sleep-well-at-night money serves two purposes. Its primary function is to allow the investors to be secure in their lifestyle. Bills are paid and critical activities are maintained. The second function is to allow the investor to be opportunistic. At the time of greatest dislocation in the market there are the greatest opportunities. Investors that lack "dry powder" will find themselves forced to be on the sidelines. While these periods may be the most psychologically difficult times to invest, having the wherewithal to do so is a critical element of successful investing.

How fat should this pillow be? This depends on the circumstances. The size of known liabilities and the reliability of income streams are the key factors. A school that draws 30% of its operating budget from its endowment should want more safe assets than another that only draws less than 5%. The retired couple living entirely off their savings and Social Security would similarly want more security than the employed 30-year-old single person.

The other key consideration is the individual's or institution's attitude toward risk. Individuals vary greatly in how financial risk affects them, and there is no simple measure of this trait. Risk-averse people buy insurance at a known premium in order to avoid the chance of a catastrophic loss. Risk-loving people buy lottery tickets. Some people do both in an apparent contradictory action. There are complicated models of human behavior that try to describe this phenomenon, but the easiest conclusion is that people are different in unpredictable ways, and each needs to determine how unhappy they would be if their wealth or lifestyle fell suddenly below a certain level.

Many institutions probably now realize they are less tolerant to risk than they thought they were before 2008. There were many sleepless nights for trustees and administrations of institutions that had to cut staff, modify programs, or eliminate capital spending programs. The extended bull market since the crisis has healed many wounds, but scars remain for anyone who went through the worst of the meltdown.

The first step of the decision process is to assess the sources of revenue. Income needs to be considered in terms of its reliability. Mary Higgins Clark at age 91 still has over 50 published books in print. Her income stream is sitting at an extremely high and dependable level. The incomes of millions of Social Security recipients at the other end of the income spectrum are also quite likely to continue, but at a rate too low to cover many catastrophic expenses. Most individuals fall into a lower category of reliability, having considerably less security in their cash flows. If one can meet all existing and planned liabilities from a secure source of income, there is little reason to be concerned with ultrasafe assets in one's portfolio for any other reason than opportunistic investing. Few individuals or institutions fall into this category.

At the opposite extreme, foundations primarily rely on their portfolio returns for the programs they support. They often have little or no outside income. If the goal is to have a high degree of predictability in grant activity through time, there needs to be a measure of confidence that assets will be there to meet the spending. This means a larger sleep-well-at-night pillow.

Liabilities clearly matter in this decision. There are external liabilities like regular spending needs, but there are also liabilities internal to the investment process. Whenever one signs up for a private partnership where future capital calls are at the discretion of the general partner, one should treat this as an explicit liability. Until that capital is completely called or canceled by the GP, the liability exists.

Institutional consultants often advise their clients to invest in such partnerships for their long-term potential. They also typically tell those clients that they should invest the targeted funds in whatever liquid instruments represent that asset class while they are waiting for the capital calls. One might choose an equity ETF or index fund for assets waiting to be called by private equity or venture capital funds. There are ETFs for commodity indexes that can stand in for hard asset partnerships for timber or energy exploration. The thought is that once a commitment to an asset class is made, one should acquire the exposure in a liquid form while waiting for the illiquid investment to begin.

This advice violates a basic premise of the sleep-well-at-night approach. Commitments to private equity programs are made in fixed *dollar* amounts. Once the subscription documents are signed, they become known liabilities. When one then takes the money allocated and subjects it to market risk, the chance for an asset-liability mismatch is very real. 2008 provided many examples of liquid equity and commodity investments that fell dramatically below the partnership commitments they were intended to support.

There is no easy answer regarding what part of such commitments should be put under the pillow. The most conservative approach is to set aside 100%, knowing that the money might not be called for several years. Endowments that receive regular gifts or other sources of additional income might look to set aside one to two years' expected capital calls as an adequate reserve. The number depends critically on risk aversion and the investor's ability to adjust to adverse circumstances. Two years is a conservative window for many institutions that can adjust their business model, but may be entirely too short for individuals whose peak earnings period is well behind them.

The final piece of the puzzle can be thought of as dry powder. There are always going to be disruptions in markets, both big and small. Only those with safe capital are in a position to turn those disruptions into opportunities. Warren Buffet and Berkshire Hathaway were reported to be holding almost $100 billion in cash in the middle of 2017, waiting for the right opportunity.[1] If short-term real interest rates were high, there would be little pain from holding this much cash. In periods where there is ample liquidity or when the Fed is targeting low interest rates for macroeconomic policy purposes, it can be quite painful sitting patiently on the sidelines.

The sleep-well-at-night part of the portfolio can also be thought of as the "no regrets" investments. If the market takes a severe tumble, there should be no regrets that the safe pillow was not large enough. Similarly when the market screams ahead, there should be no second guessing that too much was left behind in an ultrasafe form.

---

[1]Buhayar, N. Warren Buffett Nears a Milestone He Doesn't Want: $100 Billion in Cash. https://www.bloomberg.com. (7 August 2017).

4.1.2 How to Preserve Wealth and Perhaps Make a Little Bit

The composition of the sleep-well-at-night portfolio should be driven by a safety first attitude. This essentially rules out stocks, real estate, hard assets (including gold), and longer dated bonds because the potential fluctuations in market price are simply too large. Short dated bonds should make up the portfolio, but duration alone can't be relied on for safety.

For US-based tax-exempt entities, short-dated Treasury bills are the traditional starting point for ultrasafe assets. By keeping maturities below three months, the investor is assuming very little duration risk and the instruments are backed by the full faith and credit of the US government. In extreme cases this starting point is also the ending point, as any proposed deviation away from this standard involves risk compromises.

There are many other assets that some investors feel are acceptable complements to T-bills in this portfolio. Among these are:

- Short-dated Agency Paper
- Money Market Mutual Funds
- Bank Deposits
- Short-dated Tax-exempt Bonds

Short-dated agency paper includes debt securities issued by federal agencies like Fannie Mae or the Federal Home Loan Mortgage Corporation. These bonds have historically *not* carried the full faith and credit of the US government, but instead carried the government's implicit backing. After the credit crisis of 2008 and 2009, investors learned that Congress could make this implicit backing quite explicit. This backing simultaneously assured potential buyers of the paper and prevented the collapse of the residential mortgage market. Despite the formal backing of the government, these agency issuances typically offer slightly higher yields than similar maturity T-bills.

Money market mutual funds, per se, do not enjoy any government guarantees. Rules governing investments in money market funds limit the average maturity of underlying instruments to 90 days and no instrument in the portfolio can have a maturity of more than 397 days. These rules have generally insulated money market funds from most duration risk. While money markets strive to maintain a constant $1.00 net asset value, there is no obligation for them to do so and institutional, non-government money market funds must today calculate a variable NAV just like any other mutual fund. When certain money market funds have been near to or have actually "broken the buck," it has been due to a perceived rapid deterioration of the credit quality of the portfolio. The investor must look under the covers to see which money market funds might qualify for the sleep-well-at-night category and which might not because of the credit risks they assume.

Money market funds come in different flavors: all US Treasury; all government (includes agency securities); municipal (for taxpaying investors); and general or multi-asset. The general money market funds include all the types of securities in the narrower funds plus commercial paper, which is short-dated borrowing by corporations. Before the credit crisis that began in the second half of 2007, some money market funds invested in short-dated structures that contained private and agency mortgages. While they were all highly rated securities, the ratings proved illusory as the housing market tanked and the underlying collateral decayed well beyond anyone's expectations. This caused extraordinary steps to be taken by the Treasury and the Fed after the collapse of Lehman Brothers to guarantee the underlying money market assets. Without the prompt imposition of these guarantees, non-Treasury money market funds would have likely suffered a run, as investors looked to redeem and to swap into ultrasafe T-bills. People quickly rethought their notions of what was really safe during the crisis.

As is often the case, there were managers who tried to add a few basis points of return by putting assets in their portfolios that stretched the concept of safety while still meeting ratings guidelines. If no other lessons are learned from 2007–2009, one that should be seared in the minds of all investors is that ratings for bonds are only suggestions of safety and not guarantees. When moving beyond Treasury-only money market products, each fund needs to be evaluated to see if the underlying investments meet the investor's idea of sleep-well-at-night assets.

Bank deposits are fixed in notional value and term deposits carry a fixed interest rate. These deposits form the foundation for loans and security purchases and therefore usually pay rates that are lower than those available in other instruments. Current limits on Federal Deposit Insurance Corporation (FDIC) insurance are $250,000 per depositor, per FDIC insured institution. Since the FDIC is backed by the full faith and credit of the US government, deposits up to this limit are comparable in credit worthiness to US Treasury bills, notes, and bonds. Anything above that limit is theoretically at risk should the bank fail for any reason. Even insured deposits are not always replaced promptly by the FDIC, so while the assets may not be at risk ultimately, there may be liquidity issues to consider.

Short-dated *tax-exempt bonds* are issued by states, counties, municipalities, various revenue agencies like toll roads and bridges, and a vast array of not-for-profit entities like colleges and hospitals. There are general obligation bonds that are supported by taxing authority and stand high in the obligations of the issuer. There are even *pre-refunded bonds*. These bonds hold escrowed collateral in US Treasury securities large enough to pay off the issue, so there is virtually no chance of default. But not all tax-exempt bonds are so safe, as headlines about Puerto Rico remind us. The range of credit qualities is vast and the investor looking for tax-exempt ultrasafe money should be quite selective in building a portfolio.

4.1.3   The Temptation to Reach for Yield

There is always strong demand for ultimately safe assets. The investments that genuinely meet that characterization will carry little return relative to riskier opportunities. At times when either central bank policy or market forces produce extremely low real interest rates, these ultrasafe assets will provide little or no return. But whether the risk-free rate is near zero or meaningfully higher, there also always seems to be the temptation to try to reach for yield.

History is full of both well-meaning and under-handed individuals who have peddled "low-risk" assets offering incremental return. *Auction rate securities* and *structured notes* (discussed more fully in Chapter 9) are just two examples of investments that were advertised as being highly liquid, highly secure and offering premium returns. The range of risks, in these investments for which there was too little up-front compensation, is almost beyond imagination. Such instruments in the crisis of 2007–2009 destroyed entire liquidity pools.

There are legitimate ways to reach for incremental yield without destroying the concept of the sleep-well-at-night fund, but they are limited. Every return enhancement opportunity should be evaluated in terms of the *potential* risk and not on its historical behavior. Auction rate securities, for example, performed without a hitch for years until the market suddenly froze in the crisis. Investors who had believed they were in a highly liquid, safe asset quickly learned they owned term bonds that did not have a bid. The dealers that had backed these bonds sometimes offered their clients lines of credit against the auction rate securities, but many did not.

While there were many investors trapped in these securities, more careful people early on saw the potential problems in the structures and simply avoided them. It is rare that one cannot see the design flaws that can create problems, but it is almost certainly true the salesmen flogging these products will spend more time on the advertised benefits than on the risks.

A good rule of thumb is that if an investor cannot explicitly identify the risk in an investment that gives rise to the higher return, that security should be avoided. There are professionals in both the fund manager and advisor communities who can accurately assess the risks and returns of these assets. Unless one can do their own work, or has a highly trusted partner, the temptation to reach for yield should be resisted. By definition, if there are lingering questions about an investment, that asset cannot allow a good night's sleep.

4.2 THE ELEMENTS OF THE GROWTH PORTFOLIO

Once the size of the safe assets has been established, the balance of wealth should be thought of as the growth portfolio. There is considerably more latitude in the allocation of this part of the portfolio, but the ultimate recipe will still be shaped as a balance between performance targets and risk tolerance.

This section will be discussed in terms of a hypothetical 30-year-old that has $25 million in inherited wealth. Even if the reader doesn't match that profile, and very few will, the process is perfectly generic to any individual or institutional investor. The specific examples here will help to establish context.

The company built by this young person's grandparents still exists, but there is no active participation by current family members. Public stock in this one company makes up 40% of the subject's $25 million portfolio. Through careful thought along the lines discussed at the start of this chapter, it was decided that there should be $5 million in sleep-well-at-night money.

The next step of the analysis is how to allocate the $20 million growth portfolio, of which half is currently in the stock of a single company. Assuming there is no restriction other than a sentimental attachment to the family's past efforts, the entire $20 million should be thought of as a blank canvas on which to paint the best portfolio.[2]

Before outlining what that allocation might look like, it is useful to identify what colors are available on the palette. Broadly speaking, the choices will include bonds,

---

[2]Taxes on deeply appreciated stock almost always play an important role in any asset allocation discussion for a taxpayer. This is usually the biggest distinction between wealthy individuals and institutional investors.

stocks, alternative investments, real assets, and variations across the capital structure that could include currencies, loans, and other opportunities. These labels are about as broad as blue, green, yellow, orange, and red. The actual variations across the rainbow are almost limitless.

4.2.1 Bonds

Bonds are issued by sovereign governments, government agencies, corporations, and a host of not-for-profit organizations like universities and hospitals. Bonds are superior to stocks in the *capitalization structure* of a company, meaning that the obligation of the company to pay off the bondholders trumps any residual claim of the equity holders.

Investors who add bonds to their growth portfolio should do so only on a forward-looking perspective and not on the basis of any historical record. This seems obvious and intuitive, but tens of billions of bond funds were sold in 2010 on the basis of short-term, outsized returns created by declining Treasury rates and shrinking credit spreads that were extremely unlikely to be repeated in the future.

There are only so many ways one can make money from a bond. Assuming the bond is performing, the expected return consists of the interest payments plus the return of capital at maturity. Before the bond matures, its mark-to-market value is increased if interest rates decline, which can occur from the risk-free rate falling or the *credit spread* over the risk-free rate shrinking.

Bonds held to maturity can lose nominally only if there is a default. One can lose anything up to 100% of the investment if there are not enough assets at the issuer to cover the defaulted obligation. Before maturity, rates and spreads can also increase leading to mark-to-market losses.

Evaluating the role of bonds in the growth portfolio requires a realistic look into the future. A 10-year Treasury note yielding 2.5% can only be expected to earn that rate of return over its life. A highly rated corporate bond of the same maturity may earn 3%. Neither rate of return may be consistent with the growth objectives of the investor. When interest rates are falling, there will be mark-to-market gains in a bond portfolio, but unless one thinks rates will continue to fall that total return is not relevant to any forward-looking evaluation.

When considering a bond's potential role in the portfolio it is helpful to segregate the concepts of a *real yield* and a *nominal yield*. The nominal return is what we see every day. A one-year certificate of deposit may advertise a 1% yield, which says that at the end of the investment period the bank issuing the CD will return the principal plus 1%. The bank makes no promises what that principal and interest may be able to buy a year from now.

The real yield adjusts the nominal yield for the effects of inflation. For traditional bonds, the real yield is only known after the fact. In the CD example above, if inflation over the year was 3%, the buyer of the CD would have lost ground as the 1% nominal yield would fall short of the rate of inflation. The real yield in this example would be close to −2%.[3]

---

[3]In fact the real yield would be even lower if the holder of the CD was a taxpayer.

If you believe in a growing economy, you should only hold traditional sovereign bonds if you also believe that inflation or real interest rates will be declining from what is implied in the price of the bonds today. If correct, you will earn the current yield plus a capital appreciation as yields fall and the prices of the portfolio of bonds increase. That is a combination that served investors well for almost 40 years after 1980 as the United States enjoyed secular declines in both inflation and interest rates. That track record is not, unfortunately, an endorsement of future prospects.

You also want to hold these bonds if you expect the economy to slide into recession or if the traditional pattern of inflation shifts to deflation. With declining real rates because of slack economic activity or actual deflation, the value and purchasing power of a traditional sovereign bond portfolio should also benefit. High-quality, long-duration bonds are often held as a form of hedge against shocks to the equity side of the portfolio caused by economic downturns or geopolitical shocks.

This was clearly seen in late 2008 and 2009 as investors flocked to US Treasuries for safety. For a short window of time that probably felt a lot longer to investors, Treasuries proved to be the only asset class that offered any protection against the equity and credit disruption then being seen.

Not all sovereign debt is created equal. Ten years after the global financial crisis began, Japan and the European Central Bank were still pursuing zero and even negative interest rate policies. At the other end of the spectrum are emerging economies that have much higher interest rates. In the summer of 2017, Brazil's yield curve ranged from 8% for overnight funds to around 10% for 10-year government paper. These rates might seem high for a country just recovering from a serious recession and regular headlines about government corruption, but the central bank has used high policy interest rates as a tool to control inflation. The net result has been inflation squeezed down to under 5% per year. In this instance, Brazilian local currency government debt offered investors a meaningful after inflation rate of return against which all other possible investments needed to be judged.

There are also emerging market sovereign bonds denominated in hard currencies. Argentina issued 100-year, dollar-denominated debt in June of 2017, less than a year after it had resolved its most recent sovereign default. In a world of generally low interest rates for the best sovereign credits, Argentina's bonds yielded close to 8% and were three times oversubscribed. Given Argentina's multiple defaults over the past 100 years, the buyers seem to be counting on the 5% premium to long-dated US treasuries to give them enough cushion to protect them against possible defaults down the line. Many investors would not touch these bonds.

Investors place a wide range of instruments under the big umbrella called "Bonds." At the safest end of the credit spectrum are the sovereign bonds of the wealthiest and most financially secure nations. Then come a variety of private and public debt instruments that are generally considered *investment grade*. Below that are bonds and loans of troubled borrowers. If these instruments are performing, they are categorized simply as *below investment grade*. Otherwise they are classified as *distressed*. Below investment grade bonds are often also called *high-yield* or *junk bonds*.

All of the bonds discussed above are traditional in that they specify a coupon, a maturity, and little else. There is a special class of bonds that allows investors to fix the real rate of interest in advance. These inflation-linked notes, sometimes called *linkers* or in the United States, *TIPS* (Treasury inflation protected securities), pay a fixed coupon, but also periodically adjust the principal of the bond to an inflation index. These bonds overcome one of the biggest risks of traditional bonds, which is an unanticipated increase in inflation eating away purchasing power and driving up nominal yields in the short run.

With such a wide variety of bonds available to the investor, it is not obvious which bonds should be used in a growth portfolio or in what percentage. Chapter 9 explores the subcategories in greater detail to help the investor understand the specific characteristics, but at a high level there are two major dimensions to keep in mind. The first is credit risk, and the further down the credit scale one goes, not only is absolute risk greater but the risk transforms to look more like equity risk and less like interest rate risk. The second dimension is defined by whether the bond is traditional or inflation-linked. Traditional bonds do well in a world of declining inflation or actual deflation, while linkers are more attractive in a rising inflation world.

Most portfolios allocate to bonds in one of two general ways. Some portfolios restrict their bond holdings to highest-quality sovereign debt in both traditional and inflation-linked form. Others reach further and target something that is benchmarked to a broad index like the Barclays Aggregate, which includes investment grade governments, agencies and corporate bonds. High-yield and distressed bonds might play a meaningful role in one's portfolio, but they are more often thought of as special allocations, or opportunistic fixed income, and are not part of the core bond allocation. We discuss them later in Section 4.5 in this chapter.

There is an active and open debate whether one should have anything other than sovereign bonds as a permanent part of one's growth portfolio. History has shown that some large institutional investors, facing restrictions on how much total non-bond exposure they can hold, sometimes try to cheat by owning bonds that have equity-like risk while holding out the promise of larger returns than sovereign debt can offer. Given the massive amounts of capital that large institutions allocate, their behavior may, on average compress credit spreads to a point where the return potential fails to compensate for all of the risks.

This was certainly the pattern of spreads leading up to the credit crisis that started to emerge in the second half of 2007 and erupted in 2008. Huge sums were invested over a period of years in supposedly safe bonds that saw ever-tighter spreads. Despite years of apparent safety as evidenced by low monthly volatility, there was extreme risk building by the very tightness of the spreads. Bond investors, who had significant spread product in that part of their portfolios, realized too late that the potential losses could be much larger than anything previously seen.

This argues for sovereign debt being the core of one's bond portfolio, but with the highest-quality issuers like the United States, Germany, and Japan offering nominal rates at or below the rate of inflation, this can be a challenge. *There will be times when the interest being promised is so low that it is better to stay in cash and ultra-short maturities rather than risk large mark-to-market losses in longer duration bonds if interest rates should rise.*

In that world, allocations to spread product can be done selectively and opportunistically. In what might appear to be an anti-intuitive posture, allocations to spread product are less attractive when the safety of the bonds appears greatest as evidenced by very tight spreads. It is at precisely these times that the correlation to the equity market is the greatest. And any downward shocks to stocks will likely ripple through to produce a potential for losses in the credit portfolio as well.

It is perhaps not surprising that when credit spreads blow out in times of crisis investors cut positions because of their losses and the perceived risk, only adding to the positions after spreads have come back in. But this is upside down. Corporate bonds should be more attractive when the incremental return is wider than average because it is only then that there is reasonable compensation for the equity-like risk. If an investor routinely buys high and sells low, and it appears that many people and institutions in corporate bonds do just this, the entire area should be avoided.

4.2.2 Stocks

Stocks represent the residual claim on a corporation, which sounds like a bad place to be for an investor. It is, however, the only place to be to participate in the growth of a corporation. Banks that lend to the corporation or purchasers of the company's bonds have their returns capped at the return of capital plus interest. If one believes in growth of a company or a market, stocks will be the core of the portfolio.

Jeremy Siegel's book, *Stocks for the Long Run*, is considered one of the definitive arguments for why stocks should play a central role in growth portfolios.[4] It was first published in 1994 and included a statistical analysis of the US stock market reaching back into the early nineteenth century. The central premise is simplicity itself. Over virtually any 20 or 30-year window, US stocks have appreciated. There were many examples of large swings in shorter periods, but *if one had the ability to look past these fluctuations*, stocks showed themselves to have a higher return than other choices without being all that risky.

Siegel's argument for stocks is based on sound finance theory. Since equity is lower in a company's capitalization structure, it should be expected to earn a *risk premium* to more secure assets. Link this to a generally growing economy and private sector and one has the recipe for long-term compounded outperformance relative to other investment opportunities.

There are criticisms of the Siegel thesis that deserve note. The first four editions of his book are largely US-centric. A 200-year history may seem like a massive data set, large enough to divine the market's secrets, but it can actually be thought of as a single data point. What stocks did from 1802 to the present in the United States was the product of an actual set of events in a single country. The investor should ask, "What is the chance the next 200 years will look like the last?"

Siegel did not dwell on the fact that stock markets sometimes go to zero because that has not been the US history. There have been harsh crashes, wiping out large percentages of the market's total capitalization, but in the vast scope of US history, they have only been dramatic, but ultimately temporary, setbacks. Subsequent events have always repaired the damage and investors who had staying power eventually made up the losses.

But this is not the experience of most countries of the world. Wars, revolutions, and nationalizations have all played a part in taking most of the world's stock exchanges to zero at some point in their histories. It does not matter that many of these markets have risen again like a phoenix after their calamities. Once an equity investor is wiped out, no amount of "market" return after the restart can create

---

[4]Siegel, J. (1994). *Stocks for the Long Run*. McGraw Hill: New York.

wealth. Zero compounded at any rate of return is still zero. From a global perspective, the continuous US history is a rare case and not the norm.

Markets do not have to go to zero for doubts to arise about the Siegel thesis. Japan is perhaps the most dramatic example of a major market downturn that has not come close to recovering in almost 30 years. The chart in Figure 4.1 shows the monthly closes for the Nikkei 225 from 1970 through 2018.

Examining this record, things began changing in a dramatic fashion for Japan in the mid-1980s. The United States was coming off a short but deep recession and it was far from obvious that the inflationary malaise of the 1970s was truly in the past. Japan seemed to be on a much better trajectory. Exports and the economy in general were booming. Books were being written about the superiority of corporate Japan from a global perspective. Money was pouring into the country, as local and foreign investors alike could not get enough exposure to Japanese stocks.

Looking closely at the chart, one can see that Japan had its own October 1987 stock market crash, but it was corrected within months. From 1985 to the end of that decade, the Nikkei 225 average appreciated over 200%, topping out at almost 39,000. At that point Japanese stocks represented about 60% of the capitalization of all stocks outside the United States.

The tumble from the peak was fast and steep. Within two years of the top, the index had lost more than half its value. When Siegel's book appeared in 1994, the index was around 20,000. Some, reading Siegel's words and seeing how far Japanese stocks had fallen, may have concluded that it was a great buying opportunity for long-term investors. In the next 10 years the average fell in half again.

Twenty years after the top value, Japanese equities had lost over 70% of their value. Put another way, from the last index level in the chart of 19,700, stocks would have to nearly double to regain their high water mark. It takes an investor with a very long term horizon to argue that stocks for the long run has been a good rule for Japanese investors at all points in time.

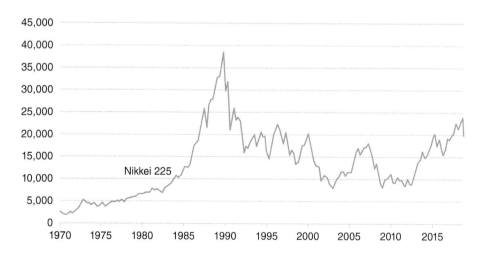

FIGURE 4.1   Nikkei 225 Stock Index 1970–2018
Source: Bloomberg

People have carried Siegel's basic theme to the point of silliness arguing in favor of a large allocation to stocks at all points of time. Perhaps the most extreme view was found in Hasset and Glassman's book, *Dow 36,000*, published in September 1999.[5] The authors argued that, because stocks were a superior investment vehicle, capturing growth while being almost immune to losses if held long enough, they warranted a very low-risk premium over US Treasury bills.

They translated this conclusion directly into a prediction. When they made their case, the Dow Jones Industrial Average was just over 10,300, trading at an average P/E ratio of over 44.[6] To them, this multiple was much too low and did not recognize either the growth potential created by technology and the Internet or the inherently safe nature of stocks held for the long run.

They believed the historical risk premium for stocks was too high, with the risks for a long-term diversified equity portfolio being comparable to T-bills. This in turn would justify much higher P/E ratios, which supported their view that the previous 20-year bull market was just a prelude to the tripling of stock value that would occur by 2002–2004. Their methodology appeared well grounded in finance and their conclusions reinforced the emotions of a broad range of enthusiastic investors.

It turned out they were quite wrong. As shown in the chart in Figure 4.2 the Dow was just slightly above their launch point a dozen years later, and twice in the intervening years, it touched points that represented over 30% declines. In an editorial in *The Wall Street Journal* in 2011, Glassman admitted that they had erred.[7]

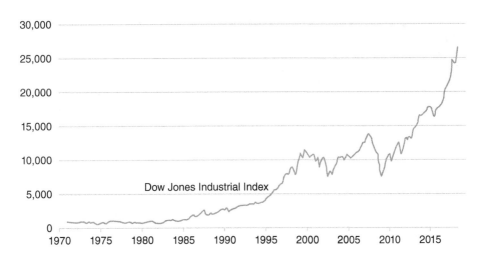

FIGURE 4.2 Dow Jones Industrial Stock Index 1970–2018
Source: Bloomberg

---

[5]Hassett, K.A. and Glassman, J.K. (1999). *Dow 36,000: The New Strategy for Profiting from the Coming Rise in the Stock Market.* Crown Publishing Group: New York.

[6]Saint-Leger, R. What Is the Long-term Average PE of the Dow-Jones? http://finance.zacks.com/longterm-average-pe-dow-jones-3619.html. (31 March 2019).

[7]Glassman, J.K. (2011). Why I Was Wrong about "Dow 36,000". *The Wall Street Journal.* (24 February).

Glassman's revised view was that the error stemmed from equating risk with volatility. Since 1999 he and the market had discovered that events like 9/11 or the flash crash of May 2010 demonstrate that statistical volatility does not always capture true risk. He also claimed that these kinds of risks have increased over time (an assertion that can be actively debated). Once one accepts that there are extra dimensions to risk, the valuation of the stock market in 1999 was not too low then and projections for continued growth were wildly optimistic.

This is a considerably different tune from what was being said by him and many others in 1999. But one does not have to argue from some theoretical peak whether stocks should fundamentally play the core of an investment portfolio or not. It is allowed, and should be encouraged, to walk down from that mountain to the valleys of reality and ask whether stocks make sense at their current valuations.

Robert Shiller was the most vocal academic in the second half of the 1990s about the price of stocks being too high.[8] But he was not the only voice on that side of the discussion. Noted value investors like Jeremy Grantham also cautioned against what they saw as a mania that was gripping much of the stock market. Cautious managers like Grantham were largely rewarded for their insights with investor redemptions, as people abandoned funds that "did not get it" in favor of the tech-based rally.

The message is not whether stocks should always play a key part of a growth portfolio or not. It is that valuations matter. In 1999, a very large number of defined benefit pension plans could have liquidated their stock portfolios entirely and placed the proceeds into traditional Treasuries and TIPS, and thereby completely covering all of their future liabilities at virtually no risk. Why few plans actually did this is illustrative of challenges every investor faces.

The most important reason why pension plans did not sell their stocks and buy bonds to immunize future liabilities is that they lost track of what they were trying to achieve. The primary goal should always have been to cover their obligations, but private and public plans alike got greedy. Relying on books like *Stocks for the Long Run* and *Dow: 36,000*, they thought their organizations could save on future contributions to the plans by riding the equity gravy train well into the future. Assets normally devoted to funding pensions could be put to other uses. Corporate boards and elected officials all were seduced by the prospects.

Similarly, pension plans found themselves being graded on their performance against their peers rather than how they did against their internal objectives. Since almost everyone had succeeded in becoming overfunded, that in itself was considered a small accomplishment. Top decile fund managers, who all got there by taking larger equity and technology bets in the bull market, were given awards by the financial press. Bull market investors were all smart. Leveraged bull market investors appeared smarter.

When valuations corrected violently after the peak, there was a collective realization of what might have been. Previously overfunded plans fell into deficit and the next decade brought little relief from stocks that swung wildly but produced virtually no return in total. Discussions turned to the costs of severely underfunded plans as Baby Boomer workers marched closer to their retirement dates. Ironically, fixed income holdings were consciously raised by many plans *after* the credit and liquidity

---

[8]Shiller, R. (2000). *Irrational Exuberance*. Princeton University Press: New Jersey.

crisis of 2008–2009 at just the time when the risk/reward profile had swung back in favor of equities.

A great deal of energy is spent determining the allocations to equity subsectors. Large, mid, and small caps have their followers in almost every geographic area. Some break the categories further into growth or value styles. All of this is designed to insure appropriate diversification and coverage.

Much of this effort is displaced. As global markets have become more integrated, deciding whether to put a dollar into equity bucket A versus equity bucket B is less important to long-term performance than how many dollars one allocates to all the equity buckets. That is not to say that all equity categories will perform equally or that intelligent tactical allocation can't produce a meaningful benefit. It only says that fine-tuning long-term asset allocations across many equity categories will likely not produce the meaningful reduction in volatility that one might have expected 40 years ago. Equity risk is much more highly correlated across categories than it once was.

The heightened correlation across subcategories only adds to the total risk of holding an equity portfolio. On the surface this is neither good nor bad, but needs to be considered when arriving at the total target equity exposure. There are other choices for the growth portfolio, which leads logically to the discussion of alternative investments.

4.2.3 Alternative Investments

You sometimes hear the question, "How much of your portfolio is in alternatives?" The questioner might be trying to get a perspective on the aggressiveness of your portfolio, but he might as well have asked how many of your managers have brown eyes. Giving any percentage answer, either high or low, may shed light on how much you are paying managers, but it says almost nothing about the exposures or risk profile of your portfolio.

Alternative investments taken in the broadest sense are not an asset class. Equity hedge funds, venture capital partnerships, pools of direct loans and funds holding farm land all fall under the alternative investment umbrella, but they have very little in common in terms of their sources of returns or risk. Saying that half your portfolio is in alternatives conveys very little information.

Chapter 9 discusses in more detail the characteristics of a wide range of alternatives. The key question in this chapter is what alternatives add to the portfolio allocation process. Given that they are not a distinct asset class, it is almost impossible to answer this question analytically. Yet there must be a major contribution because the trend over the past 50 years, led by some of the most successful institutional investors in the world, is to allocate more and more to nontraditional investments.

There are some alternative investments that offer exposures not available in traditional form. An example would be a portfolio of direct loans. Venture capital and most private equity funds fall into this category as well. The thesis is that the investor can add value, creating an attractive rate of return. Since these investments tend to be more concentrated and less liquid than what one could get from a stock portfolio, "attractive" in this context should mean superior to that expected from the public markets.

There are other alternative investments that package publicly traded securities in nontraditional ways. *Long/short equity hedge funds* and *commodity trading advisors (CTAs)* typically trade in stocks or liquid futures contracts that could be bought or sold by any investor. What makes their approaches fall into the alternative category is the use of shorting and leverage. Almost always, these funds will have higher fees and tighter liquidity terms than their traditional counterparts, though a growing category called *liquid alts* is beginning to challenge that.

Because of the ability to go short and to use leverage, these funds can differ dramatically from long stock and bond portfolios in terms of their expected risk. Intuitively from the name, one might expect a hedge fund to be less volatile than a long-only equity fund. By using leverage, hedge funds can actually target a higher volatility than the market. This does not happen very often by design, but the history of alternatives is filled with examples where low volatility was promised and disastrous volatility was delivered.

Specific alternatives are added to portfolios to exploit three potential benefits:

- Higher rates of return than public markets can provide.
- Lower volatility than the public markets.
- Diversification benefits from less correlated returns.

It may be impossible to find a single alternative that rings all three bells. Usually an opportunistic collection of alternatives is assembled that together offers the chance to achieve the above goals. The price one generally pays for those benefits includes higher expenses, less liquidity, and less transparency. Long-term investors are often willing to give up liquidity for a portion of their portfolio if the after-expense return pattern improves their portfolios. But there is no analytical way to neatly define what transparency should be worth.

Since alternatives cover such a wide range of asset classes and risk exposures, no discussion of portfolio allocation can be completed with just the top-level question, "How much should be allocated to alternatives?" Instead, investors should start with an investment theme and then ask what the best vehicle to execute that theme is. Everything should be considered on an after-liquidity, after-transparency, and where relevant, after-tax basis. Only then can one determine what role alternatives might play in the portfolio.

The biggest mistake investors make when it comes to alternatives concerns categorizations. Too often managers sell their strategies as substitutes for other traditional assets based on historical return and risk distributions. Leveraged market neutral long/short equity hedge funds or fixed income arbitrage funds can have long periods of realized volatility that is less than the stock market. This does not make them "bond substitutes." Spectacular losses in 1998 and 2008 for many of these funds demonstrated that if one wanted bond exposure, these funds did not provide anything like it.

Another major error comes from equating lack of transparency or clear mark-to-market values to low risk. Everyone's stock portfolio might seem less volatile if it was only priced once a year. Not being able to price direct loans, real estate or private equity investments on a continuous basis masks, but does not eliminate, the market risk in these alternatives positions.

4.2.4 Real Assets

Unlike the vague nature of alternative assets, real assets have one characteristic in common. Whether one invests in residential real estate, timberland, bars of gold, fine art, or barrels of oil, there is an undeniable tangibility about the investment. But tangibility does not equate to value. It has value only when there is a bid.

In a minor scene in the great 1942 movie, *Casablanca*, a couple is trying to raise funds for their exit visas from the city by selling the wife's diamonds. A somewhat shady-looking dealer disappoints them by saying that diamonds are a drug on the market; everyone has diamonds. In the particular situation of Casablanca during the depths of World War II, there was very little demand relative to the desperate desire of those willing to sell.

Some real assets like fruit farms, commercial real estate, oil and gas wells, or stands of timber can be expected to produce regular income, but that income can be highly variable either because of high costs of production or low selling prices. In 2010, with over 20% of retail space in America vacant, much of that subset of commercial real estate became a "store of value" rather than a source of current income.[9]

The sources of return from real assets come largely from appreciation through time, though, as noted above, some real investments produce income. Whether real assets work as an effective portfolio investment over any given span of time depends entirely on supply and demand. With growing economies and incomes it can sometimes seem that expanding demand will drive the prices of real assets to the moon. History shows that every time people begin to believe in that kind of trajectory, gravity takes over and brings prices back to earth.

Real assets are quite different. Unlike stocks and bonds, where the issuers control the supply, real assets are more democratic. You may have never grown soybeans in your life, but if the price got high enough, you might be tempted to learn how. Supply for most real assets responds to price increases. It might take some time for this to occur, but whenever a spurt in demand causes the price of a product to increase past what it costs to produce, you can count on someone stepping forward to try to bring more to market.

Time is the key dimension. If a scientific study appeared that said a diet of avocados and kiwis cut the chance of cancer in half, you could certainly expect the prices of those fruits to explode, at least in the short run. Farmers would try to sell more, but once the current season's crop was marketed there would be no more opportunities to meet the expanded demand. Even if the number of trees could be doubled in the next few months, these trees would bear no fruit for years. The best farmers could do is add fertilizer and pest controls to the next crop in hopes of expanding yield.

In the short run, the expansion in demand swamps the existing supply of kiwis and avocados. Prices have to go up to discourage some of the demand and reach equilibrium. After the study was announced, some previous consumers simply dropped their demand because of expense. Others paid up to buy the same or in some cases smaller amounts. Others still, who may have never eaten fruit before the study, became consumers because of the study.

If one had owned avocados, kiwis, or the land on which they grew as a real asset, there would have been a large and immediate gain to the investment. This is the kind of investment return that should be considered a windfall that is very unlikely to be repeated.

---

[9]National Association of Realtors. (2017). *Commercial Real Estate Outlook*, (30 May).

Next year's crops might be similarly attractively priced, but when the new plantings come on line, supply will rise up to meet demand and prices will once again fall. *Real asset price swings can take years to play out, but eventually supply adjusts to demand and there are no extraordinary returns available to investors.*

Unusually low prices also get corrected through time, frequently with a lag. Natural gas properties are a prime example. The chart in Figure 4.3 shows the spot price of natural gas at the Henry Hub in Texas from 2000 to 2018. The first run-up in price in 2005 was due to supply disruptions caused by Hurricanes Katrina and Rita. This is the kind of supply shock that causes temporary windfalls, but few persist to create a long-term profit opportunity. The build up from 2007 to the middle of 2008 was something else.

It was widely reported at the time that all energy prices were being driven by the growth in emerging market real incomes and the demand for auto fuel, fertilizers, and almost every other product related to the wider energy complex. This was perceived as a broad and permanent shift out of the demand curves to which potential suppliers eagerly responded. A similar pattern was seen in crude oil prices up to mid 2008 as shown in Figure 4.4. This was not a hurricane-induced disruption, but a fundamental change that appeared to spell opportunity for investors.

Natural gas and oil are obviously related energy markets, but have distinct characteristics. The biggest difference is that natural gas is much harder to transport between continents. Pipelines are more efficient than the process of liquefying the natural gas for transportation by tanker. This means that prices of natural gas are more local in nature. Crude oil prices are much more integrated globally.

The price paths of the two commodities were equally brutal in the second half of 2008. Oil fell from $147 to $35 a barrel, a decline of more than 75%. Natural gas went from near $13 per million cubic feet to around $2 briefly, a fall of over 80%. Suddenly the prevailing wisdom of a growing global economy and a near insatiable demand for

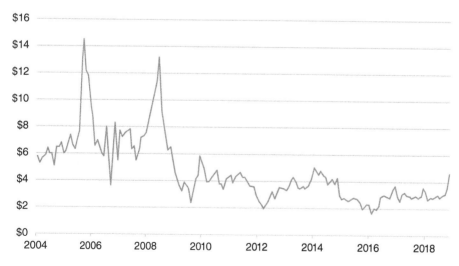

FIGURE 4.3   HH Texas Natural Gas Spot Price 2004–2018
Source: Bloomberg

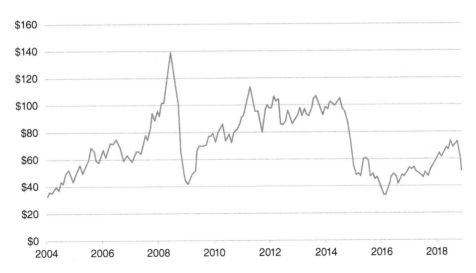

FIGURE 4.4 West Texas Intermediate Crude Oil Spot Price 2004–2018
Source: Bloomberg

energy was replaced with the reality of macroeconomic uncertainty and staggering supplies caused in part by the emerging US fracking industry.

The divergent behavior of crude oil and natural gas prices after the credit crisis speaks to the importance of supply and demand. As China, India, and Brazil led a broad group of emerging economies back to a stronger growth path, crude oil regained a balance of supply and demand. In early 2011, political and military turmoil in Libya and other parts of the Middle East once again brought into question how reliable some sources of oil supply really were. Crude oil pierced the $100-a-barrel barrier where it more or less stayed through 2014.

The path of natural gas prices could not have been more different. As prices increased in 2007 and early 2008 there was a natural supply response of more wells being drilled. But this action coincided with the widespread adoption of new horizontal drilling techniques and recovery technologies that made each new well many times more productive than the old traditional wells. When prices collapsed in 2008, these new drilling projects were well under development and vast new supplies of natural gas were in the proverbial pipeline.

Once the capital expense for drilling projects or new mines has been spent, those costs are in the past tense. Economists like to say, "Sunk costs are sunk." The only relevant question going forward is how much it costs to produce the next unit of output. In the case of natural gas, the answer is not very much. Despite the rebound in much of the global economy and rising crude oil prices, the supplies of natural gas were ample enough to push prices to their lowest levels in almost a decade.

Oil was not to be left out of the technology game. Oil wells using the similar fracking techniques, especially in West Texas and other shale basins, began expanding quickly with crude prices above $100 a barrel. US production grew to levels not seen since the early 1970s. This new supply along with aggressive OPEC output pushed the world into an oversupply situation and crude prices fell by more than half in 2015.

This digression into energy prices demonstrates some of the major challenges to investing in real assets. Most of these opportunities involve business elements that call for specialized knowledge to evaluate. Translating a macroeconomic theme like "Emerging market demand for energy is rapidly expanding" into a tradable investment idea is not a straightforward matter.

One way to limit the influence of new entrants into the supply chain is to try to acquire only those real assets where new entry is impossible. Oil paintings by Monet or Picasso, or those of any other dead artist, fall into this category. The problem with these items as an investment is that while their supply is fixed, the demand can fluctuate for a whole host of reasons. Wars have typically not been good for the price of fine art. More recently the fortunes of hedge fund managers have been a bigger driver. Then again, tastes can simply change. The Titian painting that J. P. Morgan bought 100 years ago at the height of that artist's popularity is still great art. It may have been a less successful investment over the last 50 years than a painting of a soup can by Andy Warhol.

Some suggest that land is the ultimate real asset investment because, "they're not making any more of it." This is true, but land can always be made more productive, easing much of its scarcity value. Farmland can be planted more intensively using more fertilizer. Urban residential land can see high-rise apartments replace row houses. The acres may not change, but new supply is effectively created through changes in utilization.

Probably the most frequently heard argument for real assets in a portfolio is that they act as an inflation hedge. There is perhaps no more intuitive investment argument to be made. As the value of paper money falls, the value of "stuff" must increase. There are many problems with this argument, however, not the least of which as we saw with the natural gas example above is that not all "stuff" is created equal and the time frame for investing really matters. Direct commodity investments are a particularly difficult class of real assets for the long-term investor.

Care needs to be taken when thinking about commodity investing for long-term portfolios. *Over long periods of time, because of technological advances, prices of commodities fall in real terms.* This is a natural part of the development process. Advances in yields for crops and in the efficiency in using industrial materials have been systematically positive since at least the nineteenth century. It is also true that as incomes rise, demand for higher value-added goods and services rise relative to basic products.

This is most clearly seen in the history of the United States. Beginning as an agrarian economy, as the United States developed, manufacturing eventually came to dominate agriculture. Manufacturing, in turn, faded in relative importance to services in the second half of the twentieth century. The chart in Figure 4.5, taken from the Commodity Research Bureau, shows inflation adjusted wheat, corn, and soybean prices from 1960 to 2018, all benchmarked to the last CPI.

But within this long-term, technology-driven pattern are periods of supply-and-demand imbalance that can produce great increases in commodity prices. The upward spikes in the middle 1970s is an example of how the trend can be temporarily and dramatically broken.

Energy, precious metals, and industrial metals are the three other broad categories of traded commodities, and they exhibit similar behavior over very long periods. Given that investors like real appreciation in their portfolios, the case for commodities must be made using other arguments beyond simple real returns.

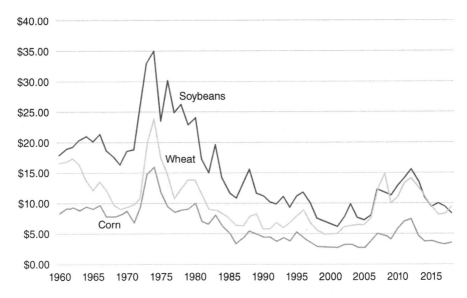

FIGURE 4.5 Inflation-Adjusted Soybean, Wheat, & Corn Prices
Source: Commodity Research Bureau

The key arguments for commodities are:

- Multiyear periods exist where increases in global demand outstrip the ability of suppliers to expand production, leading to rapidly increasing prices (The Global Growth Story).
- Commodity prices, and other real assets, should provide some protection against the general level of inflation (Inflation Protection).
- Commodity price movements are generally unlinked, or negatively linked, to the price movements of equities and bonds. They also hedge against declines in the dollar (The Diversification Story).

Each of these arguments will be expanded upon below.

4.2.4.1 The Global Growth Story – Commodity Super Cycles

In the past 30 years there has been a sea change in global growth. The emerging economies of the world have moved from a story of great potential to one of great achievement. Asia, Eastern Europe, the Middle East, and Latin America have all seen remarkable increases in their rates of growth. Today, emerging market economies are roughly 30% of world GDP based on market exchange rates. Adjusted for purchasing power parity, they account for almost 50%. A good part of this story is commodity related.

As impressive as these growth figures have been, more important is the fact that more than 80% of the global population lives in the emerging world. As the move toward freer markets gained momentum around the globe, the real incomes of hundreds of millions of people have risen, creating rapidly growing middle classes and different consumption patterns.

Diets move toward more animal proteins as incomes grow, which in turn leads to greater demand for both animals and feeds. Transportation becomes more oriented to the individual family, rapidly increasing demand for automobiles and fossil fuels. Infrastructure development shifts out the demand for industrial commodities. All of these factors come from the rapid growth of incomes and demand in the developing world. While there is talk of actual recession in North America and Western Europe, the developing economies are still growing at rates between 3% and 6% a year.

In the past much of the developing world's growth was dependent upon the economic health of the United States, Western Europe, and Japan. Today much of this growth is self-financed and sustainable without much help from the developed world. The growth rates are large enough to double real income in these countries in 15–20 years. Countries from China to Russia and much of the Middle East have also accumulated massive foreign reserves and are largely self-sufficient in their ability to produce capital for future investments. By any standard, there is still considerable force behind the global growth story.

But demand is only one blade of the scissors. It must be considered against the backdrop of supply. As noted above, over long periods of time, technology has changed at a pace to more than supply any growth in demand. The result has been real declines in commodity prices over decades. Over shorter time periods, however, supply cannot be adjusted quickly because of the nature of commodity production.

Whether you are speaking of industrial metals or energy, investments necessary to expand production require massive amounts of capital and considerable spans of time. In economics, this is called an *inelastic* supply curve in the short run. It is simply not feasible to expand the production of aluminum or crude oil by 10%, let alone achieve greater growth, in a short period of time. Should demand increase quickly, the only way to allocate scarce supply is through meaningful increases in price.

One would think that annual crops like soybeans or wheat could change their supply relatively quickly, and to a degree this is true. However, agricultural production is still the most highly controlled industry in the world, with much of world's production determined without regard to market prices. Even in the United States and Canada, farmers do not have complete autonomy in their planting decisions because of a myriad of government programs affecting the agricultural sector.

The result of these natural and artificial forces is a positive supply response, but one that can take years to make a noticeable impact on demand-driven higher prices. For example, one expects Canadian tar sands and Brazilian deep-water wells to produce significant quantities of new oil supply, but these producers will not reach full production for many years. As the decline of crude prices after 2015 showed, by the time such massive, capital-intensive projects come on line, the once-promising price environment to sell that new supply may have passed.

Historically, this dynamic has produced "super cycles" in commodities. People old enough to remember the 1970s understand well how quickly supply disruptions caused oil prices to accelerate from the single digit prices typical of the previous decades. These high prices encouraged the energy industry to explore and develop new sources of supply, which took years to bring on line. When the supply response was fully felt, it was against a backdrop of slightly greater demand, leading to a long period of depressed prices beginning in the mid-1980s and extending into the late-1990s that were disturbed only by periodic scares of politically induced supply shocks.

Figure 4.6 expands on the earlier chart of crude oil prices to include history back to before the effectiveness of OPEC and calibrates the price axis in log scale to emphasize percentage changes. The percentage gain in 2007 when oil flirted with $140 per barrel was similar to earlier price spikes.

What this means for the commodity investor is that there is an important tactical element around the long-term asset allocation. Long-term successful commodity investors like Harvard and Notre Dame have been known to vary their exposures considerably at different points of the super cycle. It also suggests that the form of the commodity investment is important to allow one to exploit the different stages of the cycle.

4.2.4.2 Inflation Protection

Perhaps the single greatest misconception about commodity investing concerns how much inflation protection it provides. The source of this misconception is confusion about the nature of inflation itself. Inflation is the *sustained* increase in general prices. It is almost always a macroeconomic phenomenon caused by more liquidity available than that needed to support any level of real economic growth. In hyperinflationary environments like those experienced in Germany in the 1920s and parts of Latin America in the 1970s and 1980s, investments in any real asset, whether it was commodity based or not, would offer a measure of protection against inflation.

Americans have no real experience with this type of inflation. Instead, we look back to the period of the mid-1970s and early 1980s for the last period of unacceptably high levels of price changes across goods, services, wages, and assets. History has shown that this inflation was, at its core, similar in nature to the hyperinflations of history, but it was radically different in degree. It was concerted monetary action

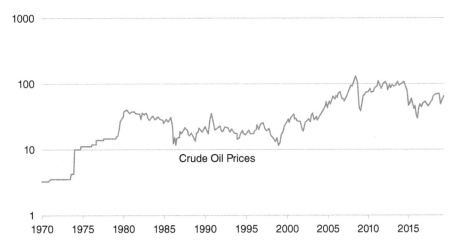

FIGURE 4.6 Crude Oil (Spot) Prices 1970–2018
Source: Federal Reserve Bank of St. Louis (FRED)

taken by the Federal Reserve under Paul Volker that dramatically lowered liquidity creation and ultimately reduced the rate of inflation.

It is perhaps unfortunate that this inflationary era corresponded with commodity supply shocks that were exacerbated by poor policies that constrained outputs of grains and energy products in this country. This led many people to believe the commodity price changes caused the inflation, and that commodity-based investments would provide good protection against future bouts of inflation. While it is certainly true that commodity price increases get reflected into price statistics, and in the case of the 1970s made the basic inflationary experience worse, commodity prices by themselves are very poor indicators of future general inflation.

The subject is further complicated by the degree of relevance of the inflation statistics to different investors. The Consumer Price Index, or CPI, is the most widely followed general measure of price change. It is constructed to reflect the cost of a basket of goods and services that a typical American consumer buys. For other organizations like insurance companies or colleges and universities, the relevant factors that pose inflation risks do not correspond well at all to headline CPI.

The primary conclusion from years of observations is that unless there is a significant period of sustained inflation, commodity prices do not provide any meaningful protection against changes in the rate of inflation. And in the event that there is sustained inflation, any investment in real assets will help the investor.

4.2.4.3 The Diversification Story

Perhaps the most often cited benefit of commodity investing is the relatively low and sometimes observed negative correlation between most commodities oriented investments and other traditional investments. The table in Figure 4.7 gives the simple correlation between monthly returns between the GSCI, the S&P 500, MSCI EAFE, and the Lehman Intermediate Government Credit Index.

There is essentially no correlation between the commodities index and either of the stock indexes. There is a small negative correlation between commodities and bond returns. This is a reflection of the weak positive link between

Correlation Coefficient 1970–2018	GSCI Commodity Index	Lehman Intermediate Government-Credit Index	MSCI EAFE - Net	S&P 500 Index
GSCI Commodity Index	1.00	−0.06	0.03	−0.03
Lehman Intermediate Government-Credit Index	−0.06	1.00	0.13	0.19
MSCI EAFE - Net	0.03	0.13	1.00	0.57
S&P 500 Index	−0.03	0.19	0.57	1.00

FIGURE 4.7 Commodity Investing Correlations
Data source: Commodity Research Bureau

commodities and inflation and the generally negative impact that inflation has on bond returns.

From a portfolio construction perspective, this is the most significant benefit from adding commodities to the asset allocation. If the returns from an activity are acceptable in the long run, and they are lightly or negatively correlated to the other assets in the portfolio, there should be on average a meaningful reduction in the period-to-period volatility of portfolio performance.

The trade-offs can be looked at in another way as well. If the risk of the current portfolio is deemed acceptable, commodities investments can allow the addition of other higher risk/higher return potential investments without changing in a meaningful way the overall risk in the portfolio.

Since the vast majority of commodities that trade internationally are denominated in dollars, commodities also provide a measure of diversification against other dollar assets. When the dollar is weakening, non-US-based consumers see the cost of commodities fall in their local currency terms, which in turn raises the demand. This has the effect of increasing the dollar prices of the traded commodities. The effect is also there when the dollar is strengthening, but in reverse. Investors that have their liabilities denominated in dollars should understand that the addition of commodities to a portfolio already containing meaningful amounts of non-dollar assets may provide overall diversification benefits, but may increase the total currency risk within the portfolio.

In the language of modern portfolio theory, commodities improve the "efficient frontier." For every level of potential return, risk is reduced, and symmetrically, for every level of risk, return is enhanced. This is the most compelling argument for commodities in a long-term portfolio. *But it should be emphasized that the cost of this diversification varies depending on where the market is within the commodity super cycle. Investors who have successfully implemented commodities investment programs almost always have some commodities exposure for diversification, but the allocation changes over time.*

The execution of any real asset investment plan is a highly specialized process if done properly. The investment industry has tried over the years to make things easier for investors with the introduction of indexes, ETFs, and structured products. The innovation has paid off, at least for the creators of the products. The specifics of how these products deliver or fail to deliver for investors is discussed in detail in Chapter 9.

4.2.5 Further Variation Across the Investment Landscape – Currencies, Credit, etc.

Investment options are not constrained to bonds, stocks, alternatives, and real assets. There are many choices that share some of the characteristics of investments in the broad categories, but do not fit neatly into any bucket. Stand-alone portfolios of foreign currencies and high-yield or distressed debts are two examples of such investments that still might play an attractive role in a portfolio.

When you own a stock or a bond it is an expression that you prefer to own that asset versus holding cash. Buying currencies is somewhat different. Every position in currencies is a relative value trade. You are never simply long Japanese yen. You are long Japanese yen *versus* the US dollar. While the vast majority of the multitrillion dollar daily foreign exchange market is done relative to the US dollar, a meaningful amount of activity happens between pairs that do not involve the United States.[10]

You can think of a currency holding as an ultra-short duration sovereign liability that carries no coupon. That would lead one to place it in the bond category, but it has no yield. Fiat money, which has been the norm for over 50 years around the globe, is also a strange kind of liability in that if you present it to the central bank that issued it, the bank would simply replace it with another identical sheet of paper with a different serial number. There is no other backing for fiat money. Its value is only a function of what people are willing to pay to hold it at any point in time.

Currency acts as a store of value and as a medium of exchange. In those ways it is similar to gold, though it is much more convenient. The only time people seem unwilling to hold their own currency is when inflation erodes its purchasing power. Even then, if the inflation is not too great, the convenience factor offsets many of the disadvantages.

Investors usually think of holding their own currency as simply their cash position. Things get more interesting when you consider holding another country's currency as part of the investment portfolio. Then you must ask what the sources of potential return and risk are as you consciously take a position against your own currency.

It is this relative value nature of a currency trade that makes it impossible to categorize currencies as a distinct asset class. Owning Japanese yen is different from owning Australian dollars or Brazilian reals. Looking at historical returns for various currencies might give you an idea of the future, but any history was the product of macroeconomic policies that may never be repeated. Certainly the citizens of Germany hope they won't repeat the destruction of the deutschemark that occurred a few years after World War I. Many other countries that have also experienced hyperinflation first hand feel the same.

Most portfolios have currency exposure indirectly in their global stock and bond holdings. The currency risk is frequently much smaller than either the equity or duration risks of these assets, so it is sometimes overlooked. This is a mistake. Just as you should have well-grounded expectations for returns and risk for your bond and stock portfolios, you should also have an opinion whether the currency effect will help or hurt. If there is a positive opinion on the asset in general but a negative view on the currency, it is possible to hedge out the currency risk.

As the United States continues its budget deficit and expands the basic money supply, it is a fair question whether US investors have enough non-dollar exposure in their portfolios. This is a similar question that led investors in emerging markets to hold a great deal of wealth in the United States when questions arose about their currency.

A desire to hold more non-dollar exposure does not need to lead to larger international stock or bond holdings. It is possible to hold foreign cash or its equivalent to isolate the foreign exchange element. There are two elements of such an investment: 1) the interest earned on the foreign cash holdings, and 2) the change in the value of the currency.

---

[10]The Triennial Central Bank Survey of foreign exchange and OTC derivatives markets in 2016 of the Bank for International Settlements estimates daily foreign exchange turnover globally at over $5 trillion, of which almost 88% are trades involving the US dollar as one of the trading pairs. www.bis.org.

The interest earned is easily observable but it may not always be accessible. Many experts have said for years that the Chinese renminbi is undervalued leading perhaps to a desire to hold renminbi deposits. The Bank of China tightly controls currency transactions involving the renminbi, so it is not a trivial exercise for foreigners to set up bank accounts in this currency. Branches of the Bank of China in New York and Los Angeles allow US citizens to have renminbidenominated accounts, but these are retail accounts not generally practical for institutional-sized transactions.

Currencies are like any other asset in that they appreciate when there is excess demand for them. This usually happens as part of a growth story. Growing economies attract capital from not only domestic investors but also foreigners. These foreigners sell their currency to buy the local currency, causing appreciation if the flows are meaningful enough.

Figure 4.8 shows two widely followed dollar indexes from 2005 to 2017. The light gray line is the dollar against a basket of developed country currencies including the euro, yen, sterling, and the Swiss franc. The dark gray line is a basket of emerging market currencies from Asia, Latin America, Eastern Europe, the Middle East, and Africa. Both indexes are arbitrarily scaled to equal 100 at the start of the series. A rising line equates to a weaker dollar.

Over the first five years that the chart covers, the dollar versus the basket of developed currencies fluctuated, but was rarely more than 10% above or below the starting point. This is actually what one might expect when comparing mature, low-growth economies. As long as all of the central banks pursue responsible monetary policies, there is little reason to favor one currency over the others. One other conclusion from this is that if such an environment is expected to persist, there is little reason to go to the trouble of hedging away what appears to be a small currency risk.

The dark line is a different story. Over those first five years, the basket of emerging market currencies appreciated against the dollar by almost 60%. This was completely

FIGURE 4.8 Dollar Indexes 2005–2018

a result of higher growth rates in the developing world and the desire of investors in more mature countries to move money into these countries.

The path can be a volatile one around the trend. In the credit crisis that began in late 2008 the flight to the safety of US Treasury securities was from all perceived risk assets, and that included emerging market currencies. The drop in the index over a short period of time was over 25%. But when the growth paths of China, India, Brazil, and much of the developing world were seen to be largely intact, the drop was quickly recovered and the trend for these currencies reestablished. It was not until 2014 with macroeconomic concerns about China and political scandal and a slip into recession for Brazil did the longer term trend reverse.

Investors can participate in this market in a variety of ways. Where capital flows are relatively unrestricted, it is possible to open bank accounts in the target countries. This can be fairly cumbersome. Other avenues include forward contracts for the currencies, non-deliverable forwards (a very liquid type of derivative contract), ETFs, and customized OTC structures. These are discussed in more detail in Chapter 9.

A basic, unleveraged position in developed market currencies should have a volatility someplace between cash and an aggregate bond index. Emerging market currencies have historically been more volatile, but still considerably less than equity markets. But most investors do not hold such basic currency exposures. They either avoid the class completely or invest through macro hedge funds or CTAs that apply leverage to boost expected returns.

Suppose you are optimistic about the currency of a certain developing country and you also note that sovereign interest rates in that country are meaningfully higher than what you are earning at home. By buying the higher yielding currency you have the potential to profit through both the extra interest earned and any appreciation, if your view is right. This is known generically as a *carry trade*. Leveraged traders who borrow money in the low interest rate currency, and then convert to the higher interest rate currency to earn the spread have often used them. Some people think of this as free, low-risk money. Nothing could be further from the truth.

The carry arising from the interest rate differential should be thought of as a buffer. For example, in 2011, the overnight deposit rate in Brazil was greater than 11%, while in the United States it was close to zero. Traders converting dollars that were earning nothing in the United States and investing in Brazilian real deposits should look at the 11% earned as the margin of safety. The Brazilian real would have to fall by more than 11% versus the dollar in the coming year before you would actually have a loss.

Unfortunately for the carry traders, it did just that. In June 2011 it took R\$1.55 to buy \$1. By December, the real had fallen by 19%, well beyond the 5.5% interest one would have earned in six months on local deposits. From 2012 through 2014, the annual declines in the real against the dollar were −11%, −15%, −12%, just slightly more than the interest rate differential. Then the wheels fell off in 2015, with the real tumbling 50% as Brazil's economy fell into recession amid a growing political corruption scandal. 2016 saw an 18% rebound in the real, leaving it still well below its value in the rosier days of 2011.

Such risks are not confined to developing country currencies. Investors in Japan have been pursuing such carry trades in an attempt to escape their market, which has been characterized by near-zero interest rates for decades. A popular destination for such funds has been Australia, which has experienced good growth and has offered much higher rates of interest. The potential peril from such trades can be seen in the chart in Figure 4.9.

The chart shows the number of Australian dollars needed to buy 100 Japanese yen. A declining line signifies a falling yen/rising Aussie dollar. From 2000 to the summer of 2008 the carry trade for Japanese investors was largely a win–win. Though there were moments of volatility, the trend was in favor of the Aussie dollar, the higher yielding currency.

Then the financial crisis of 2008 happened. The Aussie dollar fell by 60% against the Japanese yen. It was likely that Japanese investors trying to repatriate their foreign savings exacerbated this move. Picking up an incremental 4–5% of interest rate carry suddenly did not look like such a great proposition.

The height of the crisis in early 2009 was the best time to reestablish the Aussie dollar carry trade, though it would have taken some strong conviction to jump into a currency that had just fallen 60%.

Getting currency exposure through investments in foreign stocks or bonds is more common. Stand-alone, unleveraged investments in currencies are quite rare. Investors who are seeking out dedicated currency exposure often execute on the theme by employing an active manager who can adjust positions quickly and change leverage to modify the target rates of return and volatility. As in most investments, there are many ways to get any desired exposure allowing investors to tailor their portfolios quite precisely.

Another area that does not fit neatly into a traditional asset allocation category is credit. Most investments involving credit are part of the bond allocation, but when one begins looking at bank loans, high-yield bonds or distressed bonds, there is much less in common with sovereign debt than investment grade corporate bonds possess.

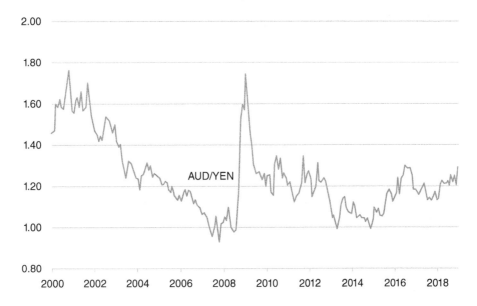

FIGURE 4.9   Australian dollars per 100 Japanese yen
Source: Bloomberg

There are times when credit should be thought of as a distinct and highly equity-like opportunity.

The chart shows the path of credit spreads over comparable maturity US Treasuries for a variety of fixed income investments from 2007 to early 2011, a particularly volatile time for the strategy. The top line reflects high yield, next is bank loans, the light gray is a basket of emerging market sovereign debt, and bottom is for investment grade corporates. The dashed horizontal line is the historical average credit spread for high-yield bonds placed on the chart for reference.

Prior to the credit crisis the world was a kind and gentle place. There appeared to be little risk, and the vast sums of liquidity that were being deployed in non-equity assets squeezed credit spreads tighter than their historical norms. As is often the case in such benign-looking environments, some people were tempted to boost yields by applying leverage. Hundreds of billions of dollars were funneled into CDOs and CLOs (discussed in detail in Chapter 9), which were then sold as "safe" investments based on past low default rates. Additionally, some hedge fund managers also levered up these trades in the quest for yield.

When the first rumblings of the credit crisis appeared in the second half of 2007, all spreads widened, but high-yield spreads moved out more quickly as is often the case with lower rated credits. The forced marriage of Bear Sterns and J.P. Morgan in March 2008 added further to the market's anxiety. But it was the Lehman bankruptcy that opened the floodgates. As investors in CDOs, CLOs, and hedge funds all rushed for the exits, spreads widened to unprecedented levels. Some bank loans, representing the highest part of the capital structure, traded to yields well above 20%.

In the greatly disturbed environment of late 2008 and early 2009, credit was so distorted that investors could project returns that were considerably higher than historical equity averages while having the added protection of being in a superior position in the capital structure. This was not to say that credit could not deteriorate

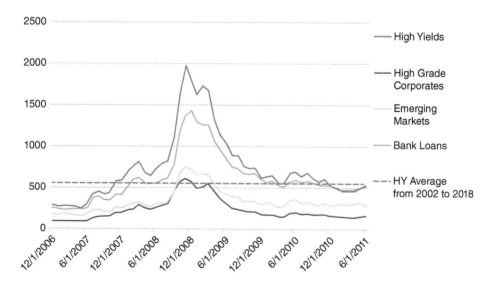

FIGURE 4.10 Credit Spreads 2007–2011
Source: Bloomberg

further. It did imply, however, that carefully researched credit portfolios could be built without leverage, and have the prospect of returns that had rarely been seen in most investors' lifetimes.

When it became clear that the world was not coming to an end, investors who were not upside down in liquidity used some of their dry powder to begin buying credit. As seen in Figure 4.10, the decline in spreads was almost continuous after March 2009. Two years later high-yield spreads were back below their long-term average.

The credit crisis of 2008–2009 was a particularly dramatic episode, but hardly unique. Investors should expect the credit cycle to correspond to the business cycle and to a large degree the equity market. Every time there is a shock to the system, one should expect corporate distress and bankruptcies to grow. With this heightened perceived risk often comes much wider spreads, and if the pre-crisis market was characterized by large amounts of leverage, those spreads will reflect not only the higher risk but also technical selling pressure. In 2008 and 2020 the technicals in the market became so large that they overwhelmed the fundamentals.

If major credit swings are correlated with the equity market, one might argue that there is little reason to own both assets. This ignores the different positions of the two assets in the firm's capital structure. In March 2009 when the S&P 500 dipped to 665, it was not clear that the macro economy could avoid a severe depression or that stocks would not fall lower. What was clearer was that buying bank loans at 60 cents on the face dollar amount of performing companies with many assets beyond their loan liabilities had a high probability of paying off.

This is pretty much what subsequently happened. Many still-shocked investors did not immediately jump back into the equity pool, preferring instead the risk/reward profile of bank loans and high-yield bonds. With perfect hindsight, that money should have been deployed in Brazilian or some other developing country's equities. Unfortunately we have to invest looking forward. Credit appropriately became a critical part of many investors' portfolios early in 2009, allowing them a safer path to expand their risk budgets opportunistically at a time when emotionally it was extremely hard to put more money to work in stocks.

Two years after the credit crisis the role of credit in portfolios was somewhat less obvious. The class is always correlated with equities, but bank loans trading near par offer less margin of safety than when they are trading at 60 cents. Credit could still potentially play a role relative to high-quality sovereign and corporate debt, but it was a considerably different one than it was in 2006 or at the height of the crisis.

The lesson from this is that environment matters. There are many investments like credit that can quickly and dramatically change in nature. And it seems investors are often out of step, emotionally more inclined to invest when the reward/risk profile is weak and avoiding the market when the opportunities are the greatest.

There are other investment opportunities that don't fit neatly into specific asset categories. Preferred stock has characteristics of both bonds and equities. Convertible securities explicitly blend both directional and volatility dimensions of stocks with an interest payment from bonds. These are specialized instruments that like credit and currencies can have widely different appeal depending on the market. The wise investor keeps all of these less-traditional options on the radar screen, avoiding them when they have become too popular and embracing them when they are shunned by the majority.

4.3   THE FUNDAMENTAL LIQUIDITY QUESTION

The traditional approach to liquidity in the finance literature was to identify what was dubbed the *liquidity premium* in less liquid securities.[11] Researchers discovered that as bid/ask spreads, which are good indicators of liquidity, widened, stock prices fell. Given that the economic activity of the companies probably had not changed, this meant that returns going forward were likely going to be higher than average. The conclusion is that investors demand a higher expected return in order to hold less liquid investments, and on average they receive it.

The thrust of most of this research was to dwell on what investors were missing. Liquidity should only really matter to short-term traders and not to long-term investors. Given the power of compounding discussed in Chapter 2, it seemed that investors should flock to illiquid assets and let any liquidity premium work for them through time.

That perspective changed abruptly after the credit and economic crisis of 2008–2009. Instead of asking why liquidity premiums were so large, academics should have been asking why so much liquidity had been given up prior to the crisis in return for so little.

Investors have demanded and received a liquidity premium through time for four basic reasons:

- The circumstances of the investor can change.
- The market can change.
- Having the option to change one's mind is valuable.
- The credit market is not always available when you need it.

Each of the cases above is an acknowledgment that we invest in a dynamic world. The academics chiding investors for demanding too high a payment to assume illiquidity are placing their faith in long-term asset allocations that real-world investors have learned through experience to not trust completely.

The common factors in each of the bullet points above are time and uncertainty. These are the same factors that determine any option's value, and the liquidity premium demanded by investors is easily thought of in these same terms. Investors are willing to pay the equivalent of an option premium in the form of lower expected returns in order to keep their investment choices open and liquidity high. As was amply demonstrated in the depths of the credit crisis, having dry powder and the ability to change one's portfolio can be incredibly valuable.

It is precisely at such times of crisis that the demand for liquidity spikes. There are always plenty of market participants who scramble around trying to find liquidity that they previously thought unnecessary. Nobody smiles at times of crisis, but those who planned ahead for the possibility of bad times can exploit these moments. These investors have degrees of freedom in their investment choices that can quickly make up for the past lost premiums they were supposed to earn from less liquid choices.

---

[11]A good example of this type of study is Eleswarapu, V. (1993). Cost of Transacting and Expected Returns in the NASDAQ Market. *Journal of Finance*, 2, no. 5, pp. 2113–2127. It shows that stocks with high bid/ask spreads also demonstrate greater long-term returns.

The stream of actual investment returns does not tell the whole story. It is hard to place a value on the peace of mind that liquidity provides. Whether an investor changes anything in their portfolio during a time of market flux is irrelevant. The fact that they *can* change their allocations is highly valuable emotionally. It appears that people are willing to give up quite a bit for that degree of control and comfort.

Perhaps the most significant trend among institutional investors starting in the 1990s was the shift toward less-liquid partnerships. Trustees saw institutions like Yale and Harvard increasing their allocations to private equity and venture capital and enjoying great success. During the bull market of the 1990s it was assumed that these outsized returns were the rewards of perpetual endowments exploiting the liquidity premiums such investments offered.

Individual investors participated in this trend, but to a much lesser extent. Wealthy individuals often have meaningful assets in their personal real estate or in the equity of a company that created the wealth. This can already be highly illiquid, so the temptation to add more in the form of private partnerships can be more easily resisted.

But it is not clear that the outsized returns of these partnerships in the 1990s were primarily a reward for illiquidity. Many of these funds deployed leverage at the financing or operation levels. *Any* leveraged index stock investment would have shown outsized returns over this period. If the strategy were executed using futures contracts or leveraged mutual funds, there would have been near perfect liquidity as well.

This began to become evident in the first years of the twenty-first century. When the stock market broadly retreated from 2000 to 2002, many partnerships suffered more than the market in general. The only significant solace to investors was that because there was little transparency, it was not possible to observe the retreat in real time.

There is another issue with private partnerships that are structured with committed capital. Once the commitment is made, the actual timing of capital calls is at the discretion of the general partner. This makes the calculation of the ultimate rate of return *for the investor* less than completely straightforward.

Any general partners reading the above paragraph are no doubt protesting loudly. Each of the funds keeps very precise records regarding when capital is called, how it is invested and how much gets returned and when. Internal rates of return (IRR) are calculated according to widely accepted procedures. What could possibly be imprecise about that?

From the GP's perspective, everything is well defined and buttoned up. But consider an investor who commits $1 million to a new partnership. His or her total return is more complicated than the fund's IRR. Since the $1 million can be called at any time, the commitment is a liability for the investor that has to be provided for. If the investor takes the most conservative approach and puts the $1 million in cash, there is an expected opportunity loss for the period prior to all the capital being called. The modest return on the cash holding should also be considered as part of the total return of the investment, but it is likely much lower than what the fund is expected to earn. In fact, the reason the GP does not call all of the capital at once is because he doesn't want that cash drag to be reflected in *his* performance.

Many investors try to minimize the cash drag by investing the $1 million in a related liquid investment waiting for the capital calls. For example, funds allocated to private equity might go into a stock index fund. Funds allocated to a real estate partnership could go into a pool of REITs. Commodity partnerships could be temporarily mimicked by a commodity index investment. The primary advantage of this approach is that once a commitment to an investment area is made, some form of the exposure begins immediately.

The ability to be fully invested may sound virtuous, but it only works well in a rising market. Suppose you made a $1 million commitment to a private equity program that you expected to be called over two years at the start of 1998. If you then put the money to work in an S&P 500 Index fund, you would have made a return of 28.6% in the first year and 21.0% in the second as the money was being drawn. You would not only have your $1 million to cover your commitment but a tidy profit as well.

But suppose you made the commitment on the last day of 1999 and similarly invested the $1 million. You would have lost 9.1% in 2000 and 11.9% in 2001. The pain continued in 2002. Given that the market was deteriorating, your GP may not have been anxious to make investments and might have postponed the majority of the capital calls beyond year three. Any money waiting patiently in the S&P 500 fund for all three years lost a total of 37.6%, which brings up another difficulty.

Commitments to private partnerships are fixed in dollar terms. They are not variable based on an underlying index. In the extreme, at the end of 2002, the investor would still be on the hook for $1 million whenever the GP gets around to making the call. The money invested in the index fund would be worth $625,000, a shortfall of more than 50% of the remaining dedicated investment. That commitment would have to be met from other resources of the investor.

Anybody who goes down this path should recognize that by fixing the future liability in the form of a commitment while leaving the assets at risk is creating one-way leverage in the portfolio. And it is in the wrong direction. To see this, let's return to the imaginary portfolio that is 100% committed to a partnership and then the proceeds are invested in an index fund.

If the market rises, the total return will equal the market (no leverage). There is more than enough money to meet the liabilities as the calls occur through time. But if the market falls before the calls happen, the investor will have to borrow (creating another future liability) to make up the difference. This is leverage, pure and simple. Many institutions have been following such a program without ever thinking consciously of it in these terms.

The credit crisis of 2008–2009 hit some of the most sophisticated institutions particularly hard on this score. They had massive private portfolios in place. They also had commitments for considerably more investments of this type. And they had most of their more liquid assets exposed to the market. When the stock and credit markets collapsed after the Lehman bankruptcy, they were left with portfolios that were in some cases overcommitted and certainly upside down when it came to liquidity.

The only good news in this history is that after the crisis the pace of capital calls slowed to a crawl. This lessened the immediate weight of the future capital calls, but it didn't remove it entirely. Trustees were still often confronted with choosing between trying to sell illiquid private assets at distressed prices to raise liquidity or borrowing at wide spreads over treasuries. Once again the tortoises that had previously lagged behind because of the lower return from their liquid investments found themselves to be winners of the race over the more aggressive hares.

The fact that pace of private equity and venture capital investments fell immediately after the financial crisis raises another potential negative from these programs. General partners find it hard to transact because credit is scarce and expensive. Potential sellers of businesses often are hesitant because the market shock has pushed bids for their companies well below what the current owner thinks they are worth. It takes months and sometimes years of market recovery before private transactions get back to normal. In the interim little capital is called for these partnerships, and much better returns are being earned in the public markets.

In every case where an investor is considering any kind of illiquid investment, the question must be asked whether the prospective gain is worth the loss of liquidity. Can the exposure be replicated with liquid instruments? If there were a change in the investment thesis or environment, how costly would it be to modify or eliminate the investment? How much value an option's liquidity provides to investors is a completely subjective exercise, but it is one that should be done before that liquidity is required.

4.4   ESTABLISHING YOUR STRATEGY OBJECTIVES AND PORTFOLIO MIX

4.4.1   Determining Your Goals for Return and Risk

If you don't know where you are going, almost any road you take will do. The first step in the investment process is to set realistic goals. Saying you want to earn 20% a year without taking any risk of capital loss when the risk-free rate of return is under 1% is perhaps a noble objective, but such a goal is almost delusional. It is important to be realistic within the relevant opportunity set in setting your goals.

Endowments and pension funds sometimes have an easier job of setting objectives than individuals. The pension plan has a good idea of their liabilities through time. Most perpetual endowments work toward preservation of real wealth while spending from the endowment in a way that provides intergenerational equality. Both of these goals help define the investment targets, which then guide the portfolio mix.

Individuals have to first force themselves into determining their objectives and risk tolerances. A young person who just received a large inheritance has different questions to address than a retired septuagenarian who is more concerned about making future inheritances. Is wealth to be preserved, grown, or diminished through time? Is the wealth acting to supplement a lifestyle, or is it the entire foundation for that lifestyle? If the stock market falls by a third in a year, how much loss could your portfolio sustain before it would be "too much" from an emotional perspective?

These questions are hard, and sincere answers made in a quiet, contemplative moment may not prove correct when the world shows its chaotic side. This is where the wisdom gleaned from the analytics of modern portfolio theory can let us down and the best parts of behavioral finance can offer some guidance.

Invariably people give themselves higher marks for certain skills and behaviors than they deserve. Hardly anyone describes themselves as a "below average" driver, saving that rating for nearly everyone else on the road. Similarly, after being taught in modern portfolio theory about risk/reward trade-offs across portfolio choices, we understand that long-term outperformance requires investing in high potential ideas and then being willing to slog through the inevitable volatility along the way.

It is the slogging part that people underestimate. A 10% loss at the portfolio level hurts. A 20% loss hurts almost beyond imagination. Once the losses total 30% or more it matters little what your head may have told you when the portfolio was constructed.

Every fiber in your body is screaming to get out and stop the bleeding.[12] In the jargon of stock analysts, the market is a balance of fear and greed, and a bear market never turns around until most people have capitulated to their fears. Ironically it is those investors who try hardest to stick to a long-term discipline before giving up who suffer the greatest losses and miss out on any market rebound.

An endowment may set its goals in pieces. It may want to keep the real value of the assets intact, so beating the rate of inflation is a minimum. It may also want, or in the case of some foundations be required, to contribute 5% of the endowment to programs supported by the not-for-profit. Then it may want to cover the costs of the investment program including staff, advisors, lawyers, auditors, and custodians. This may lead to a goal of inflation plus 6–7% over a long horizon.

Individuals will also go through this kind of analysis, but will not have an infinite time horizon. While the individual is still working, there may be no need for a draw from the assets to cover spending. Similarly, during those working years, there may be more tolerance for volatility as current investment results have little impact on current lifestyle. If one's risk tolerance allows it, this can lead to more aggressive positioning of the portfolio even though there is no minimum return needed to support current spending.

Every part of the problem changes through time. One curmudgeonly individual I met once said that if there were a dime left in his portfolio when he died he would think of it as a failure of estate planning. Most people, however, think more about legacies and a margin of safety. After all, it might not be a great outcome if that last dime gets spent while the meter is still turning.

Many retirees worry appropriately about outliving their assets or not being able to provide for family members or charitable organizations in the way they would like. These attitudes should get factored into a portfolio's goals as much as anything else.

Perhaps the first question you should ask yourself is, "Am I really a long-term investor?" There is a spectrum of behavior among buyers and sellers of stock. At one end are regular traders who act on a variety of signals and information. There are professionals who do this well, but the vast majority of amateurs destroy value. At the opposite end of the scale are long-term investors who are disciplined in their purchase plans and rarely try to time the market. The story below is about an individual somewhere in the middle of the range.

Several years ago, Ben Carlson, a financial writer, penned a piece entitled "What if You Only Invested at Market Peaks?"[13] It is an easy read that can be accessed in the footnote link. Instead of going through a pile of dry analysis, Carlson presented a metaphor about Bob, the world's worst market timer.

The story begins with Bob as a young man in 1970, determined to save and invest for his retirement 45 years away. He would save $2,000 a year in the 1970s and he

---

[12]Ariely, D. (2008). *Predictably Irrational*. Harper Collins. Describes a series of experiments where subjects are asked to *predict* how they would behave when confronted with choices (e.g. practice safe sex or no?) during a state of arousal. He then retested the subjects in the actual state and discovered their responses were considerably different than what they predicted. One might argue that investing is a much more intellectual activity than sex, but behavioral economists in general would strongly support the notion that decision-making under any kind of excitement or anxiety is much different than choices made in a calm state.
[13]https://awealthofcommonsense.com/2014/02/worlds-worst-market-timer/.

planned to ratchet this up each decade as his career progressed: $4,000 annually in the 1980s, $6,000 each year in the 1990s, and then $8,000 a year until he retired 15 years later. To save the reader some arithmetic, the total amount set aside over the 45 years would be $240,000, with half of that coming in the last 15 years.

This money was not just going to be stuffed into a mattress. The idea was to be a long-term equity investor owning the equivalent of the S&P 500 in the cheapest form available to him. There was only one problem. While Bob was a disciplined saver, he was very nervous in general about the stock market. In fact, the only time he could put money to work was after the market had enjoyed a nice run. In this contrived example, he put his first $6,000 to work at the end of 1972, right before the market turned south, losing about 50% in 1973–1974. Scared back into his hole, he decided just to set his cash aside until the environment improved. It took him until August of 1987 to make another stock purchase, and then the market tanked 30% right after. The next buy was at the end of 1999, right before the tech bubble burst, sending the entire market down more than 50%. The final purchase was in October 2007, immediately before the financial crisis and another 50% decline. Four market peaks; four purchases of the index.

This story sounds like a disaster, but by being a genuinely long-term investor, *never once selling stock*, when Bob retired in 2014 the $240,000 he had set aside over the years had grown to $1.1 million. Bob eliminated half of the emotional decisions by avoiding rash sales. Because of this, even his poorly timed purchases did not destroy the earnings power of the portfolio. Of course, if Bob had been a more disciplined purchaser, he would have enjoyed even more compounding over time and an even better outcome.[14]

A disaster would have been if Bob sold after any market crash. Being out of the market at the wrong time carries its own risks, as shown in the next artificial example. The dark line in Figure 4.11 shows the path of buy and hold S&P 500 investors from 1988 through Q1 2019. The compounded annual return over this period was 10.5%. The lower gray line shows what the returns would have been if those investors were simply out of the market on the single best return day of each calendar year. Missing that one day drops the average return to 6.6%. Compounding is critical here too. In the example, not only did the unlucky investors miss the great one-day return each year, they forever lost the future gains that would compound upon it. In aggregate, the impact of missing out on those good returns grows exponentially over time.

The ideal recipient of this analysis is the young person just starting on their path to saving and retirement. The message is clear. Contribute to your retirement fund continuously. If you are fortunate enough to have an employer supplement your contribution, use it to the fullest. Don't say the market is too expensive to invest right now unless you believe all of corporate America's growth is in the past and not ahead. If you are holding that dark view, you are fighting history.

Older readers may not have a 45-year horizon, but the lessons here are still germane. Trying to be clever about entry points may make you feel great when you

---

[14]If Bob had just mechanically invested his savings every year along the 45-year time line, his sum would have grown to $2.3 million. Buying at the completely wrong time does have its costs.

FIGURE 4.11   Long-Term Impact of Missing Best Trading Days
Data source: Bloomberg

happen to be right, but being wrong by sitting out and missing the good moments can be permanently costly. There had to be people who sold stocks in despair in December 2018 after the worst Q4 since the financial crisis. Some of them may have only gotten back in after the January 2019 rally. For the vanilla S&P 500 investor, that wasn't just missing one good day but an 8% deficit that can never be replaced in the long or short-term track record.

Most foundations and endowments believe they are organizations that will serve generations of grant recipients and students, making them the ideal perpetual investor. Yet many are governed by trustees that have the same behavioral biases that drive individuals to make emotional in-and-out trading decisions. The priority should always be a focus on asset allocation questions and not the nuances of trade timing.

These examples were contrived to emphasize a few key points. They may be artificial, but they are accurate in their message. Investors are human beings, and as human beings we are influenced by our psychology. If you are really a long-term investor, history and analysis suggest that whenever you want to make an equity investment you should do it all immediately. Because we generally believe in the growth potential for equities, even buying at a peak every time will likely turn out ok. But it is also ok to be worried when stocks are trading at apparently full valuations, and to average into stock purchases over a few months. You won't be buying at the low or the high, but you will be eliminating the risk of an emotional body blow if, in the days immediately after your one-time purchase, the market cracks.

Nowhere in the first example did we learn how Bob felt after each stock purchase and subsequent market crash. In the real world, Bob might have given up on stock investing completely after any of the dramatic events. We engage in suboptimal trades because the chance of immediate, intense psychological pain weighs upon us much more than any promise of good feelings years in the future. The trick is to avoid destructive habits in portfolio management. Averaging into or out of positions to achieve the target asset allocation may not be optimal, but it is in most cases pretty good, and consistent with program success. By embracing these kinds of approaches and avoiding the ones that can truly destroy value, you not only think you are a long-term investor, but you act like one.

This discussion might prove disappointing and frustrating for readers looking for firm direction and a single answer. Unfortunately, there is no single "best portfolio" that applies for individuals or institutions. Beyond admonitions to save while you are young and not spend more than you can afford from your portfolio, there are no hard and fast rules as to what is right. Thinking carefully and anticipating as many of the emotional challenges that might arise in your investment life are the only way to set your portfolio goals. Once you think you know where you want to go, it is time to pick a road.

4.4.2 Broad Assumptions About the Risk and Return of Investment Options

By definition a portfolio is a collection of different investments. Just how different the investments are determines what you can expect from it. As an extreme example, a suitcase filled with $100 bills with different serial numbers is technically a portfolio. Unfortunately, the difference in serial numbers does not change the way each bill responds to inflation or the rate of exchange to another currency. One may be able to distinguish the bills, but there is no meaningful difference. This is what we want to avoid in investment portfolios. Going to the effort and expense of acquiring different assets, we do not want to discover that they all behave the same way when markets move.

The world is filled with investment choices that truly differ from one another. Once the opportunity set is identified, three questions need to be asked:

- What is the expected return?
- What are the risks of this investment?
- How should this investment interact with other investments in the portfolio?

The expected return question is the least taxing of the three, but it is far from easy. Is the expectation for a day, a month, a year, or a decade? Guessing the return for the next trading session is basically a coin toss, and should probably not concern investors building a growth portfolio. Individual active managers that base their buy and sell decisions on precise entry and exit points certainly care a great deal about what prices do on any given day, but the most candid ones will admit they have little skill in guessing the shortest-term returns.

Having a view over a week, a month, or a quarter will perhaps affect the tactics of portfolio construction, but should have little impact on what the portfolio targets should be. These targets should be a function of what is expected over the next one to five years, which is a horizon that is long enough to capture the major forces in macro economies and markets. It is also not so long that the road ahead is completely dark.

Scholars like Jeremy Siegel and many investment advisors say your allocation should be based on returns expectations over decades. This supports the notion that portfolio allocations should be set broadly and kept in place through market cycles. Having gone through an overextended bull market in the 1990s, a sharp correction in the first three years of the new century, and a credit and liquidity crisis in 2008–2009, it would appear that more investment mistakes have been made following this advice over the last 20 years than at any other point in history when modern portfolio theory did not hold sway.

If you had no prior knowledge or expectation of what an investment should earn, you might ask the question, "What did it earn in the past?" Dimson, Marsh, and Staunton did just that looking at the annual after-inflation returns of stocks, bonds, and cash for 16 countries from the twentieth century.[15] Table 4.1 summarizes their high-level findings for the United States.

These data paint a pretty good picture, supporting Siegel's notion that stocks should be the core of a long-term investment program. The authors' extension of this kind of analysis to 15 other countries pointed out that the history was not always as consistently favorable as the US experience, but it still reinforced the idea that long-term investment allocations should earn positive real returns.

So which piece of history should be the basis for your return expectation? In the 10-year period immediately after the study was completed, stocks in the United States as measured by broad stock indexes earned *nothing*. Bonds and cash were positive, but were well below the 1975–2000 experience reported above. What happened?

It is a poor answer to say to investors who earned nothing for 10 years had not waited long enough for the averages to kick in. Over that period there were multiple opportunities to make thoughtful adjustments to one's portfolio that would have performed better.

Do not believe that because you are a long-term investor, you should not care about what happens in shorter periods. Before markets began to correct in 2000, Peter Bernstein, Robert Shiller, and others were presenting a strong case that stocks had become grossly overvalued both on an absolute basis and relative to bonds. Not only did many people ignore this and not trim back their stock allocations, some people came into the market based on the previous 20+ year strong record and advice from others that stocks were an all-weather investment.

Advocates of setting a long-term asset allocation and holding onto it through thick and thin often say that to do anything else is "market timing" and that on average most people are fairly poor at this task. There is absolutely no debate about this for most people when it comes to intraday movements of prices. It is likely also true for weekly and monthly changes as well. Trying to be right on such short swings is incredibly hard, with the only certainty being the transaction costs from higher frequency trading. Not only will trading costs eat up returns, but also the emotional side of investing makes it more likely that we will buy high and sell low.

TABLE 4.1 Real Returns to Stocks, Bonds, and Cash in the United States 1900–2000

Period	Stocks	Bonds	Cash
1975–2000	10.2%	4.9%	2.1%
1950–2000	8.2%	1.9%	1.2%
1925–2000	7.4%	2.2%	.7%
1900–2000	6.7%	1.6%	.9%

Source: Dimson, Marsh, and Staunton, page 52

---

[15]Dimson, E., Marsh, P. and Staunton, M. (2002). *Triumph of the Optimists*. Princeton University Press: New Jersey.

This does not, however, imply that no changes beyond rebalancing should ever be made. Imagine the Japanese investors in 1989, coming off more than 30 years of economic and stock market growth. If they had looked at historical valuations as a guide to the future (or if they had read something called *Nikkei: 100,000*), they would have maintained a dominant equity weight in their portfolio. Twenty years later, their equity portfolios would have been off more than 75% (see Figure 4.1). Having a long-term plan and sticking with it may be a good idea, but only if the plan actually makes sense!

Bonds can similarly offer the prospect for weak returns if one begins at the wrong starting point. After the credit crisis in late 2008, the Federal Reserve pursued an aggressive monetary policy designed to be supportive of the US economy coming out of a severe recession. Unemployment throughout the period was more than 9%. As the economy inched forward, the target Fed Funds rate was kept near zero, which put considerable pressure on savers to try to enhance yields.

Investors who would normally have focused on short-duration paper crept out the yield curve, buying up longer dated notes and bonds. The interest rate experience of the five-year note shown in the chart was repeated at every part of the yield curve. By the fourth quarter 2010, rates had declined to levels below those seen at the depths of the crisis.

The demand for traditional Treasuries spilled over into TIPS. Some investors were worried that the easy monetary policy and large fiscal deficits in the United States would lead to inflation down the road, but other investors bought TIPS because all US sovereign debt was being bid up. Whatever the motivation, as Figure 4.12 shows, prices of the five-year TIPS got so high that the implied real yield fell to −1.5% by the end of 2012.

This means that someone buying that five-year TIPS note would be *locking in* a return that was 150 basis points below whatever inflation would ultimately be for those five years. This is an extraordinary price level that one would normally

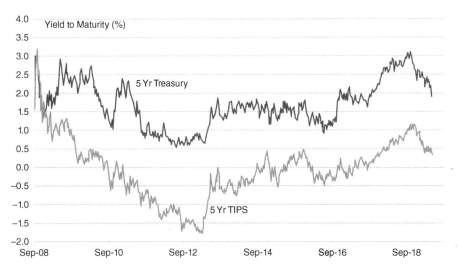

FIGURE 4.12   Five-year Interest Rates 2008–2018
Source: Bloomberg

associate with a period of surprise upward shocks to inflation. CPI inflation for the years leading up to 2013 were among the lowest on record, so it is hard to see the imminent threat that would propel TIPS pricing to these extremes.

The irony is that five years later neither the traditional nor the inflation-indexed bond paid their owners anything that could be called an attractive return. Inflation surprised many by staying stubbornly low so that both bonds earned about 1% annually over that period. When those bonds matured, the prospects for the next five years were only marginally better.

This is a case where based on recent returns TIPS might look good *relative* to the traditional bond of the same maturity, especially for anyone concerned about inflation, but the prices were bid to such extremes that looking between the two bonds is the wrong comparison. *Both* TIPS and traditional bonds offered poor risk/return profiles. The traditional bonds offer too little yield to compensate for the duration risk should rates rise. TIPS were priced so high that there were likely much better inflation hedges available outside the bond arena.

The US Treasury 10-year note is often considered the best benchmark for US interest rates and Figure 4.13 shows vividly why any historical average returns can be so misleading. Table 4.1 shows that the average return on bonds from 1975 to 2000 was 4.9%. Over the first seven years of that period, rates rose from under 8% to a top near 16%. As rates doubled the prices of bonds tumbled and the notion that 4.9% was an achievable return may have appeared remote indeed.

The major jump in rates occurred when Paul Volker as chairman of the Federal Reserve mounted a concerted effort to stop the inflation that had been haunting the nation for more than a decade. The policy of tight money worked, but at a cost of a recession and a decimated bond market as rates spiked.

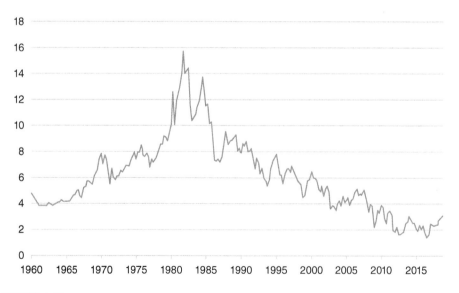

FIGURE 4.13 10-year Note Interest Rates 1960–2018
Source: Bloomberg

1982 to the present is an entirely different story. Volker's medicine to cure inflation led to severe volatility in the bond markets for a few years, but by 1985 interest rates had started a 30-year downward trend. It was this period of high and declining coupons that created the bulk of the 4.9% average return reported in Table 4.1.

The lessons from this history are hard to ignore. In 1982, coming off more than a decade of rising rates and lousy bond returns, it was the best possible environment for bond investors. 2018 may turn out to be the worst time for a bond investor, despite the stellar 30-year track record for the group. The environment clearly matters and relying on historical returns as the determinant for asset allocation decisions effectively erases all the current environmental detail from the picture.

A good starting point for guessing the return to bond investments is today's current yield. If 10-year Treasuries are yielding 2.25%, that is exactly what you should expect to earn over the next 10 years. If 10-year TIPS have a real yield of 0.50%, it is baked into the cake that you will earn whatever the inflation rate is plus one-half of 1% per year. If your investment goal is to earn at least inflation plus 5% for spending, it is difficult to see how either of these bonds has very much a role to play in your portfolio.

A lot of attention is paid to the relative attractiveness of these two bonds. The difference in the nominal 10-year yield and the real TIPS yield is roughly the market's perception of what the *break-even inflation rate* is. If the next 10 years see inflation average more than 1.75% annually, the TIPS will have proven to be a better purchase. Otherwise the traditional note wins. The market clearly has people who believe inflation will be higher or lower, but the bigger point is that relative attractiveness is small potatoes compared to the poor overall prospects for both bonds.

The careful reader may at this point protest, saying that traditional bonds and TIPS are just components of the entire portfolio. The other parts of the allocation could more than pick up the slack, so that the investment pool meets the return objective while still operating within tolerable risk bands.

Perhaps but this gets to be an increasingly difficult task as the prices of the bonds get higher and higher and yields move toward zero. If your goal is to earn inflation plus 5% overall, you need to find investments that are expected to earn inflation plus 9.5% for every dollar you allocate to TIPS with a 0.5% real return. Such investments may exist, but they are not readily available, they come with significant risks, and they may involve considerable sacrifice in terms of liquidity.

There will likely be times when your best guess for future returns falls short of your investment goals. At times like these, it is a challenge to accept the truth that the investment environment is posing a huge headwind to your goals. But a bigger challenge comes when there are no plausible scenarios where you win.

Suppose your return goal is 7.5% annually for the next five years. For a 10-year note yielding 2.25% to have a total return that matched your goal, interest rates would have to drop by 58 basis points each year.[16] The problem, of course, is that interest rates cannot fall that far from a 2.25% yielding bond without rates going deeply into negative territory. For the 10-year TIPS to reach that return would require a similar

---

[16]The duration of a 10-year note with a 2 1/4 coupon priced at par is about 9.0. This means a 58 basis point drop in rates should produce a 5.25% increase in the bond's price. That plus the coupon each year would provide a 7.5% return.

drop in the real yield. The circumstances that would produce these drops would almost certainly include massive deflation and a major recession.

If either of these bonds plays a role in your portfolio, and the world does not produce a deflationary recession and negative interest rates, the balance of the investments will need to do extra duty if the overall return target is going to be met. If the bad macro economy does occur, it is highly unlikely that other investments like stocks and real estate will show positive returns. The bonds may have been successful in "diversifying" the other parts of the portfolio, but the entire plan has a poor probability of reaching your goals.

When the best possible outcomes still produce failed results, the allocation plan is critically flawed. Investors should have been paring growth and index equity exposure to the bone in 2000. They should likely be doing the same thing with US Treasuries at historically low rates. No amount of reliance on past average returns will eliminate the poor balance of risk and return these markets can demonstrate.

Risk is the next dimension to assess. As suggested in the previous paragraphs, there is more to risk than just monthly volatility of returns. There is the risk of permanent loss from some investments. There is also the risk that you will fail in meeting your goals. Both of these are much harder to gauge than a simple statistical measure like standard deviation of returns, but are vital to consider.

Each of the prospective investments in a portfolio should be considered independently and as it is expected to behave within the portfolio. Because both dimensions can shift dramatically over short windows of time, a cautious assessment of risk is called for. An example will demonstrate the issue.

Equity market neutral hedge funds had an enviable track record before the credit crisis of 2008. In the decade prior to the crisis, the average manager in the space did not have a down year. Returns fluctuated between 6.1% on the low end and 15% on the high. More attractive was the fact that in the years 2000, 2001, and 2002, when the S&P 500 returned −9.1%, −11.9%, and −22.1%, respectively, equity market neutral managers averaged, 15.0%, 9.3%, and 7.4%.[17] Not only were the returns respectable on an absolute basis, the diversification benefits were impressive.

Then 2008 happened. In a year when the S&P 500 fell over 37%, the supposedly market neutral strategy *lost* more than 40%. Not only did the strategy's risk fall well outside any normal range of expected returns, its apparent negative correlation to stocks disappeared in an instant. Subsequent years were little better. Unlike stocks in general, there was no rebound for the average equity market neutral manager. Equity market neutral's 2009 return was only 4.1% and the strategy lost −0.9% in 2010.

For the investor who counted on equity market neutral to deliver a steady, uncorrelated return, the events of 2008–2010 were nothing short of a disaster. The strategy's history had given no hint of the potential problems that ensued. What could an investor have done to foresee the actual risk?

Risk can sometimes be proxied by historical data, but that should never be the end point of the exercise. Risk analysis means contemplating what *could* happen even if it has not yet happened. Then one needs to ask what the consequences of those events are. If the consequences are completely unacceptable (e.g. losing 40% in a strategy when the equity market falls 37%), then this should be a factor in sizing the position.

---

[17]Source: Dow Jones Credit Suisse Hedge Fund Indexes.

We make these kinds of decisions every day in real life, but somehow resist them in our asset allocation choices. Anyone who has been a pedestrian in New York City looks before crossing a street with the light because they know there is a pretty good chance that a car might drive through its stop. While the probability might be low that a car will illegally violate the pedestrian's right of way, the potential consequences are so bad that most people take the extra precaution. In fact, experienced New York pedestrians often look both ways on a one-way street to be perfectly cautious.

The warning here is not to place too much reliance on historical volatilities or correlations. Both can change quickly. If a strategy is being sold as having "equity-like returns with bond-like volatility," there is the temptation to substitute it for both stocks and bonds. The returns are an improvement over bonds while the volatility seems to be less than stocks.

In such cases there is almost always a risk factor or two in the strategy that has not been revealed yet in the historical data. It could be the strategy involves writing options or other derivatives. There could be problems with liquidity. There could be fraud. Each of these risks needs to be considered and the question asked, "What if it goes wrong?" In almost every case the right answer is to allocate more carefully than the statistical history would suggest.

4.4.3 The Fallacy of Relying on Optimizers

The two questions to be answered in the portfolio allocation process are:

- What instruments should be in the portfolio?
- What weight should be assigned to each?

Assuming you are starting with a complete blank slate, at a minimum you need to array each of the expected returns and volatilities of the investment options. The most direct way to proceed from there is to build a sample portfolio of likely candidates using some nearly uniform allocation. Then calculate the average expected return and average expected volatility, *assuming no benefit from diversification.*[18] This exercise provides the first cut of reasonableness against your overall target return. If the first portfolio falls short of your objective, change the weights to increase the higher potential earners until your goal is reached. To check on whether your goal is realistic within your personal framework, look at the resulting expected volatility. If the implied volatility makes you weak in the knees, you might not have compatible risk and reward goals.

Going back and forth, raising one allocation and lowering another, is a tedious process, and not one likely to show rapid improvement toward your goal. Such a mechanical process also ignores what are likely to be diversification benefits because

---

[18]By assuming there is no benefit of diversification you are saying that it is possible for all of the investments in the portfolio to gain or lose money at the same time. This is as bad as it gets when it comes to the impact on portfolio variance. Both the expected return and the expected variance of the sample portfolio are weighted averages of the individual returns and variances. In the real world the average volatility should be expected to be less, and perhaps meaningfully less, than this.

the available investment options are almost certainly not perfectly correlated. Since there are unlimited combinations available to construct a portfolio, investors have embraced tools to help this daunting process along.

Portfolio optimizers have been developed over the years, which use the techniques of linear and nonlinear programming. The name sounds so convincing. "Optimizer" gives the aura of fine-tuning a car engine to achieve maximum efficiency. The intuition is equally convincing. Each potential investment, at different weights, is evaluated in terms of its contribution to expected return and portfolio risk. To run such an optimizer requires not only the array of expected returns and volatilities mentioned above, but also a matrix of expected correlations between all the pairs of assets.

It is not essential to understand the math behind the optimizers to get an intuition about how they work. Most use the basic mean variance model discussed in Chapter 3 and create a risk-return surface composed of all the possible combinations. Figure 4.14 shows stylistically that all the possible portfolio combinations create a "cloud" of return and risk outcomes. This is the multi-asset version of Figure 3.10 that describes the benefits of diversification.

The spirit behind the process is that if Portfolio A has a lower expected return but the same expected volatility as Portfolio B, then it is *suboptimal* compared to B. Similarly if two portfolios have the same risk, the one with the lower expected return is suboptimal. The comparisons proceed until what is left is a set of portfolios where there is no gain in expected return unless there is also an increase in expected volatility. This set is called the *efficient frontier* and is shown in Figure 4.14 as the line drawn above all the individual securities.

To complete the optimization process requires knowing the risk-free rate of return. The tangent line from the risk-free rate to the efficient frontier identifies the optimum portfolio available (Figure 4.15). There is no imaginable combination of the available investments that improves upon the risk-reward features.

It was shown in Figure 3.13 that the optimum portfolio changes if the risk-free rate changes. This is the first hint that the search for the best long-term portfolio might not be as easily achieved as one might like.

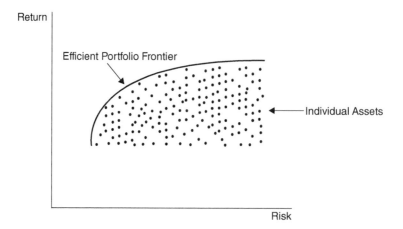

FIGURE 4.14   Discovering the Efficient Frontier

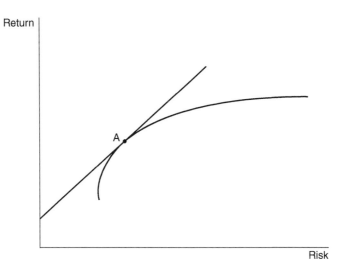

FIGURE 4.15   The Optimum Portfolio

It is perhaps not too disturbing that the optimum portfolio changes through time as the risk-free rate moves around, until you note that the typical list of potential investments being optimized includes both liquid and illiquid investments. The optimizer does not care that some investments need to be held for many years. It assumes all adjustments are possible at no cost.

This is just the tip of the iceberg, however, when it comes to the problems with optimizers. The more troubling elements concern the reliability of the inputs used in the calculation and the tendency of optimizers to reach *corner solutions*. A brief visit to history will demonstrate both problems.

Almost 40 years ago there was a PhD student at a major West Coast university who had set out for his thesis the optimization of the cropping pattern for all of Indian agriculture. He had diligently collected data on yields, crop prices, prices of labor, land, and fertilizer and virtually every other relevant factor. He also had the advantage of working with faculty who had done some of the world's best research on both linear and nonlinear programming techniques. By most dissertation standards, this was an ambitious goal, but he had as good a chance as any to succeed.

After many months of programming, as this was long before the availability of prepackaged software to do the optimizations, the first results came in. The major conclusion was that more than 75% of Indian cropland should be planted in cucumbers! This was something of a surprise for a country that historically devoted much of its arable land to wheat, rice, pulses, and cotton.

What had happened? The optimizer used all of the information available to it, and discovered that the profit margins for Indian farmers growing cucumbers were far superior to their other choices. The model had no way of understanding that if its prescription was followed, the price of cucumbers would likely fall to zero and people would pay a king's ransom for a bag of wheat or rice. None of the assumptions behind the model would hold if the model were followed!

There was no practical way to incorporate the shapes of the supply and demand curves for all of the crops being considered, so the student did what legions of users of optimizers have done for decades. He put in a constraint. He told the model that he did not want its best global answer, but its best answer subject to the limit that no more than 1% of the land could be devoted to cucumbers. Not surprisingly, the next optimized solution said that 1% in cucumbers was just right. The model had reached a *corner solution* settling in on the constraint the researcher specified.

One might not be surprised to hear that after cucumbers were limited, melons caused a problem and had to be limited too. Each time the constrained optimization used up all the acreage the new student-imposed limits would allow. Soon the solution began to be dominated by these limit-induced corner solutions.

The reader might ask what this has to do with his or her portfolio. The answer is that the same problem appears again and again with portfolio optimizers, but the users of these models don't necessarily have as good an intuition as we all have when we suspect that 75% of India should not be planted to cucumbers.

Another real-life example will show the problem as it relates to investments. Portfolio analysts working at the end of the 1990s tried to identify the optimum growth portfolio composed of all the usual suspects: US large and small-cap stocks, international stocks, Treasury securities, corporate bonds, etc. To populate the optimizer they used 30 years of monthly return data for the indexes that could proxy for each of the asset classes. No assumption was made that active management could add value.

The tests were run, and the initial efficient frontier consisted entirely of bonds and large-cap US stocks. The 30-year history of large-cap US stocks was so dominant that the model could find no room for US small-cap stocks or any stocks offshore. This result flew in the face of the theoretical idea that investors should own the market.

One approach to adjust this outcome would be to force the model to have a certain percentage of small-cap and international stocks. Minimum limits can be specified for optimizers as well as maximums. The corner solutions created are just as sharp.

The other approach was to question the historical data. It is often assumed that 30 years of data is a generous sample, and usually in science we believe more data is better, but in this case running the model with less data could offer important lessons.

The modelers next pretended that it was 1989 instead of 1999. Granted, only 20 years of monthly data were available for the new calculation, but this is still a good number. This time the efficient frontier consisted of bonds, small-cap stocks, and international stocks. *The optimal portfolio constructed using data only up to 1989 contained no large-cap US stocks.*

Imagine being an investor at the start of 1990 with no large-cap US stocks. This would have been one of the biggest errors that could have been made for the next several years. Sometime during the 1990s the data would have started to tilt the model toward including large-cap stocks, but by the time they showed up in the optimal portfolio the best returns of the decade could have already occurred.

Similarly, those who were 100% in large-cap US stocks beginning in 2000 had a "lost decade" where total returns were essentially zero. Investors who had more representation from small caps and international stocks, especially from emerging market equities, enjoyed reasonable returns.

The lesson here is that corner solutions can occur whether the model has limits or not. Frequently optimizers harshly penalize asset classes that look just a little weaker than the more favored class. Given the way historical data leans toward the most recent winners, portfolio optimizers have a disturbing tendency to start advocating asset classes at just about the time they should be most avoided.

Practitioners trying to avoid this problem modify their historical data to keep expected returns and volatilities across asset classes more in alignment. Unfortunately this is just a variation of the exercise of installing limits into the model. The solution to the model is invariably shaped more by the input assumptions than by any fundamental truth.

The second major problem with mean-variance optimizers is that those are the only two dimensions of the investment puzzle that are considered. When investment options like private equity or real estate partnerships are considered, it is usually assumed that there will be a higher investment return because of the premium paid to give up liquidity. Given that these investments have a similar measured risk profile that is no worse than their liquid counterparts, it is not surprising that the optimizer wants to invest there to the exclusion of everything else.

Of course there are all kinds of risks to illiquid partnerships that the optimizer ignores. The only way to try to level the playing field is to make ad hoc assumptions that lower the return expectation or raise the estimated volatility. Once again the solution to the puzzle becomes more dependent upon the shape of the assumptions rather than a body of objective evidence that users of the models wish they had.

Despite these defects optimizers enjoy a broad popularity. Many investors seek an analytic legitimacy for their long-term models that optimizers appear to provide. But optimizers are terribly fragile in their calculations, shifting from corner solution to corner solution with modest changes of the inputs. Trying to smooth out this model volatility invariably leads to the use of constraints or underlying assumptions that so shape the results that it is almost unnecessary to run the actual calculations. The assumed inputs perfectly predict the output.

4.4.4 The Fallacy of Relying on Simulators

As more experience developed highlighting the problem with optimized portfolios, an alternative approach was developed that was somewhat less grand in its pronouncements. There would be no attempt to optimize anything. Instead different portfolio combinations would be simulated over a broad range of statistical outcomes to see how results would compound over long periods of time.

A popular approach is called Monte Carlo simulation. If you could not figure out algebraically the probability of any given number coming up with the throw of two fair dice, you could actually throw the dice thousands of times and carefully record each outcome. Before long, the observed distribution of outcomes would begin to approximate what we would expect from probability theory. Why shouldn't such an approach work for investments?

Monte Carlo simulations typically build up from the risk-free rate of return using expected returns, volatilities, and correlations, as you would employ in an optimizer. In fact, simulators are a first cousin of optimizers, with the major difference being that simulators make no pretense of identifying an efficient frontier.

Instead, a portfolio allocation is established as a test case and hundreds or thousands of simulated return paths are created, typically extending out many years. The foundation for these simulations is usually based on decades of real-world return experience. Expected returns, variances, and correlations are the building blocks used to create the analysis. One starts with a certain base asset level, applies a random market outcome to the next investment period, and then repeats for as many years as one might like. Figure 4.16 shows a typical output from a portfolio simulator of a basic 70/30 mix of US stocks and bonds over 20 years, but these models can be constructed over many asset classes and time periods.

The chart reflects a number of summary statistics based on the distribution of the simulated results. Consider the year-one values. The middle at year one gives the average of all the simulated outcomes. Since on average we expect stocks to make money through time, it is not surprising that the average is a positive number. The top line of the cone marks the point where only 10% of the outcomes are above it. The bottom line marks the point where 10% of the observations are lower.

The reader might ask, "Why not just look at the whole range? Aren't we interested in our potential maximum profit or biggest loss?" Experience with these models suggests that with thousands of simulations being performed, the absolute extremes can be wildly away from the far more likely results. Psychologically, people looking at Figure 4.16 focus on the average and the boundaries. If the chart included all the observations, it would give a highly distorted view of the potential volatility. For exposition purposes it is useful to trim these extreme simulations, but we will discuss the downside of this in a little while.

The simulations progress from the previous year's value. A good outcome in year one is more likely to produce a positive two-year return than the simulation that came out of the blocks with a loss. Over time the central tendency to have a positive return dominates and even the low performing outcomes show a positive return if you wait long enough. The band of outcomes gives the answer to the

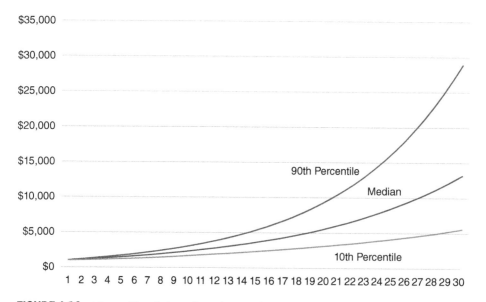

FIGURE 4.16 30-year Simulation of a 70/30 Portfolio

question, "What is the range of outcomes I should expect 80% of the time from this portfolio?"

The most extreme top and bottom results are excluded because tails of even a normal distribution can extend quite far. If the absolute minimum and maximum outcomes defined the cones, it would be quite difficult to distinguish between competing portfolio options, which is the ultimate goal of the exercise.

Figure 4.17 shows how this can be done with two competing portfolios. In the early years the cones of the two portfolios overlap considerably, making it difficult to choose between them. But as time extends, the earning potential of portfolio A improves to the point where not only the average return is better but the lower limit of the cone is higher than the upper limit of cone B. It appears that if you hold Portfolio A it should beat Portfolio B in almost any circumstances.

To get such clear-cut distinctions requires radically different portfolios. In the illustrative example in Figure 4.17, we start with the same 70/30 portfolio from above, and its range of outcomes captured from Figure 4.16 are now just the gray shaded area. The second is 30/70, stocks and bonds, and this is the dark path. A very close look at the chart shows that the 30/70 portfolio sits inside the range for the 70/30 one. The ninetieth percentile lower bounds are almost on top of one another. It shows the clear expected advantages of equity investing over long periods of time, but we really didn't need a fancy simulation program to understand that idea.

This kind of tool is often used to support what can be gained by adding high potential investments like venture capital or leveraged hedge funds to your portfolio. Faced with this kind of graphic, investors tend not to care that the expected volatility of the 70/30 portfolio is greater (as shown by the absolute width of its cone). All they focus on is the apparent conclusion that the higher volatility gets washed away through the power of compounding at a meaningful higher rate of return.

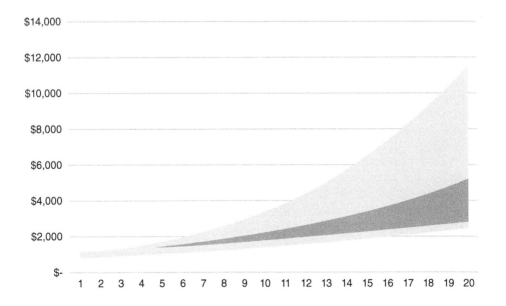

FIGURE 4.17 Competing Simulated Portfolio Outcomes

A superficial look at Figure 4.17 would lead to question why anyone would choose a 30/70 blend over a 70/30 blend since the average return for the stock-heavy portfolio is so much higher and the downside risk seems comparable. The fact of the matter is that what is not on the chart can make a big difference; especially as the investment horizon shrinks to a few years from 20. The shaded areas only capture the middle part of the expected return distribution. If we were never concerned about the 10% of the events that lie sometimes materially below the visible chart, the conclusion to go heavy in stocks would make sense every time.

This is exactly the kind of reasoning that led to the conclusion that stocks are not risky if they are held for the long run. It completely ignores the myriad of risks that can arise during the tail events that are beyond the cones and unseen in these figures. Portfolio simulations have probably led more investors into a false sense of security than almost any other analytical tool in use today.

The perils of simulators were vividly demonstrated during the market and liquidity crisis that began after the Lehman Brothers bankruptcy. Investor after investor experienced portfolio losses that were not only beyond the 90% limits, they were below calculated limits that supposedly captured more than 99% of outcomes. These events are not supposed to happen! Of course, the footnotes to the simulators carefully explained that they did not define the limits of actual experience. The 2008 reality was apparently just an incredibly unlucky break.

The most troublesome part of this story is that many advocates of simulators barely missed a beat. After experiencing outcomes that were completely off the simulation's charts, they simply reset a lower starting point for the next tests and adjusted their assumptions to have higher volatility and correlations. Instead of fundamentally questioning the validity of the approach, they made tweaks to the assumptions.

This biggest reason to doubt Monte Carlo simulations is that before enough time has passed for the simulation to clearly play out, it is highly likely that there will be a few major shifts in the underlying assumptions. Investors need to always remember that market prices do not unfold as a random chain of events. They are dealing with dynamic markets and not the throws of well-behaved dice.

There is one type of simulation that can be highly instructive, but it too has limitations. Historical simulations ask the question, "How would this portfolio have behaved during the events of _____?" People often look at the stock market crash of 1987, the rapid rise of interest rates in 1994, various emerging market crises through time and, of course, the credit and liquidity crisis after the Lehman Brothers bankruptcy.

These kinds of simulations are instructive because they reflect what really happened and not some theoretical outcome without context. The problem with this approach is that each of the extreme events listed above was quite different than the ones that came before it. Like generals that sometimes plan for the last war, investors who rely on historical simulations may find they own risks in their portfolios that are unprecedented.

The best kind of simulations combine historical events with a series of "what if" exercises. What if interest rates suddenly rise by 100 basis points? What if stock markets around the world fall by 25% *and* the US dollar is not viewed as a safe haven? What if liquidity dries up for more than 90% of the assets I own?

There is little point in trying to assign precise probabilities to any of these events. Such an exercise does not lend itself to careful statistical analysis. It is, however, quite important to ask the question, "If any or all of the 'ifs' occurs, can I live with the damage that would result?" Any time the answer is no, you need to think more about that portfolio.

Optimizers and simulators have become crutches for investors seeking analytic certainty in a highly uncertain world. They have been shown time and time again to be highly unreliable at the worst times. That is why your sleep-well-at-night part of the portfolio should be established first. There is nothing in the investor's toolkit that can be relied upon with such a high degree of confidence to be a good substitute.

4.4.5   Establishing the Target Growth Portfolio

To establish a target growth portfolio, the investor needs to remember three basic truths:

- Expected returns are a function of market environments and not historical averages.
- Volatilities and correlations can change dramatically and rapidly.
- Illiquidity has both direct and indirect costs.

These factors only modify and do not replace the basic tenets of modern portfolio theory. Diversification still matters. It is not easy to outperform "the market." Fairly priced risky assets should be expected to earn a premium through time.

From this "reality-based" modern portfolio theory, one can build an array of stocks, bonds, alternative investments, and every other imaginable money making choice the investor prefers. A projected return may be guessed, but no investor should be surprised if the actual outcome differs from the anticipated.

Since you have first established your safe assets separately from the growth portfolio, volatility should not be the primary concern. Of course you want a portfolio that has a chance of reaching your target while avoiding undue fluctuations, but fluctuations are a fact of life. How you respond during any period of extreme market moves speaks volumes about how good a fit your initial portfolio really was and how accurately you judged your own psychological makeup.

Once the portfolio array is set up, it should be reviewed periodically to see if it is *generally* meeting your expectations. If it is lagging behind your goals, is there a flaw in the portfolio, or would any realistic choice you might have considered instead lagged as well? On the opposite side, if it is doing much better than expectations, should some profits be taken off the table, with the new portfolio structured to better preserve the gains?

Real-world elements like taxes and liquidity matter in the allocation process. The portfolio benefits provided by many hedge funds for not-for-profit investors may evaporate for the taxpayer facing short-term capital gains tax rates. Similarly, certain partnership and trust structures, with their typically tax advantaged income streams, should play a more active role relative to other dividend paying securities if the investor is also a taxpayer.

Transaction costs also can influence the portfolio. Theory says an investor should only care about total return, and not whether those returns come from interest and dividend income or from capital gains. The reality is that if the investor relies on regular draws from the portfolio, interest and dividends arrive at virtually no cost. Sales of appreciated assets to achieve the same income stream occur at some expense, which, in the case of illiquid stocks, can be meaningful. The transactional elements of portfolio should influence the target asset allocation.[19]

Once an allocation is set, not a great deal of effort should be spent on small adjustments through time. Shifting 2% of your funds from small-cap equities to large-cap growth stocks after small caps have had a modest run might make you feel better, but probably won't move the dial in terms of a meaningful change in returns. *Unless there is a strongly identifiable dislocation in asset subcategories*, it will be hard to distinguish between the performances of portfolios that are similar in their broad category allocations.

There is no single "right" answer when it comes to portfolios. In fact, the more people say that one recipe is right, the more likely it is to prove wrong. Joining the investment herd today means placing your exposures alongside some of the biggest pension plans and sovereign wealth funds in the world. Individuals moving thousands of dollars demonstrate no better herd behavior than institutions moving billions.

Develop a portfolio that is realistic in terms of your goals and resources. You are probably not a major endowment with the ability to borrow billions of dollars when things go wrong. And if you are, that is still no reason to copy the institution down the street. Any competition should be against your own finish line and not against some peer group. It is the fund manager competing for your business that needs to demonstrate he is smarter than the rest. Your risk is failing to have the financial resources to do everything you want.

Having a plan is just the first step. Executing the plan by picking managers and specific investments is another big task. Our best portfolio theories don't help very much beyond this chapter. It is time to roll up your sleeves and prepare to get dirty in the details.

---

[19]This conclusion is strictly true only for investors facing no tax consequences from interest, dividends, or capital gains.

Building the
Modern Portfolio

CHAPTER 5

Executing the Plan:
The Devil Is in the Details

5.1 HOW MUCH DIVERSIFICATION IS RIGHT?

5.1.1 Do You Have Special Information or Skills?

Great wealth has almost always been created by taking concentrated risks. No successful entrepreneur in the midst of growing a business ever steps back to question whether their wealth portfolio is "sufficiently diversified." The concept is alien to the entrepreneurial process. So why does modern portfolio theory insist that investors should "own the market" and have complete diversification?

The answer lies in the fact that investors typically do not have an entrepreneurial edge in picking stocks, bonds, or other investments. The efficient market hypothesis strongly suggests that whatever information one receives about a stock or a bond is likely to be widely known and already built into the prices of the securities. Since there is no specific edge for an investor, loading up on any particular investment simply increases risk without increasing the expected return.

At a high level this is very good advice, but if it were universally true there would be no entrepreneurs, venture capitalists, or successful long-only or hedge fund managers. Capital would be allocated unemotionally and without regard to sector, geography, or form. Everyone would hold essentially the same risk profile and returns would be driven precisely by the pace of economic activity.

The world obviously does not work this way. Academics have tried to explain both how the world works and how it *should* work. There are three broad approaches that capture the competing philosophies. The modern portfolio theorists, discussed in some detail in Chapter 3, believe that in most environments information gets accurately incorporated into market prices. This makes it very difficult to get an investment edge. Behavioral finance economists argue that many market prices are more driven by emotion than by information, because humans are irrational actors. They make decisions precisely because of emotion and pay the price in terms of high-risk, high-cost portfolios.

The third school actually predates the other two. John Maynard Keynes, more often thought of as a macroeconomist than a finance specialist, was typical of his age in arguing that portfolios should be shaped according to the edge of the investor.

Like an entrepreneur focusing on an area of specialty, an investor should load up on things that he or she understands well and avoid those investments where others have an edge.

A couple of examples demonstrate this approach and its difficulties. Three-card Monte is a game where a scam artist offers to pay a nice premium if his mark can guess where the "money card" is located among three shuffled cards. The game often includes a confederate to the scam artist who only pretends to help the mark. This produces a situation where the mark believes they have an edge. The mark bets and loses with great regularity.

The second example can be found in the casino scene from the movie *Casablanca*. A young Bulgarian, desperate to leave Casablanca for America with his recent bride, is trying to win enough at the roulette wheel for passage. He is down to his last chips. The sympathetic café owner, Rick, played by Humphrey Bogart, goes over to the young man and asks him in a whisper if he has tried 22 black. The young man places all of his chips, Rick winks to the croupier, and the ball lands on 22. Rick tells him to leave the winnings on 22 and the scene is repeated. Rick then tells him to cash in and not come back.

The only difference between these two situations is in the quality of the information. Both "investors" believe they have superior information. Only one does. If one's information is truly better than everyone else's in the market, there is no reason to diversify. But how is one to be sure, and what is the right action if there is uncertainty?

In the Casablanca example, the Bulgarian had essentially nothing more to lose. Why not trust the man in the white dinner jacket? The first winning spin reinforced his confidence in the quality of his special information. The three-card Monte player's safety net comes from not betting more than he can afford to lose, so that if the information turns out to be poor, he can learn his lesson at a reasonable tuition rate and then move on. Pity the player who goes "all in" only to find the error of his judgment.

While Keynes's approach probably has the greatest intuitive appeal, the problem of uncertain information makes it incredibly difficult to model. How does one know if one has an edge or not? How big is it relative to everyone else? All these elements are cloaked in uncertainty, which opens up the opportunity to fall back on emotion. It was precisely this kind of investing that Sharpe and Markowitz were trying to improve upon with their disciplined approach and the behaviorists criticize as a basic human failing.

Perhaps the biggest behavioral failing is overconfidence. People learn something of which they have not been previously aware and it is as if the world has revealed its secret for the first time, and only to them. Whether the information comes from brokerage house economists or financial media analysts, messages are rarely thought of as genuinely new. The chance that the information is at least somewhat reflected in the market price already is quite high.

Answering the question, "how much diversification is appropriate?" therefore boils down to a candid appraisal of one's information set. Putting aside for the moment material nonpublic information, against which it is illegal to trade, if one genuinely has special information, or a perspective on how that information will play out, there is a strong argument that concentrated positions should produce above-market, risk-adjusted returns.

The vast majority of investors today are not entrepreneurs who have created great wealth by building and selling a company. Most individuals have simply been regular savers, often in their retirement plans, converting the earnings power of their human capital into investment assets. Institutional investors whether they are pension plans, insurance companies, or endowments have widely different sources for their wealth. The example of the entrepreneur creating, modifying, and transferring wealth may seem to be an odd starting point for this discussion. It is, however, highly relevant as it provides the starkest demonstration of the forces at work.

Begin with the first-generation entrepreneur. They often place all their eggs in one basket while the entrepreneurial edge is the strongest. The investment in the business is not only concentrated, but it is also highly illiquid. It may or may not produce enough cash flow to support consumption normally thought to be commensurate with that level of wealth. Of all the individuals that boldly go down this path, most will fail. To avoid the sin of overconfidence, it is essential to always remember this group. They do, however, have little to add to the story of investment portfolios, so they will be set aside at this point.

Some entrepreneurs never leave this illiquid phase. The small farm owner may have a great asset by any objective standard, but be unable to monetize the wealth. The phrase "land rich, cash poor" was often heard as farm generations sold out and moved to other vocations. These entrepreneurs may have desired a different composition of their wealth, but their lifestyle did not allow it.

Now consider the subset of entrepreneurs who get to the point where there can be a liquidity event. There is an initial public offering, or a private transaction with a financial or strategic party. It is rare that there is a complete cash-out by the entrepreneur. While a large percentage of the wealth has been transformed, a meaningful part remains concentrated in the equity of the company. If the entrepreneur maintains an active management role in the new company, this is a logical and desirable outcome.

Focusing on the growth portfolio, and not the sleep-well-at-night money discussed in Chapter 4, the entrepreneur should take great care that any new investments are not all subject to the same risks as the core equity holding.

For example, the founders of General Motors would want to add banks, insurance companies, and agricultural-related companies to their stock portfolios as they diversified. Buying other car manufacturers like Ford, Toyota, and Daimler, or global stock indexes that have these names as a major representation, would not be the best way to round out the portfolio.

Too many times when there is a concentrated stock position, there is a temptation to ignore it and build the "ideal" portfolio out of the remaining assets. The theory is that as the company stock is sold through time, assuming that is the plan, the proceeds can be apportioned across what will be the ultimate long-term portfolio. This is a major mistake. It may be difficult to conceptualize all of the risks of the concentrated position, but since it will likely be the major factor in portfolio return and volatility for as long as it is there, the balance of the growth portfolio should be selected to complement the core.

The process gets more complicated as generations are added to the discussion. Unless the founding generation has been extraordinarily good at transferring specific knowledge and the entrepreneurial spirit to subsequent generations, the argument for maintaining a concentrated position grows weaker. As hard as it may be emotionally to part with the most tangible link to the family's wealth, those shares should be sold unless there is a strong advantage in keeping them. By the time the wealth is transferred to the third or fourth generation, any connection to the original entrepreneur's edge is largely sentimental.

The worst possible conclusion is for an heir who is not integral to the founder's company's operations to hold the stock on the basis that it must be a good investment simply because it was the source of the family's wealth. A stock certificate is only a sheet of paper. It does nothing by itself. The founder's skills and energy were what created the wealth and they may have passed many years ago. There is little to suggest a permanent edge to the distant generations that would justify maintaining a concentrated position.

Charitable foundations or endowments that receive large blocks of equity are a variation on the multigeneration investment problem above. History is filled with stories of such not-for-profit investors that consciously choose to hold massively concentrated positions from the original grant. Trustees and administrations of these organizations are often under severe pressure not to diversify. The donors could still be alive, holding a large concentrated position themselves. Selling the asset could be viewed as an act of disloyalty, jeopardizing future gift chances.

If the donor is still involved in the company and sits on the board of the not-for-profit, the potential for conflict is severe. All trustees owe the not-for-profit a *duty of loyalty* and a *duty of care*. The benefit to the organization from reducing a concentrated risk position ought to be a higher priority than keeping an individual board member happy, but maintaining that priority can be a difficult task.

The not-for-profit community around Atlanta provides a good example of these forces at work as many of them benefited from the generosity of early executives and investors in Coca-Cola. Nobody should need a reminder about one of the iconic brands in the world, but a few pieces of this history can prove enlightening to the portfolio story.

According to data on the company's website, one could have purchased a single share of stock in 1919 for $40. If one had held that stock, and systematically reinvested the dividends, the value of that investment at the end of 2009 would have been almost $7.2 million, or an increase of 1,888 times. As mind-boggling as that multiple seems, it translates into a compounded rate of return for the 91 years of 14.2%. Any firm should be thrilled with that long history of success.

But the path has not been a straight line up. Coca-Cola was a rare stock during the Great Depression in that it enjoyed some success. The 1970s saw it almost double in value in the first few years, only to fall completely back by decade's end. But it was the 1980s and 1990s that defined this story. In the 1980s the stock value increased tenfold. From 1990 to the stock's peak in 1998, the value increased another eight times. $84,000 of stock at the start of 1980 was worth over $6.6 million 18 years later. Figure 5.1 shows the relative performance of Coca-Cola's stock price and the S&P 500 from 1985 through 2000, with both series scaled to equal 100 at the start of the period.

It seems that scores of institutions in the area had been given Coca-Cola stock in contributions over the years. Emory University, as just one example, saw its endowment grow into the multiple billions of dollars riding largely on the back of this stock advance. As Coca-Cola moved up faster than the market, its share of the portfolio would naturally increase if nothing were done to adjust the holdings. It is widely understood that the trustees of Emory followed a policy of trimming back the Coke stock position during this period, but the stock remained an extremely large fraction of the endowment.

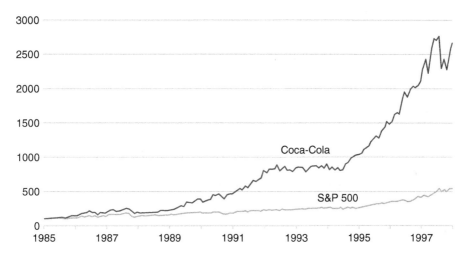

FIGURE 5.1 Coca-Cola versus S&P 500, 1985–1997
Source: Bloomberg

Other institutions took a different approach. "We've never sold a share of Coke stock, and we never will" was heard frequently around town from trustees who were intensely loyal to the company. Most of these institutions had spending rules that had allowed them to greatly increase their operating budgets as the value of Coke stock skyrocketed. In hindsight, their duty of loyalty seemed more directed to the company and the community than to the institution they were serving.

Figure 5.2 repeats the previous story but covers the eight years, 1998 through 2005.

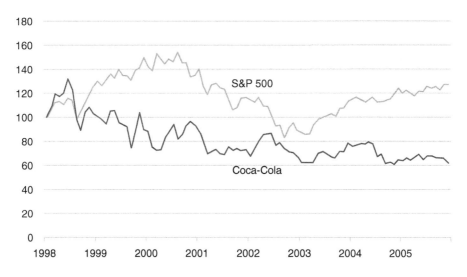

FIGURE 5.2 Coca-Cola versus S&P 500, 1998–2005
Source: Bloomberg

Between 1998 and 1999, a period when the US stock market earned almost 20%, the value of the Coca-Cola holdings fell by nearly 12%. After a nice bounce up the next year, Coke resumed its rocky path. By the end of 2005, the $6.6 million that one started 1998 with had fallen to just over $4.5 million. The S&P, in contrast, was up a few percent over the same period.

Emory's trustees probably felt some relief and satisfaction that they had managed the Coca-Cola exposure before this period. In hindsight, they might have wished for even greater diversification. But it was the institutions that made no active portfolio decisions in the 1990s that likely had the hardest conversations.

One can imagine in 1999 that as Coke stock lagged, these trustees who had been so blessed for so long simply said that the underperformance was an aberration that would correct itself quickly. As the years of underperformance accumulated, the virtue of holding such a concentrated position would be debated. Some groups would stay the course, but others, feeling pressure to add more appreciating assets would begin diversifying only after Coke stock had declined.

What was probably never discussed was whether any of these institutions had an informational edge that would argue strongly for a concentration in one stock. Instead, a pleasant historical accident shaped an environment of expectations that were simply unrealistic in the long run. Systematic overestimation of future prospects is a classic behavioral error that often takes a great deal of costly experience to overcome.

The experience of Atlanta not-for-profits with Coca-Cola stock is illustrative of the challenges everyone faces regarding diversification decisions, but it doesn't really suggest the right answer because each experience is a unique history. Depending on when the assets were acquired, the concentrated approach proved wonderful or disappointing. And Coca-Cola's long-term history perhaps paints a rosier picture than what anyone should rightfully expect in general.

DeWitt Wallace founded the *Reader's Digest*, another twentieth-century success story. The Wallace family, through their foundation, was famously generous with stock gifts to a wide range of not-for-profit organizations. Each of these organizations faced the issues discussed above with Coca-Cola beneficiaries once *Reader's Digest* stock began trading publicly in 1990. Unfortunately, this is a less happy tale (Figure 5.3). After more than doubling in the three years after the IPO, the stock price foundered until the company was taken private in a leveraged buy-out in 2007. The LBO price was about half the IPO value 17 years earlier. Even that was better for the public shareholders than the ultimate fate. In 2009 *Reader's Digest* declared bankruptcy and the LBO private equity was wiped out.

Only those organizations that had transformed their stock gifts into a diversified endowment were able to fully benefit from the Wallace generosity. Unlike the experience of most Coca-Cola beneficiaries, there were few truly great stories among the holders of *Reader's Digest*. Those organizations that lived through this transition will long remember the importance of not having most of one's eggs in a single basket.

Risk aversion plays an important part in finding the ultimate right decision. The more risk averse an individual or organization is, the quicker should be the path toward diversification. Even with an informational edge, any advantage is not enough to fully compensate for the ill feeling the concentrated portfolio creates for the risk-averse investor.

Risk aversion is entirely subjective. Individuals can be quite aggressive in their investing patterns for their own wealth, but overly cautious when responsible for

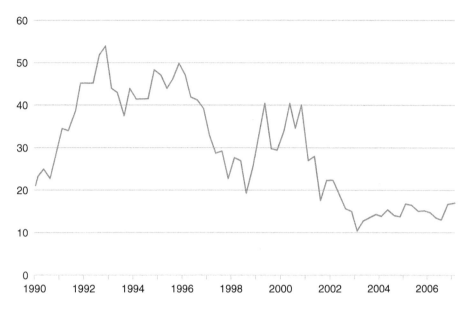

FIGURE 5.3   RDA Stock, 1990–2017
Source: Wall Street Journal.

the funds of a not-for-profit for which they serve. This could be driven by a fear of failure in a highly public setting. Anyone who has served on a not-for-profit board knows there can be no shortage of second guessers within the community whenever something goes wrong. Taking a "You can't be too careful" approach to investments may not be the best approach, but it minimizes the possibility of having to explain large mistakes.

5.1.2   Can You "Own the Market?" Do You Want To?

At the opposite extreme of the diversification spectrum is owning a representative sample of every asset available. Many people equate this to index investing, but the concept is much broader. If one truly owned the market, the portfolio would include not only every stock and bond that is traded, but also a pro rata share of the equity and debt of privately held companies, real estate, stocks of physical commodities, and every other actual store of value. Anything thought of as an asset would be held.

Not included in the portfolio would be hedge funds or other trading vehicles like *Commodity Trading Advisors* (CTAs). Neither hedge funds nor CTAs are an asset class, per se. They are simply vehicles to try to exploit asset classes from both the long and the short side, and as such would play no role in any effort to own the world.

At a practical level, implementing such a plan faces ridiculously high hurdles. First of all, there are no national boundaries. Is one to try to buy a fractional interest in every private real estate market in the world? How about a Serbian private bus company? A great deal of the wealth of rural Chinese comes in the form of pigs and chickens. Does Markowitz optimization require having those assets in one's portfolio as well?

In executing the theoretical optimal portfolio, compromises are made everywhere. First, with the wave of a hand, the practitioner says they will limit their portfolios to the *investable* universe. This rules out most of the world's real estate, private companies, and farm animals. It can also rule out stocks where foreign ownership is either not allowed or is greatly restricted or taxed. This leads to the outcome that one's optimal portfolio depends in which jurisdiction one is operating. The American investor looking into China gets a very different perspective from the Chinese investor looking out.

The construction of indexes for trading has tried to appeal to those attracted to the idea of "owning the market." Both stock and bond indexes have been introduced that include greater representation of their target universes. What sometimes gets lost is the idea that there is a cost to broader coverage, and it might not be worth the bother.

A good example can be seen in the case of US stock index products. Vanguard is widely regarded as a high quality, low cost provider of mutual funds. On their webpage in August of 2017, one could find information on 13 broad US stock index funds, 9 international stock index funds, 1 index fund covering the globe, and 13 index funds covering various bond indexes.

Most of these products have different share classes for individual and institutional clients (with widely different minimum investments) and several are offered as ETFs. Among the US index offerings is a family based on the well-known S&P 500, representing large-cap stocks and another based on the MSCI US Broad Market Index, which purports to capture "approximately 99% of the capitalization of the US equity market and includes approximately 3,100 companies.[1]

At a theoretical level, one might assume that the MSCI index would be the preferred choice for maximum diversification among US equities. If one had no informational edge suggesting large-cap stocks would do better than the total market on a risk-adjusted basis, *and the portfolios could be executed at equivalent costs,* modern portfolio theory would indeed point the investor in that direction.

The equal cost assumption is a big one. Transacting in small and micro-cap stocks faces much worse liquidity, which translates into wider bid/ask spreads. Simply building a "complete" portfolio could incur costs large enough to offset the expected diversification benefits.

Hints of how important this is can be found in Vanguard's descriptions of their funds. For the family based on the S&P 500 Index, Vanguard describes their portfolio construction process as "full replication" meaning they buy and hold every stock in the index at the index weight. If one wants to run an index fund that minimizes tracking error due to price moves, this is the only effective approach.

It is not the approach taken with the funds based on the MSCI US Broad Market Index. There a highly quantitative approach called "index sampling" is employed. The Vanguard team buys the vast majority of the names in the more than 3100 stock index, but they omit the least liquid and most expensive to trade. The individual stock weights are then adjusted to try to minimize the tracking error between the

---

[1]Source: MSCI.com (Accessed 24 February 2021).

fund and the target index by adding extra shares in industries that look most like the omitted companies. Vanguard has made a business judgment that they can produce a better tracking fund against this index by using statistical sampling than from full replication.

Vanguard has been doing index investing successfully for a long-time and their judgment is well founded in experience. Other index providers face similar tradeoffs and usually reach similar conclusions. There is no theoretical right or wrong way to build index funds in the real world. The practical elements of running index funds, trading off the precision of full replication against the painful certainty of trading costs, reinforce the importance of not immediately embracing full replication for every index investment.

Similar considerations can help guide individual portfolio construction decisions. Index investing did not begin to gather momentum until the 1990s, and in the early years there were a relatively small number of alternatives to consider. Today it seems that every financial institution understands that it is a fairly low-cost business to offer index funds in either mutual fund or ETF form. The range of alternatives is staggering and every product has a story.

One of the standard stories draws on the spirit of modern portfolio theory to argue that more stocks means more diversification, which in turn should produce better risk-adjusted returns. Index providers want to help investors achieve their goal of "owning the market."

One demonstration of how far this trend has progressed can be found with FTSE Russell, an independent company owned by the London Stock Exchange. FTSE Russell bills itself as "Your Global Index Partner." In 2016 in a brochure describing the combination of FTSE and Russell that occurred the previous year, its web site noted that "FTSE Russell is a leader in innovative index design, calculating over 700,000 benchmarks daily, covering 98% of the investable market globally that it created and managed."[2]

As the complexity and liquidity of the wide range of indexes changes, index firms like Vanguard must plan their investment strategy with all the practical elements considered. The objectives of running a fund are very different from those investing in them. The ultimate question becomes, "Does it make a meaningful difference?" Figure 5.4 shows the path of the S&P 500, and Figure 5.5 shows the MSCI Broad Market Index from the latter index's inception to the end of 2010.

Without the labels it would be hard to identify which series represented which index. One might think that the S&P 500 with 500 stocks would exhibit more volatility than the MSCI Broad Market Index with more than 3,300 names, but this is clearly not the case. Part of the problem is that the stocks in the indexes are weighted by their cap size. The top 10 names in the S&P 500 make up 20% of the total capitalization.[3]

---

[2]London Stock Exchange Group plc, FTSE Russell. (2016) *Your Global Index Partner*. ftserussell.com. p. 15.

[3]As of 31 July 2017, the top 10 holdings in the Vanguard S&P 500 Index Fund were: Apple, Microsoft, Alphabet, Facebook, Amazon, Johnson and Johnson, Exxon Mobil, AT&T, Berkshire Hathaway, JP Morgan Chase, and Wells Fargo. Source: Vanguard.com (Accessed 21 August 2017).

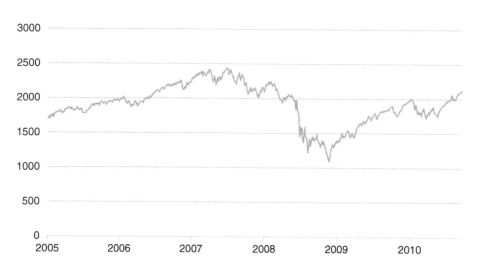

FIGURE 5.4   S&P 500 Index, 2005–2010
Source: Bloomberg

Nine of these ten names are also at the top of the list for the MSCI Broad Market Index, with MSCI breaking Alphabet into two names and omitting Berkshire Hathaway.[4] One might think that with 3,900 stocks in this index, the influence of even the biggest 10 would be muted, but this intuition is incorrect.

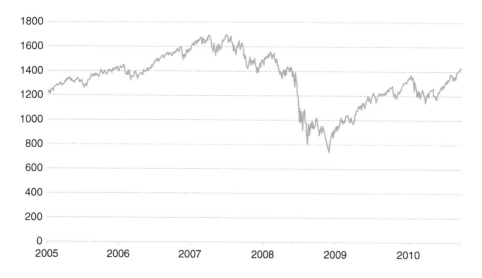

FIGURE 5.5   MSCI Broad Market Index, 2005–2010
Source: Bloomberg

---

[4]MSCI.com. Holdings as of 31 July 2017 (Accessed 21 August 2017).

The weight of the top 10 names is 15.4%.[5] There are literally hundreds of the smaller companies in the index that taken together are not as big as Apple or Microsoft.

Given the dominant influence of the largest companies in any of the cap weighted US indexes, there should be little surprise that it makes very little difference which of the broad indexes one chooses. *After the* fact there will be differences in performance, but those differences will not be predictive of future advantages. What is important is despite one's best efforts to live up to the spirit of modern portfolio theory to achieve the best risk-adjusted returns, there is very little difference in the apparent volatility of any of the indexes.

While the creators have strong arguments for why their index is superior to the competition, it seems that whether one is talking about the S&P 500, the Russell 3000, the MSCI Broad Market, or the Wilshire 5000, for the investor there are many more distinctions than true differences.

The true believer in modern portfolio theory should protest at this point and say the test is biased because it is US market-centric. As mentioned already, Vanguard also offers a family of funds based on the FTSE All-World Index. Figure 5.6 shows this index for the same time period previously examined.

The top 10 names in the FTSE All-World Index Fund make up 8.8% of the total capitalization.[6] Nine of the names overlap with the S&P 500, with Nestle nudging out Wells Fargo for tenth place on the list. Forty-nine countries are represented among

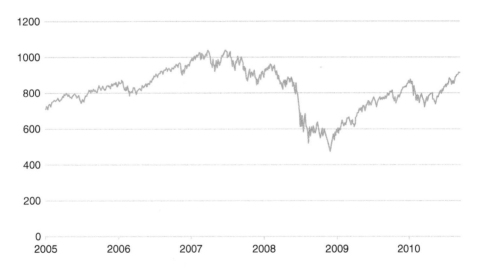

FIGURE 5.6   FTSE All-World Index, 2005–2010
Source: Bloomberg

---

[5]Ibid.

[6]As of 31 July 2017, the top 10 holdings in the Vanguard Total World Stock Index Fund were: Apple, Microsoft, Alphabet, Facebook, Amazon, Johnson and Johnson, Exxon Mobil, AT&T, Berkshire Hathaway, JP Morgan Chase, and Nestle. Source: Vanguard.com (Accessed 21 August 2017). By the time the reader looks at this list some of the top 10 names will likely have changed, but the conclusions remain the same.

the 7,845 names.[7] This is a very different sampling of the world's equity markets and yet the degree of co-movement is remarkable. Looking at all three charts, one might think that Bloomberg, which is the source of the data, is running the biggest scam in the world by providing the same data series but only changing the labels and the starting points (it most assuredly is not!).

The explanation for the similarities lies in the close integration of the world's capital markets that has been fostered by institutional investors following the prescriptions of modern portfolio theory. When Sharpe and Markowitz first developed their rules for maximizing risk-adjusted returns, there were no index funds, ETFs or any other institutional mechanisms for investing in the entire market. As these approaches have become the dominant way of investing for institutions, the net effect has been such a tight linkage across stocks that many of the diversification benefits that were once achievable by owning individual stocks have become somewhat illusory.

One might be tempted to try to identify the best index by simply looking at risk-adjusted returns. This would be a completely backward-looking exercise, which depending on the time period chosen might suggest that large caps are better than small, US stocks are better than Japan, or value stocks are better than growth. Ten years later it might suggest the reverse.

If one has a preference for any one of the three indexes above, it would have to be on the basis of an opinion that the included stocks in the broader indexes will perform better on a risk-adjusted basis in the future. But this brings the discussion back to whether one has an informational edge or not. Knowing that China and India are growing faster than Japan does not necessarily mean that those stock markets will outperform in the future. Absent an informational edge, there is little to choose from across broad-based indexes.

The investor looking to employ an index strategy should therefore first identify the area of interest, whether it is all-cap US stocks or a global mandate, and then sort the opportunities by costs. Manager expenses are at the top of the list, but are not the only costs to consider. Trading expenses, including the impact of owning less liquid names, only reveal themselves through time as underperformance to the index.

If one finds an "index" fund that outperforms the underlying benchmark, one should be cautious unless the manager describes the strategy as "enhanced" and the method for enhancing the index makes sense. Pure index funds should always slightly underperform because of trading costs. Outperformance is likely a sign of a mismatch with the underlying index stocks and can just as easily be a negative to the return in the future.

The bigger philosophical question is whether you really want to own the market as presented by the index providers. Consider the following three facts from different market environments:

- In 1989, Japan represented 21% of world GDP outside of the United States, but accounted for 60% of the EAFE Index.[8,9]

---

[7]Ibid.

[8]http://data.worldbank.org.

[9]Lawton, P. and Jankowski, T. (2009). *Investment Performance Measurement: Evaluating and Presenting Results*. John Wiley & Sons. p. 152.

- In 1999, the top 10 companies in the S&P 500 accounted for 25.4% of the total capitalization of the index and had an average P/E ratio of 130.[10]
- In late 2006, financial stocks represented 23% of the S&P 500, roughly 50% higher than the historical representation of that sector in the index.[11]

These market milestones were not chosen at random, but with the benefit of hindsight. Each marked the rough conclusion of heavily trending markets, over which there was much debate as events unfolded.

Beginning with the Nikkei 225, the index grew at an average of 19.5% annually in the 1980s to reach a valuation at the end of 1989 of 38,915.[12] At the end of 2010, the Nikkei 225 stood at 10,229, meaning it would have to increase 280% to get back to the 1989 level. By 30 June 2017, it had advanced almost 100% to 20,026, a respectable run over seven and a half years, but still needing another 94% gain from current levels to close the gap to the old high water mark. Only with the benefit of understanding how extreme market statistics like P/E and P/B had become in the late 1980s is it possible to pass judgment that the 1989 level was wrong.

The tech bubble in the United States is the singular defining event in equities trading in the 1990s. Professor Robert Shiller from Yale began noting that the market was overvalued by statistical metrics in the early 1990s. In a paper released in July 1996, he argued that because of inflated valuations, the S&P 500 would likely earn nothing over the next 10 years.[13] It then proceeded to climb 130% to the end of the decade.[14]

The growth of financial engineering at the start of the twenty-first century touched almost every facet of American life. From activities as diverse as stock trading, investment banking, off-exchange derivatives, and securitized mortgages, financial companies' profits were growing rapidly on the backs of their leveraged balance sheets. The prices of these stocks grew by much more than the average company equity, taking the weight of the financial sector to historical highs.

In each instance above there were sincere people who argued that the market, before the subsequent correction, was simply reflecting a new reality. Japan was the emerging global economic juggernaut in the 1980s, PCs and the Internet would revolutionize everything about our lives in the 1990s, and financial engineering would continue to spin more profits out of every real transaction by making each trade more efficient. In each case there was strong intuitive support for how the market actually behaved.

---

[10]S&P Corporation database.

[11] "Historical Sector Weights of the S&P 500." https://seekingalpha.com/article/99924-historical-sector-weights-of-the-s-and-p-500 (15 October 2008).

[12]The 1979 year-end Nikkei average was 6,569 and it finished 1989 at 38,915. Ignoring the effect of dividends, which were relatively small, the index compounded at 19.5% annually for the decade. Source: Bloomberg and NKS.

[13]Shiller, R.J. (1996). Price–Earnings Ratios as Forecasters of Returns: The Stock Market Outlook in 1996. (21 July). http://www.econ.yale.edu/~shiller/online/peratio.html.

[14]The 10-year total return from August 1996 through July 2006, the decade after Shiller's prediction of zero return was 134%, *almost all of which occurred in the three years immediately after the prediction.*

One does not have to debate the existence of market bubbles to arrive at a commonsense conclusion. In each of the examples cited above the market indexes became incredibly distorted from their historical norms. Did one want to own the EAFE benchmark when Japan represented more than 60% of the capitalization? Did an investor seeking broad US representation really want to own the S&P 500 when it had morphed into a large-cap tech index in the late 1990s or a financial industry proxy in 2006?

The efficient markets camp would say that the market simply reflected the best understanding of current information available to all. This may have been true, but it does not change the fact that as the market concentrations of Japan, tech stocks and financial stocks each exploded, the risk profile of any index investment changed profoundly.

This is perhaps best seen with international investors and their Japan exposure in the 1980s. As the Japanese markets took off, many institutional investors simply defied the index convention and decided to hold less Japan. Enough did this that it prompted MSCI to produce a half Japan weight international index, informally dubbed "EAFE-Lite." Despite urgings to "own the market," many investors found the risk profile of a Japan-majority EAFA beyond their tolerance.

In retrospect this was wise. More than a few managers made almost all their "alpha" versus EAFE in the 1990s by simply being underweight Japan. But whether one began the underweight precisely in 1989 or several years earlier when the Japan bulge first appeared, the point is not about the timing of directional moves. The EAFE index simply stopped being an attractive bogey from a risk standpoint for many international investors.

The cases of the distortions to the S&P 500 Index were apparently less evident to many investors. People who argued hard that the run up in tech stocks was a momentum-based frenzy, turned around and bought the S&P 500 thinking that by owning a broad market they were avoiding the excesses. It was a small victory when the S&P 500 *only* fell 43% between the end of 1999 and September 2002 as many tech stocks fell by more than 90%. Only active managers that were not targeting index sector weights managed to avoid major losses over this period.

When broad indexes deviate so profoundly from historical norms, one should question whether an index approach continues to serve its purpose. Unfortunately, there are no flashing lights signaling whether an index is in the range of normality or not. Judgment needs to be constantly applied to assess the attractiveness of the index approach over active management. At moments when the deviations from history are extreme, and the pundits' best rational is that, "This time it is different," are the times when common sense active managers add their greatest value.

5.1.3   Real Diversification Versus Owning a Bunch of Different Names

At the opposite end of the indexing spectrum are portfolios containing a wide variety of active managers. Some investors are quite specific in categorizing the portfolio by style box, wanting to include for equities small, medium, and large-cap stocks in a particular geography, and sometimes dividing those categories even further into growth and value approaches. There may be more than one manager in any given category like large-cap US stocks. At the conclusion of the exercise, all boxes are populated and the target portfolio is considered complete.

In general, there is more opportunity for true diversification in asset classes that demonstrate less correlation across individual investments. For example, if one gives a group of fixed income managers the task of managing a benchmark of the one-year US Treasury bill, there is very little any manager can do to differentiate their portfolio without adding investments far from the spirit of the mandate. Treasuries with 9, 12, and 15 months to maturity trade with a high correlation to each other. Having two or more managers with this type of mandate does little to help diversification, but may lose cost savings available from having a larger investment pool with one manager.

For basic strategies like high-quality domestic fixed income, unless one is worried about operations failures with a manager, there is little to argue for more than one manager. Beyond exhaustive due diligence, the only sure fire way to lower the potential impact of an operation failure or fraud is to have multiple managers.

As asset classes present more opportunity for seeking alpha and also present greater market risk, the argument for multiple managers becomes more persuasive. Employing multiple equity managers is quite common. Having multiple hedge fund managers is considered best practice because of the range of market, operational and liquidity risks hedge fund managers present.

Adding multiple managers to any task is done because one expects returns better than the target benchmark, but also because of the benefits that the combined portfolios can provide. If the individual investments are lightly correlated, their combination will produce a total with better risk characteristics. How much benefit comes from this diversification is an empirical question that can be explored, but not definitively predicted, in advance.

Testing the hypothesis of improved diversification requires more than comparing portfolio holdings and looking for overlaps in names. One manager holding Coca-Cola while another holds Pepsico offers a basic level of diversification, but not one that is likely to help the portfolio if Congress passes a federal tax on sodas and snacks. If one hires several active managers in any style, it is important to see if those managers share sector or cap size biases that will cause their performance to be linked.

The number of stocks in the portfolios matters as well. If one hires three large-cap growth managers, each of whom invests in 100–200 stocks, the end result may be a collection that acts like an index with active manager fees. This would tend to point toward managers with concentrated positions as being the best candidates to combine in a portfolio. The challenge here is that such managers tend to have higher individual volatilities and tracking error to the benchmark so they get downgraded by the traditional methods of evaluation, discussed further in Section 5.3 of this chapter.

No matter what one does, there are certain market events that are difficult to avoid through diversification. The credit and liquidity crisis of the second half of 2008 and early 2009 affected all long-only stock managers negatively. Every sector declined, and even the most carefully crafted diversified portfolios tumbled. The hopes placed in hedge funds to protect against the market decline were largely disappointed, with only funds that were long volatility or outright short the market able to really help offset the losses in the equity and credit markets. The only true diversifiers in the crisis were Treasury bonds and cash.

While those events need to be considered and planned for (recall the sleep-well-at-night funds in Chapter 4), they cannot dominate the thinking about growth portfolio construction. Outside of crisis times, correlations across investments do not run at extreme levels, and one usually benefits from thoughtful diversification.

Real diversification requires not only different holdings but also different trading styles. A stock portfolio that contains only deep value managers will at times find itself totally out of step with the market. Even though different stocks were chosen, the basic selection methodology would be the same, which makes the entire portfolio subject to the same kind of shocks. Ideally, one would employ both growth and value style managers that are expected to outperform over time, helping to ensure that one of the styles is favored by the current market.

Once the truly diversified portfolio is built, the problem of valuation begins. By definition, in a diversified portfolio not all investments will be at the top of the class. At times when large-cap, high dividend stocks are underperforming the average, managers working in that style will look less capable. It is often difficult to stay with these managers despite the fact that they are executing their craft in exactly the same way that created their strong track record. Section 5.3 of this chapter discusses the challenges of the evaluation process in greater detail. The key conclusion here is that a well-constructed, long-term diversified portfolio will demonstrate its superiority over the long run and not on a month-to-month basis.

5.1.4 Real Diversification Versus Owning Offsetting (and Expensive) Trades

The Holy Grail of diversification is found with two assets that individually offer greater than the risk-free rate of return but show a perfect negative correlation. Consider the following:

- Asset A has an expected return of 5% and a standard deviation of 10%.
- Asset B has an expected return of 4% and a standard deviation of 8%.
- The correlation between the two assets is –1.0 exactly.

Investing in either asset alone produces a reasonably high probability of a loss in any given period.[15] The combination of putting $1 in each asset produces a much better picture. Not surprisingly, the expected return of the portfolio is 4.5%. But because of the perfect negative one correlation, the portfolio standard deviation is only 2%.[16] This portfolio can be expected to have an actual loss in a bit more than 1% of the outcomes.[17] Clearly, experiencing losses 1% of the time versus almost 30% of the time

---

[15]The probability of any loss for either investment taken alone is about 30%, using normal distribution assumptions. The "tail loss" statistics are also relevant. In just under 2.5% of the outcomes, Asset A can be expected to lose at least 15% and Asset B will lose 12%. Lee, C.F. (1993). *Statistics for Business and Financial Economics*. D.C. Heath and Company. p. 257.

[16]The standard deviation of the sum of two correlated, normally distributed variables is given by the following equation:

$$\sigma_{X+Y} = \sqrt{\sigma_X^2 + \sigma_Y^2 + 2\rho\sigma_X\sigma_Y},$$

where ρ is the correlation between X and Y and the σs are the standard deviations of the variables. Plugging the stated values into this equation yields the standard deviation of the sum of X and Y. In the example, this is equal to the square root of (100 + 64 – 160) or the square root of 4, which is 2. Markowitz, H. M. (1959). *Portfolio Selection*. John Wiley & Sons, Inc. p. 87.

[17]A loss occurs when the return is negative, which in this distribution, is 2.25 standard deviations below the mean. The probability of that event in a normal distribution is 1.22%. Lee, C.F. op. cit.

is a big improvement and one most investors would gladly take versus even the best single investment alternative.

Perfect negative correlation is virtually never found between two assets that both have a positive expected return, but if one finds even less than perfect negative correlation, overall portfolio risk can be greatly mitigated. The Holy Grail of investing can be extended again and again if more investment options can be found that also negatively correlate to the portfolio. This is the principle that drives the quest for diversification.

This quest can be driven to foolish levels with unfortunate consequences. Too many investors look first to a negative correlation as their guide and then argue that the addition of this investment acts as a "hedge" against existing portfolio exposures. The fallacy here is in ignoring the impact on expected return by adding a portfolio hedge. The clearest example can be seen when adding a dedicated short equity manager to a portfolio already having a major long stock position.

The expected return of the long stock portfolio is the beta of the market plus any alpha the active managers produce. Over time in a growing economy, one expects this total to be positive. The dedicated short manager's expected return is minus beta plus any active manager alpha. If one places $1 in both the long and short buckets, the positive and negative betas cancel out, leaving the expected returns to be the sum of the anticipated alphas. This, coincidentally, is the principal of a long/short, market-neutral equity hedge fund.

One would never think to do such a trade with an index product on the long side and another index product on the short. The betas would cancel and one would be left with a negative expected alpha simply due to costs. There would be little or no volatility to such an "investment" but there would also be no positive long-term return.

Too often institutional portfolios carry these kinds of offsetting positions in the name of hedging and reducing volatility. Sometimes they come in the form of expensive long or short hedge funds that have performance fees, which is the ultimate folly. Whether the market goes up or down, one of the managers is getting paid on the profits, while the other simply receives the active management fee. For hedge funds that charge 20% profit participations, unless there is a phenomenal amount of alpha generated by both managers, such a combination is a recipe for losing 20% of any subsequent market move in either direction.[18]

This is analogous to walking into a casino and placing a dollar on black and another dollar on red at the roulette wheel. In every instance one of the bets will win and the other lose, offsetting one another. Since roulette wheels in many locations also have 0 and 00 slots on the wheel, the expected outcome over long periods of time is negative. Black is the market increasing and red is the market declining. The zeros are the equivalents to manager fees. One might as well write a small check to the casino at the beginning of the night and go enjoy a floor show.

---

[18]Consider two active managers with betas to the market of one. One is long-biased, the other short. Each charges only 20% of the profits; there is no straight management fee. If the market moves up 10%, the short manager loses 10%, but does not charge a performance fee. The long manager makes 10%, but subtracts 2% performance fee. The net is a 2% loss. If the market moved down by 10%, the result would be identical, but the short manager would collect the fee. The best result for the investor comes from the market not moving at all!

Rarely are misguided diversification attempts as obvious as the examples discussed above. Looking at how a prospective manager is expected to affect the portfolio in terms of risk and return based on historical data cannot identify a direct conflict. To highlight the costly problem areas, one also needs to look at how such a manager's portfolio interacts with each existing manager and subset of managers in the mix. If one identifies a group that largely cancels each other out, this suggests that part of the portfolio is essentially dead money or worse. If the investor primarily seeks to lower portfolio volatility, a better solution would be to eliminate the entire group and then put that capital into T-Bills.

There is one instance where one should seek out offsetting trades. Owning a successful illiquid partnership creates risk management issues. There may be no opportunity to sell any of the exposure in order to rebalance. This happened on a mark-to-market basis with many investors in venture capital and private equity in the late 1990s. They saw their wealth grow dramatically, but there was no mechanism to directly take some chips off the table to reduce an outsized exposure.

In those instances the best way to adjust exposures might be from a short index futures position or from the purchase of a put. This is intentionally establishing the maximum opposite position in order to reduce exposures with the highest confidence. But this should not be confused with a long-term portfolio allocation.

Too many investors allowed allocations to the tech sector, intentional or otherwise, to grow almost without bound in the late 1990s. They might have made allocations to venture capital and private equity funds that were heavily oriented to tech in the middle and latter parts of the decade. Given the raging bull market in the space, these investments prospered on a mark-to-market basis. On a parallel track there were also tech gains in the marketable growth equities and index fund parts of the portfolios. Given the growth of the overall portfolio, no one sector might have been considered overweight versus the guidelines.

In this case there was only the appearance of diversification. Different asset buckets had been allocated. Historical simulations suggested that by owning different types of equities, the risk/return profile was improved. In fact, the venture capital, private equity, active growth equity and the index fund investments were completely linked and dominated by exposure to the tech sector. A sage investor looking to take chips off the table might have sold all of their liquid equity investments and bought puts to cover some of the remaining private risk. This would have produced a very unbalanced portfolio from a traditional asset allocation perspective, but the risk profile would have been much more aligned to the investor's original goals.

5.2 ACTIVE MANAGERS VERSUS THE INDEX

5.2.1 What Is the Source of Alpha, and Can You Identify Its Presence?

Alpha is the most discussed and perhaps least understood concept pertaining to active management. In its most basic form, alpha is simply the extra return earned beyond that from owning the market basket. Every manager with a good track record talks about how they produce their alpha. It is usually described as a somewhat mysterious process combining deep research, market intuition, and a strict discipline that, in theory, avoids the most extreme negative market events while exploiting market opportunities. Every investor that uses active managers should make it a high priority to understand a manager's claimed alpha generation process. Without such an understanding, it is virtually impossible to judge whether the process is likely to be repeated in the future.

When everything is boiled away, there are only three real sources of alpha:

- The manager has better information than the market.
- The manager analyzes market information better than other investors.
- The manager executes the investment with lower costs.

Headlines about insider trading leave the impression that there are only two kinds of information: legal, public information and illegal, material, nonpublic information. While it is certainly true that trading on material, nonpublic information might give one an edge (at least until the Feds catch on), it is not necessary to cross this bright line for one to benefit from better information.

The simplistic view of the world suggests that information sprinkles down on the world like raindrops in a steady spring storm over a meadow. The drops fall more or less equally across the ground, leaving all the grass better off. A company announces its last quarter's earnings and perhaps provides some guidance and the investing world is uniformly informed.

This is rarely the reality. While some information is announced this way, there are so many relevant pieces of the puzzle that are not under the control of the company. What are competitors doing? How will changes in factor costs affect future margins? Is the financing environment getting tighter or more favorable? Each of these items is potentially a key data point. They do not appear simultaneously or with press releases attached. Most importantly, it is costly to identify the relevant pieces and collect them.

George Stigler won the Nobel Prize in Economics in 1982 for many contributions, but at or near the top of the list was his work in the economics of information.[19] Stigler demonstrated that people would invest in acquiring new market information only to the point where the marginal benefit of the information justified its marginal cost. His examples were from labor market searches, explaining why the unemployed don't search every possible job opening in order to find the single best position, but the principles are universal.

Certainly it is always possible to do more research on a company or an industry before one makes an investment, but to what benefit? If the extra research takes a year and the stock price has already moved up by the time the research is completed, the "benefit" from the additional information would be negative. At some point each investor has to make a decision that they have enough information with which to make a decision. Those with the better information should have superior results.

In an important extension of Stigler's path breaking work, Sandy Grossman and Joe Stiglitz proved that it was impossible to have markets that were perfectly, informationally efficient.[20] If market prices already incorporated all the relevant market

---

[19]Stigler, G.J. (1961). The Economics of Information. *The Journal of Political Economy*.
[20]Grossman, S.J. and Stiglitz, J.E. (1980). On the Impossibility of Informationally Efficient Markets. *American Economic Review*.

knowledge, private investors would have no ability to profit and there would be no incentive to trade. One could watch the prices bounce around randomly as new information immediately became revealed in the market price, but there would be no trading volume as no one would have an edge that they could expect to exploit. The market would become about as interesting as a game of Go Fish played with all the cards face up. Even small children get bored.

Markets simply don't exist unless there are traders who believe they have superior information and are willing to risk capital to exploit that advantage. Of course, there is uncertainty around this distribution as well. One may strongly *believe* that they have an informational edge, but be entirely mistaken. A basic observation of behavioral finance is that many more people think they have an informational advantage than really do.

But some investors work hard to find the best information and they do it at a speed and cost that is superior to the rest of the market. Grossman and Stiglitz know that these people are essential to an active market and they will be rewarded with a return to their efforts. This is the alpha from having superior knowledge.

The second potential source of alpha is from the superior analysis of available information. The principle here is that most market information is known broadly, but market relevant information does not come with a user's manual. Seasoned judgment can make a big difference. Consider the example of data on inflation. Suppose you tell 10 people that the CPI to be announced the next day would reveal last month's inflation was running at a 2% annual rate. Those 10 people would then need to analyze that data for its relevance. Even for something as simple as the price of an inflation-indexed bond, one might get several different views. Good analysis and judgment translates to superior performance.

When one does due diligence on active managers, superior analysis is the area most often advertised as being their source of alpha. Their analysts have better models, incorporating more data in highly creative ways. The analysis is their "secret sauce" that differentiates them from other investors in the market. Whether this is true or not is a subjective judgment that one must challenge continuously. Section 5.3 of this chapter discusses uses and abuses of performance statistics by managers to support their case.

Trading style is one dimension of this analysis edge. Graham and Dodd deep value managers, argue that their strict analysis and discipline in not overpaying for assets may not prevent losses on any given investment, but it does give their portfolios a better chance to make money through time. While having adherents going back decades, deep value investing is not the only style people believe in. Momentum investors in both stocks and commodities have large followings and there are numerous other, more-specialized styles that managers follow.

Not every style or type of analysis can be superior to the market. In a very real sense the world is a zero-sum gain with the winners and losers balancing out. While the potential for alpha from superior analysis of data is always present, a manager asserting that it is present does not make it so.

The one source of alpha that is virtually indisputable is from the reduction of execution costs. If two managers have the same information set and perform the same analysis, but the first manager pays two cents per share commission, while the second manager pays only one cent, that second manager will have generated relative alpha. More importantly, that alpha is much more repeatable than the performance that comes from getting one or two lucky bits of information.

Asset allocators see this effect all the time. There are big differences in the performance of active managers, but the average manager can be expected to just reflect the market. The reality of higher active management fees makes being average a losing proposition. The average US large-cap mutual fund over long periods of time underperforms the same benchmark index fund by the difference in their fees. It is pretty much as simple as that.

Each active manager wanting an investor's business will argue that their sources of alpha, either from superior information or superior analysis, justify their fees. It is the investor's job to challenge those assertions and question the likelihood of ongoing truth.

There is a special case of an active manager that tries to be "benchmark disciplined." These managers appeal to allocators who have precisely defined categories of investment and they don't want any managers that subject them to style drift. The analogy would be a music director that wants to cast all the parts in Puccini's *La Boheme*. The composer had a pretty strong opinion about how many sopranos, altos, tenors, baritones, and basses were needed to have the ideal impact on audiences. Hiring a random bunch of people with pretty good voices might get the job done, but the chance for a great performance is low.

Similarly, there are active managers that advertise themselves to be disciplined to the benchmark. Many employ sophisticated analytical programs to guide them to stay within a certain range of the benchmark, sometimes as narrow as 1% or 2%. Sector and capsize allocations must look very similar to the benchmark.

While these steps are helpful in minimizing surprises against the benchmarks, they are also terribly constraining. Even if the manager believes he or she has superior information on a company, the extra dollars that can be placed into that name are limited by the benchmark orientation. These managers see the potential for wide performance variation to the index as a source of business risk and they seek to avoid it.

If potential alpha is limited because of the benchmark orientation, the specter of the active manager's fees grows higher. Is it reasonable to expect that a benchmark-disciplined manager can add enough alpha to overcome the cost disadvantage? This is a question that can only be answered subjectively. How different is the manager's portfolio from the index, and how much would the underweight and overweight positions have to be to generate such a profit? At some point there is so little difference in the portfolios that it is much easier to throw in the towel and go passive at the lowest possible costs.

The three items above are the core elements that can create extra value for an active manager. They are so general that it is hard to find value-added activities that don't fall into one of the three categories. There is one area, however, that falls outside of traditional finance theory that can make a difference. Behavioral finance proponents suggest that investors routinely make mistakes that cost them returns in the long run. They chase fads. They sell losing positions and fire underperforming managers at the wrong time. One can debate how much such behaviors affect the bigger investment landscape. What is undeniable, however, is that there are always investors who make such mistakes.

In such a world, the more disciplined, less emotional manager can take advantage of others' poor decisions. Before the financial crisis, there were a handful of investors who believed that the housing market was in a bubble and that the market was offering extremely cheap options that would protect against a downturn. When the crisis occurred many other investment opportunities appeared that took advantage of emotional selling or forced liquidations. One might argue that these are all just examples of superior analysis of available information, but it seems there is an added dimension to the story.

Anyone who ever carefully watched the floor of a futures or securities exchange in the days before most transactions became electronic would have seen that not all traders are created equal. Like poker players or tennis professionals, the truly adept take advantage of those prone to mistakes. The skilled make good livings. The less capable either regularly compensate the winners or stop and fall by the wayside.

Unlike the first three sources of manager value added, this last element is less tangible and harder to pinpoint analytically. One can say that legendary investors like Warren Buffet are as likely to have this edge as Serena Williams does on the tennis court, but moving beyond such obvious examples is a big challenge. Consistency and longevity are two traits to look for, but even then such managers don't win every point, game, set, or match. Great players with $100 million in AUM may not have the same edge at $10 billion. In the end this evaluation is another judgment call.

Alpha is a most elusive concept. Managers marketing their products will point to their past success as demonstration that their alpha generation process works. This might be true, or it might be that the manager got lucky. Investors will want to look well beyond the simple numbers to determine which of the three sources of alpha generation are present, if any.

5.2.2 Beta and the Reality of Costs

Most investments are ways to access the fundamental growth in value that comes with a growing economy. Bonds offer promises of interest that can be paid only if the borrower's resources expand enough to meet those promises. Stocks are the residual claim on earnings. Without growth, stocks are claims on a depreciating pool of assets. Whether one owns bonds, stocks, real estate, or other assets, the existence of growth is what creates the fundamental return. Looked at from the level of the broad asset class, this growth is what is known as *beta*.

Each active manager that has an identifiable style also has a beta to that style. Previously discussed "benchmark disciplined" managers probably have a beta to that benchmark that is close to 1. That is to say, if the index goes up or down 1%, the manager will on average move similarly. Managers in this style pride themselves on the fact they have a beta of 1, while simultaneously arguing for their ability to produce alpha above the standard.

Not all stocks are created equal with regard to their place in the overall market. Some stocks move less dramatically than average and other stocks are more volatile. Managers can find themselves, either deliberately or not, with a portfolio where the average beta is either significantly more or less than one. There is no right or wrong level of beta before the fact. The investor should simply be aware of the risks involved from portfolios that deviate meaningfully from the target market so that they can position accordingly and not be surprised by performance deviations that are simply expressions of beta.

Managers that hold some proportion of their portfolios in cash dilute the beta effect of their stocks. This is a common complaint of investors that seek tight definitions around their manager mandates. A 10% cash holding would be a "drag" on the beta of the asset class. Paying active management fees on top of a watered down portfolio makes it doubly hard to have superior performance.

If cash in the stock portfolio is frictional, cash used to support transactions of a manager that would otherwise be fully invested, this concern is valid. If, however, the active long-only manager uses cash as a defensive or opportunistic tactic, then one should simply view this activity as part of the manager's attempt to add alpha through market timing. If enough incremental alpha is created, the beta drag might be worth it.

The proportion of prospective alpha to beta in any long-only portfolio depends critically on the size and type of deviations the manager takes against the benchmark. Without meaningful deviations, there can be little alpha, and without alpha the argument for active management fees evaporates. One often is left with expensive beta and the promise from the manager that the future will be better.

As important as this discussion is with long-only managers, it is even more critical as it pertains to hedge funds. The standard hedge fund fee structure of charging between 1.5% and 2% on the AUM and then taking 20% or more of the profits creates a high bar for performance. Significant alpha needs to be present to make these fees workable and funds that have a high proportion of beta are in a very tough spot.

Consider the hedge fund manager that for each dollar of client money buys a dollar's worth of a diversified portfolio of large-cap US stocks. He then selectively shorts five cents worth of high conviction names he thinks are severely overvalued and ready for a quick collapse. The fees are 2% annual management and 20% of the profits of the fund.

If the short stocks on average have a beta of 1, the overall portfolio beta is 0.95. Now suppose the stock market falls 10%. The pure beta of the portfolio would suggest a decline of 9.5%. If the manager's shorting skills did not produce any alpha, the total net return would be –11.5%, equal to the portfolio loss less the 2% base management fee.

Even if the portfolio's shorts fell to zero there would not be enough profit to overcome this loss. If the shorts completely collapsed, the total portfolio return for the period would comprise a 10% loss on the longs, a 5% gain on the shorts, and a 2% loss from management fees, for a total net return of –7%. Since there was a loss there would be no performance fee.

This would be a meaningful improvement over the index, but not realistic to expect. The crossover point at which this hedge fund actually does better than an index alternative is if the shorts fall by more than 40%, which would be large enough to cover the management fee. Expecting the shorts to go down four times more than the market is a pretty tall order.

The story when the market goes up is even more discouraging. Let the market appreciate 10%. With no alpha from the shorts, the beta of the portfolio should produce a gross return of 9.5%, but this must be adjusted for fees. Subtracting the 2% management fee plus 1.9% performance fee leaves a net return of 5.6%. The alpha shorts would have to fall by around 90% (in an up market!) to get back to the index return.

The final observation is that hedge fund performance fees typically have high water marks, but are not otherwise symmetric. The order of the gains and losses matters; if there is a loss first followed by a gain, absent a lot of alpha, the fund would not get back to its high water mark and no performance fee would be charged.

But consider the case of a 10% market gain followed by a similar loss. The market is essentially flat for the two periods, but the fund with no alpha gains only 5.6% in the first period while losing 11.5% in the second, which is roughly a 6% loss! This hedge fund manager has to demonstrate superhuman stock picking skills to keep up with a simple, but fluctuating, index.

The villain in this story is the performance fee being driven by the beta of the market. There is not enough portfolio deviation from the benchmark to expect the hedge manager's skill to overcome this head wind. The reality of the 0.95 portfolio beta also means there will not be much difference in volatility between the manager and the index. There's simply not much "hedge" in this hedge fund.

At the opposite extreme are hedge fund managers that try to stay market neutral by keeping the beta of the portfolio near zero. While this avoids the problem of paying too much for beta, it poses another set of challenges. Can there be enough alpha generated for an acceptable level of risk to justify the fees?

Most hedge fund managers fall somewhere between the market neutral and the high beta extremes. They attempt to mitigate a large part of the market risk of a high beta portfolio but leave some degree of market exposure to express their market views. The successful ones are good enough at this balancing act to add value net of fees.

5.2.3 Bucketing Strategies and Managers into Narrow Categories: What Is Achieved, and at What Cost?

There is a popular trend in institutional money management to divide investments into narrower and narrower product categories. Asset allocation is not made simply between stocks and bonds. Bonds can be subdivided into sovereign debt, investment grade corporate debt, high-yield debt, and distressed situations, which are then further divided by geography. Stocks are often broken up by cap size, value and growth disciplines, sectors, and geography. The index industry has supported this activity by offering literally thousands of benchmarks against which managers can be compared.

The trend has been reinforced by applying tons of historical data to hypothetical portfolios, and by "discovering" the benefits of diversification. Investors believe that once they adopt a long-term, precisely defined asset allocation, and then rebalance to those targets with discipline, history will carry them to a successful outcome. This belief relies on the past being a good indicator of the future in terms of how the subsectors behave individually and as a group.

Portfolios are not like sugar cookies, however. The same proportion of baking powder, sugar, flour, salt, butter, vanilla, and eggs can be used year in and year out to produce a great cookie. But there is nothing to suggest that the ratio of international small-cap stocks to US large-cap growth stocks that produced the best risk-adjusted returns over the past 30 years will work at all for the next 10. Trying to follow such a finely tuned portfolio recipe has some advantages, but numerous pitfalls.

The primary advantages come from the discipline such a process brings. If categories are precisely defined and allocation ranges are followed religiously, there is little chance of finding oneself in a radically different risk position. Trustees at institutions take comfort in this, believing that if the original formula is not too far away from what is considered standard, there is little chance they can be blamed if the outcome is not good. If one is going to lose money, it is best to lose it conventionally and with company.

The discipline of only hiring managers that fit within narrow buckets also minimizes the chance that any manager "leaves the reservation" in terms of their risk profile. By mandating that an equity manager only invest in stocks of a certain cap size, in a specific geography, and within certain valuation parameters does not eliminate the chance of losing money. It just minimizes the chance that the loss will come from something the investor does not expect.

There are many active managers and index solutions out there if one wants to follow this precisely defined path. Disciplined rebalancing assures that there is little market timing involved in the decisions. The portfolio's returns are baked into the recipe and can only be improved on if the ingredients are of a particularly high quality.

But there are disadvantages as well. If the active managers' boxes are too narrowly defined, it is extremely difficult for them to exercise enough judgment to create an alpha net of fees. This is a problem similar to the high beta hedge fund manager discussed in the previous section.

Whether one employs active managers or narrow index solutions to fill the buckets, the resulting portfolio may add up to little more than owning "the market." If that is the case, one needs to demonstrate why creating the portfolio with small building blocks is superior to owning a broad index covering the entire class. Once again, execution costs versus the index solution should be a key consideration.

But the major disadvantage is that a narrow, recipe-driven approach forecloses opportunities that are outside the recipe, or it forces the inclusion of ingredients that just should not be included. Two examples demonstrate this.

Because of the credit and market dislocations in late 2008 and early 2009, leveraged bank loans were sold almost indiscriminately from some structured products and hedge funds. These first lien claims on a firm's assets traditionally trade very near par for all but the most stressed of companies. At the height of the crisis these loans traded down to 60 to 70 cents per dollar, even for highly credit worthy firms.

Investors may have owned CLOs or hedge funds that had bank loans as an underlying investment, but it would be the very rare asset allocation that had "bank loans" as a category of fixed income investment. They are hardly traditional securities. They have no CUSIP number. They trade and settle differently than stocks and bonds. They are not included in any of the main line bond indexes. There were many reasons why they didn't fit in a well-defined recipe. There was one big reason, however, why they should have been part of the portfolio. At the height of the crisis they perhaps offered a once in a lifetime opportunity.

When the crisis erupted, thoughtful managers realized that they could do careful credit analysis on the underlying companies and make informed decisions as to which loans to acquire. Being high up in the capital structure offered considerable protection to the buyers of these loans. Risks were certainly present, but many correctly believed that prices had reached extremely low levels more because of technical selling and not company fundamentals spiraling out of control.

Portfolios with tightly defined little buckets of investments never considered the opportunities in bank loans. There was no portfolio category for them and any manager that reached outside his or her defined area to take advantage of them would be guilty of "style drift." It was like seeing $100 bills on the sidewalk but not being able to pick them up because the mandate restricted you to harvesting $5 bills.

The other side of the coin comes when risk builds up in one of the buckets and cannot be shed because of the highly defined mandate. It matters not at all that the risk/reward profile of the bucket may be completely different from the historical record used to support the allocation. The investment is held in a disciplined fashion.

There are many examples of this kind of blind investment rigor. Already discussed Japanese stocks in 1989 or US tech stocks in 1999 are two well-known, high-risk situations that many investors "trimmed" to stay within guidelines as they rallied, but they could not cut because of their tight portfolio construction mandates. A less well-known example comes from the fixed income market.

A Treasury inflation-protected security, or TIPS, is a US government bond that pays a fixed coupon and is periodically indexed to the changes in CPI calculated inflation. They were introduced by the US Treasury in 1997 and have become a popular holding in many institutional portfolios. TIPS, because of their unique inflation protection features, are sometimes given their own allocation within a larger fixed income bucket.

In the middle of October 2010, interest rates on all Treasury securities, including TIPS, were near historic lows. Prices had been bid up by people seeking the safety of US government bonds and TIPS offered protection against any surprise increase in inflation. From the start of 2010 until the October high, an investment in the Vanguard Barclays' iShares TIPS fund showed a total return of 9.9% (capital appreciation of 8% plus 1.9% in dividends). By any objective standards, it had been a very good year, but not one that on the surface would attract much attention.

But beneath the surface, trouble was lurking. The TIPS index contains bonds of every maturity held with passive weights. By mid-October every bond in the index with a maturity of less than seven years was priced to yield a negative return after inflation. No matter what inflation became, the owner of these bonds was locking in a loss in real terms.

TIPS have been issued in the United States since 1997, so the historical record of performance is relatively short. Still, the average real rate of interest for TIPS has been between 1.5% and 2%, which intuitively seems to be a reasonable rate of return for someone lending money to the US government. A negative real yield says that lenders are *paying* the government to borrow from them.

As TIPS prices rallied through most of 2010, most investors sat by passively and made no adjustments to their allocations. This was likely due to the fact that regular US Treasuries and most corporate bonds had also advanced in price, leaving the percentage of fixed income allocated to TIPS not too far away from where it started the year. Being naturally accepting of gains, investors seemed able to avoid any critical discussion of why they had just earned almost 10% in a low interest rate, low inflation environment, and whether such gains posed outsized risks going forward.

The rest of the fourth quarter was not so kind to TIPS investors. In the two months after the peak, the TIPS index lost over 5% as the market tumbled back from its extreme valuations. A 5% loss over two months in a US government bond is well outside the range of expectations of most investors.

The investor sticking to a style box discipline throughout this story would likely rationalize their behavior by saying it was impossible to know when to get out of the TIPS market and that the volatility that resulted from the correction back toward more reasonable pricing is just part of the price one pays for being invested in these assets. That is an attitude that almost guarantees the investor will be part of the herd and receive mediocre results.

One could have also argued that because of their inflation protection feature TIPS were still attractive relative to traditional Treasuries that were also offering historically low rates but no protection. Arguing this line ignores the fact that a third option, cash, is always available. TIPS were figuratively the prettiest horse at the glue factory in October 2010. Investors who eliminated longer duration Treasuries and TIPS in favor of cash in the fourth quarter of 2010 saved their portfolios from significant losses.

Examples like the extreme TIPS mis-pricings do not happen very often. They are like large trucks speeding down an almost empty road in the country. A person wanting to cross that road knows that there is little chance of being struck by a passing vehicle, but the smart person still looks in both directions. If there is a truck speeding toward you, it is a good idea to step aside.

Long-term successful investing involves both identifying growth trends, but also avoiding major, unrecoverable losses. The 5% loss in two months for TIPS investors may not seem like a major loss compared to the equity risks most investors regularly assume. But it is a huge loss for its asset class, and nobody should expect real interest rates to retreat back into negative territory as a natural market move. This is a loss that is almost certainly not going to be recovered. Narrow style box asset allocations create these types of risks with unfortunate regularity and predictability.

5.2.4 Passive Investing Is Great If You Want to Own the Index at That Point

It was shown earlier in the chapter that owning the market is a fine high-level concept, but that executing on that concept can be a tricky business. There is no single index that captures the investable universe, though there are many that make claims why they should have a superior status. Given that there are literally thousands of indexes being calculated regularly, and investment products trading against many of them, the question about passive investing can be discussed at almost any level.

There are many studies that suggest the majority of active managers do not beat their respective benchmarks. Intuitively, these findings have great appeal as managers who trade close to their benchmark's securities while charging active management fees are fighting tough odds that they will find enough alpha to overcome the fee disadvantage.

The debate is somewhat stacked in favor of the conclusion that passive investing is better by the way these tests are done. Managers are put into categories, to which they themselves have agreed to manage. People who manage to a benchmark with limited tracking error can have difficulty overcoming their fees, but this does not imply that active management is a failed industry or that investors should completely simplify their lives and allocate across an array of passive strategies.

The biggest challenge is coming to the conclusion that you actually want to own the index in which you are investing. Most people never even ask the question, and instead assume that the benchmark is a desirable target. It often is not.

Take, for example, the issue of emerging market stocks. By the end of 2010, China became the world's second largest economy and grew at a pace that made the number one slot a real prospect in most of our lifetimes. Yet the wizards that create stock market indexes include China in the emerging market category, if they include it at all. Moreover, the total capitalization of all stocks traded in Hong Kong, Shanghai, and Shenzhen was $6.7 trillion, roughly 60% more than the capitalization of stocks traded in Tokyo and Osaka.[21]

Hong Kong traded stocks are typically included in developed market indexes. Shanghai and Shenzhen stocks are represented in emerging market indexes, even though there is considerable overlap of companies between the H shares traded in Hong Kong and the A shares traded inside China. As somewhat arbitrary are some of the categorizations, the representative index weights make up another set of problems.

The FTSE All World Index and its Vanguard index funds were discussed earlier in the chapter. Another all-world passive basket of stocks is the iShares product based on the MSCI All Country World Index Fund known as ACWI. The top five countries and their representative weights for the two indexes coming out of the financial crisis are in Table 5.1.

There are a number of curiosities in and out of this table. French companies make up about 4% of the indexes even though there is little stock trading done in France anymore. These companies are listed across several European exchanges. This highlights the increasingly global nature of stock trading and is of little practical importance to investors. The other inferences from the table are not so benign.

The most obvious conclusions are that the indexes are very similar to one another, but there are meaningful differences between the indexes and the capitalizations of the local stock markets. The major overweight in US stocks has to do with the concept of *investability*, which captures how freely a company's stock trades across global capital markets. Because US stocks can be purchased by nearly anyone, they pick up extra weight from countries that restrict access. This gives US stocks a disproportionate impact on the index values relative to their global share of capitalization.

China and Hong Kong are much further down on both lists, totaling about 4% of the index weights despite their combined capitalizations exceeding 12% of the global total. This is the flip side of investability. Almost 10 years after the table data, most global investors still do not have completely free access to the Chinese traded shares,

TABLE 5.1 Country Weights FTSE All-World and MSCI All Country World Indexes 31 December 2010

Country	FTSE Weight	MSCI Weight	WFE Weight
United States	41.4%	41.7%	31.5%
Japan	8.2%	8.7%	7.5%
United Kingdom	8.1%	8.3%	6.6%
Canada	4.1%	4.6%	3.9%
France	4.1%	3.6%	–

Source: FTSE, MSCI, and the World Federation of Exchanges.[22]

---

[21]http://www.world-exchanges.org/statistics/.
[22]http://us.ishares.com/product_info/fund/overview/ACWI.htm.

so the index creators haircut the Chinese weight to a level they believe is reflective of international access.

It is perhaps not surprising that the index providers build their products this way. Indexing is a business and not a theoretical academic pursuit. The major potential buyers of index services are only likely to pay for indexes they can actually act upon. But this does not make the asset allocation that results the correct one.

Imagine that you did not have the benefit of the above table. Instead suppose that you were only told that China was the world's second largest economy on a path to be number one in 30 years, and that its stock market capitalization today was more than 40% of the United States. In what ratio would you hold US and Chinese stocks?

Modern portfolio theory would suggest that 2.5:1 in favor of the United States might be the best answer, arguing that today's relative capitalizations have largely captured the growth trajectories of both economies and stock markets. Someone might choose a higher China weight if they were more optimistic than the market, or a lower weight if they were more concerned with China-specific risks. But in almost no situation would one come up with 10:1, which is the ratio suggested by indexes.

Similar arguments can be raised for smaller emerging markets and so-called frontier markets that are typically not included in any of the "all-world" indexes. Chile, Indonesia, Israel, and Poland together total about 1% of the FTSE All-World Index. That creates a ratio of 40:1 in favor of the United States versus this collection. It is certainly debatable whether that ratio is too high or too low today.

The broad passive investing discussion implicitly assumes that there are easily identifiable, superior indexes for each investment category. This is not the case. Indexing is a much younger industry than many realize and it is an industry that is constantly confronting investors with alternatives. This only adds to the challenge of getting passive investing right.

Over the years, the industry has grown in a number of ways. First and foremost, the number of indexes from which to choose has exploded. Forty years ago the Dow Jones Industrial Index was almost the only US stock index people could name. The broader S&P 500 gained a much greater following after stock index futures began trading in 1982. In the years since there have been thousands of new indexes created, many of which are available to investors as mutual funds, ETFs, and structured products.

The most popular form of trading vehicle for many years was the open-ended mutual fund. Since the vast majority of the passive stock index funds were cap weighted, the fund providers could build the funds at current market weights and pretty much set them aside. Market changes affect the underlying stocks and the indexes identically, making the funds truly passive, requiring action only when there are names inserted or removed from the index or when dividends need to be reinvested. New investments or redemptions are treated on a proportional basis.

The next major trading innovation was the creation of Exchange Traded Funds, or ETFs. These are nearly identical to their mutual fund cousins except their price is determined in the marketplace throughout the trading day. In a way ETFs are like closed-end mutual funds, but with one important difference. The creator of the ETF generally agrees to monitor the trading price versus the value of the underlying securities. If the ETF price is too high, the sponsor creates and sells new ETF shares while simultaneously buying the underlying securities. If the ETF price is too low, the sponsor buys up ETF shares and sells the underlying securities. Both of these activities are done in an attempt to keep the price of the ETF in close proximity to the underlying index value throughout the day.

Both passive index mutual funds and ETFs are generally tax-efficient for the buyers. There is no active management of the portfolios, so there is little reason to trade the underlying stocks unless shares are being created or redeemed. This also allows for extremely low management fees. If one wants to own the index, it is a very efficient model.

The industry has prospered over the past 30 years to the point where hundreds of billions of dollars are invested in passive index strategies in their various forms. New ETFs appear in the market every week and investment companies continuously innovate in an attempt to win part of this huge market from the older, longer established firms like Vanguard, State Street, and BlackRock.

The range of offerings can be daunting to investors. Each product has a story and an advertised advantage. Lately a great deal of innovation has come from alternative forms of indexes that supposedly fix flaws in the earlier products that command the lion's share of the market. Stock indexes have been created that are price, earnings, and even dividend weighted. Each is designed to improve on the traditional cap weighted model. In the increasingly popular commodity space, new indexes have appeared that avoid the reliance on near month futures contracts characteristic of the Goldman Sachs and Bloomberg "first-generation" products.[23]

To analyze the competing entries from which to choose, the investor can benefit by looking at the product from the eyes of the creator. The business challenge is this:

A new firm wants to enter a well-established space.

Copying the industry leader won't work because those products already enjoy the cost-efficiency benefits from their large scale.

To attract business one must come up with a major improvement.

This is ultimately no different than selling toothpaste or laundry detergent.

Unlike toothpaste or laundry detergent, however, financial indexes can be dreamed up by running nearly limitless simulations using historical data. Goldman Sachs did this with historical futures prices before they created the Goldman Sachs Commodity Index (GSCI) in the early 1990s and every index provider since has followed along. Given that each year provides a new set of data points, the claim is the ongoing research can only be moving us closer to the truth.

Or is it? The genius of these sales pitches is that they play upon the same human emotion that led alchemists in the Middle Ages to attempt to transform everyday objects into gold. There must be a "right" formula and with enough careful thought and experimentation it can be discovered. Alchemists believed that finding the formula had to be easier than digging in a gold mine, and many financial engineers think similarly about indexes. Unfortunately, the reality is something else again.

No index provider is going to introduce a new product with a simulated track record that is worse than the prevailing standard. Each stock, bond, or commodity innovation will appear to be an improvement. But there is little to suggest that these improvements will persist through time, or that the new indexes won't suffer from some other inefficiency.

---

[23]The Bloomberg Commodity Index was once known as Dow Jones-UBS Commodity Index and before that the Dow Jones-AIG Commodity Index.

Investors need to remember that creating an index is a very different business from running an investment product based on that index. The beauty of a capitalization weighted stock index is its low maintenance. Using any other weighting scheme requires periodic rebalancing, which comes at a cost. For commodity indexes, liquidity is usually superior in the nearest contract month. Creating a trading product out of deferred contracts can require trading into the teeth of a wide bid/ask spread. Few simulated trading results include these very real factors.

Innovations away from the basic model tend to move closer to active management, and with those moves come higher costs of trading and usually higher management fees. One of the primary arguments in favor of index investing is diminished. But the issues are more fundamental than that.

Every discussion of index investing implicitly assumes that there is no connection between investing according to an index and the behavior of the component prices of that index. In the jargon of economists, everyone is a *price taker* and has no impact on the market. This is simply not true.

Perhaps the best example comes from commodities. So much money poured into the GSCI and Bloomberg in the first years of this century that the underlying price structures of the index commodities were profoundly changed to the disadvantage of the commodity index investor. The new commodity indexes try to avoid the problem of overcrowded trades caused by the first-generation index investors, but if they are successful in attracting meaningful assets, they will create similar problems of their own. There is no fundamental problem to be fixed, but only market dislocations that can move around with the investing herd.

Active managers sometimes close their funds when they believe the size of their assets can become a detriment to creating investment returns. Index providers never do this. Their goal is not a solution to a difficult puzzle or a public service information campaign. They are in an economies-of-scale business that is driven by volume. If one index stops delivering as expected because too much money has been attracted to it, another index will attempt to take its place.

This does not produce better investing. Instead it raises questions about the promise versus the reality of index investing. It also argues indirectly for active management that is not benchmark constrained to avoid the market distortions occasionally caused by the investing crowd. There is no easy way to create gold from lead, or from any special recipe of securities.

You may not want to own an index because of these fundamental challenges, but there is also the previously discussed problem of extreme valuations that occur within indexes that become seriously distorted. Japan's monster equity weight in 1989 global indexes and tech stocks in 1999 have already been mentioned. This issue is exactly the same as the TIPS and bank loan problems discussed earlier in the chapter. There are often things you should own that are not represented in the indexes and there are things that you should run away from that are prominently featured.

One is left with the conclusion that *if* one is seeking the general exposure covered by an index, and *if* that index is a good expression of the desired exposure, and *if* there are no extreme valuation issues with either included or omitted assets, then there is a good chance that a passive investment is the most efficient investment option. That is a lot of "ifs." Is one capable of reaching the right conclusion? Going through the process of evaluating those questions can lead one right back to active management.

5.2.5   The Case of *Smart Beta*

There is now a label on one of the more recent innovations in equity index investing. *Smart Beta* is a generic term that covers a host of efforts advertised to improve on traditional capitalization weighted index investing. It is an approach that consciously tries to appeal to the efficiencies of index investing, while differentiating itself from fundamental active investing by stressing the analytical mechanics of the portfolio construction process. In the post-financial crisis era it has gathered hundreds of billions of dollars in assets.[24]

Smart Beta uses empirical research to identify factors that are claimed to provide extra return relative to their risk and then construct mostly passive strategies designed, on average, to beat traditional capitalization weighted indexes. The factors that Smart Beta proponents advocate can include smaller size companies, value companies, low-volatility stocks, or stocks that display momentum. While the spirit of the models is straight forward, the implementation of the strategies is not necessarily so, leading to many competing products in the marketplace.

One of the major challenges of Smart Beta index portfolios is that they require periodic adjustments. As previously mentioned, capitalization weighted index portfolios virtually maintain themselves as market price changes automatically are reflected in index weights. Smart Beta indexes can be equal weighted or "fundamentally" weighted, but in either case there will be times when actual portfolio holdings differ meaningfully from the index weights. This requires periodic rebalancing and produces transactions costs. To date, management fees and expenses for Smart Beta products are generally less than those for classic active managers, but are still meaningfully above the largest truly passive funds.

Without exception, proponents of Smart Beta are intelligent people, often with highly impressive academic credentials. But the track record of actual returns using these strategies is so short that much of the discussion is carried out like a university seminar. Models are debated and competing historical simulations compared. Apparent profitable factors are often explained as being the result of some anomaly from behavioral finance. This has led to a growing body of papers on the subject that largely concludes Smart Beta is an improvement, but it is a strategy that continues to evolve.

Investigators at EDHEC-Risk Institute surveyed the state of the discussion in 2013 and discovered that investment managers who had a horse in the race generated the bulk of the "literature."[25] Smart Beta models seemed similar but were often incompletely specified to protect the proprietary nature of the research. The authors note:

"In our opinion, this similarity in the investment process raises a major question. What is the minimal level of information which the Smart Beta investor should possess in order to evaluate genuine performance and risks? In the area of Smart Beta indices, one is forced to conclude that the situation is currently inadequate."[26]

The EDHEC researchers called for more transparency in an honest attempt to move the academic discussion forward. Given the huge amounts of money at stake, it is unlikely that many of the Smart Beta practitioners are likely to cooperate.

---

[24]O'Connell, B. (2017). Smart Beta ETFs Surpass $500 Billion in Assets, and Financial Advisors Better Understand Why. www.thestreet.com. (13 March).

[25]Amenc, N., Goltz, F., and Martinelli, L. (2013). *Smart Beta 2.0*. EDHEC. (April).

[26]Ibid. p. 32.

Other noted academics are less patient. Bill Sharpe, who created many of the pillars of modern portfolio theory, is particularly skeptical. Speaking at a CFA Institute Annual Conference in May 2014, he was quoted as saying, "When I hear smart beta, it makes me sick."[27] His concerns are more basic in nature.

Sharpe won a Nobel Prize in part for explaining carefully how it is impossible for everyone to do better than the market as a whole, and after transaction costs, the average investor should be expected to do worse. It should therefore come as no surprise that, in his attempt to "own the market," Bill Sharpe holds capitalization-weighted indexes in his portfolio.

He argues that if the Smart Beta people really are smarter than the market, the world is made up of those smart people, dumb people like him and, then the really dumb people who are underweight the stocks the smart people are overweight. If the smart people really end up winning over any period of time, at least the really dumb people should abandon their approach. Some of the traditional indexers may shift too. As this happens the prices of those preferred stocks will reflect the additional attention, and eventually the Smart Beta portfolio will look more and more like the market and the advantage of the approach will be eliminated.

Sharpe's criticism notes that many of the profitable factors that appeared in the back tests for one country either don't appear in other markets' data or that they fail to be predictive of the future. Once again, back tests are either revealing the appearance of an effect that is not really there, or that if enough people try to act on an anomaly it gets priced out of the market. This conundrum leads logically to the question of how any investing that is actively choosing to be at variance with the market can ultimately succeed.

5.2.6 Active Managers Can Avoid Major Pitfalls If They Are Not Benchmark Constrained

Active managers are often placed in a difficult situation. They are told to manage to a benchmark so that they can play a required role in the portfolio. Then they are told to go out and beat that benchmark on a regular basis, presumably by making decisions at odds with the index holdings. Managers get fired if they stray too far from their style box or if they have a stretch of underperformance.

Yet there is a huge industry of extremely large, benchmark-hugging managers that serve institutional investors wedded to the formula of filling buckets in a precisely defined asset allocation. The secret of their success seems to be to do everything in their shop from research, to trade execution, to operational reporting in a highly professional fashion and keep their performance within a band of respectability. This may be a great business model, but it is not a formula for outstanding success for their investors.

Creating a superior performance record requires an ability to avoid the trucks rolling down the highway toward you while looking for moments of opportunity. Active managers operating against broad mandates as compared to narrow style boxes are best positioned to do this. Having a broad mandate does not guarantee a

---

[27]Huebscher, R. (2014). Bill Sharpe: "Smart Beta Makes Me Sick." *Advisor Perspectives*. (13 May).

great performance, but it provides the necessary degrees of freedom to allow superior skills to shine through.

There are stock managers that have the ability in their funds to invest globally and go up and down the cap size range. They may be willing to hold cash if market volatility indicates caution or if there is a shortage of stocks to buy that meet their discipline's criteria. These managers drive the data services crazy. Their portfolios may look like they should be compared to a large-cap US benchmark for some periods and against small-cap foreign stock benchmarks for others. How does one calculate alpha? What is the manager's relative performance? What is the relevant peer group?

A statistic, called *active share,* has been developed to help guide investors through this thicket. Starting with some agreedupon benchmark like the S&P 500, the manager's performance is decomposed into what part was due to owning stocks in the index at the index weight versus the rest of performance. The ratio of the non-index performance relative to the total is the manager's active share. A manager with an active share in the single digits is likely a benchmark hugging closet indexer. Someone with an extremely large calculated active share may actually just be compared to the wrong index.

As eclectic as these high active share managers appear, some of them enjoy a common feature that over long periods of time they make money and beat most of the potential benchmarks. When one looks at the attribution behind such a record it usually comes from a balanced blend of seizing on opportunities and avoiding train wrecks.

The more regimented investors who avoid these managers do so out of a concern that the track record was created by taking risks inconsistent with the investor's goals and objectives. *This is an entirely appropriate and valid concern.* Managers can say they are invested primarily in a diversified universe of bonds or stocks and compare themselves against broad standard indexes, but their behavior may actually include leverage or risky derivatives strategies that have nothing to do with those benchmarks.

It is, however, somewhat inconsistent that these investors reject any highly active long-only stock and bond managers while simultaneously investing with hedge fund mandates that have extremely broad mandates. It would seem that if a hedge fund manager is given extra degrees of freedom in the quest for return, that courtesy should be extended to the long-only managers as well. The challenge lies not in the mandate, but demonstrating that a manager's process has integrity and is repeatable.

It is incumbent upon the investor to do enough due diligence on how money has been made or lost in the past, and how the portfolio is likely to be positioned in the future before a track record is accepted at face value. This is hard work with few real shortcuts available. Managers selling their products will try to help prospective investors along with a sheaf of statistics that supposedly demonstrate their skills. The next section explores those tools in detail to determine which statistics genuinely help and which statistics can be used to hide the truth.

5.3 LUCK VERSUS SKILL

5.3.1 Evaluating Managers

Several years ago when the universe of active hedge fund managers was probably around 5,000, a noted CIO of a state pension plan commented during a presentation

	2008	**2009**	**2010**
January	3.67%	−1.22%	
February	8.32%	4.82%	
March	9.31%	2.12%	
April	3.35%	4.52%	
May	2.27%	2.93%	
June	2.16%	1.66%	
July	14.39%	3.12%	
August	4.12%	−2.98%	
September	1.12%	7.96%	
October	5.50%	1.63%	
November	5.10%	−7.72%	
December	8.42%	10.34%	
Year	**91.91%**	**29.27%**	

FIGURE 5.7 Ebullio's 2008–2009 Performance

that she thought there were 16,000 hedge funds actively trading. When challenged about her estimate, the CIO stated she came to that conclusion because she had been approached by at least 4,000 managers, all of whom had claimed to be top-quartile.

Evaluating manager claims of superior performance is one of the greatest challenges investors face. Even when one identifies a manager who appears to have outperformed either benchmarks or peers, the analysis has just begun. Was the extra performance achieved by taking extra risks? Were those risks identifiable and of the type the investor was willing to assume? Consider the following actual track record:

Ebullio, based in the United Kingdom, advertised itself as a *Commodity Fund*. According to National Futures Association records, it categorized itself as an *exempt commodity pool*. This meant that while it probably traded futures and options contracts as its primary activity, it only had qualified investors in a private partnership structure and therefore was exempt from all the rules normally required of *commodity pool operators (CPOs)* or *commodity trading advisors (CTAs)*.

Prior to October 2008, the fund noted in its records that its performance was based on the returns of a *managed account*. This means that the actual fund available to outside investors did not exist until that date, but the manager claimed that the performance of the strategy executed for the separate account was indicative of what the fund would have accomplished. Assets under management at the end of this period were somewhat under $100 million (Figure 5.7).

Anyone remotely aware of the turmoil in 2008 and early 2009 would likely be impressed by these returns. 91% total net returns with no down months in 2008 had to place the fund among the elite performers of all global hedge funds. 2009, which was not an easy year for many CTAs, was quite strong as well. This manager was actively raising assets from new investors on the back of this track record and the apparent ability to make a lot of money under a wide range of market conditions.

Then 2010 appeared. In two months the fund lost almost 96% of its assets, entirely on directional bets on nonferrous metals prices (see Figure 5.8). Since copper, nickel, and tin prices did not fall by that amount in January and February, there

	2008	**2009**	**2010**
January	3.67%	−1.22%	−69.65%
February	8.32%	4.82%	−86.25%
March	9.31%	2.12%	
April	3.35%	4.52%	
May	2.27%	2.93%	
June	2.16%	1.66%	
July	14.39%	3.12%	
August	4.12%	−2.98%	
September	1.12%	7.96%	
October	5.50%	1.63%	
November	5.10%	−7.72%	
December	8.42%	10.34%	
Year	**91.91%**	**29.27%**	**−95.83%**

FIGURE 5.8   Ebullio's 2008–2010 Performance

was evidently a fair degree of leverage being applied to these trades. Nowhere in its basic communication did the manager describe in any detail the risks that were being taken to produce either the strong positive returns in the first two years or the ruinous losses of the last two months.

This is an extreme example proving that past performance is no indicator of future returns, and it is easy to see in hindsight that whenever one has outsized gains there is usually a chance of outsized losses as well. But nobody gets to invest in hindsight. This section discusses what to look for when considering the marketing materials of managers so funds like the above can be avoided just at the time when the story seems the most appealing.

Investors should always expect performance to be presented in the most favorable light. If a manager outperformed a benchmark by 200 basis points over the previous five years, that fact will be prominently featured. The manager has no obligation, for example, to inform the potential investor that the average manager in the same strategy beat the benchmark by 500 basis points over the same period.

Comparing managers within peer groups requires assurance that the investment styles are comparable. This is somewhat less of a problem with vanilla, long-only stock and bond managers than it is for the more loosely defined groupings of hedge funds. Yet mutual fund rules in the United States and some other countries can allow some use of leverage or derivatives, which rarely are prominently disclosed when they are part of the portfolio.

Careful performance attribution is the only way to begin to answer whether a manager's performance was due to luck or skill. Some managers provide detailed breakdowns of their sources of returns. Long/short equity hedge funds can easily document their average gross long and short exposures monthly and how much profit or loss can be attributed to each. In this way the investor can compare the actual results to hypothetical outcomes that would have been produced by a manager owning a comparable index basket. A simple example can demonstrate the process.

Assume Manager A's stated policy is to be usually 100% long a portfolio of large-cap US stocks, but some amount of cash can be held as a defensive step. In the most recent month, the S&P 500 lost 4%. The manager averaged 80% long stocks and 20% cash for the month, and posted a loss of 3%. While the fund outperformed the index, how did it really do?

Holding a large cash position in a declining market was clearly a good idea after the fact. If the portfolio had owned 80% stocks exactly replicating the S&P 500 for the month, the loss would have been 3.2% ($= 0.80 \times 4.0\%$). The good timing decision of raising cash can be described as adding 0.8% or 80 basis points of value. Since the total advantage over the index was 100 basis points, there was another factor at work as well. The extra 20 basis points can be attributed to security selection and any interest earned by the cash in the portfolio. By choosing, on average, stocks that outperformed the index, the manager also added value.

A manager's actual returns do not always show positive contributions from either timing or security selection. It is unrealistic to expect managers to add value in every reporting period. A track record that suggests such could be a warning sign of fraud. Ideally one would look at this kind of attribution over an extended period and, preferably, one that includes both bull and bear markets.

Average outperformance is a useful statistic, but the pattern through time should also be assessed. It is not unusual to see strong outperformance in the early years of a track record only to be followed by smaller outperformance or even lagging performance. If such a pattern emerges, one would want to see if the assets under management grew dramatically or whether there were any important changes to the team or the investment process.

Figure 5.9 is a stylized "Growth of $1" chart that is frequently part of manager presentations. It is often accompanied by tables focusing on "since inception" statistics. In this and several examples that follow in this chapter, the data is entirely fictitious, but developed around a period of stock market history, 1999–2009, that saw two serious corrections surrounding a strong bull market.

FIGURE 5.9 Hypothetical Manager Stock Returns

Over the entire life of the fund, which spans 10 years from the last quarter of 1999, the manager added a great deal of incremental return over the S&P 500 Index. The total outperformance was over 40%, and the manager would likely remind any potential investor that the period 1999–2009 was the "lost decade" for S&P 500 Index investors.

Decomposing that return suggests a more nuanced story.

Figure 5.10 rescales the manager's and the S&P 500's returns to cover just the last five years. In this picture there is a close parallelism that suggests the manager's beta to the index is virtually 1, and in the period after the market top of October 2007, the manager seriously fell behind the index, lagging over the entire period by more than 20%.

Which is the accurate characterization? Perhaps neither. The next steps of due diligence would try to ascertain why such a divergence of performance might have occurred. A good place to start is assets under management. It is not unusual for a promising new manager to begin small, often starting with seed capital that includes his own money, friends and family assets and perhaps funds from an entrepreneurial institution that is trying to get in at the ground floor. In this hypothetical example, let's say the manager started with $100 million.

In the first few years it is difficult to raise additional outside money. Track records are short. Assets under management are small. The manager has yet to prove to the world that he or she can be trusted with someone else's money. As time passes, however, a real record of performance begins to unfold.

By the three-year mark in Figure 5.9, a positive picture can be described. Despite starting the fund just before the breaking of the tech bubble, the manager stayed above water. At the three-year anniversary the fund was essentially flat, but the index

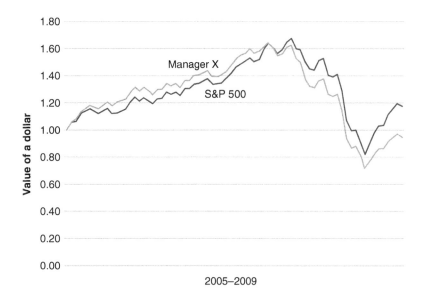

FIGURE 5.10 Hypothetical Manager 5-Year Performance

had fallen by a third, a major victory. This is the kind of performance that is difficult to ignore, and outside capital becomes much easier to attract.

The recovery phase of the market after 2002 was equally kind to the hypothetical manager. In the next 30 months as the index worked to regain its high water mark, the fund earned over 80%. By the end of 2005, with a total return since inception of almost 100% while the index was up 7%, the manager could be seen as a rising superstar. The biggest problem of marketing such a fund is having time to answer all the incoming calls. In this story, assets at the start of 2006 stand at $10 billion, with a client base composed of high-net-worth individuals, foundations and endowments, pension plans, and a large percentage of funds of funds.

Given the different sized portfolios in the two five-year periods, are the return patterns really comparable? It is difficult enough to compare investment performance across different market environments, but when there are such radical changes in the business model of the organization, more questions than answers appear.

Fund size is not the only variable that might have changed. Staffing probably grew dramatically over the 10 years. The founder might be a tremendous stock picker, but a terrible manager of other stock pickers. There can be illnesses of children, divorces, and a score of other factors that can influence the firm management and fund performance.

Successful fund managers get reinforcement every day that they are truly brilliant and have energy without limitations. Sometimes they begin to believe it themselves. They begin new funds, expand their range of business ventures, and have been known to buy sports teams. In short, they can increasingly spend time doing everything except that which created their success. Step by step, the alignment of interests between the fund manager and the investors becomes strained.

The hypothetical picture painted above is too obvious. Everyone can see the pitfalls, and most investors would like to believe they would avoid them. However, the real world rarely has bright flashing green or red lights to instruct investors. Imagine one is told that the AUM of the manager above never exceeded $1 billion, the professional staff was only 20% bigger than the fund started with, and none of the senior partners of the firm had departed. Add that the founding partner remains married to his college sweetheart and they are actively awaiting the arrival of their first grandchild. How does one explain the fall off in performance in the second five years?

It could be bad luck. Or it could be a combination of good luck in the first half of the record, and bad in the second. *Most people want to believe that outperformance is always due to genius and that underperformance is caused by colossal mistakes.* While some of that perception is true, there is more randomness to investing than anyone readily acknowledges. Managers that remain disciplined, grounded to the realities of the market, and humble seem to have the best opportunity for long-term success.

5.3.2 Classic Performance Measures and Their Limitations

Over the past 50 years, investment management has moved smartly from being a lightly analyzed art to being presented as a highly quantitative science. Like all quantitative sciences, there is a tool kit of statistics that is used (and abused) in the presentation of results. Most investors receive reports that are loaded with statistics, many of which are beyond intuitive description. The following section attempts to demystify several of the more popular measures and describe their advantages and limitations.

5.3.2.1 *Compound Returns*

At the end of the day most investment questions boil down to, "How much did I make?" The most direct answers come in the form of *compound annualized returns* calculated over the investment horizon. To calculate this return only four pieces of data are required:

1. The value of the assets at the start of the period (V_t).
2. All income, like interest and dividends, over the period (I_t).
3. All costs associated with the investment over the period (C_t).
4. The value of the assets at the end of the period (V_{t+1}).

The simple returns calculation is given in Equation 5.1:

$$R_t = (V_{t+1} - V_t + I_t - C_t) / V_t - 1 \tag{5.1}$$

The numerator contains the change in the value of the asset, plus all income received, less the costs associated with the investment. Dividing this by the starting value and then subtracting 1 produces the net percentage change for the period.

If the period of the investment is exactly a year, the answer above is the annual return. If the period is shorter than a year the convention is to annualize the return by dividing the basic return by the fraction of the year it represents. For example, a net percentage return of 3% for a calendar quarter would annualize to 12%. Note that this convention assumes no benefit from continuous compounding of returns.

For periods longer than a year, the calculation to determine the annualized returns is somewhat more complicated. The goal is to determine what single annual return, if held and compounded for the entire period, would produce the actual investment result for the period. It is the compounding assumption that complicates the calculation.

Suppose an investment is held for exactly two years and produces a total net return of 8%. It would appear on the surface that the annual return averaged 4%, but that ignores the effect of compounding. The true rate is derived from Equation 5.2.

$$(1 + R_t)(1 + R_t) = (1.08)$$
$$(1 + R_t) = (1.0392) \tag{5.2}$$
$$R_t = 3.92\%$$

The difference between 3.92% and 4% may seem trivial enough, but as shown in Chapter 2, small differences in rates can lead to major final results when compounding comes into play. When comparing the results across managers it is essential that each is reporting in a consistent fashion. This type of calculation can be applied to annualize any total return over any investment horizon.

One might think that there are few games that can be played with something as simple as returns, but that would be a mistake. While it is difficult to manipulate the stated returns from regulated mutual funds, the world of partnerships and separately managed accounts is a different story. The massaging of results can be done in many creative ways. Some managers report gross returns, ignoring the fund costs, which can be substantial. Other managers have been known to "cherry pick" their best results and downplay their less-successful periods. They have also compared their actual returns to inappropriate benchmarks in order to improve the appearance of their relative performance.

To try to establish some measure of order to what can be a chaotic landscape, the Association for Investment Management and Research (AIMR) in 1987 established a voluntary code of reporting standards. The not-for-profit organization AIMR, which is now known as the CFA Institute, decided that investors would be best served by transparent and consistent reporting. The AIMR standards initially applied to only US and Canadian money managers, but through the years the scope has expanded. In 1999 the first Global Investment Performance Standards (GIPS) appeared and they have been refined in the years since. In 2011, a revised GIPS was approved, which created a single global standard of investment performance reporting and increased minimum standards worldwide, replacing the previous array of various country-specific performance standards. Thirty years after the first standards there were more than 40 countries around the globe that had sponsored the GIPS standards.[28]

Compliance with the GIPS standards is entirely voluntary. It is not a violation of any rule or regulation to report performance differently, but it is a violation to claim GIPS-compliant reporting when it is in fact not the case. Firms that choose to follow the GIPS path must use standardized disclosure language in their reports. Quite often to assure investors of their compliance, investment managers engage independent specialists to examine their processes and results and to certify them as GIPS compliant.

The GIPS rules are quite detailed. There are many legitimate reasons why a firm might not report its results under those guidelines. Young firms cannot be formally GIPS compliant simply because they lack a long enough track record. While being certified as GIPS compliant may give potential investors some comfort about a manager, non-GIPS-compliant funds should not be rejected out of hand. The lack of GIPS reporting means that investors need more diligence of their own to confirm that the returns advertised are reflective of the investment program's prospects.

Returns discussions are virtually worthless without accompanying data on risks. Before the financial crisis of 2007–2009 many managers with steady returns dutifully reported their results in detailed monthly tables. After the crisis, and some major drawdowns, some managers choose to replace the tables with summary statistics highlighting average returns over long periods, conveniently drawing attention away from their most dramatic monthly losses. It is perfectly within reason for potential investors to ask for, and receive, detailed return performance. In addition to such a table, *standard deviation* and other volatility-related measures of performance like the *Sharpe* and *Sortino Ratios* discussed below should be considered.

5.3.2.2 *Standard Deviation*

Figure 5.11 shows two investment managers that managed to produce the same total return over their life. Manager A is the same hypothetical manager from the discussion earlier in this chapter. Manager B is another manager that may or may not have been following a similar investment program. The two most obvious things about

---

[28]CFA Institute, https://www.gipsstandards.org.

FIGURE 5.11 High and Low Volatility Return Managers

the chart are that the managers produced exactly the same total return *over the entire period,* but the paths that produced those returns were wildly different.

Standard deviation is the most widely used statistic to describe the volatility of an investment return stream. The formula for standard deviation is given in Equation (5.3):

$$\sigma = \Sigma(R_i - \mu)^2 / (n - 1) \tag{5.3}$$

where σ is the symbol for standard deviation, μ is the calculated average of the sample of periodic returns (R_i) and n, is the number of observations in the sample.

The calculated standard deviation will be expressed in the same terms as the units of observation. That is, if the returns are monthly, the standard deviation will relate to those sized returns. Similarly for daily or quarterly return series. How then does one compare two managers if one reports performance monthly and the other quarterly?

Like the basic returns calculation, standard deviation also has a convention for annualizing the values.

$$\text{annualized } \sigma = \sigma / \sqrt{(1 / T)} \tag{5.4}$$

where T is the number of sample periods in the year. For monthly returns streams, T is 12, and for quarterly data T is 4. This means that the annualized standard deviation is twice the standard deviation calculated from quarterly returns streams and roughly 3.46 times the standard deviation derived from monthly data.

Since the calculated 10-year returns are identical between the two managers, how does one best distinguish the two? For the first third of the experience, there appears to be little to differentiate them. Manager A's performance seems a bit choppier, but it is hard to have a very strong opinion between the two. The next five years seem to belong to Manager A. The monthly volatility is much larger, but it is good volatility, primarily on the upside. Most investors when comparing the two managers through 2007 would intuitively pick the better performer.

The last two years tell a completely different story. Not only is Manager A still more volatile, but it is primarily on the losing side. If the last part of this experience were the only data available, most investors would run away from Manager A. So what is the true story?

Looking at the entire 10-year period, we know the managers' average returns are the same because they started and ended at identical points. The calculated annualized standard deviation for Manager A is 15.3% while for Manager B the value is 6.1%. Given that most investors are risk averse and they prefer getting their returns with as little risk as possible, Manager B would appear to be the superior choice.

The investor comparing the two managers today has an advantage over another investor who made the decision three years ago. That investor saw Manager A as the clearly more volatile manager, but it was mostly "good volatility." Managers with strong runs of outperformance are prone to downplay their absolute levels of volatility and emphasize instead their large absolute returns.

Investors *never* have access to the right data set with which to judge managers for the simple reason that it does not exist. Looking at the two managers today, one might be tempted to hire Manager B on the basis of the apparent superior risk adjusted returns, but there is literally nothing in the data alone that can indicate that this edge will exist in future investing periods.

It will be repeated throughout this section that relying on simple statistics as the primary tool for manager selection is a fool's game. The phrase "Past performance is not an indicator of future returns" is much more than a regulatory necessity. It is the truth. Investors can use return statistics as a guidepost, but they must first understand a manager's investment process if they are going to build informed and effective portfolios.

5.3.2.3 Beta

The general concept of beta was developed in earlier chapters. Managers use beta as a descriptive measure for their portfolio. Hedge fund managers, in particular, are often asked how much beta their portfolios hold against standard factors like stocks, bonds and credit.

Calculating beta is done one of two ways: bottom-up and top-down. The more complicated route is to estimate the beta of each position in the portfolio and then aggregate the estimates. Only someone having access to every position in the portfolio can do this bottom-up approach. It also implicitly assumes that there are no diversifying benefits from holding a multi-asset portfolio. As such, this approach to beta estimation may be conservatively high.

Since each item in the portfolio has its own estimated beta, there is the risk that these backward-looking estimates will vary meaningfully from what the future actually produces. One might expect that errors in estimation happen both high and low, producing an aggregated estimate that is on average pretty close. Too often, however, the betas on entire groups of securities move in the same direction in response to market shocks. The only effective defense against such an event is to run "what if" scenarios against the portfolios to see if potential outcomes present acceptable levels of risk.

An extreme example of how severe these changes can be occurred in March 2020 as the stock market had its quickest retreat into bear market territory ever. Bloomberg, like many data vendors, has a beta function for the various securities it tracks. Their default approach regresses the price of the security in question against the reference index using daily data over the past two years. Today's beta estimate for a stock differs from yesterday's estimate by adding the most recent and dropping the most distant price changes from the equation. Since the entire sample is slightly over 500 trading days, under normal circumstances the beta estimates move glacially.

This was not the case with the COVID-19 bear market. Figure 5.12 shows the calculated betas from October 2019 through early October 2020 for Amazon (AMZN) and General Motors (GM). Before the crisis both stocks performed as intuition suggested. Amazon was considered a classic growth name deserving of a beta greater than 1. GM was smack in the middle of the pack, neither growth nor deep value. Its calculated beta of 1 reflects this. Then March happened.

Over the month of March, the S&P 500 fell by 12.4%. Amazon's beta going into the month of 1.5 would have predicted a decline of 18.6%. In fact, Amazon gained 3.5% in March. If GM's beta had been a good predictor, GM would have fallen right with the index. It fell 31% for the month. The deviations from past patterns were so large that GM's beta leapt above 1.2, while Amazon's fell down near 0.8. The calculated betas post-March 2020 would suggest GM is now the growth stock and AMZN the demure value company. Both characterizations are nonsense and highlight the challenges of using historical data to shape trading decisions.

The shift to betas greater than 1 was not unique to GM. Scores of old economy value companies saw large market losses create outsized calculated betas. Classic value stock funds used to be embraced because buying companies at a perceived discount to fair value usually provided a margin of safety not enjoyed with growth stocks. Lower volatility and a measure of defense in the portfolios were expected.

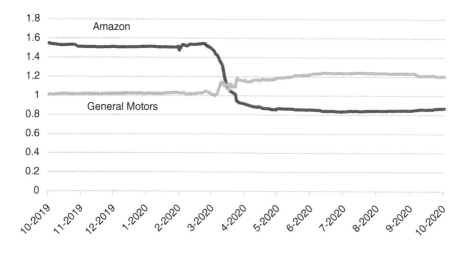

FIGURE 5.12 Shifting Betas
Source: Bloomberg

This pattern was shifting before the COVID-19 bear market but accelerated as value managers in general endured severe drawdowns and slower recoveries than their growth manager counterparts.

Trying to pin down exactly what to expect from any given fund manager is equally as challenging as predicting an individual security. That does not stop people from trying. A top-down estimation of beta can be done by anyone with a time series of historical returns. Using simple or multivariable regression tools, a fund's returns are regressed against the returns of the target factors. Stock managers that report a fund beta typically estimate it against their fund's benchmark. As shown in 2020, past estimates of fund beta may be poor predictors of how a manager or sector will perform in the future.

Beta does not just apply to long-only portfolios. Hedge fund managers will often calculate a logical beta against their style. Rarely does a manager seek to emphasize a high beta. More often managers use low estimated betas as evidence of their fund's low correlation to other potential investments found in the portfolio. This is a stretch. Low beta managers can still be highly correlated. As the discussion about the hedge fund Amaranth in Chapter 2.5 highlighted, great caution should be taken before accepting historic low beta calculations at face value.

5.3.2.4 *Correlation*

Consider again the managers in Figure 5.11. While their standard deviations were quite different over their 10-year histories, a casual look at the chart of their respective returns suggests they were *correlated*. That is to say the general directions of gains and losses were similar.

Equation 5.5 gives the formula for calculating the correlation between two series, A and B. The value can range from +1.0, which implies perfect *positive* correlation, to –1.0, which is a perfect negative correlation. A value of zero suggests no correlation. That is, if someone told you that Manager A made 1% last month, that information alone would give you no guidance to help predict whether Manager B made money or not.

$$\text{Correlation (A, B)} = \text{Cov (A, B)} / \sigma_A \sigma_B$$
$$= E\Big[(A - \mu_A)(B - \mu_B)\Big] / \sigma_A \sigma_B \qquad (5.5)$$

Running this calculation for the monthly returns of the two managers in Figure 5.11 gives a value of 0.51, which suggests the managers are somewhat connected directionally, but not overly so.[29] It is not unusual for long-only equity managers to have correlations to their benchmarks and to each other of over 0.9. Hedge fund managers typically tout their meaningfully lower correlations as evidence of the diversifying benefits from adding them to a portfolio.

---

[29]There are standard statistical tests to help determine whether the calculated values of correlations and other statistics discussed in this chapter are reliably different from zero or any other value. A fuller discussion of this topic is found in Lee, C.F. op. cit.

An interesting challenge is to decide what data to use in calculating correlations. With today's high-speed data gathering capabilities, one could consider using minute-by-minute returns. Most managers trading in liquid markets have their portfolios linked to market data feeds to get a "real-time" picture of profit and loss. This data is rarely shared with investors, but it is theoretically available to create a correlation calculation.

The smaller the unit of time in the correlation calculation, the greater the chance the result will be predominantly a reflection of noise. Two managers that show no statistical correlation on a minute-to-minute basis might be much more linked on a day-to-day or month-to-month basis. If one could have enough time series to compare decade-by-decade returns, it would be the extraordinary manager that was not highly correlated to any subset of peers.

A general practice is to perform most of the calculations in this chapter on monthly returns. The data are generally available, with the biggest exception being returns from partnerships in private equity, venture capital, and real estate, which more typically report quarterly. Monthly data has the advantage of filtering out much of the short-term noise in the experience, but is not so long a period that it blurs important distinctions across managers.

Figure 5.13 adds hypothetical Manager C to the two previously considered managers.

Manager C seems to be a very different animal. After the initial five years when the first two managers were up 50–80%, Manager C was down almost 20%. If all three managers had started in the portfolio, chances are good the investor within that period would be having serious doubts about Manager C's future.

The great thing about hypothetical examples as compared to real-world decision-making is the ability to "cheat" by not only seeing the future clearly, but creating it!

FIGURE 5.13 Three Hypothetical Managers

In this case, over the entire 10-year span, Manager C performs identically to the other two hypothetical managers. What about correlation?

Visually there is little connection, though in the last two dramatic years it appears Manager C was taking almost completely opposite positions to Managers A and B. Calculating the 10-year correlation between C and A is –0.17 and between C and B the estimate is –0.15. Here there is a weak negative correlation over the whole period, though because it is close to zero, one should feel considerably less confident that any relationship is reliable looking forward.

The benefits of diversification, using managers with low and ideally negative correlations, are shown in Figure 5.14. One could have begun the decade with an equal blend of the three managers. Without rebalancing at all over the decade, that would have produced the return pattern marked Blend in the chart.

Notice how many of the bumps and wiggles in the return paths of the managers are smoothed out in the blend. The total return of the blend for the decade is by definition the same as the three equally performing managers. The calculated annualized standard deviation for the blend is 7.3%, as compared to 15.4%, 7.5%, and 7.5%, respectively, for Managers A, B, and C. This simple example shows how combining managers or strategies with the right correlation characteristics can produce a portfolio that is superior on a risk/return basis to any of the individual components.

A practical factor that can affect the calculation of both standard deviation and correlation is the accuracy of the investment's reported net asset values (NAV). If a fund only contains actively traded securities, there should be no issue with a fund's NAV. If, however, there are illiquid, hard-to-price securities, the calculation of the fund's NAV may be based on stale prices, and not reflective of actual market conditions.

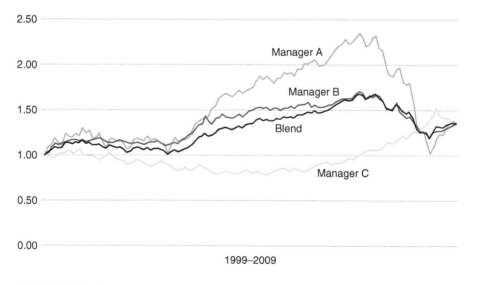

FIGURE 5.14 Three Hypothetical Managers plus an Equal Blend

Real estate partnerships can be extreme examples of this problem. A partnership buys a building for $10 million dollars and puts it on the books. Where is it priced the next quarter? There is an excellent chance the price used for NAV calculations will be $10 million. Carried on quarter after quarter, this behavior gives the impression that there is not much risk in real estate investing, which is contrary to everyone's experience that has ever done it.

Partnerships are loath to mark up a position unless there is a material event to justify it. Marking a property down for NAV purposes may be more common, but even then the fund manager might not be aggressive in the pace of write-downs. FAS 157 accounting rules have created more pressure to be accurate in the annual marks of illiquid investments, but this cannot create a precise market time series when none otherwise exists.

While the example of the real estate partnership is extreme, there are many less obvious examples. Hedge funds and even mutual funds can put illiquid securities and derivatives alongside their liquid book. The majority of the prices might be fluctuating daily, or even minute-by-minute, but any meaningful exposure to "sticky-price" assets can dampen the estimated standard deviations and the correlations.

The importance of any underestimation in this area cannot be stressed too much. Managers routinely sell themselves on the basis of their "risk-adjusted returns" and their contribution to portfolio diversification attributable to their low correlations. If the statistical foundation for these claims is suspect, investors might add these managers or weight them more highly in a portfolio on the basis of these doubtful claims. Hidden volatility and correlation is still real, and many investors learned this profoundly in the crisis of 2008 and early 2009.

The next statistic, autocorrelation, is a useful tool to help detect whether the estimated correlations and standard deviations are biased downward.

5.3.2.5 *Autocorrelation*

Autocorrelation is a special type of correlation statistic used with time series data. As its name implies, it is the correlation between data in a series and that same data lagged a number of periods. The most popular, and perhaps the most informative in the analysis of investment returns, is *first-order autocorrelation*. This is the correlation between any given return and the previous period's return.

Generally if data moves in a choppy fashion, with negative moves being followed regularly with positive ones, the calculated autocorrelation is negative. Time series that roll smoothly will have positive moves that are more likely followed with another positive change and the autocorrelation is positive. Random time series have no predictable relationship between observations of different dates.

$$
\begin{aligned}
\text{Correlation}\,(A_t, A_{t+n}) &= \text{Cov}\,(A_t, A_{t+n})/\sigma^2 A \\
&= E\left[(A_t - \mu_A)\,(A_{t+n} - \mu_A)\right]/\sigma^2 A
\end{aligned}
\tag{5.6}
$$

Equation 5.6 gives the formula for autocorrelation, focusing on the correlation between a series and itself n periods in the past. Financial researchers get most of their useful information in the case where n = 1, first-order autocorrelation. This addresses a question like "Can the return for a stock on any given day help us predict the return on the next day?" Not surprisingly, this equation looks very similar to the basic Equation 5.5 for correlations. Returning to a set of hypothetical managers in Figure 5.15, however, will demonstrate the principle.

Once again, we use the period from 1999 to 2009 because of the wide range of outcomes, but the principles demonstrated are completely general. The light gray line in the chart is the S&P 500, scaled to begin at 100. Visually, managers X and Y track the index perfectly over the 10 years and show reasonable correspondence in most periods. But the summary statistics tell a different story. The annualized standard deviation of the index, calculated using monthly returns data, is 16.2%. Manager X's returns look choppier and in fact come in with a standard deviation of 25.0%, while steady Manager Y can claim a standard deviation of 8.4%.

Stepping back and looking at the entire history anyone can see that the two managers and the S&P 500 are reasonably closely related over this period. The calculated correlations, however, based on monthly returns tell a different story. Choppy Manager X can claim a correlation to the index of 0.37 and smooth Manager Y's correlation is 0.42. What are the correlation estimates missing?

The answer lies with autocorrelation. Monthly changes in the S&P cannot be distinguished statistically from a random process. The calculated first-order autocorrelation in the index is only 0.18, not meaningfully different from a perfectly random 0.00. Manager X, however, shows a strong negative autocorrelation of –0.57, which says that if the manager shows a positive return in a given month, one can reasonably expect it to be followed with a loss in the following month. This back-and-forth pattern throws noise around the bigger trends, which in turn reduces the calculated correlation with the index.

FIGURE 5.15 Autocorrelation of Hypothetical Managers

Manager X's sales materials may try to paint the fund as a diversifier, given the low correlation to the index. Cautious investors, however, would spot the meaningfully higher standard deviation, and be worried about potential risk. In this case, ironically, if the manager is rejected, it is probably for the wrong reason. The negative autocorrelation makes the manager's risk seem higher than it really is. The best reason for rejecting the manager is that one is just buying a noisy index.

Manager Y poses greater challenges for evaluation. That fund will claim a low correlation to the index *and* a meaningfully lower standard deviation. This is the perfect diversifier! But the diversification benefit is a complete illusion. The positive autocorrelation has reduced both statistics, and as the chart clearly shows, Manager Y is simply a smoothed index manager.

It is extraordinarily rare for a manager to self-report an autocorrelation statistic. Fortunately anyone armed with a time series of returns can calculate one on a spreadsheet. The easiest diagnostic to perform is to calculate the autocorrelations for the fund and its benchmark. If the fund's statistics are meaningfully different, especially with the fund showing strong positive autocorrelation, one should ask closely about the portfolio holdings and the fund's pricing policy. If there are private holdings that are irregularly priced, or priced to a model, the returns history may be hiding more volatility than is actually present.

Outright frauds often have highly autocorrelated returns, but a more common problem is poorly priced portfolios. Investors should be very skeptical of any investment strategy with low standard errors and correlations to benchmarks. The risk may be quite real, but hidden in smoothed marks.

5.3.2.6 Sharpe Ratio

William Sharpe created what he called the "reward-to-variability" ratio in 1966.[30] Sharpe was trying to respond to the common sense problem that if one does not know how much risk a manager is taking, it is impossible to fairly compare the returns of different managers. Long before Sharpe was awarded his Nobel Prize in economics in 1990, other academics and practitioners dubbed this statistic the *Sharpe Ratio*.

Both the concept and the calculation are straightforward. Sharpe was first interested in *excess return*, that is, the return above a benchmark asset. Typically the benchmark is the risk-free rate of return, which is proxied in the calculations by short-dated Treasury bill yields. The second critical factor is risk, which is estimated by the standard deviation of the return stream. The higher the excess return per unit of risk, the higher the Sharpe Ratio. The formula is given below:

$$S = E(\bar{R} - R_f)/\sigma \qquad (5.7)$$

The numerator is the expected excess return of the manager ($\bar{R}$ is the manager's return and R_f is the risk-free rate) and σ is the standard deviation of the returns series. Both are estimated from historical data, typically a time series of monthly returns.

---

[30]Sharpe, W. F. (1966). Mutual Fund Performance. *Journal of Business*, 39 (S1), pp. 119–138.

Ranking investment managers by their Sharpe Ratios is an exercise that leaves many open questions. Sharpe himself recognized several limitations.[31] Perhaps the biggest criticism over time has been that Sharpe used standard deviation, a symmetric measure, as the single metric of risk. There are many managers with strong track records who will claim this unfairly penalizes them. After all, if the volatility is primarily to the upside, why should investors be concerned about that?

At a concept level, investors should seek out volatility if it can be guaranteed to be upside, or good, volatility. The reality, however, is that managers who have historically high upside volatility also seem to have a higher probability of downside volatility *sometime* in the future. The bad volatility simply may not have shown up yet. Still, to address this concern, the Sortino ratio discussed in the Section 5.3.2.8, distinguishes upside and downside volatility.

Managers sometimes calculate and report their own Sharpe Ratios. While one might expect there to be little disagreement on such a basic calculation, there can be differences in what is used for the risk-free rate. If Treasury bill yields are used, which maturity is appropriate? Some managers simply plug in an average level, like 3%, for all observations. As short-term interest rates plunged in 2008 and stayed near zero for years, most managers were quick to incorporate this low bar into their calculations, yet standards vary. One should either calculate the Sharpe Ratios across a group of managers oneself, or make sure the assumptions behind each manager's calculations are comparable to the rest.

A bigger concern with the Sharpe Ratio is related to the concerns about smoothed NAVs and low estimated volatility, the same problem first encountered with positive autocorrelations. If the NAVs are based on stale or smoothed prices, the estimated standard deviation will appear lower than it actually is. A too small σ means an estimated Sharpe Ratio that is too large. Ranking managers by Sharpe may give the advantage to those trading illiquid assets or smoothing their returns.

The only solution to this issue is to only compare Sharpe Ratios across managers who one knows are pursuing similar strategies with similar investments. Checking the autocorrelations of those managers may also provide help in determining if a manager's attractive Sharpe Ratio is a creation of smoothing. Even then, the Sharpe Ratio, like all of the summary statistics discussed in this section, is a creation of past data, which may or may not be reflective of what the future has in store.

5.3.2.7 *Information Ratio*

The *Information Ratio* was developed to address the concern that different investment strategies have different objectives than the risk-free rate referenced in the Sharpe Ratio. Bond managers may say they are trying to add value relative to a portfolio of Treasury securities, but rarely will one find an emerging-market equity manager with that stated objective. It is basically assumed that one would not pursue fundamentally risky strategies unless one expects to beat the risk-free rate over time.

---

[31]Sharpe, W. F. (1994). The Sharpe Ratio. *Journal of Portfolio Management*, 21 (1), pp. 49–58.

Calculating the Information Ratio for a manager is identical to measuring the Sharpe Ratio, with one critical exception:

$$IR = E(\bar{R} - R_b) / \sigma \qquad (5.8)$$

The Information Ratio calculation is exactly the same as the Sharpe Ratio except that the *benchmark* return, R_b, is substituted for the risk-free rate. In the case of an emerging market equity manager, this would typically be a broad emerging market stock index.

All of the criticisms of Sharpe Ratio regarding asymmetry of risk and managers self-selecting their calculation assumptions also apply to the Information Ratio.

5.3.2.8 Sortino Ratio

The Sortino Ratio appeared some 15 years after Sharpe introduced his metric.[32] There were two major concerns that the Sortino Ratio sought to address. The first was that investors were more concerned with *Minimum Acceptable Return* (MAR) than they were with the risk-free rate. The second was the belief that only downside volatility should concern investors.

$$Sortino = E(\bar{R} - MAR) / \sigma_D \qquad (5.9)$$

Downside risk, σ_D, is calculated identically to standard deviation except that any time the observed return is greater than the MAR, the actual value is replaced with 0. For example, suppose the series of excess returns for manager A were:

$$-4\%, +2\%, +3\%, +5\%, -1\%, -2\%, +5\%, +3\%, +2\%, -1\%$$

The series used to calculate downside risk would be:

$$-4\%, 0, 0, 0, -1\%, -2\%, 0, 0, 0, -1\%.$$

The standard deviation from the original sample is 3.0% while the downside standard deviation is 1.3% as all of the "upside risk" is removed from the calculation.

Over time the concept of MAR in the Sortino Ratio has gravitated in one of two directions. There is a camp that wants to emphasize the asymmetric risk dimension of the calculation. These people use the same numerator as the Sharpe Ratio, replacing MAR with the risk-free rate. Another group, who are much more concerned about whether a strategy is profitable over the long run in absolute terms, sets the MAR at zero. One can also plug in a market benchmark for the MAR, which has the effect of transforming the Information Ratio to account for asymmetric risk.

Once again there is no standard approach, leaving investors with the task of tracking down a manager's calculation assumptions. Short of calculating all of the ratios oneself, one must be completely informed about all the steps a manager has taken before comparing these statistics across managers.

---

[32]Sortino, F. A. and van der Meer, R. (1991). Downside Risk. *Journal of Portfolio Management*, 17 (4), pp. 27–31.

5.3.2.9 *Omega Ratio*

Keating and Shadwick in 2002 proposed a performance ratio that was general enough to apply to any statistical distribution of returns.[33] In the true spirit of the finance literature, they named their ratio one thing, but it has become known as something else. The statistics behind this measure, which is now known as the *Omega Ratio* *(Ω)*, are well beyond the scope of this book, but the basic intuition can be shown in Figure 5.16, taken from Keating and Shadwick.

Suppose the black and gray lines are the return distributions for two managers, A and B. Manager A has a symmetric return pattern that averages a return of 10, with a standard deviation of 12.3. It is a classic normal distribution. Manager B's pattern of returns defies simple description. The most common outcome is zero, but in contrast with Manager A he never loses more than 10. It turns out that when one calculates the mean and standard deviation, Manager B has a mean of 10 and a standard deviation of 12.3. In terms of Sharpe and Information Ratios, these two managers are identical!

Clearly something is amiss, as these managers are only the same in terms of mean and standard deviation. Many investors if shown the two diagrams would say they had a strong preference for Manager B because of the nice average return and the strong downside risk control. Statistics that implicitly assume symmetrical distributions of returns cannot capture even these crude and obvious differences.

The Sortino Ratio and other measures designed to distinguish between downside risk and total risk could differentiate between Managers A and B, but there are many possible situations where these ratios are fooled as well. The solution was to identify a ratio that captures all the characteristics of the underlying distribution. The answer is the Omega Ratio.

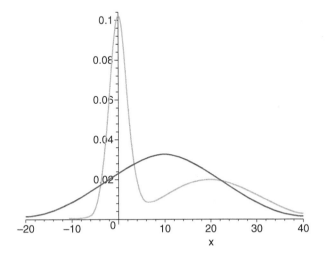

FIGURE 5.16 Two "Identical" Distributions

---

[33]Keating, C. and Shadwick, W.F. (2002). *A Universal Performance Measure*. The Finance Development Centre: London.

On a theoretical level, there is very little to object to with this ratio. With a normal distribution of returns, the Omega Ratio collapses to the Sharpe Ratio. With any other distribution, however, the Omega Ratio tries to rank managers by rewarding higher average returns and fat tails above the mean, while penalizing fat tails below the mean. That is, managers that can achieve a certain return while skewing results away from bad outcomes achieve a higher Omega Ratio.

There is one major stumbling block, however, in the execution of these tests. If one *knew* with certainty what a manager's underlying return distribution looked like, the calculated ratios could be compared with confidence. Unfortunately, history unfolds one observation at a time. Whether it is the Sharpe, Sortino, or Omega Ratio, each new data point might reveal a brand new pattern.

The hedge fund manager Amaranth was first discussed in Chapter 2. Begun as a relative value hedge fund primarily engaged in convertible arbitrage, Amaranth evolved its strategy and risk as it grew. Figure 5.17 shows the frequency distribution of Amaranth's returns from its inception in 2000 through June 2005.

Throughout its more than five-year history since inception, Amaranth showed a pattern of steady monthly returns with no losses in a month of more than 3% or gains more than 6%. Even with more than five years of data, it is difficult to confirm that the returns approximated a normal distribution, but all of the performance ratios were quite solid relative to other managers.

Figure 5.18 superimposes nine more months' experience to the above chart. This was the period when the fund grew to near $8 billion in assets under management.

There appears to be an improvement in the return pattern. There are no additional losing months and the winners are larger. This is the "fat tail above the mean" that the Omega Ratio is looking for. By all the backward looking measures, Amaranth looks like a stronger manager in April 2006 than it did just nine months earlier. Some investors used statistics like the Omega Ratio to "prove" that Amaranth was a superior manager deserving of their investment dollars.

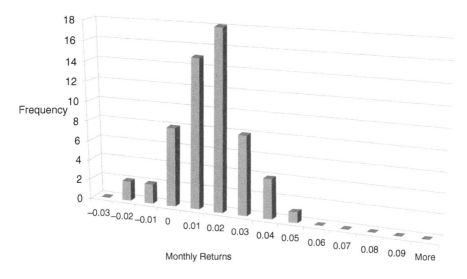

FIGURE 5.17   Distribution of Returns 2000 – June 2005

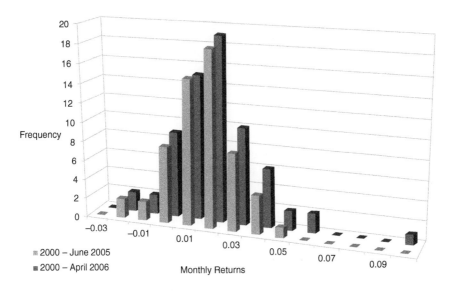

FIGURE 5.18   Distribution of Returns 2000 – April 2006

Figure 5.19 is the final look at Amaranth's history. It contains all the information in the previous two charts, but the scale had to be radically expanded. The full experience is given by the light gray bars and includes monthly losses of –12% and –66%. After that last return Amaranth closed its doors.

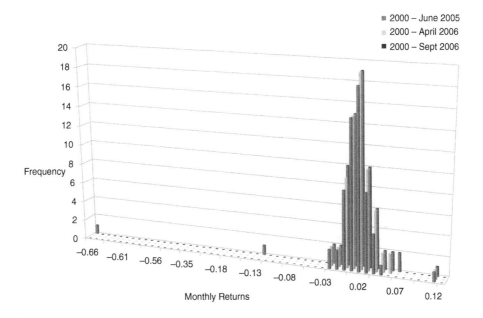

FIGURE 5.19   Distribution of Returns 2000 – Sept 2006

The calculation of Amaranth's Omega Ratio after September 2006 no doubt produced a very different value, and painted a different conclusion than the estimate just six months earlier, but by then it was too late for investors.

5.3.2.10 Final Comments

The statistics in this section vary in ease of computation and understanding, as well as acceptance among the investment community. Each has been developed to help investors answer the basic question whether a money manager is skilled in their craft. Novice investors tend to place too much emphasis on these measures for the following reasons:

- The statistics by definition are calculated looking backward, and the past is not necessarily a predictor of the future.

Each measure is itself a statistic subject to uncertainty. If two managers have Sharpe Ratios of 1.5 and 0.9, for example, it is unlikely that one can distinguish between the two with any confidence. This is true for all of the statistics discussed above.

While GIPS may have made progress in the reporting of returns, there is no standardization in the use of performance ratios or any other metric. Managers that choose to report such figures do so because it is advantageous to their marketing. There is no other light in which to view this information. Further, any investor that relies on manager reported summary statistics for comparison purposes must make the extra effort to verify the calculation assumptions. Differences of opinion about something as seemingly straightforward as the risk-free rate of return can make meaningful differences in the calculations.

Sorting and selecting managers on the basis of performance ratios may be an interesting exercise, but it should be, at best, only a starting point of a complicated process. Investors who rely heavily on these measures are demonstrating a great deal of faith in science and predictability. When it comes to investment managers, too much of the wrong kind of faith can lead to folly.

5.3.3 IRR Calculations and Multiples of Capital Returned

The statistics discussed above are almost always calculated in terms of time-weighted returns. This is the standard throughout the mutual fund industry and most investment programs involving highly liquid assets. There are, however, many important programs involving buy-out funds, venture capital, real estate, and other less liquid investments for which time-weighted returns can paint a very distorted picture of actual results. For these types of investments it is more common for funds to report an *internal rate of return*, or IRR.

The IRR differs from time-weighted returns in that it accounts explicitly for when capital is invested. An example will show the difference. Suppose on day one you invest $100 in a mutual fund. As long as that money is invested it will be subject to all of the ups and downs of the market and the manager's decisions. The series of periodic returns that we have discussed in the previous section give a highly accurate picture of the investment performance as long as the returns are truly net of all fees.

Contrast that to an investment you make in most private equity partnerships. On day one you commit $100 to an investment. Capital may or may not be called at the first "closing." Over the life of the investment period, the manager calls capital to deploy into specific investments. Depending on the richness of the investment environment, the pace of capital calls may be fast or slow. An accurate return measure will account for how many dollars you have at work at any given point in time as well as the specific return on those investments in each marking period.

Figure 5.20 stylized three-period investment. You can think of this as the simplest kind of investment that private partnership to do all the time. Of course they invest in many underlying opportunities and rarely invest on a strict schedule, but the example shows the challenge of getting an accurate return picture when investments vary through time.

Suppose you buy one share of stock for $10 at the start of the exercise. After one period, you are pleasantly surprised to find the price has doubled to $20, and you decide to buy another share. After the second period, your genius is confirmed as the stock has once again doubled to $40. Knowing you are onto a good thing you buy another share. In the last chapter of the story, the CEO is found to be a crook, and the stock collapses to $4. What was your return?

In each of the first two calendar periods you made 100%, but you lost 90% in the period after your final purchase. On a time-weighted basis your investment lost a total of 60%, which would be precisely accurate if you had simply bought a single share at the start of the exercise as your only investment. But you did not do that. You continued to add to the position at higher and higher prices, which meant when the price ultimately fell the damage was applied to a much larger sum of capital.

The IRR of the entire investment turns out to be –73.9%, meaningfully worse than the –60% time-weighted return. This should make sense as the terrible loss at

Time-Weighted Versus Dollar-Weighted Returns

Time Weighted

Period	0	1	2	3
Price	10	20	40	4
Return	100%	100%	–90%	
Total Return	–60%			

Dollar Weighted

	Buy 1 Share	Buy 1 Share	Buy 1 Share	Sell 3 Shares
	IRR = –73.9%			

FIGURE 5.20

the end of the investment affected all three shares that were purchased at increasingly higher prices.[34]

Another measure often used in these kinds of investments is the *multiple of invested capital*. This is a very basic concept that simply says how many multiples of each dollar invested did you ultimately have returned to you. In the example above, the total investment was $70 and the return was $12. This means the multiple on this investment was 0.17, not such a great result.

Managers who are responsible for funds with drawdown structures insist on this kind of return reporting because to do otherwise would unfairly penalize them. If the return meter started clicking on the day the commitment was made, there would be a long string of negative numbers as costs accumulated without any investment returns. By only counting returns on called capital they minimize that drag.

While the IRR and the multiple on investment are both descriptive measures of returns, they need to be used with caution and not directly compared with other investments that are typically reported in time-weighted terms. This is because the managers do not have to concern themselves with the overall organization of the client portfolios.

Suppose you allocate equally to two investment choices. The first puts $100 to work in a mutual fund immediately. The second is a $100 commitment to a drawdown structure fund. While you don't expect all of the $100 commitment to be called at once, you should think of that obligation as a liability that needs to be funded. Suppose you are quite conservative, and you set aside $100 to eventually meet that commitment. From your perspective the performance of the drawdown structure fund should actually be the combined return of the manager plus the performance on any money waiting to be called.

If you are ultraconservative, you will keep all uncalled monies in the highest safety, cash-like assets. This means that compared to your mutual fund investment there is a likely expected opportunity cost from lower returns. Of course it does not always work out this way as markets can go up or down, but presumably your low-risk asset has a more modest expected return. When you ultimately ask which investment was superior, you will want to compare the time-weighted return of the mutual fund to the blended return of the drawdown structure fund and whatever the uncalled assets ultimately produced.

More assertive investors, seeking the beta exposure of the private program, might take any uncalled amounts and invest them in an index fund covering a similar space. For example, if $10 was immediately called from a new $100 partnership commitment for large-cap private equity buy-outs, $90 could be invested in an

---

[34]Calculating the IRR of an investment involves finding the rate of interest that equates the present value of all cash flows from the investment to the stream of outlays. In any multiperiod investment, the calculation can be quite cumbersome. Fortunately there are many IRR calculators available to investors where all that is needed is a careful account of the timing of inflows and outflows. Unfortunately, not all of these calculators are equally rigorous in their approach, and they can lead to different results. When comparing the investment returns across different programs it is vital that you use the same model for all of your calculations. A good introduction to the topic that provides a simple IRR calculator can be found at http://www.datadynamica.com/irr.asp.

S&P 500 Index fund. The theory here is that once you make a commitment to an area, you want to have exposure.

The problem with this approach is that the total commitment to the private program is a fixed dollar amount, and is not a sum indexed to the stock market. Institutions that took this approach in the first half of 2007 saw their stock investment fall by over 40%, as the size of their private equity commitment remained unchanged. While their overall investment returns certainly reflected the stock market, they created an asset liability mismatch with this approach.

The IRR approach to reporting returns should therefore be viewed as only applicable to the narrow investment program to which it applies. You as the investor need to integrate these values into the total return pattern of your portfolio.

Another way IRR calculations can be deceiving is when they are applied to investments where there is a distribution in kind. Some venture capital and private equity programs distribute stocks in the underlying investment companies to their limited partners. It is the responsibility at that point for the investors to keep or dispose of the stocks. The general partner calculates its IRR based on the value of the stocks at the time of the distribution. Of course, distributing stocks carries with it very low costs. If the general partner had first sold all of these stocks and distributed cash, the return would have been net of the transaction costs and any bid ask spread. By passing that responsibility on to the limited partners, the calculated IRR is an overstatement of the actual performance of the program.

The IRR and the multiple of invested capital measures of returns are the best available to these kinds of private programs. That still does not make them perfect, nor does it make it easy for investors to compare performance across different classes of investments. There is no magic bullet here. Investors simply must show great care when evaluating all of their investments within the context of their portfolios.

5.3.4 Peer Rankings of Managers

If objective statistics are not always helpful in identifying future top performing managers, are there other ways to complete the task? Many investors look to large databases of manager performance, classify the managers by investment style, and then construct peer rankings. This too is a backward-looking exercise that has limitations in its ability to guide investors in the future.

Because the databases are larger and go back further in history, peer rankings among mutual fund managers are more commonly used than in other investment areas. But such rankings exist for hedge funds, private equity funds, commodity trading advisors, and every other category of investment one can imagine.

The process of creating peer rankings seems direct enough:

- Identify the set of managers that comprise the group.
- Determine the relevant comparison period (months, quarters, years).
- Rank order the managers by net performance.

In practice, everything but the last mechanical step involves considerable judgment.

The challenges here are many. Suppose one is interested in identifying the best large-cap US stock managers. It might seem to be a straightforward task to classify large-cap US stock managers, but even here questions arise. How many mid-cap or small-cap stocks can one have in the portfolio before being disqualified? How about foreign stocks? Usually there is no hard and fast rule and managers often self-select their categories. But this raises other questions. If the top ranked manager in the US large-cap category for the past three years held 92% of his portfolio in classic US blue chip names and 8% in emerging market stocks, was that an act of great foresight or was it cheating?

There is a tendency to divide and subdivide the categories. All US equity managers are broken down by their typical cap sizes. These groups are then broken down into growth or value styles. Among growth managers one finds GARP (growth at a reasonable price) and momentum managers. As this process continues it sometimes seems like the process is designed with the goal of finding some categorization that places the manager in an attractive light.

Identifying the right time frame is equally challenging. A year intuitively seems too short, but 10 years eliminates a great number of managers that don't have that long a track record. Three- and five-year groupings tend to get the most attention, but here too there are issues. The five years of the raging bull market from 1995 through 1999 painted a considerably different picture than the markets from 2005 through 2009. The best managers in the first period may have had exactly the wrong skill set to navigate successfully the second.

Consistency of databases is also a problem. Managers can change their investment styles through time. Registered mutual fund returns are in the public domain and can be gathered independently, but the opposite is true for hedge funds and private equity partnerships. All public reporting is voluntary and it is not surprising, perhaps, that as performance lags funds are tempted to stop releasing their data. This has strong implications for hedge fund index construction that go well beyond the construction of peer group performance.

There is a rich and useful academic literature on peer rankings for mutual fund managers. The evidence for strong predictive power for future manager success is slim. Researchers at Standard & Poors, drawing their data from the University of Chicago's CRSP Survivorship Bias-Free Mutual Fund Database, found that 24.3% of large-cap US equity funds with a top-quartile ranking over the five years ending September 2004 maintained their top-quartile ranking over the next five years.[35] A completely random outcome would have produced a value of 25%. Similar results were found for other categories of US equity mutual funds.

Where did the other top-quartile managers in the second five years come from? They had previously been second-, third-, and sometimes fourth-quartile managers. Selecting mutual fund managers based on their current top-quartile standing may be little better than a random draw across all managers.

The S&P study does note one area of predictive power from the rankings, however. Fourth-quartile managers are much more likely to be merged or liquidated in the next five years than the higher performers. Mutual fund companies clearly don't want to have to explain a high percentage of underperforming managers in their stable.

---

[35]Srikant, D. (2010). Do Past Mutual Fund Winners Repeat? *S&P Indices Research Insights* (January).

The biggest criticism of the simple ranking of managers by average returns is that such a process completely ignores risk. Bill Sharpe was trying to address this issue when he developed what came to be known as the Sharpe Ratio. As demonstrated in the last section, the most common estimates of risk are backward looking and often not predictive. Still, there have been serious attempts to adjust simple peer rankings for risk.

The most widely known and researched efforts for mutual fund managers come from Morningstar, which was founded in 1984 by Joe Mansueto. He recognized that there was a scarcity of objective information about performance and holdings of mutual funds. Morningstar's first publication, the *Mutual Fund Sourcebook*, covered 400 US mutual funds. By 2018 they had grown to have operations in 28 countries covering hundreds of thousands of investment products.

Morningstar does not rank funds along a simple return metric. Instead it rates funds with a star system that attempts to capture risk-adjusted returns. Ratings across funds are roughly symmetric, but it is not a system designed to capture quintiles. The distribution for all the ranked US equity mutual funds in 2019 is in Table 5.2.

Having a Morningstar five-star rating is one of the most coveted possessions in the mutual fund industry. Most fund families prominently feature their four- and five-star funds in their marketing efforts.

Because of the transparency of Morningstar's process and data, its rating system has been the subject of numerous research studies over the years. These studies began early in Morningstar's life and generally focused on the question whether the star ratings had any predictive power for future returns. The results over time have been mixed at best.[37] Top-rated funds don't do materially better than funds with two- or three-star ratings. One-star funds tend to lag in the future, but this may be more a function of high fees than inferior gross returns.

Morningstar works continuously to improve its analytics. Morey and Gottesman (2006) revisited the forecasting power of the system after Morningstar announced enhancements in 2002.[38] Unlike most previous studies, this one found a small positive link between a fund's rating and its performance from 2003 through 2005. This

TABLE 5.2 Distribution of Rated Morningstar US Mutual Funds

Rating	Number of Funds	Percentage
5 Star	635	10%
4 Star	1429	22.5%
3 Star	2223	35%
2 Star	1429	22.5%
1 Star	635	10%[36]

[36]Morningstar company website: http://www.morningstar.com/.
[37]Parwada, J.T. and Faff, R.W. (2004). Pension Plan Investment Management Mandates: An Empirical Analysis of Manager Selection. (20 September). http://ssrn.com/abstract=593226 or doi:10.2139/ssrn.593226.
[38]Morey, M.R. and Gottesman, A.A. (2006). Morningstar Mutual Fund Ratings Redux. Working paper, Pace University. https://ssrn.com/abstract=890128.

period, however, captured a highly directional bull market, leaving open the question of predictability in choppy or bear markets. Kraeussl and Sandelowsky's 2007 paper looked at later periods as well and could identify little predictive power.[39]

There is one effect of the star rating system that is unambiguous. Investors act on changes in a fund's ranking. In a 2007 study, Del Guercio and Tkac reported that in the six months after a fund went from four to five stars, new inflows were 25% higher than average, a statistically significant difference. Flows from funds dropping from five stars to four, showed little change, but another drop to three stars caused outflows twelve times normal for these funds.[40]

Such marketing success can come with a price. Morrey (2005) studied the performance of mutual funds for the three-year period immediately after they received their initial five-star rating.[41] He found that, on average, these newly anointed funds *underperformed* their benchmarks. This could have been due to style drift by the managers. It could also be due to an inability to sustain superior returns after an influx of assets chasing the promotion in ratings. More recent research has confirmed that high star ratings convey little useful information about future performance, but low ratings can be a useful warning sign.[42]

Despite the questionable value of ratings for mutual funds, similar efforts are now being applied to hedge funds. The experience is too short to evaluate whether these ratings are any better, but numerous questions can already be raised. As mentioned above, hedge funds report voluntarily, so there is a tremendous bias toward recent strong performers reporting their results. Underperforming efforts are often closed with their managers working hard to bury the evidence. Also, unless the ratings process can somehow avoid the backward-looking nature of risk measures like the Sharpe, Sortino, and Omega Ratios, the process of risk adjusting ratings will be biased as well.

It is often claimed that among private equity and venture capital partnerships, quality managers persist. The logic behind this is that the best managers in these spaces are better able to develop management teams or restructure businesses, and this is definitely a value-added proposition that should persist from company to company. Like the top-rated mutual funds, these top managers have been able to attract more and more investment dollars as their funds have tended to grow dramatically through time. The open question here is whether the strong performance is really due to superior skill or whether these managers took more risky or leveraged approaches in the 1980s and 1990s when they were certainly helped by the strong bull market. The same questions can be asked for investments made during the prolonged bull market after the financial crisis of 2008–2009.

---

[39]Roman, K. and Sandelowsky, R.M.R. (2007). The Predictive Performance of Morningstar's Mutual Fund Ratings. Working Paper, VU University, Amsterdam.

[40]Del Guercio, D. and Tkac, P.A. (2007). Star Power: The Effect of Morningstar Ratings on Mutual Fund Flow. http://ssrn.com/abstract=286157.

[41]Morey, M.R. (2005). The Kiss of Death: A 5-Star Morningstar Mutual Fund Rating? *Journal of Investment Management*, 3 (2) (Second Quarter). http://ssrn.com/abstract=712187.

[42]Haslem, J.A. (2014). Morningstar Mutual Fund Measures and Selection Model. *Journal of Wealth Management*, 17 (2) (30 July), pp. 19–30, Fall 2014. https://ssrn.com/abstract=2474225.

If neither percentile rankings nor risk-adjusted ratings systems like Morningstar's star system are useful predictors of future performance, then the question must be asked why investors continue to base allocation decisions on these measures.

In the complex world of investing, decision makers are constantly seeking out efficient ways to summarize a sea of information and come to conclusions that would otherwise be difficult to reach. They *want* to believe that today's top performers as measured by rankings will persist. They *want* to believe that thoughtful and technologically sophisticated firms like Morningstar can sort out the good funds from the bad. They want to please clients that come to them asking why they are not seeing more five-star funds in their portfolio. But wanting those results and actually getting them are two different things.

If the rankings and ratings have little predictive ability, portfolio returns of those who follow the rankings should be little different from those that do not. In fact, actual investor behavior suggests that there are big differences, and the results are not encouraging.

Institutional investors have been studied to assess their skills in timing manager selection.[43] The results suggest that for traditional equity strategies lagging managers tend to be fired after a particularly weak period. Similarly "top" managers are put into portfolios after the bulk of their outperformance has occurred. In both cases, on average, there is a reversion toward the mean after the firing or hiring decision. *Manager hiring and firing decisions typically detract value among institutional investors.*

It should be stressed that these are average outcomes and not a pattern that repeats with certainty. If it did, investors should only fire top performers and hire new managers from the bottom of the pack.

The psychology of active investing is at the heart of the problem. Investors want to associate with winners, and they believe that winning comes from skill and not luck. It actually comes from both. Skillful managers have a better than average chance of showing their craft in the future, but they can also have it hidden by bad luck. There are no simple ways to sort skill from luck. Instead one must make a deep dive into the manager's process to become informed.

Underperforming active managers pose as big a challenge to investors as anything. Why isn't the manager picking better securities? Why shouldn't we just invest in an index and save the active management fees? There is a constant questioning of past decisions by investors that can erode the entire discipline of the investment process. If the decision-making body is an investment committee and not a single individual, the interpersonal dynamic makes the problem considerably worse.

The first question to ask is whether the manager's process is broken. Have the assets under management grown rapidly or fallen precipitously? With larger assets, the manager's process might not work as well. With smaller assets the manager might be distracted from the investment work because of worries about the economic viability of the firm.

Has there been staff turnover? Have there been changes in regulatory structures like restrictions on short selling or a large increase in margins that impact the trading model? Internal and external forces all come into play.

---

[43]Stewart, S.D., Neumann, J., Knittel, C.R., and Heisler, J. (2009). Absence of Value: An Analysis of Investment Allocation Decisions by Institutional Plan Sponsors. *Financial Analysts Journal*, 65 (6) (15 December). http://ssrn.com/abstract=1523736.

When one invests with an active manager, it must be acknowledged that it is entirely a human business. The fund manager struggling with a divorce or the illness of a family member might not be totally engaged as they have in the past. Successful managers that start new businesses, engage actively in politics, purchase sports franchises, or build second or third houses with second or third spouses may simply overtax their bandwidth. It is of course possible that nothing in the investment process will be lost as these managers evolve personally. But common sense suggests that a manager's early success was probably achieved when there was a laser focus on the investment process. Remove that focus and something important could be lost.

It may be uncomfortable for an investor to ask about anything other than portfolio composition and attribution. But there are so many things that can affect performance that it is incumbent to do so. Any underperforming manager worth his or her salt will want to convince his or her investors that the investment team is intact and focused.

There is an opposite problem with top performers. Investors tend to believe good results are a natural outgrowth of their obviously well-refined manager selection process. Not enough scrutiny is placed on how these top performers reached their standing.

In the second half of 2007 credit markets began to show the signs of strain that would ultimately lead to the near meltdown of the financial system a year later. It also provides a textbook study on the fallacy of relying on top quartile managers.

From 2003 to early 2007 credit spreads tightened. As liquidity dominated markets, investors aggressively bought all kinds of credit instruments, including ones that implicitly or explicitly used leverage to boost yields. Intermediate bond fund managers were caught in a bind. To earn higher returns, many managers sought out nontraditional fixed income investments that carried higher yields for their given ratings. In most cases the managers did not violate any of their investment guidelines for either duration or credit quality.

The top-quartile managers for the period 2003–2006 almost all took extra risk by purchasing CLOs, CDOs, or exotic mortgage securities. By doing so they beat their benchmarks and their peers who shunned such instruments. The more cautious managers were rewarded by being branded as laggards and behind the times. They also lost assets to the top performers.

In July and August 2007, everything changed. With the first cracks in the credit market appearing, some investors scrambled for liquidity by redeeming from all managers. The bids for the more exotic instruments tumbled and the once top managers posted the absolutely worst results. Some investors claimed there was no way to anticipate such a bad outcome as they had only invested in the highest-ranked managers.

The error came from equating ranking with quality. Results achieved by taking bad risks were quickly reversed. Simple measures like standard deviation of returns over calm periods like 2003–2007 were poor predictors of potential risk. Investors caught in that storm had been far too willing to accept statistical summaries and rankings rather than really understand what was going on in their portfolios.

Intermediate bond managers provide a particularly valuable object lesson in this case because the gap between the best and worst managers is usually quite low. A top-quartile manager might only be 10 or 15 basis points of return above the mean. Most investors believed that skinny margin was due to repeatable skill. In the end they lost hundreds of basis points absolutely and relative to the benchmarks because of this mistaken belief.

5.3.5   Shaping Your Own Expectations for Managers and Their Role in the Portfolio

The limitations of statistical summaries and peer rankings in effectively grading the performance of managers are severe. Given the ongoing desire to evaluate one's active managers, how does one proceed? The best way, though challenging, is to establish one's expectations for how an investor or manager will contribute to the portfolio, and then objectively judge that performance in that light.

Two examples will demonstrate the concept. In the second half of the 1990s, the boom in tech stocks created two broad classes of equity investors: those who pursued growth and momentum strategies and those who did not. It was relatively easy to decide in which camp any given manager fell, but evaluating them along the way was a bigger challenge.

Investors who wanted to participate in the rally flocked to growth managers, and the managers who had the highest beta in their portfolios looked the smartest during the bull market run. There were many managers with more of a value orientation that stuck to their disciplines and never bought any of the high-flying stocks at lofty valuations.

These value managers may have been doing *exactly* what their investors had asked them to do, but they almost all suffered from major redemptions. The reason? They failed to stay abreast of the S&P 500. Investors claimed to understand that the value style was out of phase, but became frustrated when those value managers severely lagged *the overall market*.

The bigger problem, however, was a failure to see how the S&P 500 had transformed itself, because of the rapidly increasing capitalization weightings of tech stocks, into a high tech growth index. The S&P 500 could no longer be viewed as a fair representation of the market as a whole, but investors have a great deal of difficulty coping with situations where the standards of measurement are themselves shifting.

The value managers typically earned very solid absolute rates of return, but because they lagged not only the apparently smarter growth managers but also the broad indexes, investors penalized them. The investors that terminated the value managers either shifted to growth if they were aggressively chasing returns, or they put the money into an index fund if they thought they were being conservative. The irony in this example is that both choices were essentially the same, but with the index funds having a slightly lower beta. From the top of the market in 2000 until the trough in 2002, both investments showed massive losses.

If those investors had originally invested consciously in value style managers, the evaluation should have been done against a relevant set of stocks. There are value and growth labeled indexes that may be an improvement, but even these have been known to shift their composition through time. The fact that so many people shifted out of these managers just before their style came back into favor is a testament to the poor timing decisions by most investors.

The second example comes from fixed income funds. From 2004 through the start of 2007, credit spreads compressed on the back of easy liquidity and a belief that default probabilities were quite low. Typically, bond managers that had high credit exposure in the period outperformed their benchmarks and peers. As spreads got to their tightest levels, many of these managers saw great inflows from investors seeking out higher returns.

The credit crisis that began in 2007 crushed many of the "smartest" managers as spreads widened dramatically. Investors who had deserted more conservative managers once again were about 180 degrees off in their timing. To add insult to injury, the best credit oriented managers were rejected in late 2008 and early 2009, just at the time spreads were widest and their portfolios had the greatest potential.

The investor error here was to misunderstand the fundamental bet. Bond managers hold essentially two risks: interest rate (duration) risk and credit risk. If interest rates double, all bond managers will be hurt, but those with the greater duration will be hurt more. If the managers all have approximately the same duration, the relative rankings will be determined by how much credit risk a manager takes and the movement of credit spreads.

Investors should naturally want to avoid credit-focused managers at times of very tight spreads because the slight extra return is potentially too small a reward for the risk posed by spread widening. Looking backward at the good returns achieved as spreads tightened is useful as a guide as to which managers to *avoid*, not to make new investments in.

Too many investors have no clue what their bond manager's duration or credit exposures are. When these managers outperform or underperform the index, there is little understanding as to why and, more importantly, less guidance as to what one should do going forward. At the end of 2008 when credit spreads were at historically wide levels it was the time to embrace one's credit-oriented bond managers and not to terminate them for underperformance.

There are even important nuances within the credit category that need to be acknowledged. In March of 2009, with the stock market at its cyclical lows and many people thinking the macroeconomy worldwide was ready to fall into depression, there were still investors looking for opportunities. They could have simply bet on stocks, but buying on dips in the previous 18 months had proved disastrous. Many turned to bank loans and bonds.

Bank loans and corporate bonds had been severely sold off, with prices between 60 and 70 cents per dollar of par for corporations that had reasonably strong balance sheets and prospects of performance. Some credit managers decided that with careful fundamental research they could build an unleveraged portfolio with a high return potential but also with a margin of safety should the equity markets and the economy continue to tumble.

A typical manager pursuing this strategy over the last three quarters of 2009 might have made between 25% and 30%, a strong absolute return by any standard. However, the Barclays High Yield Index, which is the closest established benchmark to the strategy, went up over 50% as equity and credit markets rallied around the globe. This index, however, contained many of the "junkier" names that a cautious investor probably wanted to avoid in the darkest days of the market crisis.

The investor with an ability to see what a conservative manager was doing over this period could appropriately evaluate the performance. Someone relying on an index would end up making an unfair apples and oranges comparison.

The ultimate evaluation has to be against the investor's own expectations and guidelines. There are investors who tell their active equity managers and hedge funds that they expect to earn all of the upside in a bull market while avoiding all of the downs. These investors will be disappointed on a regular basis and no manager will measure up. If one has realistic goals and a good understanding of the process, however, there is a good chance that ongoing manager evaluations will be fair and the decisions to hire or fire can add value through time. Ten years after the financial crisis with equity markets at historical levels and credit spreads similarly tight, these same topics appear in real-time testing whether investors can learn from the past.

5.4 PORTFOLIO CONSTRUCTION AND MARKET TRADING REALITIES

On 6 May 2010, US stock market investors experienced their first, but perhaps not their last, *flash crash*. After drifting lower over the course of the trading day, at 2:42 in the afternoon the market began falling precipitously. In just five minutes the Dow Jones industrial average lost 600 points, or more than 5% of its value. Twenty minutes later the market had largely rebounded from the extreme drop. But during the episode large stocks like Accenture traded at prices as low as a penny per share, and other stocks traded at $100,000 per share. Clearly this was market volatility in the extreme, shaking investor confidence in the stock market as a dependable institution.

Immediately in the wake of the flash crash, regulators and market participants began searching for causes. There had been market crashes before, but it appeared this time that technology played a headline role. Never before had blue chip stocks individually traded at such extreme levels at one brief moment, only to recover back toward their earlier prices in the next.

Many months after the event the SEC and CFTC issued a report that suggested a large index sell order, by a Midwest mutual fund in the CME S&P 500 E-mini futures contract, had been a precipitating event. The CME subsequently argued that this customer had not been unusually large, nor had the orders been placed in a manner that should cause disruption. What seems clear well after the fact is that there was a confluence of events including this order that produced the flash crash. The question before investors is whether the event itself should cause such concerns that they question the market, or alter their long-term investment strategy.

Whenever markets gap significantly it is a clear sign that liquidity has left the market, but it does not explain why liquidity was absent at that point in time. It appears in this instance that electronic market making, which now dominates almost all markets, was in the middle of the story. To better understand the dynamic in the marketplace, one needs to at least identify the major players.

The most easily identified participants in the stock market are retail investors. This group represents a tiny fraction of all trading volume, but catches the attention of the media and regulators. They may be frequent traders or buy-and-hold investors. Given the active attention of dedicated news channels, this group represents the public face of the market. As a rule, however, retail investors rarely are the force in the market that precipitates any dramatic move. They are much more reactors than actors.

More important in terms of their market impact are institutional investors representing pension plans, insurance companies, and other large pools of capital. Some of these investors primarily operate through external managers, but many build their own equity portfolios in order to save costs. By and large, these investors also do not trade actively but instead set up long-term asset allocations and manage their cash flows against the manager. By their sheer size they need to be sensitive to how they trade in the marketplace, but once again they are not a group of traders that typically moves a market in the short run.

Active fund managers come in many varieties. There are long-only managers in mutual funds, or as sponsors of the wildly popular ETFs. The trading of these managers is largely a function of their own cash flows. Some may change their opinions about an individual stock or sector, but most of these participants do not actively trade their portfolios. Unless their client base is entirely not-for-profit, these managers are usually sensitive to the tax status of their investors. In the crash of 1987, evidence suggests that mutual fund managers selling aggressively on the mornings of 19 and 20 October were in part responsible for the large-order imbalances present on those days. This was due to the large redemption requests they had received over the weekend. Under normal circumstances these managers trade in a much more controlled fashion, but their size can create disruptions.

The Midwest mutual fund placing futures sell orders on the day of the flash crash falls into this category. Under most market environments there would be little difficulty or market impact in placing that order. On 6 May, however, the market was already under pressure and additional selling caused unusual stress. It is one of the important skill sets of institutional investors to be able to gauge the impact of their actions and moderate their trading decisions when necessary.

Passive mutual funds and ETFs represent a significant portion of all stock market activity. Managers of these funds only trade in response to their own fund flows or if the composition of the underlying index changes. Either of these events can be significant, though in general the trading of these managers is not viewed as containing meaningful market information. These managers are buying or selling a sector or the entire market, which can convey important macro sentiment, but does little to pressure one stock versus another in any group or market.

In addition to long-only funds there is a large class of managers who trade from both the long and the short side. These are typically hedge funds and their trading activity can be much more active depending on their underlying styles. Discussed in more detail in Chapter 9, these managers sometimes look like fundamental buy-and-hold long-only managers, but others can sometimes turn their portfolios over several times a day. One of the key skill sets of hedge fund managers is assessing their underlying liquidity and pacing their trades accordingly. They are often looking for price distortions caused by other traders who have moved aggressively or clumsily into the market.

In an ideal world both retail and institutional stock traders would come together in an open and highly liquid market process. The real world has rarely worked this way. In the days when the traditional stock exchange was the center of the universe a group of professional market makers acted as facilitators to the flow of buy and sell orders. They would gather all of the orders on both sides of the market and sense the direction that the price needed to go to produce a balance. Stock exchange specialists had affirmative obligations to make markets on both the buy and sell side. It was a skill in understanding when to build inventory and when to sell it that differentiated the profitable specialist from the one who had no future in that profession.

Other markets like the early days of the NASD had competing market makers who would provide two-sided markets. When there were many NASD members who had an interest in a stock both the bid side and the offer side would be deep and the *bid ask spread* would be tight. In neither the NASDAQ model nor the exchange specialist model did the rules of the organization always ensure that the market makers would be there with large amounts of liquidity. Despite rules that said there was an affirmative obligation to make two-sided markets, there were many stocks on the New York Stock Exchange and in the NASDAQ marketplace during the crash of 1987 for which there were no bids. Telephones were not answered. Computer screens were ignored. While generally supportive in highly liquid markets, neither market model guarantees liquidity at all times. It is simply impossible to expect rules to create liquidity.

The biggest change in market structures in the twenty-first century has been the automation of order flow and matching. As technology improved in the last 20 years of the twentieth century, telephone and written buy and sell orders were largely replaced with computer-generated trade tickets. The stock exchange specialist was mostly reduced to a manager of a database supplementing a highly automated process with his own purchases and sales in order to maintain balance. Intricate rules were developed at the NASD in order to integrate the order flow with the electronic markets made by the competing market makers. In general, technology allowed volumes to expand and the markets to become much more democratic in terms of access to the best bids and offers.

With this change in technology came a new type of market participant. Electronic proprietary traders develop software to analyze and act upon the flow of orders. This was the beginning of high-frequency trading in the stock market, where human intervention was at the programming level and not at the actual trade execution level. While this class of traders was evolving there were other development steps going on. Various market venues emerged to compete with the traditional stock exchange or the NASDAQ system. These "dark pools" were developed to try to provide large institutional traders less public trading venues so that they could execute larger size transactions without having to advertise all of their market intentions.

In essence, these new trading platforms were an attempt to circumvent long-standing trading rules that were designed to protect public participants in the stock market. The theory was that these large institutional traders could not execute the size transactions they required in the public markets without severe economic disadvantage. Some of these concerns were quite valid. Once broker-dealers learned of the intentions of their large institutional customers, the orders were not always held in confidence. Positions were front run or otherwise traded in a disadvantaged way. The theory behind these alternative venues is that anonymity was assured and large institutional buyers and sellers could cross their trades without undue interference from other market participants.

Figure 5.21 how dramatic these changes have been. Growth in total volume of stock market transactions has far outpaced any growth in the real economy as shown by the value of stocks traded relative to GDP. The volume of trade away from the traditional stock markets has also grown at an explosive pace, with a very large percentage coming from high-frequency traders operating both within and across trading venues. It is this activity that one suspects is at the heart of the 2010 flash crash.

As trading volumes have expanded dramatically in the past years, many institutional and retail investors probably view the liquidity in the market as being greatly enhanced. The number of executions that occur between the publicly advertised bid and offer is much larger than it ever was under the specialist system. On-line brokers sometimes report how much *price improvement* their systems have generated for the

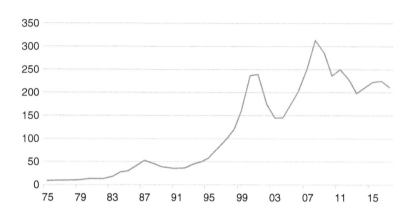

FIGURE 5.21 US Stock Market Value Traded as % of GDP
Source: St. Louis Federal Reserve (FRED)

customer's trades. That is what increased competition is supposed to do for a marketplace. The problem with this development is that none of these high-frequency traders is obligated to be present in a marketplace at any point in time. In fact, the best high-frequency traders all have intricate risk controls in their programming that shuts down their activity whenever extreme conditions and volatility appear.

What is likely to have happened in the afternoon of 10 May 2010 is that when there was large institutional selling of futures contracts to hedge stock portfolios, arbitrageurs tried to take the other side of those orders while simultaneously placing large, automated sell orders in the individual stocks comprising the index. It appears that in many instances the sell orders were so large and came so rapidly that they exhausted all of the standing bids in the market. The time frame under consideration here is measured in tiny fractions of a second.

The reported transactions for individual stocks at one penny per share were the result of what is known as "stub quotes" where a market maker will simply hold a place in the market by making the smallest bid possible, never expecting a transaction to occur there.

This does not explain why some stocks melted up and traded at $100,000 per share. Here a more complete understanding of all market participants is essential. Long/short equity traders often place *stop loss orders* for both their long and short positions. If the total market is trading significantly down, this can prompt those managers to try to sell their long holdings to avoid even bigger losses. Those managers that insist on holding equal exposures of the long and short side must also put in buy orders to close out their short positions. These buy orders can be as disruptive in their individual names as the broader sell orders were in the marketplace. If the high-frequency traders retreat from their activities, they will neither buy nor sell stock. Hence, liquidity can evaporate on both sides. The absurd prices that were seen on 10 May are the results.

Market regulators and the exchanges quickly came together after the event and voided the most extreme prices that were posted that day. Still, individual stock volatility was higher than few had ever seen, and confidence about the system was shaken. The public wondered whether this was just another sign that our financial system was broken. Many scrambled for policies or technical solutions to avoid a repeat of this event.

At a very high level the basic problem seemed to be that electrons move much faster than human beings. Long before anyone could respond in a fundamental way to an idea the price was either too high or too low the automated systems had moved prices even further. What was likely needed was a bit of electronic sand in the trading machinery to slow things down.

The crash of 1987 produced a set of rules known as *circuit breakers*. Any time the stock market in general falls or rises by an extraordinary amount within a trading session trading can be halted across the stock market, the options market, and the related futures markets. 1987 proved that it was essential to have coordination across all possible trading outlets. When the market is in a pause mode, it allows fundamental traders time to assess value and to decide whether a trading opportunity exists or not.

If the cause of the market decline is fundamental in nature (e.g. a tsunami, a terrorist attack, an extreme surprise in economic data), circuit breakers simply postpone the ultimate necessary market correction. In those circumstances the rules get in the way of market efficiency. In other instances, like was seen on 10 May, the volatility seems to be more a function of the trading environment than any change in fundamental news. If there had been individual circuit breakers on single stocks there is an excellent chance that buyers would have appeared well before prices fell to one penny per share, or sellers would have offered their holdings well below $100,000 per share.

As technology progresses in the marketplace the organizers and the regulators are in constant race to anticipate all of the impacts of technological change. It appears from the results of the flash crash that nobody could foresee how quickly electronic liquidity could evaporate. The good news is that as traumatic an event the afternoon of 10 May was, it was ultimately a highly transitory happening. Lacking any fundamental reason for moving in such an extreme way, stock prices moved back toward their previous levels. To the long-term investor the events of 10 May look like a disappointing day, but nothing out of the ordinary.

That is the fundamental lesson that investors should take away from these brief moments of extreme volatility. The world has been blessed with great technological strides that in the vast majority of cases have improved liquidity, reduced trading costs, and generally made markets superior to what they were years ago. While this is a great benefit, it should in no way change the way long-term investment portfolios are constructed. Similarly, the kind of short-term volatility caused by the flash crash should have no impact on our basic game plan. The long-term capital formation process has not been altered, and the benefit from owning stocks versus all other assets is not materially changed.

It will be demonstrated in later chapters that different types of active managers will try to exploit these evolutionary changes in the stock market, but this is just an effort to develop a trading advantage over other market participants. While it may affect which managers are hired in a portfolio, it probably should have little impact on overall asset allocation decisions. Long-term investors need to focus not on the day-to-day wrinkles in the market, but on systematic opportunities that exist. While market structure is ultimately quite important for the long-term success or failure of the system, history has shown that generally there is considerable progress, but with some bumps along the way.

5.5   MANAGER DUE DILIGENCE AND SELECTION

Once the asset allocation is established the process of populating the portfolio with actual investments begins. In some cases this will involve acquiring particular securities, or index funds, but in many cases it will involve hiring a manager. Success or failure in this step contributes meaningfully to the ultimate performance of the investment process.

One can think of this as trying to execute a complicated recipe. The cookbook author has carefully given you the proportions and all the necessary steps for putting the ingredients together, but success is certainly not assured. Unless quality ingredients are purchased and the construction steps followed carefully, the end result could be a major disappointment. Manager due diligence and selection are the steps equivalent to going to the grocery store and carefully picking among all of the available options. The better work that is done here, the better the final dish will be.

The analogy with recipes breaks down because the complexity of the manager selection process has many more dimensions to it than simply finding the ripest fruit or the best-marbled meat. This section is devoted to a discussion of the major steps that need to be considered before hiring a manager. There are several broad areas covered in due diligence. The first is to thoroughly understand the investment process. Investors who confess that "I'm not really sure how Manager X makes money, but the numbers have been really good" are asking for trouble.

After establishing the investment thesis, you should learn as much as you can about the firm as a business. Who are the owners? How are team members compensated? What is the alignment between the interests of the investors and the people who control the fund?

Due diligence can then turn to the historical sources of returns and risk. How did the fund make and lose money? What were the market forces at work over this history? The returns might be good on some absolute scale, but have the investors been compensated enough for the risks being taken?

If this initial due diligence is not promising, there is no reason to spend any more effort on the manager. If, however, the investment thesis and business proposition of the manager make sense, the next level of diligence begins. Non-investment due diligence covers all operational aspects of the firm. How are trades executed? Confirmed? Money transferred? How are securities in the portfolio priced and net asset values established and audited? Is the firm registered with a regulatory body and what has been their regulatory history? What are their internal trading rules, and who enforces them? Do they have appropriate disaster recovery procedures? What are their legal, accounting, brokerage, and administration relationships? The list goes on and on.

Too many investors find this entire exercise complicated and more labor-intensive than they like. They often accept the recommendations of friends whom they believe have done their own due diligence. This is one of the biggest potential mistakes that investors can make. Even if someone else's basic due diligence was adequate to his or her needs, there is no guarantee that the manager will be a good fit for you.

Why is it that we rarely ask someone else to buy a pair of shoes for us? While we can describe the basic style we want, the price range, and our usual size, that goes only part of the way to finding the right pair of shoes. Ultimately it is best to try the shoes on, walk around a bit, and decide if they would be a wise purchase. Taking someone else's recommendation on a manager is even more problematic. No matter how good the manager's returns may appear, they might ultimately be the wrong style and size, and create many more problems than just blisters.

Due diligence is more than just a checklist of activities. It is a process designed to make sure the manager fits properly into the needed role. While there may be a limited number of ways from an investment perspective to lose money from a given trade, the nontrade aspects of the manager's performance can disappoint in almost limitless ways. The categories of due diligence listed below are extensive, but not exhaustive. Every ongoing relationship with a manager is a learning experience, and the preliminary due diligence is just the first step to determine if it makes sense to go further with them.

There are many ways for a manager to fail due diligence. Sometimes you discover information that should be an immediate deal killer. However, when the manager's past returns are attractive enough, there is always the temptation to rationalize the due diligence problems. This can end badly. It is hard enough to understand all the important issues you will face with a manager before you invest, but when you discover troubling information beforehand you should count yourself lucky and move on. No manager is so special, or even remotely unique, that you should compromise in this area.

Due diligence would be easier if every question had a yes or no answer. Typically this is not the case. What usually happens is the answers fall along a scale and you have to decide whether the aggregate result is a passing grade. If you have concerns in an area, they should be communicated to the manager. It is possible you did not grade the manager fairly, or it is possible that the manager is less concerned about, or even unaware of, a deficiency that you find. It is an informative exercise to see how managers respond to your concerns. An attitude of "this is how we do things" should be a major warning sign. If the manager is not responsive to you before you are an investor, it is unlikely that you will be in the front of their mind after you have sent them your money.

Reasonable disagreements between managers and investors occur all the time. Managers should not try to cater to every whim of every investor. But good managers want to have well-functioning operations that are responsive to their investor base, and if they are seriously lacking in areas, they should show a willingness and ability to improve. If the due diligence topic is important to you, but not of interest or importance to the manager, it is again time to move on and find a better fit.

It cannot be emphasized enough that just because other investors find a manager's practices acceptable does not mean that that manager is right for you. History is filled with examples of wildly successful managers with broad followings who ultimately destroy large amounts of wealth or even blow up completely. There may be some comfort in having a lot of company if you were involved in such a situation, but it is far better to have avoided the problem beforehand. Time spent on preliminary due diligence is an invaluable investment.

5.5.1 Understanding the Investment Thesis

It is remarkable how often managers or their marketing representatives approach investors with the introduction consisting entirely of a claim that they have "good numbers." Apparently there are enough investors who chase returns that this approach is effective. But a return history without an understanding of how those returns were created is essentially worthless. The first step in any due diligence process is a thorough understanding of the manager's investment thesis.

One should not confuse investment objectives with the investment thesis. For example, saying your objective is to beat the Barclays Aggregate Bond Index simply expresses a goal, not a means to achieve that goal. Some bond managers will say that their advantage against the index is from credit selection. Others will say they have skill in market timing movements of interest rates. There are times of market dislocations when a particular sector or trade is attractive. Managers who build their entire approach around such dislocations should be recognized as having finite potential. Once that dislocation leaves the marketplace, who is to say other dislocations will appear that will allow that manager to prosper?

An equity manager could have as their investment thesis the idea that they do better fundamental research than the majority of other managers on the street. It is rare to find an equity manager who doesn't have confidence in their research. The investor needs to ask the question, "Do I believe that this manager has the resources and the insights to perform?" Other equity managers claim to rely on analytical screens to identify the best companies and the best stock values. Again, with literally thousands of individuals sorting through the same publicly available data, one needs to assess whether this manager can stand out from the crowd.

After the credit disruptions in late 2008 and early 2009, there were literally scores of credit managers who had as an investment thesis that prices of high-yield bonds and bank loans had been beaten up to the point where they offered unusually strong values. It was believed that the bonds of well-run companies could be identified that had a high probability of payoff, which could be purchased for $0.60–$0.70 on the dollar. The thesis was absolutely basic. Even if the economy continued to struggle, there was a good chance that these bonds would perform. The investment thesis at that point in time could easily be described as a pure beta play.

This investment thesis turned out to be one of the best trades available. Anyone who had long exposure in the space made serious money over the next 18–24 months. As the credit market moved back toward historical spreads, it was actually difficult to lose. The hard part was making the decision to invest during the darkest moments of the crisis. Many investors in the first quarter of 2009 simply did not want to take any more risk at any price. Everyone who missed out on this major move was offered an opportunity to invest later.

The highest-integrity managers in the credit space acknowledged after two years that the bulk of the correction had already occurred. They warned investors that the best opportunities were in the past. While they believed sincerely that they could add value to a credit portfolio, they cautioned investors that the previous two years' returns would likely not be repeated. Those were the most honest managers.

Other managers took their two-year track record to less discerning potential investors and tried to impress them with their ability to create outsized returns in any environment. They were selling track records, pure and simple. What was not fully disclosed was the fact that the environment had changed dramatically and that the likelihood of repeating that outsized performance was almost zero.

In evaluating a manager's investment thesis it is the investor's responsibility to gauge both the environment and performance within that environment. In the example above, the 2009 investment thesis was opportunistic. There is absolutely nothing wrong in trying to exploit opportunities. The problem arises when one confuses a simple opportunity with a long-term ability to make money. Many of the successful credit managers in 2009 and 2010 seriously lagged that performance in the subsequent more normal environment, an outcome that should have been expected. Investors who fail to distinguish between two very different states of the world are likely to enter the trade at the wrong moment and with the wrong expectations.

"Past performance is no indication of future returns" is the standard disclaimer that every manager places in their marketing material. Given that law requires it, the phrase has almost reached the same status as health warnings on cigarette packages. Everyone knows the message is there and they probably believe it is true, but it does not change many behaviors. We have become numb to the standard investment boilerplate, but it is the one message that we should think about every day. A good track record is not an investment thesis. There is very little one can do analytically to test whether a manager's stated investment thesis is valid or not. What is required is a subjective evaluation of the manager's claims, coupled with a thorough scrubbing of the historical record to see if it adds up to a consistent story. This is where thoughtful attribution analysis comes in.

5.5.2 Determining the Sources of Returns and Risks

In Section 5.3 of this chapter, measures like correlation, standard deviation, beta, and the Sharpe Ratio were discussed as popular ways managers characterized their own performance. These measures, however, are only descriptive statistics. While they can be suggestive, they fall short of being a true attribution analysis. When doing due diligence on any manager, an essential step is as thorough as possible scrubbing of past returns. Managers tend to love to talk about the ways they have made money in the past. They may be less enthusiastic talking about their losses, but most understand that this is a point of keen interest on the part of potential investors.

Long-only equity managers form an interesting case study of attribution analysis. After seeing the monthly return history, the first step is to compare it to the benchmark that the manager is working against. Suppose the manager builds his portfolio from large-cap US stocks, and uses the S&P 500 Index as his benchmark. Suppose also that the manager claims to hold a concentrated portfolio of under 30 stocks and does not try to match the sector allocations of the index. Historically the manager has held only a few percent of the portfolio in cash for transaction purposes.

Given the relatively simple nature of this portfolio, there are only two sources of underperformance or outperformance: stock selection and sector selection. As an example, suppose in a month when the S&P 500 Index increased by 2%, the manager returned 3%. If you know the portfolio for that month, you can see where the sector overweights and underweights were. If the manager had an extra allocation to industrial stocks relative to the index, and that sector did well in the month, part of the manager outperformance was due to that decision. If the manager's individual stocks within the industrial sector outperformed the average, then another part of the attribution came from stock selection.

Underperformance is similarly analyzed. In addition to knowing how much of the attribution was due to stock or sector selection, it is frequently helpful to understand how much of the attribution was due to a particular stock or sector bet.

If almost all of a month's underperformance can be traced to a single stock mistake, this is only potentially a problem. One might think that active managers should be able to avoid such major mistakes, but that is a pipe dream. Baseball players go to the Hall of Fame if they bat 0.300 for their career. Stock managers have to have a much higher batting average than that to stay in business, but even the best managers fall well short of batting 1.000.

Sometimes investors who have a particular expertise in a business or industry can be hypercritical of managers who invest in their area. Suppose the manager takes a large position in a company that might have been a former competitor of the investor. Natural emotional forces lead the investor to view this stock position in the same way they used to view them when they were going head-to-head. They don't expect the stock to be a superior performer, and they question the motivation and intelligence of the manager.

This is an entirely natural reaction from investors who know something about a particular area. While they may have a very solid, well-founded opinion of the business, they may not have a good foundation for evaluating the stock or its place in a portfolio. Great companies can be a very bad investment if the stock is too expensive when it is purchased. Similarly, okay companies can be a great investment if their stock price is cheap relative to its potential. While the investor may be an expert in the industry, it is the stock fund manager's job to decide where there is investment value.

Every track record of any length that spans market cycles will have lots of examples of mistakes. It is essential in evaluating the track record to try to determine if these mistakes show any pattern, or if they are the result of the occasional piece of analysis gone wrong, or just bad luck. Similarly, profitable trades can show a pattern as well. Good managers learn from both. A track record that shows a long history of adding value on average through both stock and sector selection is exactly what one looks for in an active equity manager.

The track records that deserve additional scrutiny are those that contain one or two spectacular periods, followed by a majority of results that look entirely average or worse. When this happens managers can stress the average returns over the whole period in their marketing materials. If the manager's average alpha was largely created by one or two trades, there are real questions whether that kind of outperformance can be expected in the future. One often sees track records of managers that have large outperformance in the early years of their history when they had much smaller assets under management. Being nimble is a huge advantage. Even if one finds the same great stock names after the fund has grown, it may be much more difficult to realize the outperformance when the stock holdings become so large.

The main benefit of this kind of attribution analysis is that it provides a solid foundation on which to base your future expectations. Only if the market conditions and the business conditions of the fund are similar to those that were in place when the track record was created should you have confidence that past performance may be indicative of future returns. If the market environment has changed, if the operations or size of the fund is radically different, or if the fund manager has simply grown so wealthy that he is occupied with a score of other potential distractions, it becomes a probability assessment whether the past is a good indicator of the future. Investors tend to want to believe the best about a manager before they make an investment, but it is essential to be as objective as possible.

Long-only equity managers are perhaps the easiest type of manager on which to perform attribution analysis. The same type of procedure can be followed for long-short managers, with the obvious added complication of doing separate attribution for the short positions. It is really quite remarkable when one does attribution analysis on long-short equity managers, how few of these managers actually add value from their short positions. They may be great stock pickers on the long side, or they may have a particular skill in adjusting risk prior to the market correction or advance, but actually picking stocks to fail has historically been a very difficult skill to demonstrate.

The attribution of fixed income managers typically gets broken down into decisions about duration and credit quality. Did the manager pick the direction of interest rates correctly? Did they buy cheaply priced credits of companies that were of fundamentally sound quality? The major challenge in evaluating fixed income managers comes from the fact that the spread in performance between the best and worst is usually quite small. A top-quartile intermediate-term fixed income manager might be no better than 10 basis points superior to the average.

In such a world it is critical to understand where those 10 basis points came from. In the run-up to the crisis in 2007 and 2008, many fixed income managers tried to add value by relaxing their credit standards and by using structured instruments to add yield. This was exactly the wrong thing to do in an environment of tight credit spreads. When the crisis occurred many of these managers moved from the top to the absolute bottom of the performance rankings. People who believed that the previous outperformance was a result of the manager's fundamental genius were shocked with this outcome. Those who understood the source of the manager attribution as well as the current market environment could make more informed choices across managers and avoid these problems.

The biggest challenges in attribution come from those managers who consciously try to cheat. In the go-go days of the 1990s, a very popular source of return from mutual fund managers was from "flipping" IPOs. The largest mutual funds often did huge business at brokerage houses, and were given preferred positions in the allocation of new *initial public offerings*. There is absolutely nothing wrong with taking advantage of these opportunities for the benefit of their investors. It is wrong, however, to suggest that a manager's outperformance was attributable to superior stock selection in these instances. There were managers in the 1990s running funds that had nothing to do with tech stocks, but who used the proceeds of their IPOs in that sector to boost their returns. If these transactions were established and liquidated before quarter end reports, there was virtually no way for the investors to understand what the true source of profits was.

Another way managers have enhanced returns is through the selling of *options*, *credit default swaps* (CDS), or other derivative structures that collect premium. This can be a perfectly legitimate strategy or it can be a way to try to smooth over returns in rough months. It is difficult to play too many games with exchange-traded derivatives, but over-the-counter products provide managers with much more latitude. While all fund managers have extensive and apparently ironclad pricing policies, they are primarily designed to protect the manager. Unless the investor can confirm that the pricing of over-the-counter derivatives reflects actual market conditions, it is a safer policy to assume those prices are set to improve the appearance of the manager's returns. It may yet be an even safer policy to minimize the use of mutual fund managers who populate their portfolios with products that are not actively traded on a public exchange.

Attribution becomes increasingly difficult when applied to hedge fund managers. Returns could be ascribed to stocks, bonds, real assets, and any other investments. Typically this is impossible to do without the help of the manager. The best managers understand the needs of their investors and try to give good descriptions of their attribution. Other managers are more opaque. One must decide how much transparency is necessary to make an informed analysis. When transparency is not complete, there are some statistical tools available to close the gap. Applying the concepts of alpha, beta, and factor decomposition that were developed in the previous section can go a long way in objectively determining a manager's sources of returns.

5.5.3 Alpha versus Beta: Factor Decomposition

Given the proliferation of index mutual funds and ETFs, it should be a basic proposition that you must not pay too much for beta. The main point of performance attribution from active management is to see how much alpha is being created, and to assess whether it is large enough to justify the active management fees. If position level data is available, the kind of attribution analysis discussed above is readily performed. Bigger problems arise when one either does not know any position information, or only receives a list of positions at the end of a quarter or year. It is never a reasonable assumption to believe these snapshots accurately characterize a portfolio for the entire period.

If a track record looks reasonable but there is not good data available on which to perform attribution analysis, the investor can make inferences from that return history. The primary tool to do this is regression analysis. If this level of statistics is beyond the investor it is probably a good idea to reach out to someone who has the skill set to find the answers.

There is little need here to go into the details of how to perform this statistical analysis. The basic proposition is to regress the fund manager's returns against market variables. For example, as discussed earlier in this chapter, regressing a large-cap US stock manager's returns against the S&P 500 Index can give simple estimates of both the manager's beta and alpha. For hedge fund managers who can invest in a broad range of products the exercise is only slightly more complicated. In those cases the returns are regressed against multiple market variables. For example, a simple test might look for a relationship between the fund's returns and the returns to stocks, bonds, and credit instruments. This way if any of the market movements contributed to the manager returns, they should show up as significant variables in these tests.

Even managers who claim to be market neutral can have major exposures to different market factors. Long-only and hedge fund managers who trade in equities can have regular biases in terms of cap size or sector exposure. It is great for active managers to identify potential value across a wide range of stock opportunities, but if the portfolio is always positioned in a similar fashion the investor may not be getting much more than partial benchmark exposure. As ETFs have expanded their coverage across market sectors, any specialized coverage can be purchased today at a very low cost. Active management fees should only be paid for truly active decisions.

The hedge fund Amaranth was discussed in detail earlier in the chapter. In addition to being a good example of why summary statistics are not always predictive, it proves why attribution analysis needs to be extensive. In its communication to its investors Amaranth was relatively open about the areas in which it was trading. However, it did not share with its investors precise data discussing attribution or risks. Investors doing due diligence on Amaranth were left to try to develop the picture themselves.

If one had done a simple regression analysis on Amaranth's past returns in the early part of 2006 the results would have been highly encouraging. Over the history of the fund Amaranth had shown a near zero beta with respect to the stock market, the bond market, and the credit market. If one truly believed that story, the entire return history could be attributed to trading alpha. For many investors this was their Holy Grail: a high-performance fund with no correlation to the other assets in their portfolio.

Experienced investors looking at this result did not accept it at face value. It is extraordinarily rare to find any investment history that has no market influences. Regressing Amaranth's returns against commodity prices revealed a potentially troubling pattern. Despite starting life as a low-volatility, relative value hedge fund manager, Amaranth had evolved as it grew into a fund dominated by the movements of just one of its underlying strategies. That strategy was highly dependent upon spreads in energy prices. As discussed earlier in the chapter, just because the fund had not experienced large volatility did not mean it could not be exposed in the extreme.

A regression analysis on Amaranth's returns that included energy prices showed that the fund was hardly market neutral. Rather than being a low-volatility, market neutral fund, the majority of risk revealed in the returns history was in the energy sector. There is nothing fundamentally wrong with investing in macro managers that are energy oriented. There is a big problem if you think you are investing in a low-volatility, market neutral strategy, and you are in fact investing in a natural resources macro fund. Thorough due diligence on this fund saved many investors from participating. Many more, however, were lured by the high return pattern and the lack of correlation with stocks and bonds.

As previously shown, beta can be calculated in terms of almost any market factor. True alpha is a very scarce commodity. If the first examination of a manager's history suggests that the majority of the returns came from alpha, there is a good chance that further examination will show something else. Despite wanting to believe in the superior abilities of every manager we invest in, we should remain skeptical and always examine that record. If the bulk of the returns come from easily duplicated market factors, one must question whether the expected returns in the future are going to be large enough to justify the fees and any lockup that may be associated with the fund.

5.5.4 Do the Returns Justify the Risk?

Repeating a common theme in this book, just because a loss has not happened yet does not mean it cannot happen. Risk is not past volatility. It is the potential for future loss over the investment horizon. When doing due diligence on managers' history, the question should always be whether the investor was adequately compensated for the risks that were taken in the portfolio.

Very few managers who approach you will have poor track records. Almost anyone with any experience will have rough patches, but by the time they come to talk to you there will be a positive story on the return front. For managers who have a very short track record, it will almost always be spectacular in absolute terms. Losers tend not to do a lot of marketing. Given that everyone you look at will have good returns, the obvious question becomes are they good enough for the risks that were taken?

For long-only managers in stocks and bonds, this question can easily be examined in terms of the portfolio holdings and the attribution that you do on those returns. If the stock manager working against a large-cap index derives a significant amount of his or her return from micro-cap stocks, or from emerging markets stocks, it may be that the manager did not earn enough to justify the risk from these types of equities.

This is actually a much larger problem with bond managers. To be a top-quartile performer in any peer group for a short-duration mandate usually only requires a handful of basis points versus the average. History is full of examples where the best manager in a group only made 5 or 10 basis points more than the average manager, but on the basis of that track record was able to amass large amounts of investor capital. It was only later, after some severe adverse event, did the investors come to learn that a great deal of risk was required to earn that meager edge.

This kind of problem has been around for as long as managers have compared themselves to each other or to benchmarks. The comparisons are almost always done by looking at returns. Whatever work is done examining the risk space is almost always backward looking. As we saw earlier in the chapter, the statistics meant to capture this risk have little capability of actually looking at the potential causes of loss. The only way to do that is through a thorough understanding of the portfolio, and a subjective understanding of what can go wrong.

More esoteric managers pose even more challenges in this area. Decomposing all the risks in a hedge fund is a major challenge for anyone. In addition to both the long and the short market risks, one must also frequently wrestle with the issue of liquidity. In another truism of the investment world, there is rarely any liquidity risk in a bull market. It is only when a manager is forced to liquidate a position that the true risks are revealed. The due diligence challenge therefore is to anticipate those risks in advance.

An area that is particularly hard to assess are partnerships where there is significant vertical integration within the fund. Suppose, as an example, a manager initiates loans to small businesses to finance their inventories. The manager then takes those loans into a pool to pay back the fund investors who supplied the capital. To enhance returns the manager might apply a certain amount of leverage on top of the limited partners' capital. In addition to a management fee for organizing the fund, the manager could pay himself a fee for originating the loans, and another fee for servicing those loans.

The risk profile of this kind of fund is very difficult to pin down. The underlying loans do not have an active market price, and they are therefore typically held at cost unless one of the borrowers defaults. While the various layers of fees should be disclosed in the fund prospectus, they are rarely highlighted, and there is no way of knowing whether the fees being charged are at competitive rates or not. A sweet spot in the market seems to be funds that advertise a "mid-teens" net return to investors, which sounds very attractive.

The problem is that with the leverage being applied on top of the investors' capital the gross returns should be very much higher. Even though the net returns look attractive on some abstract basis, the investors who are risking their capital should be receiving a larger percentage of the total return since they are assuming all of the market risks. Here there is no substitute for careful examination of fund documents, and a thorough scrubbing of where all of the proceeds go. An apparent good return for investors might be a very poor return per unit of risk taken. But you can count on such situations as providing a great return for the organizers of the fund.

Nowhere is this a bigger issue than in the area of hedge fund and private partnership fees. There are many managers who have successful track records and decide they can charge fees well above the industry norm. A hedge fund manager that charges a 3% management fee and takes 30% of the profits is charging what the current market may bear. Investors in these funds often say that they do not care about what the manager charges if their net returns are satisfactory. They should care a great deal.

How did the "satisfactory" returns get generated? It could very well be that the manager has exhibited continuous superior insight and execution in his investments. That is what everyone would like to believe. Another hypothesis is that the manager took outsized risk, got away with it, extracted large fees, and then sent the remainder to the investors. Unless you can clearly distinguish between these two explanations, there is a chance that at some point down the road the combination of luck and outsized risk will run out. Once again it is the investor who is bearing virtually all of the risk while receiving a disproportionately small part of the gain.

There is only so much objective analysis that can be done on the portfolios, return attribution, and estimation of risk. Investors who rely solely on these analytical tools may be missing some of the biggest risks in the fund. There are many subjective elements to taking the evaluation to the next level. The best place to start is getting to know the people responsible for your fund investments.

5.5.5 Getting to Know the Team

Ideally, before you make an investment you should have the opportunity to meet many of the key players who are responsible for your fund. This is fairly easy in the case of small, boutique hedge funds, unless, of course, some of the key decision-makers choose not to make themselves available. In larger organizations there are many more challenges. In funds with literally thousands of customers and tens of billions of dollars under management, it is extraordinarily rare to have access to the actual portfolio managers. Much more typical is the model where there is a team responsible for all client contact, and if they cannot provide detailed answers immediately they will act as an intermediary between the client and the investment decision-makers.

Having direct access to the portfolio manager is incredibly valuable. Not only do you get first-hand impressions of market opportunities and risks, you also have much easier access to the investment philosophy of the fund. How are investment ideas sourced? Who is involved in the ultimate buy or sell decision? Are positions scaled into? What are the sell disciplines? Is the risk management process integral to the investment process, or is it simply a control that sits on top of the investment decisions? There are literally scores of topics that quality portfolio managers love to talk about so that their investors have a complete understanding of what they are trying to accomplish.

Communications with clients is a delicate balancing act. Every client wants to have good access to the decision makers, but they don't want those decision makers distracted by being away from their main mission too often. As the size of the fund grows and the number of clients increases, many portfolio managers find that they have to place barriers between themselves and their clients. This is entirely understandable, and investors should be respectful of the portfolio manager's need to focus on the main mission.

Some highly presentable portfolio managers limit their client-facing time to new business acquisition. They understand how important it is for a potential client to be comfortable with the investment process and the leadership of that team. Investors should have some natural caution about the "star" manager who makes a great deal of time available to them before they are an investor. Don't be afraid to ask how much of the portfolio manager's time is being spent on new business acquisition. Also ask how decisions are made and how overall supervision is carried out when the main individual is otherwise occupied with these new business efforts.

People who are very poor marketers run some of the best funds in the world. Their investment process may be highly disciplined and sophisticated, but they have little ability to sell themselves or their funds. Potential investors should not be turned off by less than polished presentations. Looking past the lack of polish, one might discover a diamond in the rough. If you do, there is a further advantage that the manager is unlikely to raise too many assets in too short a period of time while you are taking advantage of his or her strong investment skills.

One of the most important reasons to want to speak to the portfolio manager is to get a thorough understanding of how they run their portfolio. The manager should be clear and not condescending. While there may be considerable technical sophistication to the investment process, an inability or an unwillingness to describe that process completely should be a major red flag. Sometimes portfolio managers forget that they are not extending invitations to a party where everybody already wants to attend, but they are asking to be trusted with your hard-earned wealth. This is a position of responsibility that is not bequeathed to anyone, but is instead earned.

Trusting the portfolio manager is a crucial first step, but it is only a first step. If possible, you should also try to meet independently with analysts, traders, and anyone else that contributes to making investment decisions. It is often said that the best investment funds are not democracies, but are closer to monarchies. However, there are both good and bad monarchs. You want strong leadership at an investment fund, but you also want a well-functioning team. There is no perfect way to assess how well teams work together before you make an investment. Typically it takes a long time of watching the team at work before your impressions can be complete. But the initial interview process of as many team members as possible is an important way to try to make an assessment.

Investment decisions are not the only areas that need to be examined. Talk to the back-office people. How are trades executed? How are they confirmed? Who has the ability to move money or securities? Where are the controls, and how are they exercised? The more complicated the investment fund, the more capable the operational team needs to be. If the portfolio manager is trading intricate derivative securities, you will want to assure yourself that the back-office staff has equally deep experience with these instruments.

The legal and regulatory elements of fund management have never been more important than today. Is there a full-time risk officer, or is this a part-time function performed by another professional? Major organizations have the luxury of having lots of headcount. Younger, smaller funds are often highly resource constrained, and people have a range of functions. As responsibilities get concentrated in a smaller group of people, the dimensions of team cooperation become increasingly important, and well-disciplined controls are essential.

Having a chief risk officer is almost mandatory in today's environment, but that person may have other duties as well. The important thing to determine is that risk-monitoring obligations are taken seriously by the firm with adequate internal or external resources.

Registered investment advisors, which include the fund managers of all mutual funds, are required to have a chief risk officer. For unregistered partnerships, very few institutional investors will invest unless this function is present. In the twenty-first century, having somebody responsible for risk is considered best practice.

Having a chief risk officer is one thing. Having a chief risk officer that makes a difference is quite another. The standard communication to both potential and actual investors is often that the risk officer has great latitude to step in, modify the portfolio, and protect investor capital. The actual working model is sometimes quite different. Dominant portfolio managers can have a very strong sense of the risks they are taking in the portfolio. They also frequently have a great deal of their own money in these trades. If they believe their portfolio positions are prudent given the opportunity before them, they may strongly disagree with a contrary view made by the chief risk officer.

Ultimately the chief risk officer reports to somebody in the firm. If that somebody happens to be one of the founding partners, who is also a portfolio manager, the organizational structure is ripe for conflict. When getting to know the team, potential investors should spend as much time as they can with the risk officer. Ask for specific examples of situations where the officer believed that portfolios needed to be adjusted because of inappropriate risk. Get as much detail as possible on how that process actually evolved. What one looks for is a chief risk officer who is a respected member of the team, and whose views on managing risk in the portfolio are actively encouraged.

Too often the risk officer is something of an appendage to the process. Risk officers may be sincerely attempting to do their job, but the risk takers do not genuinely value their input. Ask about the history of this position. When was the first risk officer hired? How many risk officers have there been? This is not a history that some funds like to advertise. Having multiple risk officers in a short period of time is usually a sign that they were delivering messages that the controlling partners did not want to hear. This is almost worse than having no risk officer at all.

The head legal officer of a fund has two primary functions. The first duty is to protect the fund by creating documents and communications that do not expose the fund or the principals to potential litigation. The second, and increasingly important, function is to assure regulatory compliance. This has never been an easy job, but the market events in the first decade of the twenty-first century and the subsequent response by Washington and the states have made it a lot worse. As some of the rules mandated by the Dodd-Frank legislation are still being finalized a decade after the crisis, there is genuine concern about what the ultimate obligations will be.

Regulatory uncertainty places amazing burdens on all investment managers. Even private placements, which have traditionally enjoyed a more sheltered position against the imposition of regulators, are devoting considerable resources to trying to understand and live up to the myriad of rules they face. Once a fund manager gets large enough, the chief legal officer often assumes the role of unofficial lobbyist to try to shape the rules under which they will live. Few of these activities make any productive contribution to the process of making money for investors.

The last group of people to be evaluated is the client service specialists. Who are the people with whom you will have the most contact? Oftentimes in early meetings before an investment is made, these individuals play relatively minor roles compared to the more senior people you meet who are trying to earn your business. Since the vast majority of your future contacts will be with these individuals, evaluating how they fit into the overall team will help determine how successful the ultimate relationship might be.

The interaction of client service individuals and the investment team is a key dynamic to explore. The best client service people have a skill set that is just short of, if not equal to, those of the portfolio managers. They sit in on team meetings as investment ideas are discussed. More importantly, as the public face of the investment fund, they have the opportunity to gather information from informed investors and bring it back to the attention of the portfolio management team. If you discover in your due diligence process that the client service people basically read from a script, you should expect there to be many lags in communications as the questions you are most interested in may not have already been answered in that script.

While this phase of the due diligence process should primarily be focused on evaluating all dimensions of the investment process, it is equally important to explore the business elements of the fund. While everyone should be motivated to earn money, the ways the fund owners and investors prosper could be in severe conflict with your goals.

5.5.6 The Business Model of the Fund

In an ideal world the team you meet at a prospective investment fund will be highly motivated toward your success. Since all you really care about are solid, risk-adjusted returns, the business of the fund should be oriented so that there is a strong alignment of your interests with the fund owners. Sadly, we do not live in an ideal world.

Toward the end of the great bull market that closed out the 1990s, John Bogle began sharing his concerns about the mutual fund industry, an effort he pursued for over 20 years until his passing. In one brief book he described how many of the most prominent institutional features of the mutual fund industry worked against the best interests of investors.[44] While much of the thesis can be viewed as his rationale for founding the Vanguard Funds in the mid-1970s, the message is actually much broader.

---

[44]Bogle, J. (2007). *The Little Book of Common Sense Investing: The Only Way to Guarantee Your Fair Share of Stock Market Returns*. John Wiley & Sons, Inc.

Too many institutional fund managers profit primarily from the collection of fees, which are almost always directly related to the size of assets under management. Even if the best investment practice would call for a limit on the size of a fund, the economic pressures to grow assets often win out. A young manager may build a very impressive track record on a modest level of funds under management, and then use that track record as a marketing tool to grow AUM to levels that cannot reasonably sustain that performance.

Most investors do not have the capability to find the small, hungry manager, or perhaps they do not choose to take the risks associated with the less institutional organization. Instead they wait until a track record is established, and hope that it can be repeated, even with assets that are many times larger than were in place when the early record was created. As understandable as this behavior is, it plays right into the hands of the fund manager.

A good part of the Bogle book is devoted to fees. Explicit, up-front sales fees, known as "loads," and 12b1 fees are a particular object of his scorn. These charges have only one purpose and that is to compensate the gatherers of assets. They do nothing to add value to the investment process. Bogle cites considerable data showing the strong negative relationship between the size of these fees and ultimate performance.

The basic management fee also receives criticism. Here Bogle asks a simple question, which is, "How much is enough?" He notes that as a mutual fund grows from $1 billion in assets under management to $10 billion, for example, its costs almost certainly do not grow tenfold. Yet there are few examples in the mutual fund industry of funds reducing their basic management fee, which are always expressed in basis points per dollar under management, as their fund sizes have grown.

Beyond the explicit fee schedule there are issues about trading costs. A portfolio manager should have a fiduciary responsibility to execute trades at the most efficient prices and at the lowest costs. If, however, the manager is not careful about trade execution, the full burden falls on the investment performance and not on the pocketbook of the manager. Doing appropriate diligence on the mechanics of fund execution is essential to understand whether the manager is working hard to minimize these expenses.

High turnover managers, by definition, experience greater drag from costs versus the buy-and-hold manager. Managers operating in less liquid markets are usually quite sensitive to this liquidity drag that can occur from frequent trading, but everyone should be thoughtful in understanding that these implicit costs can be a meaningful detriment to performance.

Taxpayers of course feel this pain twice. While execution costs affect everyone, high turnover portfolios produce ordinary income gains and losses for taxpayers. Portfolio managers who have a large amount of their personal worth invested in their funds may be more sensitive to the tax efficiency issues than those managers who are less personally exposed. In addition to finding out how much of the portfolio manager's wealth is invested in the fund, another way to check alignment of interests for taxpaying investors is to ask about the composition of other investors in the fund. If a large percentage of the assets are from pension plans, foundations, or other non-taxpaying investors, there may be little incentive for the manager to even think about tax sensitivity of the portfolio.

All of Bogle's complaints about the cost and fee structure of mutual funds can be applied to almost every investment option available today. Hedge funds that charge both a management fee and a performance fee typically argue that the performance fee creates an alignment of interest between the general partner and the limited partners. On an abstract level this is true, but one needs to look carefully at the real economics of the business.

A $10 billion hedge fund that charges a 2% management fee and 20% on total performance is an amazing economic engine. The general partners effectively receive $200 million a year for turning on the lights. Whatever they receive from the performance fees is almost gravy. Even if the senior general partners have several hundred million dollars of their own money invested in the fund, it is not obvious that they have a strong incentive to take the risks necessary to earn their limited partners an adequate net return after fees and taxes.

Hedge funds are an area where the objectives of taxpaying investors and not-for-profit organizations can seriously diverge. The low-volatility hedge fund that earns 4–5% above the risk-free rate may be extraordinarily attractive to the not-for-profit investor. But once one considers the typical lack of tax efficiency in hedge funds, the low net return and the limited liquidity can make it very hard for these funds to have an effective role in individual investor portfolios. Just like in mutual funds, individual investors should ask about the composition of the investor base. If institutions dominate it, the fund manager may cater the risk and return profile to those clients to secure a steady income stream from the management fees. Alignment of interests to one group of investors does not assure alignment of interests to all.

An area where fund terms seem to show stronger alignment can be found in private equity funds. Perhaps because of the highly illiquid nature of these investments, general partners have usually offered their limited partner investors fund terms that have several desirable features. While there is frequently a management fee on *committed capital*, increasingly some managers are charging the flat fee only on capital that has been called. There is almost always a performance fee, but unlike most hedge funds, private equity partnerships typically only calculate performance fees on realized transactions. This is highly advantageous to the limited partners as it prevents the fund managers from receiving compensation on paper gains that can later reverse. More funds are introducing *preferred rates of returns* and other investor friendly economic features. Given the multiyear nature of these investments it is perhaps not surprising that the general partners of private equity funds have realized how important it is to keep the economic terms aligned.

Most other areas of the investment landscape are less inclined to move in this direction. In 1997 *The Wall Street Journal* columnist Jason Zweig gave an address to a group of mutual fund executives in which he challenged those present about how much they were really working toward the welfare of their investors.[45] In the middle of one of the great bull markets of most of our lives, it was easy to downplay some of his criticisms, as everyone was making a lot of money, investors included. Many years later, which have included long stretches where few investors have been profiting, his observations are as timely as they were when they were originally made.

---

[45]Zweig, J. Putting Investors First. (1997). Presentation to the Investment Company Institute (May 1997). http://jasonzweig.com/the-difference-between-an-investment-firm-and-a-marketing-firm/.

Every investment manager is primarily motivated to advance his or her own best interests. There is nothing wrong with that. But the degree to which they extract wealth from their investing clients varies widely, and one of the main goals of your due diligence process should be to identify those with whom you have the greatest common interests. Typically those managers are harder to find, because they do not employ a large sales force. But the search for these managers can be worth a great deal in terms of your investment success.

Once you believe you have found the managers with the right investment process and business model, the due diligence process shifts to another arena. The "business of the business" is only worth exploring in detail after you believe you have found a viable candidate. The next sections of this chapter go over the wide range of topics that you will want to explore.

5.5.7   Reporting and Client Communications

Once the manager has your money, the dating period is over. From the day you make your investment you should think of yourself as being married. And like almost all marriages, poor manager communications to investors can absolutely sink an investment relationship. How often does the manager report? How long does it take after the reporting period does it take to receive the report? How much detail is contained covering both return and risk attribution?

The prospective investor should ask for a sample client communication that contains real data, sanitized of course to protect any confidential information. People's opinions on what they want to see in client communications vary, but the best reports typically display a great deal of forethought and planning to make them complete, but readable. Blaise Pascal once apologized to a correspondent about the length of the letter he was sending, stating that he did not have time to write a short one. Fund manager letters often should have this apology. There are a number of prominent fund managers whose letters are worth tracking down, but that club is much smaller than most managers think.

Good client communication should contain a prominent mention of net returns for the time period being covered. There should also be a description and as much supporting data as necessary covering the attribution behind those returns. Both winners and losers should be discussed. Any meaningful changes in the risk profile of the fund should be revealed. Anything beyond these basics should be considered editorial, and valuable only to the extent that it is educational or entertaining.

There are some institutional investors who have made position transparency a precondition for investing. This is a topic subject to debate. If you think it is important to know every position in a portfolio, ask yourself what you will do with that data. Collecting complete position or transaction data is a little bit like buying, but not watching, a lot of exercise videos. Unless you do something with the information, it is not going to make much difference in your life.

Mutual funds are required to disclose all holdings periodically, though with a lag. This data is a snapshot in time, falling short of complete transparency that would reveal all purchases and sales. It would be interesting to see what fraction of the investors in these funds look at even this limited information. It is probably quite low.

The clearest advantage of complete position transparency is that nothing is hidden from the investors view. Unless you take the time to really study the data, bad things could be hiding in plain sight. You must be willing to invest in the considerable effort needed to analyze position data. Making complete real-time transparency a criterion for investing could greatly restrict your access to good managers. Only establish this restriction if you are serious about using the data.

Many managers agree to share a summary of their internal risk reports. High-quality managers typically are quite proud of their risk management efforts, and if you show an interest in the process they will be responsive. When summary risk data is not routinely provided in client reports, it is more likely the case that the manager is concerned about the investors' interest and understanding, than any concern about releasing proprietary information. Ask for this data if it is not provided.

Mutual fund managers are constrained by law to provide all investors the same information. This can sometimes be quite frustrating to the investor trying to get basic questions answered that are not covered in the standard materials. The best mutual funds leave few questions unanswered, covering returns, attribution, and risk in their reports. Other mutual funds seem to hide within forests of data that by their volume give the impression of being comprehensive, but in actuality leave key questions off the table. It is not hard to judge mutual fund reports before you become an investor. Ask for a past report from a disappointing, losing quarter. Imagine that you have just received this report and ask yourself whether it satisfactorily addresses your concerns. If you can't really tell how money was lost, or how the portfolio has been repositioned as a result, you will likely not find future reports to be that helpful either.

Tax reporting is a service that is relevant only to taxpaying clients, but it is an important consideration for that group. Hedge funds and other private partnerships pose the most challenges with the filing of their annual K-1 reports. There is nothing that can differ meaningfully in substance in these reports, but the timing of their release seems to vary widely. Hedge fund investors as a rule should expect to file extensions on their federal and state tax returns, because it is unlikely that all of their K-1s will be received sufficiently before 15 April each year. Given the complexity of many of the hedge fund portfolios, this is not entirely out of line. But it seems that some hedge fund managers end up distributing their K-1s well into the third quarter of the calendar year, adding additional complexity and annoyance to the taxpaying process.

Hedge fund of funds are perhaps in the worst spot of all. They cannot file their K-1s until they receive all of the K-1s of the underlying managers. Typically their accountants are almost scratching at the door waiting for the last manager. Investors in fund of funds that have K-1-issuing private partnerships should understand this practical problem before they make any investment. It may seem odd to have a decision hinge on something so far removed from the investment process, but many people avoid whole classes of funds and managers because they don't want to be bothered by the added tax filing complication.

5.5.8 Operational Due Diligence

The difference in personality between those who analyze and trade investment ideas and those who actually execute, clear, account for, and report those trades is sometimes quite striking. The back office at an investment fund should be made up of hard-working professionals with a strong attention to detail, and little concern for the big picture. The questions you ask when reviewing the back office are consequently much different than those involved in evaluating the investment professionals. For many, this is not a fun part of the due diligence process, but since great sums of money have been lost through error or fraud in the back office, your operational due diligence efforts are critically important.

No book can teach anyone how to do operational due diligence. It is a skill set that is acquired by learning from those who have gone before. The more you do operational due diligence, the better you get at it. Some of the best practitioners of this art formerly worked in back offices themselves or at auditors of such funds. They know the day-to-day challenges and can focus their questions on potential trouble spots.

Some people argue that you need only limited operational due diligence for funds that are registered with a regulatory body. This is a risky belief. The periodic reviews of the regulator will go over processes and procedures to assure that they appear to be consistent with best practices, but there are no guarantees that the actual behavior of the manager meets your standards. The number of frauds that have been unearthed in previously reviewed, regulated entities suggest that even well-intentioned regulators will not catch everything of importance.

The 12 topics in this part of the chapter cover most of the key operational diligence areas. Each section suggests the type of questions that should be asked. Whenever possible the answers should be in writing, and then followed up with additional interviews. Getting to know and trust the back-office professionals is as important to an investor as forming a good relationship with the investment principals.

5.5.8.1 *Trading and Trade Allocation*

The mechanics of trading is the first broad area of operational due diligence. How are trades executed and by whom? Once the trade is executed, how is it confirmed and financed? If the trade involves securities, where are they custodied? If the transaction involves derivatives or other non-CUSIP securities, what are the *prime broker* relationships that assure the smooth execution of these trades?

The simplest example one could consider involves a portfolio manager overseeing one commingled fund vehicle. Every transaction that is done is a purchase or sale for all of the investors in the fund. Later we will relax that restrictive assumption, but even in this simple environment there are challenges to be monitored. Some funds have dedicated traders who do nothing but execute instructions given to them by the portfolio managers. Many smaller funds, especially those that have low turnover in their portfolios, will have the trading done by the portfolio managers themselves. The reason that this is an important distinction is that the skills needed to select good trades and to actually execute them are quite different. Many portfolio managers have improved their fund's performance by stepping back from trading and giving that chore to a dedicated professional.

The actual process of trading today is largely a function of the security in question. Most stocks, futures contracts, currencies, and many fixed income instruments can be traded on automated networks. The desirability of having an independent broker to execute transactions depends entirely on the liquidity in the marketplace. For many actively traded securities and derivatives, reasonable size orders can be filled at the bid or the offer almost instantaneously. Paying someone extra to "work" the order produces very little in net return. If the trade is of a large size, closer attention can have a big payoff.

Every manager should have a process to analyze the quality of trade executions. If they trade electronically, how good are the prices relative to others available during the trading day? If they use outside brokers, the broker should be able to qualitatively evaluate where those transactions occurred versus the bid or the offer. Since bad fills detract directly from performance, the portfolio manager will want to see that everything possible is being done to keep deviations to a minimum. One might assume that the portfolio manager's best interests are aligned with those of the investors in this area, but as will be seen in the next section this is not always the case. Sometimes there are relationships between managers and brokers that trump the damage that bad execution causes.

Once the trades are executed, the process is fairly mechanical. Every trade should be reconciled, as should the cash accounts used to finance the trading. With the advent of electronic trading, much of the matching process has been streamlined, but it is still the case that actual executions should be matched against where the trader believed the transaction occurred. *Out trades*, where the two sides of the transactions believe they have done a trade at a different price or quantity, are still an issue that need prompt attention and resolution.

The back office of the fund manager will be responsible for confirming that securities are delivered against sales, or the new purchases get placed in the appropriate custody account. Here the greatest virtue is attention to detail. Getting to know the back-office personnel, and understanding their experience and culture, can help you evaluate whether this part of the fund manager team is an asset or liability.

If the portfolio manager has more than one account into which trades may be placed, the issue of *trade allocation* arises. Managers who have multiple separate accounts that operate under the same mandate should have a fair and impartial way of allocating trades across those accounts. The due diligence process should explore the allocation methodology, and also ask for evidence that the allocations are working as fairly as possible. Usually this is done through an examination of the returns dispersion across accounts. There will always be minor differences in performance across customers having separately managed accounts, since it is literally impossible for everyone to get transactions done at exactly the same price. But if the allocation process is a fair one, some days you will receive a good price and other days you will receive a below average price. Through time these pluses and minuses should balance out, and the experience across customers should be very close.

A risk in separate accounts is that the manager will give the best trades to his or her best customers. In the case of managers that have both separate accounts and registered mutual funds, the bias is almost always to favor the mutual fund to enhance its public record. When there are differences between a separately managed account and the manager's mutual fund, this can be a major warning sign that the allocations are not as fair across customers as they should be. When discrepancies happen, the manager can always fall back to the idea that the funds had different mandates or investment restrictions. This is why it is vitally important for anyone setting up a separate account to make sure their investment guidelines are as closely aligned as possible to the other clients or the public funds run by the manager.

While not strictly a trade allocation question, if the personnel of the fund are allowed to trade for their own accounts, one needs to be assured that the internal regulation of that behavior protects the outside investor. Evaluating the internal trading rules of the manager is a point of emphasis for external regulators, but for unregistered partnerships one must rely heavily on the integrity of the principals.

The trading of off-exchange derivatives or non-listed securities requires the use of a broker or a dealer. Here it is particularly difficult to determine the quality of the pricing. Areas of potential abuse occur when a manager trades too frequently with a particular counterparty. The smart manager will request quotes from several qualified counterparties, and remind every one of them how intent he or she is on getting the best execution. All of the same trade allocation issues discussed above for securities apply equally to OTC derivatives or special structures.

5.5.8.2 Brokerage Relationships and Soft Dollars

Commissions paid for the execution of stock or bonds trades vary widely. Prior to 1975, stock trading commissions were fixed by agreement across brokers. Not surprisingly, this collusive behavior produced fairly rich rates. When the SEC banned fixed commissions, rates fell as natural competitive pressures came into play. But since most people do not choose a broker on price alone, the resulting landscape was not uniform.

Some brokers provide execution services only, while others advertise additional value by also providing research. *Street research*, as it is called, is still widely used as part of a marketing pitch by many brokers. While many institutional fund managers believe their internal research is far superior to that of the street, there are others who find access to this information of value. It is therefore not an obvious problem when Manager A pays less than one cent per share to execute stocks while Manager B pays three cents a share to another broker.

The subjective question is whether there is any real value given to the investor from these increases in execution costs. Such execution costs are as much a drag on performance as any management fee, and it is difficult to assess whether there is any alpha associated with research that is provided. The picture is further clouded by the existence of *soft dollar* payments from the broker to the fund directing trades to them.

Soft dollars are potential rebates of commissions to be used for research. They are not paid directly to the manager but are used as a kind of prefunded expense account for certain activities and services. A first cousin to this practice is known as *commission recapture*, which is a literal rebate on commissions once volume hits a certain level.

Regulators have for some time made this area a priority for their examinations. They want to assure that the manager only spends the soft dollars on the narrow range of allowable research expenses and not on general administrative outlays. But the regulators are not in a good position to evaluate whether the expenses are reasonable or not. Is $20,000 too high a price to pay for a weekend investment seminar in Napa Valley? The world is filled with such opportunities that are advertised as being eligible for soft dollar payment.

Many managers no doubt view their soft dollars as a subsidy to their business, primarily shedding costs onto their investors. Other managers take the opposite extreme position in this area. They say that they negotiate their trading fees as low as possible with every broker. For those brokers that charge a premium commission, but allow the investor to recapture part of the commission through rebates, the manager credits the fund that generated the trade with the rebate. 100% of any benefit accrues to the fund and its investors. Managers who can document this practice have little trouble with that part of their regulatory review. Investors should acknowledge and reinforce this behavior whenever possible.

Some large funds pride themselves on paying fees that are not rock bottom on the theory that the more important they are as brokerage customers the better treatment they will receive from their brokers in terms of execution and information flow. This borders on the unethical. Brokers have a fiduciary responsibility to treat all their clients fairly. Wall Street is a large information machine, and if you ever get the impression that you are the last to learn some important news, or worse, that information about your trading intentions is not being treated confidentially, it is time to change brokers. Managers who encourage such broker behavior are likely to be also cutting ethical corners elsewhere in their process.

Hedge funds and many other investment managers often require services beyond those of traditional brokerage firms. Prime brokers typically offer all the traditional services but they also provide credit and some administration that go meaningfully beyond the basic model. Given the comprehensive nature of the business relationship between an investment manager and its prime brokers, competition is strong to get the best hedge fund managers signed up. At times when market liquidity is great and credit conditions are easy, prime brokers will aggressively court even small and midsize hedge funds.

There are two schools of thought concerning prime brokerage. Some investors think it is a virtue for an investment manager to have an exclusive, all-encompassing prime broker relationship with one firm. The advantage of this approach is that the brokerage house extending credit to the investment manager in theory sees all of the transactions and can apply their risk management discipline to the process. The downside comes from having less competition across brokers and the risk that something should happen to one's prime broker that could interrupt critical business during times of market volatility.

Most significant hedge funds have decided that the business risk of having a single prime broker is simply too great. They instead have competing prime brokers that offer a degree of redundancy should any one of the brokers experience an interruption of service for any reason. Savvy investment managers beginning in 2007 began expanding their relationships across brokers in anticipation of potential volatility and risk. While few clearly forecast the actual difficulties that were experienced, when the credit and liquidity chaos reached a crescendo in the first quarter of 2009 those who had planned ahead and established multiple lines of credit were in a superior position to assure their own business and investment continuity.

Investors doing due diligence in this area should ask for a list of all the prime brokers that the manager actively uses. You should also ask for a history of the relationships to see if there have been any changes and why those changes took place. Ask for contacts at the prime broker who can be used as a reference. It is unlikely that a current prime broker contact will say anything negative about a client, but it is still important to verify the basics of the relationship.

Different parts of the institutions that act as prime brokers may often serve an additional function as a swap counterparty to the investment manager. Over-the-counter (OTC) derivatives are an important part of many modern portfolios, and prime brokers often provide their basic service at very low profit margins in order to get an introduction to the more lucrative swap business. Not all investment managers participate in these kinds of transactions, but for those who do a new set of due diligence questions arise.

5.5.8.3 ISDA Relationships and OTC Derivatives

Financial derivatives have been an important implement in an investment manager's tool kit for decades. Exchange-traded derivatives have highly organized clearing and settlement procedures, at least on par with listed stocks and bonds. OTC derivatives share many of the investment features of their exchange-traded cousins, but the trading and administration of OTC products is another world. Too many investment managers begin trading these products with an inadequate appreciation of the complexities involved.

The first question of due diligence in this area covers the extent of the business.

Is it a primary activity or just an occasional thing? If it is the latter, ask the manager why they are doing it at all. There are many ways to express an investment opinion using securities and exchange-traded instruments. Adding OTC derivatives as a sideline may be an indication of laziness or ignorance of the space, where the manager is willing to implicitly pay a swap dealer a handsome structuring fee rather than build the exposures from scratch. Since any OTC activity carries with it extra burdens on the operations side, you want to be convinced that the activity is worth the bother.

The *International Swaps and Derivatives Association*, commonly known as ISDA, largely organizes activity in OTC derivatives. ISDA serves many functions, but perhaps its greatest contribution to the industry was in the standardization of many terms in a *swap agreement*. It is standard operating procedure today to establish ISDA agreements with all of your potential counterparties before trading begins. A common question using the jargon of the trade is to ask a manager, "How many ISDAs do you have, and how many are active?" This is asking the manager how many counterparties can he or she do business with in OTC instruments and how many are currently being used.

This is relevant from a number of dimensions. If the investment manager only executes OTC trades with one counterparty, poor prices may result. Swap dealers understand quite well whether their counterparties are aggressive in seeking out the best bids and offers or are merely looking for quick execution without being sensitive to price. A little competition goes a long way in this business and can make a great deal of difference in the ultimate performance of the trade.

The other important dimension in the counterparty equation is credit risk. If your only counterparty in the summer of 2008 was Lehman Brothers, the concentrated risk position could have jeopardized any profits in your OTC derivatives. The failure of Lehman Brothers in September of that year would have also left you without any active counterparties with whom to trade. Trying to establish new ISDA agreements in the fourth quarter of 2008 was a daunting task. It is far better to have multiple potential counterparties already established before any crisis befalls one of them.

In the early days of OTC derivatives, there was more reliance on credit evaluation and extension and less reliance on collateral standing behind the positions. It was assumed by most swap dealers that they had essentially a banking relationship with every one of their clients that was managed along fairly traditional banking lines. As people learned how these products could swing from profit to loss very quickly, *collateral* began to play an increasingly important role.

Today most OTC derivatives have initial collateral requirements for the clients. They also have precisely defined limits describing how much a position can lose before additional collateral must be posted. In the majority of circumstances the contracts are structured implicitly assuming that the swap dealer is credit worthy and the client is less so. If 2008 taught us anything, it is that swap dealers can pose considerable risk to their customers.

Serious swap counterparties, and this should include almost all fund managers, should negotiate swap agreements that have highly symmetric collateral requirements. As profits build up for you as a client, you should have the right to remove excess collateral from the position. You need to remember that embedded profits in an OTC swap are a liability of the swap dealer. If that dealer were to declare bankruptcy, those profits would become an unsecured claim on the bankruptcy estate. Keeping excess profits from building up by periodically sweeping excess collateral away from the dealer is the best protection a manager can have.

Any investment manager with a large OTC derivatives book should be able to describe in great detail how they manage their collateral arrangements. Those who live with asymmetric ISDA contracts are putting themselves at a disadvantage relative to the swap dealer. This can ultimately have meaningful negative implications for the portfolio's returns.

Marking an OTC derivatives portfolio for the purposes of calculating a net asset value for the fund can be a difficult area of due diligence examination. Unlike marking exchange-traded securities where obviously independent prices are available, marking OTC swaps can be subject to considerable subjectivity. The simpler the swap, the less challenging is the task of coming up with a good price. But swaps that incorporate leverage, optionality, or complicated pricing triggers can be quite complicated, and counterparties often disagree on the value. Understanding what latitude or influence the manager may have in coming up with OTC derivative prices will shed additional light upon how much reliance you can place on the manager's NAV.

OTC derivatives are of increasing interest to regulators around the world. The Dodd-Frank legislation placed great emphasis on trying to get more of the best practices from the exchange-traded world into place for these OTC products. The goal had been to get more swaps traded on *swaps execution facilities* (SEFs) and to have them collateralized and cleared much like futures contracts. A good due diligence question to managers using OTC derivatives is to determine what fraction of this activity is taking place with cleared swaps. The higher the number, the more mainstream the activity.

Even to the extent that these ongoing regulatory efforts are successful, the challenges of OTC derivatives remain. While it may be tempting to try to avoid investment managers using these products, this by itself would be a mistake. OTC derivatives have become much too powerful of a tool to avoid completely. Managers who avoid these instruments where they would be useful are probably limiting their abilities to make money.

Like many things in life, OTC derivatives represent a trade-off. Managers who use them well and responsibly can add value for their investment clients. Without skill and a strong ethic, however, the risks to investors can be meaningful. Understanding all of the dimensions of the OTC derivatives process is an increasingly important part of any due diligence process.

5.5.8.4 *Custody and Administration*

It was not that many years ago that paper shares of stocks and bonds, from which investors clipped coupons, were the norm. *Custody* of those assets involved keeping them safe and accounted for. With the world now characterized by electronic book entry of almost all securities, how custody services are provided has changed, but the basic principle has not.

Investment managers should have the ability to work with a wide range of global *custodians*. These institutions will range from global financial banks like J.P. Morgan and State Street to major brokers like Charles Schwab and Fidelity. The quality of custody of stocks and bonds relies heavily on checks and counter checks to assure the existence of securities in the appropriate accounts. To assume that all custodians around the world operate at a high level of accuracy and efficiency would be naive.

In addition to the major firms listed above, there are a large number of smaller organizations around the globe. Every investment manager that deals with such custodians must be prepared to have their back office confirm every transaction and movement of securities. They should also be willing to work with the investor to let them know if there are any difficulties in the custody relationship. While not technically their responsibility, any deviation from perfect service at the custody level will taint that investment experience and indirectly reflect poorly on the manager.

Investors should be particularly cautious about organizations that custody their own assets. Many of the great frauds in history were built on such a model. An independent custodian provides a natural check on the activities of an investment manager and offers another source of audit control. Investment funds that claim that their securities are so special that traditional custodians are not well-suited to the task should be questioned closely. The usual argument for self-custody is an economic one. The big firms charge too much for delivering such a basic service and there is no reason for that expense. There are many economical custody solutions available to investors. This is a very small expense relative to the protection it affords.

Global investing in stocks and bonds offers additional custody challenges. Even the largest global custodians don't have operations in every place that stocks and bonds are traded. In those instances they have *sub custodians* that have local resources, knowledge, and expertise. Like all chains, the total is only as strong as the weakest link, and due diligence in this area must make judgments about all of the participants in the custody process. Questions should be asked about liability assumed by the master custodian versus the sub custodians. If shares should go missing in a foreign jurisdiction, what is the process to protect the interests of the ultimate customer?

If everything in investment portfolios were a security, the custody and administration process would require great attention to detail, but at a fundamental level would be straightforward. Unfortunately many of the best investment opportunities cannot be custodied in the traditional sense. OTC derivatives, direct loans, real estate, traded bank loans, and physical commodities are a sampling of the things that find their way into investment portfolios. Each transaction involving such investments must be recorded and all the legal documentation behind them must be maintained. This is usually a cooperative effort between the fund manager and the *fund administrator*.

Fund administrators, like custodians, come in a variety of sizes and sophistications. Part of the due diligence process will evaluate the capabilities of the fund administrator. What is their asset base? How complicated are the instruments that it handles for fund managers? What types of investment managers make up the administrator's core business? While it is relatively rare today to find managers who self-custody their assets, you still find investment managers who self-administer their funds, using similar arguments. The portfolio is too complicated. An outside administrator doesn't really understand our investments. We do most of the work anyway, so why pay an outsider?

Increasingly, investors are more skeptical of self-administration. Like a strong custodian, a good outside administrator is a value-added check on the entire investment process. That is not to say that every administrator plays that role. There are too many administrators who allow the investment manager more latitude and input than they should. Unfortunately for the investor, the administrator sees himself or herself as working for the investment manager and not the ultimate investor. When disagreements arise, it takes a strong administrator with a solid economic foundation to push back and threaten the business relationship. From the due diligence perspective, the prospective investor should evaluate the manager's choice of administrator as critically as they do any service provider. One of the biggest areas of potential conflict is in the pricing of individual securities in the portfolio, which is the specific topic of a later section.

5.5.8.5 *Cash Movement*

An important subcategory of custody and administration concerns the movement of cash. How are clients' initial investments recorded? In what form are cash assets in the fund maintained and where? When securities are purchased, how does money move to pay for them? When securities are sold what assurances are there that cash returns to the fund? Who can authorize the actual removal of cash from the fund account and where can it go?

The reconciliation of *cash movements* should occur every day. What securities are bought or sold and what cash is used for those transactions, the deposit or withdrawal of customer funds, and any paid expenses from the fund should all be accounted for. Some funds may think that less frequent reconciliations are adequate, but daily cash reconciliations are an important first line of defense against inappropriate activity or outright fraud.

The fund manager should have well-documented procedures for who may authorize the movements of cash. Ideally, the movement of cash out of a fund should require two independent signatures, with neither signer being a party to the transaction. Where fund money can be sent should be established in advance of the transfer request. For example, all eligible customer accounts to receive redemption proceeds should be recorded well before the client asks to redeem.

In general, you would want to see separate cash accounts for the fund and for the management company of the fund. The first would contain all of the investment cash flows, which include customer subscriptions and redemptions, interest rate payments, and dividends. The second would be used to manage the expenses of the management company. Whenever the management fees are debited from the fund, there should be an explicit and documented transfer between the two accounts.

Fund managers that deal only in listed securities will have accounts at different brokers. These accounts will of course include cash balances. It is generally considered good practice today to not leave large sums of cash within a brokerage account. While there are protections available from SIPC and ultimately the bankruptcy code, a regular cash sweep from these accounts minimizes the chance of problems. The downside of this practice is the cash sits outside of the brokerage account and must be carefully accounted for.

Commodity trading advisors and many hedge funds regularly trade in exchange traded and OTC derivatives for which only a good-faith margin deposit is required. In these circumstances the funds generally maintain very large excess collateral pools of cash. Since the leverage employed by the fund manager can vary over time, it is possible for this excess collateral to be reduced without affecting the trading positions. This is a due diligence area of great importance. Who is allowed to move money from the excess cash held outside of the derivatives transactions? Unfortunately, there are many examples of fraudulent fund managers who have dipped into the excess collateral pool for their personal use. Sometimes these transfers are disguised as loans to shell companies. Sometimes the fraud is less elaborate. Whether the manager ever had the intention of repaying the withdrawn funds is immaterial. As excess collateral leaves, the limited partner investors are put at risk as their money is being employed in ways they never envisioned or authorized.

Everyone doing due diligence on a fund manager should find the cash management practices completely transparent, subject to independent verification and control, and almost annoying in their attention to detail. This is Fund Operations 101, and every high-quality fund manager places great emphasis on being completely buttoned-up in this area. Falling short is an invitation to error and fraud. Investors should accept no compromises in this area.

5.5.8.6 *Pricing of Securities and the Calculation of the NAV*

Fund managers who only own liquid, exchange-traded stocks should be able to calculate the *net asset value*, or NAV, of their fund holdings literally seconds after the market closes. Today's modern communications and high-speed computers allow virtual real-time calculations of profits and losses in any such investment portfolio. Investors in these funds have come to expect this kind of precision in all of their investments. The sad truth is that most investment funds are far different from this ideal. Focusing on this element of operational due diligence allows investors to establish confidence that when they make an initial investment, or execute a redemption, it will be done at a fair price.

Consider a hedge fund that has in it exchange-traded stocks, privately negotiated bank loans, OTC derivatives, and real estate. The exchange-traded stocks are trivial to price on a regular basis. The bank loans and OTC derivatives may have several dealers that make a market in these types of transactions, or they may be "traded by appointment." The real estate holdings are likely to have at best an appraisal done at irregular points in time. Combining all of these transactions into one portfolio makes calculating NAV a genuinely challenging process.

All fund managers should have well-documented policies for the calculation of their NAV. If exchange-traded prices are not available, there will usually be efforts made to acquire broker quotes as the best indication of investment's value. For bonds that trade irregularly, matrix pricing may be used where historical spreads to other more actively traded bonds are used to establish a price. As investments become less and less liquid, like real estate, there may be policies in place to hold these investments at cost until there is a tangible market event to adjust them.

Since all purchases and sales of units of the fund happen at calculated NAV, it is essential that this number be accurate. If the NAV is too low, new buyers get to come into the fund at a discount, disadvantaging the current investors. If the NAV is too high, redeemers similarly get to take more out of the fund than they deserve. Anyone investing in a mature, ongoing fund has a strong interest in seeing that the NAV is broadly fair.

In the last several years pricing categories, or levels, of investments have been established. *Level one investments* are those with readily available public market prices. Level two consists of securities that do not trade on a formal exchange but typically still have active dealer markets. Many bonds fall into this category. Level three, the final category, includes all other investments, which covers a wide range of liquidity and price availability. The investor will want to know how much of each type of investment a portfolio typically holds, and the manager's pricing procedures for each.

Just because a manager has formal procedures in place, it does not mean that the calculated NAV is a true reflection of value at any given point in time. The savvy investor will want to look at specific examples of pricing on days when there was a meaningful market move, and then ask why a particular investment was or was not priced in line with the market. This is particularly relevant for large mutual funds that have fewer opportunities for bets away from their competitors. If all but one or two mutual funds in an asset class are having an off day, week, or month, particular scrutiny should be placed on the actual pricing of assets by the outliers.

One should be particularly aware of opportunities by managers to influence brokers or supposedly independent third-party pricing sources when it comes to evaluating highly illiquid securities. Some managers are large enough to buy entire issues of a bond, or build customized derivatives that only apply to them. If the independent source of data wants to mark these investments down, they may meet resistance from the manager. If the manager is an important source of revenue for the broker, then there is always the potential for business pressures to overcome the independence of the information.

Private equity funds pose fewer issues in this regard than partnerships or mutual funds that allow continuing investments or redemptions. Usually the NAV of a private equity fund is simply an indication that allows the investor to mentally assess how the fund is doing. Since the commitment lasts many years, and the ultimate payout is a function of transactions in the portfolio, interim NAV calculations don't materially affect the economics of the investment.

It is a completely different story for hedge funds. Not only do new investments and redemptions get made at the calculated NAVs, but also the fund manager's performance fees are regularly calculated on these values. This means that before any actual realizations occur a fund manager can be getting paid. If subsequent valuations show a loss there may not be a facility to claw back already paid performance fees. This makes the calculation of the NAV of even greater importance.

Possibly the worst abuses in the calculation of NAV come from portfolios that are *marked to model*. The Granite Fund in the early 1990s was a highly leveraged fund specializing in esoteric mortgage-backed securities. Its PPM clearly stated that these were potentially illiquid securities that may not have a continuous bid. In the event that bids were not available from the broker community the fund had the right to estimate the NAV from its proprietary models. In February 1994, when the Federal Reserve began raising interest rates, virtually every bond fund in America showed a loss on their portfolio. The Granite fund for one month showed a gain. True believers thought this showed the superiority of the fund's investment process. More experienced investors were skeptical and began to redeem. When the fund needed to sell securities to meet those redemptions the actual bids were well below what the model said was fair. The fund quickly lost virtually all its value and went out of business.

Model pricing generally works well when the markets are calm and there are no liquidity issues. Unfortunately, no one is ever concerned about the accuracy of the NAV in times like these. The due diligence starts with close examination of the fund documents to determine the pricing process. That must be followed up with actual examination of the process in action to see if reality matches the promise.

This can be particularly challenging when it comes to regulated mutual funds, since they have fairly limited transparency requirements, and a lot of window dressing of portfolios can occur before the end of a quarter. It would be nice to believe the SEC offers the investor some protection against pricing shenanigans when they do their periodic fund reviews. It is more realistic to expect a deceptive mutual fund manager to be three steps ahead of the regulator when it comes to understanding market dynamics and pricing. As long as the formal pricing policies are being followed and documented, the regulator is likely to sign off, even if there are fundamental inequities occurring.

Some hedge fund managers have begun to engage their audit firms to help them check their pricing on a quarterly basis. The idea is to give investors more comfort that the NAV calculations are done fairly. If the auditor has a large database of transactions done by their institutional fund clients, such an independent check can be an important source of finding pricing anomalies. But once again, the auditor must be viewed as working for the fund and not the clients of the fund. One's own due diligence is more important than the work of any outside vendor.

5.5.8.7 *Audits of the Firm and Fund*

Audits of both the fund and the management firm are important sources of outside control. They are certainly not a complete deterrent of fraudulent activity, but they act as an important check that the process controlling the investment fund is intact. But not all audits are created equal. Due diligence in this area requires a review of the work product and the firm conducting the audits. Experienced investors learn that they can rely more on certain auditors, but just seeing a familiar name as the fund auditor is not enough.

The expenses involved in a fund audit are almost always passed on to the investors of the fund. Young managers operating with smaller pools of capital may be unwilling to incur the larger expenses that the name brand auditors usually bring with them. Every dollar of expense is potentially a noticeable drag on net performance. There are many fine auditing firms that do work for the investment community. Some investors believe that you should avoid anything but the largest and most experienced firms, but such an approach may unfairly penalize the smaller or specialty auditor that can do honest and excellent work.

The key is to determine that the manager is using an auditor that has experienced resources and is capable of fairly reviewing all of the activities within the fund. It is perfectly acceptable to reach out to the auditor and perform due diligence on them. How many investment fund clients do they have? What types of funds and investments do they audit? How long have they been engaged with this manager?

If you discover that an unknown firm is auditing a multi-billion-dollar investment fund, this is a potential problem. Once the investment fund gets to a certain size the fixed cost of doing an audit becomes quite small in terms of basis points of NAV. While you always want your manager to be thoughtful in the expenses that are charged to the fund, large and complicated investment pools probably require one of the top-tier auditors. On the flip side, if a meaningful part of an auditor's income comes from a single large family of funds, there is less assurance that objectivity can be maintained.

The primary objective of a fund audit is to verify the transactions that took place over the period of review, the assets and liabilities in the fund at the end of the period, and the pricing of those assets and liabilities. The location and movement of cash is an important subset of this examination. Some fund audits use a sampling approach to transactions made over the year. That is, they do not do a complete reconciliation of all trades, but instead spot check transactions to verify their accuracy. A more expensive but obviously more thorough approach is to do a complete census of all trades. Ask the manager and the auditor which approach is used for the fund in question and why they have taken that route.

As previously mentioned in the calculation of NAV section above, a still somewhat rare, but highly attractive, activity is the periodic review of fund pricing outside the regular annual audit cycle. Some large, complicated funds have begun to ask their auditors to review the pricing of the portfolio on a quarterly or more frequent basis. This not only has the advantage of providing extra confidence to investors that the monthly NAV calculations are on a firm foundation, but also eases some of the burden that would normally accumulate over the year before the audit. By having the auditor engaged continuously during the year, there is a better chance of a smooth functioning annual audit and a timely report.

Investors should ask whether the funds received a clean audit, or whether there were any reportable conditions. If you can examine a copy of the audit's final report, then that is even better. Your due diligence is searching for evidence that there were any deviations from standard trading, pricing, or custody practices. The timing of the audit is also of interest. Uncomplicated funds can be typically audited in a reasonable time. Delays in the release of the final audit report can be red flags. But one must also keep in mind business reality when it comes to timing. A fund manager with many funds will typically instruct the auditor to prioritize the largest and most successful funds first. Smaller fund managers may find that their audit firms prioritize larger clients in front of them. If you invest in a small fund, or a startup manager, you should perhaps not be too concerned if your audit is not at the top of the stack.

Many investors stop their due diligence with the fund audit. This is a mistake. One should also investigate the audit of the management company for the fund. This is an important source for data about the viability of the investment company. Again one wants to see a clean audit, with no reportable conditions. Of particular concern would be notations about lax cash management practices, or deficiencies in financial controls.

Sadly, the existence of good audits for either funds or management companies is not definitive. Frauds are usually perpetrated by people who work very hard to keep their activities hidden from view. Auditors primarily work with the data they are provided. They are rarely in a position to act as forensic experts. Good auditors have enough experience to identify environmental warning signs and dig more deeply. But some of the best fraudsters in history have come from back office and accounting backgrounds, and they know how to avoid these telltale signs. Everyone wants to blame the auditor after a fraud is discovered, but in reality nobody should expect perfection from this review.

5.5.8.8 Legal and Regulatory Due Diligence

The legal and regulatory foundation of a fund manager relates to a type of risk that has nothing to do with market price movements or volatility. An investor should think about this as evaluating the question, "What can happen to me and my funds if bad things happen in the market or to the manager?" The answers to this question lie buried in a mountain of documents that legally define the fund and the management company. These documents were created for one reason, and one reason only, and that is to protect the fund manager. They are universally written to the fund's advantage. The prospective investor can try to negotiate the terms that they believe are most problematic, but in many cases this is a take it or leave it world. Investors must be prepared to walk away if the terms are too onerous.

At the top of the stack are the documents that define the fund. *Registered mutual funds* will have a *prospectus*. *Private partnerships* will have a *private placement memorandum*, or PPM. These documents define the investment strategy, any investment limitations within the fund, the liquidity terms, and the fees. They should also explain what expenses are paid by the fund versus the management company. These documents will explain what the manager may do with investments if the fund must be liquidated. During the most severe times of 2008 and 2009 too many investors discovered that their funds had the right to distribute investments in kind, or to create *side pockets* or *liquidating trusts* where less liquid investments would reside until the manager decided at their sole discretion that it was an opportune time to sell them.

It is perfectly understandable why a fund would place language in its documents that gives it maximum flexibility. It is common sense that you do not want to establish grounds in your legal documents that would allow your investors to sue you if there is a market outcome that disappoints. Having said that, these documents are typically so dense that many investors treat this language as boilerplate and do not think about the implications for them at a time of market crisis.

The evaluation of the fund's legal language should always be done in terms of what is reasonable for the investment process. A manager who actively trades large-cap stocks or other completely liquid securities may find it desirable to have a long lockup, infrequent redemption dates, and long notice periods, but these are features entirely for his or her convenience and not for the protection of the investor. There are many other investment pools that trade genuinely illiquid investments for which such features are absolutely essential.

Mismatches between the fund's liquidity terms and the underlying investments in either direction should be a cause for concern. For example, if a manager builds a portfolio of privately negotiated loans and then turns around and offers daily liquidity, the investor should ask whether those liquidity terms could be met in any realistic fashion at a time of market volatility. Some new fund managers trying to raise capital after the financial crisis designed their funds with extremely attractive liquidity terms because, in their words, "investors were demanding it." Each of the funds offering easy liquidity protected themselves with language later in the document that allowed the manager to withhold redemption proceeds if the underlying investments did not support an easy liquidation. It is the investor's responsibility to see that the day-to-day headline fund terms are realistic.

It is in the prospectus or the PPM where one is likely to learn what expenses get charged to the fund. This can be an eye-opening experience. Some managers who by any objective standard already charge large management fees also succeed in letting the investors pay for a wide range of expenses that go beyond the normal investment practice. For some funds it seems that the word "management fee" is a synonym for "manager profit." When you visit a manager's office and you see a luxurious coffee bar or exercise facility, it is perfectly acceptable to ask whether those expenses are coming out of the manager's pocket or your fund investment. If such practices are disclosed in the fund document, the investor has no one to blame but himself or herself for allowing it.

There are many other documents in which investors should show great interest. For partnerships and separate accounts there will be a *limited partner agreement* and a *subscription document*. These define the terms under which investments are made. The manager should also have *articles of incorporation* for the firm. Any regulated entity will have documents that they file with their regulators. *Part II* of the *ADV* is the public version that managers are required to update with key information about their firm and funds. It is there where one gets the most accurate information on fund flows, and personnel changes.

As stated at the start of this section, the legal team of the manager, working only for the benefit of the manager, produces all of these legal and regulatory documents. It is perfectly acceptable to review them closely and challenge terms with which you do not agree. In such cases you may request an amendment to any document, which is typically called a *side letter*. Many managers, attempting to be fair to all of their investors, make it a policy not to execute side letters. In these circumstances your ultimate choice is whether to invest or not at terms you see as less than ideal.

Many institutional investors make it a practice of sending all of the manager documents to their counsel for review. This is a sound practice designed to protect everyone, but it requires supervision from people whose priorities are on the business side. For example, suppose you are a New York–based investor looking to begin an investment relationship with a Chicago-based manager. It is highly likely that the manager's documents will have a clause that says in the event of a dispute it will be adjudicated in Illinois. The outside counsel for the New York investor will argue that it would be better for a New York jurisdiction. One can burn up many basis points of return letting stubborn lawyers debate this topic. At some point in time, the investor may want to acknowledge that Illinois courts respect precedent as well as New York courts and move on. If the alternative jurisdiction in the manager's documents was Zimbabwe or North Korea, there may be a better case for raising a fuss.

By the time you are reviewing legal documents you have usually reached the stage where you want to make an investment. A big challenge is not to let that emotion get in the way of sound judgment. All the terms should be carefully reviewed to see how they potentially impact you from both a legal and a business perspective. There are some things worth fighting for, and ultimately if they are not fixed they could become a deal breaker. There are too many good managers out there to accept fund terms that are grossly disadvantageous to the investor.

More and more often investment managers are regulated entities. The Dodd-Frank legislation decreased dramatically the number of managers who could operate outside regulatory oversight because of their status as providers of private partnerships. While many managers have been regulated for years, many more are new to this environment. The careful investor can use this regulatory experience as part of their overall due diligence process.

Ask the manager when their last regulatory audits occurred. Be direct in your questions. Ask whether deficiencies were found and what actions were taken by the manager to correct these deficiencies. It is not unusual today for managers to be registered with the SEC as a Registered Investment Advisor, or RIA, but not yet have an SEC audit in their experience. The SEC has quite a backlog of firms that it needs to review. In these instances ask the manager what they are doing to prepare for the eventual visit. Some managers engage private consultants to review their documents and perhaps even conduct a *mock audit*.

To the extent that these managers make their regulatory compliance a priority, this is a good thing. One should be careful of firms that appear to be simply going through an exercise without the dedication to run a high-quality firm.

The SEC is not the only potential regulatory overseer. Some management companies register as broker-dealers and also have FINRA as a regulator. The CFTC requires registration of commodity trading advisors and commodity pool operators. Much of the regulatory oversight in this area is delegated to the *National Futures Association (NFA)*. Audits by these bodies cover somewhat different territory than SEC examinations of RIAs, but can be similarly revealing of the firm's deficiencies.

Regulatory due diligence should be open-ended. Ask the firm about their history of regulation with any domestic or foreign body, and then investigate the experience with that body. Firms sometimes drop their registration because of a change of business, but sometimes they are trying to avoid a checkered past. Brokers and locals banned from trading futures because of extreme abuse of public customer orders or mishandling customer funds have been known to reinvent themselves as hedge fund managers or registered investment advisors. Most regulators today have extensive websites that can be used to help verify the information given to you by the manager. As much as we would like to believe that regulated bodies operate with superior protections to unregulated ones, history shows this to be false. Use the information gathered by regulators to your advantage, but do not rely on it exclusively.

5.5.8.9 Anti-Money Laundering

A point of special attention in the last several years has been the use of investment funds to illegally move money. A simplistic scheme would have questionable money deposited into offshore bank accounts, which then are used to fund legitimate investment programs. Once those investments reach their maturity and capital is returned, it is sent back and has become entirely legitimate. To stop this behavior requires strong *anti-money laundering* (AML) policies at the investment manager.

"Know your customer" is a basic tenet. The manager should understand enough about the customer to satisfy fundamental questions about whether the funds being used are legitimate or not. The conflict here is that the manager seeking new investments may not want to offend the potential customer with too many questions. There are, however, appropriate ways of getting this information and the highest-quality managers are all dedicated to doing the right thing in this important area.

Anti-money laundering monitoring does not end once an investment is made. Any effective program watches cash flows carefully from all existing accounts, but does not require rocket-science complexity. How often are new investments or redemptions made? Are the sources of new funds different from the location where redemption proceeds are sent? Suspicious activity needs to be examined, and if enough questions remain unanswered authorities need to be alerted. The investment manager may not believe that such a program is a great way to keep investors happy, but no investment manager should want to be associated with investors using them as a conduit for illegal activity.

Regulators are increasingly tough on this part of their examinations. There are real links between attempts to launder money and terrorist activity, and financial regulators have been made sensitive to the need to be vigilant. What may appear to be a low-level risk for many money managers is in fact an area where the regulators will cut little slack. Potential investors will want to associate themselves with those managers that take all parts of their regulatory responsibilities seriously, but are particularly careful in this area.

5.5.8.10 *Internal Compliance*

Every money manager must have procedures in place to assure compliance with outside regulations and the fund terms that are offered to investors. All of these should be described in an internal *compliance manual* that employees are required to read routinely and attest that they are following the rules. Prospective investors should ask to see a copy of the internal compliance manual. Some managers will decline that request stating that their internal procedures are proprietary. In such instances the investor needs to somehow get comfortable that the document is a serious one and that it is being followed in practice.

Some compliance manuals only contain the bare minimum required by the regulators. Other managers have manuals that are quite thoughtful in that they go beyond the minimum to describe the culture that the manager seeks to establish. For example, many fund managers have very precise personal trading rules to avoid the possibility, or even the appearance, that the manager's staff can take advantage of information that would normally be used to benefit the investor. Such rules are effective only if there is a process in place that permits verification of compliance.

The due diligence process here needs to explore which employees are covered by the rules, and what part of the organization does the monitoring. An independent compliance officer is increasingly a part of the landscape, though many small firms lack the resources for such a stand-alone function. The Dodd-Frank legislation has greatly expanded the role and potential liabilities of a regulated firm's chief compliance officer (CCO). No matter what formal structure an investment manager has, enough independent checks and balances must be in place to assure that compliance is a real activity and not just window dressing.

Anyone who has gone through the training and examinations for broker licenses would tell you that there is a great deal of detailed information that needs to be learned. At the end of the day, however, most of the rules boil down to two general principles. You don't lie to your customer. You don't steal from your customer. One might assume that there is no need to be reminded of such basics, but history seems to suggest differently.

Consider a firm that has a strong investment history, but has a background that includes serious regulatory sanctions of a principal and sketchy internal policies. One school of thought says that as long as the firm is making money then everything is fine. A more cautious view would ask under what circumstances might the manager do something to take advantage of existing investors. A compliance manual will not prevent such behavior or guarantee an ethical organization. It will, however, be a regular, positive reminder to an organization that has established a strong culture of compliance.

Contrary to the impression left from headlines touting illegal and fraudulent behavior, there are many honest, hard-working money managers available to you. Avoiding firms that have the potential to do you harm through unethical behavior should be a priority of your due diligence.

5.5.8.11 *Technology*

It seems trite to say that technology has changed our world. But nowhere is this truer than in the world of investments. Today's portfolio manager has access to more fundamental and market data than was possible to analyze even 20 years ago. There are many good investors who rely on traditional analysis to make their decisions, but every day they face more competition from managers who deploy the most sophisticated technologies available. This part of operational due diligence will determine whether your manager is operating at a significant disadvantage or not.

The evaluation of technology should be broken into two parts. The first, covering the evaluation of trading opportunities, is considered much more interesting to some. The second covers the more mechanical elements of the investment process ranging from trade execution and allocation to accounting and reporting. This basic blocking and tackling is in many ways just as important as the technology that helps determine what trades happen and when.

In Section 5.2 of this chapter we discussed how there were only three basic ways of creating alpha: 1) having better information; 2) analyzing information better than the competition; and 3) lowering the cost of trading. Technology may not get you better information in the marketplace, but it can have a meaningful impact on the second two sources of alpha.

Some managers try to impress you with the vast resources dedicated to the technology of trading. This is vitally important in strategies that require active purchases and sales, but is less important for long-term buy and hold strategies. Any manager that claims to be adding alpha from *high-frequency trading* is engaged in an incredibly competitive arena where firms routinely spend tens of millions of dollars to keep their technology near state-of-the-art. This type of trading is constantly in need of updating and refinement to stay competitive.

Evaluating this technology is quite difficult. Not surprisingly the managers who have made such investments are rarely willing to pull back the curtain and show investors how the process works. While one can appreciate the secretive nature of any black box traders, the trust-me nature of the relationship puts investors at a meaningful disadvantage. What inefficiency in the market does the model exploit? What protections are embedded in the technology to prevent risk limits from being violated? How does the trading model respond to sudden changes in market volatility? These are fairly basic questions.

One sometimes is introduced to early-stage managers who claim to have developed trading systems that generate consistent, outsized returns. Since information on how this technology works is almost always highly proprietary, the prospective investor is in a tough spot. If an investment is made and the fund works, the manager collects a nice performance fee. If the promise is not fulfilled, the manager makes an apology and returns what's left of the money.

Perhaps if the technologically intensive training programs are so superior, their inventors should not need any outside capital. This is in fact how many high-frequency trading firms operate. They have such faith in their systems that they only use proprietary capital, and consequently avoid all of the complications of dealing with outside investors. When these firms, after many years of successful trading, decide to open their activities to outside capital or they sell their firms to larger, well-established financial giants, it is usually a sign that whatever technological edge they once had has waned.

The more mundane side of the technology ledger involves the tools to trade, settle, account for, and report the investment activity. Here the due diligence should cover whether the technology employed is adequate to the complexity of the investment process. It is not absolutely essential to have the most modern or most expensive technologies employed, but it is important that the tools are up to the task.

Anyone who has ever gone through a major technology project knows how much pain is involved. Major transitions of either hardware or software often cause great disruptions and should be undertaken only when the advantages of the transition are large. This means that systems covering accounting and reporting, where strong programs have been available for years, probably require more evolutionary enhancements steps than they do revolutionary change. But other areas can become quickly out of date.

The volume of trading activity across all securities and derivatives has literally exploded through time. The combination of investors, like hedge funds that can have a shorter trade horizon plus automated, high-frequency trading platforms, has made it imperative that technology be able to keep up with both the speed and volume of transactions. This environmental change has not affected all investment firms, but all managers should be able to take advantage of the technological improvements that have accompanied these changes.

One area where technology has made a big difference is trade allocation. In the old days managers had fairly mechanical rules, but it often relied heavily on human intervention that was subject to error or worse. Managers who have responsibility for separately managed accounts should be using highly automated software to code individual fund guidelines and the methodology used to allocate trades as fairly as possible across the accounts.

The other elements of due diligence relating to technology involve the processes the firm uses to manage change. Are the computers used for development segregated from those in production? Are the new systems run in parallel beta mode before they are implemented and for how long? You want to try to determine how sophisticated the manager's technology team is and how likely are any disruptions caused by that team dropping the ball.

Some smaller organizations have chosen to largely outsource their technology function. This is a highly practical solution that, if executed with a quality firm, minimizes the fixed cost investments in technology as well as the likelihood of a major service disruption. While technology is a special area of inquiry in the due diligence process, the final objective is to establish that this critical element of business operations is efficient and secure.

5.5.8.12 Cybersecurity

Cybersecurity at managers, brokers, and custodians has taken on outsized importance in recent years, as criminals scattered across the globe look for computer vulnerabilities everywhere in the financial chain. This is a cat-and-mouse game where there never seems to be an end to increasingly clever mice. This special subset of technology due diligence should focus on several topics. What has been done to protect access to critical data? Is that data encrypted securely so that in the event of a breech no critical information is lost? What are the risks that someone gaining unauthorized access can hold data hostage for ransom?

The biggest vulnerabilities to any firm's computer systems usually come from trusted employees. Someone opens an email attachment that contains malware and the system is compromised, perhaps not obviously so. Invasive pieces of software can sit quietly in a system, undetected, as they gather information that can be used for financial gain. The best defense is thorough and ongoing training of all staff members to minimize the chance of these incursions.

Regulators are stepping up their efforts to check on cybersecurity efforts of their regulated entities, but nobody should expect miracles simply because the government has taken an interest. Every entity in the financial chain already has a strong private interest to protect their customers' assets and their own reputation. Insurance against loss due to cybersecurity breaches is increasingly common and due diligence should check on its existence and scope.

5.5.8.13 Disaster Recovery

Service disruptions can come from a variety of sources both natural and man-made. Hurricanes periodically strike financial centers disabling entire communities. But we have also seen terrorist attacks in various financial capitals around the world. Power outages and failures of communications and transportation can act separately or in combination to severely disrupt the operation of any investment manager. Some think due diligence on disaster recovery plans is largely a technology exercise, but it has a much more important human dimension as well.

Every investment manager and advisor should have a detailed *disaster recovery plan* to minimize disruptions. Such plans will typically involve data backup and recovery sites well removed from the main location of the firm. Increasingly cloud solutions are being employed as well. But these plans will also discuss how key employees will continue to stay in contact with the market, clients, and each other. Larger firms will typically have much more intricate plans that can involve alternative sources of power and telephone service, or even remote locations where key employees can gather to continue working.

Part of the due diligence process should be to ask how the firm performed at different times of crisis. Firms well beyond lower Manhattan were affected on 11 September 2001 when the World Trade Center was attacked. While it took several days to resume trading on the US stock markets, other markets around the world continued to trade. Some investment managers were quickly able to resume their key activities operating in the available markets. Others had difficulty and operated only with greatly reduced capacities. Ask the manager about its experience and what changes were made subsequently as a result.

Japanese-based firms can be asked about the impact of the 2011 tsunami and subsequent nuclear reactor concerns. It is a rare manager who has not had to deal with some kind of serious disruption. It is appropriate to ask details about how trading and custody of assets was affected in such times and what the firm learned from those events. It is also important to know if and how communications with clients was suspended or delayed.

From the investor's perspective it is perhaps less important to have seamless trading opportunities across any disruption, and more important to emphasize the basics. Are the assets in the fund intact? Can they be appropriately valued? In some sense a short disruption in trading is comparable to adding an extra holiday in that the biggest risk is a lost opportunity to trade. For most long-term investors this will not make or break performance. Losing assets or seriously mispricing them in an NAV calculation can lead to a permanent loss.

While most of a firm's disaster recovery plan will focus on their own trading and operations, part of it must deal with their relationships to brokers, swap counterparties, administrators, and custodians. Investing is a highly interrelated activity and even the strongest investment manager may be damaged by links with ill-prepared service providers. Your due diligence of an investment manager should discover a healthy understanding of where the linkages may be faulty, and the steps the manager has taken to protect their assets.

Disaster recovery plans are one of the "check the box" items in any regulatory review of the manager. Knowing that a regulator has acknowledged the existence of a disaster recovery plan provides only minimal comfort. There is a big difference between adequate disaster recovery plans and genuinely thoughtful ones. This difference likely only becomes evident in the middle of a crisis, but that is a very poor time to update your due diligence files.

5.5.9   Background Checks: Public and Private Sources

Every investment manager should be able to provide a strong list of references that can attest to the quality of the firm and the senior people involved. At a minimum these references should represent relationships that have been long-standing, and ideally span both good and bad market environments. These references should all be checked carefully with an emphasis on trying to discover any potential deviations between what you expect and what is likely to be delivered. If possible, try to get some names of people who are no longer clients of the manager and ask them why they have left.

Everyone should expect these references to be favorable, even the ex-clients, since the manager supplied them. Since all good managers are quite circumspect about proprietary relationships, it should not be easy to find other current or past clients with whom to have independent conversations. But the investment management world is finite, and it is perfectly acceptable to reach out to other investors or managers you know with broad inquiries, which may or may not produce relevant information.

For regulated entities there are a number of public sources for background information. Who must be regulated and by whom is something of a patchwork quilt of complexity, but the landscape is not so jumbled as to be unworkable for an outsider. Registered investment advisors, mutual funds, commodity pools, commodity trading advisors, broker dealers, and some private partnerships all get regulatory oversight by one or more bodies. The SEC, CFTC, FINRA, and the NFA all maintain public, searchable websites to allow investors to examine public filings and, most importantly, disciplinary histories of both firms and individuals.

Some private partnerships have voluntarily decided to be registered with the SEC in order to give investors extra assurance about their operations. As all of the Dodd-Frank provisions have become fully effective, many more partnerships are now registered and fully complying with the rules. However, some prominent hedge funds like the one run by George Soros decided to return all outside money rather than jump through the regulatory hoops. Through time the database on which to do background checks will become a much richer source of information for potential investors.

Anyone doing due diligence should be creative with these resources. A hedge fund or private equity manager might have no formal regulatory obligations today, but that does not mean there are not relevant facts in these databases from the past. History includes examples of individuals essentially banned from a regulated market that reinvented themselves as private investors and then unregulated hedge fund managers. Caveat Emptor is the operative motto in these instances.

Particularly discriminating due diligence should go beyond the publicly available regulatory resources, but this may be beyond the scope of most investors' abilities or resources. Specialty firms, sometimes founded by ex-FBI personnel or other security specialists, offer a wide range of background checks. For particularly important investments, or those with long lockups, an outside background check might be warranted.

In this area the sky's the limit. Practical questions need to be answered about how many of the investment firm's employees should be reviewed and to what extent. Basic checks verify education and employment history, public filings and litigation, arrest records, and data that can be gleaned from an intensive Internet search. With much more expense, you can get interviews with neighbors and past colleagues, plus examinations of less public records. Imagine what the FBI would look at in your past if they were interested in you for a job. That's how extensive some of these checks can be.

Is this really necessary? Maybe. There are venture capital and private equity firms who perform the most extensive (and expensive) checks on all of the top management team members of companies targeted for investment. Any serious red flags can kill the deal. But these firms are preparing to commit millions of dollars of the

LPs and their own money to investments that can span many years. Missing a behavioral flaw in a key person because they were unwilling to spend several thousand dollars for a thorough background check would demonstrate a false economy.

For the average investor background checks are a matter of costs and benefits. It may be worth some effort and resources to get a basic check on a mutual fund team, but there are other protections in place, including the right to redeem on any day, that might mitigate the need to go overboard on such a check. On a big, illiquid private investment, the extra expense of the full-bore approach might make a lot of sense.

The biggest failing in this area is laziness. You might actively want to send money to a fund. The track record is right. The market feels right. The prospects look great. As a bonus, you discover a respected friend who has been an investor for a while and has had a good experience. That's all you needed to hear. You are in.

It is hard to estimate how much money has been avoidably lost in situations like this. Never assume that someone else has done your homework for you, or has done it as well as you would have liked. There are no investments so wonderful that they have to be executed today. Check references, scan public websites and do background checks where appropriate. Certainly, it is an expense and a bother, but sleeping better because you have well-founded confidence in a manager is worth a lot.

5.5.10 Confidence and Trust

Confidence and trust are the two requisite characteristics that should be in place before any investment is made. You build confidence and trust through the due diligence process. In a successful investment relationship both traits should grow through time. This is your ultimate goal and at any 40,000-foot level it is a straightforward concept. The actual execution contains many practical challenges.

Investors must decide for themselves what level of confidence in a manager is enough to start a relationship. This is perhaps the most introspective topic in this book. Some investors put the highest priority on making money without much regard for how it is done. They are looking for the smartest, toughest, and scrappiest managers who succeed perhaps by staying just on the right side of the law and ethics. Some might say it is okay to cross those lines as long as you don't get caught. It would be naive to suggest that there are not a great number of investors in this camp, and many managers that respond to them. The fact that these kinds of managers sometimes fail in their goals and also create problems from the way they do business is viewed as just another form of investment risk.

It is almost impossible to gauge the ethics and motivation of any investment manager. Many individuals with spotless track records and resumes filled with civic good deeds have been found to be amoral fraudsters. That is why extensive due diligence on their process of investing is so important. Understanding how money is made and what risks are being assumed is more important in building confidence than any track record. There are no sure things in the investment world except for the fact that there will be periodic disappointments. Understanding what might create those disappointments beforehand allows one to make reasoned decisions.

The Madoff fraud is as good an example of the challenges as any. Bernie Madoff ran a broker dealer that like many such organizations not only executed stock trades, but also had a number of discretionary trading accounts for clients. History is not completely clear about when the fraudulent behavior began, but at some point the brokerage statements depicting stock and option sales and purchases became largely fictitious for a large group of customers. The returns for these customers were steady, if unspectacular. When asked about the strategy behind the accounts, it was broadly characterized as a synthetic option spread strategy. This label was more complicated than most of the clients could understand. It sounded impressive and the results were good. No more inquiries were made.

Clients probably took comfort from the fact that the NASD, later rebranded FINRA, regularly audited the Madoff broker dealer. They received regular brokerage statements that may not have appeared as polished as those they received from Merrill Lynch or Fidelity, but they showed cash flows that appeared to be consistent with their experience. Later in the fraud, investment managers became brokerage clients of Madoff and then sold investment products based on the scheme. To add another layer, some fund of funds added these products to their portfolios. None of the investors in these funds could have any knowledge of what was going on underneath, relying almost exclusively on past and, as it turns out, fraudulent track records.

A decade after the fraud was revealed, Madoff is in jail and through considerable effort from the bankruptcy trustee, investors have received back more of their original investment than they might have originally expected. Madoff is only different from the countless other fraudsters who take advantage of people's hopes and aspirations by the magnitude of his fraud. Some of his victims no doubt believed in the perceived merits of his investment plan. Others actually admitted that they had no idea how he made money, and suspected that a source of his profits was trading on information embedded in the buy and sell orders of his brokerage customers. This did not sound particularly virtuous, but as long as the trading program made money and the regulators gave him a clean bill of health, who could complain?

Madoff's investors had great confidence in his approach and trusted him personally. Both confidence and trust were terribly betrayed. While there may have been warning signs and many questions along the way, there was no history of bad behavior to send up obvious warning signals. Not all fund managers start with such a clean slate.

In the United States and in many cultures around the world, it is generally acknowledged that people can make mistakes. If the mistakes are severe enough they might lead to civil or criminal penalties. In principle, we generally like to believe that people can learn from their past behaviors, and once they have paid their debt to society, they can move on and lead productive lives. That is a fine principle, but it need not be the defining rule of behavior when it comes to deciding where to invest your money.

Imagine doing due diligence on a long-standing, successful private partnership hoping to ultimately make an investment. In this process you discover that one of the principals who has primary responsibility for risk management received a severe regulatory sanction when he was working at an exchange many years earlier. The offense involved working with other brokers to defraud customers, and the penalty was essentially a ban from the industry. What should you do?

Some might say the past is the past and the more relevant history is the one of producing good returns for his clients. Others might be more wary and ask themselves whether the first episode was an example of poor judgment in one's youth, or a manifestation of a fundamental character flaw. The key question is whether this person would try to steal from current investors or indirectly damage them through some bad behavior if the chips were down today.

Every potential investor will answer the question of whether or not to invest with the aid of his or her own moral compass. When you hire an investment manager you are not looking for a dinner companion or someone with whom to discuss current events. You should not expect them to be part of your inner circle, but the relationship is so important that you should expect to be able to trust them in any circumstance. If you do not, and you rely on a belief that you can somehow extricate yourself from a bad situation before it happens, you probably are kidding yourself and should not invest.

There is a small chance you might sniff out trouble at a mutual fund and liquidate your position before the majority of investors, but with hedge funds and other private programs, the liquidity terms work against the likelihood of getting out before the fire alarm sounds. And in the case of actual frauds like Madoff, even those investors who withdrew money in the years prior to the scheme imploding were dragged back into the litigation and had to return at least part of their assets.

There is no simple rule to follow when deciding to invest or not. Only a total evaluation can help you answer the question, "Am I completely comfortable trusting this manager with my money?" Reputations are difficult to establish and easy to tear down.

Once an investment is made, it is no time to rest. Each manager should be evaluated continuously to confirm that the original confidence and trust were well placed. That is the topic of the next section.

5.6   ONGOING MANAGER EVALUATION

There is no "happily ever after" when it comes to investments. Once a decision is made to begin an investment relationship, the learning period has just begun. Deconstructing returns as they are announced and getting to watch the portfolio team work in real time are both important parts of the ongoing evaluation.

Before you made the first investment, you should have established how often you would communicate with the manager and in what form. Well-established mutual fund managers typically have large conference calls or web casts to try to make their communications as timely and uniform as possible for their client base.

These group efforts may or may not be sufficient for your needs. Some institutional investors insist on regularly scheduled calls of their own to further explore topics introduced in the group effort or to explore topics not otherwise addressed. All investors should be aware of the fact that rules governing mutual funds restrict their ability to give pertinent information about the portfolio to one group of investors and not another. If your question crosses the line, expect the manager to respectfully but appropriately decline to answer.

Discussions covering the *process* of the investment decisions in the period can be particularly useful. What made the manager change his opinion on interest rates? Why was a stock sold in the past quarter and not six months earlier when earnings started to decline? Questions covering liquidity and other important environmental topics can be asked privately and answers compared to those given by other managers.

As much of the initial investment due diligence involves the evaluation of historical returns, a good place to start is the analysis of returns in real time.

5.6.1 Evaluating Returns in Real Time: Positive and Negative "Outliers"

The first returns from the new manager are awaited with some anticipation. There's a good chance that any manager you hire will have a strong historical track record, but that is of no practical use to the new investor. The first returns will come in and be immediately compared to benchmarks and to expectations. In an example of what might be a special case of Murphy's Law, it will seem like early returns provide more disappointments than successes. This is unlikely to be true, and is more a function of our selective memories and unrealistic expectations.

No matter what the return, care should be taken to understand the sources of attribution. What made money and why? Were the losing positions due to general market movements, or were there security specific surprises? Most of the time if the preliminary due diligence has been thorough, then this attribution analysis will reinforce the previous work and not suggest any surprises.

Eventually there will be a positive or negative return that will stand out as an "outlier." Both require extra examination. Too often investors readily accept a surprising positive return as a sign of the manager's genius. This can of course be true, but such returns can also be the result of excessive risk-taking and a nice stroke of luck. If your portfolio manager were to reveal to you that last month's 20% return was due almost entirely to his fund buying a lottery ticket and succeeding, you would properly be suspicious about the chance of that event repeating itself. There are many less evident lottery tickets in the investment world, but it is important to try to differentiate between luck and repeatable skill in your portfolio.

Negative outliers cause the greatest consternation. It is likely that several times in your investment history you will have a manager who experiences his or her worst return ever in a given period. When that happens everyone is looking hard for an explanation. The first and most important question asks about the risk profile in place before the loss occurred. Was it typical for the environment? Had it grown suddenly in an attempt to take advantage of a perceived market imbalance? Or did it in fact have less expected risk than historically typical, but was overwhelmed by extreme market events?

If the extreme loss was caused by a sudden deviation from normal behavior or your expectations of what the manager would be doing, this can be a cause for termination. Many times, however, the extreme loss is a result of past disciplined practices not being completely appropriate for actual market events. The investor who likens paying active management fees to clairvoyance is bound to be disappointed time and time again. No manager bats 1.000. Even the best managers sometimes strike out with the bases loaded. The question you want to ask yourself is whether you want that manager to be at bat at critical times in the many innings that are yet to come.

Nobody likes to lose money. But there is a brighter side to the event if it occurs for legitimate reasons. The occasional losing streak is remarkably effective in discouraging ill-informed, short-term investors from trying to chase the "hot hand." Finding quality managers and sticking with them through good times and bad is a lot easier if they don't have massive swings in their assets under management.

Another advantage of the periodic loss is the ability to add to an investment at an attractive price. This is one of the hardest things to do in all of investing, but actually has great potential to add value through time if it is done with discipline and after a solid analysis of the fundamental opportunity. Some of this activity falls under the heading of rebalancing, but it also involves the opportunistic use of dry powder. The challenge when adding to a temporarily underperforming manager is trying to gauge what other investors will be doing. If the manager is facing large redemptions, the business headwinds may actually trump any investment opportunity that might be available. In such instances it is probably better to try to find similar investment themes elsewhere in the market rather than to risk going down with a sinking ship.

Investors must always be aware that portfolio decisions are made in the context of a dynamic market environment. The world that created a track record may not exist today. That is why ongoing attribution analysis never stops. A good manager is constantly learning and adjusting in sometimes-subtle ways to the market. The manager that claims to invest exactly the same way he or she did 20 years earlier is either oversimplifying or is dangerously unaware of how market dynamics change through time. The ability to have fear of the marketplace is a wonderful characteristic that helps managers stay current. Highly confident managers, who "know" that their process is right, run the risk of being swept away.

5.6.2   How is the Manager Doing?

Once you understand how a fund made or lost money, it is natural to try to give the manager a grade. Just like in school, the scale can be absolute or on a curve. As discussed in the previous sections, managers will grade themselves in their marketing literature in the most flattering terms possible. It is important for investors to have their own standards and to apply them consistently.

The two most common ways of grading are against benchmarks and against peers. Both need to be used with caution. If you ask an active manager to run a highly concentrated portfolio, not constrained by the terms of a benchmark, you can hardly fault that manager when their actual returns vary meaningfully from that standard. On the flip side, investors who expect their managers to be highly disciplined against the benchmark can be legitimately critical if they are off by too many basis points.

Peer rankings are relevant if you have confidence that all of the managers in the comparison sample are genuinely operating with similar risk and return goals. More typically what happens is that managers get combined under broad umbrellas without being truly comparable. Take for example fixed income managers. A manager who has been given the mandate to first and foremost preserve wealth in all market environments will likely have shorter duration and less credit risk than other fixed income managers working off of a short-duration benchmark. In periods of falling interest rates and shrinking credit spreads the capital preservation manager will lag the peer group. This does not mean the fund should receive a below average grade. Instead, it needs to be evaluated relative to the original mandate.

There will always be elements within a portfolio that explain differences between a fund and its benchmark or other funds in the asset class. Some of these factors are discretionary and getting them right should be a signal that the manager is doing the job asked. But for nondiscretionary factors the evaluation should be concerned with the execution of the mandate and not whether the environment was ideal for that strategy. For example, once you decide to invest in a fixed income manager who by design owns treasuries and agency securities, you should not fault the manager if high-yield bonds perform better.

The evaluation of hedge fund managers is always more challenging. By definition these managers are expected to remove certain market risks. Consider two managers in 2008. One manager preserved capital by eliminating most risk positions in the portfolio. The other made money by shorting key sectors of the market that were subject to great deleveraging. Which manager did a better job?

In a sense both managers did a good job, but the first manager's success was due to an ability to get out of the way of a speeding train. The second manager not only did this, but also managed to jump on board, and in that sense had the better performance. But investment decisions typically come in pairs, and subsequent events are essential in any complete evaluation. There were more than a few managers in both camps above who failed at the next level. Some who drove their exposure toward zero never got seriously reinvested as the markets rebounded after March of 2009. There were others on the short side of the market who believed quite sincerely in global economic ruin, and gave up much of their gain from 2008 on the rapid reversal.

This is why ongoing communication and evaluation is essential. Stopped clocks are correct twice a day, and just because you outperformed the market and peers in a tough period does not mean that future success is assured. Especially after good performance, investors need to re-underwrite each investment manager to ensure that the thesis and process is intact looking forward.

From a behavioral standpoint it is very difficult to objectively grade one's own managers. The bias is always to believe better things about people you have chosen, whether they are underperforming or outperforming. This makes it more difficult to pare back outperforming funds or sectors, because there is the belief that the good result was a result of fundamental genius that should repeat. It also makes it very difficult to terminate underperforming managers. Even when logic says termination is the best path, there is a strong tendency to want to wait until the loss is recovered. Eliminating as much emotion as possible from the investment decision should be an ever-present goal. There will be times when parting company with a manager is absolutely the best course of action. It is rarely easy to end a once well-functioning relationship, but there are a variety of reasons why it should happen.

5.6.3 Deal Breakers: Time to Terminate

Investment managers have a number of legal and contractual obligations to their investors. But investors usually have a much higher expectation for their managers than simply meeting the letter of the law or their investment agreement. There are times when the manager's shortcomings are so severe that termination is the only viable outcome. There is no definitive list of actions that should trigger a termination, but there are critical areas where failure to meet high expectations often lead to this outcome.

5.6.3.1 *Is the Process Broken?*

Every manager falls short of return expectations at some time. The discussions above highlight the challenges in sorting out whether such shortfalls are due to fundamental deficiencies or simply bad luck. But a fair question to ask is, "How long should an investor wait before pulling the plug on an underperforming manager?" Unfortunately there is no simple answer.

We have seen how statistics can only be partially helpful in this process. There is no magic number for returns, standard errors, or Sharpe Ratios that unambiguously signals that a decision should be made. Each investor needs to evaluate the process and the results to determine whether the manager in the future has a good chance of exceeding their goals and expectations.

Presumably you would not have invested originally if you did not believe in the process. To terminate the manager, you must conclude that either your original analysis was flawed or that the process has become broken along the way.

There are many ways that this can happen. Some of them are completely outside the manager's control. History is full of examples, particularly in the hedge fund space, where certain arbitrage opportunities produced wonderful returns for a while, but then were competed away. There was nothing you could point to that the manager did wrong. It was simply the case that the environment changed and the profit opportunity was eliminated. In these situations the investor must apply careful analysis to the current environment. Historical returns are of virtually no use. While there are some managers who will raise the white flag and acknowledge that the approach is no longer appropriate, most will try to keep their businesses together and press arguments for why they are likely to be successful going forward. This is a bit like asking a barber if you need a haircut. You are more likely to get an objective answer by looking in a mirror or asking your spouse.

Another way the process can break is from the weight of assets. Managing the size of an investment pool is one of the biggest challenges every portfolio manager has. There is no doubt that investment funds can be operated in the hundreds of billions of dollars, but there are many doubts that all successful, alpha-generating strategies can operate at a fraction of that size. The typical story has the successful manager building a track record on a modest base of assets. After years of working in relative obscurity they may be discovered and become an overnight success. Money comes in from all corners.

At the early part of this process there is usually excess capacity and the new investments do not hinder performance. If the manager is trading in big-cap stocks, sovereign debt or currencies they may believe that they have effectively no capacity constraints. This is almost always a mistake. Even the largest markets are not infinitely liquid and positions need to be scaled so that they can be managed with the dexterity they were when the fund created its track record.

The pace of growth also matters. Managers that grow very rapidly because of strong investment returns often attract "hot money" that can leave as rapidly as it arrived. Building portfolios as assets are coming in the door is a lot easier than managing asset sales to meet redemptions. Since fund flows can be a function of both individual performance and macroeconomic events, investors need to be aware of which of their managers are potentially vulnerable to big asset swings.

The negative impact on performance from rapid liquidations can erase many years of good outperformance. Sometimes it is best to exit or trim growing managers, even while their performance is strong, to avoid the risks that are potentially developing. This can be one of the hardest calls in all of investing.

If the manager has a strong history of adding value through security selection, but falls into a prolonged period of benchmark-like performance, the research process may be somehow broken. This is extremely difficult for an outsider to evaluate. People usually do not become stupid overnight, and before terminating such managers you should look for any other possible reason for their shortcomings.

Long-short equity managers, for example, may be suffering through a phase of high correlation between stocks. If you believe this is a passing phase, the investment should be maintained. If you believe it is a permanent part of the environment, the entire strategy and not just your manager should be questioned.

Investments in many hedge fund managers often come with some lockup and limited liquidity. These partnership terms define a natural minimum evaluation period. Unless one is willing to try to sell their interests in the secondary market, often at steep discounts to NAV, the investor will watch at least until there is a liquidity date. In fact, one of the things you implicitly sign up for in all private partnerships is an agreement to be as patient as the partnership terms require.

This, perhaps ironically, makes liquidity dates much more dramatic in terms of forcing decisions than investors face when they own liquid investments like mutual funds. As the deadline for the notice period approaches, the investor must either liquidate or agree to another term for their investment. They may not be entirely sure that they want to terminate the manager, but they know that once the opportunity is passed they will be once again locked in until the next available notice date. Many questioning investors pull the plug rather than sign up for another hitch where the performance could be as bad or worse.

There is a reasonable chance that anyone who terminates a hedge fund manager would give a manager in a liquid or mutual fund structure more time. This is the source of the irony. The manager with daily liquidity options ends up with more sticky money than the hedge fund with only periodic liquidity dates. This is not to suggest that any hedge fund should offer more liquidity than can be supported by the underlying investments, but it does suggest that overly restrictive terms can create liquidation decisions that might not otherwise occur.

Consistency of the investment approach demonstrates at a minimum the manager's discipline. If you detect meaningful shifts in the investment profile, this can be a key indicator of another way that the manager's investment process can be broken.

5.6.3.2   *Has the Risk Profile Changed?*

Suppose you begin an investment with the manager who created an effective track record with a heavily long-biased portfolio, but who had never used leverage. It is highly likely that the fund's documents would be flexible in terms of what was legally allowed, but by practice the manager had never used the leverage latitude allowed in the documents. It is also likely that this approach and history would have been discussed at length in the initial due diligence process. You probably had an expectation that this would be the risk profile going forward.

Now suppose when you review the manager's risk documents you discover that the long bias is now even greater by the use of 50% leverage. The first thing you should do is reach out to the manager and discuss why this change of approach was made at all. And specifically why it was being made at this time. While within the manager's legal rights, this would appear to be a major deviation from history and from most investors' expectations.

The manager will likely respond that the shift was due to the most favorable opportunity set that he or she has seen in his or her many-year career. When you see fat pitches, you are supposed to swing at them. This may or may not be a well-founded and persuasive explanation to you.

You hire an active manager to make decisions, and you are explicitly paying them a premium fee to have them act on their best thinking. But this always should be within the agreed-upon context. A long-biased manager who begins employing maximum leverage, or at the other extreme a traditionally fully invested manager who turns 70% of the portfolio into cash, are both operating legally but at variance with expectations. Investors who are confronted with such radical shifts in risk profiles only has two choices. They may trust implicitly the decisions of the manager or they may terminate.

Deciding between these two paths is largely a function of the role you anticipated for the manager. If your expectation was that they would fit a tightly defined bucket in order to complement all of the other elements of the portfolio, there is a good chance that the new behavior could be working at odds with the larger scheme. If, on the other hand, the original mandate was much broader, the manager's deviation from history may be welcome.

But it is the ultimate responsibility of the investor to hold the reins on the risk profile of the total portfolio. Managers that dramatically cut risk can be expensive from an opportunity cost basis if the market rallies, but no one has ever gone hungry by preserving capital while others are making money. The flipside does not hold. Adding leverage to a portfolio can be done to an extreme so that the long-term viability of the investment corpus is risked. If a well-intentioned manager pushes your portfolio beyond your comfort zone, it is time to terminate.

There are many examples of fund managers who increased their risk profile after a period of poor performance. Doubling up to catch up is an unfortunate temptation for managers who find themselves in a hole. Sometimes it actually works, but it is the rare manager who has succeeded in this plan actually swears off the practice after it is initially successful. Too often managers are encouraged by early success and believe they can trade out of any problem with simply more trading. This is a well-trod path to ruination.

One might think that managers have a strong incentive to be disciplined in the investment of customer funds, and generally that is a correct assumption. But there is a certain "heads I win, tails you lose" element at work here. If the manager takes excessive risk and succeeds, he or she benefits from performance fees and from additional management fees that come in from new clients. If the risk gambit does not succeed, it is largely the client money that is lost. The manager might be genuinely apologetic after the event, but apologies do not replace lost assets.

While there are many cases of dramatic losses stemming from too much risk-taking, it is also possible to have serious problems in the other direction. Investors need to be particularly cautious about historically successful managers who have reached such a state of success that their highest priority is not to lose assets and the management fees that go with them. Many people talk about financial institutions that are "too big to fail." But in the investment world the problem of "too big to succeed" is just as relevant.

The major line of ongoing due diligence in this area comes from regularly examining risk reports and comparing them to historical patterns. All major shifts should be clearly communicated to investors with the rationale for any adjustment well advertised. If the manager seems to be reticent in this area, don't be afraid to ask.

5.6.3.3 Changes in the Team

High value-added investment teams usually consist of individuals with a strong company culture. This culture shapes every element of the investment process from the creation of ideas, to execution, and ultimately to client communication. Like a successful sports team everyone knows their role and executes efficiently. When changes come to the team, as they inevitably do, investors must ask how this will affect the group's ability to perform.

The original due diligence process should have identified all of the key players and their responsibilities. Part of that due diligence should have been an examination of contingency plans should any of the key employees not be able to perform. This does not have to be an ironclad blueprint, but it should demonstrate a strong forward vision to ensure that all bases would be covered in the event of a personnel change. This is far too important to be a subject of improvisation.

There are three broad categories of personnel changes. Voluntary termination happens when people leave for better opportunities. Involuntary termination happens when the management of the firm decides that a lineup change is necessary. The last category involves unplanned changes that are the result of an untimely disability or death. Thoughtful managers in any organization are thinking about all of these possibilities on a regular basis. Each category, however, raises somewhat different issues for the investor evaluating the portfolio manager.

Every regular due diligence review call should include operational questions. One category of inquiry should concern staff arrivals or departures. In a well-functioning, growing investment management firm the response usually involves discussing the addition of the next batch of analysts. Occasionally there is a report that a younger staff member has left the firm, but typically the conclusion is that all key team members are in place.

Sometimes, however, the news reveals an important departure. If a key person has left the firm because they were asked to, the conversation should explore the circumstances of the departure. In lean and volatile times, tough decisions often have to be made regarding which parts of the team are contributing the most. Sometimes with involuntary departures the individual who left the firm will reach out to investors or other important parties. This can be the first step in a new job search or it can simply be their interest in telling the story from their perspective. All of this information is relevant in the ongoing evaluation of the firm. You want regular reinforcement that your investment managers are viable businesses with well-functioning teams focused on the job of making money.

Voluntary departures of key people are sometimes really involuntary terminations that are packaged more politely. Again the circumstances of the departure should be explored in whatever detail is possible. Unless the departed employee has contractual restrictions against speaking to clients, you should make an attempt to connect with him or her to perhaps get a slightly different perspective. If the departure was truly voluntary and was a result of the search for more responsibility, higher pay, or broader experience, this is all relevant to the evaluation of your existing manager.

Effective investment teams often take years to develop. If the environment of the manager is not conducive to building such teams, it can hold back performance in the long run. It is not unusual for high return managers to splinter over the subject of compensation. Everyone feels like they contribute at a high level, but even objectively, some team members can view princely compensation levels as inadequate. In today's highly competitive environment for investment talent, departures that have their roots in compensation disputes can be expected

Some investment managers seem to embrace a culture of turnover. Senior management is constantly evaluating the entire team, with perceived underperformers being pared away. These can be incredibly intensive places to work. Not every personality type is well suited to this kind of environment. As investors, we should recognize that there is no single model of effective investment management. The judgments need to be made as to whether the model in place is likely to produce superior results in the future. Monitoring employee turnover can give you some insight on this topic. Too much stirring of the personnel pot suggests that not 100% attention is being paid to the research and trading process.

5.6.3.4 *Changes in the Relationships with Clients*

Every part of the client relationship should be discussed before an investment is made. The liquidity provisions, fees, and the frequency and content of client communications are all areas of either implicit or explicit agreement. Relationships can and do change over time, and sometimes these changes are sufficient to lead to the termination of the manager.

It is unusual for a manager to reach out to clients with a suggestion that fees are increasing or that liquidity terms are being tightened. Typically these features are explicitly set out in partnership agreement or in the prospectus, and changing them can take a major effort. Instead managers will often start new funds with the terms they feel better reflect their needs and then encourage existing investors to transfer their funds. This is an entirely voluntary effort, but in the extreme the manager can always liquidate the first fund and return all client monies.

More surprising to investors is when the manager elects to use certain terms in the agreement that had never been used before. Examples in 2008 and 2009 include payouts in kind, liquidating trust, and gates limiting the size of total redemptions. Managers at the time always said that they were invoking these options to protect the ultimate value of the fund for all investors. But in the moment many investors saw them as a unilateral abrogation of their rights.

While being on firm legal ground given the language in their documents, at a minimum the managers acted at strong variance with investor expectations.

Most funds that were so affected had already suffered large losses, so there were low expectations by the manager of collecting performance fees anytime soon. Some managers went further and declared that they would not collect management fees for funds in liquidation, but this behavior was rarer than one might have hoped for. Instead it often seemed that some fund managers were dragging their feet in the liquidation process in order to maintain the stream of reduced management fees.

Many hedge fund investors left 2008 and 2009 with very sour memories. What they had perceived as a relationship in good times devolved into a legal agreement when times became tough. Many investors sought to terminate relationships only to find that their assets were held captive. While it is understandable that such flexibility should be contained in legal documents to protect the manager and the fund, abuses of these terms have turned off whole groups of investors. These people will avoid such partnership structures in the future no matter who is running the fund because of the perceived chance that the terms of the relationship will change at the worst time.

Another area where the relationship can change is in client communications. Young, growing managers often go out of their way to communicate with existing and potential clients. As assets under management grow, each of those individual relationships falls in importance. The portfolio manager may add investor relations staff to take on more of the communication chores. Taken at the macro level, every investor should applaud the portfolio manager's wise use of his or her time. But at the individual level it can hurt to learn your access to the PM is no longer as readily available.

Once again there is no single right answer on this topic. If intimate, frequent communication is important to you, and it is no longer being offered, it may be time to terminate the relationship. But if the manager is performing well, investors must be objective in deciding whether the new forms of communication are adequate to their needs. Different is not necessarily worse, and terminating a well-performing manager for this reason may be a triumph of ego over common sense.

A great deal of the evaluation has to rest on how well the IR people do their jobs. Going from the completely knowledgeable and controlling PM to an ill-informed, out-of-the-loop IR person may simply not be acceptable. Little is as frustrating as trying to do ongoing due diligence with an IR person who lacks critical information or understanding about the investment process. If you had a strong, long-standing relationship with the PM, you should alert them to your concerns. While they understand that they may not be able to spend as much time with clients as they once did, they also want to see solid communications across the firm. The PM may not understand that this side of the business has tumbled without feedback from investors. If sufficiently remedial steps are not taken, it may be a sign that you should move on.

5.6.3.5 *Legal and Regulatory Issues*

Investment managers are not immune from scrapes with the law or regulatory organizations. Normally one would expect reasonably open dialogue on such topics that are of great concern to investors. In fact, more often than not it requires great initiative on the part of investors to get the complete story. While managers are required to update their ADV forms in a timely basis, and regulatory websites update their disciplinary files regularly, it is the rare investor who is routinely monitoring all of these sources of information. If the manager does not volunteer pertinent data, the investor should make periodic inquiries as to whether any issues have arisen.

The easiest way to do this in a nonconfrontational manner is to ask a regulated manager when they last had an audit or a review. There are a large number of managers who have never had a visit by a regulator. A subset of this group may have shown initiative and arranged for a mock audit performed by a private firm well-versed in compliance and regulatory matters. It is permissible to ask what the outcomes of these reviews were, and what steps if any the manager has taken to be responsive.

Suppose you discover that the manager was found to be in violation of either a governmental or self-regulatory organization rule. Some of these violations are minor in nature and lead to nothing more than a warning, while others can be quite severe and are resolved in the extreme with fines, suspensions, or outright bans for the parties responsible. Between these two extremes where the decision to remain an investor or leave is clear-cut, lies a vast gray area that requires subjective evaluation.

Investment managers should operate under the assumption that their clients are highly interested in these regulatory matters. A fund accused of *insider trading* would seem to have an affirmative obligation to let the investors know of this action early in the process. The manager may vehemently deny all wrongdoing, but communicating in any way that is not honest and open is a sign the manager has little respect for the investors that have trusted the fund with their money.

Communicating the information selectively to a small group of investors, but leaving the others in the dark, is perhaps the worst behavior. The manager is worried about one group of investors and tries to minimize that business risk by talking to them. The manager either fails to respect the rest of the client base enough to inform them or believes they will never catch on. While it is always expected that the best clients will receive more attention, it should never be the case that one group of investors is implicitly pitted against the other in these critical communications.

Litigious is probably one of the best adjectives to describe society in the twenty-first century. Suits are filed on a regular basis, almost to the point where word of new civil litigation hardly raises any alarms. Still, if your investment manager is on either side of such action you should take note. As soon as litigation becomes publicly known it becomes a fair topic for discussion in your due diligence calls. You should establish whether your investment is truly without risk should a judgment go against the manager. Even if your funds are protected there can be serious business risk to the manager, and at a minimum there is the diversion of attention and energy that could prove detrimental to investment returns.

Some managers by their strategy are activists and they welcome litigation as one of their key tools. Most managers are not in this camp. Prolonged litigation rarely adds value to the investment process, and investors must determine how severely the funds may be affected. Any time you believe the distractions are too severe it may be cause for termination.

A special case of criminal and civil legal issues is fraud. By the time a manager is wrestling with criminal or civil trials, it is usually way too late for investors to make a painless decision about the future of their investments. Investment fraud is as old as time itself. Dealing with this risk goes well beyond the questions discussed in the section, and deserves its own treatment.

5.7   FRAUD

In investments there are so many honest ways to lose money that it seems tragic to have to consider the risk of fraud. But fraud is always with us and investors are their own best line of defense. Unfortunately, no amount of due diligence or ongoing monitoring can prevent frauds. The best one can hope for is to minimize the probability of the event and to detect any fraud early in the process before the damage is too extensive.

Background checks can reveal evidence of fraudulent behavior in the past. While we would like to believe that everyone can move on from past mistakes, there are many examples of serial offenders who never seem to learn how to operate on the straight and narrow. Placing your money in trust with somebody who has a documented history of fraud is an extreme act of confidence, which may or may not be rewarded.

Not surprisingly, most fraudsters have no record of getting caught before. The more sterling the character in the past, the more likely the success in raising funds from trusting investors. One might logically think that a long track record of unblemished service would be a strong indicator of character. But the Bernie Madoff experience demonstrates that frauds can go on a long time undetected. All of the due diligence steps discussed in the sections above are important in minimizing the chance of being in a fraud. But nothing in those activities can guarantee that you won't be affected.

Independence of function is perhaps the greatest path to minimizing the chance of fraud. Auditors, fund administrators, and lawyers all need to be genuinely independent and accountable if inappropriate behaviors occur. Within the firm there should be as much separation as practical between the trading, back office, and reporting functions. Each should be in a position to question activities of the others. In the 1990s, the collapse of Barings brought on by the fraudulent trading of Singapore-based Nick Leeson, his wife oversaw the operations department of that office.

In retrospect a lack of checks and balances can be quite obvious. But why are these situations allowed to exist? In most cases the operations are small and a lack of division of labor is justified on the basis of it being economically impractical. Small investment management companies by necessity have to assign multiple tasks across a small group of people. In these cases investors need to have more confidence that the outside service providers are truly independent.

Issues of inadequate control are not unique to small companies. When Barings collapsed, over 25% of the previous year's revenue for the firm worldwide was attributable to Nick Leeson's trading. There was no budget constraint getting in the way of best practice. In this particular case, senior officials of the firm did not want to rock the boat and do anything in terms of additional controls that might upset their star trader.

There are frauds that are done out of desperation, to try to eliminate or cover-up trading losses. These situations start out with otherwise honest people who see no other solution to a problem that either they or the market created. The portfolio manager who says "I can trade out of this" has already crossed the line into fraudulent territory, but may not consciously acknowledge it himself or herself. When a web of deceit begins to grow in an attempt to hide the original problem and any subsequent issues the trader has likely started down a one-way path.

One might find some sympathy with the fraudster who is trying to rectify previous mistakes. The more extreme class of individuals set out consciously to steal. This group plays upon the hopes, aspirations, and confidence of investors. From the very first page of the fraud, they work hard to keep their activities hidden. Placing these people in a highly controlled environment where their every action can be monitored is one of the only deterrents. Not surprisingly, the majority of frauds occur in small operations run by the fraudster.

Since the probability of fraud cannot be eliminated completely, every effort should be made to have regular checks designed to catch frauds quickly and to minimize their impact. Best practice at banks for generations has required extended vacations for key personnel, during which time they can have no access to their accounts or internal communications. Complicated financial institutions have thousands of moving parts and it is usually a full-time job to hide illegal activity. Periodic absences when there are fresh sets of eyes applied to the books present good opportunities for fraud detection.

Regulators can be of some use here, but they should not be considered insurance against fraud. Perhaps the best thing a regulator can do beyond their regular audits and reviews is to be prepared to respond to investor questions or concerns about fraud. If you have difficulty getting your money back from a regulated investment advisor, you should immediately call the relevant regulator and describe your plight. Failure to return client capital in a timely way can be a strong signal of fraud. Regulators can act on these tips, sending in forensic accountants who will check the accuracy of client records in the existence of assets and cash. Many small time frauds have been discovered in this fashion and stopped before the damage was too great.

While regulatory auditors should be more sensitive to potential problems than the average investor doing due diligence, fraudsters with foresight are often clever enough to hide their activities from this group as well. The element of surprise is particularly valuable to the regulator who has the authority to demand books and records in real time. Unless there is an effective conspiracy to maintain parallel books and records, a spot audit has a reasonable chance in identifying missing assets.

Investors reasonably have an expectation for higher returns if they assume more market risk. In the case of the risk of fraud there is rarely any incremental compensation. Obvious Ponzi schemes that promise extraordinarily high rates of returns do not in fact compensate any but the earliest participants for the almost certain likelihood of fraud. The reality is that most frauds look like every other investment alternative. The returns are okay. The investment risk seems reasonable. When there are no obvious warning signs, fraud detection becomes even harder.

Section 5.3 of this chapter described many statistics including standard deviation and autocorrelation. It was stressed in that discussion that these statistics are at best diagnostic tools to guide investment due diligence, but they can also often be used to help detect frauds. Funds that have return histories that are too smooth may have some kind of manipulation going on. Not all low standard deviation, high autocorrelation funds are frauds, but most frauds share these statistical traits. To dupe their victims the fraudsters try to maintain an appearance of control and stability.

The only way to truly protect oneself from the effects of fraud is through diversification. This is simply a probability game and an assessment of damage. If you do careful due diligence on all your investments you should have minimized the chance that any single one of them is a fraud. But if that low probability event happens in any area, can you withstand the impact? This is why some investors impose internal limits on how much of a portfolio can be under the control of any given investment manager.

A general rule that no exposure can be more than some arbitrary level like 5% may make an investor feel more protected but may also lead to unreasonable expense and complications. For example, a fixed income manager charged with building a treasuries-only separate account where the securities are custodied in the investor's name may be as close to bulletproof as possible from an operational risk perspective. Capping that relationship at the same level as a self-administered hedge fund makes little sense. There can be a big difference in fraud risk between different types of investments and these variations should be considered in setting any limits.

Avoiding damage from fraud heavily depends on following the adage about not having all your eggs in one basket. If having most of the eggs safe is important, three baskets might not be enough. However, having a separate basket for every egg only makes sense in the fantasy world where there are no costs associated with building baskets. In the real world, investors will want to make practical trade-offs between the benefits of avoiding frauds and the costs of extra diversification. The information necessary to make those informed judgments should become available as you do your initial and ongoing due diligence.

By now, some readers might be throwing up their hands and saying "There must be an easier way!" An entire industry has evolved that suggests that they can make your life easier. Funds of funds construct diversified portfolios, perform due diligence, and perform ongoing monitoring. This is of course done for a fee. Whether a fund of funds is right for you and adds value above its fees are the questions explored in the next section.

5.8   FUNDS OF FUNDS

As portfolios moved from simple combinations of stocks and bonds toward more complex recipes containing hedge funds and other private partnerships, investors were challenged to make informed decisions. Some traditional investors wanted to participate in what were viewed as evolutionary improvements, but felt inadequate to the task. The *fund of funds* industry came into being to address these needs.

The fund of funds model is fairly basic. Instead of picking individual stocks or bonds the portfolio manager builds a collection of other funds. Hedge and private equity fund of funds are particularly popular because of the underlying complexity of the individual investments. Investors seem to place less value on portfolios of long-only equity or bond managers and these fund of funds represent a much smaller part of the total market.

5.8.1   Advantages of Funds of Funds

Funds of funds advertise a meaningful list of advantages to potential investors. At the top of the list is usually the seasoned judgment of the portfolio manager. A fund of funds team is typically composed of experienced people who have had exposure to many strategies and the operations that support them. With literally thousands of underlying funds available from which to choose, finding a fund of funds manager that can improve on your selection skills may be worth paying for.

If you believe that the due diligence of private partnerships is fundamentally more complicated than that performed on long-only stock or bond managers, you have to ask yourself whether you as an individual investor are up to the task. Funds of funds often have dedicated research staff members who specialize in the due diligence of their underlying managers. They are implicitly providing economies of scale in their due diligence activities to their many underlying clients. This too is a valuable service.

Unless you are an investor who counts your investments in the tens of millions of dollars, building appropriately diversified hedge funds or private equity portfolios can be an issue. Placing all your alternative partnership assets into one or two partnerships is an invitation to concentrated risk. Such concentration is always wonderful when the risk is to the upside, but this is certainly not assured. Funds of funds are often built with 15, 20, or even more managers. In the hedge fund space this allows diversification across managers within subcategories like long/short equity or global macro. In a meaningful investment in a fund of funds, there may be 20 or more different ultimate exposures, none of which would reach the individual manager minimum size on their own.

Not only is the portfolio diversified, but also it is actively managed. The fund of funds manager should be overseeing all of the underlying investments and aggregating the risk profile across the fund. If one sector becomes overweight, investments may be pared back and the assets redeployed. Whenever managers need to be terminated, that is also part of the active oversight process.

A major benefit to the fund of funds process comes from consolidated accounting and reporting. If an investor sought to replicate the exact holdings of a fund of funds they would receive regular account statements from all of the underlying managers, which would have to be aggregated to arrive at a hedge fund category return. Spreadsheets were designed to do this task easily, but anyone who has dealt with a lot of line items in their portfolio accounts knows that there is attractive efficiency from aggregation.

Tax accounting is also made more efficient. Instead of 20 or more K-1 reports, the investor receives a single consolidated tax return. This is not only easier, it also should lead to a direct reduction in tax preparation charges where accountants typically charge for every such report that they have to incorporate into the taxpayers return. Of course the expense of creating the fund of funds' K-1 gets passed along to the underlying investors, but there are economies by spreading out this expense across all of the investors.

Some funds of funds will argue that they provide access to underlying partnerships that would be otherwise unavailable to the individual investor. This argument was much more prevalent in the 1990s when all kinds of hedge funds and private partnerships had closed themselves to new investors. After the bear market in 2001–2002 and the financial crisis in 2008–2009, access to specific managers has rarely been a problem. Even the most elite managers seem to be finding capacity. The fund of funds manager who includes access as one of the main selling points is probably overstating the importance of this advantage.

There is a subset of funds of funds that goes beyond the simple exercise of aggregating managers into a portfolio. They actively monitor the risk profile of the fund, including measuring the betas to equities, interest rates, and credit. If these risks move beyond certain limits, the fund of funds manager will independently put an overlay trade in place. This is often done with exchange-traded derivatives or with OTC swaps contracts. Some managers have a history of routinely buying out-of-the-money puts no matter what the aggregate exposure is in the portfolio as a form of ongoing tail risk insurance. Funds of funds that pursue such overlay strategies should be able to demonstrate the benefits to their investors.

5.8.2   Disadvantages of Funds of Funds

While the fund of funds manager will emphasize the advantages of this approach, the investor should be aware of the other side as well. At the top of the list is the question whether the diversified portfolio of underlying managers is actually appropriate for the investor at every given point in time. Funds of funds tend to be somewhat formulaic, and it is not obvious that the emphasis within that formula is desirable for all investors in every market environment. Since the underlying investments in private partnership based funds of funds range from somewhat to highly illiquid, it is not reasonable to expect these aggregations to change their exposures in response to markets for any individual client's needs.

Funds of funds in the private equity or venture capital space often make a point of raising their next fund based less on market opportunity and more on the schedule of their preferred underlying managers. They will tell you that they are striving for manager and vintage year diversification, and that it is very difficult to evaluate what years should be embraced or avoided.

Given the amount of funds that were raised at the height of the tech bubble into the teeth of extraordinarily high valuations, this seems to be an abrogation of one of the duties of a good fund of funds manager. Private partnership managers who are raising new funds will never tell you that it is a lousy time to make new investments. Once the fundraising is completed, the GPs may actually be quite disciplined in their approach, and slow to call capital as they seek out the best opportunities in a bad environment, but they will typically be collecting fees continuously as you wait. Even the best fund of funds will find it difficult to put their business expansion plans on ice, even though it may be in the best interest of investors to do so.

Some fund of funds follow a formulaic schedule of their new fund launches geared to underlying manager calendars because they fear losing access to their best relationships. If an "A+" manager is beginning a new fundraising, failure to participate may jeopardize future opportunities to invest. This approach places a great deal of confidence in the consistency of top-level private partnerships, which is open to question. Even if this hypothesis has substance, placing customers into long-dated investment vehicles with very poor risk return profiles seems to be a way for funds of funds to detract value.

Given that markets tend to run in cycles, there are clearly better or worse times to be exposed to any trading strategy. Funds of funds by their very business model have to ignore this reality. The substandard performance of many hedge and venture capital fund of funds in the first decade of the twenty-first century can often be explained by this philosophy that you must always be invested. The fund of funds manager is not immune to business pressures that want to see you make new allocations.

For buy-out and venture capital fund of funds, the timing of investment gets extended in these tough times. Each of the underlying partnerships has its own investment schedule, and not all of the managers in the fund are identified and committed to instantaneously. It can take anywhere from quarters to years to fully populate such a fund of funds. If each underlying manager has a three-year investment window and a five-to-seven-year window for realizations, you should expect the life of the fund of funds to extend well past a decade. Some have been known to stretch out to two decades before the final distributions are made, during which fees continue to be paid.

Since both the underlying managers and the fund of funds report their returns on an IRR basis, it is actually of less concern to them how quickly their investments get made and completed. But given that the underlying investor has many alternative opportunities in the market, that calendar drag can be meaningful. Managing the implicit liabilities of uncalled capital over many years is a challenge that investors face, but that most fund managers downplay.

Some funds of funds can be accused of over-diversification. Extremely large, institutionally oriented funds of funds may see the number of underlying managers grow not because it is a good idea from a portfolio sense, but simply because they need many places to send their client capital. Academic studies suggest that the diversification benefits of adding hedge fund managers fall off quickly after 40 or 50 names. Any funds of funds with more exposures than that should be asked to explain what the added benefits are. At some point, the investor gets the equivalent of a hedge fund index, but with an additional layer of fees.

All of the advantages discussed above of the fund of funds approach come at a cost. Some funds of funds charge a flat management fee, typically ranging between 50 and 100 basis points per year. Other funds of funds start with a somewhat lower management fee, but also add a performance fee ranging from 5–10% or more of total performance. These kinds of expenses can add up very quickly in a world where the risk-free rate is near zero and all investment return expectations are muted.

If the underlying hedge fund managers are charging 2% management fees and 20% performance fees, adding even 50 basis points and 5% performance is a major hit. You also need to remember that inside the fund of funds there is no netting of performance. If one manager makes 20% gross, the net return will be 14% (20% minus the 2% management fee and the 4% performance fee). If another manager loses 20% gross, the net will be −22%. If these two managers had operated within a single fund structure and had equal capital allocations, their gains and losses would have canceled out and the investor would have simply netted −2%, reflecting the management fee. Instead, because a performance fee was paid to the winning manager, the investor nets −8%. And this is before the fund of funds fee.

Investors need to receive a great deal of service and superior returns to justify this economic structure. The due diligence requirements of the investor do not go away, they simply change form. Performing due diligence on a fund of funds requires the evaluation of their process as well as all of the operational aspects of their business. It is a sad fact that among the largest investors in Bernie Madoff were large institutional funds of funds. A long track record and a large AUM are no guarantee that the fund of funds managers are thoroughly doing their job. Too often the emphasis has been on fundraising and finding new managers in which to place those funds, rather than a thorough scrubbing of the manager's investment thesis, procedures, and integrity.

A final cautionary tale is worth mentioning. Paul Capital, a San Francisco–based firm that manages funds of secondary investments and private equities funds of funds, announced in early 2014 that it would be greatly cutting back its operations, stop new fundraising, but still maintain oversight over the existing funds.[46] Out of a staff of 65 employees across six offices, all but a few operational staff would be laid off. All but the main office would be closed.

---

[46]Primack, D. (2014). Paul Capital's Real Failure is in the Fees. *Fortune*. (21 March).

Paul Capital was just one of many victims of the financial crisis that began in 2007. Once managing several billion dollars across multiple funds, its holdings got hit particularly hard in the crisis and attempts to raise new funds in the post-crisis environment were unsuccessful. Investment teams left to find greener pastures, and Paul sought out a strategic partner or a buyer. When those efforts failed, the firm made the strategic decision to cut costs to the bone while letting the remaining portfolios run out their natural life cycle. They also decided that they would continue to collect the management fee stipulated in their subscription documents.

Investors in these funds of funds had little recourse. They will receive regular valuation reports that any well-trained clerk with a spreadsheet could put together from the reports of the underlying managers, but there will be no meaningful investment oversight as there are no investment professionals remaining at the firm. LPs will be paying a full management fee for a basic clerical function.

This is almost certainly not what these investors expected when they signed their subscription documents. All of the advantages of diversification and professional oversight that were no doubt advertised during Paul's fundraising days were reduced to an orphaned collection of investments. These investments might do well or poorly, but Paul Capital doesn't care. The general partners are content to let the portfolio evolve in any way it does, all the while collecting their management fees until all of the partnerships are mature, an event that could take many years.

This is an extreme example of a zombie fund of funds that likely holds a number of underlying zombie funds, given the vintage of most of the investments. LPs that went to Paul were investors who probably needed the professional expertise of the GP more than most, and they are left with a damaged portfolio and almost no services. As the *Fortune* article describing this episode noted, "It's things like this that give private equity a bad name."[47]

Many institutional investors avoid fund of funds for all of these reasons. The business model should not be dismissed out of hand, however, simply because some large investors have chosen another path. There are numerous quality providers in the market giving their investors more than their money's worth. But each investor must evaluate their own needs, the services they expect to receive, and the costs. Picking a fund of funds as a shortcut to reach alternative investments without doing careful due diligence and analysis is the wrong approach.

5.9 REBALANCING

Rebalancing a portfolio periodically is absolutely necessary to maintain discipline to the long-term investment goals. Knowing that you have to rebalance is the easy part. Figuring out when and to what degree portfolios are actually rebalanced can be more of a challenge.

Rebalancing is necessary because the return patterns of different asset classes and managers never match each other. You can start with your desired asset allocation and as soon as the market moves you will be away from your original

---

[47]Ibid.

target allocation. Moving assets around as part of the rebalancing exercise to regain those target levels usually involves some costs, which can quickly add up if you try to maintain your targets on a continuous basis.

A simple example will demonstrate the problem. Suppose you have a three-asset portfolio. The first is large-cap US stocks, with the weight of 40%. The second consists of small and medium-size US stocks with the weight of 35%. The last category is emerging markets stocks with a target of 25%.

In a largely "risk off" month, let the large-cap stocks stay flat, the smaller-cap US stocks fall 3% and the EM stocks fall 8%. The total portfolio pie has shrunk from 100 to 97 and the shares for the three classes are now 41.2%, 35.1%, and 23.7%. While not far off from the original plan, large-cap stocks are now over weighted relative to EM. So what should you do?

If there were no costs associated with buying or selling the stocks, you would sell off part of the large-cap US exposure and use the proceeds to buy more EM stocks. This would get you back much closer to your preferred asset allocation, which presumably reflects the risk return profile that you want. In the real world, however, there are costs to such transactions. You may conclude after such a month that you are close enough to your goals that the best decision is to do nothing.

But what does "close enough" really mean? Some investors try to analyze this by looking at historical simulations that optimize the rebalancing process. This is a difficult exercise because it typically assumes away most of the practical features of the rebalancing exercise like direct trading expenses and bid/ask spreads.

If rebalancing could be done without any friction, there would be the temptation to rebalance continuously, making a string of small purchases and sales to maintain the target allocation. Since this is obviously an impractical outcome, trade-offs need to be made. Some investors fall back on a two-step process combining how far they are away from the target and the dimension of time.

In the simple example above the target allocation was 40%, 35%, 25%. One can assign bands around these targets, so that the allowable ranges become something like: 35–45%, 30–40%, 20–30%. Analysts sometimes use historical data to try to establish the best bands, but the process is actually more subjective. Make the bands too narrow, and you discover you are adjusting by small amounts all of the time. If they are too wide, rebalancing trades almost never happen.

There is also no reason to have the rebalancing bands equal for all asset classes. Big equity allocations might do well to have plus or minus 5% as the range, but a 4% total allocation to an investment like high-yield debt should be held within a narrower range to maintain the overall risk profile of the portfolio.

Similarly, you will want to have a rebalancing discipline across managers as well. A target allocation of 3% to a hedge fund manager who is running a high-octane, low-correlation strategy can quickly become a 6% or 1% weight. Disciplined investors trim outsized winners to control overall risk. They also add to underperformers as long as the thesis and process is intact.

The psychology of such decisions can be pure torture. If a manager earns a massive outsized return, investors immediately believe that it is a reflection of great insight and execution skill. Everyone wants to be associated with winners, and after a good streak it is easy to rationalize why you want a bigger allocation. It can also be awkward to answer the questions of the manager inquiring why you are redeeming from such a well-performing fund.

The right answer in all of these instances is to say that you are performing the same kind of risk discipline that you hope the manager exercises. You thank them for the outsized returns. You then go on to say how you have every bit as much confidence in them today as you ever had, but there is simply too much risk represented in a now outsized position. If you had lost confidence in them, you would be making a total redemption.

The harder decision comes from the opposite situation. After a major loss, it is natural to assume that something in the process is broken. Even if you cannot identify the flaw, the very act of a loss plants the seeds of doubt. It is almost impossible to add to the losing manager, even if every logical thought points in that direction. Large losses that are within the range of objective expectation are always disappointments, but they should not be on their surface a cause for reevaluating the investment thesis of the manager. If that thesis is intact, it is desirable to rebalance on down performance in order to maximize long-term success.

The wild card in this analysis comes from the fact that you are rarely the only investor in the underperforming fund. In these cases you need to assess not only the manager's process, but you also want to anticipate the behavior of the other investors. Even if you are still a strong believer in the manager, there may be other less confident investors who decide to pull their money out. Selling large parts of the portfolio to meet redemptions can be disruptive in itself, leading you to conclude that at a minimum you do not want to add more funds to this position.

Rebalancing to target allocations once allocation bands are violated is perhaps the most disciplined approach to this problem. It does, however, require continuous monitoring and the ability to act on short notice. In volatile markets, deviations away from the allowable ranges can be fleeting. If they are not acted upon, the market can rebalance the portfolio for you eliminating any opportunity to buy low and sell high. For many investors, this is too intensive an activity. When this is the case, calendar-based rebalancing is an alternative solution.

Investors following this approach pick a schedule and on the designated dates buy and sell assets in order to bring the asset allocation back to the target levels. If calendar rebalancing is the only rule followed, you may find yourself making small adjustments in very quiet markets, or find yourself quite far away from target levels in volatile markets. For these reasons, many investors use a combination of the approaches. They will evaluate their allocations, say, quarterly, and readjust the portfolio buying or selling only those assets that are beyond their target bounds.

Many investors like this approach because it gives them a regular discipline, while avoiding potentially inconsequential moves in the portfolio. There are only two major drawbacks to this approach. The first is that extreme market moves shortly after a rebalancing date can lead to a portfolio significantly at variance with the targets for a long period of time. The second drawback is that if you choose dates that are widely followed by other investors, you have a good chance of wanting to buy asset classes at the same time as those other investors, and similarly your sales will occur with the crowd. Year-end rebalances are perhaps the worst in that they can be very crowded times for trading when market liquidity is well below the norm of other times of the year.

Despite the convenience of matching up rebalancing dates with reporting dates like calendar or fiscal year-ends, there is virtue in running a rebalancing program "off cycle" to avoid the crowd. Picking the end of January, April, July, and October for rebalancing would likely avoid the most serious competition from other rebalancers in the marketplace.

Rebalancing always "works" in the sense that portfolio exposures stay reasonably aligned with the desired risk profile in the investment policy. This is why we rebalance, but often investors are tempted to evaluate rebalancing in terms of added return. For example, in the long bull market that characterized the 1990s the investor who never rebalanced looked like a winner. That is, until the market collapsed after 2000. In fact, investors make the common mistake of continuously adding risk in a bull market, and a disciplined rebalancing program avoids this.

The most advantageous environment for rebalancing is one that exhibits highly volatile, but independent, asset class movements. If markets are volatile, but highly correlated, the entire portfolio moves up and down together, potentially leaving the percentage allocations of individual asset classes little changed from their targets. In contrast, for example, if international stocks rise when small-cap US stocks are falling, there is a greater chance that these allocations can fall outside their allowable ranges. If these investments eventually revert back toward the mean, selling the over weighted assets and buying the short-term losers is a great way to stay disciplined and to add return over the cycle.

Throughout this discussion there has been an implicit assumption that rebalancing occurs back to the target levels. There is nothing that requires this. Go back to the example where the target allocation was 40%, with an allowable range of 35%–45%. If the market moves have resulted in the current allocation being 47%, that asset should be sold down. It could be sold back to the target of 40%, or it could be sold to any level within the range. Some investors use this flexibility to shade their asset allocations to reflect their market expectations. Investors who do not believe they have enough skill to add value in this process should follow the most disciplined path of going back to target.

Investors who have periodic cash inflows or needs to withdraw assets to meet spending needs can use these activities in a way to create more continuous rebalancing. Even if an asset class is within the allowable range, new monies in or out should be allocated in such a way to nudge the allocation back closer to the targets.

The most important part of the rebalancing process is to establish a discipline, and stick to it. The rebalancing rules can be incorporated in the investment policy statement. It should be clearly articulated when rebalancing occurs, how the plan is executed, and who has the authority to make the portfolio changes. For not-for-profit organizations, it is not unusual for the investment committee to set the rebalancing policy, but then authorize the staff to automatically execute it as market conditions evolve. Any rebalancing transactions should be reported back to the committee as a matter of good control. This way the investment committee can see on a regular basis that the policy is being followed.

5.10   INVESTMENT ADVISORS: GETTING HELP WHEN YOU NEED IT

In the latter part of the 1990s the investment process seemed easy. In many ways it was fun. With the stock market growing 20% a year with great regularity, the only question seemed to be how much of your portfolio should be exposed to the seemingly endless bull market. Trustees at endowments debated earnestly about why their

18–19% returns were falling short of their peers' returns, which were racing ahead at more than 20%. There are worse problems to have.

The first decade of the new century changed all of that. The overall stock market corrected severely in 2001 and 2002, with tech bets often falling more than twice as fast as the overall market. The middle years, helped by easy money from the Federal Reserve and other central banks around the world, seemed to signal a return of the bull market trend. This abruptly changed with the credit crisis of 2007 and 2008 that once again severely depressed equity prices. The decade proved that investing was not easy. And there were very few moments of fun along the way.

The scars from this history have a way of lasting. Despite decade-long bull markets in both stocks and bonds, investors still remember the more trying moments. Few with these experiences are cavalier in their attitude toward investing today.

Investors come to the process with different goals and attitudes. For the professionals in the industry, investing is their vocation. Whether it is easy or hard on any given day, this is what they get out of bed to do. Like all professions, some people do their jobs better than others. This group is a small percentage of the overall investing public. The vast majority of investors have other day jobs, and investing is simply a means to a bigger end.

Some in this larger group find the process recreational. They enjoy the dynamic of the market and look forward to their active participation. These people may or may not show any particular skill at the task, but they derive enjoyment from the activity. Other investors can be completely intimidated by the process or view it as a total nuisance.

Whether you view investing as a vocation, an avocation, or a nuisance, you may actually benefit from the services of a professional advisor. Such advisors shape a long-term portfolio to be consistent with your investment goals and risk preferences, and then aid in execution through individual security and fund manager selection. All of this advice comes with a fee, and like all investment expenses must be evaluated versus the benefits the advisors provide.

Anyone who recognizes that their investment portfolio is a meaningful part of their overall wealth should ask themselves whether they need help or not. For the family that is intimidated or annoyed by the investment process, an advisor is likely to be a necessity unless one resigns themselves to mediocre returns or worse. These individuals would look to the advisor as someone to absorb virtually all of the pain of the actual investment process.

For the individual who gets recreational benefits from their investing, an advisor can still play an important role. Many amateur investors fall short in their analysis of their portfolios or specific investments. Professional advisors can fill in these gaps, point out potential deficiencies in the portfolio, and hopefully help avoid important errors. In these cases the advisory relationship complements rather than completely substitutes for the activities of the investor.

One might assume that all investment professionals would manage their own portfolios. But many of these individuals are specialists, and have little ability to deal with broader portfolio issues. As an analogy, talented house painters might still find it beneficial to hire an interior decorator to deal with the overall design plan before the painting begins. Here again, the advisor would complement the professional investor and try to balance out the strengths and weaknesses of the client.

There are at least as many types of investment advisors as there are portfolio managers. No matter which type of investor you are, you will want to do extensive due diligence on any potential advisor you might engage. Your primary evaluation will be to assess the quality of the services and products provided versus the fees paid. The next question will assess whether you have the opportunity to develop a solid working relationship based on trust in your advisor.

5.10.1 Types of Investment Advisors

Investment advisors come in different varieties. There are those who charge a direct fee for their advice. There are others who are paid through the commissions they generate from securities purchases and sales or through a share of the profits of the funds or products they recommend for clients. There are hybrid models that include both types of fees. The different models can produce seriously different incentives for the advisors, which should be a major consideration when evaluating what type of advisor to employ.

Broadly speaking, some advisors charge a fee and then populate portfolios with investments at the lowest possible costs in order to maximize investor returns. The mirror image model has no or a very low explicit advisory fee, but an implicit one where the costs of the investments imbeds that advisory expense. The virtue of the first approach is that the client sees exactly what is being paid for. The second model may appear less expensive, though without a careful accounting of the internal costs it cannot be determined for sure. Hidden costs eat into returns just as effectively as explicit ones. The two approaches may, however, create very different incentives for the advisor, posing alignment of interest challenges for the client.

5.10.1.1 *Brokerage/Product-driven advisors*

For as long as there have been stockbrokers, there have been individuals who label themselves advisors, but whose major activity has been generating commissions through stock purchases and sales. These advisors recommend specific security transactions, which are typically executed through the broker–dealer for which they work. These advisors may or may not charge an explicit advisory fee based on the assets in the portfolio, but it is not unusual for the majority of the compensation to be based on the commissions generated. These advisors are almost always registered as security salespeople.

Broker-dealer regulations have recognized for decades the temptation to *churn* such accounts. Abusive advisors are not that hard to identify and drive out of the industry, but the question always remains with these types of broker advisors whether their recommendations are primarily based on the client's welfare or on their desire to generate revenue. Evaluating performance of these advisors must always be done on a net of fees and commissions basis.

As the advisory industry has grown, so have the varieties of commission-based advisors. Investors will want to understand how the advisor relates to their underlying firm, whether it is an insurance company, a bank, or a mutual fund company. In many of these cases the activity labeled advice is in actuality commission-based sales.

Some financial institutions have tried to minimize the appearance of conflict by offering a menu of investment options beyond those provided by the advisor's firm. If Bank A's advisor is recommending Fund Company B's mutual fund, it appears to be independent advice. In reality, many such institutions have distribution relationships with a wide range of fund managers who split their management fees with the advisor recommending them. Investors doing due diligence on a prospective advisor should be very explicit with their inquiries about all of the sources of income for the advisory firm.

There are no truly free advisory firms or costless investments. Advisors who recommend structured products that have no explicit charges are getting paid somehow. Either there are distribution fees paid to the advisor by the creator of the structured product, or there are large embedded profits in the structure that are shared with the advisor. Again investors need to explore in great detail the compensation structure of the advisor in order to truly understand all of the potential conflicts that may be present.

5.10.1.2 Institutional Consultants

A massive industry has evolved over the decades to provide institutional clients consulting services. These services range from advice on asset allocation to the evaluation of individual investment options. Many of these independent consultants pursue non-conflicted business models where their only source of revenue is from their advisory clients, but the investor too should verify this.

Some consultants charge a flat negotiated fee. Others charge on the basis of assets under advisement independent of the underlying portfolio. Some other advisors charge different fees for different types of investments. It is not unusual to charge a premium for hedge funds and other alternative investments on the theory that these activities require greater due diligence and therefore come with greater cost. There may be some justification for this approach, but when these fee differentials enter into the schedule it introduces an incentive for the advisor to recommend the higher fee activities. Only when independent advisors do not receive different fees depending on the investments recommended, can clients take complete comfort that suggested portfolio changes are motivated by a desire to improve portfolio performance rather than generate a new commission or fee.

Some institutional consultants have decided to package recommended fund managers into internal funds of funds. The rationale for this is that it allows for consolidated reporting of activities like private equity or hedge funds, and makes the overall investment process easier. Sometimes, however, advisors have added incremental general partner fees that can create an incentive to recommend these products. Even if these funds of funds are passed through to investors at cost, there still may be a conflict. The research departments of these consultants may be instructed to keep the most promising, capacity-constrained partnerships for the internal fund of funds and not share it broadly among the advisory clientele.

Relationships between consultants and brokerage houses are not uncommon where stock and bond trading activity is directed to the broker in exchange for part of the commissions. Similarly, some fund managers offer consultants a break on their management fees in order to be placed on the consultant's approved platform. If the ultimate client does not receive 100% of the benefit of this fee break, these discounts become indirect and sometimes undisclosed compensation for the advisor.

In the extreme, there have been examples where portfolio managers have used consultancy or placement agents as a conduit to inappropriately rebate fees back to pension fund employees or trustees as a form of a kickback to get the business.

When discovered, this kind of activity questions the integrity of the entire investment process.

Truly independent advisors can demonstrate that 100% of their revenue is derived from fee income paid by their advisory clients. These advisors charge explicit fees that should be completely transparent. They can often appear more expensive than the advisors following other business models, but clients should make sure that they are making appropriate comparisons when looking across approaches.

5.10.1.3   *The Special Case of the Outsourced CIO*

Advice can be partial, applying to only parts of the portfolio, or comprehensive. A special subset of advisors has appeared in the last several years that goes by the label *outsourced CIO* (OCIO). These advisors typically do all elements of the investment process: asset allocation, portfolio construction, ongoing due diligence, and reporting. Families or institutions may think of the outsourced CIO as an alternative to having their own investment staff. Given the high cost of staffing many investment positions, it can often be a more economical alternative to "rent" an investment staff rather than "buy" one for all but the largest investors.

There are different approaches to this model as well. Some outsourced CIOs believe they have identified a strong portfolio that can apply to a wide variety of clients. They create a single investment program as if they were acting on behalf of a single idealized client. Every participating advisory client receives a pro-rata share of the overall portfolio. If the client decides that this portfolio represents too much risk, they would reduce their outsourced CIO portfolio and place the extra proceeds into a risk-free asset. Clients who believe they want more risk would actually have to enter into a leveraging transaction.

Firms that have taken this approach tend to attract similar clients. Groups of endowments, for example, may find it attractive to know that their assets are being managed in ways that are identical to many of their peers. While this is a very efficient model for the advisory firm, it does require some compromises to be made by the clients that invariably would prefer some customization on the standard model.

The closest analog to this approach can be found in a *multifamily office*. Different families recognize that the expense involved in running their own investment company can be quite high, so they pool resources and share the expertise of their staff. Even in these circumstances, it is rare for each family to have identical portfolios, which is why many outsourced CIOs take a more customized approach.

5.10.1.4   *Independent, Custom Advisors*

The advisory firms that are independent of all managers, brokers, and other financial institutions have a simple business model but a complicated actual business. They construct custom portfolios for each advisory client based on all of the factors discussed so far in this book. Any economies of scale they enjoy come from their research and reporting efficiencies. Adding a new client can be quite labor-intensive, as the existing client portfolio needs to be evaluated, the preferred portfolio identified, and then the actual transition executed. This model is the highest form of custom service available in the advisory world. In its purest form it should be conflict-free with the interest of the client and the advisor in complete alignment.

The downside of this approach is the difficulty in identifying value added by the advisor. In the outsourced CIO model where everybody shares the same portfolio, it is easy to see where the gains and losses occurred. When every client has an individualized portfolio that can reflect widely different investment needs and risk tolerances, it is challenging to say how the advisor is doing at the firm level. Individual clients should have access to custom benchmarks and their own expectations to evaluate whether the advisor is doing a good job, but there is no single analytical figure that outsiders can access to provide an easy summary of performance.

5.10.1.5 *Robo-advisors*

Technology never stands still anywhere and one of the newer applications has appeared in the form of *robo-advisors*. These firms have attempted to marry the finance theory discussed in Chapter 3 with elements of behavioral finance to guide clients toward low-cost portfolios often populated entirely by *exchangetraded products* (ETPs). The founders of these firms rely on science, technology, and an assertion that passive investing is always superior to appeal to investors.

The typical robo-advisor has a website where the client is asked a number of questions about their age, income, and asset levels. There might be a panel of questions designed to elicit insight into the client's risk appetite. The data is fed into a program designed to match the person with a number of model portfolios developed by the advisor. It is usually asserted that years of research have crafted a highly precise program useful to anyone, without the fees and expenses from traditional advisory models.

The market inroads these firms have made are impressive, especially among younger, more tech-savvy investors. This has caught the attention of the major brokerage houses that are beginning to offer their own versions of these programs. For many investors who might not have the resources to hire a personal independent advisor, asset allocation advice from a robot may be a useful starting point for creating a portfolio.

There are issues to consider, however. All of the caveats to modern portfolio theory discussed in Chapter 3 apply to robotic advice. Just because a process is computerized does not make it more complete or thoughtful. The biggest challenge is incorporating all of the idiosyncrasies of a client into the portfolio. Human capital and other non-liquid assets like real estate are almost impossible to model generally. It seems like the case of the outsourced CIO with a single portfolio a lot is being assumed away largely for the benefit of the advisor.

Robo-advisors as a group are still a young industry. While the science of portfolio construction may appear to be reasonably direct, in practice the construction of algorithms can create meaningful divergences. The Financial Industry Regulatory Authority (FINRA) in 2016 published a report on the robo-advisor industry, which they called *digital investment advice*.[48] In it they reported on a survey of seven well-established robo-advisors and summarized the recommended portfolios they produced for a stylized 27-year-old investing for retirement.

---

[48]The Financial Industry Regulatory Authority (FINRA) (2016). *Report on Digital Investment Advice*. (March). Washington, D.C.

The range of advice was striking. Recommended equity allocations ranged from a high of 90% to a low of 51% of the total portfolio. Fixed income went from 10% to 40%. One firm recommended a dedicated 14% allocation to a portfolio of commodities. Foreign stock allocations went from 22% to 50%. One robo suggested a 5% allocation to gold.[49] These are wildly different portfolio suggestions all based on supposedly objective and highly scientific foundations.

As more and more investors move toward index mutual funds and ETPs, the pricing of these products will also be affected, to the disadvantage ultimately of the herd. Cost advantages can only go so far to offset pricing inefficiencies, and completely foregoing a wide range of active products will likely come at a cost to ultimate performance.

Behavioral finance reminds us that investing is a very human activity with layers of psychology at work. Robo-advisors may suggest that their programs have been designed to avoid the biggest psychological pitfalls, but they cannot take emotion out of the process. A robo-advisor will not spend time with a client who is distraught about a sudden market decline or the results of an election. There are times when the guidance of another seasoned human being is called for.

In the end, the decision is very much like the one between active and passive fund management. You either get value from the totality of your active manager relationship to justify the fees or you don't.

As the bull market of the 1990s has given way to the more challenging, volatile start of the twenty-first century, more and more investors are seeking the help of investment advisors. Financial salespeople often carry the additional label of advisor in order to enhance their appeal. Non-conflicted advisors are increasingly being sought out as the challenges of the market make it more important than ever to avoid excess fees and frictions in an investment portfolio. Even if you decide that you have a strong preference for completely independent advisors, there is one major decision that you still have to make. Should you give your advisor discretion over portfolio changes?

5.10.2   The Question of Discretion

The ultimate advisory relationship involves giving legal authority over your portfolio to someone else. This can be as basic as giving your stockbroker authority to buy and sell shares within your account. It can be as complex as giving someone the ability to sell bonds in order to buy real estate or any other transaction that they believe appropriate within your investment guidelines. Before you give discretion at any level, you should have complete trust in the advisor's abilities and integrity.

Some of the best advisory relationships are built exactly like this. Sadly, some of the worst abuses also arise from them as well. Clients who have a strong dislike or fear of investments naturally gravitate toward this model, but unfortunately they are often in a poor position to do an adequate evaluation of the advisor beforehand.

When one combines discretion and actual control over the assets, the potential for fraud jumps dramatically. Advisors or managers who have control over the cash and securities and where they may be sent can perform all manner of mischief.

---

[49]Ibid, pp. 3–4.

Independent custody arrangements and administrators provide one level of protection against the worst frauds of cash just disappearing, but cannot prevent an advisor with discretion from making investments that are entirely inappropriate to your goals or wishes.

A good compromise between total discretion at one extreme and the investor making all decisions at the other is the outsourced CIO model with "virtual discretion." The advisor offers suggestions to the client as if they had trading discretion over the portfolio, but they neither have final decision-making authority nor control over the assets. In such a model the client can always say no to any investment suggestion, and at no time can funds be moved in or out of their control without their knowledge.

For the client who recognizes his or her limitations in making investment decisions, but wants to stay engaged with the process, this can be a good solution. Over time the dynamics of portfolio adjustment make the advisor smarter about the needs of the client, and the client smarter about the abilities of the advisor. As trust is developed in a good working relationship, both parties should become more efficient in conveying their views and executing any portfolio adjustments.

For clients who are less attached to the process, it is important for the advisor to be as transparent and low hassle as possible in executing the investment steps. Without having complete discretion, the process can still appear to be almost running on autopilot for the client. But it is also important to maintain good lines of communications. If the client signs off on every recommendation without having at least a basic understanding of the goals and the risks, there is a high probability at some point there will be a mismatch between expectations and actual results.

The goal should be a smooth running process with minimal inconvenience to the client, but with a continuous flow of enough information to keep everyone on the same page. The client receives the strong direction they are seeking from their advisor, has a good understanding of whether the investment program is performing as expected, and always maintains ultimate control of their assets.

5.10.3 Choosing the Best Approach

Every investor should take some introspective time and ask whether they need an advisory relationship or not, and what form it should take if they do. This is highly subjective, and it is not a time to overestimate one's abilities. Bull markets tend to make people more confident in their skill set. Volatile bear markets heighten people's anxieties and fears and make them susceptible to unrealistic sales pitches. Neither environment is necessarily the best for an unbiased assessment of your needs and wants.

Investing has both intellectual and emotional components. There are many smart people who are completely unequipped emotionally to be good investors. There are also people who have the right temperament, but lack the knowledge base or inclination to do a good job. There may be people who are well-equipped in both areas, but who simply have much more productive activities to occupy their scarce time. All of these people are likely candidates for an advisory relationship.

Choosing the right approach involves establishing an alignment between emotions and objectives. If you are incredibly risk-averse and cost-conscious, you will want to avoid aggressive advisors who profit from active trading within the portfolio. If you have the ability to stomach short-term portfolio volatility and are actively seeking growth, you will likely not be happy with an advisor who stresses capital preservation. The good news is that there are many flavors of advisors available and you should be able to find one that is a good match.

It is impossible to discuss advisors without also discussing costs. There are low-cost advisors that try to achieve economies of scale in their own businesses by advocating standardized model portfolios for all their clients. Like index fund investing, if what is being packaged and sold is what you want there is no reason to seek out higher cost advisors who offer customized products. Someone looking for a genuinely customized solution should expect to pay higher fees for that service. In every case the ultimate question is whether you get enough value to justify the expense.

Value comes in many forms. There is the obvious value of a portfolio that does better than what you could construct yourself. But there are other values as well. For the investor who does not get recreational pleasure out of the portfolio construction process, the savings in their own time by delegating investment activities to an advisor can be large. Even those investors who enjoy their active engagement in making high-level allocation decisions are probably not well-equipped to identify or do extensive due diligence on the individual managers or investments in the portfolio. Here the advisor saves both time and hopefully adds needed expertise that can help avoid the more catastrophic outcomes.

One of the biggest challenges of evaluating different advisory options is to identify all of the costs of the relationship. As pointed out above many of the advisory models rely either on explicit commissions that can vary with the level of activity, or on structured products or other financial instruments being sold that have embedded cost structures that can be highly expensive to the client. "No fee" advisors cannot stay in business if their advertisement is literally true. All advisors try to make a living, and if it is not from transparent, direct fees, then it is from a combination of charges that may be hard to identify.

How do you know whether your advisor has done a good job? If the advisor has a standard model portfolio that all clients use, one can use the same evaluation techniques on the advisor that were discussed when it comes to evaluating individual managers. Benchmarks can be established. Historical performance can be matched to those benchmarks.

Advisors who create customized portfolios are much harder to examine quantitatively. In severe bear markets, clients with lower risk portfolios are likely to have preserved capital much better than those with more aggressive goals. The reverse is true in bull markets. An advisor who cites one or two clients who outperformed the market averages in any given period is probably using the same kind of selective presentation methods that were discussed in the section on managers.

For such advisors, prospective clients should ask about the range of client experiences over both bull and bear markets. The primary focus should be on the portfolio performance, but it is appropriate to dig deep into individual manager performance within the portfolio. How have the existing managers in client portfolios performed against the benchmarks and against the managers already in the client's portfolio? How many managers have been terminated over the last year or more? What were the clients' worst manager experiences?

For advisors who provide highly customized services, ask for references from clients that the advisor believes are most similar to you. A highly satisfied endowment client's ringing endorsement of an advisor may not be relevant to a multigenerational family. Speak to the reference about all elements of the relationship. Everyone will naturally want to speak about performance, but you should also assess their satisfaction with reporting, communications, and all operational aspects of the relationship.

Avoid the temptation of evaluating an advisor based on one or more examples of strong client outperformance in the most recent period. Advisors understand that prospective clients often shop for new providers after a poor recent experience, and they attempt to attract new business with the simple suggestion that if the client had been with them they could have avoided that disappointment. That may or may not have been the case. The strong performing portfolio being advertised may have been completely inappropriate for the client in question. It is always a possibility that the new advisor could have been as bad or worse in real time.

The ultimate evaluation is holistic. Does the advisory relationship work for you? A portfolio that meets the risk and return criteria of the client may be necessary, but it is probably not sufficient for a good advisory relationship. The results have to be there and they have to be delivered in a way that meets your practical and emotional requirements. The same kind of confidence and trust discussed for managers applies even more so for advisors.

We can return to the metaphor earlier in the chapter about buying shoes. You can describe what you are looking for in great detail. You can see someone else wearing a pair that looks attractive to you. The salesperson will say the store has just what you need. But until you take more than a few steps yourself, you cannot really tell whether the shoes are both flattering and functional to you. A good advisory relationship is like your favorite pair of shoes. They do the job you are asking of them and you look forward to putting them on.

CHAPTER 6

Tactics for Enhancing Returns

In Chapter 5 we discussed the basic ways that active managers can add alpha versus an index. They can have better information than the competition. They can process market information more intelligently than the competition. They can have lower costs of operation. Literally every money-making idea can fall into one of these three broad categories.

Despite this basic simplicity, investors are regularly bombarded with pitches from managers claiming that they can enhance returns over any given benchmark using a variety of potentially complicated techniques. Usually these claims are made with the backing of at least some historical record, adding to the credibility of the approach. It is the responsibility of the investor to sort through the claims and the history to evaluate the likelihood of success in the future.

It is difficult to identify the source of alpha for most programs that claim to enhance returns. Usually, one risk is being substituted for another. If such a substitution made sense, and created outsized returns in the previous three years, there is no reason to believe necessarily that such a trade will work in the future. Too many investors evaluating managers by historical track records fail to recognize the perils that may be embedded in the investment strategy they are considering.

This chapter will discuss two approaches that fall under the category of processing market information more intelligently. The first is the basic skill of market timing, where the manager adds to or reduces risk in anticipation of market moves. It is impossible for all investors to be superior market timers, as there must always be winners and losers in every market trade. But such individuals exist who combine market knowledge and discipline and have demonstrated the long-term ability to add value this way.

The second approach exploits the dimension of volatility to enhance portfolio construction. Options strategies including *covered calls* and *fully collateralized short puts* recognize that time is a diminishing asset and that selling it can add meaningful revenues compared to portfolio strategies that do not use options.

A third approach for taxpaying investors involves the management of the portfolio to periodically create tax losses that can be used to offset gains elsewhere in the investor's life. This is not some aggressive interpretation of the tax code to avoid taxes, but a long-standing and accepted practice that allows one to be smart about how to minimize one's tax obligations. It is the embodiment of the adage, when dealing with lemons, make lemonade.

The chapter concludes with a longer section itemizing various flawed strategies that are routinely offered to investors. These approaches appear to add value under certain market conditions, but usually hide risks that can ultimately destroy any promised enhancement and more. Investors who are often struggling to find adequate yield in their portfolios are susceptible to these claims. When these approaches reach their height of popularity, they are often most vulnerable to the hidden risks. This discussion will point out what can go wrong, which will likely happen at the worst possible time.

6.1 MARKET TIMING

Market timing is one of the skills that some academic economists and market practitioners claim cannot exist.[1] The view is that between every buyer and seller there will ultimately be a winner and a loser. The market in total is a zero-sum game. It is expensive to trade. Add this to the fact that markets tend to process information quickly and efficiently, and it is easy to be suspicious about the existence of sustainable market timing skills.

Despite this, any examination of published analysis throughout history shows that the world is obsessed with market timing. Whether the trading suggestions are derived from technical analysis of past prices or from fundamental data in the marketplace, commentators are always making suggestions on how to adjust your portfolio by using market timing. For something that supposedly doesn't exist, a remarkable amount of time and energy is spent pursuing it.

Just because something is difficult does not mean that it cannot be done. The trading floors, and now computer rooms, in New York and Chicago are liberally populated with individuals who have made an above average living through timing the markets. Just as there are extraordinary tennis players and pianists, there are some individuals who process available market information far better than the average. Some of these individuals manage portfolios for outside investors.

There is a group of long-only managers who run their funds insisting on the flexibility to raise at least some cash whenever they think the opportunities are limited or the risk is high. Many of these managers claim that they add value through time by such opportunistic decisions. Sometimes only narratives concerning specific trades support these assertions. In Chapter 5, techniques were described that allow one to test these claims more definitively.

Many institutional investors choose not to allow their active long-only managers any latitude on the subject of cash. While they expect these managers to be able to opportunistically add value by picking the right time to buy and sell stocks, they choose to control when they are in or out of the asset class. For investors who rigidly adhere to long-term portfolio allocations, allowing any other approach might

---

[1]Vanguard founder John Bogle, in a presentation to the Investment Analysts Society of Chicago in 2003, claimed not to know anyone who could market time successfully, nor did he know anybody who "knows anyone who has timed the market with consistent, successful, replicable results." Bogle, J. (2003). The Policy Portfolio in an Era of Subdued Returns. Bogle Financial Markets Research Center. (June 2003). Mr. Bogle seems to categorize market-timing success as near-perfect foresight. With this narrow definition, he was no doubt correct.

jeopardize the investment discipline around the entire portfolio. If you are sure you are pursuing the one, true portfolio allocation, then this is the correct policy. If you acknowledge that there may not be a single best recipe for all points in time, you may be unnecessarily tying your active managers' hands.

An irony in this is that many of these same investors make significant allocations to hedge funds, which have been specifically charged with making all manner of market timing decisions. Unless one believes that hedge funds form a distinct asset class (and there is ample evidence to the contrary on this topic), such an approach is the equivalent of saying one group of active managers has market timing skills while another group does not. It is actually quite hard to imagine how labeling oneself a hedge fund imparts any particular skill.

Market timing can be done within a narrow asset class, across sectors or parts of the capital structure, or between large categories of investments. As the tech bubble expanded in the late 1990s, two schools of thought emerged. One group saw these stocks as wildly overvalued and moved resources into perceived better-opportunity areas like bonds and the stocks of cyclical industries. The other camp stressed the fallacy of market timing and maintained market weights both as the market advanced and as it rapidly declined.

Not every market timer got those decisions correct. Highly disciplined value investors started cutting risk several years before the ultimate collapse. As the market continued to disagree with their fundamental views, disgruntled investors withdrew, sometimes imperiling the funds' franchises. It is a lonely business being a market timer who is out of step, but investors should recognize that no fund managers are 100% accurate in their market timing calls. It is the averages over long periods of time that demonstrate skill or lack thereof.

Market timing skills can vary considerably depending on the time horizon. There are some traders, most typical of the old fashioned floor traders at the commodities exchanges and the modern high-frequency computerized traders, who focus on trades lasting from fractions of a second to a few minutes. There is no way these people can be called investors in any meaningful sense of the word. They are market participants who excel in their ability to make, on average, lots of short-term gains. In return, they usually are the primary liquidity providers to others in the market.

Some investors believe they can add value by shading their portfolio over periods of days, weeks, or months. Famed investor and philanthropist Bernard Baruch said that the definition of a liar was someone who says they bought at the low and sold at the high. Such precision isn't necessary for effective market timing.

As the length of the timing horizon for individual securities increases, it becomes increasingly difficult to distinguish those security-specific contributions from the bigger beta moves in the market. Ultimately, the longer the decision horizon, the more the timing decision becomes a market call and less an opinion on the individual securities.

Successful market timing around crisis events requires a strong contrarian bent and discipline. Many people saw the impending crisis in the US housing sector in the middle part of the first decade of the twenty-first century. Some market timers placed their bets in 2005 and 2006, and were completely disappointed as the market forged ahead against them. Others, who had lived for a long time with tight credit spreads and low volatilities, jumped into bigger long positions at the first sign of a reversal in the second half of 2007. Some of these traders decided to use leverage in order to make a good opportunity into a great one. When the real calamity of 2008 unfolded, these market timers, who had been quite right in principle, were forced out of the market with great losses.

As these forced liquidations in many markets continued through the fourth quarter of 2008 into early 2009, the general popular view was that the world was coming to an end. Financial institutions around the globe were threatened, and central bankers were employing their full tool kit of remedies to stop the crisis. The contrarian market timers at this point had one important fact on their side. Prices of many assets had fallen so low that unleveraged investments could be made that had higher than average expected returns seen in most markets.

While most investors were completely pessimistic, these individuals saw long-term opportunity. They understood that things could get worse, but they also viewed the risk reward trade-off in the marketplace as being the most favorable perhaps in their lifetime. Assets were put to work at attractive prices, but with an understanding that short-term volatility would likely be high. Being on the other side of the fence from the investing herd was essential. Sizing the position with discipline so that future bumps in the road would not force them out was just as important.

There were many investors who brilliantly navigated the 2008–2009 crisis. Some of them are quite realistic, acknowledging that their extraordinary returns were in part the creation of an extraordinary environment. Others have used their track record from that period to lure new investors who hope that the manager's past market timing exploits can be regularly repeated. Some of these managers have more new assets than was previously imaginable. Almost without exception they have not met the lofty expectations of their new investors since. The post-crisis environment after the quick snap-back in markets has been conducive to solid returns, but not extraordinary ones. The weight of massive AUM in some of the aggressive strategies has made the likelihood of success even lower.

Enhancing returns through market timing is just like every other value-added pursuit by active managers. A good average performance and consistency are the keys. Picking one great stock does not make the manager a genius when it comes to building long-term portfolios. Buying extraordinarily cheap options against the possibility of the mortgage crisis in 2006 does not ensure that such opportunities will always be available. Each investor must evaluate the manager's record and make an objective assessment about the probability of future success. Then you must be willing to live through periods where mistakes are made.

Like all activities to enhance value, market timing is not a certainty. Associate yourself with managers who have strong, long-dated track records of success in the area, and who continue to operate in an environment where their skills can be demonstrated. This means that assets under management can't be too large and that the marketplace needs to be supportive. One way the market can help is through the pricing of volatility, and the next section describes options-based strategies that can help toward that end.

6.2   VOLATILITY: THE OVERLOOKED DIMENSION

Investors' primary market focus is almost always on direction. We want to know if our investments made money or lost money. Few investors actually spend much time thinking about *volatility* except when they have just experienced a particularly large series of moves. That is an omission that can cost returns. The volatility in the marketplace may be no more controllable than the direction of stock and bond prices, but there are ways to use volatility to enhance portfolio performance.

For many, the complications of stocks and bonds are great enough. When the subject of options comes up, they profess that it is a topic well beyond their capabilities. Investors should not be so quick to dismiss these important trading instruments. Chapter 10 includes a description of options and outlines key trading strategies that can be effectively implemented depending on one's outlook. In this section we shall discuss two basic approaches that exploit a fundamental truth about options. Options expire at some point in the future, and you can be certain that time will pass.

There are two components to an option's price. The first is *intrinsic value*. This reflects the value of the option if it were to be exercised immediately. The second component is called *time value* and this is what gives options their unique characteristics. While Chapter 10 goes into some detail about the various forces that contribute to an option's price, the only element that is necessary for this discussion is the acknowledgment that all options' prices reflect the market's expectation for volatility in the underlying instrument and that as options approach expiration their time value goes to zero.

Calls, which convey the right to purchase the stock at a fixed price, and *puts*, which give the right to sell the stock at a certain price, are the two basic types of options. If the underlying price of the stock were never expected to change, neither option would have any worth beyond the intrinsic value of exercising the option today.[2] But, of course, the prices of all securities change through time, and the market knows this. This expected volatility is reflected in the time value of options. Critically, the greater the expected future volatility, the more expensive the options. Investors with an awareness of volatility use this information as part of their portfolio construction strategies.

To the less well initiated, discussions of options and other derivatives usually make them think of more risk in their portfolios. While it is certainly true that there are many derivatives strategies that add to risk and reinforce this perspective, there are other approaches that have the opportunity to enhance returns without meaningfully increasing risk. Two, covered call writing and fully collateralized writing of puts are the subjects of this section.

6.2.1 Covered Calls

People who buy calls receive the right, but not the obligation, to buy the underlying security at the agreed-upon strike price during the life of the option. For this right the buyer pays a *premium* that is determined in the market. For every buyer of a call there must be a seller. The seller's obligations are considerably different. In return for receiving the premium, the seller of the call agrees to provide the security at the

---

[2]Suppose a stock is trading at a price of $50 per share. An option to buy that stock for $60 within the next three months would be worthless if the market consensus was that there would be no variation away from today's price. An option to buy that stock for $40 within the same time would be worth $10, which is both the intrinsic value and the total value, under the same assumptions of no stock price volatility.

strike price if the buyer selects his or her option. If the call buyer chooses not to exercise his or her rights, the seller of the call does nothing except pocket the premium. Of course, if the buyer exercises the call the seller must deliver the security.

Selling *naked calls*, that is selling calls without already owning the security that might need to be delivered, is a speculative activity that exposes the seller to considerable losses if the price of the security rallies. If, however, the seller of the call already owns the securities to be delivered, the position is hedged against a price increase. These calls are covered.

Suppose you own a large block of stock currently priced at $50 per share. You have made the portfolio decision to sell half of that position if the price reaches $55. Most investors would make a mental note of that decision and then when the price had risen enough they would place their sell orders. Other investors might plan ahead a bit more and place *resting orders* in the market to make their sales at that price. Neither of these investors is exploiting the opportunities embedded in the options on the stock.

As an example, suppose further that there are call options on the stock with a strike price of $55 and a current premium of one dollar per share. Also suppose that these options expire in four weeks, though there is nothing about this specific date that changes the fundamentals of the example. Instead of planning to sell the stock at $55 or placing a resting order to do the same, you could sell these call options in a quantity representing half of your holdings.

If the options expired when the underlying price exceeded $55, you would expect the buyers of those calls to exercise their rights and you would deliver the stock. The net proceeds in this example would be the $55 sales price plus the one-dollar option premium you collected. If when the options expired the price was less than $55, the buyers of the calls would not exercise their option and you would remain the owner of the stock. But once again you would have received the one-dollar option premium.

In both instances, whether the call option was exercised or not, your net outcome was one dollar per share higher than it would have been if you had not used options. *Given that you had already decided to sell half of your holdings if the price reached $55*, the risk profile of the covered call strategy was exactly the same as you would have had if you had simply placed limit orders to sell the stock.

In this example, covered calls have increased the total return while offering the same risk profile. It is not a panacea, solving all of the risk problems of owning stock. Your $50 stock could easily fall dramatically, and the only silver lining would be the one-dollar premium you collected. After the fact you might have wished that you simply sold the stock directly at the current market price.

Covered calls can be used to reshape risk dramatically. In the example above, after writing the $55 calls and collecting the one-dollar premium, you could use that premium to buy puts, which protect you against severe downside. In this simple example, suppose you could buy a similarly dated $45 put option for the dollar you collected. Now you have a *collared position*. If the price fluctuates between $45 and $55 you will have the exact same outcome as if you had held the stock without any options. If the price goes above $55, it will be called away from you just as you had hoped. If the price falls below $45 you have the right to sell that stock to the put writer, which limits your downside risk.

There is a range of prices between the put and call strikes, and you will experience the same return as the holder of the stock who chose not to use options. While you may not have enhanced your realized return as you did in the simple covered call strategy, you have greatly reduced the downside risk of holding that stock. This can certainly be considered an enhancement to the portfolio.

Critics of this approach will say that the covered call eliminates your flexibility to change your mind and not sell the stock in a rising market. This is of course true. But the example was established on the assumption that you intended to sell stock at a price of $55. If that is true, the covered call strategy is always superior to liquidation plans that do not use options. If you write the $55 calls and later change your mind, you can always buy back the options at the current market price. If enough time has passed and the market perception of volatility has not increased dramatically, you might still receive some profits from your options transaction.

6.2.2 Fully Collateralized Short Puts

The flipside of the covered call program is acquiring stocks using fully collateralized short puts. In this approach the investor has a target price for stock to be purchased. Instead of mentally identifying the price at which they want to buy, or actually placing a limit order below the current market, puts at the target price are sold with 100% of the value of the purchase set aside in assets that are not exposed to market risk.

The spirit here is identical to the covered call strategy. Instead of simply thinking of directional decisions, the fully collateralized short puts strategy combines the sale of the wasting asset of time with that decision to acquire the security at a below market target price. Again, the more the market is concerned about volatility, the higher the premia for the puts, and the greater the benefit to the strategy.

If the price of the security never falls to the strike price, the short puts will expire worthless, but the writer will have received the premium, which of course enhances total returns. If the price of the security drops through the strike price, the security is purchased at a net value of the strike price less the premium collected. In all outcomes the strategy adds value relative to placing virtual or actual limit orders.

In the covered call strategy, security came from already owning the shares that could be called away from you. Here it is absolutely essential to have cash equal to the purchase price of the stocks that may be put to you should the buyers of the options decide to exercise their rights. Lacking this 100% collateralization in cash means that you are adding leverage to your portfolio, which produces a potentially highly risky outcome in the case of severe market declines.

There is one meaningful risk that all investors pursuing either covered calls or fully collateralized short puts should be aware. Markets can gap, meaning that the price path of the security does not move smoothly from value to value. If either unexpected good or bad news is announced, the price of the underlying security may jump past the strike price of either written option. This can cause the options to be exercised at prices well away from the current market price.

Consider the earlier example of the covered call. You have written $55 calls against your portfolio that has a current price of $50. After the close of the market one afternoon the company announces that it is being acquired at a price of $70 per share. You can be assured that the market price the next morning will be much closer to $70 than to $50. If you had taken the approach of placing a limit order to sell your stocks at $55, there is at least a chance that you would receive what is known as a *price improvement* when your sell order was executed. If you had simply made a mental note to sell your shares at $55, you would gladly adjust your price to market conditions and sell them near $70. The covered call strategy absolutely locks in the $55 sales price.

The same effect applies to the collateralized short puts. Suppose you wanted to buy 1,000 more shares of the company above at a price of $45, and suppose also the $45 strike price put is trading in the market at $1.25 per share. You set aside $45,000 as your collateral, and you sell 10 puts.[3] You can think of the $1,250 you receive in premium as a partial subsidy to your purchase.

But imagine if after the close the company announces that it will miss its earnings target because it has suffered accounting irregularities. Depending on the severity of the announcement, the stock could be cut in half or worse. The next morning when the market opens your short puts will likely be deep in the money, with the buyers of those options being only too happy to sell you their stock at a price of $45.

Again, if you had placed a limit order instead of writing the puts, you would almost certainly be a buyer of the stock, but there might be some price improvement. If you had simply placed a mental reminder to buy when the price reached $45, you would enjoy the opportunity to rethink your decision and either purchase at the new market price, or decide to avoid the situation entirely.

Since meltdowns in stock prices seem to be more likely than melt ups, the risk of prices gapping seems to be a bigger concern for the fully collateralized short put writer than for the seller of covered calls. But it is also true that *gap risk* is well recognized in the marketplace and should be reflected in the values of the puts and calls you may be writing. That is, the risk here is more a psychic cost after a mistimed decision than an economic one.

For the organized and disciplined investor, buying and selling stocks at target prices is usually fundamental to their success. For those investors the covered call and 100% collateralized short put programs can meaningfully enhance returns over what would be experienced with limit orders. In times of high market volatility such approaches take on even more potential importance. The premia collected are higher in such environments and the option writing adds more certainty to the actual execution of the buy and sell decisions.

6.3   TAX-LOSS HARVESTING STRATEGIES

This technique is only useful to taxpaying investors, but it can be a meaningful contributor to net returns for anyone regularly facing large capital gains tax liabilities. Most tax-oriented strategies promoted by the street try to exploit nuances in language in the tax code, are heavily promoted as miracle cures, and more often than not get rejected by the tax court. These should be avoided no matter how many lawyers hired by the brokers say they believe the strategy is consistent with current law. Those lawyers never pay your tax bill or penalties when your claims are rejected.

There is, however, one approach that has been used for decades and passes all the agency's tests. It is called tax loss harvesting and it is particularly useful after volatile periods in the stock market. Suppose you purchased a large-cap US value

---

[3]The typical convention for exchange-traded options is for each put or call to represent 100 shares of stock.

mutual fund in the summer of 2018. In Q4, concerns over global geopolitics and the chance of recession pushed the S&P 500 down almost 20% and value stocks fell more. How can you maintain your portfolio exposures while realizing a trading loss that you can use at tax time to offset other gains?

The strategy would have you sell the recently acquired mutual fund, creating a loss, while taking the proceeds of that sale and placing them into another index fund or active manager mutual fund. At the end of 31 days, you could either reverse the trades to restore the original positioning, or you could simply keep the new funds if they were proving adequate to your portfolio needs.

Two things must be met to allow for the loss deduction. The first is that any replacement position must be sufficiently different from the one sold for a loss so that the service does not view the sale as a sham transaction. This is easier to meet than it might seem. An active value manager that doesn't hold the same stocks as the fund being sold clearly has the same style, but different risks, so that trade is allowed. Competing index funds with different benchmarks can also be substituted.

The second criterion is that the loss position cannot be reversed for at least 31 days. This is the window that defines a wash trade in the eyes of the IRS. Once the two criteria are met, the taxpaying investor is on the solid ground of tax minimization and not of the slippery slope of tax avoidance.

The previous example was developed around fund investments, but the principle is much broader. Suppose you had a loss in Coca-Cola stock. You could realize that loss with a sale and then turn around and buy Pepsi. There would be no question that those two stocks create different risks, but if your primary goal were to own positions in the soft drink and snack space, either company would play that role. The two stocks should be positively correlated, but there are enough idiosyncratic risks that it is entirely possible for Pepsi to lose big while Coke rallies in the wash sale window. It is this risk that demonstrates the trade was an economic one done for more than just tax minimization reasons.

Quantitative fund managers who actively adjust portfolios through time to create periodic trading losses have institutionalized this broad approach. You can give cash to one of these managers and instructions to match the S&P 500 through time. They start with a replicating portfolio just like the big indexers, but as the market fluctuates they may sell some stocks for losses while buying another basket of replacements.

The logical question is how does this succeed against the index mandate if you no longer own the index basket? The answer comes from the manager's analytical framework where the key market factors (industry, cap size, etc.) of the sold stock are replaced by other stocks with similar factors. While the index may no longer be owned exactly, the factors behind it are.

These differences create tracking error to the benchmark, but the best practitioners in the space have admirable track records in controlling that tracking error even through events like the financial crisis. The long-term return is very close to the benchmark plus any ancillary tax benefits along the way.

These strategies are at their most powerful when the portfolios are newly created. As losses are realized in the portfolios it is likely there are unrealized gains building as well. Through time it becomes harder to find candidates for loss harvesting. The solution to this is to periodically refresh the portfolio with new cash, which long-term users of this strategy incorporate into their ongoing allocation process.

As always, fees matter in this activity, and different providers can vary widely in what they charge. If you go with a formal tax loss harvesting plan, select a manager that has a strong record of tracking the target index while charging reasonable fees. The fees will never be as low as a vanilla index fund, but they can be meaningfully lower than those charged by the average active equity manager. After all, it makes little sense to pursue such a strategy if the manager receives most of your tax break.

Tax loss harvesting is an activity that is never going to turn a bad portfolio into a successful one, but it will add after-tax returns at the margin. This is the ultimate meaning of enhancement.

6.4   MORE CHALLENGED STRATEGIES FOR ENHANCING RETURNS

One sign that index-oriented investing has become mainstream is the prevalence of *enhanced index strategies* being offered to the public. Why settle for index returns when you can easily beat them? There are multiple enhanced index funds available, each offering a special path to improved returns. In almost every asset class, fund managers have developed enhancements that they believe will provide superior returns to the benchmark and implicitly improve their relative standing among all managers in that style . The history of these programs, however, suggests that most of the enhancements create at least one new risk that may or may not be well understood by either the investor or perhaps even the manager.

When confronted by the opportunity to invest in an enhanced program, the investor should analyze how the enhancement is designed to work, and how it might behave in a wide range of market outcomes. It is certainly not sufficient to rely on past returns because this history may have been created in an ideal environment that might not be representative of market conditions in the future. Too many of these programs are sold on the basis of simulated returns based on the fund managers' models. While one cannot fault researchers for trying to identify past market inefficiencies that could have been exploited, such historical simulations always run the risk of being no better than curve fitting exercises to the data. Believing in a model and actually seeing it work in real time are two very different things.

Most such programs start with the benchmark and then identify either fundamental or technical variations to create the enhanced return. You evaluate these processes the same way you would evaluate any active manager. How is the manager going to outperform over long periods of time? Their claims either have credibility or they do not. There are some enhancement programs where the extra return comes from a black box system that is highly quantitative and not revealed to the investor. Accepting these approaches requires a large measure of faith since neither the source of return nor the potential risks can actually be directly evaluated.

What follows below is a short list of ways some fund managers have tried to create enhanced returns. Nearly all of these have failed, sometimes spectacularly, at some point in time. Some have fooled different generations of investors multiple times. None of the strategies, per se, are lacking foundation. They merely pose risks that can ultimately unwind the total promised enhancement of the program and more. There may be times when these are perfectly desirable approaches, but to advertise them as all-weather enhancements is inaccurate. We will start with bond index enhancements and then move to a variety of stock index strategies.

6.4.1   Extending Durations in Low-Interest-Rate Environments

One of the constant challenges facing fixed income investors is the search for adequate yield. For the safest part of one's assets, the objective is always to get as much as possible without exposing the portfolio to too much risk. An upward sloping yield curve can be a powerful temptation to try to enhance returns by extending duration.

Movements in the US Treasury yield curve from the start of 2017 to the end of 2018 will be used to demonstrate some of the challenges. This period is far from typical in history, but the thought process in evaluating it in real time can be applied to all interest rate environments. At the start of 2017, Treasury bills with three months to maturity were priced to yield 80 basis points. The total return to a holder of similar securities in the previous year was 60 basis points. Even with headline inflation running under 2% on a year-over-year basis, real interest rates on the safest assets were significantly negative with little prospect for near-term improvement. Figure 6.1 shows the Treasury yield curve as it existed at the start and midpoint of 2017.

Rather than be content with miniscule returns with the shortest maturities, the investor might try to enhance yields by going farther out on the curve. Rates had started moving higher the year before, and the three-month bill started the year around 50 basis points. The two-year was yielding 125 basis points per year, and the three-year was yielding just under 150 basis points per year. Even with the Federal Reserve advertising its intention to raise policy interest rates into 2018, there was a strong temptation to lock in three times the three-month yield by buying the three-year paper.

The problem with this strategy is that three times very little is still a terrible rate of return when inflation is running meaningfully higher. This leads to looking out to even longer maturities. The five-year notes paid 1.8% per year, and the 10-year notes paid 2.3% annually after enthusiasm for potential economic growth post-election caused rates to start moving higher.

Investors trying to evaluate such a move sometimes get the wrong kind of reinforcement from recent history. In the first six months of 2017, long-dated interest rates did not continue to march higher as many predicted, but instead fell back a bit.

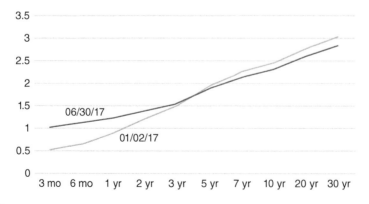

FIGURE 6.1   1/2/2017 versus 6/30/2017 Yield Curves
Source: Bloomberg

Over that window the total return on 10-year notes was over 2.5%, a meaningfully enhanced return over the shorter maturities.

This is precisely the kind of story that attracts new investors, especially those who may have reached the point of ultimate frustration with the continuing low returns on their short-dated treasuries. But just because a note had a strong total return in the prior period says nothing about the likelihood of success going forward. In fact, the positive return in the first half of 2017 may have actually biased the future toward a weaker outcome unless macroeconomic events deteriorate at some point or geopolitical events like North Korean war scares or trade conflicts with China cause a sudden flight to the perceived safety of US Treasury debt.

Figure 6.2 shows what happened for the entire year of 2017. The entire curve moved up for maturities under 10 years and dropped a bit for longer dated maturities. The curve flattened dramatically. Anyone who bought two, three or four-year papers hoping to pick up additional yield actually had price declines in their bonds that ate up much of the interest income earned. The ultraconservative investor that bought a series of three-month bills ultimately was earning meaningfully more than the two-year note that was purchased a year earlier.

The process did not stop there. By the end of 2018, with the Fed systematically raising interests for the previous two years, the yield curve had become essentially flat. Figure 6.3 shows that the investor who bought the two-year note at the start of 2017 hoping to pick up 80 basis points of yield over the three-month rate, actually did worse than someone who just bought a three-month bill and repeated eight times.

This example is just one of many that could be given. Not all penalize the buyer of extra duration. Owning long-duration bonds worked well on a comparative basis in Europe and Japan as sovereign rates fell into negative territory for durations even longer than 10 years. One should not evaluate any strategy by asking how it did in the recent past, but instead one needs to ask whether the risks taken by extending duration are being compensated by the yield being offered. The following example of duration risk should be committed to memory as a reminder of what can go wrong.

Extending duration is a strategy that works brilliantly until it stops. Suppose the yield curve is upward sloping like it was at the start of 2017 and you buy a newly issued 10-year note with a coupon of 2%, with the intention of gradually reaping the

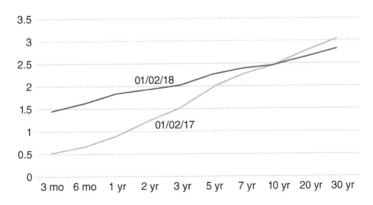

FIGURE 6.2   1/2/2017 versus 1/2/2018 Yield Curves
Source: Bloomberg

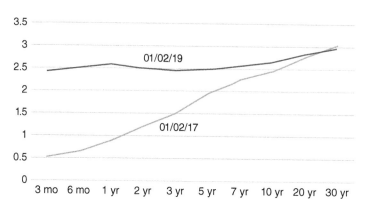

FIGURE 6.3   1/2/2017 versus 1/2/2019 Yield Curves
Source: Bloomberg

incremental yield over the shortest term Treasury bills. If you hold that bond for two years, you now own an eight-year bond with a 2% coupon that must be compared with all the other bonds available in the market. The US Treasury does not issue new eight-year notes, but there are many existing older maturity notes and bonds that have rolled down to that maturity. Now consider what happens if during the time you held the bond, market interest rates for those treasuries moved up to 4%, a rate that is close to historical norms.

Given the increase in rates, your Treasury note will have fallen in value. But the size of that decline may surprise you. An apparent modest increase in rates to 4% means that a new investor would only have to invest 50 cents to earn the same interest that you are earning on every dollar you invested in notes two years earlier. Your note will not have fallen in value by 50% because the government has still promised to pay you back your principal in eight years, but your mark-to-market loss would be 13.5%, and if interest rates stay the same for the next eight years you will earn 2% less income each year versus the current market rate.[4]

We have seen this story before. At the start of 1994, the Treasury market was coming off a multiyear bull market. Ten-year rates fell from 7.1% at the start of 1992 to 5.8% at the end of 1993. While this rate seems generous to the post-financial crisis investor facing ultralow interest rates, at the time it was the lowest interest rate investors had seen since the 1970s. Frustrated investors reached for yield by extending maturities.

In February of 1994 this all suddenly changed. The Federal Reserve sensed that the economy was recovering from a mild recession two years earlier and began raising policy interest rates. This caught many investors and traders flat-footed. Bonds of all maturities were rapidly sold and yields began a multi-month climb. By the end of 1994, the investor who hoped to earn 5.8% in their 10-year note experienced a

---

[4]The price of a bond is given by the following formula: $P = \sum_{t=1}^{n} C_t/(1+r)^t + F/(1+r)^n$ where C is the coupon received in each of the remaining n periods of the bond's life and F is the face value of the bond, which is returned at maturity, and r is the current yield. For a 2% coupon, eight-year bond with a current yield of 4%, the price is $865 per $1,000 face value.

total return of minus 15%, wiping out multiple years of any "enhancement" that they might have targeted from extending duration.

As previously noted, there may be many good reasons for holding extended maturities in one's bond portfolio at any given point in time. Certainly there have been investors since the end of the financial crisis that firmly believed in a US deflationary story, which would support owning longer duration treasuries at even historically low rates. But this is a different argument than placing such bets in an attempt to improve the return on one's cash.

Cash is traditionally thought of as the safest of assets. Extending maturities in any interest rate environment adds the dimension of *duration risk* that may or may not be consistent with the investor's goals. What is unquestionably true is that as interest rates fluctuate, the market value of a longer duration portfolio will move around as well, which may not be consistent with the desired risk profile of a client's cash.

6.4.2 Lowering Credit Quality

The first cousin of the extended duration strategy among bond managers trying to beat the benchmark is buying bonds of lower quality credits. It should almost always be the case that the debt of less credit-worthy companies and governments should have a higher yield than better credits. This incremental yield is the market's way of protecting the buyers of such debt from the higher probability of nonperformance. Some bond managers will argue that they can apply superior credit analysis and identify those bonds that are mispriced relative to their probability of default.

In constructing their portfolios, these managers may try to match the average credit quality of the index, but there may be significantly lower rated bonds sprinkled in to try to boost returns. Again, this is less of an enhancement strategy than active trading strategy against the index. If we were considering an equities manager benchmarked against the S&P 500, the comparable behavior would be the addition of micro-cap stocks that the manager thought were particularly undervalued and attractive relative to the large and mega cap names in the index.

As an example of how this approach can be applied, consider the case of a bond manager who is asked to outperform an AA index. Suppose the AAA bonds are yielding 2%, the AA bonds are yielding 2.1%, and A bonds are yielding 2.5%. It is not unusual for the differences between bond grades not to be equal as bond quality goes down. The index fund in this example matching the AA index should be expected to yield 2.1%. A manager could place half the portfolio in AAA bonds and the other half in A bonds and have an average yield of 2.25%. That manager could argue that the index has been enhanced by 15 basis points.

The extra yield earned by the active manager is reliable only if the interest rates across all credit qualities remain stable. When either the interest rate level or the specific spreads change, what once appeared to be an enhancement can actually become a detractor. The approach taken by the active manager may be a perfectly effective trading tool, but it is not without risk, and should not be considered a basic enhancement.

If one believes in the general accuracy of credit ratings, the simple example above probably does not entail a great deal of risk in that all bonds rated A or higher have a very high probability of performing. But a blended portfolio could be more extreme.

The manager could put 80% to work in AAA bonds and the remaining 20% in below investment grade bonds to achieve a much higher blended yield while keeping the average credit rating at AA. Such a portfolio could expose the investor to considerable risk if the equity or credit markets deteriorate quickly.

After the experience with credit ratings in 2007 and 2008, one should be highly skeptical of bonds that have meaningfully higher yields compared to other similarly rated securities. Yet a popular practice prior to the crisis was to build portfolios of bonds of certain credit qualities with only instruments or structures that had higher yields. For example, there was a large industry creating securities based on pools of mortgages or bank loans. These pools were often segmented and prioritized in terms of their bankruptcy standing, and then sold to investors who showed specific needs in their fixed income portfolios. On the simple theory that a portfolio of mortgages should be less risky than the individual securities, the ratings agencies at the time often gave these structures higher ratings than any of the underlying securities.

This produced an entire new class of AAA assets to be sold in the market. Managers who operated against benchmarks, largely defined in terms of ratings, added them to their portfolios and picked up incremental yield. Some advertised their products as enhanced versions of the low-risk indexes. This all fell apart quickly starting in 2007 as the crisis in the housing market began to unfold. Investors who placed too much reliance on bond ratings and on managers who were supposedly making only modest enhancements found that their expected safety was an illusion.

In general, the market does not rely exclusively on bond ratings to set value. In the case of the housing crisis, these structures all carried modest premiums to their yield that should have been more of a warning that it was. Investors and managers, on average, got this very wrong. What little premium was offered in the marketplace was a tiny fraction of what it should have been if the true risk of these instruments had been better understood. Instead, there was a multiyear history of modest outperformance before the crisis. As each successful year passed, more people bid for these apparently safe structures compressing their yields even more. Whatever incremental enhancement was achieved in the good times was destroyed many times over in the crisis.

6.4.3 "Insured" Portfolios

Many years have passed since the heyday of one of the most widely followed enhancement strategies, *portfolio insurance*, was being widely discussed by academics and actively sold by brokerage houses and specialized investment managers. The promise of these programs was simple. Drawing on well-established arbitrage relationships in the options market, providers of portfolio insurance claimed that they could dynamically trade portfolios in ways where they were always exposed to market advances, while simultaneously avoiding declines. In this way they would lead to an enhanced return over the basic index.

Normally to insure an equity portfolio requires the purchase of put options. As discussed in Chapter 10, purchased puts establish a floor on the valuation of the security. The price of this insurance is the premium paid for the option. Two University of California, Berkeley, finance professors, Hayne Leland and Mark Rubinstein, in the early 1980s argued that they could use the same arbitrage principles that Fischer Black and Myron Scholes employed in their option pricing model to create synthetic put options without incurring the expense of the premium.

They would target loss limits and as the stock index declined they would sell stock index futures against the portfolio holdings. This would synthetically raise cash and limit the impact of further declines in the market. The amount of futures to be sold could be determined analytically from the option pricing model. It was quite eloquent. Peter Bernstein in his book *Capital Ideas* called it "the ultimate invention."[5]

Leland and Rubenstein joined forces with John O'Brien, who had extensive financial marketing experience, to form Leland O'Brien Rubenstein Associates, Inc., more commonly known as LOR, to develop and sell portfolio insurance products. Because of the complexity of the product, success was not immediate, but business grew throughout the decade. It also attracted imitators, with Wells Fargo being the largest established institution offering portfolio insurance products. At the peak before the crash of 1987, it is estimated that perhaps $70 billion of stock portfolios had purchased one form of portfolio insurance or another.[6]

The theory behind portfolio insurance was almost unassailable, as long as the assumptions behind it held. The key assumption was that the market moved continuously. That is, prices flowed from level to level without gapping. The second assumption was that the adjustments to the portfolio could be done in any quantity necessary to keep the arbitrage relationship intact. A third assumption necessary to the LOR approach was that market arbitrageurs would always keep the stock index futures contracts lined up with the underlying stock market. These are perfectly reasonable assumptions for any investor that is a tiny part of the market. When portfolio insurance grew into the tens of billions of dollars in the 1980s, it was anything but a tiny part of the market.

Events began to deteriorate in the third quarter of 1987. The US stock market peaked in August and then began a slow decline that accelerated in early October. Through Friday, 16 October 1987 the stock market had one of its worst weeks in history with the Dow Jones falling by 250 points or almost 10%. The worst was yet to come. Asian stock markets opened on Monday, 19 October with massive selling in response to the weak US Friday close. The panic rolled westward tsunami-style through the European markets and headed back to the United States. Sell order imbalances left many stocks untraded hours after the opening bell on that day. The stocks that did trade tumbled with abandon.

There were almost no relief points during the day, with afternoon declines being greater than the morning's. At the closing bell the Dow Jones Index had fallen 508 points (23%) for the day. Throughout the carnage, portfolio insurers had been active sellers of index futures in an attempt to deliver on their promise of protection.

Historians debate whether portfolio insurance selling caused the 1987 Crash. A commission headed by Nicholas Brady exhaustively looked at all the market participants over the period of greatest stress. The key finding was that there were many

[5]Bernstein, P. (2005). *Capital Ideas*. John Wiley & Sons.
[6]Ibid.

sellers of all stripes during the crash. Identifiable portfolio insurance programs were quite active sellers, but were not even close to being the majority.[7]

The objective here is not to establish blame for the 1987 Crash. The question on the table is whether portfolio insurance actually delivered on its promises. Here the record is unambiguous. Throughout the day on 19 October, S&P 500 futures traded at the Chicago Mercantile Exchange were priced at a significant discount to the stocks. Part of this could be attributed to the staleness of prices on a barely functioning New York Stock Exchange. But much of the discount was due to the fact that there were significant imbalances to sell futures and that traders taking the other side required meaningful price concessions.

Almost all of the assumptions behind portfolio insurance failed badly in practice. Prices did not move continuously, but instead gapped widely. It was impossible to get the volumes of trading required executed even remotely close to the target prices. There was virtually no arbitrage activity possible between stocks and futures to hold the prices of those two markets together. Every single one of these failings made it more expensive for the portfolio insurers to trade and dramatically cut into the promise of portfolio protection.

The story of portfolio insurance as practiced by LOR and other firms is a familiar one. The early adopters had strong, positive experience as the programs were executed in small sizes and in liquid markets. Early success attracted more participants eager to enjoy the benefits. Once the size of the program grew to be a significant part of the market, all of the promises were broken because they simply could not be fulfilled in the magnitudes that they were made.

Another familiar part of the story is the compensation to the providers of the portfolio insurance schemes. While the models said that they could replicate a synthetic put strategy without paying explicit premiums, there were of course meaningful fees paid to the providers of the insurance to administer the plan. The first consumers of portfolio insurance very likely got well more benefit from the program than their fees totaled. The latter adapters, as is often the case, paid their hefty fees and received negative results.

After the crash of 1987, the explicit portfolio insurance industry basically dried-up and disappeared. There had been too much pain experienced by too many investors for them to go back to that well. But the spirit of portfolio insurance lived on. Regularly, investors are offered investment programs designed to enhance returns based on some dynamic trading strategy. Some have considerably less theoretical foundation than the LOR programs. But the appeal is the same. Investors may not understand the process by which the enhancement is supposed to occur, but they are highly attracted to the prospect of getting a better return at little or no expense. The word "insurance" is often loosely used in the sales pitches to amplify the appeal.

True insurance for a portfolio can only be achieved by buying real puts and paying the premium required by the market. Once that put is paid for, it does not matter

---

[7]Presidential Task Force on Market Mechanisms, US Department of the Treasury, *Report of the Presidential Task Force on Market Mechanisms: submitted to The President of the United States, The Secretary of the Treasury, and The Chairman of the Federal Reserve Board.* (1988). Readers who go to this reference are encouraged to read the entire report and not just the executive summary. There are multiple instances of conclusions in the summary that are either not supported or are outright contradicted by the actual data in the study.

in the short run whether markets gap, trading becomes illiquid, or the futures market diverges from the underlying stocks. Purchased puts are an explicit contract that will perform the desired function as long as the financial institutions standing behind them are functioning.

While owning a put offers protection against extreme downside events, it costs real money. Just as we saw in the covered calls and fully collateralized puts section of this chapter, because options are wasting assets, their time value decays. We have seen that writers of calls and puts should expect additional returns from this time decay. Conversely, buyers of insurance should count on doing worse than the index on average.[8]

There may be extensive benefits from buying insurance on your portfolio and reshaping the range of expected outcomes, but enhanced return is not one of them. Just like insuring your house or your life, portfolio insurance is an expense. If you cannot identify the explicit expense involved, there is a good chance that your insurance program will not perform the way you expect it to at a critical point in time.

The lessons of portfolio insurance are not complicated or profound. There are no free lunches. The major beneficiaries of these programs turn out to be the firms selling them. If too many people are doing the same thing you are doing, there is a good chance that the program will fail in unimaginable ways. These lessons are not unique to portfolio insurance, but have been repeated again and again throughout financial history.

6.4.4 Portable Alpha

Another type of enhancement program that has similar academic roots to portfolio insurance is called *portable alpha*. The spirit here is that if the manager can identify *any* source of outperformance in *any* market for which there are futures or swaps contracts traded, that alpha may be transported to another similar market. For example, if you find a bond manager who can create a reliable alpha over the Lehman Aggregate Bond Index, you can combine that manager with a package of derivatives and create an enhanced index program based on the stock index of your choice, less fees, of course.

The academic foundation for portable alpha is much simpler than any option pricing model. All that is required is the identification of the beta of an asset class. Any performance beyond that beta is called alpha, and with the development of a wide range of derivative securities, investors have the ability to isolate both components of the investment return.

The key evaluation by the investor has to be on the alpha generation prospects and accompanying risks. The mechanics of transporting that alpha are quite direct, as shown in Figure 6.4. There are definitely some practitioners that have developed thoughtful, risk controlled ways of generating alpha, but there are many others who pursue alpha strategies with considerable tail risk that can occur at just the wrong moment. Examining past returns without having a good understanding of the source of alpha is a path ripe for disappointment.

---

[8]Petzel, T.E. (1989). *Financial Futures and Options*. Quorum Books. Pages 177–178 discuss the expected return of a put protected portfolio. It is the same as the unprotected portfolio less the time value of the purchased put.

The derivatives behind this program are discussed in detail in Chapter 10, but a simple example can be constructed to demonstrate the basic principles. Suppose active Manager A has shown an ability to beat the Barclays Aggregate Bond Index by an average of 75 basis points annually. For the sake of this example assume you are trying to find an investment that will enhance the S&P 500. Manager A can still come in handy.

The portable alpha program would include the following steps:

1. Invest $100 in Manager A.
2. Enter into a *total return swap* that pays the Barclay's Aggregate Bond Index and receives the S&P 500 Stock Index on a notional value of $100.

Suppose the Barclays Aggregate Bond Index increased in the investment window by 2%, and the S&P 500 Stock Index increased by 7%. Let Manager A earn 2.5%, slightly less than her historical average but still an alpha for the period of 50 basis points.

In this example, the return from Manager A was $2.50. The return on the swap would be a positive $5, the difference between the stock and bond index returns. The total return would be 7.5%, equal to the S&P 500 Stock Index return plus the manager's 50 basis points of alpha.

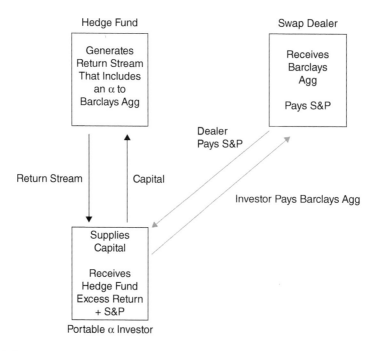

FIGURE 6.4   Equity Total Return Swap to Create Portable Alpha Program

Suppose everything in the example above is the same except that the S&P 500 Stock Index fell by 7%. The return from Manager A would still be $2.50. But now, instead of receiving money on the swap, you would have to pay a total of $9.[9] Combining the inflow from Manager A and the outflow paid on the swap gives a net loss of $6.50. This is again exactly equal to 50 basis points better than the stock index.

This simple example makes it appear that no matter what the stock index does, the portable alpha strategy will enhance its returns. Given the unstated assumptions in the example, this is certainly true, but a few adjustments to account for reality will qualify that conclusion.

The most important assumption is that there is an alpha to transport. In the example above, the fixed income manager had a track record of 75 basis points of outperformance. The actual outperformance of the 50 basis point varied from the historical averages, but it was at least still positive. There is nothing to guarantee that the alpha would not be considerably less or even negative. Many portable alpha strategies discovered during the 2007–2008 crisis that the abilities of their alpha generating managers were correlated to the overall market. This translated into negative alpha being added to the equity beta losses making the problem worse.

The second risk concerns managing *collateral*. In an equity total return swap, the receiver of the equity return actually pays twice when equity markets fall. They pay their expected interest rate part of the swap to the swap dealer and then they "receive" a negative stock return, which means they pay on that part of the swap as well. Where does that extra collateral come from?

As the stock market falls, the alpha engine needs to be partially liquidated to meet the obligations under the swap. If the alpha trading strategy is perfectly liquid, there should not be much of a problem, but if it is in a hedge fund structure with quarterly liquidity or worse, there can be a serious mismatch between the call for funds and their availability. Typical notice periods with hedge funds also make the careful management of cash flows more difficult.

One effective solution to the collateral management problem is to hold cash outside the alpha engine to support collateral calls. If one invested, say, 80% of one's capital in the alpha engine, put 20% in cash, and then executed a 100% notional value total return equity swap, there would be a ready cushion against market drops up to 20%. The cost of this is a meaningful dilution in the size of the net alpha since one can expect the returns to cash to fall well below the regular required interest rate payments on the swap.

Another possible solution is to have a dedicated line of credit against which one could draw needed cash in the event of a collateral call. The cost of such lines also eats into the alpha of the program, and the loan terms may give the lender more control over the assets of the alpha engine than one might desire.

Other considerations include the expenses of the swap and the reliability of the counterparty. When Lehman Brothers declared bankruptcy in 2008, outstanding swap arrangements were valued using the latest possible data, and then canceled. Investors in the middle of programs like portable alpha strategies found

---

[9]You are obligated under the swap to pay the return on the Barclays Aggregate Bond Index, which is 2%. You receive the return on the S&P 500 Stock Index, which had a loss of 7%. Receiving a loss results in you paying out that 7% on the swap, making the total payment to your counterparty 9%. On a swap with a notional value of $100, the payment would be $9.

themselves scrambling to put in place new derivative contracts at a time of maximum confusion and market disruption.

6.4.5 Leveraging Small Alphas to Reach Acceptable Returns

In the world of modern portfolio theory there is almost no alpha that could be considered too small. As was shown in Chapter 3, the primary goal is reaching the efficient frontier. Once there, access to the capital markets allows you to maximize your risk-adjusted returns. If this requires using leverage, there is nothing in the theory that prevents it.

Presumably if large profit opportunities exist, almost everyone can identify and quickly exploit them. Hidden well below this surface are supposedly more riches in the form of small profit opportunities that most people overlook. Oftentimes, quantitative approaches seek out these small profits, which taken on an unleveraged basis may not be interesting enough to attract investor capital. As soon as these returns are leveraged, however, they look highly desirable. Leverage, large or small, is often advertised as an enhancement to the underlying benchmark.

By regulation, US mutual funds under many circumstances may employ up to 1/3 leverage with the major requirement being that the leverage is disclosed in the listing of the holdings. There is nothing in any finance textbook that suggests that 1/3 is the magic number beyond which terrible things begin to happen. Regulators have simply decided that below this level, risk is low enough to be acceptable for most mutual fund investors.

Hedge funds through most of their history have operated under completely different rules. As long as they did not explicitly violate the *Regulation T* margin requirements set by the SEC, they could and did employ considerably higher levels of margin. This was constrained primarily by their counterparties' willingness to lend against their positions.

In the case of fixed income arbitrage, where the trader buys one debt instrument and sells it against another, the amount of allowable leverage has been quite large because the market believed that under most circumstances the risk in the spreads was minimal. But many firms, including the hedge fund LTCM and futures commission merchant MF Global, learned the hard way that supposedly low-risk trades levered up can become lethal.

The problems from this approach to enhance yield stem from modern portfolio theory, ignoring most of the risks inherent with great leverage. It is generally assumed that small mispricings cannot become large because there is a limitless supply of arbitrage capital to keep the prices in line. This assumption has broken down time and time again whenever the size of the positions has gotten large versus the market or when liquidity has been squeezed by some financial crisis. Until we can outlaw concentrated positions and liquidity crises there will be considerable risks that MPT doesn't consider.

Investors should treat these forms of enhancements the same way they do any stand-alone investment opportunity. The trades need to be considered both in terms of their inherent worth on a micro level, but also on their potential macro risks. Past histories are suspect unless they include experience with all potential stress environments. Long track records through quiet times should be particularly suspect because they are likely to attract large pools of new assets that can badly tilt the future risk return profile.

6.4.6 Writing Uncovered Options to Sell Time

Earlier in the chapter, the decaying nature of options was described as a potential source of enhancement in both covered call and a fully collateralized short put strategies. Since you can always count on time to pass, the premiums received from the short options are, on average, a wasting asset. If these two strategies can enhance portfolio returns, are there other strategies involving selling options that can do the same?

One strategy that is sometimes sold during bull markets combines a long portfolio of equities with *short out of the money puts*. This is something of a hybrid between covered calls and collateralized short puts, with the important difference being that the downside risk is amplified. Typically the manager of such a strategy will state the obvious, which is that stocks have a high probability of increasing in value through time. The manager will then add that by writing out-of-the-money puts, the fund will add incremental value from the ever-present time decay. There will always be an assertion that the short put part of the portfolio is rigorously monitored and that the manager can eliminate this risk by buying back the position if the market signals the need to do so.

This can be an attractive argument during a bull market because the investor not only benefits from being long the market, but has incremental returns from those nervous investors who purchased the unneeded puts as insurance. While acknowledging the existence of downside risk, the manager assumes most of it away with the assertion that superior modeling and trading skill can avoid most of the problems.

The single biggest risk to the strategy is a market that gaps down. Not only do the stocks in the portfolio lose value, but also the short puts get exercised, and the manager receives additional equity exposure as the market is collapsing. As was shown in the section on portfolio insurance, even the most sophisticated option models fail to provide assurance that the portfolios can be adjusted dynamically during a market crash.

This approach to enhancing portfolio returns suffers from many of the same problems discussed above. While it is working, it adds a small amount above the benchmark. But when it fails, the losses can be multiples of any previous gains. Rather than be seen as an enhancement strategy, this should be classified as a risky market timing strategy with highly asymmetric outcomes.

When evaluating the investment thesis of such programs, ask the manager what the fund return would be if we woke up tomorrow morning with the stock market down 20%. This kind of gap move would prevent any dynamic trading program from easing the loss. A typical answer to this question might be, "That can't happen," or "That has never happened before, so we don't have to worry about it."

These events have happened to a greater or lesser degree, destroying large amounts of capital and shutting down funds. Victor Neiderhoffer had his first enhanced fund following this strategy close in 1997 on the heels of a 7% one-day market loss. He started a second similar fund, which advertised improved risk controls, as the stock market began to recover in 2003. After receiving industry accolades for the best fund early in its run, it was shuttered in 2007, after suffering a similar extreme decline.

Pursuing such strategies reveals the kind of mindset that suggests a triumph of arrogance over wisdom. We have discussed frequently how statistical modeling of markets can fail spectacularly. Given the highly asymmetric nature of uncovered option writing, and the periodic episodes of price changes that do not conform to the standard portfolio models, we should expect these strategies to fail at some point.

There is a reason why people pay real money for the protection offered by purchased calls and puts. Just like insurance on a house or car, people are willing to pay a known amount to protect against a much larger, unknown risk. While there is a certain element of probability embedded in the pricing of stock market options, that world is a far cry from the actuarial regularity involved with insuring houses and cars. While the writers of naked options should expect on average to earn the time value of the option, the moments of loss can occur suddenly and be staggeringly large. These are not the features most investors want in any enhancement strategy.

6.4.7   Buying Out-of-the-Money Options to Capture Tail Events

If writing naked out-of-the-money options fails as an enhancement strategy, then perhaps doing the opposite would succeed. Why not regularly buy out-of-the-money puts and calls in order to receive the benefit when extreme market moves occur?

In general, this strategy suffers from being on the wrong side of the time decay path. One should expect that out-of-the-money options will expire worthless. The money devoted to these options are like lottery tickets that have a chance of paying off big, but on average the returns are below what is spent for the options. We typically do not see financial managers sprinkling lottery tickets into their portfolio as a form of enhancement, yet we sometimes see managers claim that there are always good options available that can do that job.

Part of this story has its roots in 2006 and 2007 when an excess of liquidity and a severe misjudging of market risk caused many options to be severely underpriced. A subset of managers recognized how cheap these options were. Despite the fact that even cheap options suffer from time decay, some of these managers like John Paulson made major allocations, which resulted in some of the greatest returns in the history of investing.

After the crisis of 2007 and 2008, the belief in cheap options may have lived on, but the reality suggests that the world got a lot smarter about the pricing of risk. No longer could you risk five basis points in order to earn 300%. Since most investors struggle with even the basics of option pricing, they are vulnerable when funding managers who assert that they can always find underpriced options offering a tremendous prospect for returns.

Without an ability to regularly find mispriced options, the manager trying to enhance returns by being long puts and calls is fighting an uphill battle. Time decay is an absolute certainty, and unless pricing mismatches regularly exist, buying options will be a drain on returns and not a plus. Investors may want to buy the equivalent of a financial lottery ticket periodically, but they should understand that the expected return is negative, and in no way is this any part of an enhancement strategy. "Black Swan" portfolios designed to exploit tail events are the subject of the next chapter.

Enhancement strategies in general are as attractive as they are because of the highly benchmark-oriented methods of most managers and consultants. Once the benchmark is held out as the ultimate goal, there is a great temptation to focus only on alpha relative to that benchmark. We have seen that there are a few ways that might be successful in achieving that goal, but there are many other apparently promising paths that are actually likely to fail. Like all active strategies, enhancements must be dissected by the investor and critically evaluated. Those that rely on dynamic trading strategies and sophisticated models have demonstrated periods of success punctuated by moments of great failure. Investor skepticism is as vital here as it is in any element of portfolio construction.

CHAPTER 7

Black Swan Portfolios

In 2007, Nassim Taleb's book *The Black Swan* introduced to many investors the notion that markets regularly deviate from the assumptions of normality embedded within most finance models.[1] He squarely attacked many of the major tenets of modern portfolio theory. Both portfolio and risk managers, and by implication millions of investors, were being badly led astray by defective models developed by the latest generation of financial engineers.

The industry response was mixed. Few tried to refute the basic claims because their general foundation was firmly established in market observations. Some argued that the traditional models were still useful, but one needed to be mindful of their limitations. Others jumped right onto the Black Swan train and began to develop investment strategies designed to exploit extreme market moves.

The metaphor of the Black Swan is based on the eighteenth century notion that all swans were white because nobody in Europe had ever seen anything else. Then sailors returned from Australia with evidence that black swans existed. A black swan event is something that nobody can predict based on past experience, but it happens anyway.

Financial markets may have a few genuine black swan moments, but mostly the term has been applied to any extreme market move that caught investors off guard. Before the twenty-first century, there had never been a time when massive amounts of subprime mortgage debt had been packaged into securities that were subsequently sold to highly leveraged buyers. When that trade collapsed, was that a black swan? There have been countless examples throughout history of mispriced, leveraged securities exploding and creating massive market losses. Focusing only on the narrow situation of subprime securities, there may have technically never been a black swan seen before, but there were plenty of really dark brown swans that hinted that black ones might exist.

The point of this chapter is not theology or sorting out precise definitions. The point is that since the market crisis that began in 2007, a sub industry has evolved to provide investors portfolio solutions to the problem of extreme market moves. These solutions can take many forms. Some are dedicated hedge funds designed to do well in times of stress. Others involve overlay programs that may or may not involve dynamic trading strategies similar to portfolio insurance that was discussed in the previous chapter.

---

[1]Taleb, N.N. (2007). *The Black Swan*. Random House: New York.

7.1 TAIL RISK IN THE OVERALL PORTFOLIO

Risk in many individual investments and portfolios is often described in terms of statistical distributions. Figure 7.1 two stylized views of how returns can be distributed. The dark line is a *standard normal distribution*, the backbone of most statistical modeling in investing. It has many virtues, not the least of which is that it is mathematically tractable. More importantly, so many activities across all walks of life seem to be nicely approximated by it.

The chart is a representation of *probability*. The most likely outcomes are clustered around the *mean*, or average, value. Lower probabilities are associated with events away from the mean. The normal distribution allows the analyst to guess how likely any particular outcome will be.

Unfortunately, as Taleb emphasized in his book, trying to model market behavior with the standard normal distribution is a bit like trying to force the evil step sister's foot into Cinderella's slipper. The normal distribution has been used largely because of computational ease, and not because it actually captures market price reality on a regular basis.

The gray line distribution in Figure 7.1 is also symmetric around the mean, but contains more observations clustered around the middle while there are also more extreme observations on both sides. This distribution is said to have *fat tails* relative to the normal.[2]

The major challenge to any statistical representation of markets is accepting the notion that there is a stable distribution of returns that can characterize future

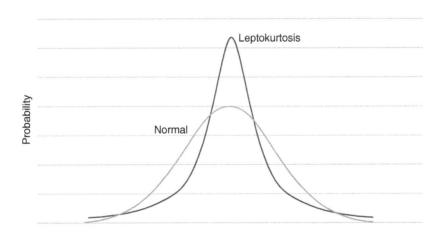

FIGURE 7.1 Normal versus Leptokurtosis

[2]Every statistical distribution has *moments*. The first moment is the mean, and the second moment is the standard deviation. Both are widely used in the analysis of portfolios discussed in Chapter 5. Going beyond these measures leads to less well-known territory. The third moment captures *skew* and the fourth moment is called *kurtosis*. Kurtosis captures how likely extreme observations are, and in the jargon of the statistician, fat tailed distributions are said to be *leptokurtic*.

events. Taleb's contribution is to remind us that even if a long history of returns suggests a wellbehaved, symmetric distribution of outcomes, markets can change rapidly and produce results that appear almost impossibly improbable when considered in terms of the standard models. Fat tails can be much fatter than originally expected.

One might think that if the standard normal distribution is a poor proxy for reality in statistical models, the solution is to replace it with another algebraic formula that shows fatter tails. It is not that easy. If the history of returns has never contained any extreme movements, what should guide the analyst in determining the proper analytical distribution? What is the actual probability of an event the standard normal distribution says is a one in ten million chance? Ultimately one is left with the task of asking the question, "What can go wrong?" This is a vital question, but not one that leads to a precise analytical formulation of the problem.

Reality is actually much more complex than a question between symmetric fat tail distributions and normal distributions. Figure 7.2 gives two examples of distributions that are not symmetric. The gray line in the chart displays what is known as *positive skew* and the darker line shows the reverse distribution where the outcomes are skewed negatively.

Investors would love it if their portfolios showed a return pattern with positive skew. This would mean that their losses were typically limited while there were many opportunities for large positive returns. This is the outcome pattern that people are looking for when they buy options. The losses are limited to the premiums spent for the put or call, but if the market moves in the right direction, the gains can be many times larger than the expense of the option. Not surprisingly, to achieve positive skew distributions one needs to pay an up-front premium.

Negative skew is the investor's nightmare. There is a ceiling on gains, but the downside is unlimited. After a particularly unlucky streak in the market, investors might think that this is the world they are facing, but in reality to create such an extreme negative skew requires writing options either directly or indirectly in the portfolio. For the explicit writer of puts and calls, there is a premium received as compensation for taking on this very unattractive risk profile.

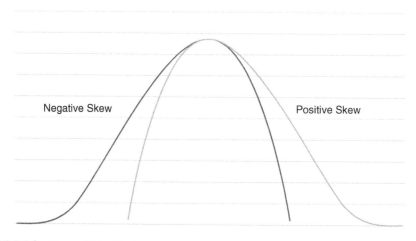

FIGURE 7.2 Skewed Distributions

These concepts are critical to understanding portfolio risk, and any responses one might take to reshape it. Portfolio managers actively selling tail risk protection typically do so without considering how severe the overall risk really is. They instead play upon the emotions of investors who may overestimate the risk within their portfolios and not carefully consider the cost of the protection against adverse moves.

Going back to the basic portfolio construction problem discussed in Chapter 4, one needs to consider the risk profile of each element, but more importantly anticipate how the elements will combine in different market environments. The sleep-well-at-night money should be almost isolated from any extreme, adverse moves. On the growth side of the portfolio there can be considerable risk of great loss, and it is likely in times of major stress that these losses will correlate positively across the different asset classes.

Suppose for the purposes of discussion that you own 1/3 of your portfolio in bulletproof, sleep-well-at-night money. Let the remaining 2/3 be distributed across a wide range of growth assets including global stocks, corporate credit, and real estate. In crisis periods like 2008, the bulletproof assets reign supreme, while all of the growth assets fall to varying degrees. Portfolios that contained traditionally defensive assets like gold and hedge funds also suffered as these areas were liquidated as well in the crisis, and provided minimal protection against the other declines.

This is the environment that set the stage for the growth of Black Swan portfolio techniques. Investors who had been disappointed that their traditional diversification failed to protect them in a meaningful way sought out new approaches. Many providers have appeared in order to meet this demand. While the specifics of any given Black Swan product vary, the general approach is to construct portfolios that are anticipated to do well during moments of great stress. The sections that follow describe three types of products that share the trait that they all did well in the past crisis. Unfortunately, they were not widely employed before the last crisis, so it remains to be seen how they will do in the next crisis if they become widely popular.

7.2 PROTECTIVE EQUITY PUTS

Buying a put to match the size of your long equity holdings is the most basic form of insurance. Just like your house or car insurance, you pick a deductible, establish the term of the policy, and the market tells you how much the insurance will cost. Put protection is the ultimate Black Swan portfolio hedge in that no matter how much the market falls, the profits on the put will replace all losses beyond the deductible. The challenge is to assess whether the cost of the insurance makes sense relative to the risks that you actually face. When the market's perception of risk is extraordinarily high, it may be better to self-insure and save the premium expense.

An example can show how challenging this decision can be. In the middle of 2019 the S&P 500 stood at 2964, nearly a record level. At that time you could buy various puts on the S&P 500 Index that would provide almost a full year of protection. The cost of those puts is in Figure 7.3.

If you own the index at 2964 and want to buy insurance, you have a wide range of choices. The figure shows a range of strike prices from 2400 to 2950. Buying the 2950 put means that you are trying to get insurance from just below the current index level. The deductible works out to be 0.5%. Any decline below 2950 in the stock portfolio is

FIGURE 7.3   Cost of One-Year S&P 500 Put Protection 30 June 2019

Spot Index = 2964		Options expire 20 June 2020		
Strike Price	Deductible	Premium	Premium as a %	Maximum Loss
2950	0.5%	160.4	5.4%	5.9%
2850	3.9%	129.4	4.4%	8.3%
2700	8.9%	92.4	3.1%	12.0%
2400	19.0%	45.2	1.5%	20.5%

Source: Bloomberg

made up for by the increasing value of the put. The premium for the 2950 put on that day was 160.4, representing 5.4% of the total value of the index. This means you are paying a certain expense of 5.4% in order to insure against any declines beyond 0.5% of the index. Since the time value of the option is a wasting asset, this translates into a maximum loss of 5.9%, the sum of the deductible and the price of the premium.

If you believe that that is expensive insurance, you can lower the premium by increasing the deductible. The figure gives many options, and focusing on the 2400 strike price, the cost of the option falls by almost 75% versus the near-the-money 2950 strike price option. Of course the deductible is meaningfully larger. In this case you are self-insured for the first 19% decline. In worst-case, you could still lose 20.5% of your portfolio.

It is difficult to make an absolute judgment as to whether or not this is expensive or cheap insurance. A great deal depends on your expectation about risk in the marketplace. It is unambiguous, however, that a willingness to pay over 5% of your portfolio annually in order to protect against most declines in the index places a great burden on the expected equity returns. On average, following this approach when the stock market has historically returned 8–10% annually means you are willing to give up more than half the expected return in order to minimize the downside.

Just like your car insurance, you can reduce the up-front expense by increasing the deductible. Being self-insured for almost a 20% drop, which is a pretty dramatic event, still costs 1.5% of the portfolio value every year. Since these quotes came directly from the market, at that point in time they reflected the balance of opinion across real investors. Concerns about volatility were clearly on many people's minds.

This is not just a one-time expense. Every year that passes where the market does not fall brings up a new decision moment. The insurance was not needed last year. The market still has not corrected or collapsed. Do I buy a new batch of insurance for the coming year? A multiyear bull market as in the decade after the financial crisis can result in a long and quite expensive path of insurance premiums being paid.

Campbell Harvey and his coauthors looked at put protection as a strategy over a much longer period than the single observation contained in the above example.[3] Applying a systematic program of buying one-month, at-the-money S&P 500 puts

---

[3]Harvey, Campbell R. and Hoyle, Edward and Rattray, Sandy and Sargaison, Matthew and Taylor, Dan and van Hemert, Otto. The Best of Strategies for the Worst of Times: Can Portfolios Be Crisis Proofed? (17 May 2019). https://ssrn.com/abstract=3383173 or http://dx.doi.org/10.2139/ssrn.3383173.

from 1986 through 2018 created a 7.4% average annual drag on returns. Options purchased with large deductibles created an even worse cost–benefit trade-off because they offer no protection during long, gradual declines.

There are Black Swan funds and trading programs that are based on the approach of *always* owning puts. It does not matter whether the price of the insurance is small or great, the attitude is that the market accurately reflects the probability of extreme moves and the price is generally fair. Since people who buy insurance are those who are particularly sensitive to the risk of extreme loss, they should always want protection.

This may not, however, be an accurate interpretation of tail risk and the cost of insurance. Exchange-traded options on stock indexes have been trading for over 30 years. That history shows that the cost of put insurance spikes *after* the market has experienced a large downward move. It could be that the writers of puts, having been burned from the drop, refuse to write more insurance at the same premiums. It is also likely that some investors who had no insurance before the decline decide that it is now a good idea, even at a higher cost.

Markets go through cycles. During prolonged bull markets like the 1990s and 2003–2007, investors become complacent about potential risks, and option writers get greedy after a string of expirations where they effectively pay no claims. Option premiums fall despite the fact that the fundamental risk may be growing with the heightened valuations. The moral of the story is that it is probably better to buy an umbrella during a string of sunny days than to try to find one in the middle of a storm.

This is illustrated in the next two figures. Figure 7.4 shows the path of the S&P 500 from 2003 through 2013, and Figure 7.5 presents *VIX*, the market measure of volatility calculated from the value of S&P 500 options over that same span. Bull markets are never straight-line affairs, but as the stock market trudged higher from 2003 through the start of 2007, investor confidence built. VIX, which had started the period over 20, drifted down to near 10 over the same four years.

FIGURE 7.4   S&P Index 2003–2013
Source: Bloomberg

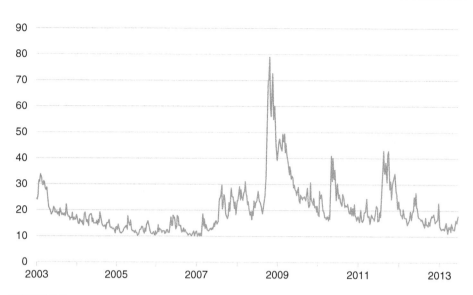

FIGURE 7.5 VIX Spot Price 2003–2013
Source: Bloomberg

VIX began to grow as storm clouds gathered over the US housing industry in 2007. When Lehman Brothers collapsed, VIX exploded. Three years after the event, investors were still wary about potential volatility and priced options above historical averages. But as the stock market moved steadily higher, more comfort was felt and VIX drifted lower until it was approaching record low territory in 2013.

The best period to have bought almost any options for the purpose of insurance stretched from 2006 into the first half of 2007. Markets were ebullient. Liquidity was plentiful and writers of options asked for small premiums because their models showed that many investment products carried almost no risk. There were a few hedge funds that positioned themselves well in anticipation of what would become a perfect storm of bad news. Some of them used their spectacular returns through the crisis as a marketing springboard to later gather large sums of new assets.

The pitch was basic. Buying protection worked, as could be plainly seen from the returns that in some cases exceeded 100%. The world will always be a risky place. Insurance will periodically pay off, and you will always be glad you owned some. The Black Swan fund industry was born. Rarely do the marketing presentations of these funds spend any time describing how cheap the pre-crisis options were that created the track record. They also fail to warn adequately of the potential cash drag that comes from the cost of insurance held through noncrisis periods.

While the principles behind Black Swan funds are most easily seen with puts used for insurance, the marketing genius of the most successful Black Swan funds came from the fact that the managers had typically not had to buy options, but instead executed the same strategy with OTC credit default swaps, or CDS. Almost no non-professional investors have a thorough understanding of these relatively new instruments, adding to the mystique of the managers who employed them so adroitly.

A final word is that just because options are relatively cheap, reflected in a low level of VIX, does not mean the market is about to crash. The ongoing bull market after 2013 is a great example of how low VIX levels are sometimes correct. While it is usually better to buy cheap options for protection rather than highly expensive ones, a cheap option says little about the chance that the insurance will be needed.

7.3 CREDIT DEFAULT SWAPS (CDS)

Credit default swaps (CDS) are a relatively new class of derivatives that seek to protect the buyer from the event of a default in a single bond or in a pool of bonds. They are described in detail in Chapter 10, but the basic structure looks very much like buying options for insurance previously described. The buyer of CDS pays a one-time premium in return for the promise that if the bond experiences a default (as determined by a special committee of the International Swaps and Derivatives Association), the seller of CDS agrees to make up the difference between the defaulted bond's value and par.

CDS might have begun as contracts to protect against the default of specific sovereign or corporate bonds, but it was quickly expanded to cover indexes of bonds and other fixed income structures like CDOs and CLOs. In these cases, it became a portfolio problem where each of the underlying components of the package contributed to an overall performance standard of the structure. The specifications of what constituted a default and the subsequent required compensation gained considerable complication as the industry evolved.

By most objective standards, protective put options based on stock indexes were fairly cheap in late 2006. But in comparison to CDS on pools of mortgages, they seemed outrageously expensive. Financial engineers had resorted to models of mortgage structures that relied heavily on the idea that while one family in Florida might default, their experience was independent of families in Illinois, Connecticut, or Texas. By building structures containing a diversified portfolio of underlying mortgages, one could actually improve the performance of the pool relative to any of the individual components, lowering the risk to near zero.

These models were based on many years of history that "proved" that the pools were essentially riskless by design. Of course, that history did not have any evidence of the housing crisis that was on the horizon. Ratings agencies and practitioners used the complicated models and the benign history to convince themselves that these were essentially riskless instruments.

If a security is truly riskless, the CDS on that security should be free. For quite a while in 2006, a great deal of CDS traded hands at near-zero prices. The writers trusted their models and believed that anything they collected in premiums was essentially free money. In hindsight, the models that predicted no chance of default were horribly flawed and the writers of these CDS contracts lost billions of dollars when the true risk was revealed.

That was the sellers' problem. The buyers of these CDS contracts owned cheap lottery tickets that paid off big as the mortgage market tumbled. These turned out to be the ideal Black Swan investment vehicles since they produced returns that were many multiples of their cost at a time when most traditional risk assets suffered.

Imagine risking less than 1% of your total portfolio to earn a 50x return. Such trades existed and those who held them actually saw their total wealth increase through the worst of the crisis.

These are the stories that marketing wizards can usually only dream about. Since they actually happened in some cases, the histories were packaged and actively sold to investors who had not previously heard of Black Swans, but who had recently paid a high tuition to learn about them in real time. Of course, the future was unlikely to look like the past for multiple reasons.

The biggest impediment to repeating the extraordinary returns was finding anyone to write such cheap CDS after the crash. Previously unmodeled risks were revealed in the crisis, and CDS prices quickly calibrated to the higher, more accurate risk profile. Sellers learned the hard way that their earlier offerings were too cheap. They did not need a lot of reinforcement to avoid that mistake going forward.

The second reason CDS paid off so well came from the depth of the crisis. Almost everyone involved in credit badly misjudged the mortgage market. CDS was not the only area that suffered from excesses. Investors used too much leverage in acquiring these assets. Homebuyers severely extended themselves to buy houses they could not afford. When the crisis erupted, everyone ran for the same exit door and the market impact was extreme. That kind of extraordinary move may not happen again for many years until the lessons learned from the crisis have been forgotten or ignored by a new generation.

An analogy can be found in forest fires. In an unmanaged forest, a lot of things build up through time. Mature trees gain mass. Dead trees fall over. Underbrush builds up. Layers of leaves accumulate. If lightning strikes such a forest, there is a good chance there will be a fire. Because of all the potential fuel, the fire can expand rapidly, ultimately causing massive destruction. Now imagine that lightning strikes the same forest the following season. There may be a fire but because there is so much less fuel, the damage is contained.

It is not like the forest "learned" from its first experience and therefore was smarter in avoiding the destruction from the second lightning strike. Instead, the first, horrible fire cleaned out most of what made the catastrophe possible. The financial and credit crisis of 2007–2009 had a similar effect on the investment landscape. Of course investors were smarter after the event, but the financial destruction that accompanied the crisis also eliminated a great deal of dry tinder that could fuel another massive sell off.

CDS became appropriately more expensive after the crisis. And if a new insurance event is triggered, the size of the payoff will likely be smaller, reflecting less damage. What does this mean for Black Swan portfolios using CDS at their core? It means that meaningfully bigger Black Swan positions will be needed to offer the same level of protection and they will be more expensive. This is yet another case where past experience is probably a poor indicator of future results.

7.4   OTHER MACRO TAIL RISK BETS

Most investors understand the broad concept of tail risk. Financial panics usually manifest themselves with extreme stock market declines, often followed by a drop in value in other growth assets like real estate. As shown above, the most direct way to protect against such an event is to buy out-of-the-money stock index puts, but this direct insurance can be quite expensive if the market is in a fearful mood. For a while in 2005 and 2006, the CDS market offered extremely inexpensive indirect insurance, but as the link between risk markets became better understood, the cost of this insurance rose meaningfully as well. In response, some managers have tried to identify other, less crowded trades that might serve as insurance against tail risk events.

These are usually expressed using macroeconomic positions in interest rates or currencies. In the extreme crisis of 2008 and early 2009, as people ran from risk assets, a large part of their proceeds were spent on short-dated US Treasuries. This, in turn, caused the dollar to strengthen in almost all foreign exchange markets.

Holding Treasury bills is rarely thought of as an integral part of Black Swan portfolios because their short duration precludes any meaningful price increase. They certainly fulfill the role of sleep-well-at-night money, but preserving capital in one part of the portfolio is not the same as insuring against major losses in another. There are, however, related trades that might serve this role.

A common chain of events during times of crisis has anxious investors and central banks alike buying up the shortest-dated sovereign debt, pushing interest rates down on the front end of the yield curve. This has the immediate impact of making the yield curve steeper. Other investors, in an attempt to increase yields, may sell some of their Treasury bills and buy longer duration notes and bonds. This increase in demand raises prices and lowers those yields as well. Implicitly, the immediate spike in demand for Treasury bills radiates out to all maturities along the yield curve.

Declining interest rates in the longest-duration Treasury bonds can have a meaningful impact on the price. This means that a portfolio of the longest duration Treasury bonds can be expected to act as a counterbalance to declines in other parts of the portfolio at times of crisis. But one does not need to stop with a basic portfolio of bonds.

A more energetic approach would involve buying a leveraged basket of long-dated bonds. Since the yield curve is often upward sloping, the financing costs for obtaining the extra leverage should be less than the interest earned on the bonds themselves. This is a classic carry trade, but one that is designed to do well at times of stress.

There is no perfect answer as to how much leverage is appropriate, or how large this part of the portfolio should be. One would have to estimate the sensitivity of the bond price to any potential crisis event and then scale the position to fit the estimated potential loss. The effective limit to leverage for most investors would be a fully margined position in US Treasury bond futures traded on several exchanges around the world.

Since this is usually a *positive carry trade*, one might be tempted to assume that there are few risks from this approach. This is not true. Interest rates can and do fluctuate for many reasons and any meaningful shift up in the yield curve could generate powerful losses at a time when the other assets in the portfolio are not necessarily rising. This would almost certainly be the case if market expectations for inflation shifted up suddenly. Treasury bonds would fall as interest rates increased, and the stock market might also be challenged with the bad news.

The natural response to this kind of risk is to try to limit the downside of the bond portfolio by executing the trade using options instead of futures. This solves one problem, but at the expense of a continuing stream of option premium payments. Like all long option positions, the erosion of value from time decay is a consistent drag on performance.

Trying to get tail risk protection in the currency market is also challenging. While the dollar has had a history of being a safe haven at times of market stress, the overall pattern of currency trading is one of extreme volatility at many times. You could say you wanted to be long the US dollar against a basket of both developed and developing country currencies as a crisis hedge, only to discover that the regular ebbs and flow of value swamp any notion of protection that you think you are receiving.

Gold is often touted as an asset for extreme crisis times. There has sometimes been truth to this, especially in highly inflationary environments or moments of geopolitical stress. But changes in inflation typically do not fit the pattern of a Black Swan event. Inflation evolves. It doesn't spring upon the world suddenly.

Experience in 2008 suggests gold is a very poor tail risk hedge against the events of the worldwide financial crisis. Figure 7.6 shows the history of gold prices from 2005 through 2018. While there was a strong upward trend over the first six-year period, gold lost almost 1/3 of its value during the peak of the crisis. For whatever reason, investors decided to run away from gold almost as rapidly as they left global equities, but unlike equities, they were not quick to return.

One might argue that gold in the last five years of the chart points out the perils of trying to find Black Swan investments. As the stock market marched steadily upward, gold trickled downward, with no assurances that it would bounce back if equities took a tumble.

Finding innovative trades that can act as a Black Swan tail risk hedge is a difficult proposition. It is not hard to hypothesize how an asset *might* behave at a time of crisis, but the actual experience can be meaningfully different from what was originally expected. If you are truly trying to protect against a small probability event called a

FIGURE 7.6 Gold Price 2005–2018
Source: Bloomberg

stock market crash, the cleanest way to do this comes from the outright purchase of an equity index put. This, however, is almost certainly the most expensive way to get protection.

As investors evaluate Black Swan strategies, the trade-off between expense and precision must always be considered. If the tail risk hedge appears inexpensive, there is a good chance it is due to the fact that its probability of success in a pinch is low. Managers touting their approach will sometimes draw on historical track records taken from a time when very few people were actually doing the trade. There may be an appearance of consistency between the hedge instrument and the market at risk. But future reliability is not assured, either because there was no fundamental connection in place to begin with, or that the trade has become unworkable as it became more and more crowded. The Harvey paper cited earlier in the chapter analyzed all of the strategies discussed above and found them all lacking to one degree or another over many market cycles.

When evaluating the wide range of Black Swan fund alternatives available, the first question should not be, "How will they work?" The first question should always be whether your portfolio would be better or not with their inclusion. This is a basic insurance question that you face in many walks of life.

7.5   WHAT IS INSURANCE WORTH TO YOU?

If it is difficult to make one's portfolio crisis-proof, what explains the appeal of Black Swan strategies? The major appeal is highly emotional. It is the same emotion that causes people to pay high premiums for specific accidental death airline flight insurance. We think about the severity of the event vividly. It is extraordinarily difficult to get a good estimate of the probability of that event. Even when we are told that it is a miniscule probability, we end up believing that for us it is higher simply because it is an activity that touches us personally.

There will always be unpredicted events in the marketplace. Some of them will be severe. They fit the definition of a Black Swan. But while we might not anticipate exactly the events that trigger a sudden drop, we can certainly understand that such drops can and do happen. That is why we started the discussion of portfolio construction with determining how much money has to be set aside for you to sleep well at night. If that exercise was done properly, the risks in the balance of the portfolio, including Black Swan event risk, should be manageable.

It is nonetheless tempting to look at how well any particular manager did in the depths of any crisis and say, "If I had only owned some of that fund ...". This is an exercise in *counterfactual history* where the only variable that changes is the inclusion of one different investment.

The world does not work that way going forward. Today's portfolio is not the same as the one you owned before Lehman Brothers collapsed and the Fed began a giant plan of adding liquidity to the economy. The Black Swan fund you are considering is operating in a different environment too. The portfolio you are contemplating, with Black Swan insurance, is almost certain to behave differently in the future.

That does not automatically mean you should not add Black-Swan-type managers. You need to determine what impact there will be on your financial plans or your lifestyle if another financial crisis occurs. Would the impact be temporary or permanent? If it is likely to be temporary, can you stand the emotional swings before you recover? If the impact is permanent, how much are you willing to pay to avoid even that small chance of loss?

There are some events that are so expensive to insure against that it is better to assume the risk by being *self-insured.* This was definitely *not* the case in 2006 when equities options were historically cheap and many types of CDS were almost being given away. But environments change and so does the cost of insurance.

A question that does not have an obvious answer is, "Would you be willing to spend 2% of your assets each year to avoid any chance of loss exceeding 10%?" By taking this insurance you are assuming the first 10% loss. That is your deductible. Once the insurance is in place, it is theoretically possible that the market could drop every year by 9% without receiving any benefits of the coverage. Whether the market falls a modest amount or increases, you know with certainty that 2% of the portfolio, the premium, will be permanently lost. Repeat that for five years in a row and imagine how you would feel.

Long-term investors who believe in the growth potential of their countries and their stock markets would likely not be attracted to such an insurance policy, but that does not mean it has no place in any portfolio. If the potential impact from a catastrophic event is great enough, a Black Swan insurance fund might have a role.

Before going down that path, however, consider all of the other alternatives. Increase the size of the sleep-well-at-night pillow. Reduce the allocation to the most susceptible risk assets. Think about how any possible tail event could impact the entire portfolio and objectively evaluate your own emotional stability during such an event. Black Swan funds are like every other investment you consider. They have their own risk and reward profile. What was cheap and worked well in 2007 and 2008 may not be so today. Having them aggressively marketed on the back of what might be a once-in-a-lifetime event does not make them the right solution for all investors.

CHAPTER 8

Market Bubbles and Crashes

The history of investment is also a history of *market bubbles*. Human nature seems destined periodically to create markets that are meaningfully out of sync with any notion of long-term stability or value, and when these markets adjust, they do so with a suddenness and magnitude that absolutely shocks the imagination. If the market in question is large enough, there can be systemic implications that ripple through the entire economy.

There is a long list of great market bubbles. A far from exhaustive sample includes:

- Seventeenth-century Dutch tulip bulbs
- Eighteenth-century South Sea and Mississippi land speculations
- General stock market crashes in 1929 and 1987
- Silver in 1980
- Japanese stock and real estate markets 1989
- Tech stocks in 2000
- Real estate in 2007
- Selective small-cap stocks in 2021

The dates on this list note the time the bubble popped. In most cases there was a multiyear build up that kept inflating prices. This chapter will not try to dissect the past episodes. Volumes have already been written on those subjects. We shall try to better understand how bubbles are formed, why they pop, and how investment portfolios should be positioned along the way.

The key word in the prior sentence is *pop*. All market bubbles have high prices, but not all high-priced markets are bubbles.[1] In well-functioning markets the best solution to the problem of high prices are those prices themselves. High prices encourage existing suppliers to produce more and often encourage new suppliers to come into the market. This extra supply signals to demanders that their needs will be amply met, lowering at some point their eagerness to bid excessively. Market adjustments can overshoot. If too much supply comes to the market, prices will fall until new demanders are coaxed into the market. This describes normal market dynamics, which operate every day without the dramatics of a price bubble.

---

[1]While it is certainly possible to have a "bubble" with extremely low prices that "melts up" when it corrects, the far more likely event is a bubble with high prices. Examples throughout this chapter will be of this kind, while acknowledging that mirror image situations can happen. Low-price bubbles are not that common, and are therefore of less practical interest.

So what constitutes a bubble? Some observers insist that bubbles imply irrationality on the part of the participants. It cannot possibly make sense, for example, as Charles Mackay notes in his book, *Extraordinary Popular Delusions and the Madness of Crowds* (1841), that the following list of items make up a reasonable price for a single, even quite rare, tulip bulb[2]:

- Two lasts of wheat
- Four lasts of rye
- Four fat oxen
- Eight fat swine
- Twelve fat sheep
- Two hogsheads of wine
- Four tuns of beer
- Two tuns of butter
- One thousand pounds of cheese
- A complete bed
- A suit of clothes
- A silver drinking cup[3]

Peter Garber has studied the tulip phenomenon more carefully than most and is not so quick to conclude that human emotion and irrationality intersect as often as most writers suggest.[4] He makes the excellent point that market pundits calling any extreme market move a bubble have taken the easy path. Markets are much more complex and when looking at a situation in real time rather than with the benefit of perfect hindsight, it is rarely easy to pinpoint what might actually be a bubble.

Charles Kindleberger and Hyman Minsky focused almost exclusively on market bubbles that created macroeconomic chaos or systemic financial crisis like much of the world experienced in 2007–2009.[5] They cite leverage as a necessary ingredient. Easy credit implicitly encourages buyers to pay more than they ought, which when aggregated across a large number of participants creates momentum in the market and severely inflated prices in at least a few markets. Few worry about borrowing or lending in this environment as the value of the collateral rises in the inflating part of the bubble cycle. These are the kinds of market bubbles that are of most interest to macroeconomists and policy makers. But by emphasizing the macroeconomic dimension of the issue, the critical microeconomic foundation of the bubble phenomenon may be missed. Irrationality and leverage are not absolutely necessary to the creation of a bubble. It is true, however, that for a bubble to create systemic issues, easy credit and leverage seem to be essential ingredients.

While stock markets and real estate attract most of the attention in bubble discussion, the issues can arise in any kind of market. Beanie Babies, created by the

---

[2]Mackay, C. (1841). *Extraordinary Popular Delusions and the Madness of Crowds*.
[3]For those needing help translating seventeenth-century Dutch measurement units, a *last* is about 4,000 pounds, a *tun* is 252 gallons, and a *hogshead* is ¼ of a tun. Source: Wikipedia.
[4]Garber, P. (2000). *Famous First Bubbles: The Fundamentals of Early Manias*. MIT Press: Cambridge, MA.
[5]Kindleberger, C. (1978). *Manias, Panics, and Crashes: A History of Financial Crises*. John Wiley & Sons. Minsky, H.P. (1986). *Stabilizing an Unstable Economy*. Yale University Press.

firm Ty, Inc. in 1993, are small plush toys filled with plastic beads rather than more traditional batting used in stuffed animals. Anyone who saw a small child with one in the 1990s immediately saw the appeal. They were reasonably priced, and no doubt considerably cheaper to produce. There was a large natural demand among the pre-teen crowd.

Ty's genius was to create specific characters and limited editions, which meant that after some unspecified production run, the character would be "retired." This had the effect of suggesting scarcity and created an aura of collectability. In short order the demand shifted from what was predominantly a kids' toy market to one driven by adults buying the babies primarily as a collectible. Prices soon reflected the adult world. Particular characters that had sold originally for $5 sometimes traded hands in the late 1990s at prices over $2,000. Holiday season 1997 saw the publication of the book *Beanie Mania: A Comprehensive Collector's Guide.*[6]

Ty did not directly benefit from the overheated market, as they neither raised their initial offering prices nor tried to sell more of the characters to eliminate the sense of scarcity and value that had evolved. They did, of course, profit mightily as the number of children and adults alike demanding the next newly issued toys expanded dramatically with the promise of easy riches.

There may have been some individuals who borrowed in order to acquire Beanie Babies expecting that continuously rising prices would justify the leverage, but it is more likely that the key driver came from middle-class families who were also enjoying regular 20% annual returns from their stock market investments. Feeling flush with success, some had no problem spending the equivalent of an upscale New York City apartment's monthly rent on a few cents worth of cloth and plastic that they were confident would continue to appreciate.

One might question what the story of Beanie Babies has to do with real investment markets. While most serious investors never considered this market to be anything other than a somewhat nutty phenomenon in the low-end collectible space, there are a number of insights that can be learned from how this history unfolded.

The phases of a market bubble can be summarized:

1. Initially there is a normal market made up of traditional suppliers and demanders.
2. For some reason, rational or not, a new group of demanders enters the market pushing up the price beyond the normal equilibrium. This often happens in markets where supply in the short-run is either naturally or artificially constrained.
3. The simple act of the price increase begins a *momentum* phase in the market. New demanders continue to arrive, primarily driven by the trend and perceived trading opportunities. The price in the market grows well beyond the maximum value that any of the traditional demanders would be willing to pay. The first group can be said to be priced out of the market.
4. Some event occurs that breaks the momentum. It could be the appearance of new supply that is attracted by the extreme prices. It could be a change in sentiment as some of the participants themselves begin to question the prices and decide they want to realize profits. It could be an external event that greatly curtails or eliminates the buyers' ability to keep purchasing.

---

[6]Phillips, B. and Estenssoro, B. (1997). *Beanie Mania: A Comprehensive Collector's Guide.* Dinomates Inc.:Naperville, IL.

5. The market begins to correct, but discovers that there are few or no buyers at prices just below the peak levels. The traditional demanders are nowhere to be found and some of the second group of demanders flip sides and become suppliers as they try to exit the market. The market hits an *air pocket* and prices fall dramatically. The bubble has popped.

6. Prices often need to fall below the initial normal equilibrium in step 1 to attract the return of the traditional demanders. Because of the sudden, large decline in price, they are as cautious as anyone. They require a margin of safety in their price before they return to the market. The recovery phase has begun.

Let's put the Beanie Baby story into this framework.

1. Ty, Inc. (traditional supplier) provides a delightful toy to millions of children (traditional demanders) at a price many of them can afford.

2. Ty, Inc. decides to "retire" characters on a regular basis, giving a new group of demanders (adults) the idea that there may be value in collecting these characters. This in principle is no different than the strategy followed by Lladro, Wedgewood, or Hummel when they create limited editions of their artworks. It was only executed at a different initial price point.

3. Prices of retired Beanie Babies progress into the hundreds and then thousands of dollars for the perceived rarest and highest-quality examples. Few nine-year-olds can afford to participate in anything but the new issue market and they are sometimes denied access as total demand outstrips supply. New character supply is rationed by queuing or lotteries.

4. Nearly simultaneously with the break in the tech stock bubble, the demand for Beanie Babies pulls back dramatically. People appear to reevaluate the prospects for further appreciation. Ty has not done anything radical to expand supply, but it becomes clear that there is no obvious end to the creation of new characters. Once perceived extreme scarcity becomes less obvious. Styles and fashion change.

5. The person who paid $2,500 for a rare, early-edition baby discovers that there are not multiple bids right below that price at $2,490, as there would be in a normal *continuous* market. Bids exist, but are present only several hundred dollars lower. The market gaps down as the bubble pops. Some earlier buyers decide not to sell, but instead wait for a recovery. Many of those collections likely exist intact 20 years later.

6. Once the surplus collectibles work their way through the market, traditional equilibrium reappears with children being the primary demanders from Ty, Inc. who continue to offer a wide array of cute toys priced with a reasonable profit margin in mind. The bubble is gone, and it is not likely to reappear in this particular form.

There is no better way to describe the general process than to rely on some simply microeconomic supply and demand charts. Figure 8.1 is laid out in three panels to show how the prices evolve through the different phases. What is harder to show is the time line of the resulting prices.

Figure 8.1a depicts a simple supply-and-demand equilibrium. Traditional suppliers (Supply) will offer increasing quantities to the market as the price rises.

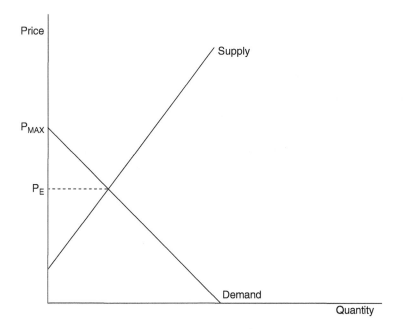

FIGURE 8.1A   "Traditional Equilibrium"

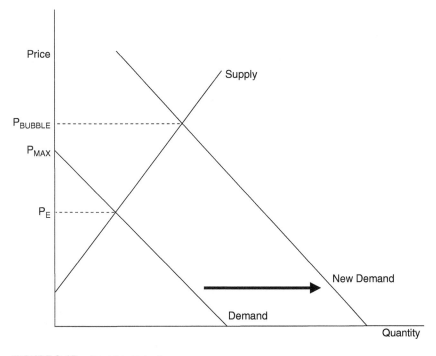

FIGURE 8.1B   "Bubble Price"

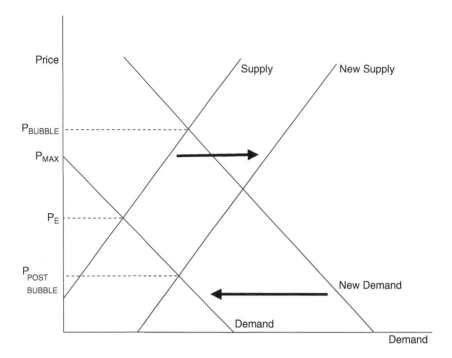

FIGURE 8.1C   "Post Bubble Price"

Traditional demanders (Demand) respond to price in the opposite direction, desiring more as price falls. Any price above P_{MAX} in the chart is too high for these demanders. Nothing gets sold above this price. The traditional equilibrium is shown where supply just equals demand with a resulting price P_E.

The end result of the next phase is shown in Figure 8.1b. New demanders come into the market, typically in stages over time. The aggregate demand curve becomes the sum of the traditional demanders plus the new entrants and the whole demand curve shifts out (New Demand). As this aggregate demand curve moves out, the equilibrium price grows steadily from P_E to P_{BUBBLE}. Note that in this figure P_{BUBBLE} is well above the old P_{MAX}, meaning that at the bubble price all of the traditional demanders have been priced out of the market. The new demanders have essentially taken over. Their interaction with the supply curve determines the market price. Little kids who just want a cheap, lovable toy are out of luck.

This is where the dynamic of price bubbles really kicks in. The bubble price logically encourages the suppliers to find more of the expensive product to bring to market. This should moderate price, but often demand keeps growing at a good clip while supply takes longer to adjust. The result is an inflating bubble.

Eventually bubbles pop because new supply not only catches up to the speculative demand, it expands right past it. Prices begin to drop. People who were buyers because they believed prices could only go up begin to have second thoughts. Some, and possibly most, of the new demanders change their minds. In the next chart, the extreme case of all the new demanders leaving the market is shown. Demand shifts all the way back to its traditional core constituents. Further, some of those new demanders have decided that they would actually be sellers, and the supply curve shifts out to New Supply. The intersection of Demand and New Supply produces a cleared market price of $P_{POST\ BUBBLE}$, which is meaningfully below the previous traditional equilibrium.

Unlike the more gradual path taken as prices moved up from P_E to P_{BUBBLE}, the drop to $P_{POST\ BUBBLE}$ can be sudden and often disorderly. The bubble has burst and it can take months or years to sort out the disruptions and distortions in the market that the bubble has created. Eventually, however, adjustments occur and the cycle is completed as prices are once again determined by the original suppliers and demanders. Beanie Babies are priced as toys and tulip bulbs are once again seen as plants instead of objects of speculation.

Academics have spent a good bit of time and effort looking at the pattern of prices across many markets hoping to determine whether a bubble exists, and when it might pop if it does exist. To date, this has not been terribly fruitful because market dynamics are not physics.

Consider two widely acknowledged market bubbles, silver going into 1980 and Japanese stocks at the end of the 1980s. The price pattern for silver prices from 1978 to 1981 (Figure 8.2) bears some resemblance to the prices of the Nikkei 225 Japanese stock index from 1987 to 1991 (Figure 8.3), but not a lot. Silver's run-up and subsequent collapse were both more acute than the Nikkei's moves. Silver's price dropped below the starting point of the most rapid ascent, but in subsequent years has traded in a broad range both above and below the original equilibrium. The Nikkei, in contrast, continued to drift lower for years after the history in the chart, and found itself more than 75% below the peak value 20 years later and still down 50% after almost 30 years. Try as one might to define a precise mathematical pattern that defines a bubble, it does not exist.

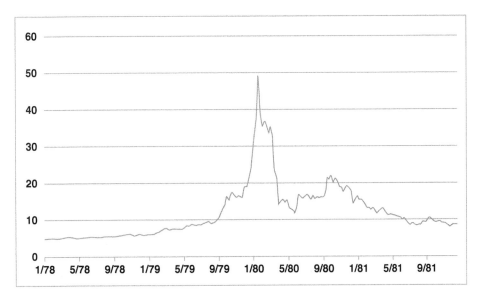

FIGURE 8.2   Silver Spot Price 1978–1981
Source: Bloomberg

FIGURE 8.3   Nikkei 225 Index 1987–1990
Source: Bloomberg

The futility of attempts to define mathematically a market bubble stems from the fact that while the basic phases of a bubble that were described above exist in every case, the specific components are different in each market and they can evolve at different speeds. Some industries are able to adjust supply to high prices more quickly than others, which make it difficult to create large bubbles. And when they do occur, they pop more quickly. Similarly, investor psychology about a market as important and deeply personal as residential real estate will adjust more slowly, and more painfully, than opinions about Beanie Babies. The basic conclusion is that not all of the data points will fit neatly into a predefined model.

8.1   IRRATIONALITY IS NOT NECESSARY TO CREATE A BUBBLE, BUT IT HELPS

While it is tempting to generalize broadly about the irrationality of market bubbles, it is not always "the delusion of crowds" that creates the problems. Markets can become segmented and move sufficiently far away from their traditional equilibriums that bubbles can form and pop. A less studied example can be found in the *convertible bond* market.

Prior to the 1990s the convertible bond market was largely the domain of mutual fund managers and other professional long-only investors. These hybrid securities, which make regular interest payments while simultaneously offering call options on the company's stock, are little understood or held widely by the investing public. The traditional buyers of convertible bonds typically analyzed them in a somewhat old fashioned way. What were the prospects for the stock price? Was the interest coupon attractive enough considering the default risk of the company? Was the embedded option to convert the bond into stock attractive?

In the 1990s, thanks to the Black-Scholes and the *binomial option pricing models*, a new group of demanders entered the market for convertible bonds. Specialty hedge fund managers realized that the embedded options in the convertible bonds were frequently mispriced relative to the arbitrage equivalents in either the stocks or listed options of the companies. They would buy the convertible bonds and then sell an appropriate amount of stock or options to capture the spread and sometimes attain a positively convex portfolio. The mispricing translated into a greater than risk-free rate of return for what was essentially a low-risk trade. As more of these arbitrageurs entered the market, and pricing became more accurate around the arbitrage values, increasing amounts of leverage were used to achieve the target total fund returns.

The convertible arbitrage space was fairly well established by the late 1990s, but did not really take off until 2000–2002. As the stock market in general was tumbling from its tech bubble-induced highs, the average convertible bond manager earned 25.6%, 14.6%, and 4.0%, respectively, in those three years.[7] This was the kind of performance that secured hedge funds' reputation in the minds of institutional investors. Assets under management at convertible bond hedge funds exploded. Apparently not all of it was from long-term investors.

As assets rolled in they had to be deployed. Convertible bonds were bid up, and yields fell further. Traditional buyers were not interested in the arbitrage characteristics of the paper, and many of them left the space as they viewed absolute levels of yields and the relative yield to comparable quality bonds as unattractive.[8] It was estimated that by 2003, 60% of all convertible bonds were being purchased by hedge funds.[9] Two years later researchers claimed that hedge funds accounted for up to 75% of the market.[10]

After earning a robust 12.9% in calendar year 2003, the next year showed a disappointing 2% total return. Worse, 2004 started reasonably well, but the returns were strongly negative in the second half of the year. Many of the short-term-oriented, returns-chasing investors decided to get out. Assets at convertible arbitrage hedge funds that had peaked at over $40 billion in mid-year 2004 tumbled to near $25 billion 18 months later.

$15 billion may not sound like a large sum to raise to meet redemptions, but given the inherent leverage that these hedge funds deployed, bonds equal to many

---

[7] Dow Jones Credit Suisse Hedge Fund Indices.

[8] Lucchetti, A. and Lauricella, T. (2003). These Funds Are Making a Conversion of Sorts. *The Wall Street Journal*, (27 June). Note that several large mutual funds that had historically specialized in convertible bonds were changing their names by dropping the word *convertible*. The managers did this because of an SEC rule that says that the funds must invest at least 80% of their assets in securities that correspond to their names. Managers were quoted in the article saying that the prices of convertible bonds had gotten so unattractive that they could no longer meet their investment goals without expanding their mandate.

[9] Ibid.

[10] Mitchell, M., Pedersen, L.H., and Pulvino, T. (2007). Slow Moving Capital. *AEA Papers and Proceedings* (May), pp. 215–220, describe the convertible bond market in 2005 when large redemptions caused severe price declines in the average price of the bonds. Their primary observation was that when the hedge fund industry came to largely dominate the convertible bond market, it left that market vulnerable to disruptions and severe mis-pricings.

multiples of this number needed to be sold. A few of the most highly leveraged funds performed so poorly that they closed. The convertible bond market did not react well to this period of adjustment.

The price movement in this market did not attract a lot of broad attention because it touched a relatively small number of professionals, but it affected them severely. According to pricing estimates after the fact, the bonds traded down to a discount of 2.7% relative to their theoretical value.[11] This was almost three standard deviations away from equilibrium, a very big number in a world that was supposed to be easily held together through arbitrage.

Was this episode a bubble? It fits the general pattern described above, but it wasn't very big in the grand scheme of things. The key distinguishing features were the shift from traditional owners of convertible bonds comfortable in a lower price neighborhood to the arbitrage buyers willing to pay much more. When the price fell, it fell quickly and to levels that were meaningfully below what was perceived as appropriate versus alternative investments used in the arbitrage. But the prices did not fall so far that traditional long-only buyers flooded in to pick up bargains. Instead, other hedge funds that were not experiencing redemption pressures came in and began to build new arbitrage positions. This may have been an example of a bubble losing a good bit of its air, but not popping completely.

That bubble popped with the credit crisis of 2007–2008. Then it wasn't just convertible arbitrage hedge funds that faced redemption pressure. Big multi-strategy funds that held large convertible bond arbitrage portfolios were also hit with large requests for redemptions. As these funds tried to liquidate all kinds of leveraged credit securities, there were almost no potential hedge fund buyers with dry powder available to pick up the bargains.

Prices at the end of 2008 and early 2009 fell like a stone. This was not unique to convertible bonds. Bank loans and high-yield paper were also dumped at indiscriminate prices. Early in 2009, traditional long-only buyers started to return to the market and the recovery phase began. In every dimension, the price action of these securities during and after the crisis confirmed that we had just gone through a bubble experience.

Nothing in the convertible bond experience required irrationality or extremes of emotion. Arbitrageurs simply did what they always do. They identified mispriced securities and then hedged out various risks. At no time did the prices seem crazy viewed through the lens of the arbitrageur.

The fact that the trade was getting crowded or that one group of demanders was dominating the marketplace could have signaled that the potential for an extreme move was increasing and caution should be taken. After all, this was not a new circumstance. The space faced a similar set of issues when LTCM collapsed in 1998 creating great concerns among managers and prime brokers, as well as severely distorted prices that persisted until new arbitrage capital appeared to take advantage of the crisis.

The lesson from this episode is that at some point behavior, that is completely rational (and unemotional) when viewed in the isolation of an individual trader, creates different risks in the aggregate. The challenge for all traders and investors is to take off the blinders that restrict one's range of vision about what risks may be present. Risks evolve from specific and individual to general and collective.

---

[11]Ibid. p. 217.

Bubbles require at least some collective behavior. Even the most irrational and misguided individual cannot distort a market. A crazy person bidding absurd prices will be ignored if the bids are well under the market and will be met with a flood of offers if the bid is too high. It is only when a new group of demanders together moves a market well away from the traditional equilibrium that a bubble forms. When it does there is also collective risk that the bubble will pop.

8.2 MARKET BUBBLES, COLLECTIVE RISK, AND SYSTEMIC RISK

Collective risk is not the same as *systemic risk*. Collective risk arises from common action by a large number of market participants that, when reversed, can create large and sudden price changes in a market. Unless the market or its participants in question are large relative to the economy as a whole, there is little chance that a market bubble will create a risk to the financial system.

The Beanie Babies phenomenon is a good example of this. There is little doubt that the prices of Beanie Babies in the 1990s formed a bubble that popped near the end of the decade. The change in collective attitude and behavior of the participants also, no doubt, created meaningful losses among the late-cycle buyers. It appears, however, that there were no examples of losses being so great as to threaten financial institutions or the state of the economy. Even if Ty, Inc. had failed as a company as a result of the bubble bursting, it would have only been a tragedy for the owners and workers of Ty, and not anything that would have elevated itself into a systemic event.

The story is similar with convertible bonds in 2005. Hedge fund losses were in the billions of dollars and several firms closed their doors, but at no time was there a risk that these losses would radiate out and threaten the financial institutions that financed the arbitrage, let alone the financial system or economy as a whole. So what is it that changes collective risk into systemic risk?

The two simple answers are size and leverage. Even large bubbles in small markets are not likely to create systemic risk when they pop simply because the losses involved may be absorbed in the bigger picture of economic activity. The major systemic risk issues caused by market bubbles are almost always characterized by large market positions financed with leverage provided by a preponderance of financial market institutions. Everybody is playing in a meaningful way and when the music stops there are not enough sources of capital to take the other side and keep a leveraged meltdown from happening.

This is why convertible arbitrage in 2007–2008 was meaningfully different than the same market in 2005. Granted, nobody blames the financial crisis on the convertible bond market bubble bursting. It was just one piece of a big puzzle that included several bubble markets (housing, CDS, bank loans, and high-yield bonds). But collectively the largest financial institutions on the planet were highly leveraged themselves or providing massive amounts of leverage financing to other bubble participants. This is the classic recipe for systemic risk and financial crisis as described in Kindleberger and Minsky.

Given the infrequency of financial bubbles that create systemic risk, one might argue that there is little for regulators, central banks, or government to do except wait for the event and then react to contain the damage. Some extreme thinkers would push this further and argue that there should be no bailout or damage control response to a financial crisis ("How else do you teach a lesson except to make the foolish directly responsible for their actions?"). But this would create great pain on large parts of society that had nothing to do with starting or escalating the bubble. The externalities created by imposing the strictest market discipline would be unacceptable at a societal level. This is why the Fed and other central banks around the world acted so strongly beginning in 2008 and again in 2020.

The typical response over many centuries of history has been for some kind of adjudicated solution. When the tulip bubble collapsed, Dutch courts ruled that unfilled forward contracts could be settled at 10% of the agreed-upon price.[12] In the many instances where the value of the tulip bulbs had fallen to an even lower value, the courts said that any defaulting buyer would be liable for the difference between the actual price ultimately secured by the seller and the benchmark 10% value.

What the courts were trying to achieve was a balance of liabilities. They understood that if they imposed a 100% performance standard they might have achieved a high moral plane by forcing buyers to stand by their contracts. But the practical consequences of that posture would have been ruinous to the financial system, since none of the often leveraged buyers would be able to perform. By wiping out most of the liability for buyers on unfilled contracts, and simultaneously erasing most of the windfall profits for the sellers, the courts tried to minimize the aggregate damage to the system.

Such solutions are never perfect and critics can easily find targets after the fact. Lehman Brothers was allowed to fail completely in September 2008 after Bear

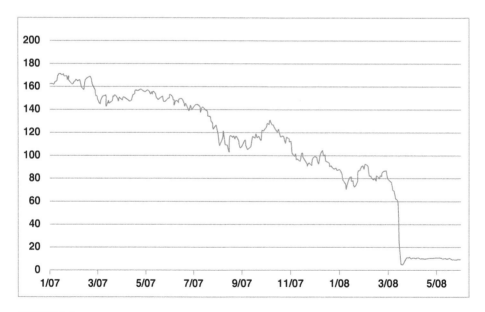

FIGURE 8.4 Bear Stearns Stock Price 2007–2008
Source: Bloomberg

---

[12]Mackay, op. cit

Stearns, another collapsing broker-dealer, was forcibly married off to JPMorgan earlier in the year. AIG was rescued immediately after Lehman Brothers failed with a series of loan guarantees that opened the door to meaningful government ownership and control.[13] To an outside observer, there was absolutely no consistency in this chain of vastly different decisions. Yet it highlights the fact that there is little science to these decisions in real time and any given decision can be heavily dependent upon the outcome of a previous action.

JPMorgan acquired Bear Stearns in March 2008. In the process, the uncertainty surrounding Bear Stearns' extensive liabilities was removed, and market anxieties eased. There were many who criticized the intervention of the federal government and the Federal Reserve for their roles in facilitating JPMorgan's acquiring Bear Stearns. The most principled critics argued that the market should have been allowed to work and if that meant Bear Stearns failed, it would serve as an important lesson to other financial institutions to be more cautious about their affairs.

The outcome may have been criticized, but it was no bed of roses for Bear Stearns shareholders and employees. Figure 8.4 shows the price of Bear Stearns stock from the start of 2007 through 2008. From a high of over $165, it dipped below $5 a share before the final take over price near $10 was agreed to. Meaningful numbers of Bear Stearns employees were also made redundant in the process.

By September when the effects of the crisis were spreading and Lehman Brothers looked threatened, there were public cries for more market discipline in the event of a failure. As a practical matter there were not that many strong hands around the table that might have been able to absorb Lehman Brothers and their complicated book of liabilities in September. Lehman failed on 15 September 2008 and the macro-learning process really began.

It appears that even the most senior banking and Treasury officials had no real appreciation of the vastness and complexity of the financial linkages that a firm like Lehman would have. Almost immediately one of the oldest money market mutual funds in America announced that they would *break the buck* because of their holdings of now heavily discounted Lehman commercial paper. This led to participants in other money market mutual funds to request redemptions in a "shoot first and ask questions later" type of behavior. The prospect of a full-scale run on the industry was averted only after the Federal Reserve quickly stepped in and guaranteed the holdings of all money market mutual funds.

Then the question of credit default swaps, or CDS, took center stage. This over-the-counter market included tens of billions of dollars in notional protection against the event of a Lehman Brothers default. Because there was no central administration or clearing facility through which CDS trades were placed, no regulator or industry watchdog had any clear notion of how much liability existed from the CDS contracts and who held it. This is where AIG came onto center stage in this play.

---

[13]AIG repaid all of the capital it received from the government along with $17 billion in interest in December 2012. The rescue of AIG may be debated in socioeconomic and political terms, but as a financial proposition it was a clear winner for taxpayers. In fact, with the exception of the funds extended to General Motors, Chrysler, and some smaller banks, payments under the Troubled Asset Relief Program (TARP) were all paid back with above-market interest. Bennett, R. (2012). A Happier Ending Than I Anticipated, AIG Pays Back TARP Money, 17 Billion in Interest. *Deseret News*. (17 December).

AIG's financial products division had been an active participant in the relatively young CDS market. Despite the obvious similarities with other traditional lines of insurance (you collect a premium and pay up when a bad event happens), CDS was so young that any concept of actuarial risk was on a very uncertain foundation. Large-scale macroeconomic failures had not been part of the US landscape since the Great Depression. Several generations of market participants believed that such macroeconomic shocks had been engineered out of the system. Decades of experience reinforced this positive view.

The firms that had purchased this protection from AIG and other CDS writers included some of the biggest financial firms on the planet. Firms like Goldman Sachs, Merrill Lynch, and JPMorgan Chase all had billions of dollars of counterparty exposure to Lehman, which in many cases was hedged with purchased CDS. If the insurers could not perform on their obligations, this would leave these large banks with massive holes in their balance sheets. Once such financial contagion began to spread, there would be no telling how far the damage to the system would go. The Federal Reserve and the Treasury decided to act.

The *Troubled Assets Relief Program*, or TARP, began with the primary goal of solidifying bank balance sheets but was quickly extended to provide relief to AIG, Chrysler, and GM. The motivation for these actions may have been different, but in AIG's case it was no doubt driven by an understanding that a failure there would have had serious knock-on effects for major participants in the national banking system. TARP arranged for loans and the purchase of distressed assets from the AIG balance sheet. Within four years a more-focused AIG had repaid all of the obligations arising from TARP plus a meaningful profit for the Fed and the Treasury.

This brief history is provided to suggest how deep the troubles from large bubble markets can become. Even with emergency action by the Fed and the Treasury, the disruptions from the collapse of the credit fueled bubble are still being felt in some parts of the market a decade after the event. Investors that navigated these waters successfully shared some common characteristics.

The most prominent investors were those who saw the bubble forming and took positions to exploit the moment that it popped. John Paulson and other hedge fund managers set up portfolios that were long volatility at a time when most of the market was unconcerned about credit spreads that were too tight, an overheated housing market and equity prices at all-time highs. Given the sanguine attitude of most market participants, option prices were cheap, reflecting an expectation of low volatility going forward. CDS on many financial instruments that had never had a history of default were being sold at prices that ultimately were shown to be way too cheap for the resultant risk.

The market was set up beautifully for the contrarian managers, some of whom bought massive exposures for a few pennies on the dollar. When the bubble popped and market volatility exploded the payoffs were lottery-like to those so positioned. These were the rare participants in 2007–2008 who enjoyed outsized gains at a time most investors showed meaningful losses.

Investors responded as they usually do. People who had no understanding of volatility trading rushed to invest with some of the biggest winners on the theory that if these managers could make money in such a severe crisis they would most certainly be able to succeed in any market environment. Too many managers in this camp accepted all of the new money, and the fees that went with it, without explaining carefully how market conditions had changed.

Markets quickly incorporated all of the new information about the volatility just experienced. Once insanely cheap options and CDS now were priced as if the crisis would repeat itself each calendar quarter. Even though the bubble had already popped, it was assumed that further catastrophes were possible in the near future and protection was priced accordingly. Managers who built their strategy around buying cheap insurance soon found there were no cheap alternatives available. They paid up for protection against terrible events that never happened. Peoples' lottery winnings turned into an expensive lottery habit.

The more flexible managers tried to avoid buying overpriced insurance. They instead shifted focus to macro-themed strategies like gold and defensive postures in the equity markets. Given that in many cases they had built their entire reputation on superior performance in a bear market, it was difficult to change course too radically and embrace the recovery phase of the cycle. It was not uncommon for investors who were extremely damaged when the bubble popped to flee into these high-profile managers only to find that their losses continued more slowly as they bought expensive insurance against events that were not going to repeat, or into bear market strategies in a recovering market. This is almost exactly the wrong way to invest through a bubble.

There were other investors who took a steadier course. Throughout the buildup phase of the bubble they resisted the temptation to join the crowd. As credit spreads compressed well inside historical norms, they reduced their exposure to long credit. They avoided fancy structured products that leveraged up low-yield instruments while promising the highest quality. Importantly they did not extend exposures or give up liquidity while the bubble built momentum. They did nothing dramatic with their portfolios, but they kept cash on hand in the event that future opportunities would become available.

When the bubble popped and the crisis unfolded these investors suffered losses from the growth-oriented parts of their portfolio, but the losses were not devastating nor did the investors become liquidity constrained. This meant that they avoided having to sell at the trough of the market in order to meet other obligations. Not only did they have staying power, the dry powder in their portfolio allowed them to exploit some extraordinary opportunities.

The importance of liquidity in these events cannot be stressed too highly. Many sophisticated foundations and endowments, that had convinced themselves they were investors with a perpetual horizon, went into the crisis with a majority of their investments in illiquid partnerships. The theory was straightforward. Illiquid investments were expected to earn over their life 1–2% more than liquid investments in the same general area. That may not sound like much, but given the power of compound interest first discussed in Chapter 2, even a small percentage edge can be expected to produce meaningful dollar gains through time.

Consider an extreme example of an endowment that emphasized long-term growth. Their asset allocation may look like the following: 70% growth assets; 30% risk reduction assets. On the surface that might not appear too aggressive. Assume the targets for the growth assets are: 30% global liquid equities; 40% venture capital and private equity private partnerships. The risk reduction assets could be divided 20% hedge funds and 10% general fixed income. In steady state the portfolio would be 40% liquid and 60% semiliquid (the hedge funds) and completely illiquid (the partnerships).

That may be the steadystate goal, but one cannot simply snap one's fingers and own such a portfolio. Because partnerships call capital over a period of years, it is not unusual to only have part of the partnership's committed capital at work at any point in time. Suppose an endowment started with such a target portfolio at the beginning of 2007, but only half of the partnership commitments had been funded. What should the endowment do with the assets that had not been called?

Keeping the uncalled commitments in cash was often viewed as "dead money." Many decided that since they were long-term investors who wanted 70% of their portfolio to be exposed to growth assets they would place the uncalled funds into the liquid equity markets. The theory was that as capital calls were received, liquid parts of the stock portfolio could be sold to meet the requests. Such an approach works fine in normally flowing and upwardly trending markets, but it fell terribly apart in the crisis of 2007–2008.

In the example above, the endowment following this plan would start out owning 50% of the endowment in liquid equities, 20% working in private partnerships (with another 20% committed), 20% in hedge funds, and 10% in fixed income. *The total working and committed assets equal 120% of the endowment.* Whether the endowment actually thought they were doing this or not, they were assuming a fixed dollar liability (the 20% of the portfolio committed to future capital calls) and simultaneously funding it with liquid equities that would fluctuate with the market.

Assume the endowment started with $100 million and consider what actually happened in the crisis. Global stocks fell by about 1/3, or a loss of $17 million. The "risk reducing" hedge funds fell less than the equity market as a whole, but they still lost around 20%, which translates to another $4 million. Assuming fixed income was in the most conservative sectors and returned 10%, this only translates to a gain of $1 million. Whatever change occurred in the existing illiquid partnerships was probably meaningfully negative, but since there is no occasion or ability to liquidate any of those assets the mark-to-market on that part of the portfolio is largely academic.

The net effect of the above market moves is a loss of $20 million on the liquid and semiliquid parts of the portfolio. All of the assets that were earmarked to be available to fund the uncalled commitments had been lost to the market. The portfolio has become considerably less liquid, leaving few options for future asset allocation decisions. If any capital calls come in they have to be met by selling liquid equity assets at distressed prices, by liquidating part of the already small allocation to fixed income, or by borrowing.

This problem doesn't even consider the reality of the planned regular contributions from the endowment to support the operation of the organization. In the real world, many of the largest educational endowments choose to borrow sometimes billions of dollars to support their operations through the tough patch rather than sell more liquid assets at distressed prices and skew their portfolios even more.[14]

---

[14]Harvard Borrows $2.5 Billion: The Costs and Rationale. (2008). *Harvard Magazine.* (19 December).

The crisis that began in 2007 and extended through the first quarter of 2009 was an important but painful learning experience of how investors need to think about the possibility of a bubble breaking and creating systemic risk. Long-term asset class average returns and correlations don't help the portfolio when virtually everything except risk-free assets is being sold. It was not enough to avoid the big bubble markets directly. Because of the systemic effects and the sudden rise in volatility and correlations, even good citizens who believed they were not participating in any of the excesses got swept up and damaged.

The single most important lesson deals with leverage. Systemic events tend to be built on leverage and when the bubble pops not only do the directly affected markets implode, but virtually all activities that use leverage are affected. The endowment described above may not have thought of themselves as using leverage, but that was exactly what they ended up doing when they had 100% market exposure and another 20% of the endowment in uncalled capital commitments. As the systemic crisis accelerated, they were caught as surely as if they had been directly purchasing residential real estate through borrowing.

A corollary to this is that when borrowing is extraordinarily cheap, it may be the wrong time to use it for investment purposes. Any borrowing that is done should be done at fixed rates of interest and at terms no shorter than the maturity of the financed obligation. It is a fool's logic that argues for buying something that is twice too expensive simply because it is easy to borrow at apparently low financing rates, or with an expectation that funding will always be available. That logic only works while the bubble is still inflating.

Some investors work hard to try to identify bubbles before they pop and then buy appropriate insurance against the event. This can be done by buying options or appropriate CDS. They work to become *long volatility*. Only in rare instances, like in 2006, is the available insurance arguably cheap, which then creates a lottery-like payoff when it works. Usually the picture is more balanced with the insurance premiums creating a meaningful drain on the resources of the investor. Timing in these instances is vitally important. Being too early can mean prolonged negative cost from insurance. Being too late is potentially fatal.

The only fool-proof approach to preparing for bubble markets or the systemic events that may ensue is to keep some capital handy to exploit the situation when the bubble pops. This was certainly the case from October 2008 to March 2009 when investors with dry powder were able to buy unleveraged portfolios of high-yield bonds and bank debt at fire sale prices much more draconian than the actual default probabilities would imply. This may have been a once in a lifetime opportunity, but it was only available to those who were not digging through the rubble themselves or were upside down in terms of liquidity.

This is what makes dealing with market bubbles so challenging for investors. There is no flashing light on the wall signaling an imminent danger zone. Close attention needs to be paid to the fundamentals in the market to identify potential imbalances, and less emphasis should be placed on recent price moves. Investors need not abandon a market as soon as they suspect prices are inflated, but they should adjust risk according to the likelihood of a rapid decline. Most importantly, they need to resist the temptation to join a party that is desperately close to running out of drinks and having the band pack up. That is the time to get into the car and safely drive home before the last revelers hit the road.

8.3 MARKETS: ALLOCATORS OF CAPITAL OR SOCIAL REENGINEERING?

Websites like Seeking Alpha, active since 2004, offer investment-minded individuals a loosely structured forum allowing for an exchange of ideas. Contributors are supposed to disclose positions that they own or anticipate having for full disclosure. Most contributors appear to be aspiring stock analysts and traders, unconstrained by the limits that come with working for a regulated entity like a broker or a bank. The reality is that everything listed in Seeking Alpha should be assumed to be someone talking about their book until proven otherwise.

As 2020 was drawing to a close the intersection between stock market investing and social media grew much larger. Participation in Reddit-hosted groups began to explode with activity. Like Twitter, almost anything can be said, and often is. A theme that began to get traction was that small traders linked by social media could be strong enough to take on Wall Street hedge funds. Their targets were often identified through regulatory filings that large owners or sellers of stock are required to file with the SEC.

One such target was GameStop, a Texas-based retailer that built its business primarily as a reseller of used video games played on consoles like Xbox and PlayStation. Over time more and more of the commerce in video games migrated to digital downloads, eroding the size of GameStop's market. These changing fortunes were reflected in its share price. At the start of 2016 GameStop (ticker: GME) was trading at $32 per share. By January 2017 the stock was at $24. During 2017, a year when the S&P 500 was up every month, GME fell over 30% to $17. The decline continued over the next two years, with GME starting 2020 in the $6 a share range. For many, GameStop was a classic example of a "melting ice cube" company.

It did not get easier for GME in early 2020. When the reaction to the pandemic started to hit the stock market in February, the drop of 34% in the S&P 500 in five weeks was the fastest drop for the index of that size in history. For all of Q12020, the S&P 500 dropped almost 20%, and GME dropped by almost half, not atypical for small-cap stocks at the time that suffered more than the largest, best capitalized companies. There was a 30% rebound in Q2, but the true change in fortunes was yet to come.

At the June 2020 annual meeting of GME, two candidates backed by activist investors won board seats, a sign of shareholder frustration with the direction of the company. Additional activist interest built, and on 11 January 2021, the company announced that it was expanding its board from 10 to 13 and planned to add Ryan Cohen, co-founder and former CEO of Chewy.com and two other previous Chewy senior colleagues. This was the spark that began a tumultuous three-week period.

The stock quickly jumped higher on the Cohen announcement, but there was more at work than just optimism for an e-commerce veteran breathing new life into a traditional brick-and-mortar retailer. Over a prolonged period that began before the COVID-19 disruptions, GME had been one of the most shorted stocks in the market. Many long/short hedge funds had embraced the melting ice cube thesis and built sizable short holdings, sometimes in ways with considerable embedded leverage like writing out-of-the-money calls.

Financial regulations in the United States require large position holders on both sides of the market to make disclosures. Some managers work hard to stay below the reporting thresholds, while others use the disclosure as a signal to less-informed investors that influential and historically successful hedge funds have a strong opinion. Whether the specific owners are explicitly disclosed or not, the total short-open positions are pretty much public information.

Enter Reddit and the investors connected by social media. The news of the Cohen involvement was paired with discussion of the size of hedge fund short-open interest. Most messages discussed the positive fundamental developments of the company, but there was also a serious undercurrent talking about how small investors acting together could teach Wall Street, and the greedy, destructive hedge funds in particular, a lesson.

Figure 8.5 shows the price action of GameStop for the first weeks of 2021. The dynamic was breathtaking. The price for GME as 2020 drew to a close was $18.84, and it stayed in that neighborhood until the Cohen announcement. On 13 January, the stock closed at $31.40 and a week later the stock had more than doubled for the year, closing at $39.12. The ride was just getting started.

Exactly a week later, on 27 January, the closing price was $347.51, an increase of 788%. The next day the stock touched its intraday peak at $483, but traded as low as $112.25 before closing at $193.60. A week later the stock was at $92.41 and heading lower. The social media messages as the stock price was roaring higher included cheers of support like, "We're Winning!" and "To the Moon!" On the decline, "Hold the Line!" and "Don't Give In" were posted, possibly by investors trying to cash out and lock in their profits while discouraging other sellers. Two weeks after touching its all-time high, GME was trading near $50, more than 2.5 times its price at the start of the year, but down 90% from the peak. The most active Reddit conversations had by then switched to cannabis stocks.

During the run-up there was genuine pain across the early short sellers. Hedge fund Melvin Capital lost 53% in January for its entire fund from its leveraged short bets on GME and other trades. Contemporaneous reports suggested that it covered the last of its GME shorts in the final week of January. As the population of forced buyers trying to control losses shrank, some of the opportunistic longs exited

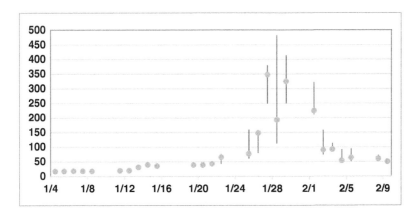

FIGURE 8.5   GME January 4–February 9, 2021
Source: Bloomberg

understanding that the impetus for the momentum trade might be shrinking. Others, later to the game, made unfortunate purchases at those highs.

Amidst the frenzy, some brokers suspended purchases of the most volatile names as the Depository Trust Company appropriately raised collateral requirements for everyone. Voices across the political spectrum decried an alleged collusion between Wall Street hedge funds and the brokers restricting the trade of "the little guy." The SEC and the Secretary of the Treasury both weighed in that every element of the episode would be examined to see if there was manipulative or collusive behavior.

What transpired may have been aided and abetted by illegal behavior, but illegality wasn't necessary for it to occur. This was a short-lived bubble of the classic kind. People bid up the price well beyond any reasonable prospects for the company simply because they believed it would go higher yet. When the demand ultimately waned, the stock price tumbled back with little resistance. Just like the progression in Figure 8.1, the fundamental demand for owning GME was at prices far below the bubble peak.

If there is any irony in the GameStop story, it is that the company itself was just an observer. Unlike some other highly volatile companies at the time, GameStop did not try to issue new stock or raise debt at the high prices to improve its balance sheet. Perhaps it all transpired too quickly for their executives and board to act. The net effect was no change in the capital structure of the company but massive transfers of wealth from the losers to the winners in the secondary market.

The GameStop episode is a classic example of the difference between trading and investing. All the while the price is rising there is a steady stream of commentary that attaches sensible sounding investment theses to what is simply a momentum trade. These stories are most often told by early winners, sometimes sharing screen shots of their brokerage statements to verify their success. Their motivation is not to educate readers on investment fundamentals, but to persuade new traders to join the party.

In 2021 the bubble story took on the added dimension that it was supposedly a virtuous refutation of the entrenched Wall Street elite and their greed. What was learned was that a large, focused group of amateur traders could be marshaled to push a small-cap stock price from $20 to $483. What they could not do was make GameStop a $483 company.

The Building Blocks for a Modern Portfolio

CHAPTER 9

Traditional Portfolio Investments

The range of investments that can make up the modern portfolio is almost limitless. Long gone are the days when assertive investors added equities to spice up their bond portfolios. Even the most conservative portfolio managers today typically venture beyond the core holdings of stocks and bonds. "Traditional" portfolio investments now include multi currency assets, different kinds of credit exposures, real estate, other real assets, and a wide range of private partnerships including hedge funds.

The addition of many of these investment choices has gathered momentum over the last 30 years largely because of the efficiency in the most traditional stock and bond markets. Investors questing for superior returns have sought out once esoteric investment options in the belief that they offer both less efficient markets and less correlated opportunities. The experience has not been 100% positive. There are many types of risks available today that go well beyond those embedded in stocks and bonds. Understanding all dimensions, return and risk, of investment alternatives is critical to effective portfolio construction.

This chapter is designed to provide background information on most of the popular areas of investment today. Much of this material may be familiar to the reader, but could provide background information to fill in any gaps in understanding. Other topics may be relatively new. More and more often we see investors, both institutional and individual, being coaxed into making investments in areas where they lack a good foundation of understanding. The frequent argument is that all of the major, well-regarded institutional investors have these kinds of positions in their portfolios, which supposedly justifies everyone owning them.

Nothing could be further from the truth. As has been repeatedly argued in this book, investing must be a highly customized activity designed to meet the needs of the particular family or institution. Most of us are not the endowment of an Ivy League university or a state pension plan. Many investments designed to pay off 30 or 40 years down the road have no role to play at all in the portfolio of the family. But more importantly, the ability to weather the ups and downs of market cycles depends greatly on understanding beforehand what risks are being assumed. Without a good understanding of why each investment is in the portfolio, there are likely to be times when poor buy and sell decisions are made on the basis of incomplete information.

The portfolio you are building could contain stocks, bonds, real estate, and cash. For some investors this would be all that they owned. Many others think of these as the foundation for their investment program, on which they add other items in an attempt to enhance returns. This chapter will give background information on a wide range of investments that today can be considered traditional. The next two chapters explore derivatives and other investment structures that have been created in the last several decades to make the investment process more efficient. They are not yet so widely used or understood that they can be considered traditional. These chapters can help you decide what kind of a role, if any, these investments should play for you.

9.1   CASH

There is nothing complicated about the concept of cash. It consists of all assets that are immediately available to spend that are fixed in notional value. The tightest definition of cash includes only the money in your pocket and your checking account balance. You might also include your "on-demand" savings accounts, but the list is really not much longer. Certificates of deposit or short-dated Treasury bills may be highly secure assets, but they fail the cash definition because of their somewhat limited liquidity.

Because cash enjoys the highest level of liquidity, it frequently has no investment return. People hold cash for the convenience of immediate access, not because it offers the chance to become richer. This immediate access can be thought of in two ways. The first is the obvious benefit of being able to buy something anytime you want. Cash allows this transaction to occur with virtually no costs attached to it.

The second benefit from immediate access comes from having the option to act quickly when unexpected consumption or investment opportunities arise. This could be as mundane as seeing the perfect pair of shoes marked down 90%. Or it could be as meaningful as having cash balances in your brokerage account on the afternoon of 6 May 2010. This was the day of the infamous *flash crash* when the Dow Jones Industrial Average fell by almost 1,000 points in a few minutes. As frightening as the moment was, many opportunistic investors who were armed with cash identified the event as a temporary aberration and were able to buy equities before they bounced back.

Not all opportunistic needs for cash are as fleeting, but the point is that there will always be transitory opportunities that might disappear in the time it takes to sell other assets in order to acquire the purchasing power needed. This can be a powerful motivation for always holding a certain amount of cash.

Cash has the critical property that it is fixed in nominal terms. All a one-dollar bill guarantees is that it will purchase one dollar's worth of goods or services. It guarantees nothing about how many of those goods or services it can purchase. This is the downside to cash. Unless you happen to live in a deflationary world, the purchasing power of cash declines through time.

Everyone should at some point in his or her life experience hyperinflation (hopefully briefly). Watching prices increase by 1% per day, which was Brazil's inflation rate for a while in the mid-1980s, dramatically changes your willingness to hold cash. Few people in these environments hold anything other than the bare minimum cash necessary for immediate transactions. Tourists exchange small amounts of hard currency every day at steadily improving exchange rates.

This kind of inflation experience indelibly imprints caution onto the mind of the person holding cash. There can be no sloppiness about how cash is handled because the consequences are too great. Instead, the transaction benefits of holding cash are constantly weighed against the costs from eroding purchasing power.

People living in a low inflation world, say 1–2% annually, can be distracted from declining purchasing power because it is so slow. It is like patients in the eighteenth century who were leeched by their doctors. They suffered slowly from the loss of blood over time, but there was nothing so dramatic to cause them to reject the therapy that had been prescribed by their trusted physician.

Because of inflation, which is the normal state of affairs for almost all nations with fiat currencies, cash is not universally good. It always has desirable transaction properties, but can fail as a store of value. It is therefore not surprising that the role of cash in investment portfolios, or in daily life, should depend critically on the rate of inflation. As people try to move away from cash holdings, the next resting place is the massive category called bonds.

9.2 FIXED INCOME

Fixed income investments cover an extremely wide range of opportunities. They can vary by maturity and credit quality. When you include floating rate debt obligations, you get investments that are often still called fixed income, but really are not. The key characteristic that defines this class of investments is that they are all promises to pay, in one form or another. The original transaction has the lender giving the borrower a sum, to be repaid over an agreed-upon period of time at some rate of interest. This can include overnight deposits at banks and 100-year bonds issued by a university, and everything in between.

Like most broad asset categories, saying that you have 20% of your portfolio in fixed income says very little. The range of investment assets is so broad that a 5% allocation to long-duration, low credit quality fixed income could be a lot riskier than a 25% allocation to short-dated Treasury bills. Understanding the types of instruments available and the various risk factors is necessary to forming an appropriate portfolio allocation for you.

9.2.1 Varieties of Fixed Income Instruments

Fixed income securities come in various forms. In the most vanilla format, the borrower agrees to pay the lender a fixed rate of interest periodically over the life of the loan. The interest payment is known as the *coupon*, a name that can be traced to a time when paper bonds had physical coupons that the bond owner clipped and submitted to the issuer for payment. At maturity, the last interest payment is made and all of the capital borrowed is returned. The money to pay off the obligation might have come from revenues collected along the way, or it might be raised from a new debt issue. The lender does not care. As long as the interest is paid in a timely way and the principal repaid in full, the bond is considered performing.

Short-dated instruments like Treasury bills do not have an explicit coupon payment. Instead, they are sold at a discount to face value. A $1,000 face value one-year instrument might be issued at a price of $900, or a discount of 10%. A year later the full face value is returned to you. The *yield* of that bill is 11.1%, which is the $100 gain divided by the initial purchase price.

For one-year discounted paper the yield calculation is simplicity itself, as shown above. For maturities less than a year, the simple percentage return is often converted into an annualized rate for ease of comparison. For example, a six-month bill might be priced at $950. The $50 gain from holding the bill to maturity translates into a 5.26% absolute return. The convention for converting this return into an annual rate is to scale it up by how many return periods there are for this bill in a year. For six-month bonds, there are two such periods in a year, so the annual yield is said to be 10.52%, or twice the 5.26% absolute return.

The specifics of essential interest rate mathematics include many conventions covering even seemingly obvious things like how to count days in the year (it's not that obvious – some instruments use 365 days in a year while other calculations assume 360). While critical for fixed income traders, investors need to focus on the details only when comparing different types of investments that might be subject to different rules.[1] When in doubt about whether two advertised yields are comparable, the safest path is to look at the respective cash flows for the investments and make your own return calculations.

In addition to coupon bearing and discount bonds, there are other flavors of securities. Increasingly important in investor portfolios are bonds that have their interest payments fluctuate. Called *floaters*, these bonds pay periodic interest that is typically based on a reference rate like 90-day LIBOR. The bond is described in terms of a spread over the reference rate (e.g. 2% over LIBOR, adjusted and paid quarterly). Both the borrower and the lender face uncertain cash flows from such bonds. The advantage to the lender, however, is that if interest rates should suddenly rise, they will not be stuck with a low-yielding bond. The issuer presumably gets a lower initial borrowing yield for accepting this uncertainty.

Bonds can be adjustable in other ways as well. *Linkers* are bonds that have their principal amount adjusted according to another price or index. The most popular linkers globally are inflation-linked bonds (like TIPS in the United States) though there are bonds linked to commodity prices and equity indexes that create hybrid instruments containing multiple market exposures. The appeal of inflation-linked bonds, assuming you believe the reference index accurately measures inflation, is that with positive interest rates the principal never declines in purchasing power.

The last major feature of which fixed income investors should be aware is *callability*. Some bonds may be paid off before their maturity at the borrower's option. This feature protects them against the chance of borrowing a lot of money today at one rate, only to find that if they had delayed their decision they could have benefitted from lower rates. Some bonds are callable at any time. Others become callable after a certain date, which gives some protection to the lender. As any call feature offers protection to the borrower, lenders typically receive a slightly higher interest rate as compensation for the option they are granting.

A much less common form of bond that has an embedded option is called a *put bond*. These bonds allow the lender to force the borrower to prepay the issue at least once during the life of the bond according to a predetermined schedule. Put bonds protect the lenders against higher rates as they demand their principal back on the

---

[1]Stigum, M. (1981). *Money Market Calculations*. Dow-Jones Irwin: Homewood, IL. Anyone looking for detail on interest rate calculation conventions can find an encyclopedic treatment of the topic in Stigum, which remains the standard for the industry.

put dates, at which time they can reinvest the proceeds for a higher return. This type of bond is also known as a *multi maturity bond*, an *option tender bond*, a *variable rate demand obligation* (VRDO).

Callable step-up bonds combine different features of some of the bonds described above. Their interest coupons are not fixed over the life of the bond, nor are they completely floating. Instead they follow a custom schedule established when the bond is issued where the coupon "steps up" through time. As an example, a five-year maturity note may be issued where the interest rate is 1% in the first two years, 2% in year three, and 3% in years four and five. There is no standard format to these bonds, but they are typically callable by the issuer. With callable step-up bonds both the borrower and the lender can see some potential advantages, so they offer a rich opportunity to express different market opinions.

The above discussion was meant to be suggestive of the wide range of fixed income products available to investors and not exhaustive. The key message is that any attempt to classify all bonds into one easily described basket is doomed to failure. Each fixed income investment must be analyzed in detail to identify its risks as well as potential rewards. Different bonds do different jobs, and finding the proper mix is critical if effective portfolio allocation is to occur.

9.2.2   Duration and Credit Risk: Bond Pricing, Convexity, and Spreads

All promises to pay are not created equal. The US government saying they will pay you back in 30 days is a different risk than your brother-in-law promising to repay your loan to him sometime in the next five years. The maturity of the loan and the credit worthiness of the borrower are the two primary determinants of fixed income risk.

Bonds are typically issued for a fixed term, from as short as overnight to as long as 100 years. In 1751 the British government first issued non-maturing, or perpetual debt called *consols* (an abbreviation of consolidated annuities). These bonds simply agreed to pay a fixed coupon to the lender forever. They could be retired by the state, but the buyers of this debt could not force repayment of principal. Consols were the ultimate expression of confidence in the soundness of a nation's finances. In 1923 the interest rate was set at 2.5% where it has remained ever since. It has been many years since there were any new consols issued. Perhaps it is not surprising that there are few people willing to lend on these terms today. For this chapter's discussion, we can focus attention on bonds with fixed terms.

Most people think of a bond's term to maturity as the most relevant time dimension, but this is an imprecise characterization. Bonds may have the same maturity but different payout structures, which leads to potentially meaningful differences in the way their prices behave in the marketplace. Frederick Macaulay was dissatisfied with term to maturity as a useful measure of time, seeking instead a concept that was more effective in allowing useful comparisons. *Duration* was developed by Macauley in 1938 as a standardized measure expressed in terms of the maturity of a *zero-coupon bond*.[2]

Every zero-coupon bond has a duration equal to its maturity. Bonds that pay coupons at different points in their life return income to the owner earlier than the

---

[2]Macaulay, F. R. (1938). *Some Theoretical Problems Suggested by the Movements of Interest Rates, Bond Yields, and Stock Prices Since 1856*. National Bureau of Economic Research: New York.

maturity date and therefore have a duration that is shorter than the maturity. Duration captures the timing of the payment streams and weights them according to their importance to the overall return.

A simple example can demonstrate the concept. Consider a $1,000 three-year bond, priced today at par, paying a $25 coupon semiannually. The table in Figure 9.1 shows the cash flow that is relevant to the duration calculation.

Each of the $25 payments every six months can be thought of as its own zero-coupon bond. If you wanted to buy a zero that paid you $25 in six months and returned an annualized rate of 5%, it would cost you $24.35, which is the discounted value of that coupon back to today (column 3). The $25 payment two years from now would only cost $22.61 because there is more time for the interest to build. The big payment at maturity in three years includes the final coupon payment of $25 plus the return of the original $1,000 in capital. Its present value today is $884.08.

Adding up all of these discounted cash flows tells you what the implicit "portfolio" of zeros that make up the three-year bond is worth. Since we already said the bond is priced at par, it is good that the total of the discounted cash flows adds to $1,000.

The next two columns get to the concept of price weighting. The first coupon payment's worth today represents 2.44% of the total value of the bond. As the $25 coupons extend out into the future, their discounted present value drops, as does their weight in the bond's value. The final payment at the end of year three counts for more than 88% of the bond's value today.

Macaulay's contribution was to multiply each of the bond's payment dates by their weight, or their importance to the bond's total value. This is the last column in the table and when these values are summed the total is the Macaulay duration of that bond.

All standard coupon-paying bonds look like this example. A bond priced at par was chosen to make the relationships in the table somewhat clearer. Time and the interest rate are the important elements. As interest rates get bigger, duration falls for every maturity. If interest rates are very close to zero, duration approaches maturity. As time passes the duration of a bond shrinks to the point where it equals maturity right after the next to the last coupon is paid.

The beauty of duration is that it can be applied to any type of bond. Coupons can be paid at irregular increments. They can vary through time. If you can write down the schedule of cash flows from the bond, you can do the discounting and calculate duration. This duration calculation will allow you to compare the interest rate sensitivity across all kinds of bonds.

Time	Payment	Discounted Cash Flow	Price Weight	Price-weighted Maturity
0.5	$25	$24.35	2.44%	0.012
1	$25	$23.75	2.38%	0.024
1.5	$25	$23.15	2.32%	0.035
2	$25	$22.61	2.26%	0.045
2.5	$25	$22.06	2.21%	0.055
3	$1,025	$884.08	88.41%	2.652
Totals		$1,000.00	100.00%	2.823

FIGURE 9.1 Duration of a Three-year, $1,000, 5% Coupon Bond

The other handy feature of duration is that it gives an approximation of how a bond's price will change when interest rates change. For example, the 30-year 3 1/8 Treasury bond maturing on 15 February 2042 had a duration of 19.4 years shortly after it was issued. A buyer of this bond could expect to lose 0.194% on a mark-to-market basis if interest rates instantaneously moved up by one basis point or make 0.194% if rates dropped by a basis point from the current level of 3.078%.

Because duration changes as interest rates move, you should not depend on these price relationships to hold over large shifts in rates. A 100-basis-point move up in interest rates will drop the price of the bond in this example by 17.2%, less than the 19.4% drop naively predicted from multiplying by the duration. Similarly if the market interest rate fell 1%, the bond would pick up 22.2% in market value.[3] While the duration of 19.4 is a very good starting point for estimating the risk of a bond, there is no substitute for calculating a bond's price if you want precise answers. Still, a guess that you could gain or lose 19% on the value of your bond if interest rates move by 1% gives a pretty good notion that this long bond has a great deal of interest rate risk.

As suggested in the example above, duration not only applies to individual bonds but also to portfolios. If you own $1 million in bonds with a duration of 10 years and $4 million in bonds with a duration of five years, you can estimate the duration of this portfolio by taking the weighted average of the individual durations. In this case, 80% of the dollar weight has a duration of five years and 20% has a duration of 10, making the portfolio duration six years.

Portfolio managers constantly look at their bonds' weighted average duration, but this does not tell the entire story. The frequently unstated assumption behind this calculation is that as interest rates change, all maturities move up or down by the same amount. This is known as a *parallel shift* in the yield curve, which may or may not be a good approximation of reality.

If all yield curve shifts are parallel, the simple 20/80 portfolio described above should demonstrate the same interest rate sensitivity as a 100% holding of bonds with a duration of six years. But if the curve should get steeper or flatter around the center point the results will be different. That is why bond managers pay so much attention to valuations of individual maturities along the curve and why they will change the composition of their portfolios even as they may try to maintain a particular average duration.

In the real world the yield curve reflects the supply and demand for each maturity bond, and is rarely a uniformly positioned array of rates. But the demand for one maturity is certainly affected by the yields of others. For example, suppose the newly issued 10-year Treasury note was yielding 5%, but an existing 30-year bond that was issued 19.5 years ago was yielding 6%. The credit quality of the two securities is identical and their maturity differs only by six months. Most potential buyers of bonds near this maturity would gravitate toward the 6% instrument, reasoning that the extra 1% annual return over the next 10 years is a huge compensation for the extra six months of maturity.

---

[3]It should be emphasized that duration is an approximation. The actual bond prices used in this discussion were taken from a Bloomberg duration analysis page that calculates what the different cash flows of a bond will be worth under various interest rate scenarios. The duration of 19.4 will always underestimate the size of the up move from interest rate declines and overestimate the impact of interest rate increases.

This is such an extreme example that you never see it in reality. Long before the yield difference got that wide, demanders of bonds would begin ignoring the low-yield (high-price) 10-year in favor of the high-yield (low-price) 10.5-year security. This market action would cause the yield differential to narrow. This kind of yield spread would also likely attract the attention of *fixed income arbitrageurs* who would borrow the 10-year note to sell short while buying the cheaper 10.5-year instrument. As long as the spread was wider than the cost of financing this trade (often done with leverage), the arbitrage would continue.

Between the actions of thoughtful buyers and arbitrageurs, many of the anomalies in rates across the yield curve get smoothed out, but differences in the shape of the curve can arise that suggest different strategies for the bond portfolio manager.

Yield curve A in Figure 9.2 can be thought of as normal. The curve is smooth and the slope from short to long maturities is neither too flat nor too steep. In a stylized world where A was the yield curve, a bond manager might hold what is called a *laddered portfolio*. Nearly equal holdings of each maturity from short to the longest target date make up the portfolio. As time passes and some bonds mature off the shortest step of the ladder, they are replaced by newly issued bonds with the longest maturities. The duration of such a portfolio is the weighted average of the durations of all the individual bonds. The world is never this well behaved, but you can think of this portfolio as the base case.

Figure 9.3 adds a different shaped yield curve. It has a bulge in the middle of the maturity array, with both the shortest and longest maturities yielding less than the normal case and middle maturities yielding more. How can a bond manager

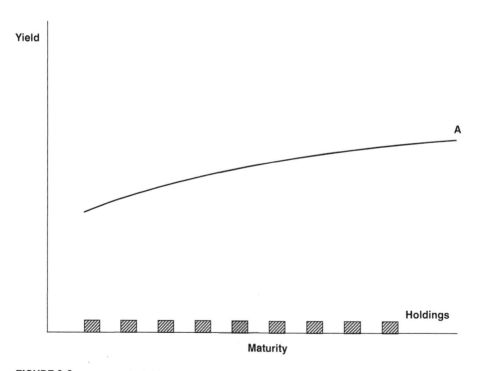

FIGURE 9.2 A Normal Yield Curve and a Laddered Bond Portfolio

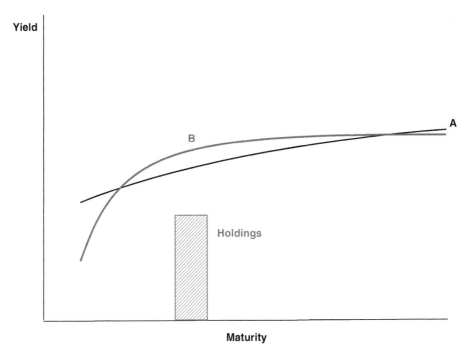

FIGURE 9.3 A Bulging Yield Curve and a Bullet Bond Portfolio

exploit this? Rather than buy the ladder, the short-dated and long-dated allocations are avoided and extra maturities in the middle years are bought where the yields are more generous. This portfolio is called a *bullet* since all of the attention is focused on a narrow range of maturities that are thought to be cheap relative to the others.

Finally Figure 9.4 presents the opposite case. Here the *belly of the curve* is expensive as rates are lower than normal, while the extreme maturities are cheap. This suggests a *barbell* strategy to the bond manager where some very short maturity bonds are combined with long-dated issues. The amount of weight placed on each end of the barbell depends on where the manager wants the average duration to be. It is easy to construct a barbell with the exact same average duration as the bullet in the previous example.

As long as all subsequent shifts in the yield curve are parallel it does not matter whether you own a ladder, a bullet, or a barbell. But in the real world, parallel shifts are rare so positioning matters. This is a major component of what fixed income portfolio managers bring to the table.

It should be emphasized that if a manager decides to pursue a bullet or a barbell strategy, this is not the same as arbitrage. Curves that are cheap in the belly can get much cheaper, and the barbell practitioner can detract value from the strategy. Managers often loosely say that they are "arbing" the yield curve when they deviate from the basic ladder. In fact they are placing relative value overweights and underweights that, like all value judgments, may or may not work out.

How does one determine the value of a bond? Start with the definition. A bond is simply a promise to pay out interest over a period of time and ultimately return the

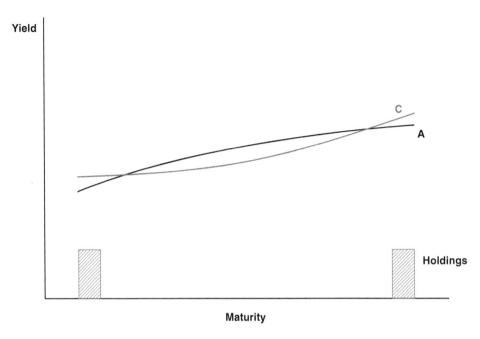

FIGURE 9.4 An Expensive Belly Yield Curve and a Barbell Bond Portfolio

principal. What you should be willing to pay for it depends entirely on what other bonds are offering. That is, you are not likely to pay the same price for a 30-year bond with a 5% coupon as you would a 30-year bond of similar credit quality carrying a 10% coupon. The stream of cash from the 10% bond is definitely worth a premium.

We began addressing this issue when we calculated the duration above. The price of any risk-free bond is the sum of its discounted cash flows.[4] Interest expected next week is worth more than interest paid years into the future, but it all has some value. Adding up all of the pieces gives the total price of the bond.

The coupon, the maturity and the amortization schedule all have an impact on a bond's price. There are other features like *callability* and credit quality that play critical roles as well, which will be discussed in more detail below.

Traditional bonds also have a characteristic that all fixed income investors should be aware of and that is called *convexity*. This term reflects the fact that as interest rates move up and down, a bond's price moves in the reverse direction, but not in a linear fashion. What this means is that the price increase that results from the first 10 basis point decline in yields is smaller than the price increase resulting from the second. Convexity is the bond owner's friend.

Figure 9.5 shows the relationship between a bond's yield and its price. The reason the curve is *positively convex* arises from the basic definition of what a bond is worth. Discounting future cash streams (demonstrated in the equation in footnote 4

---

[4]The price of a risk-free bond is the discounted present value of all of its cash flows. The formula is $P = \sum_{t=1}^{n}(C/(1+i)^t) + M/(1+i)^n$, where P is the price of the bond, C is the coupon, n is the number of coupon payments, and M is the value of the bond at maturity or its par value.

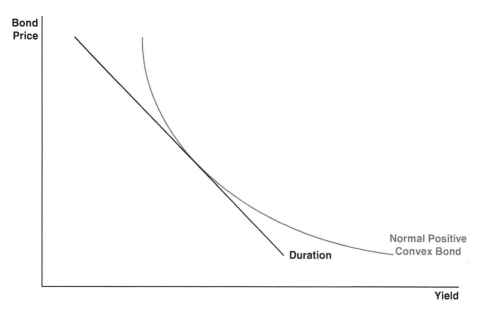

FIGURE 9.5 Positive Convexity

of this chapter) is a nonlinear process. As interest rates rise, the compounding of the discount rate grows exponentially, but the rate of change depends on where you start. A 1% increase in rates from 3% to 4% is a much bigger deal in the calculation than the same rise from 23% to 24%. At those higher levels most of the discounting damage from bringing future cash flows back to present has already been done.

The curve suggests why the longest-dated Treasury bonds can be large winners if rates fall. Start with a 30-year, 3% coupon bond priced at par. Consider times of geopolitical risk or moments like the second half of 2011 when concerns about a European debt crisis led to a flight to perceived safety. Drops of 50 basis points in such situations are not unusual, producing more than a 10% increase in the market price of the 30-year Treasury.

This is, of course, a knife that cuts both ways. Should rates increase at any time from the ultralow base, market price declines would be as swift.

Not all bonds are as well behaved in terms of convexity. If a bond is *callable*, that is, if the issuer can pay it off early, a lot of the fun from positive convexity goes away. As an example, some corporations issue debt that is callable after a number of years. If interest rates move upward after the initial issue, the corporation metaphorically puts a smile on its face and pays off the lower coupon bonds on schedule. If, however, rates fall, there should be an expectation that the corporation will exercise its option to call the now high coupon bonds and replace them with lower cost debt. The best part of the convexity curve has been taken away. Bond buyers understand this well and typically demand initially higher yields to grant a corporation this call option.

Mortgages are an extreme example of callable bonds. Because people change houses for a myriad of reasons, they need to be able to repay their mortgages at any time. Buyers of mortgage bonds must understand that there is no calendar of potential calls and that their income stream could be taken away at any time.

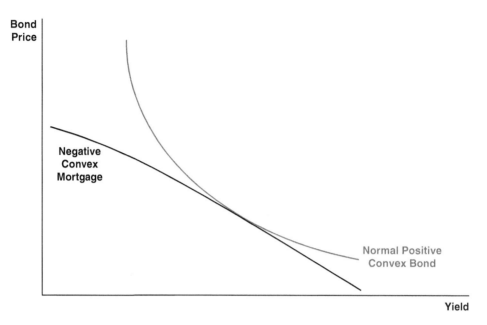

FIGURE 9.6 Mortgages and Negative Convexity

Figure 9.6 shows what the price/interest rate relationship for a mortgage might look like. As interest rates rise from where the mortgage was issued, the relationship looks normal, i.e. positively convex. There may be some prepayments of loans as people move for whatever reason, but there will be no voluntary refinancing to lock in higher rates. The homeowner who borrowed the money holds most of the cards in this game.

Falling rates are another story. If you just financed your home with a 4.25% 30-year mortgage, you might not voluntarily incur all the expense of refinancing if rates fell to 4.15%, but at 4% you might begin looking. At 3.75% the case for refinancing starts to look compelling. The bank or mortgage lender who wrote the first loan is at least disappointed. They thought they were going to get a nice stream of income yielding 4.25% for the next 30 years, but instead they got a few interest payments and then all of the principal back early. This money has to go to work again in a lower rate environment. This is simply good luck for the homeowner and bad luck for the lender.

People who write mortgages are not so naive to be surprised by prepayments. They spend great energies trying to model how their loans will behave under different interest rate scenarios and pay for them accordingly. But it is an imprecise science no matter how many finance PhD dissertations have been devoted to the topic.

The borrower wants the maximum benefit from the prepayment option in his or her mortgage, but the decision to refinance is more than just an interest rate story. After the financial crisis of 2008 and the severe decline in home prices across the country, many people would have liked to have refinanced their mortgages at lower rates, but did not have enough equity in their homes to qualify for a new loan. In these cases, the bad effect of negative convexity did not come so much into play as the simple theory might suggest and lenders got an unexpected windfall. That is, for those mortgages that continued to pay. This raises the ultimate wild card for bonds – *credit quality*.

Array a dozen bonds, each paying 5% coupon interest and maturing in 10 years, and you are likely to see them trading at a dozen different prices. Why? Perceived credit quality at every point in time is the driver of a bond's price and its projected yield to maturity. Those issuers with the lowest expected probability of default trade at the highest prices (and lowest yields). Should a negative earnings announcement come out for a company, its bonds may trade down as the world downgrades its perceived credit worthiness.

As vividly demonstrated by the unfolding European credit crisis, perceptions of credit quality can change dramatically through time. A country or a company could have a spotless history, always paying its bondholders in a complete and timely manner, and yet they could see their bonds drop in price if their future ability or willingness to pay comes into question.

In the new issue market, the initial coupon yield is a good indicator of perceived credit quality. Oftentimes there is a benchmark security, like a similar maturity Treasury note or bond, and bonds are quoted as a spread over the benchmark rate. As perceived credit quality drops the quoted spread gets larger.

This spread determined by the market is a much more consistent indicator than any ratings generated by a service like Moody's or Fitch. Investors in 2006 and early 2007 learned this lesson the hard way when they purchased AAA-rated structures that had a modest spread to Treasuries. They believed they were getting ultrasafe securities with the bonus of incremental yields. It turned out that the modest yield premium was horribly inadequate for the large incremental risk. It was no consolation that these securities were downgraded by the ratings agencies after the fact.

Bonds actively trade in the secondary market and credit worthiness can shift through time. Bonds that are upgraded in the minds of investors go up in price. Even though the best a borrower can do is to pay all coupon interest and return principal when it is due, par is not the upper bound for the price of a bond that has coupon payments left. For example, a bond of a questionable company issued to yield a premium of 5% over Treasuries might trade well above par if its fortunes improve. But no matter how wonderful a company is, at maturity the lender will only get the face value of the bond returned.

Perceived credit deteriorations work just the reverse. Bonds drop in value to reflect the probability of default, the timing of any default, and any recovery that might be paid to lenders of defaulted bonds. Assume a company issues a bond that has a coupon of 10% and a maturity of 30 years. Now assume it runs into business problems that seriously call into question its ability to repay that bond. It could trade down to 50 cents on the dollar, implying that the market now demands a 20% yield to compensate it for the perceived higher risk of default.

There is no magic scale that determines these bond prices. Everything is supply and demand. If there was meaningful concern that the company would default before its next coupon the bonds could trade down to 2 cents, implying a yield of 250% – if they pay the coupon. This is the dynamic nature of credit evaluation and bond pricing.

Duration and credit spreads are the two key factors that determine a bond's *relative value*. To establish the *absolute value* one needs to know the risk-free rate. And that, usually, comes from the yield curve of government bills, notes, and bonds. As we begin to describe the array of fixed income investments available, it makes sense to start with sovereign debt.

9.2.3   Sovereign Debt

A government for a defined territory that is supreme in establishing its domestic policies and is independent in its international relations is a *sovereign state*. In managing its financial affairs it may have reason to borrow against future revenues, issuing
bills, notes, or bonds with a wide range of possible maturities. This paper is called
sovereign debt.

Sovereign debt is often thought of as the best possible debt because the government issuing it usually has broad power to raise taxes to service the debt. For countries like the United States that have never failed to perform on federally issued debt,
there is a strong expectation that the full faith and credit of the country will continue
to back their bonds.[5] But a spotless sovereign credit history is the exception rather
than the norm. Most other governments have repudiated or restructured their debts
at some point in their histories. Some countries appear to be serial defaulters. Not all
sovereign debt can be considered *risk-free debt*.

The European debt crisis reminded everyone that the basics of credit analysis
apply to the evaluation of sovereign debt. Simultaneous with the restructuring of
Greek sovereign debt one could observe Swedish and Norwegian paper being given
the highest credit ratings by the marketplace. The rest of European sovereign issuers
were arrayed along a spectrum of perceived probability of default or restructuring.

Most sovereign debt is denominated in the currency of the issuing country. But
for countries with a history of serious inflation episodes and a desire to raise capital
from outside their borders, bonds denominated in US dollars, euros, or yen may be
more attractive to potential lenders. Of course the governments issuing these bonds
have limited ability to raise revenues in another currency, so this feature adds to the
chance that performance might not be assured.

Sovereign debt can be issued in many forms. Bills sold at discount and coupon-
bearing bonds are the most common forms. Bonds indexed to inflation are also quite
popular (e.g. Treasury inflation-protected securities, or TIPS, in the United States).
Examples of floating rate sovereign debt or bonds linked to other prices or indexes
can also be found but are considerably less common.

An important feature of sovereign debt is that it *usually* is the best-rated debt
issued in that country. The theory is that even highly profitable corporations could
be limited in their ability to repay their debt if their sovereign government gets into
trouble and tries to limit payments. Therefore the credit rating of the sovereign can
place a ceiling on how well rated other issuers in the country can be.

There are exceptions to this rule. Major multinational corporations domiciled in
Greece have sometimes paid lower rates on their bonds than the sovereign government, but most corporate borrowers in Greece are paying up directly for the sketchy
behavior of their sovereign.

Risks to owning sovereign debt are no different than for any other debt. Does the
sovereign government issuing the debt have the *ability to pay* and the *willingness to
pay* to meet its obligations? Presumably nobody would have bought the debt when it

---

[5]It should be noted that while the US government has never defaulted on its debt, individual
states have defaulted and the debt of the Confederate States of America was repudiated after
the Civil War.

was issued if they did not expect the nation to be able to somehow raise revenue to service that debt. But the world changes. Economies founder, which reduces revenue streams and the ability to pay. Regimes change. The Bolsheviks taking over Russia in 1917 felt little obligation to pay the previous Tsars' debts.

The biggest difference between sovereign debt and other debts are the legal remedies available to the bondholders in the event of a default. If the United States did the unthinkable and passed a law repudiating all of its treasury debt there would be global outrage and perhaps physical conflict, but it would be difficult to get relief in a court of law. The jurisdiction that issued the bonds is the same governing body that would handle the bankruptcy estate. The deck is clearly stacked against the bondholder.

To ease this risk some countries with a history of default like Argentina have issued dollar-denominated sovereign debt explicitly establishing the United States as the relevant legal jurisdiction. Despite this, when Argentina defaulted in 2001, they ignored several US court orders that were contrary to their administration's view of fairness. The restructuring process began in 2005 and it wasn't until a change of presidents in 2014 that the negotiations made any real progress. A negotiated settlement was finally reached late in 2016, highlighting how complicated and prolonged any resolution of defaulted sovereign debt can be.

The other major risk to holders of *local currency sovereign debt* is loss of purchasing power through inflation. Frequently through history governments have avoided actual repudiation or restructuring of their debt by inflating the currency and simultaneously shrinking the real value of their debt obligations that are fixed in nominal terms. There are dramatic examples like the German hyperinflation in the early 1920s and more subtle examples like the United States after World War II and during the 1970s. Whether dramatic or nuanced, these implicit debt restructurings extract wealth from the lenders. In response, some bondholders have demanded protection in the form of inflation-linked notes. Still, the vast majority of sovereign debt today is in the form of traditional bonds.

Reinhart and Rogoff provide a detailed history of the types of bond restructurings, repudiations and devaluations that sovereign governments have pursued for centuries.[6] They remind us that patterns of bad behavior repeat regularly. Cries that sovereign governments won't default because they would then be cut out of future borrowing opportunities lacks credibility. Investors have short memories across the generations and the credit window eventually reopens for almost every sovereign borrower. In 2017, just over a year after Argentina finally resolved its 2001 bond default, it issued 100-year, dollar-denominated bonds that were eagerly purchased by the international investment community.

9.2.4 Agency Bonds

Agency bonds are a general category of debt that falls just below sovereign debt in terms of credit quality. Two types of entities can issue them. *Government Sponsored Enterprises* (GSEs) are typically privately owned corporations that have been

---

[6]Reinhart, C.M. and Rogoff, K.S. (2009). *This Time Is Different: Eight Centuries of Financial Folly*. Princeton University Press: Princeton, NJ.

chartered by the federal government. Examples include Fannie Mae and Freddie Mac. There are also federal government agencies that have specific public policy missions. Examples include the Farm Credit Banks, Ginnie Mae, and the Small Business Administration. In each case the agency or GSE issues bonds to finance its specific activity.

The perceived credit quality of any agency bond is a function of how independent it is from the federal government. Agency bonds issued by Ginnie Mae and the Small Business Administration are backed by the full faith and credit of the federal government. The major exception to this rule is the agency bonds issued by the Tennessee Valley Authority (TVA). The revenue from power sales by the TVA back these bonds. Like TVA bonds, GSE-issued bonds are backed by the economic activities of the enterprises, without any explicit guarantee by the government.

In reality, the distinctions are rarely as black and white as the above description would imply. After the financial crisis of 2008–2009, Fannie Mae and Freddie Mac were essentially insolvent. Their main assets consisted of pools of mortgages, a large fraction of which were either delinquent or in outright default. Rather than see these enterprises go bankrupt, which would have resulted in their bondholders receiving much less than par, the Congress of the United States authorized large transfers from general revenues to keep them operational.

Many considered this action a form of implicit government guarantee. To date no Fannie Mae or Freddie Mac bondholder has suffered any losses from either delayed interest or loss of principal. Investors should not, however, view past behavior as a promise for future guarantees. As long as the guarantee is not explicit, there is a risk a democratically elected Congress could change its mind. This is an important reason why the bonds of Fannie Mae and Freddie Mac offer slightly higher interest rates than direct US treasuries.

The liquidity of agency bonds also varies from issuer to issuer. Mortgage-backed agencies tend to be the largest and most liquid of all agency debt. Smaller agency bonds have considerably less liquidity. While they may be backed by the full faith and credit of the US government, they may still carry slightly higher interest rates due to the lower liquidity.

Tax characteristics of the bonds can also vary. While many agency bonds are exempt from both state and local taxes, this is not universally the case. GSE entities like Freddie Mac and Fannie Mae issue bonds that are fully taxable. It is vital for taxpaying investors to review their holdings with their tax advisor before investing in any agency debt.

Most agency bonds pay a fixed rate of interest or coupon semiannually and are noncallable. While these *bullet bonds* are the norm, there are many other forms available to investors. Some agencies issue floating rate bonds, which can be linked to either US Treasury bond yields or LIBOR. There are also short-dated bonds that are sold like T-bills at a discount. Other more complicated structures are sometimes present in the market, but these issues tend to be purchased more by professional money managers than by retail investors.

The agency debt market in the United States is larger than the supply of sovereign debt of most countries in the world. It is a major force in the fixed income landscape, and every bond investor should be aware of the opportunities. The major attractions of agency debt are the very high credit rating and the liquidity of most of the issuers' paper. Another massive pool of government-related debt issues, the broad category of municipal bonds, is considerably more heterogeneous in terms of liquidity and credit quality, but still plays a major role in many fixed income portfolios.

9.2.5 Municipal Bonds

Municipal bonds, or "munis," include a wide range of debt instruments issued by state and local governments. While the credit worthiness of municipal bonds in general has been quite high, there are numerous examples of serious defaults that have cost investors dearly. Credit research is as important in selecting municipal bonds as it is for any corporate issue, which will be discussed in the next section.

Nonfederal government entities issue municipal bonds primarily to finance their capital investment and cash flow needs. Such bonds finance schools, highways, hospitals, sewer systems, and many other projects to serve the public. *General obligation bonds* are backed by the full taxing authority of the issuer, while *revenue bonds* are special-purpose bonds that rely on an income stream from a narrow activity. Revenue bonds issued by any jurisdiction have higher default risk than the general obligation bonds of that issuer.

Municipal bonds vary widely in maturity. The shortest-dated issues are frequently *tax anticipation notes*, which are sold to finance the jurisdictions' normal expenses before the actual collection of taxes. Longer dated maturities, which can extend 30 years or more, are typically issued to finance large capital investments.

The primary appeal of municipal bonds to many investors is their tax-exempt status. Interest from munis is typically exempt from federal income tax, though every time Congress discusses tax reform the topic is debated. To date, Congress has recognized that eliminating this tax exemption would raise the cost of debt to most cities, counties, and states in the country, and it has rejected any extreme changes in this part of the tax code. Furthermore, munis are exempt from state and local income tax requirements in the jurisdiction where they are issued. The phrase "triple tax-free" to a New York City resident implies that the bond was issued by New York City, making it exempt from federal, state, and local income tax.

This dimension of municipal bonds segments the market. A bond that is attractive on an after-tax basis to a New York City resident may have no appeal to a Florida resident that faces no state or local income taxes. Not-for-profit organizations only rarely will find interest rates on municipal bonds to be attractive enough to qualify for their fixed income portfolios. This is important because the tax tail can sometimes end up wagging the portfolio dog.

Suppose you are a wealthy resident of Arizona. In an attempt to minimize your total tax obligation you build your fixed income portfolio exclusively from Arizona municipal bonds. While there may be many good issues from which to choose, such a portfolio by construction is less diversified than one a similar resident of Texas, which has no state income tax, would own. No investor should sacrifice good diversification discipline to the single-minded goal of minimizing taxes.

Municipal bonds are offered in a variety of maturities and structures that have already been discussed for treasuries and agencies. One important subset of municipal bonds that deserves further discussion is the class called *pre-refunded bonds*. With these bonds, typically used for long-term capital projects, the proceeds of the debt issue are invested in treasury bills, which is then held as collateral against the bonds. Effectively, the bonds are completely backed and are not dependent upon tax proceeds or revenue streams to be repaid. Many investors see these bonds as being as safe as Treasury bills, but paying a slightly higher interest rate.

Some jurisdictions have used municipal bonds to promote economic development. They reach out to private corporations and propose the construction of major facilities, which are financed at least in part, with the issue of municipal debt. These may be factories, sports facilities, or private hospitals, but they all share one major feature. The tax-free feature of the municipal bond has been used to secure cheaper financing than would be available to any private borrower. The downside is that the taxpayer is very likely on the hook, at least to a degree, if the economic forecasts behind the development are not met. These bonds are among the riskiest municipal bonds in the marketplace, in many cases comparable to the next category of fixed income securities, corporate debt.

9.2.6 Corporate Bonds

Corporate bonds allow private firms to borrow directly from the public. In form and substance they are similar to Treasury securities, but have to rely exclusively on the profitability of the issuing firm to ultimately fulfill the obligation. Default risk is the single most important factor to be estimated by anyone buying a corporate bond in either the primary or secondary markets.

There is no standard form for a corporate bond. Maturities are typically shorter than that of government debt, reflecting the perceived more temporal nature of the corporation versus a sovereign state. But there are many examples of extremely long-dated issues from major corporations. These bonds may be *callable* at a specified call price, or they may be *call protected*, which assures the buyer that they will not be paid off before maturity.

Corporate bond markets vary widely around the world in terms of their size and liquidity. The United States has the most developed corporate bond market. According to SIFMA data, the US corporate bond market is larger than the agency and municipal bond markets combined.[7]

Western Europe and developed Asia have much smaller corporate bond markets. In many emerging countries there is little or no activity in corporate bonds denominated in the local currency. Corporations in these areas sometimes try to access the much larger US and European marketplaces by issuing US dollar or euro-denominated bonds. Such an approach may prove to be a fruitful source of financing, but it raises several issues.

Typically the credit rating of the corporation is capped at the credit rating of its home country. This can be a particular burden for high-quality firms that happen to be domiciled in countries struggling with their public finances. But the logic is that a country that is having problems may impose capital restrictions that could impede a corporation's ability to pay off its debt even if it has the resources and the willingness to do so. There is a further risk if the corporation's revenue is largely local currency based, while the obligation to repay is in dollars. Any meaningful devaluation of the local currency could impact the firm's ability to pay.

---

[7]The SIFMA website, Investinginbonds.com, reports that there was $9.1 trillion in corporate debt outstanding at the end of 2012, which compared to $3.7 trillion in municipal securities and $2.1 trillion in agency debt outstanding.

For an investor willing to do the necessary credit research and assume these types of risks, hard currency-denominated corporate bonds of foreign companies may provide an attractive source of incremental return. The investor must determine that the credit spread is sufficient to cover not only the basic corporate default risk but also all of the other jurisdictional and currency risks that accompany such bonds.

Many of the countries where corporations look beyond their borders for public bond funding have economies that are much more dependent on bank loans for financing. People often have an outdated view of how modern, global banking works. They believe the bank makes loans to corporate or individual borrowers, and then they hold those loans on their balance sheets as assets. This still occurs today, but the size of corporate loans has in many instances grown so large to create outsized risks for any given bank. In these cases the bank sells into the secondary market some of these loan obligations, and buys other assets with the proceeds. This activity has grown dramatically in the last few decades and has created another major fixed income investment market that is highly comparable to corporate bonds. This is the subject of the next section.

9.2.7 Bank Loans

Banks regularly make loans to individuals and companies. That is their job. Many of these loans will stay on the bank's balance sheet as assets until they are paid off or written off. If too many loans are made to a particular borrower, or to a group of borrowers in a particular region, the assets side of the bank's balance sheet may contain dangerous concentrated risks. When similar kinds of concentrated risks began to threaten large insurance companies, reinsurance was invented to allow for more diversification. Banks in the last few decades have followed insurance companies in marketing part of their loan book to outside investors. This has improved balance sheet diversification, but it has also created a new investment category for people looking to own fixed-income assets.

It does not matter why a bank seeks to sell some of its loan books. The net effect is that the buyer of the *bank loans* receives the revenue stream from the regular interest payments and simultaneously takes on any default risk. It is not unusual after a bank sells a loan that it retains the servicing function, receiving a small fee while liberating the buyer from worrying about anything other than the investment merits of the loan.

Potential buyers evaluate bank loans on all of the normal criteria. Maturity, interest coupon, and the credit worthiness of the borrower are the key elements. There are, however, several important distinctions between bank loans and corporate bonds. Bank loans are typically higher up in the capital structure of the borrowing firm. This means that in the event of a bankruptcy, bank loans get paid off before corporate bondholders. The term *senior secured debt* is often applied to bank loans that have covenants requiring the firm to maintain collateral against them. Similarly, *senior unsecured debt* consists of loans that are first in line to be repaid but have no explicit assets of the firm backing them.

An operational and regulatory distinction between bank loans and corporate debt is that loans are not considered securities by the SEC. Corporate bonds must be issued under a strict set of rules that have evolved over many decades that try to assure fair and transparent dealing. Bank loans, in contrast, are created in a private transaction between the bank and its borrower, and are then sold into the professional market of fixed income dealers and investors. There is little disclosure required, making it imperative that any buyer do extensive due diligence on both the terms of the loan and the quality of the borrower. There is a further complication that bank loans are not assigned a CUSIP number because they are technically not securities. This makes it more difficult to settle transactions and to identify active bids and offers than is experienced in the corporate bond market.

The duration of most bank loans is relatively short. A meaningfully high percentage of all bank loans are structured with *floating rate* terms. LIBOR is a frequent base rate used for these floating rate loans, though many other base rates can be negotiated. The combination of short duration and floating rates can make a portfolio of bank loans particularly attractive to fixed income investors who are concerned about a rising rate environment.

The bank loan market was meaningfully transformed over the past 20 years by the creation of *collateralized loan obligations,* or CLOs. CLOs and other forms of credit structures are discussed in detail in Chapter 11. CLOs, like the bank loans that underlie them, usually are not subject to the securities acts of 1933 or 1940. One might think that such instruments should be regulated like stocks and bonds, but the market has evolved with a number of exemptions to these acts. Like all private placements, CLOs may only be sold to qualified investors, which means this market is largely dominated by sophisticated, large investors.

The most important point here is that as the CLO market grew, the demand for banks to sell whole loans from their portfolios increased dramatically. Many financial institutions began to think of themselves more as loan originators and packagers than as traditional banks.

The peril in this transformation came from the loss of alignment of interest between the loan originator and the eventual assumers of the risk. When banks kept all of the loans they made, they worked very hard to maximize loan quality and minimize losses from defaults. In principle, banks that sell their loans should also be careful in their origination because a higher-quality package of assets should attract more demand. In practice, however, before the credit crisis that began to unfold in late 2007 more emphasis was placed on volume than on quality.

Bank loans that had been sold, whether as whole loans or as tranches of CLOs, began to move into the hands of leveraged buyers. There were many examples of faulty CLO structures, but there were also ample numbers of investors who simply could not absorb the market losses that resulted from their leveraged holdings. The challenges of transacting in the bank loan market came to the forefront at the height of the crisis. Spreads on bank loans blew out to unprecedented levels, as there were many forced sellers. The worst excesses of this market were relieved in a few months, but it was a difficult time for all market participants. Regulatory changes since the financial crisis require banks to retain more of the risk from loans they originate in order to maintain better incentives, but there are no assurances that this market won't one day experience extreme stress again.

Investors who are not qualified to participate in private placements can only access bank loans through some kind of fund structure managed by a registered investment advisor. Both closed and open-ended mutual funds are available. Unlike T-bills or short-dated corporate debt, the smaller investor may not purchase individual bank loans or CLOs. Having said that, such investors should keep bank loan funds in mind when thinking about their allocations to fixed income securities. There will be times when the advantages from the short duration and the floating rate character of loans will more than offset the management fee charged for the fund.

9.2.8 Mortgages

Mortgages are a specific type of loan that is collateralized by the physical property it is financing. Different countries around the world have meaningfully different rules concerning mortgages. In countries like the United States, the property is the only collateral behind the loan. Other jurisdictions allow the lender to pursue other assets as well to satisfy the repayment of a mortgage debt. This obviously affects the credit quality of any specific mortgage or pool of mortgages, but it does not change the most fundamental common feature.

Because people move for a variety of reasons and sell their houses, residential mortgages almost always allow for early prepayment. This is like having a callable bond with no explicit conditions on either the date or the interest rate at which the mortgage may be prepaid. Lenders therefore face great uncertainty as to what their cash flow will be, or whether they will even have a cash flow if interest rates change.

The negative convexity of mortgages was discussed earlier in this chapter. The implication of this is that any investor holding mortgages has implicitly written options to the borrower. This prepayment option should be highly valuable, meaning that lenders should receive higher coupon interest rates for mortgages than they would receive for comparable credit quality traditional loans.

That is the concept. Evaluating how much that option is worth at any given point in time is a very complicated, analytical puzzle. Just like all valuation problems, the market sometimes gets it right, but not always. If the market does not expect prepayments to be large, borrowers will have to pay a very small premium, and conversely. Small armies of highly technical researchers have spent 30 years or more trying to build models that accurately value the prepayment option on pools of mortgages. The fact that new finance PhDs are still writing dissertations describing improved approaches suggests that a final solution remains elusive.

One of the biggest innovations of the second half of the twentieth century was the concept of securitizing pools of mortgages. Like CLOs discussed in the previous section, mortgage-backed securities allowed the bundling of many mortgages into a single security, which are then sold in its entirety or in highly specialized tranches. This greatly increased the attractiveness of mortgages as an investment vehicle, and radically transformed the mortgage lending business.

Residential mortgages come in two broad flavors. Mortgages that meet a set of criteria in terms of size, credit worthiness of the borrower, and initial loan-to-value can qualify to be sold to GSEs like Freddie Mac and Fannie Mae. These organizations then create securities that represent pools of mortgages where the principal value is guaranteed by the GSE. These are often referred to as *agency mortgage-backed securities*. Residential mortgages that do not meet the qualifications to be sold to the GSEs can still be securitized, but they are done so privately. Creators of these *non-agency mortgage-backed securities* sometimes sought private insurance like that provided by the GSEs. The depth of the crisis in 2008 and 2009 quickly erased most of the anticipated benefits from private insurance, as losses rapidly grew past the ability of the insurers to pay.

One only needs to look at the collapse of the housing market and the fact that Freddie Mac and Fannie Mae seemed to be on permanent government life support to conclude that this process was fraught with numerous design and execution problems. There were the same kinds of misalignment of interest issues between the originators in the ultimate investors in the mortgages that existed with CLOs. There was also the problem that the demand for securitized mortgages was so great before the crisis, that traditional credit standards were often waived in order to issue a loan and place it in a pool.

If banks or other lenders had held these mortgages on their balance sheets, perhaps there would have been better credit work done and an improved understanding of all the risks in the loan. Instead, massive quantities of residential mortgages were pooled to create securitized products designed in a way that made it particularly difficult to do thorough credit analysis. Everything was fine as long as the housing market continued to prosper, but when that cycle broke all of the flaws and misunderstandings became evident.

This is not a problem that needs to be inherent in mortgage investments. Just because an instrument has uncertain call properties and negative convexity does not mean its risks cannot be accurately assessed. Since the crisis there has been a large and active market in which specialists sorted through the problem-mortgage loans and evaluated what they believed would be a fair price. Because of the size and complexity of the problem, there were many outsized opportunities for mortgage investors in the early stages after the crisis.

These opportunities did not quickly go away. Unlike high-yield bonds, which are discussed in more detail in the section on credit below, individual mortgages and pools of mortgages are based on much more complicated collateral. It may actually be easier to analyze the ability of a multibillion-dollar corporation to pay back its debt than it is to assess the market and the psychology behind a pool of residential mortgages. This should lead to residential mortgages being a less efficient marketplace than many other forms of fixed income securities. Liquidity might be more difficult as there are fewer participants, but investors might be compensated with somewhat higher interest rates to accept these complications and risks.

If any lessons were learned from mortgage investors during the crisis, the most important one should have been a reinforcement of the truth that mortgages are inherently complicated and require great care in analysis. They cannot easily be homogenized and marketed as a commodity. No one should assume that housing prices will always increase, improving the quality of the underlying collateral. But mortgages can provide a valuable source of investment return to those people with the skills in the appropriate risk profiles to appreciate them. The residential mortgage market is one of the biggest fixed income markets in the world. It is far too important to be avoided by fixed income investors simply because of past missteps.

Mortgages on commercial properties also form an important fixed income investment category. These mortgages can also be thought of individually or as part of a pool, called commercial mortgage-backed securities, or CMBS. Because of the size of commercial mortgages there are almost always fewer individual loans in any given pool. This often allows investors to do much more detailed research on the underlying properties backing the mortgages. Commercial mortgages also tend to be on properties that are more specialized and have had much more capital invested in them, making it less likely that they will be refinanced because the owner decides to relocate.

Because the commercial mortgage industry is more specialized and involves much larger sums per loan, lenders have typically been able to place more restrictions on the borrower's ability to refinance at will. For all of these reasons the negative convexity of commercial mortgages is less of a problem than that for pools of residential mortgages.

The prices of all mortgages in the secondary market reflect the confluence of private and public supply and demand. Because property is so broadly held across the public, there is a long history of government interventions in the housing and mortgage markets. After the housing and credit crisis left tens of millions of homeowners owing more than their homes were worth, there were multiple attempts to encourage restructuring of mortgages.

One can debate whether the government's programs to encourage broader home ownership exacerbated the housing bubble and the subsequent collapse. But what is undeniable is that the government is an active, and not always predictable, participant in the space. From the investor's perspective this means that there is an added dimension of risk to all mortgage-based investments that goes beyond simple duration and credit risk.

It is impossible to model this kind of risk. The net result has been lower prices, and higher yields for the buyers of mortgages than would have existed otherwise. Perhaps over time if the government behaves in a more predictable way, this risk premium will shrink, but in the years after the depths of the crisis, mortgages appeared to be offering slightly higher returns as compensation.

9.2.9 Direct Loans

One of the more obscure areas of fixed income investing consists of owning direct loans. The closest most individual investors get to this activity is if they partially finance the sale of their own home by extending a second mortgage to the buyer, or if they extend loans to family members. Neither of these activities is typically driven by pure investment motives. But when one considers the vast array of fixed income investment opportunities available, this is an area that should be at least acknowledged.

It perhaps goes without saying that there are meaningful risks associated with making and owning loans to individuals or companies. At the top of the list is the concentrated risk associated with whether the borrower will pay back the loan. This is not in principle different from the default risk of a corporate bond, but with a registered security it is highly unlikely that you will be a meaningful part of the total obligation. There may be hundreds if not thousands of bond owners, which in the event of a default can marshal resources in order to maximize any recovery. With a direct loan all the burden of collection falls upon the lender.

Almost as important as the concentrated default risk is the illiquidity that comes with direct loans. In theory, every loan could be sold to another investor. In reality it is quite difficult to do thorough enough due diligence to evaluate what an existing loan should be worth. This restricts the market to highly trained professionals in the credit space, and greatly limits the number of potential participants at any given point in time.

Because of the highly customized nature of the transaction, and the concentrated risk, few individuals participate meaningfully in building a portfolio of direct loans. The space is relevant, however, to all investors because of the existence of funds that attempt to add value doing just that. Frequently these funds are in the form of private partnerships, available only to qualified investors. This is actually a consistent outcome given the nature of the underlying investments. A mutual fund holding direct loans could face great difficulties in meeting redemptions without suffering large losses as they try to sell.

The descriptions of such funds emphasize two things. The first is a statement that the credit market is a highly imperfect arena, where worthy borrowers are not always able to access credit in either the bank loan or bond markets. The fund claims that it has an active network to source loans and a strong ability to do the necessary credit evaluations. These funds will typically try to hold dozens of loans in order to minimize the risk of default by any single borrower. The hoped-for result is a total return that is meaningfully higher than that available in the liquid credit markets.

Investors evaluating such fund managers face many challenges. First they must be able to evaluate the claims about the sourcing network and their credit expertise. During times of great liquidity and growing GDP like was seen from 2004 to 2007, almost every credit looks wonderful. Track records of managers from these periods may not reveal all of the true risks.

The second challenge comes from a lack of good market prices for the underlying loans. It is not unusual for such fund managers to hold the value of the loan at par as long as the interest payments are being made. Any such manager who went through 2007 and 2008 without showing a monthly loss simply failed to acknowledge that if they had tried to sell any of these loans they would have received considerably less than par. Less responsible managers in this area sometimes try to assert that this lack of marking to market is actually a reflection of low risk. Nothing could be further from the truth.

While there are some managers of direct loans who experienced relatively small default rates during the crisis, many more found themselves in the middle of the storm. These managers showed no losses until they had to write off loans as uncollectible. The pattern of returns showed steady month-to-month gains, followed by catastrophic losses.

This is a particular risk if the funds allow for regular subscriptions and redemptions. New investors could be buying into a portfolio at a much higher price than market reality. Conversely, early redeemers could receive their proceeds at a much higher than warranted NAV, similar to the Granite fund in 1994, disadvantaging all of the remaining investors who own a much smaller pool of assets. This is an argument against direct loan hedge funds and in favor of true private partnerships that do not allow new investments or redemptions on a continuing basis.

A somewhat arcane element of due diligence for direct loan funds is a need to evaluate the servicer of the loans. Some funds do their own servicing, while others outsource this activity. Either way, loan servicing comes at a cost and as much detail as possible about how this works should be obtained. An 8% net return may look attractive until one discovers that the gross proceeds were 15% on a very risky book of loans, but a combination of manager and servicer fees eroded away 7%. Too many direct loan efforts seem to be run to generate auxiliary service fees to the manager and its affiliates rather than net returns to the investor.

Leverage is sometimes a component in direct loan funds, especially at times of low interest rates, tight credit spreads, and great liquidity. This can be a deadly combination. Investors should examine fund documents very carefully regarding what types of leverage are allowed and how it is secured in the marketplace. If the manager loses access to the credit market providing the leverage, this may force liquidations from the portfolio at fire sale prices.

Direct loan funds should have the greatest appeal to investors during periods where the regular credit markets are not functioning well. When the economy is booming and money is readily available from traditional sources, there is a natural negative selection governing who must settle for privately negotiated loans. Worthy credits can go to the bank or to the bond market. It is mostly second- and third-tier credits that must resort to direct loan financing, and then the question becomes whether you are receiving enough incremental interest yield to cover this risk.

During periods of relative economic unease when the traditional sources of credit are not dependably available, direct loans may offer great opportunities to those who can evaluate and manage the fundamental credit risks. In the section below devoted to credit, the discussion is expanded to more fully explore this dimension of investment return. As one moves further out on the risk scale the investments begin to look less and less like a bond, and more and more like an equity investment. There is no single right or wrong answer as to whether or not one should own direct loans in their portfolio. It depends entirely on the price and the environment. But it is unambiguously true that these are more difficult investments to evaluate than other fixed income alternatives.

9.2.10 Cat Bonds

Catastrophe bonds, commonly known as *Cat Bonds*, are difficult to classify because they are labeled bonds, and pay a regular coupon, but are based on the performance of underlying insurance pools. In that regard they are much more like structured products discussed in Chapter 11 than they are the classic bonds discussed above. However, as the Cat Bond industry has grown they have increasingly been compared to traditional fixed income in terms of expected returns and volatility.

To understand Cat Bonds requires at least a background in insurance and reinsurance. There have been various forms of insurance policies around for centuries. The biggest risk to the person buying a policy has always been the insurance writer's ability to pay on a claim. Collecting premiums is easy. Investing those premiums wisely so that capital is available when the insurable event occurs is a bit more difficult. Living through extremely rare events when losses pile up faster than actuary tables would predict is harder still.

No insurance company keeps capital reserves equal to the maximum possible loss they could experience if all the policies they wrote filed a maximum claim instantaneously. That would be completely uneconomical. But an insurance company still has to be alert to the chance that a cluster of large loss events could prove ruinous to its business. One defense would be to keep more capital in reserve. Another would be to convince another group of creditworthy people to assume part of the negative tail risk.

To spread out some of these risks the concept of reinsurance was developed. In 1688 Lloyd's of London began as a syndicate of insurers that would stand collectively behind the risks that were underwritten by the individual members. It was the first organized structure for reinsurance.

The basic process is simple. There is a new set of insurance policies protecting against the extreme events created by the original insurance. Premiums are established and additional capital put in place to back up the original set of risks.

The problem with this solution is that it still relied on the capital within the insurance industry. Risks are diversified across insurers, but they remain inside the industry. If outside capital could be brought to bear on the problem in a manner that didn't open up new credit risks, that would improve the entire insurance environment. In the latter part of the twentieth century, innovators created Cat Bonds.

Cat Bonds are structured with limited duration, typically three to five years. They pay regular coupons determined in the marketplace. Where they differ from traditional corporate bonds is how they are paid back. When IBM borrows money in the bond market, it usually makes a broad representation that it will use its resources to pay back its obligations. IBM decides how to use the bond proceeds and subsequently how it will perform and not default.

The proceeds of a Cat Bond are typically placed into a restricted investment account associated with a specific risk pool. For example, there may be a $100 million Cat Bond issue that stands behind insured storm damage losses that exceed $300 million. That is to say, the original group of insurers are responsible for the first $300 million in losses, but if they exceed that amount the Cat Bonds will cover up to the next $100 million.

The bond proceeds can be used for two purposes, and for only two purposes. If the insurance losses are less than $300 million over the life of the bond in this example, the entire fund gets returned to the bondholders. If, however, losses break through $300 million, the bond pool is drawn upon, potentially until it is exhausted.

The difference between corporate bonds and Cat Bonds should be evident. Corporate bonds get paid back if the company does not default, which is highly dependent upon the financial wellbeing of the company. When it is time to pay off the bonds at maturity, the company either has the resources to do so or it raises new capital in the market to avoid default. While corporate bonds perform depending on the continuing health of a company, Cat Bonds behave narrowly depending on the way a finite set of actuarial events play out.

This means the entire concept of default needs to be reconsidered. It is entirely possible that a Cat Bond will pay back $0.80 on the dollar even if the insurance company remains completely solvent. All it takes is a larger number of high loss storms in the period covered by the bonds.

Since the vast majority of the value of Cat Bonds is a function of the insurance environment and not on the financial health of the underlying insurance company, one would think that the yields on these bonds would be primarily a function of the weather. Hurricanes Katrina (2005), Sandy (2012), Harvey (2017), and Irma (2017) were huge loss events, and many Cat Bond holders found that their assets were being called in under the terms of their agreements. By structuring the deductible and the limits of coverage appropriately, investors could dial risk up or down to target an appropriate return on their investment just in the way an insurance company would for its own capital account.

Sellers of Cat Bonds often point to this feature as a benefit to investors. These hurricanes did not care whether the 10-year Treasury was trading at 2.5% or 7.5%. Cat Bond returns should be mostly independent from short-term fluctuations in interest rates or changes in the stock market and therefore provide diversification benefits to the overall portfolio. History shows that not to be entirely true.

Figure 9.7 shows the spread for Cat Bonds from 2002 to 2014. The light gray line shows the implied spreads for a class of Cat Bonds that have a 2% expected

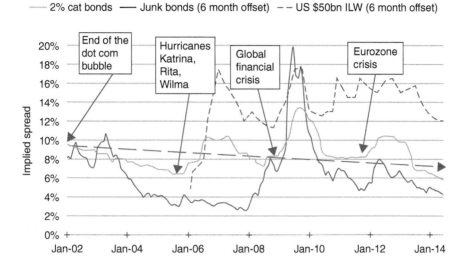

FIGURE 9.7 Implied Spread for 2% Cat Bonds Versus High Yield
Source: Adam Alvarez

loss ratio.[8] Using standardized actuarial models, Cat Bonds are categorized and sold according to the likelihood of loss. The higher the projected loss ratio, the bigger the yield paid on the Cat Bonds.

The chart shows a history of declining spreads for Cat Bonds until the severe hurricanes in 2005. Predictably after those major loss events, the cost of reinsurance acquired through the purchase of Cat Bonds went up, as did yields for new Cat Bond buyers. This is completely consistent with how this market should work. When there is a big loss paid, capital in the system needs to be rebuilt, and to attract that capital requires higher reinsurance premiums. In the case of Cat Bonds, this means higher yields.

After that the pricing varied from what the model would predict. The financial crisis triggered by the bankruptcy of Lehman Brothers seemed to push Cat Bond yields higher for many months. Later, when the European Union was threatened with collapse by the weak fiscal health of some of its periphery, spreads widened again. Neither of these events had any connection to the number or severity of storms around the world.

What appears to be the case is that the market fell victim to investors looking at Cat Bonds and traditional corporate bonds through the same lens. Once high-yield bonds tumbled in price to return more than 20%, potential buyers of Cat Bonds were lured away. Even though there had been no change in the actuarial risk, people in position to invest had new attractive opportunities elsewhere and the Cat Bonds had to be sweetened to find buyers.

---

[8]ILW in the chart refers to industry loss warranties. These are similar to catastrophic reinsurance except that they are structured to pay as a function of the losses across the entire industry instead of a single insurance company. This is a younger and smaller market and to date it appears somewhat independent from the pricing of the Cat Bond market.

This explains why Cat Bonds are not the completely uncorrelated asset that their proponents would like them to be. While this connectivity diminishes the diversification benefit of owning these bonds, it also sometimes opens up opportunities like it did in 2009. When disruption hits the traditional credit markets, people seeking reinsurance protection through Cat Bonds need to pay higher yields. Higher yields for the same actuarial risk translate into a better investment for the Cat Bond buyers.

There is a dark side to this equation, however. After a prolonged period of artificially low Treasury interest rates that followed the financial crisis, institutional and individual investors alike were starved for return. No doubt some of them were attracted to the higher yields of Cat Bonds. Money flowed into the space from people who likely lacked the expertise to evaluate the actuarial risks, and Cat Bond yields tumbled along with corporate credits. As long as the storm seasons in the United States stayed as subdued as interest rates, nobody would have minded. After Hurricanes Harvey and Irma in 2017, these owners of Cat Bonds probably wished they had paid more attention to actuarial risks and less attention to Fed policy.

9.2.10 Mutual Funds

Mutual funds are certainly not a specific subset of fixed income investing, but instead one of the most popular vehicles to access the space. Much of what will be written here is as relevant to equities as it is fixed income, but there are some important features that should be highlighted in the fixed income discussion.

Some of the largest investment funds on the planet are fixed-income-oriented mutual funds. The concept of mutual funds was created in the Investment Company Act of 1940; hence one often hears these products referred to as '*40 Act Funds*. The SEC devotes much of its regulatory oversight effort to the operation of these funds, as they are often the primary vehicle through which public investors receive exposure to a market.

There are two broad categories of mutual funds. *Open-ended funds* allow investments and redemptions every day at a *net asset value* (NAV) calculated at the close of business. These funds form the lion's share of the mutual fund industry because of their liquidity and accuracy of pricing.

Closed-end funds, in contrast, are created with an initial pool of capital and a fixed number of shares. They are typically listed on a stock exchange, so they are available to trade continuously through the day. The downside is that there is no mechanism to keep their traded prices near their net asset value, so discounts or premiums to NAV regularly appear and vary with the sentiment of the market. This uncertainty creates trading opportunities for some investors, but many more prefer the NAV certainty of the open-end model.

The well-known features of mutual funds include disclosure rules and limitations on what may be said in advertising. There are many other less appreciated regulations. These include limitations on leverage and restrictions on what a fund may hold relative to how the fund is described.

Much of the regulation to protect investors concerns the safekeeping of assets. A fund's custody agreement with a bank is typically far more elaborate than the arrangements used for other bank clients. The range of the custodian's services extends from safekeeping and accounting for the fund's assets, to the control over all of the transactions in the portfolio. This part of the fund operation is much more tightly proscribed than unregulated investment vehicles.

Mutual funds are exempt from any corporate taxes on their portfolios as long as they distribute at least 90% of their income. Since what is not distributed is taxed at ordinary corporate income tax rates, most fixed income mutual funds distribute almost all of the interest income that their portfolios produce. Many fixed income funds distribute income monthly, though quarterly payments are not unusual. Taxable investors are, of course, responsible for their own tax obligations, and reinvesting the distributions does not avoid the tax.

Mutual fund rules do not require the distribution of realized capital gains, but the corporate tax rate applies to any capital gains retained. Mutual fund companies, therefore, almost always also distribute these gains, though this activity occurs very near to year-end, so that gains and losses can be netted efficiently. Savvy investors watch the distributions' calendars closely. One should in general seek to avoid investing right before a large capital gain distribution, which would incur a tax liability for investments in which there was no corresponding investment gain.

Some degree of transparency is mandated by the regulation, and the industry prides itself on being more open than other alternatives like hedge funds. But there are limitations that can frustrate the investor trying to do a full evaluation of holdings and returns.

The mutual fund *prospectus* is required to be maintained in an up-to-date form. In it one finds the fund's investment objectives, a broad description of strategies and risks, fees and expenses, and performance. An important feature of these documents is that they have to adhere to standards of presentation that allow investors to compare funds without doing too many mental gymnastics. That's the good news.

The bad news is that there is no requirement to disclose sources of the fund's returns. Was the outperformance a result of a duration bet or good credit selection? Two bond funds that have the same stated objectives could have very different portfolios and results. The better performer would have you believe it was entirely due to his or her superior skill, when in fact it might have been the result of greater risk-taking and a run of good luck.

Positions do have to be periodically disclosed, but the minimum requirement is only twice a year, with a lag. Some mutual funds with relatively simple portfolios will list them in their quarterly or annual reports. Other more complicated funds publish summaries of positions, with the full portfolio only available to the public on request or through SEC EDGAR files available online.

One would like to believe that these semiannual portfolio lists are representative of the actual holdings through the year, but that is not necessarily the case. While the largest bond funds are like battleships that are not easily turned, smaller funds can easily make adjustments to improve the appearance of their portfolio holdings at the time of their mandatory reporting. This is called *window dressing*, and it is virtually impossible for an outside investor to know that it is going on.

One of the key '40 Act rules is that the mutual fund company may not selectively disclose portfolio information to one set of investors over another. This is a virtuous rule designed to protect the investing public. But mutual fund managers routinely use that regulation to hide information that they don't want the public to focus on. If you inquire about a specific period's holdings or performance attribution, the standard answer is to tell you to read what is in the quarterly report. If what is in that report does not answer your inquiry, the manager is not legally allowed to provide you information that they have not given others.

While the spirit of this at one level is admirable, it also allows the manager to shape the communication to all investors in such ways to downplay any problems or risks. This is not an issue for investors who have enough assets to have a separately managed account. These investors can see every transaction and holding. There are no questions about your own portfolio that are off-limits.

One of the least understood elements of fixed income mutual funds is the potential use of leverage. The mutual fund regulations limit leverage at the portfolio level to about one third. Many fixed income mutual funds do not use leverage at all, or they restrict the use of leverage to short periods of time and only for the purpose of facilitating transactions where cash flows don't match up. This is an important element that should be discussed in the prospectus and well understood by the investor.

There are other mutual funds that give themselves broad latitude in using up to maximum leverage. Sometimes this is done the traditional way through borrowing and purchasing extra securities, or it can be done with the use of derivatives. These derivatives can be either exchange traded or over-the-counter. It is up to the investor to determine whether the strategy and approach of any particular manager is consistent with their own objectives.

The regulations also require that the underlying holdings be highly liquid, with at least 85% of the securities in the portfolio being able to be liquidated at or near the current price within seven days.[9] This is a highly subjective standard that is largely self-defined by the manager. There appear to be few examples of the SEC taking an enforcement action against a mutual fund for violating the liquidity rules. It is only after the fact when a fund experiences a liquidity run that one really understands whether the holdings met the definition or not.

During the depths of the crisis after the Lehman Brothers bankruptcy, these liquidity provisions were sorely tested. After the Reserve Primary Fund announced that their holdings of short-term Lehman Brothers paper caused them to break the one-dollar net asset value of their fund, many investors tried to exit from money market mutual funds in general out of concern over the portfolio holdings. The vast majority of mutual funds were holding highly liquid, high-quality paper, but at the darkest moments very little other than Treasury bills could be sold at prices that had existed the week before.

Once the federal government and the Federal Reserve stepped into the crisis and guaranteed the value of these funds, the panic quickly subsided. In the aftermath, however, there was a careful examination of actual practice versus what was allowed in the rules. After the crisis, SEC chairwoman Mary Schapiro began a major re-examination of money market mutual fund policies. Her goal was to eliminate rules that might inadvertently lead investors to suddenly seek to redeem their shares.

The obvious way to do this is to eliminate the fixed one-dollar price that virtually all money market funds try to maintain. This convention, which is a great convenience to the investing public the vast majority of the time, is possible because of the highly liquid, short-duration nature of the underlying investments. The small variations in NAV that occur as markets routinely change can be "smoothed out" by offsetting payments of the interest.

---

[9]The liquidity regulations for money market mutual funds are much stricter, with 95% of the portfolio being categorized as liquid.

An important reason investors like this system is that it makes their accounting easy. With each share priced at one dollar, purchases and sales are made at the same price and there is no requirement to monitor tiny capital gains and losses. Fund managers appreciate the simplicity of the model and the ease of communication that comes with it.

Of course there are those rare occasions when the prices of the underlying securities change in a meaningful way. If they have appreciated there is little problem. Payouts can be adjusted upward and the one-dollar net asset value maintained. It is much more complicated if prices are falling.

If the value of the assets drops sufficiently, the fund is not allowed to continue the $1 share price. Even breaking away from the $1 price by a small amount is a devastating blow to the company. There have been several hundred instances over the decades where mutual fund companies have elected to supplement the portfolio with their own capital rather than face the prospect of lowering the reported NAV below $1. These actions do not have to be reported to the investing public directly, but the SEC needs to be informed.

As more and more assets are invested in money market mutual funds, Chairwoman Schapiro was obviously concerned that at some point a market disruption could occur that would be too large to be covered by the resources of the fund company. Like the Reserve Primary Fund event in 2008, this could spark a negative public reaction that would affect the whole industry.[10] Chairwoman Schapiro was rightfully focused on the fact that taxpayers could be on the hook for an implicit guarantee of this industry if the alternative would be a disastrous run on the funds broadly.

The issues surrounding money market mutual funds are symptomatic of the fundamental tension that exists in the regulated fund industry. Rules are established to shape the risks of the investments in order to give the investing public confidence that their assets are generally safe. But how do funds differentiate themselves from the competition if the regulations restrict everyone to the same narrow set of investment options? The answer is that every imaginable option within the letter of the rules is explored, and if they hold promise to add extra return they are pursued.

Unfortunately, perhaps, the market is a lot smarter than the regulations. The reason Lehman Brothers short-dated paper was yielding more in the months leading up to its bankruptcy is the market understood the higher risks. Most money market fund managers avoided this paper because of these risks. Some, like the Reserve Primary Fund, chased the higher yields hoping that Lehman would not fail. Or they might have believed if Lehman was about to fail, they would be pushed into a forced marriage like that of Bear Stearns in March of 2008, that created no losses for bond holders.

Virtually up to the point of bankruptcy, the Lehman short-dated paper met all of the money market fund rules for inclusion into a portfolio. It was only when the losses caused Reserve Primary to break the dollar did investors across the industry begin to question whether their money was truly safe. The key conclusion is that no

---

[10]It is important to note that the size of the loss is less important than the fact that the dollar NAV was broken. Investors in the Reserve Primary Fund ultimately got back more than 99% of their funds, but the business was destroyed.

regulations can eliminate 100% of the chance of loss. Any belief by the public that they can is bound to lead to disappointment eventually.

The anecdote to this kind of problem is not more or different regulations, but better diligence by the investing public. Just because a fund is a regulated mutual fund does not mean it is perfectly safe. It isn't. Outperformance by any manager needs to be investigated and understood. Any outperformance is more likely to be the result of taking on different risks than it is the variance in a manager's intelligence or trading skills.

Fixed income mutual funds offer many advantages to the less sophisticated investor. Many early abuses were greatly curtailed by the '40 Act, and mutual funds may very well be the best option available for millions of investors. But the rules also allow managers more latitude than one might like regarding portfolio transparency and attribution. Sophisticated investors need to be able to get past whatever communication limitations exist, and compare the mutual fund manager to other structures like separately managed accounts that might be available.

9.2.11   ETFs and ETNs

Exchange-Traded Funds (ETFs) and *Exchange-Traded Notes (ETNs)* are the single biggest investment phenomenon of the twenty-first century. The term ETP, representing the broad category of *Exchange-Traded Products*, is sometimes used generically. This broad activity has grown from being considered a relatively niche product targeting more active traders to trillions of dollars of assets working for every manner of institutional and retail investor. Like the discussion of mutual funds, much of what will be discussed here is not unique to fixed income, but applies to equity-based products as well.

ETFs were invented to be an alternative to index mutual funds. Like mutual funds, they are registered under the '40 Act, and have a detailed prospectus available to investors. Their obvious advantage is the ability to trade during the day versus being forced to use end-of-day net asset values for mutual fund transactions. To large institutions holding index portfolios, such a feature might seem to be of limited value. In fact, it might make the user look more like a speculator than a long-term investor. Through time, the tradability of ETFs increasingly appealed to active traders looking for liquid ways to express market or sector views. ETFs have grown to be comparable to traditional index mutual funds and the proliferation of new products has been astonishing. Figure 9.8 shows the year ending assets in ETFs and index mutual funds since 1998.

The basic ETF model looks just like an open-ended mutual fund. Shares are created that own a basket of bonds. But instead of all transactions being executed at the end of the trading day net asset value (NAV), ETFs are bought or sold in real time on a stock exchange. This makes the management of the underlying portfolios much more dynamic. If more buyers show up during the day than there are sellers, the ETF's price gets bid up to a premium over the value of the underlying bonds. At that point the ETF's sponsor can step in and issue more shares while simultaneously buying the underlying bonds. The two largest providers of ETFs in the early years, Barclays Global Investors (BGI) and State Street, used their well-established index arbitrage skills to profit from this kind of transaction. In doing so, they also kept the traded prices of the ETFs reasonably close to the value of the underlying assets.

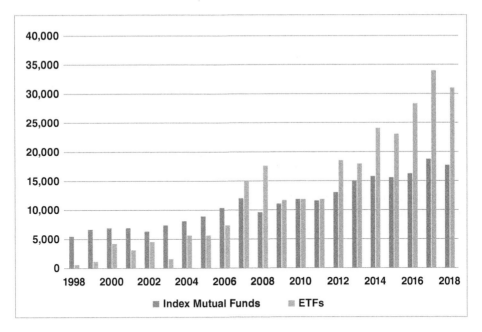

FIGURE 9.8 Net Assets in Index Mutual Funds and ETFs
Source: Investment Company Institute

From a humble beginning of a few ETF providers offering products on major stock indexes, the industry has literally exploded. Almost anyone can sponsor an ETF, but that does not mean they will be successful. According to data compiled by State Street and Bloomberg, at the end of 2008 there were 22 fund companies offering more than 700 distinct ETF products. Less than a decade later there were more than 50 companies offering over 2,000 ETFs.[11] New entries seem to appear daily. The early innovators hold a wide advantage in the market. The top three companies – BGI (now BlackRock), State Street and Vanguard – control nearly 70% of the assets in ETFs.[12] Nine ETFs are larger than $50 billion in assets. At the other end of the spectrum, more than 250 ETFs have less than $5 million in assets.[13]

The initial ETFs were structured as unit trusts, meaning the underlying portfolios *fully replicate* the underlying index of the ETF. For popular ETFs like SPY, based on the S&P 500, this means that once a portfolio is constructed the only transactions inside the ETF are when companies move in or out of the index. This structure lends itself to low turnover and transaction costs, making these ETFs among the most cost and tax efficient index products available.

Not all indexes are easy to replicate. Because of the extreme breadth of bond indexes, some truncation of the index universe is almost necessary. In these cases

---

[11]www.etf.com. (13 September 2017).
[12]www.etfgi.com. (13 September 2017).
[13]www.etf.com, op.cit.

the ETFs are set up as open-ended funds. The manager will use various techniques to try to mimic the performance of the index without full replication (e.g. the Barclays Aggregate Bond Index consists of over 8,000 bonds while the ETFs and index funds that try to mirror it will often hold less than half that number). These open-ended funds can trade more frequently and experience *slippage* (plus or minus) against the performance of the index. Each prospective investor should compare the performance of the ETF versus the underlying index as the first step of due diligence.

Another structure for ETFs is a *grantor trust*. This is most popular with ETFs backed by physical commodities like gold (e.g. GLD), and is not typically used in bond products.

You might think that this is already a bountiful array of opportunity. However, you should never underestimate Wall Street financial engineers. Once a simple idea takes hold, there is no shortage of imagination applied to create related products. In this case, the major innovations include *leveraged ETFs*, *inverse ETFs*, and the previously mentioned ETNs.

Government regulation allows open-ended mutual funds to have a modest amount of leverage, which was discussed in the previous section. Leveraged ETFs and ETNs have extended that somewhat, 2X leverage being the most popular variety. A subtlety lost on many investors is that these leveraged ETFs are designed to match the index *for a single day*. The importance of this is best illustrated in an extreme example. Suppose at the start of a trading day the index and a 2X ETF both begin at 100. Also presume that in a particularly bad day of market activity, the index falls 10% to 90%. If the 2X ETF tracks its mandate exactly, it will fall 20% to 80. So far, so good – at least in terms of the mechanics.

At that point the ETF portfolio no longer matches the characteristics of the index, so the sponsor rebalances the holdings so it is once again lined up. Now let the index increase by 10% on day 2, ending at 99. A 20% increase in the ETF takes it from 80 to 96. Looking at the two-day experience of the investor, the index is down 1% (100 to 99) while the 2X leveraged ETF is down 4% (100 to 96). *Volatility has created slippage that can build significantly over time, and this effect occurs in both up and down markets.*[14] Leveraged ETFs are designed for short-term traders, not investors.

Inverse ETFs allow the buyer of the product to make a reverse bet on the underlying index or asset. This allows retail investors to take a negative position without borrowing and shorting securities. Not surprisingly, there are leveraged versions of inverse ETFs available as well. These too can experience considerable slippage between the target index and the ETF.

While ETNs may look temptingly close to ETFs in that they are traded on exchanges, there is a huge difference. ETNs can be based on the performance of bonds, stocks, commodities, and almost anything else one might imagine. However,

---

[14]To show this, reverse the example. The market moves from 100 to 110 on a 10% up move and the 2X leveraged ETF goes from 100 to 120. If on the next day the market drops 10%, it will fall 11 points to 99. The ETF's 20% drop will be 24 points taking the ETF to 96. Volatility is a major enemy of leveraged ETFs.

the only thing backing the ETN is the promise of the fund sponsor. ETNs are much more closely related to structured notes, which created many negative headlines in 2007 and 2008, than they are to asset-based ETFs.

It should come as no surprise that the fees associated with these complicated products are often meaningfully higher than the more basic ETF funds. Liquidity in the hundreds of smallest ETFs and ETNs can be a nightmare.

The basic ETF has many potential positive uses in an investment portfolio. It can be a cost-effective short-term placeholder in an asset allocation, or be a permanent element to establish a core holding. ETFs have grown to date primarily because they are good for both the investor and for the firms that create them.

More recently the landscape has shifted. New and complex ETFs are not created as a result of huge investor demand for esoteric instruments. Instead they are created and sold in ways that are mostly beneficial to the fund managers. This is the dark side of financial engineering. Unfortunately it is only the latest chapter in a book with many unhappy stories for investors. Leveraged swaps, structured notes, CDs, CDOs, and CLOs all started as basic products that over time became more complex and the object of heavy sales efforts with inadequate risk disclosures.

Anyone looking seriously at bond mutual funds should also consider ETFs in the comparison set. While there are no hard and fast rules in this area, there are some useful guidelines to start one's inquiry into ETFs:

- The ETF's legal structure affects taxes paid. Each ETF product needs to be evaluated individually as tax efficiency can vary widely.
- If the goal of the ETF is to mimic a particular index, active trading and turnover are the enemies. Expenses from direct trading costs and bid/ask spreads can mount quickly. The most successful bond-index ETFs have stable, low-turnover portfolios.
- ETFs that use models to try to mimic an index can be subject to more tracking error and higher internal trading costs.
- ETFs that use surrogate positions – for example, trading futures or other derivatives when trying to capture movements in spot prices – tend to trade more frequently and have the potential for significant tracking error.
- Fund expenses vary widely across funds and providers. If there are fund expense caps in place, one needs to understand completely when caps might be modified or removed.
- Leveraged and inverse ETFs should primarily appeal to the short-term trader. Long-term investors are likely to find the tracking errors of such funds incompatible with their goals.
- Because of the inherent credit risk in ETNs, great care should be exercised in choosing the counterparty
- There are four things investors always need to keep in mind: return, risk, cost, and the impact of taxes. Unless one fully understands how an instrument behaves in all four categories, one cannot determine whether the product fits into the portfolio. No doubt there will be important ETFs trading on the world's stock exchanges for years to come, but many of today's offerings have little or no legitimate role to play in a careful investor's portfolio.

9.3 CREDIT

Credit has previously been discussed as one of the most important factors in determining the price of bonds. But it also deserves at least a short separate discussion because as one moves down the credit continuum, the securities begin to look less and less like bonds and take on their own portfolio characteristics. This is particularly true of nonperforming or *distressed credits*.

There are no bright lines separating these assets, but a good rule of thumb looks at interest rate sensitivity. High-quality corporate bonds tend to move in price similarly to that of treasury securities as interest rates change. The prices of lower quality credits can be more a function of the specific prospects of the borrower and less reliant on the general level of interest rates. Often, high-yield bonds are considered to be influenced as much by the stock market as they are by interest rates. They are traditionally thought of as being different enough from core bonds to be their own asset group. The range of credit investments extends from there.

Stressed debt is a loose categorization for high-yield bonds of issuers who may be on the verge of default. In these cases the bonds trade at a deep discount to par reflecting a high probability that repayment will not be made. A 10 or 15 basis point movement in Treasury interest rates has almost no impact on the price of these bonds. The investment thesis revolves around whether the borrower will default or not, and the size of any subsequent recovery if it does.

Distressed debt is a specific category of bonds that have already stopped performing. This is a highly technical area of investment that relies on both a keen understanding of bankruptcy law and an ability to evaluate the meaningful assets available to meet the obligations of the non performing borrower.

The liquidity of the bonds put into the portfolio should largely dictate the structure of any investment in this arena. There are many large, institutional high-yield mutual funds that operate easily in a daily liquidity format. Separately managed accounts of high-yield bonds are also readily available to large investors. In both of these cases the manager should select among only the most liquid bonds available in the market. When this does not occur, as was the case with Third Avenue late in 2015, there can be a run on the fund and a rapid deterioration of value.[15]

Usually the credit spreads are large enough to make the total perspective return from an unleveraged investment attractive. Sometimes, however, closed-end funds and other structures will employ up to 1/3 leverage in order to enhance returns even more. During the credit crisis of 2008 and 2009, these funds were particularly hard hit as investors fled this higher level of risk. Many closed-end funds traded at extremely wide discounts to NAV during this time.

Managers that gravitate toward less liquid high-yield bonds, stressed debt, and distressed debt usually operate in some kind of a private partnership structure. These can vary from hedge funds with monthly or quarterly liquidity to true multiyear private equity structures. The longer lockup funds avoid some of the risks of illiquidity that come during periods of crisis when some investors scramble for redemptions and cause forced selling in other structures.

---

[15]McLaughlin, T. Third Avenue Junk Fund Blowup Exposes Risks of Unsellable Assets. www.reuters.com. (12 December 2015).

The deadliest combination in credit has been from hedge funds offering reasonably liquid terms while deploying multiple turns of leverage. These funds have historically attracted hot money after a period of credit spread tightening, only to have the funds attempt to depart quickly at the earliest signs of loss. This is a classic example where you can have many years of strong, relatively steady returns, followed by a completely disastrous outcome when everyone tries to depart from the strategy at the same time.

True private equity structures are best for managers who purchase stressed or distressed debt with the expectation that the holding period will be years and not quarters. These will have well-defined investment periods during which the capital is called and put to work, followed by a time during which the deals are worked out and sold. For realizations that happen during the investment term, the funds may be reinvested in new transactions. If the realization occurs after this window, the proceeds are returned to the limited partners.

The investment environment is critically important to the length of the investment. In the market downturn and small recession around 2002, many distressed debt private equity funds were started to take advantage of the perceived opportunity. This was a particularly good environment in that there were many deals to be considered, followed by a rapidly recovering stock market that supported profitable and early exits. Some funds rapidly called capital, put it to work, and returned it to investors with a strong return within a few years, and certainly well before the allowed terms described in the documents.

The flipside can also be true. Managers who tried to raise new funds in 2005 and 2006 discovered that their investment options were quite limited, and the price of even defaulted debt was high. The more disciplined managers avoided fundraising in this environment, but some proceeded to raise large new programs on the backs of their previous funds' successes. This usually led to meaningful losses when the credit crisis of 2008 and 2009 caused some of their companies to fail completely or require large new capital injections to keep them afloat.

No matter what the form of the investment, these credit funds seem to live between the fixed income and equity allocations in your portfolio. This means they are not as sensitive to general interest rate shifts as a traditional bond fund, but they will be correlated at least somewhat to changes in the equity market. When considering what kind of an allocation to make, investors should also be sure to remember that when the stock market takes a major tumble, the correlations are likely to rise dramatically, placing the credit funds at risk of a big hit as well.

Like virtually every investment opportunity, there is a push to identify indexes covering much of the credit space. This is a tricky business. While there are literally thousands of high-yield bonds available to track, much of the population is thinly traded or reflects borrowers that would be considered dubious credits at best. While the creators of the indexes try hard to build representative products, this is an area where the investor needs to ask tough questions. If an index based mutual fund or ETF is available, is it a product that you want to own at any given point in time? Chances are good that there is a significant fraction of the index that you would want to avoid for credit or liquidity purposes, or both.

Indexes purporting to measure distressed securities are even more problematic. These securities do not trade actively, and when they do, buyers and sellers frequently confront wide bid/ask spreads. Any attempt to mimic these benchmarks will likely struggle, but the problem could reside in the faults of the index rather than problems with portfolio construction. Distressed debt indexes should be used at most as general indicators of how the space is performing, and not as a precise trading option in the way many investors look at stock indexes.

Asset allocation models that include credit indexes as an investment option routinely overestimate the diversification benefits of credit investing. Because of the limited liquidity of many of the underlying bonds, estimates of volatility and correlations based on historical values can have a downward bias. This was a major issue before the credit crisis of 2008 and 2009, with investors expecting their credit portfolio to provide a somewhat independent source of return from their stocks and bonds. During the crisis, high yield and distressed securities were highly correlated with equities and suffered greatly, offering no protection to the portfolio.

A relatively young, and still quite small, part of the credit opportunity space involves microfinance investment vehicles, or MIVs. Microfinance is practiced in many parts of the developing world and it involves the extension of very small loans to individuals or families to help them develop entrepreneurial activities. The principles of microcredit were developed in the 1970s by Muhamad Yunus, a Bangladeshi economist and professor. He noted that there was a large stratum of the population in developing countries who were entrepreneurial but were too poor to qualify for traditional bank loans. By dedicating assets to these microcredits, he identified the advancements possible for these people. In recognition of his efforts, he was awarded the Nobel Peace Prize in 2006.

Even small loans require a source of capital, and over the years various private/public partnerships have developed to direct capital to these programs. More recently, investment funds dedicated to microfinance have come to the market. As of the end of 2015, there were over 100 MIVs with a total asset base of $11.6 billion.[16] Many of these efforts began in the last decade, so track records are quite difficult to analyze.

Investors attracted to MIVs are sometimes more attracted to the social mission of the funds rather than the return potential. In a very real sense, this is an extreme expression of socially responsible investing. Providers of capital are directing their investments toward some of the most disadvantaged people of the world with the goal being a major improvement in social welfare in addition to a return on the investment. Symbiotics produces an annual survey of the space and in 2015 they found that there were more than 300,000 active borrowers, 68% of whom were women with an average loan size of $1,575.[17]

It is fair to ask what should be the expected return to an MIV. If one begins with an argument that some private capital is generally available in the marketplace, then the conclusion is that microcredit borrowers must present a combination of costs and credit risks that keep capital from flowing to these poorest borrowers. MIV sponsors, however, argue that there are major imperfections in capital markets that deprive microcredit borrowers of normal access. They attempt to demonstrate that cost-effective programs are possible that help the borrowers as well as offer a fair return to the providers of capital.

---

[16]Symbiotics, 2016 Symbiotics MIV Survey. (September 2016). symbioticsgroup.com.
[17]Ibid.

According to Symbiotics, the average return to unleveraged debt MIVs in 2015 was under 3%, and this has been the general experience for many years.[18] Some try to compare this to the return on six-month LIBOR, and in that light this is a meaningful premium. Whether this is the right benchmark is debatable. While many microfinance loans are for relatively short terms, the credit quality of the borrowers is far from the prime financial institutions captured by LIBOR.

MIVs ultimately face all of the challenges of other direct loan programs. If the goal is to be more than a transfer of wealth to some of the poorest people in the world, funds need to be judiciously employed. Costs and credit risks have to be closely monitored. The programs have to work toward the dual objectives of doing well for the borrowers and making an appropriately compensatory return for those risking their capital. Any potential investor must evaluate the MIVs in this light to see how it fits within their many objectives as well.

9.4 THE CURIOUS CASE OF NEGATIVE INTEREST RATES

In 2015 the world changed in a fundamental way with concerns about the viability of the European Union. Seeking safety against a possible breakup, many investors rushed to buy Swiss government bonds. Switzerland is certainly a safe haven, but it is a small one and the flood of capital threatened to distort the value of the Swiss franc and Switzerland's economy. To discourage the rush of capital, the Swiss pushed interest rates on their bonds into negative territory.

These were uncharted waters. Nowhere in the Markowitz or Sharpe worlds was it contemplated that investors should ever have to pay borrowers to hold their money. Macroeconomists only thought about the possibility of negative rates at times of extreme deflation, and even then as long as there was cash available as a store of value, why would anyone lend at negative rates? This made negative interest rates at most a curiosity among economists and finance professors. With the Swiss move that curiosity became real, but it was only the beginning.

The Chinese stock market tumbled 18% in the first few months of 2016 on growth fears. In June, British voters surprised all with their Brexit vote. A few months later, OPEC cut its production for the first time since the financial crisis sending oil prices higher and global recession fears soaring. The response by investors was to actively seek safety, and the debt of Germany and Japan joined Switzerland's in negative territory. By the middle of 2016 there was more than $12 trillion of sovereign debt outstanding that was trading at prices that produced negative yields.

The market trauma of Q4 2018 once again brought about another flight to safety and quickly bond prices increased again and rates tumbled. By the middle of 2019, the total amount of negative yielding debt in the world exceeded $16 trillion, mostly sovereign paper but also including some corporate debt. Investors can no longer think of negative interest rates as an academic curiosity. They have become one of the primary forces shaping both return and risk in portfolios. You may not have any such bonds in your portfolio, but their impact is still felt throughout.

---

[18]Ibid.

The mechanics of negative yields are not obvious. The best news in this story is that the world has yet to see a negative coupon bond. Nobody is being asked to write a check to the German government every year for a decade, which is a good thing, since the ensuing collection nightmare would take a serious bite out of the bond proceeds. How these bonds end up with a negative yield involves the interaction of the par value, the coupon and the market price.

In 2019 an auction was held for a German 10-year bund that had a zero coupon and a par value of 100. When the bond was issued, it came to market at a price of €102.64. This meant the German government pocketed €102.64, with their only promise to the buyers being that they would pay back €100 in a decade. A few weeks later this bond traded to €103.93, which meant if a new buyer held this to maturity they would be guaranteed to lose €3.93. This loss, amortized over the decade, translated to an annual yield to maturity of −0.37%. Later that summer, the yield had tumbled further to −0.50%.

Older bunds still outstanding all had positive coupons. The auction prior to the zero-coupon one was for a 10-year bund, with a positive coupon of 0.25%, paid annually. Given that there is a positive income stream associated with this bond of similar maturity, it should be priced higher, and it was. This bond traded at €106.60 on the same day the zero-coupon bond traded near €104. The yield to maturity for the coupon bond was nearly identical at −0.39%.

The owner of this latter bond might receive a check each year for their coupon payment, but the bond price itself would see a steeper march down as the value goes to €100 at maturity. The other slap in the face to a taxpaying bondholder is that they would owe income tax on the annual coupon.

Why do people buy these negative yielding bonds? Why not just hold cash in a safe deposit box? For the average citizen that wants to simply maintain the capital value, holding cash might be an option. For a large institutional investor this is not a practical choice. One might think of the −0.40% yield as a fee on a virtual safety deposit box maintained and protected by the German government. Any way you look at it, however, it is a tax on any person or entity that simply wants to maintain the notional value of their safest assets.

There are also speculators that buy these bonds at 102.64 at issue, hoping to sell them at 104 or higher. That is, they expect negative yields to become more negative. This has little to do with investment and a lot to do with trading.

One might assume that careful investors would simply rule out such bonds for their portfolios. After all, nobody with a positive return goal could find these instruments attractive unless the return on all other assets increased enough to make up the difference. Even with generous assumptions about diversification benefits, it is hard to tell a compelling story for why these bonds have a role to play.

There are many investments that are excluded from portfolios for a wide variety of reasons. Some people embrace cryptocurrencies. Many others do not. It might seem that the simple answer is to avoid negative yielding paper and move on, leaving the headaches to others who may be forced to own it. It is not that easy.

When considering the sovereign debt of countries as significant as Germany, Japan, and Switzerland, the prevailing interest rate defines risk-free, at least from a credit perspective. As discussed in the previous section, all interest rates build up from the risk-free rate, and by 2019 negative rates had rippled through the entire capital structure. This meant that the insurer Allianz, with an S&P credit rating of AA (just one notch below the United States at AA+), pharmaceutical company Novartis (AA−) and food giant, Nestle (AA−) all could access the credit market at below zero cost. Unbelievably, the most senior covered bonds of shaky banks Societe Generale and Deutsche Bank also had negative yields. This may be great for their shareholders, but if every project can be funded at essentially no cost, how many less than stellar investments are being made? Lower quality countries and companies also have access to funds that likely are not yielding enough to cover the fundamental risks to the lenders.

One would naturally assume with repressed risk-free rates all other expected returns would come down as well. This has to occur in the long run as investors shift assets away from the lowest yielding bonds toward lower credits, equities, and real assets. In the short run, however, there may be a boost to realized returns across the board. *TINA* is an acronym standing for There Is No Alternative. Investors pull assets from zero and negative yielding safe assets and push them toward riskier opportunities.

Any rally in risk assets should not be confused with a permanent increase in return potential. Recalling Figure 3.13, if the risk-free rate drops into negative territory the entire capital markets line shifts. The new optimum portfolio has both lower risk and lower returns. The only way to regain total return in this world is to add more leverage, a strategy that we saw in Chapter 8 can ultimately lead to systemic excesses and crashes.

Who else besides savers are hurt by negative yields? Banks are particularly handicapped by this environment. There is no practical way for them to charge regular depositors, so there is a lower bound of zero for these funds. If the banks cannot find positive yielding loans to make, they are likely pushed into acquiring the negative yielding government paper, creating a negative yield spread for that part of their balance sheet. Contrast this to the United States where the Federal Reserve has paid positive interest on excess reserves held at the Fed since the crisis. European banks face a meaningful tax, while US banks have reaped billions in subsidies. This may be one more reason why the financial services sector in Europe has struggled far more coming out of the financial crisis.

If the negative interest rate environment persists, one can expect an acceleration of the movement to eliminate physical currency. Governments today probably view physical currency as an evil made necessary by outdated cultural norms. It is expensive to produce and impossible to fully control. It facilitates illegal activity. If the IRS, financial regulators, and the Treasury had their way, every monetary transaction would occur on a fully documented electronic network, which rules out anonymous block chains.

Negative interest rates amplify all these issues. With all-electronic transactions, it would be easy to debit even consumer accounts for the negative yield as there would be no alternatives. Fortunately, we are pretty far away from that all-electronic environment at the moment, but worlds that are upside down with negative interest rates are ripe for radical change.

Are negative interest rates a permanent addition to the investment landscape or just a passing phenomenon? Investors have to see them for what they really are, which is a tax on savers desperate to have some of their funds in the safest assets and ultimately suppressing total returns. Politicians, on the other hand, have never seen interest rates too low. They can borrow and spend with virtually no impact on their current or future budgets over the relevant political horizon, which in most democracies is the next election cycle and not the long term. Fiscal responsibility has become a quaint concept since the financial crisis and so far there have been few popular downsides yet to these aggressive approaches of spending and borrowing.

Negative interest rates will end only when the apparently insatiable demand for these bonds dries up. No serious investor can contemplate adding negative yielding paper to their portfolios and expect to meet their goals. But there clearly is demand, from central banks pushing policy rates down to government pension funds that may be required to own this paper versus that of other countries or of companies with lower credit. How much of the demand and the push down in rates is due to macroeconomic speculators is hard to measure, but there are billions in momentum funds probably playing the trend.

Negative interest rates are in no way a natural state of affairs. One day they may be again seen as a curiosity and a footnote in investing history. But as long as they persist in the trillions of dollars in notional value outstanding, investors have to be aware of their impact even if they can avoid the direct effects in their portfolio.

9.5 CURRENCIES

Currencies are often thought of more as a source of risk than as a source of potential return. If one holds stocks or bonds denominated in another currency, and that currency fluctuates, there will be a gain or loss due to factors other than interest rates or equity market valuations. There is an active debate among asset allocators as to whether or not such currency exposures should be hedged out of the portfolio or not. Some argue that currency shifts primarily add volatility to a portfolio with no expectation of incremental return. Others look at historical correlations and suggest that a certain amount of currency exposure actually improves the risk profile of the portfolio.

Experience during the credit crisis of 2008 and 2009 and immediately thereafter suggests that in periods of "risk off" trades there is a flight to US Treasury securities globally and a subsequent increase in the value of the dollar against most currencies. This has tended to make currency exposure for US dollar-based investors a bad thing, as the other currencies have typically lost value at the same time foreign stock markets have fallen and credit spreads have widened.

One should be very careful about extrapolating this experience into all points of the future. There are many examples further back in history where the dollar has fallen during periods of market stress, and foreign currency exposure provided diversification benefits. This is certainly a case where picking one's historical sample can change dramatically the conclusions about the relations among the asset classes.

Since currency risk can come in many forms in a modern global portfolio, one may dial up or dial down total risk by one's choice of investment products. $1 million invested in foreign corporate bonds will have the same exposure to currency changes as $1 million invested in the same basket of the country's stocks. However, the total risk contribution of the equity portfolio should be expected to be higher than that of the bonds, leading to the obvious conclusion that you will hold fewer foreign stocks than bonds if you are only worried about your risk budget.

It is possible to have a dedicated line item in your portfolio for currencies. This would be an attempt to get pure exposure to the movements of currencies without any of the additional risks associated with interest rates or equity markets. To see how this might work, one must first understand the basic principle of *spot and forward exchange rates*. The basic conclusion is that exposures to currencies through time are primarily positions based on *interest rate differentials* between the two countries.

If the spot exchange rate is known, and one is told the interest rates in the two countries, the forward price can be determined with certainty. This is due to a principle known as *interest rate parity*, an arbitrage condition that tightly connects the markets of freely convertible currencies around the world. A simplistic example of currency arbitrage was given in Chapter 3.6. What follows is a similar example, but with more attention to specific details.

Suppose you could buy one Swiss franc for 50 US cents in the spot market. Suppose further that this same exchange rate existed for transactions anticipated one year in the future. This is known as the forward exchange rate. Now let the one-year interest rates in the United States be 7% while the same one-year interest rate in Switzerland is 5%. Where would an investor place their assets?

Someone holding 2 million Swiss francs could invest at the current interest rate at home and in one year have 2.1 million. The alternative would be to buy 1 million dollars with the Swiss francs, while simultaneously entering into a forward transaction to sell $1.07 million for 2.14 million Swiss francs in a year. You could then invest the $1 million at 7% in order to achieve the amount you promised to sell. This is clearly the preferred investment alternative.

But there is no reason to limit this transaction to someone who already owns Swiss francs. A credit worthy arbitrageur could borrow the 2 million Swiss francs at a 5% interest cost, and then enter into the spot and forward currency transactions and the US dollar 7% investment listed above. At the end of the year, the arbitrageur would have 2.14 million Swiss francs to pay off the 2.1 million due on the loan, netting a risk-free profit of 40,000 Swiss francs.

As long as Swiss francs are freely convertible into US dollars, which is certainly not a guarantee in today's world of currency market interventions, this arbitrage should go on until either or both of the following things happen. As capital flows from Switzerland to the United States, interest rates would tend to equalize. The other alternative would be for the forward dollar exchange rate to fall relative to the spot rate as dollars are purchased today and sold a year from now. The adjustment in interest rates and exchange rates would proceed until there was no risk-free profit.

When all risk-free arbitrage opportunities are exhausted the markets are said to display interest rate parity. It is simply expressed in Equation 9.1:

$$F = S\left[1 + \left(r_f - r_\$\right) / \left(B / T + r_\$\right)\right]$$

where F = forward foreign currency per dollar rate

S = spot foreign currency per dollar rate

r_f = foreign interest rate   (9.1)

$r_\$$ = dollar interest rate

T = days between forward and spot

B = base number of interest rate days in the year

Whenever the foreign currency interest rate exceeds the dollar interest rate, $(r_f - r_\$)$ is positive, and the forward exchange rate will exceed the spot rate. That is, it will take more units of foreign currency to buy a dollar in the future than it does today.

This should lay to rest the view that forward exchange rates somehow predict future values of the spot rate. As soon as you know the spot exchange rate and the interest rates in the two countries, you can immediately know whether the forward rate will be higher or lower than the spot. It is simply an expression of an arbitrage relationship and has nothing to do with forecasting.

Relative interest rates are quite important, however, in certain currency oriented investment strategies. *Carry trade* currency programs are sometimes attractive to investors living in countries with very low interest rates. Japanese investors have become quite used to near-zero interest rates since their stock market tumbled in 1990. Anxious to try to achieve a higher rate of return they purchase programs that are essentially deposits in other countries. Capital inflows from these kinds of investors were in part responsible for Brazil meaningfully raising taxes on foreigners buying fixed income products in 2010.

The essence of these investment programs is simplicity itself. The investor assumes the risk that the foreign currency will devalue and in return he or she receives a higher nominal interest rate. For example, if short-term Japanese interest rates are 1% and the same term interest rate in Brazil is 11%, the Japanese investor is a net winner as long as the Brazilian currency devalues less than 10% in the holding period. If the interest rate differential is smaller, the investor has a smaller margin of safety against adverse currency fluctuations.

One might ask whether there is a way to receive the higher interest rate while avoiding the currency risk. This is where the forward rate equation discussed above comes into play. Any attempt to lock in the value of the forward exchange rate will be done at a price that completely reflects the interest rate differential. Placing your money in Brazil and then hedging the currency brings you full circle back to your home interest rate.

This does not mean that such programs cannot play a role in an investment portfolio. Instead it means you have to have a judgment about the relative stability of the currencies. In the example if you believe that Brazil's will experience superior growth relative to Japan, its currency might actually appreciate through time relative to the yen. Placing your assets into Brazilian deposits without a currency hedge has the potential to earn in two ways. First there is the higher interest rate offered in Brazil, and second there is the possibility for currency appreciation. Of course, there is also the risk that a political corruption scandal will impeach one president, implicate scores of legislators and drive Brazil's currency rapidly downward.

Investors should be quite cautious when carry trades are combined with leverage in an attempt to amplify the apparent returns. This tends to happen when the interest rate differentials are small in absolute value. Suppose in the example above, the interest rate in Brazil was 4%, making the differential between the two countries 3%. This may not be as attractive as the original 10% spread. An entrepreneurial manager may apply four times leverage, deduct a 2% management fee, and still advertise the prospect of a 10% excess return.

This is a potentially combustible combination. If the currency exchange rate moves by only 2.5% in the wrong direction, the entire interest rate advantage is eliminated. The investor has assumed four times more currency risk for the same potential carry return. History is full of examples where carry trades have become quite popular in leveraged form, attracting more and more investors as the high returns build up. The end result is always the same. A shock hits the system reversing the appreciation of the high interest-rate currency, causing large losses to the investors entering the trade in the latter stages of the rally. People try to exit a crowded trade making the situation worse. Almost like a Ponzi scheme, the only winners are those who were early participants and then had the good sense to get out.

In a more traditional vein, there are also specialty macroeconomic-oriented managers that manage pools of currencies. This should be thought of more as a trading strategy than as investing in an asset class, because it is difficult to identify a specific return to holding a basket of currencies as you would for a basket of stocks or bonds. Still, investors may have an opinion about whether they believe the dollar will appreciate or depreciate against other developed or developing country currencies, and these funds give them an opportunity to express that view.

Not surprisingly, indexes have been developed over the years to try to measure broad movements of different baskets of currencies. These are typically expressed in dollar terms, as the US dollar remains the key currency in international transactions. If an investor believes that emerging markets will be a superior opportunity for investing over long periods of time, but there is no strong view about which country will do best, one alternative would be to buy a basket of emerging market currencies. Just like stocks and bonds, there are many products available. Some stick quite closely to the weights in the index that they're using is a benchmark, while others are more actively traded.

In the case of currency funds containing multiple nations, there will be either a positive or a negative carry depending on the average relative interest rate for the basket versus the US interest rate. If, on average, the basket has a lower interest rate than in the United States, investors should expect a regular deficit in interest payments that they hope will be offset by currency appreciation.

It should make no fundamental difference on the ultimate profitability of a currency position whether it is a positive or negative carry trade. However, psychologically, people seem to resist negative carry trades, as they do not wish to see regular debits in their account. Conversely, positive carry trades appear to offer a free return. Since all that matters is the total return of the investment, made up of either a positive or negative carry and the change in the currency value, investors should try to get past their psychological biases in order to evaluate whether the trade fits with their market expectations or not.

In conclusion, currencies can play a specific role in portfolios, but they must be a reflection of a specific market opinion. Whether that opinion is expressed with a dedicated currency portfolio or it is combined with interest rates or equity exposures is less important than understanding that this risk factor is present. Currencies are not a fundamental asset. Instead they are simply a medium of exchange that fluctuates in value relative to other currencies and the myriad of things that people buy with them. Viewed this way, currencies can become one more element over which investors have control, and are not simply a risk to be endured.

9.6 EQUITIES

Shares of common stock represent fractional ownership in a corporation. They can be listed on a recognized exchange or traded over-the-counter. As an asset class collectively they are known as equities. Since the second half of the twentieth century, equities have become the major asset in most investment portfolios. Once seen as highly speculative, they have been increasingly embraced by the long-term investor looking to participate in the growth of the market economy.

Not all equity markets are equally evolved. Many developing countries that are still establishing clear rules of law find that their companies rely much more on bank financing than they do the issuance of tradable stock. But it is a general rule that as the financial markets in a country grow in size and sophistication, the trading of equity securities grows as well.

The most important thing about stocks is that they represent residual claims for the owners. This means that the equity owners may not receive any proceeds until every other obligation of the corporation is met. Taxes, wages, amounts owed to suppliers, and interest owed to bondholders and other creditors must all be paid before the equity owners can receive any benefits. What is left over at the end of each accounting period can be distributed to the shareholders, or it may be retained by the company in the hope that it can continue to build shareholder value.

The other critical feature about equities and corporations is their limited liability nature. This means that if you invest through the purchase of stock the most you can lose is what you spent on that stock. The creation of limited liability corporations was a major step forward in the evolution of finance. Prior to that, owners of a company were partners who shared responsibility for all potential losses by that firm. Given that the risk of owning a business could extend well beyond one's monetary invest- ment, capital was more difficult to raise among those who did not have direct control over the companies' policies and activities.

Over the years different types of equity ownership have evolved. The forms are designed to attract different kinds of capital investors. What a corporation issues depends greatly on what is available in the market and how the board and manage- ment of the company want to shape the capital structure. Just like junior and senior debt, the different forms of equity can have different priorities in the event of bank- ruptcy. Before looking at various alternatives, it is best to understand the characteris- tics of simple common stock.

9.6.1 Common Stock

In the United States alone there are over 14,000 publicly listed companies in which an investor can own shares.[19] About 30% of these are listed on one of three primary exchanges, the New York Stock Exchange (NYSE, a division of the Intercontinental Exchange, ICE), the American Stock Exchange (AMEX), and the National Associa- tion of Securities Dealers Automated Quotation (NASDAQ). Exchanges themselves are now, more often than not, for-profit institutions and the trend is for global opera- tions. The most advanced markets in the world are usually part of a multinational network of exchanges to take advantage of economies of scale in technology, but due to local trading regulations remain separate entities within their respective domiciles.

---

[19]Sources include www.otcmarkets.com, the website of the OTC Markets Group. This com- pany provides a trading system for about 10,000 OTC stocks called OTC Link. The remaining 4,000+ stocks are listed on one or more of the SEC registered exchanges.

Not all companies and their shares are created equal. There are huge differences in market capitalization and liquidity. In the second half of 2017, Apple Inc. had a market capitalization of $825 billion and often had a daily turnover of over 30 million shares worth over $5 billion.[20] The vast majority of the 10,000 companies traded OTC have capitalizations below $5 million and the average daily trading volume across all of these stocks is approximately $600 million.[21]

Retail investors are the more typical participants in the OTC markets. Some pension funds and mutual funds actually have restrictions prohibiting them to hold OTC stocks, primarily because of the severe liquidity limitations compared to exchange-traded securities. There are a few hedge fund managers that specialize in micro-cap stocks, but the liquidity challenges of these equities can add challenges for the general partners to manage their own subscriptions and redemptions on a continuing basis.

In the simplest of equity capital structures there is one class of stock where the owners share the economics and the governance decisions proportional to their share of ownership. Such a simple structure is rarely the case in practice. Some companies issue various classes of stock with different voting rights attached. It is not unusual for a company like Facebook that was closely held for many years to raise new capital in a way where the economic ownership of the founding owners may be diluted without those owners giving up voting control of the corporation. Investors need to be very cautious about companies where the control of the governance is widely different from the distribution of the economics of the firm.

Equity owners get rewarded in different ways. Assuming a company is profitable, the management and the board decide what to do with those profits. If the company is in a growth phase, it may retain the earnings as a source of investment capital. Even though shareholders do not receive any of the profits directly, they should benefit as the fundamental value of the company increases. For taxpayers, this may be a preferred outcome since tax rates on dividends are almost always higher than long-term capital gains tax rates, and capital gains are not taxed until the shares are sold, a decision entirely in control of the shareholder.

In the bull market of the 1990s, growth companies seemed to take pride in *not* paying dividends. The theory was that profits reinvested in the company generally had a strong chance of enjoying a solid return on equity. Since retained profits were a cheaper source of capital than either new debt or equity issuances, promising growing companies rarely paid a dividend.

There is a critical assumption in the argument above that did not always hold true. It was assumed that there would always be reinvestment opportunities that had high returns on capital and that management was responsible in acting on them. These options would include new internal investments or acquisitions of other companies for strategic reasons. As long as the stock market was steadily marching upward, this view was rarely challenged.

The premise was found to be flawed when management teams began to force themselves into new investments that held less promise or acquisitions that were so overpriced that the company's profits flowed not to shareholders but to the owners

---

[20]Source: Bloomberg (15 September 2017).
[21]Source: OTC Markets Group, op. cit.

of the acquired company. More disciplined management took the path of retaining the profits as cash in anticipation of better opportunities in the future or to build a cushion against potential adversity.

While a certain amount of cash as a rainy day fund is always a good idea, growing cash the way some tech companies like Apple have done can naturally be questioned by shareholders. According to annual filings, Apple had over $230 billion in cash, short-term, and long-term investments at the end of its 2016 fiscal year.[22] This sum, which can be compared to their market capitalization of over $825 billion, is the result of years where the majority of profits were retained.

In a world of near-zero Treasury bill rates and historically low rates on longer duration treasuries, holding massive amounts of cash and safe investments does not generate positive returns after inflation for any investor. Companies that hoard cash well beyond their investment or precautionary needs are actually reducing the wealth of shareholders through time with those company assets.

This does not mean it is better to force new investments or acquisitions. Instead the companies should return capital to shareholders in the form of dividends or share buybacks. Apple has done just that to a degree with a cash dividend yield around 1.5% and meaningful share repurchases since 2013.[23] In total, over five years they bought back 1.4 billion shares out of a total count at the start of the period of 6.6 billion shares, all the while assuring shareholders that they were not impeding any internal investment or acquisition opportunities.

Dividends can come in many forms, some more directly beneficial to shareholders than others. Many companies declare *regular dividends* where they distribute cash to owners of record, on a specific date known as the *record date*. After that date the stock is said to trade *ex-dividend* and new buyers of the stock will receive no payments unless they hold their shares to the next record date. When a stock goes ex-dividend the price of the stock typically falls by the amount of the dividend payment, as the value of the company has fallen by the cash distributed to shareholders. This does not always happen exactly because information about the company or market sentiment can always change the underlying price.

Companies sometimes declare *special dividends* that they label as such because they do not want shareholders to believe that such payments will repeat in the future, or become regular dividends. Special dividends often occur after a major one-time transaction that generates a great deal of cash not needed in other parts of the business.

The actual payment of the dividends often lags the record date by several weeks. This can be a source of confusion for investors. They see their stocks go ex-div and the market price falls. It appears that they are worse off, but they have a receivable in the form of the unpaid dividend. Very few retail brokerage packages try to keep track of unpaid dividends, making the apparent volatility of a stock holding higher than reality. The drop in price after a stock goes ex-div has an unaccounted offset in the dividend to be paid. When the cash arrives in the account sometime later it looks like a windfall, but is not. Fortunately, institutional fund accounting rules are very clear on this point and avoid net asset value fluctuations due to the timing of cash flows.

---

[22]Source: Yahoo Finance.
[23]Pisani, B. (2017). Apple Has Been a Buyback Monster. (3 May). www.cnbc.com.

Shareholders on the record date of either regular or special dividends are owed those dividends even if they sell their shares before the payment date. It is the job of the *transfer agent* (also known as the *share registry* in Great Britain, Australia, and New Zealand) for the stock to assure that dividends get directed to the proper owners as of the record date. The transfer agent is typically an independent company designated with the task of assuring all stock ownership records are complete.

Similarly, short sellers of securities on a record date are responsible for the payment of the dividends. Buyers of stock don't care whether they are buying from an existing holder or a short seller. They have appropriate expectations that they will receive the dividends that they are due no matter who is on the other side of the trade.

It might appear that if a stock's price drops by the amount of the dividend every time it is paid, then over time the stock price would fall to zero. If a company is not profitable, but still tries to pay a dividend, this will certainly be the ultimate path. Responsible companies restrict their dividends to some fraction of the profits that they believe are sustainable through time. In this way they limit the chance that they have to cut their dividend in the future, an act with almost universal negative implications to investors.

There are some investors who are attracted to stocks simply on the basis of their high current dividend yields. These situations have to be analyzed carefully. Imagine a company that has waning fortunes, and the stream of profits that supported the previous dividends is in jeopardy. A rational market senses this and drives the stock price down before the fact. The stock's current reported dividend yield is simply the last dividend payment divided by the stock price and then annualized. If the stock price denominator drops suddenly, it appears that the yield has increased, but it has increased for bad reasons.

Savvy investors look through to the profitability of the company and ask whether the actual past dividend payments can be supported with existing or projected cash flows. There are high-dividend-yielding stocks that can maintain their payments, but an extraordinarily high-dividend yield can be a signal that the future dividend payments will likely be falling.

In one extreme example, Jason Zweig's article in *The Wall Street Journal* described a closed-end mutual fund that promised dividends of over 20%, but had very little sustainable revenues to support the payouts.[24] The fund would periodically have special stock sales to existing shareholders to raise more capital, which the fund would then use to pay the dividend. The only obvious winner in such a fund is the management that gets paid along the way. Shareholders are apparently duped into believing they are getting a great dividend return, while their ownership is continuously diluted and the vast majority of the dividends they receive are simply a return of their own money. This is the complete opposite of a sustainable dividend.

Some people believe that companies with a consistent record of high and growing dividends are actually superior picks for long term total returns (dividends plus price appreciation) versus companies that keep most of their profits for internal reinvestment. This theory says that by declaring a regular dividend and demonstrating an ability to grow it through time, the companies have made a public commitment to

---

[24]Zweig, J. (2012). High Rates? Are You Delirious? *The Wall Street Journal*. (13 July), page B1.

shareholders for careful stewardship. Growth is sought, but all internal investments are carefully weighed against the possibility of failure that could end up jeopardizing the dividend. The growing dividend is a highly public report card on the management team.

An example of this kind of approach to corporate finance can be seen in the payout pattern of Novartis, a Swiss-based drug company. Figure 9.9 shows the 15-year earnings and dividend history of the firm since it was created by a merger of Ciba-Geigy and Sandoz in 1996.

The pattern of payouts shows a conservative approach to dividends. Each year Novartis declared a higher dividend than they had the year before, but in each case their earnings were meaningfully higher than what they paid out. This left a cushion for the future. As earnings were growing quickly at the start of the new century, they also rapidly grew their dividend, but after the financial crisis and the slowing of western economies, they slowed the pace.

For a certain type of investor more interested in consistency than outsized capital appreciation stocks like Novartis can play an important role in their overall portfolios. This is especially true during periods of extremely low risk-free interest rates. The ability to grow earnings and dividends through time offers investors the opportunity to consider the cash flow from these investments *almost* like they would interest from bonds.

One of the biggest arguments against dividends is that they create immediate double taxation. Corporations pay taxes on their profits and if they declare dividends the shareholders pay another round of taxes at the individual taxpayer level. The tax code shifts around on a regular, and not always predictable, basis, but while certain qualifying dividends have at times been taxed at lower rates than the prevailing ordinary income rate, there is no escaping the conclusion that taxes are being paid twice on the same revenue. The obvious implication is that taxpaying investors need to consider the after-tax dividend yield at any point in time just as they would compare interest on municipal and corporate bonds on an after-tax basis.

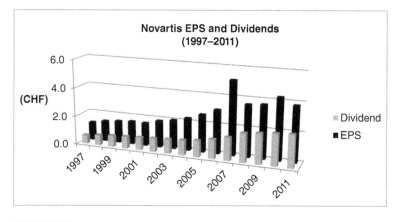

FIGURE 9.9 Novartis Earnings and Dividend History
Source: Bloomberg

There are two types of companies that by design are focused on the payment of dividends. *Real estate investment trusts (REITs)* and *master limited partnerships (MLPs)* are special legal structures that pay no income tax at the corporation or partnership level as long as they pass through at least 90% of the income they generate. There is a debate whether this gives them a competitive advantage over entities subject to corporate taxes, but there is no debate that the structures force the behavior of these firms' managements to focus on cash generation and distribution.

There are many different kinds of REITs and MLPs. The most popular REITs invest in specific income-producing properties, and are known as *equity REITs*. Some REITs concentrate in shopping malls, residential apartments, or commercial office space. Some highly specialized REITs only invest in health care facilities like nursing homes. No matter what area an REIT focuses on, the goals are to buy properties that will appreciate through time or will generate a good rate of return through the distributed rents.

Equity REITs are sometimes thought of as *liquid real estate*. They are by far the easiest way to get equity exposure to what is normally a highly illiquid investment. They were a very popular investment during the growth years at the end of the twentieth century because of the steady appreciation of property values. Like most real estate investments, they employ some leverage, which caused problems in the financial crisis on two fronts. First, declines in the underlying properties were magnified by the leverage to be larger losses on the REIT equity. Second, concerns about the ongoing availability of financing arrangements led many investors to sell their shares, cutting values further.

Once the worst of the crisis had passed, equity REITs with largely leased, high-quality properties were among the strongest recovery stories in the stock market. Investors again began to focus on their dividend paying properties, which in an environment of historically low interest rates, increased their appeal even more.

A much smaller part of the REIT market is a class of securities known as *mortgage REITs*. Instead of owning properties, these REITs own portfolios of mortgages. Here again leverage is often used to magnify the cash yield and the dividends. The source of the cash flow is quite simple. These REITs buy mortgages with their capital and also buy more mortgages with money borrowed in the short-term market using their portfolio as collateral. As long as the yield curve is positively sloped, there will be a gain from the cash flow from the mortgages exceeding the cost of borrowing.

Mortgage REITs are exposed to all of the risks that any owners of mortgage securities face. Agency mortgages from FNMA and Freddie Mac may have their principal guaranteed, but they face duration and prepayment risks. Non-agency mortgages also face the risk of default. Trying to appeal to specific parts of the market, some mortgage REITs have specialized. Annaly (NLY) is the largest mortgage REIT and for many years it historically restricted its portfolio to agency paper. Because of the implicit principal protection of these mortgages, they have lower yields, but they also have better value as collateral. Mortgage REITs typically use more leverage when investing in agency paper than non-agency securities.

The market risks faced by owners of mortgage REITs are not dissimilar to those faced by most bond investors. Rising interest rates cut the value of the underlying mortgage portfolio, lowering the net asset value of the REIT. Additionally, for REITs that use leverage, a flattening of the yield curve cuts the spread between the borrowing and lending rates. This may not impact the NAV of the REIT immediately, but it does reduce the potential cash flow through time.

Commercial mortgage REITs are a small subset of the bigger mortgage REIT pool. They differ from their residential mortgage REIT cousins in two important ways. First, their portfolios consist only of mortgages on properties like hotels, office buildings, medical facilities, malls, and warehouses. This leads to much larger loan sizes, more concentrated portfolios, and greater reliance on deep credit analysis to control the risks of default. The second differentiator is that most commercial mortgages are floating rate loans, which greatly reduces the duration risk of these REITs compared to their home mortgage counterparts.

It may not seem to make a great deal of sense, but fluctuations in the stock market can affect REITs of all kinds. While their cash flows are not directly affected by the level of the stock market, both equity and mortgage REITs prices do correlate somewhat to the general market. Investor sentiment paints with a very broad brush.

Investors need to be mindful of the current price of an REIT relative to its book value. When REITs trade well above their book value, managements of the REIT have incentives to issue new stock in secondary offerings. They take the proceeds and acquire more mortgage assets at relatively favorable prices. While these transactions may be accretive to long-term cash flow, the act of issuing new stock is dilutive to existing shareholders.

REIT dividends are treated as ordinary income for taxpaying shareholders. Since the REIT is not paying tax at the corporate level, there is no public policy motive to extend any preferential tax rates to the dividends of REITs. Individuals often place high-yielding REITs in their tax deferred retirement accounts for this reason. Not-for-profits find the high dividends particularly attractive as they have no tax liabilities from these securities.

Master Limited Partnerships, or MLPs, are similar to REITs in that if they distribute more than 90% of their cash flow in dividends or capital spending to support their projects they do not face double taxation. They are also typically traded on stock exchanges. But instead of a corporate structure, these entities are true limited partnerships. The tax code governing what qualifies as a potential MLP is complicated, but traditionally most activity has taken place in the exploration, production, storage, or transportation of natural resources like oil and natural gas.

Energy-oriented MLPs should not be thought of as a homogeneous group. Some partnerships are actively engaged in exploration and production, which leads to a large exposure to commodity price changes. Other partnerships focus on storage and transportation. In these situations the pipeline operator does not care whether the oil is $60 a barrel or $100 a barrel, since the "toll" that is paid for transportation does not vary with the price of the commodity. Well-structured midstream MLPs of this type can be an attractive source of regular dividend income.

Adding further to the attractiveness of MLPs is the opportunity to pass along depreciation of capital investments to the limited partners. For example, a pipeline MLP that makes large capital investments in expanding the network passes along the depreciation to the LPs. This, in turn, can allow the regular distributions to be treated as a return of capital and not as ordinary income, providing the opportunity to defer paying taxes. As capital is returned to the partners, the cost basis of the MLP is reduced, and when the MLPs are sold, capital gains taxes are due. Since capital gains tax rates are typically less than ordinary income rates, these MLPs offer numerous tax advantages.

The major drawback of MLPs is the existence of the K-1s for taxpaying partners, and the theoretical risk of *unrelated business taxable income* (UBTI) for not-for-profit

participants. As partnership tax forms go, the K-1s for MLPs are not terribly complicated, but they are meaningfully different from the 1099 reports corporations issue
annually. Investors should examine the K-1s of any MLP they are considering to see
if the activity generates UBTI or not. In many MLPs there is enough depreciation
from ongoing capital expenditures so that UBTI is not a practical concern at all. Still,
ultracautious investors will not put MLPs into the investment portfolios of their not-
for-profit organizations or their individual retirement accounts.

As MLPs have become increasingly common, some organizations have tried to
create mutual funds and structures like ETFs and ETNs that block the unattractive
features like K-1s and UBTI. These structures are worth considering if they do not
meaningfully dilute the positive cash flow or other attributes that MLP investors are
trying to achieve.

9.6.2 Preferred Stock

Corporations sometimes deviate from the standard model of common stock in order
to increase the attractiveness of their holdings. One version, which seems to fall
somewhere between stocks and bonds, is called *preferred stock*. The dominant feature of preferred stock is a preannounced dividend that holds preference over other
dividends that might be paid to the holders of common stock.

For example, a company might issue preferred stock with a face value of $25 per
share and a preferred dividend yield of 8% annually. This means each quarter the
owners of this stock will receive $0.50 per share before any dividends can be paid
to the common shareholders. If the price of the stock goes up the yield will fall. The
company has no legal obligation to maintain a percentage yield, but only the absolute
cash payment.

The payment schedule of such preferred stock makes it look like a bond with
no fixed maturity. At any given point in time an investor can look at the price of the
stock versus the promised dividend payment and calculate a rate of return. If interest rates are generally rising in the market, one can expect the price of a preferred
stock to fall, and conversely prices will rise with falling interest rates. Unlike a bond
however, with no ultimate maturity date there are no forces that ultimately force the
price of preferred stock back to its face value.

Some preferred stocks are called *cumulative preferreds*. This means that if the
company misses a dividend payment the obligation does not disappear. The dividends continue to be owed to the shareholders so that when dividends eventually
resume the cumulative amount must be paid before the obligation is erased.

Another variation on the theme are fixed-to-floating preferred shares. These
securities look like a traditional preferred stock for a certain period of years but then
convert to floating rate payments if the shares are not called after the call date. All
of these parameters (the fixed dividend, the time to the call date, the spread over
the reference rate once the shares move to floating) are all known to investors when
the securities are issued. The floating rate option makes these shares more attractive
when investors expect interest rates to rise.

Preferred stock may be issued by any kind of corporation in any industry, though
historically financial services firms have found this way of raising additional capital
to be particularly attractive. During the financial crisis of 2008, bank-preferred stocks
became quite volatile, breaking a long-standing pattern of relative price stability.

Traditionally solid institutions that had never been questioned about their ability to pay their preferred dividends suddenly became suspect. Prices of preferred shares fluctuated dramatically as the fundamental viability of the institutions was in doubt.

Preferred stock shareholders frequently have fewer voting rights than the owners of common equity. This is one of the trade-offs preferred owners make for their privileged position to receive cash flow. There are examples of companies that go into a stressed state, at which point they may attempt to offer voting rights in exchange for the guaranteed dividend. Most owners of preferred stock only accept this as a last resort since they obviously demonstrated a preference for the dividends when they bought the preferred shares.

9.6.3 Convertible Bonds

It may seem odd to find anything labeled bonds under the broad category of equities. But *convertible bonds*, like preferred stock, live in a gray area that is neither clearly fixed income or equities. A convertible bond is structured with a face amount, an interest rate, and typically a maturity date, so from those dimensions they clearly look like a bond. But they also have a feature that allows them to be converted into common equity at the option of the owner. Under certain market conditions this makes them trade much more like stock than any bond.

This is accomplished by embedding a call option into the terms of the bond. For example, suppose a company's stock is trading at $10 per share. It issues a five-year convertible bond with a coupon of 5% annually that may be converted into a single share of stock at a price of $12 over the life of the loan. This is equivalent to a package of a simple bond and a five-year out-of-the-money call option.

Investors are attracted to convertible bonds because of the considerable upside potential if the company's stock takes off in value. They also enjoy the protection of receiving regular interest payments from the bond. This eliminates a meaningful amount of the downside from owning the common equity.

In the example above if the company's stock price never gets above $12, the price of the bond will be largely determined by the interest payments that it offers. If the price of the stock goes up well beyond $12, the embedded option is said to be in-the-money and the primary determinant of the bond's price will no longer be as influenced by interest rate movements.

Companies that issue convertible bonds believe that they are an effective way to raise capital more cheaply than traditional bonds. The option to convert is a valuable feature, and presumably investors will accept lower interest rates on the bonds because they own the call option to convert to stock. If the owners of convertible bonds convert their shares into equity, it is a dilutive event in that there are now more shares of equity outstanding owning the same basic assets.

9.6.4 Accessing the Equity Markets

In the most developed markets around the world, investors can access equities in a variety of ways. Traditionally, investors built portfolios stock by stock. Those who chose not to create their own portfolios instead went to active managers who were responsible for day-to-day portfolio activity. Through time, regulatory structures have evolved that define specific vehicles available to investors. Mutual funds, exchange-traded funds and notes, and closed-end funds are just three examples available to investors. Because they have somewhat different features that may appeal to different types of investors, they will be described separately below.

There is no single best way to access the equity markets. Each approach has advantages and disadvantages, but primarily one must always keep in mind the issue of cost. Some expenses are carefully disclosed and perhaps readily tracked. Others are less direct and more difficult to gauge. In choosing across the options, an investor should simply ask whether he or she is receiving true value for the expenses charged. Everyone in the financial services industry will tell you what they are providing is worth the cost. You are the only objective judge of that assertion.

9.6.4.1 Mutual Funds

The structural and regulatory basics of equity mutual funds are identical to those trading bonds discussed in Section 9.2.10, and will only be summarized here. Open-ended equity mutual funds where investors are able to transact once a day at the closing net asset value (NAV) are by far the most popular. Closed-end funds that trade at market prices that may be at a discount or premium to NAV throughout the trading day have a dedicated following, but have never attracted the amounts of capital their open-ended cousins have.

Data from the Investment Company Institute confirm this. At the end of 2018 the US stock mutual fund industry had over 7,675 openended funds, representing over $10.8 trillion. This is just part of a global equity mutual fund total of $22.1 trillion. In contrast, there were only 499 closed-end stock funds, representing just over $267 billion.[25]

Globally, equity mutual funds are the most popular. Over 44% of all mutual fund assets are in equity funds and another 12% are in a category called Balanced/Mixed, which include both equities and bonds. The remainder of the funds are primarily in bonds and money market instruments.[26] Figures 9.10 and 9.11 show the distribution of mutual fund assets by type of fund and by region.

The chart showing the distribution of assets by region reflects the historical evolution of the mutual fund industry. It is largely today a North American enterprise reflecting its origins, but this is changing rapidly. While the majority of mutual fund industry assets are still in North America, the number of equivalent funds in Europe and Asia are larger and growing rapidly. This growth, along with the explosion of exchange-traded funds and exchange-traded notes, are the defining themes in the global investment industry.

It is highly likely that over the next few decades the mutual fund industry in Europe and Asia will continue to grow more rapidly than the more mature North American region. Stock ownership in many parts of the world is meaningfully lower than it is in the United States or Canada, and as both institutional and individual portfolios grow in size and sophistication, the mutual fund industry will work hard to meet these needs. Just as many people expect the stock markets of Asia to continue

---

[25]Investment Company Institute (2019). Worldwide Mutual Fund Market Data, First Quarter 2019. (25 June). www.ICI.org.
[26]Ibid.

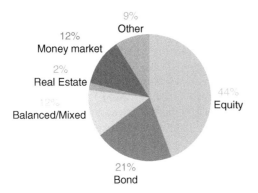

FIGURE 9.10   Style Distribution of Mutual Funds 2019
Source: Investment Company Institute

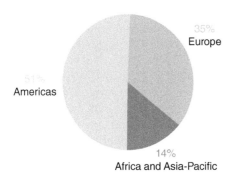

FIGURE 9.11   Geographic Distribution of Mutual Funds 2019
Source: Investment Company Institute

to represent an increasing share of global capitalization, one can reasonably expect Asia's mutual funds to become a much larger slice of the global pie.

Institutional investors have over the years looked down upon equity investing through mutual funds. There is a widely held but mistaken belief that the best portfolio managers only operate in separately managed accounts. This appears to be something of a snob effect, believing that only those investors able to meet large minimum amounts for a separate account actually have access to the best talent.

While there are literally thousands of mediocre or worse equity mutual funds around the globe, some of the best qualified managers choose the mutual fund format to assure all investors equal access to their best ideas. The regulatory obligations are not insignificant, but as previously discussed, are designed to assure a high degree of fairness to all investors in the fund. Some investors insist upon the direct ownership of securities that a separately managed account provides, but if this is not a binding factor for you, there is no a priori reason to believe that the mutual fund solution is an inferior one.

That is, of course, assuming that fees are somewhere in the neighborhood of reasonable. John Bogle, founder of Vanguard and long-term champion of the individual investor, devoted a large percentage of his message to investors in *Common*

Sense on Mutual Funds to this topic.[27] The overwhelming conclusion from decades of actual results is that mutual funds that have either direct sales charges, indirect sales charges, or basic management fees that are simply too high have an extraordinarily high probability of lagging their benchmarks.

In this regard mutual funds are no different than almost any other investment vehicle that is actively sold in the marketplace. When one deducts a direct sales charge, it creates a meaningful hole from which it is difficult to emerge.

Taxpayers must be aware, however, that mutual funds create different challenges and offer less control when it comes to the amount and timing of tax payments. There is no opportunity for the mutual fund investor to choose to harvest losses within the portfolio as part of an overall tax management plan. In fact, these investors are at the mercy of the portfolio manager who can make trading decisions without being sensitive to the tax consequences of the trades. It is perfectly reasonable for prospective mutual fund investors to ask for information on the past tax efficiency of a fund.

The turnover ratio of the mutual fund is one indicator of a manager's orientation. High turnover creates additional trading costs for both tax-exempt and taxpaying investors, but is particularly costly when it creates short-term profits for the fund that cannot otherwise be offset against losses. The general practice of US mutual funds is to have a fiscal year that ends on 31 October. To avoid paying taxes at the fund level, distributions of at least 98% of ordinary income and net capital gains in that fiscal year must be distributed to the fund shareholders in the calendar year who then bear the responsibility for any taxes due.[28]

This is primarily a timing issue. Distributions of capital gains are typically announced late in the year and paid to all shareholders of record on the record date. For example, suppose a fund began the year at a price of $10, and proceeded to have a very active and profitable trading year. Suppose the net asset value of the fund on 15 November was $12.50, and that two dollars of the increase reflected realized short-term capital gains before 31 October.

If you had been an owner for the entire calendar year, your tax obligation would reflect your experience as an implicit holder of the portfolio. Presumably you were aware of the active trading habits of the manager and were willing to face the tax implications. But suppose you were a new investor, attracted to this manager because of the impressive recent track record. If you bought the fund on 15 November for $12.50, and then discovered a few days later that a two-dollar short-term capital gain distribution was going to be made, you would have a tax liability in that year for activity in the fund that predated your investment.

Some people mistakenly see this as "paying someone else's taxes." This is actually a mischaracterization. The day after the record date for the fund the net asset value should decline by the two-dollar distribution that was made. This means that the fund you bought for $12.50 now has an NAV of $10.50. If you sold your shares, you would have a short-term loss exactly equal to the distributed gain of the fund. On net, there is no gain or loss, and no taxes owed.

---

[27]Bogle, J. (1999). *Common Sense on Mutual Funds: New Imperatives for the Intelligent Investor.* John Wiley & Sons, Inc.

[28]26 US Code 4982 – Excise tax on undistributed income of regulated investment companies.

But most people do not invest in a mutual fund in order to immediately turn around and sell it for the tax loss. In this particular example the more likely outcome is that the taxpayer will have a tax liability in the current year due to the capital gains distribution of the fund, but will also have an embedded loss in the value of the mutual fund that will have tax benefits in the future. It is less a question of the amount of taxes that ultimately gets paid, but more a question of when those taxes are due.

In general, investors interested in a mutual fund on any date other than the first of the year should try to become aware of the tax status of the fund so far that tax year. One should try to determine whether there are realized net gains that could ultimately pose a tax liability in the current tax year. Conversely, if there are losses in the fund either from this year's trading or carried forward from previous years, new investors in the fund can implicitly take advantage of those losses through their purchase.

As a general rule, tax considerations should never be the driving force behind an investment decision. But people should be aware of the current tax status of a fund and what that may imply for their own tax situation. Someone looking to purchase shares in a mutual fund in the latter part of the year may decide that deferring the purchase for a few weeks is a reasonable decision, trading off the uncertain prospect of a gain for the certainty of avoiding a liability in the current tax year.

Balanced funds are a category of mutual funds that combine stocks and bonds in an actively managed allocation. One might think of balanced bonds as the precursor to the modern wealth advisory industry. Investors would give virtually all of their investable assets to a single manager who would be charged with deciding the right mix of stocks and bonds. Given that balanced funds command over 10% of all assets of mutual funds, there is still significant demand for this one-stop shopping.

Within the broad category of balanced funds there are meaningful differences across practitioners. Some funds are traditionally active, making timing decisions about the relative attractiveness of stocks and bonds. The objective of these kinds of funds is long-term capital appreciation mixed with dividends and interest income.

Other funds have appeared over time that take a more mechanical view of the investment process. These funds target a long-term asset allocation mix between stocks and bonds. The fund may target a specific blend like 60% stocks and 40% bonds and then vary the allocation through time within relatively narrow ranges in an attempt to add extra value. Sometimes the allocation targets are based on some general assumption about the needs and risk tolerances of individuals of a certain age. The theory is that as one ages, the portfolio should gradually shift away from stocks for the relative security of fixed income.

The assumptions that go behind these models are remarkably broad and not surprisingly many times inappropriate to the specific needs of the investor. Just because someone is 47 or 77 says very little about what they need from an investment portfolio. These *lifestyle funds*, as they are sometimes called, are designed to provide intuitive appeal in an otherwise complicated subject. While they have been very successful from a marketing perspective for the mutual fund industry, the verdict is still out as to whether or not they are serving the investing public well.

A final note is in order about closed-end equity funds. Since closed-end funds trade continuously on the stock exchange, their transaction prices can vary significantly from the underlying net asset value. This offers both opportunities and challenges to the investor.

If the underlying assets in a closed-end mutual fund are illiquid and difficult to price, the market price below the reported NAV may be justified on the basis of uncertainty. But in the case of closed-end equity mutual funds, the underlying securities are almost always exchange listed stocks for which there should be little disagreement about their value. If one finds a large discount to NAV in one of these funds, it is often a reflection of negative investor sentiment about the abilities of the management team. People get frustrated with poor performance and decide they want to sell out. Lacking the daily liquidity feature of an open-ended fund, they must go to the marketplace where they may or may not find an interesting bid.

If you find a fund trading at a large discount to NAV, it might reasonably be viewed as a quality set of assets that you could buy "on sale." One should never buy a closed-end fund simply because it is trading at a discount, but if the underlying stocks are of interest, it may be the most efficient and cost-effective way to acquire such a portfolio. Some hedge fund managers monitor this world closely to look for opportunities where they can buy the closed-end fund at a discount and then short the equivalent basket of stocks in an attempt to secure the differential. The strategy is discussed in more detail in the hedge fund section below.

The problem with discounts is that they can always get bigger before they get smaller. Just because you buy a closed-end fund at 15% below its net asset value does not mean you cannot lose considerably more. The underlying stocks can fall in value and the discount can get wider. Buying closed-end funds at a discount, however, does offer some measure of protection and if the discount closes it is an additional source of potential return.

Discounts often appear in closed-end funds at times of market stress. This highlights one of the key risks. Suppose you could buy a portfolio of stocks in a closed-end fund trading at its NAV or in an open-ended mutual fund. The market risk of the underlying basket of stocks is identical, but the total risks are not. If the market suffers a serious setback, the open-ended mutual fund will fall identically to the net asset value of the underlying stocks. The closed-end funds could develop a discount to its NAV, meaning that the total loss in such a situation is greater.

Similarly, if one is attracted to a closed-end fund currently trading at a premium to its NAV, there is the risk that the premium could evaporate or turn into a discount, offsetting any potential gains in the underlying stocks. One must carefully ask why a closed-end fund should be purchased at a premium when it is possible to buy all of the underlying stocks more cheaply.

9.6.4.2 ETFs and ETNs

Exchange-traded funds and notes (ETFs and ETNs) are one of the world's fastest growing investment areas. Like mutual funds, they cover a broad landscape of product areas, but equity-themed products dominate the market. According to the Investment Company Institute, the total ETF and ETN assets were close to $3.9 trillion at year-end 2018, almost $3.1 trillion of which were domestic and global equity oriented.[29] While smaller than the total mutual fund industry, one must remember that the base was nearly zero at the start of the century.

---

[29]Investment Company Institute (2019). ETF Assets and Net Issuance, May 2019. (27 June). www.ici.org.

The broader discussion in Section 9.2.9 describes many of the general principles all ETF and ETN investors face. Early equity ETFs primarily focused on the replication of major stock indexes like the S&P 500. Their main drawing card was the ability to trade intraday. No longer did an investor have to wait until the end of day to receive an NAV for transactions purposes. Many of the advantages of low-cost passive vehicles could be available to traders throughout the day.

Some observers wondered what all the fuss was about when ETFs appeared. Long-term investors certainly didn't trade actively and nobody expected them to add much value by picking the best entry and exit points during the day for the few trades they did. Still, ETFs on the major indexes quickly caught the attention of large numbers of individual and institutional investors, growing rapidly to become among the major forces in the market and larger than index mutual funds.

Equity ETFs appeared at about the same time that two forces were gaining traction. The first was the broader acceptance of the major tenets of modern portfolio theory. Investors were beginning to embrace the conclusions about market efficiency and the attractiveness of indexing over individual stock selection. The second force was a growing trend toward day trading by individuals who had first come to the market in droves during the great bull market of the 1990s.

When the tech bubble burst in 2000 some of those people who had fancied themselves great stock pickers were sorely disappointed. Suddenly simply buying into stories that might one day have great promise was found to be inadequate. And careful fundamental analysis was discovered to be both labor and resource intensive. Day traders were in a quandary since many of them clearly enjoyed their avocation, but when it came at great expense rather than trading profits, they needed another approach.

In a leap that cannot be entirely justified by theory, many of these traders shifted their focus from individual stocks to the market as a whole or its major sectors. ETFs on broad indexes or industry sectors provided the fuel for this fire, as traders who no longer felt they could pick specific tech stocks believed they could still time the overall market or decide whether autos were going to outperform financials in the next few trading sessions.

Equity ETFs were the ideal vehicle for such traders. No longer did they have to worry about a single bad earnings announcement knocking down their favorite holding. Insider buying or selling would no longer dominate the results of traders who were clearly outsiders. It did not matter that few, if any, of these traders had any market information edge over the other participants. Just as the vast majority of individuals classify themselves as above average drivers, most day traders believe they have superior timing skills. This is another classic behavioral bias, and as long as one's losses are not too severe, it may be easy to overlook.

Finally, the ETF industry has a strong incentive to promote these products over traditional mutual funds. It is not that their stated fee structures are materially higher than those of open-ended mutual funds, but there are opportunities to trade profitably around the management of fund shares that generate large and steady streams of revenue.

The process can be contrasted to the creation of shares in an open-ended mutual fund. In the traditional fund, the manager receives indication of new investments or redemptions over the course of the day. If there is net flow in it is the manager's job to buy underlying shares of stock at as close to the final net asset value as possible so that the newly created fund shares match up well with the underlying assets. In general, any improvement in the price at which the underlying stocks are acquired accrues to the benefit of all the other fund participants as the new assets go into the pool at less than the end of day NAV. Net redemptions are simply the mirror image of this process on the sell side.

New ETF shares are created whenever the market demand exceeds the existing supply available for sale. At such times an *Authorized Participant* (AP) goes about acquiring the underlying stocks in the ETF and packaging them into new ETF shares. The shares are registered with the sponsor and become part of the float. Again, the process of redeeming shares is identical on the other side.

The key distinction, however, is that the AP does not act until there is some indication of excess demand for the ETF shares. That indication is the price of the ETF rising above the NAV of the underlying shares. This is an activity that gives rise to an arbitrage opportunity for the AP. Once the ETF price is high enough, the AP buys the lower priced securities and sells the new shares of the ETF, locking in a trading profit.

This activity is essentially the same kind of arbitrage that has gone on between stock index futures and baskets of stocks since the 1980s. In the case of stock index arbitrage-using futures, it is a highly competitive open market and long ago any excess profits were competed out of the system. It is somewhat different with ETFs. While there are many authorized participants operating across literally hundreds of ETFs, there is not complete and open competition for these services. The arbitrage spreads are not egregiously large, but they are attractive enough to encourage institutional ETF participants to promote more business.

This brings us to where we are today. The ETF market has grown to become a major force in all major equity markets around the world, with steadily expanding volumes. The lion's share of the business is concentrated in a relatively small number of major index ETFs, but new entries appear regularly. Each of the new products is trying to reach critical mass that will support the operations of the ETF and the trading opportunities of the associated authorized participants. Few people know before the fact which of the new products will become blockbusters, or in fact have any success at all. But the economics of the marketplace are such that there are many incentives to continue to create new products. Fortunately for investors the benefits of ETFs are attractive enough to justify the different layers of modest cost. It is debatable whether anyone really needs equity ETFs given the vast array of other alternatives available, but it seems without question that they are a product that is here to stay.

Equity-based exchange-traded notes, ETNs, are something of a curiosity. As with all ETNs the shareholder has a credit relationship with the creator of the ETN that promises to pay out on the basis of some equity price relationship. Investors should always ask why an ETN relationship is required versus a more directly backed ETF. For equity index-based products it is hard to imagine that there are serious market deficiencies that prevent the use of an ETF.

ETNs may be appropriate for an actively managed portfolio where the sponsor agrees to pay the equivalent performance to the ETN shareholder. But with the exception of possible intraday trading, there appear to be few advantages of inserting a middle person between the active manager and the ultimate shareholder. First there is the natural expense and second there is the additional credit risk that the ETN sponsor represents. Finally, because actively managed portfolios are more difficult to replicate at any point in time, Authorized Participants will demand and receive wider spreads when they either create or retire the ETN shares. Most investors would likely be better off going to a low-cost traditional mutual fund structure for their actively managed equity portfolios.

9.6.4.3 Completion Funds

Completion funds are a specialty area that have primary interest among institutional investors. They were created to provide investors a discipline to keep active management from straying too far from designated benchmarks. The spirit behind them is classic modern portfolio theory.

Just as in the discussion of active versus passive management, the question is whether the investor wants to own the exposures reflected in the benchmark indexes. In this particular example, the conclusion is an unquestioning "Yes." The theory comes right from Sharpe and Markowitz that the optimal portfolio is owning the entire market, and it is a short step to assume that the index captures that ideal.

The many counter arguments to this world have been discussed above and will not be repeated here. But for those investors who are still true believers, the mere existence of active management in a portfolio raises serious questions about portfolio efficiency. It is unlikely that active managers will be able to keep the exposures to key factors in the portfolio like sector and cap size lined up carefully with the characteristics of the index. When this happens the portfolio is making sector bets against the market, and the theory claims that this is suboptimal.

Enter the completion fund. These funds in their simplest formulation analyze the portfolio holdings according to investable factors and identify discrepancies with the index. These gaps are closed with an actively managed portfolio that acts as a counterweight, being overweight factors that are underrepresented in the portfolio, and underweight those factors that are too prominent relative to the index. In essence, the completion fund tries to reduce the active bets within the portfolio to pure expressions on the individual companies.

This is an example of trying to have your cake and eat it too. At one extreme, the most avid adherents to modern portfolio theory should never allow active management at all. Sharpe and Markowitz did not base their views on efficient portfolios with only cap size and sector in mind. If you owned exactly the market weight of large-cap pharmaceutical companies, but decided that you would only own Novartis and completely ignore Pfizer, you would still be making a bet against the marketplace. This according to MPT is suboptimal.

Investors still like to believe, however, that stock picking ability exists. Hence, many pursue a *hub-and-spoke approach* to equity portfolios. They build a core position around their benchmark indexes using passive vehicles and then complement that with active managers. When that produces a portfolio with factor exposures at odds with the benchmark, the completion fund is designed to bring these exposures back into line.

If this all sounds like a very complicated process, your intuition is sound. Completion funds have enjoyed some following among the largest institutional investors guided by their theory-driven consultants, but it is impossible to escape the conclusion that this is just one more layer of fees that has the effect of neutralizing some of the active manager attempts to add value.

Completion funds have never gained a great deal of traction in the marketplace, perhaps because of behavioral myopia that leads people to expect too much from their active managers. Another hypothesis, however, is that investors who hire active managers with specific guidelines in mind want to give those managers every opportunity to succeed. Active bets may be on the basis of company specific information, sector information, geography, or capitalization. They may not always be right, but asking an active manager to use his or her best judgment in all four areas, and then paying another manager to offset three of those four bets is not likely to produce any great returns in excess of the costs.

The investment industry has ample examples of products that appear contradictory to any consistent investment philosophy. The mixing of active and passive equity management is just one of them. One of the most dramatic examples is the explosion in the use of hedge funds by institutional and individual investors, many of whom firmly believe in the virtue of indexing their equity portfolio. Somehow when the fund is placed in a partnership structure that allows leverage, the shorting of securities, less liquidity, and higher fees, the manager is somehow expected to overcome all of the efficiency challenges posed by modern portfolio theory. The next part of this chapter describes the wide array of hedge funds that are out there and attempts to discover those areas that have the highest chance of investment success.

9.7 HEDGE FUNDS

Hedge funds are an industry controlling almost $3 trillion in assets in 2018. The range of strategies and risk profiles is almost limitless. There are so many investment vehicles under the hedge fund label that if you told someone you had 20% of your portfolio in hedge funds, you would have revealed almost nothing about your portfolio positioning or risk. Hedge funds are not an asset class, yet they are treated by many analysts and consultants as if they were. To better understand hedge funds today, a look at their early beginnings is useful.

Warren Buffett suggests that one of the earliest hedge funds was run by famous value investor Benjamin Graham and his partner Jerry Newman.[30] It was a partnership structure that invested in both long and short positions, and it paid a performance fee to the general partners. While the term hedge fund was still more than 20 years in the future, Buffett argues that the basic structure was in place by the 1920s.

Alfred Jones is often considered the father of the hedge fund because he dubbed his partnership a "hedged fund" in the late 1940s. It had many of the characteristics commonly found in long-short equity funds today, emphasizing the risk reducing roles of the short positions in the portfolio. In 1966, *Fortune Magazine* ran an article profiling Jones' success, noting that since its inception his fund had meaningfully outperformed almost all long-only mutual funds.[31] Some industry observers see this article as the coming out party for the hedge fund industry. But even then there were a relatively tiny number of fund offerings available, and the assets they controlled were miniscule relative to the broader stock market.

---

[30]Aquilera, K. (2012). What Was the Very First Hedge Fund? Ask Warren Buffett. www. bloomberg.com. (24 April).
[31]Loomis, C.J. (1966). The Jones that Nobody Keeps Up With. *Fortune*. (April).

Hedge funds structured similarly to Jones' efforts that focused on long and short positions in common equity, using only modest leverage, were only the beginning. Since hedge funds were only offered in private partnership format, the regulations that constrained mutual fund investments did not apply. Soon general partners of hedge funds were trading a wide variety of instruments with wildly different degrees of leverage. Not surprisingly, during periods of great market stress like 1973–1974, there were spectacular failures among the most extreme versions of hedge fund offerings. This is a pattern that has repeated itself in every subsequent market crisis.

This part of the chapter will describe the major categories of hedge funds available to investors today. The list is long and complicated, but far from comprehensive. More than 70 years after The Investment Company Act of 1940 created a regulatory structure around the mutual fund industry, the hedge fund industry is just beginning to get a measure of formal regulatory organization. Because of Dodd-Frank requirements, a large number of previously exempt funds now have to register with either the Securities and Exchange Commission or the Commodity Futures Trading Commission. That does not mean, however, that their trading styles will be radically altered, so we can expect the hedge fund menagerie to continue to grow in size and diversity.

It is easy to forget that hedge funds are essentially an infant industry. Of course there have been hedge funds around for decades, but the industry did not become a major market force until the 1990s. Even then, with the prolonged bull market in stocks that didn't end until 2000, many investors wondered what all the fuss was about. If the stock market on average returned more than 10% annually, why would you want to hedge?

The popping of the tech bubble and the accompanying decline in the large-cap indexes from 2000 to 2002 provided a clear answer. Hedge funds of most types largely preserved capital over this period and some made respectable returns. The investors who had made good sized allocations to hedge funds going into this period did meaningfully better than the more traditional stock and bond investors of the time.

Figure 9.12 how dramatically the hedge fund industry grew in the first years of the twenty-first century. Starting with only $118 billion in total assets in 1997, the total reached $1.3 trillion by 2005 and over $2.3 trillion before the market crisis in 2008. After a severe drop during the crisis, the industry quickly recovered assets, growing to about $3 trillion less than a decade later.

There was a big difference between the 2000–2002 stock market collapse and the 2007–2009 episode. In the first instance the majority of hedge funds acted as a diversifier and protected capital. In the second time period the average hedge fund may have lost considerably less than the market as a whole, but still had losses in the double digits. The exceptions to this came from short-biased hedge funds, CTAs, and some macro/credit funds like those of John Paulson that had bought extremely cheap credit default insurance prior to the market collapse. The experience was both a surprise and a disappointment for hedge fund investors. Why weren't the hedge funds hedged?

The reaction was swift and dramatic. Assets in the industry fell by 40%, partly from market losses and partly from investor redemptions. Many investors learned the hard way that what they thought were well-defined liquidity terms could be modified as necessary by the general partners. Terms like *gates* and *side pocket investments* became part of the regular lexicon.

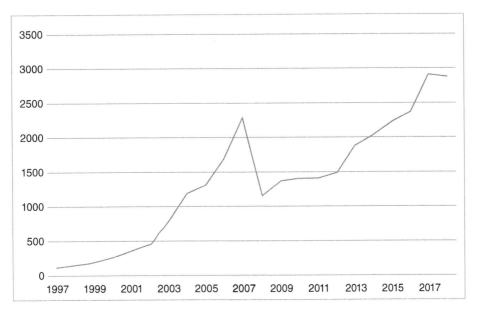

FIGURE 9.12   Global Hedge Fund AUM 1997–2018 in Billions of $

Some fund managers behaved well and did everything they could to meet the letter of their partnership agreements. In the years leading up to the crisis, other managers had placed highly illiquid investments inside their funds in a quest for extra return. These managers often had little choice but to suspend redemptions or limit them to a fraction of the requests (a *gate*) or to also segregate the illiquid investments into a separate sub portfolio that could be liquidated through time (a *side pocket*). Investors in these situations discovered that at least part of their holdings were locked up completely out of their control for an indefinite period of time. This was not what most of these investors thought they were signing up for.

Given poor market performance and creative applications of fund terms, it would not have been surprising if the hedge fund industry struggled for a while to regain the confidence of investors. But the chart shows that if some customers have sworn off the space, their loss has been more than made up for by others. Hedge fund assets quickly recovered to be higher than they were before the crisis.

The recovery is definitely not attributable to great average performance. The 2009 hedge fund bounce back was well less than the market as a whole, and the next two years showed small gains and losses. Instead, it seems that institutional investors were reestablishing asset allocations that had been disrupted by the crisis. Allocators basically assumed that the concept of hedge funds was intact, but their choice of funds had been faulty. Investors in droves poured money into managers that had experienced even mediocre returns in the crisis. The industry bounced back bigger, if not better, than ever. Today's investor is confronted by a larger and more complex hedge fund landscape than at any time in history.

Throughout this part of the chapter, strategies will be described that attempt to exploit some informational advantage or market inefficiency. They cover a considerable range of activity that can be confusing to the uninitiated investor. The goal here is to give a deep enough introduction so you can differentiate across strategies and managers. The investors who chased strong performers from 2008 have not all been awarded since. They might have been fighting the wrong fight with the wrong weapons. This chapter emphasizes once again that past returns really are not an indicator of future performance.

Before looking at strategies, a couple of basic concepts need to be established, which are central to an understanding of all hedge funds: *net exposure* and *leverage*. Net exposure tries to capture the amount of market risk for every dollar invested. Leverage describes the total positions in place for each dollar invested. While they are basic concepts, they can be calculated and communicated in different ways. The following paragraphs detail some of the challenges using equity long/short funds as an example, but the concepts are generic across all types of hedge funds.

The net exposure of the portfolio can be looked at in simple dollar terms or a beta adjusted basis. If a manager has collected $1 million of investable capital from the limited partners, and then buys $1 million in long equity exposure and also goes short $600,000 in other stocks, the net exposure is $400,000 long. If the average beta of all the stocks in the portfolio is 1, the net market exposure of this hedge fund basket should be approximately the same as a long-only manager controlling $400,000 worth of stock. Put another way, the hedge fund should only be 40% as volatile as a typical $1 million long-only equity portfolio.

Since not all stocks have the same sensitivity to the marketplace as the average stock, some managers refine their risk calculation by looking at the weighted average of all the individual stock betas within their portfolios. If in the example above the manager's long stocks on average have a beta of 1.1, while the shorts average beta is 1.0, the net beta-adjusted exposure would be $500,000.[32]

If our $1 million manager bought $2 million worth of stock while selling short $2 million, the net exposure would be identical to the unleveraged manager holding $1 million of both long and short positions. This demonstrates why net exposure is important to understanding risk, but is incomplete without an understanding of the leverage in the portfolio.

You might think that leverage is a basic and fundamental measure. Unfortunately, different managers have slightly different interpretations, and it is up to the investor to understand how any calculation behind reported leverage is done. First, one must understand that leverage can be introduced into a portfolio in different ways. The most intuitive way is through borrowing, or financial leverage. But it is also possible to use financial instruments with embedded leverage without borrowing to get the same effect. We'll begin with a discussion of financial leverage.

The simplest way to calculate leverage is on a gross basis, but this can give misleading results. Gross leverage is simply the sum of long and short positions divided by the capital in the fund. In the example of the $1 million market neutral manager holding both $1 million long and $1 million short portfolios, gross leverage would be equal to two.

The reason this is misleading is that neither the long nor the short side of the book has been levered through borrowing. Given the rules of shorting stocks, no

---

[32]($1 million × 1.1) − $600,000 = $500,000.

particularly fancy financing arrangements need to be in place for the manager to create this portfolio. The long side is purchased with the fund's capital. The short position is completely collateralized by the long stocks in the book.

Comparing different managers simply on a gross leverage basis highlights some of the problems with this approach. The market neutral manager in the example above clearly has a radically different risk profile than a hedge fund manager who has 200% exposure on the long side and no shorts, yet they have the same gross leverage calculation. For this reason many market-neutral managers with a 1 X 1 portfolio will describe themselves as being unleveraged.

These managers start with the basic concept, but modify it somewhat. They report leverage as the sum of longs plus shorts divided by the fund's capital, but then they subtract 100%. Call this *modified gross leverage.* In the example, this calculation creates a value of 1, which matches the intuition that there is no leverage being used, but this concept fails in other instances. The market neutral manager with $2 million longs and $2 million shorts has a gross leverage of 4 and a modified gross leverage of 3. Neither value seems to capture what is going on in that portfolio.

For these reasons some look at leverage strictly through a borrowing prism. If our $1 million fund manager borrows another $500,000 to go long a total of $1.5 million in stock, and then uses that position as collateral to sell $1.5 million in equity short, the leverage based on the ratio of borrowing to capital is 50%. Similarly if Manager B's portfolio was $2 million by $2 million, the borrowing ratio would be 100%. Another way this is sometimes stated is that the first manager has "a half a turn of leverage" while Manager B has "one turn of leverage."

Note that if another Manager C borrows 100% of the fund's capital and simply buys $2 million in long exposure, the fund has the same leverage as the 2 X 2 market neutral manager. This is a strong example why neither net exposure nor leverage should be used alone as a measure of a fund's riskiness.

In most instances for long/short equity managers the borrowing ratio is the clearest expression of the leverage in the fund, but it is critical that the potential investor understand what methodology is being used and not assume one approach or another.

Leverage done with financial instruments can be considerably trickier to monitor. Both futures and options contracts and OTC swaps often are based on notional values, but with considerably smaller sums of collateral posted to establish the position. Leveraged ETFs imbed a multiple of risk by design. For long/short equity managers, the first question should be, "What are all of the types of securities and derivatives that you use or are allowed to use?" If the manager only trades in traditional securities, the basic measures of financial leverage probably paint a reasonably accurate picture. If the book is populated with derivatives, structured products or leveraged ETFs, the task is much more complex.

Consider a $1 million hedge fund that buys $900,000 of long stocks and then takes the balance of the capital and uses it as margin on $3 million of S&P 500 stock index futures. While there is no formal borrowing in this portfolio, the manager has exposure to the stock market of $3.9 million with only $1 million in capital. This is instrument leverage, and the portfolio should be expected to gain or lose similarly to someone holding a $3.9 million stock portfolio.

If the fund uses options, interpreting leverage depends entirely on whether the options are purchased or written. Suppose in the example above the manager uses the $100,000 in cash to purchase $4 million of out of the money S&P 500 call options rather than as margin for long futures. It seems like there is leverage here, but it is asymmetric. If the market rallies, the profits will be based on the $4.9 million in long stock exposure, less the cost of the options. This looks like instrument leverage.

If the stock market falls, the calls will expire worthless and the fund will have lost $100,000 plus whatever losses hit the long stock portfolio. But the important difference is that if the market keeps declining, the loss is only on the original $900,000 in stocks. There is no instrument leverage to losses of more than 10% in this portfolio. The cost of that favorable asymmetry is the money spent on premiums.

Written options are an entirely different story. If our fund manager decides to write $4 million in index puts, for example, and collects $100,000 in premiums, the hope is that the market will settle above the strike price when the options expire. In that case, the fund pockets the entire $100,000 of premiums received. Should the market drop, however, the exposure is the same as owning a $4.9 million stock portfolio, which is considerable instrument leverage.

The most conservative approach is to consider the portfolio to be leveraged by the full notional amount of any written options. There is a probability that the options expire worthless, in which case there is no leverage at all. But it is possible that the market moves the wrong way turning the written options into full directional exposure. By knowing this value in advance, the investor has identified the worst case leverage scenario.

OTC derivatives will look either like futures or options, or a combination of the two. Modeling different market outcomes similar to the process above provides the best picture of fund leverage in both up and down markets.

While the calculation of net exposure and leverage is not always transparent for investors considering hedge fund strategies, the concepts need to be grasped in order to compare the returns and risks across managers. In each of the discussions of hedge fund strategies below, we shall regularly return to net exposure and leverage as differentiating factors across managers that label themselves similarly. The first place to apply these lessons is with the classic hedge fund strategy, long/short equity.

9.7.1 Long/Short Equity Hedge Funds

When people are asked, "What is a hedge fund?" most think of long/short equity portfolios. These funds meet the intuition of what a hedge fund is designed to do and generally they are the most easily understood products in the broad category. They are the essence of active equity management, identifying stocks that are expected to outperform on the long side while adding short positions that act to hedge against general market movements or profit from idiosyncratic declines.

Stock price changes can be grouped into three types. First, there are those price changes that are due to company specific information. Second, a company's shares may be influenced by news about the industry or sector. Finally, there are times when a stock price changes simply because the entire market is moving up or down. The hedge in the short equity positions comes from the ability to mitigate some of the risks of these last two types of moves.

A simple example will demonstrate the principal. A hedge fund manager after doing extensive fundamental research believes that Dell Computers is undervalued relative to its earnings potential and its peers. After establishing a long position in

Dell, the manager becomes concerned about the general state of the economy. In a downturn, sales of personal computers and tablets to both individuals and businesses are likely to fall, and there is a good chance that the overall stock market would correct. A specific hedged position against the Dell exposure could be a short in Hewlett-Packard, or in a basket of computer-related companies. If there was a downturn in the sector or the market as a whole, it is likely the long position in Dell would suffer but that the short position would profit, at least partially offsetting the loss.

Sometimes the short positions are put on primarily as hedges, or sometimes they are established as *alpha shorts*. In the latter case the manager actively tries to identify stocks that will decline in value. This is essentially a mirror image activity of the manager's fundamental research to find attractive long positions. Whether the short positions are put on primarily as hedges or as alpha seeking positions, they should still have the primary benefit of offsetting some of the directional risk in the long book.

Simply identifying the manager as a long/short manager provides little information about the exposures being taken or the ultimate risk faced by the investor. This is where the previously discussed concepts of net exposure and leverage come into play.

One subclass of equity long/short managers is known as *market neutral*. In the simplest form they will keep equal dollar amounts of long and short positions. In a more analytically driven form they will try to completely offset the estimated betas of the long and short equity positions. This is the purest form of active stock management, focusing entirely on the relative performance of individual stocks, while trying to eliminate any broader directional forces.

Market neutral strategies frequently attract highly analytical managers who believe they have found either fundamental or statistical anomalies in the marketplace that can be exploited. Whether the holding period for these stocks is measured in seconds or minutes or days or months, manager believe they have an informational edge on the relative value of the securities in their portfolio, but they have no particular information about the direction of the market is a whole.

Since a large part of the overall risk of equity investing comes from broad market moves and not from company specific information, market neutral managers can be among the least volatile expressions of any form of stock portfolios. In the early days of hedge funds there was limited competition within this somewhat specialized group of managers, and reasonable returns were achieved. Over time their success attracted many competitors, squeezing down the opportunities and with it the profitability of the approach.

In a theme often appearing in this book, some of these managers concluded that to get around modest returns, they could safely apply more leverage. The rationale was simple. Since most of the directional market risk was eliminated through the market neutrality of the portfolio, it would be acceptable to raise the risk profile by adding more positions on both the long and the short side as long as they stayed completely balanced.

While each manager would claim that they had developed their own secret sauce through years of intensive research, the reality was that for most managers the buy and sell signals were driven by a set of common factors.[33] Most of the secret sauces were in essence just combinations of financial ketchup and mayonnaise.

---

[33]The analytical factors are discussed in more detail in Chapter 5.5.

The market factors were chosen because they had been identified in historical data as being indicators of relative value. Of course this data was created before the managers began trying to trade on the relationships. As more and more assets moved into the space, different managers began unknowingly to establish common trades. Crowded positions, created with leverage, make for a dangerous situation.

The performance of different hedge fund strategies in 2008 shows just how dangerous the situation can be. Market neutral funds over long periods of time demonstrated limited volatility and appeared to be relatively low risk. In late 2007 and 2008, during periods of extreme market stress, reality varied tremendously from expectations. As shown in Figure 9.13b in 2008 the average market neutral equity hedge fund lost 40.3%, worse than the general stock market as measured by the S&P 500, which was down 37%, and the average long short equity hedge fund, which was down 19.8%.[34]

These figures, sometimes referred to as periodic tables, record the average hedge fund return by style. Emerging Market managers, for example, are always dark gray in these charts and one can watch how that style does versus all the other styles as

1997	1998	1999	2000	2001	2002	2003	2004	2005	2006	2007
Global Macro 37.11%	Managed Futures 20.64%	Long/Short Equity 47.23%	Convertible Arb 25.64%	Distressed 20.01%	Managed Futures 18.33%	Emerging Markets 28.75%	Distressed 15.62%	Emerging Markets 17.39%	Emerging Markets 20.49%	Emerging Markets 20.26%
Emerging Markets 26.59%	Long/Short Equity 17.18%	Emerging Markets 44.82%	Market Neutral Eq. 14.99%	Global Macro 18.38%	Global Macro 14.66%	Distressed 25.12%	Emerging Markets 12.49%	Distressed 11.74%	Distressed 15.58%	Global Macro 17.36%
Long/Short Equity 21.46%	Market Neutral Eq. 13.31%	Distressed 22.18%	Risk Arb 14.69%	Convertible Arb 14.58%	Market Neutral Eq. 7.42%	Global Macro 17.99%	Long/Short Equity 11.56%	Long/Short Equity 9.68%	Multi Strategy 14.54%	Long/Short Equity 13.66%
Distressed 20.73%	Multi Strategy 7.68%	Convertible Arb 16.04%	Global Macro 11.67%	Market Neutral Eq. 9.31%	Emerging Markets 7.36%	Long/Short Equity 17.27%	Global Macro 8.49%	Global Macro 9.25%	Long/Short Equity 14.38%	Multi Strategy 10.10%
Multi Strategy 18.28%	Risk Arb 5.58%	Market Neutral Eq. 15.33%	Multi Strategy 11.18%	Fixed Income Arb 8.04%	Multi Strategy 6.31%	Multi Strategy 15.04%	Multi Strategy 7.53%	Multi Strategy 7.54%	Convertible Arb 14.30%	Market Neutral Eq. 9.27%
Market Neutral Eq. 14.83%	Distressed -1.68%	Risk Arb 13.23%	Fixed Income Arb 6.29%	Emerging Markets 5.84%	Fixed Income Arb 5.75%	Managed Futures 14.13%	Fixed Income Arb 6.86%	Market Neutral Eq. 6.14%	Global Macro 13.53%	Risk Arb 8.77%
Convertible Arb 14.48%	Global Macro -3.64%	Fixed Income Arb 12.11%	Managed Futures 4.24%	Risk Arb 5.68%	Convertible Arb 4.05%	Convertible Arb 12.90%	Market Neutral Eq. 6.48%	Risk Arb 3.08%	Market Neutral Eq. 11.15%	Distressed 8.35%
Risk Arb 9.84%	Convertible Arb -4.41%	Multi Strategy 9.38%	Long/Short Equity 2.08%	Multi Strategy 5.50%	Distressed -0.69%	Risk Arb 8.98%	Managed Futures 5.96%	Fixed Income Arb 0.63%	Fixed Income Arb 8.66%	Managed Futures 6.01%
Fixed Income Arb 9.34%	Fixed Income Arb -8.16%	Global Macro 5.81%	Distressed 1.95%	Managed Futures 1.90%	Long/Short Equity -1.60%	Fixed Income Arb 7.97%	Risk Arb 5.45%	Managed Futures -0.11%	Risk Arb 8.15%	Convertible Arb 5.17%
Managed Futures 3.12%	Emerging Markets -37.66%	Managed Futures -4.69%	Emerging Markets -5.52%	Long/Short Equity -3.65	Risk Arb -3.46	Market Neutral Eq. 7.07%	Convertible Arb 1.98%	Convertible Arb - 2.55	Managed Futures 8.05%	Fixed Income Arb 3.83%
CS Hedge Fund Index 25.94%	**CS Hedge Fund Index -0.36%**	CS Hedge Fund Index 23.43%	CS Hedge Fund Index 4.85%	CS Hedge Fund Index 4.42%	**CS Hedge Fund Index 3.04%**	CS Hedge Fund Index 15.44%	CS Hedge Fund Index 9.64%	CS Hedge Fund Index 7.61%	CS Hedge Fund Index 13.86%	CS Hedge Fund Index 12.56%

FIGURE 9.13A Hedge Fund Returns by Strategy 1997–2007
Source: Credit Suisse

---

[34]Source: Dow Jones Credit Suisse Hedge Fund Indexes.

2008	2009	2010	2011	2012	2013	2014	2015	2016	2017	2018
Managed Futures 18.33%	Convertible Arb 47.35%	Global Macro 13.47%	Global Macro 8.44%	Distressed 11.77%	Long/Short Equity 17.73%	Managed Futures 18.36%	Multi Strategy 3.84%	Convertible Arb 6.60%	Emerging Markets 16.87%	Fixed Income Arb 1.1%
Risk Arb -3.27%	Emerging Markets 30.03%	Fixed Income Arb 12.51%	Fixed Income Arb 4.89%	Multi Strategy 11.19%	Distressed 16.00%	Multi Strategy 6.09%	Long/Short Equity 3.56%	Distressed 6.38%	Long/Short Equity 13.4%	Risk Arb -0.18%
Global Macro -4.82%	Fixed Income Arb 27.41%	Managed Futures 12.22%	Market Neutral Eq. 4.49%	Fixed Income Arb 11.04%	Multi Strategy 11.23%	Long/Short Equity 5.54%	Market Neutral Eq. 1.69%	Risk Arb 5.89%	Market Neutral Eq. 8.54%	Global Macro -0.11%
Long/Short Equity -19.76%	Multi Strategy 24.62%	Emerging Markets 11.34%	Multi Strategy 1.83%	Emerging Markets 10.28%	Market Neutral Eq. 9.27%	Fixed Income Arb 4.37%	Convertible Arb 0.81%	Emerging Markets 4.47%	Distressed 7.3%	Multi Strategy -1.05%
Distressed -20.48%	Distressed 20.95%	Convertible Arb 10.95%	Convertible Arb 1.13%	Long/Short Equity 8.21%	Emerging Markets 8.81%	Global Macro 3.11%	Fixed Income Arb 0.59%	Multi Strategy 4.41%	Multi Strategy 6.83%	Distressed -1.58%
Multi Strategy -23.63%	Long/Short Equity 19.47%	Distressed 10.27%	Risk Arb 0.80%	Convertible Arb 7.82%	Convertible Arb 6.03%	Distressed 2.55%	Risk Arb 0.41%	Fixed Income Arb 4.29%	Fixed Income Arb 6.52%	Convertible Arb -2.25%
Fixed Income Arb -28.82%	Risk Arb 12.00%	Multi Strategy 9.29%	Managed Futures -4.19%	Global Macro 4.58%	Risk Arb 4.92%	Emerging Markets 1.52%	Global Macro 0.17%	Global Macro 3.58%	Risk Arb 5.79%	Long/Short Equity -4.62%
Emerging Markets -30.41%	Global Macro 11.55%	Long/Short Equity 9.28%	Distressed -4.24%	Risk Arb 2.82%	Global Macro 4.32%	Market Neutral Eq. -1.20%	Emerging Markets -0.22%	Long/Short Equity -3.43%	Convertible Arb 5%	Market Neutral Eq. -4.99%
Convertible Arb -31.59%	Market Neutral Eq. 4.05%	Risk Arb 3.17%	Emerging Markets -6.68%	Market Neutral Eq. 0.85%	Fixed Income Arb 3.80%	Risk Arb -1.32%	Managed Futures -0.93%	Market Neutral Eq. -4.58%	Managed Futures 3.23%	Managed Futures -6.69%
Market Neutral Eq. -40.32%	Managed Futures -6.57%	Market Neutral Eq. -0.85%	Long/Short Equity -7.31%	Managed Futures -2.93%	Managed Futures -2.56%	Convertible Arb -1.67%	Distressed -5.30%	Managed Futures -6.84%	Global Macro 2.14%	Emerging Markets -10.16%
CS Hedge Fund Index -19.07%	CS Hedge Fund Index 18.57%	CS Hedge Fund Index 10.95%	CS Hedge Fund Index -2.52%	CS Hedge Fund Index 7.67%	CS Hedge Fund Index 9.73%	CS Hedge Fund Index 4.13%	CS Hedge Fund Index -0.71%	CS Hedge Fund Index 1.25%	CS Hedge Fund Index 7.13%	CS Hedge Fund Index -3.19%

FIGURE 9.13B Hedge Fund Returns by Strategy 2008–2018
Source: Credit Suisse

dark block moves up and down across the years. For the 22 years covered, there is no one consistently winning hedge fund strategy, reminding us that everyone managing money has ebbs and flows depending on the market environment. In the case of market neutral funds in 2008 that market environment was not only shaped by the financial crisis but the mountain of money that had been placed into managers pursuing the same strategy.

What appeared to happen in 2008 was that too many leveraged market neutral funds were trading on the same type of analytical model and had similar longs and shorts. The signals that identified theoretically overvalued and undervalued stocks were driven by the same factors across these portfolios. When these leveraged managers were asked for more collateral, or were facing redemption requests from their limited partners, they all found themselves trying to sell the same stocks from their long books and to buy back the same shorts. There was not enough fundamental demand in the marketplace for other managers to step in and keep prices aligned. There rarely is at times of crisis. Losses quickly mounted for the market neutral managers as a group.

Losing 40% in what was expected to be a low-volatility strategy is devastating to both investors and the managers. Many funds closed after 2008 and those that did not typically operated with vastly smaller pools of capital. Note from the chart that unlike some of the scuffed up strategies from 2008, equity market neutral returns did not bounce back after the crisis, earning just over 4% in 2009 and 2011, and showing a small loss in 2010. In only 2 of the 11 years since 2008 could one call the average market neutral hedge fund return respectable.

It is easy after the fact to be critical, but what did investors see before the crisis? From 1997 through 2001, the figure shows the strategy earned 14.8%, 13.3%, 15.3%, 15.0%, and 9.3%. These years included highly volatile stock markets, up and down. Investors noticed the good returns and relative stability. The next six years showed more modest returns, but there were no losses and the worst outcome was 6.1%. Market neutral equity funds as a group began to be viewed as a stable bond substitute offering a meaningful premium on the return side.

It is this kind of thinking that causes problems. Just because a strategy exhibits a similar return and volatility pattern to bonds over some period of time does not mean it is a good substitute for fixed income investing. The true risk profiles can be fundamentally different, a fact made obvious during times of market crisis.

The fund manager has no reason to try to scare existing or prospective investors by emphasizing all of the potential risks before they occur. The manager may not even recognize them himself or herself until it is too late. But leveraged strategies that attract too many assets are analogous to living along an earthquake fault line that has been quiet for years. Everything is fine, until it is not. Investors need to understand their geography when they go into an investment.

Equity long/short managers are often confronted by investors who can rarely be satisfied by what they are trying to do. If a fund is market neutral it faces questions about whether there is enough market exposure to earn a reasonable return. At the other end of the spectrum, if a fund is, for example, 100% gross long and 15% gross short, investors question why they should pay a performance fee on a portfolio with so much market beta. Like Goldilocks, investors seem to be looking for "just right" as they sample the range of equity long/short managers. It is not an easy quest.

Some of the most successful long-term equity long/short hedge funds are meaningfully over 100% net exposed to the market. 140% long and 25% short is an exposure profile of a manager with high confidence in their stock selection. If their confidence is reinforced with actual results over time, investors can be rewarded with better-than-market returns that more than makes up for the higher volatility and fees.

This is obviously a better strategy in bull markets, where the beta of the portfolio and good stock selection can be a powerful combination. The downside, of course, comes in periods of market stress. There it is almost impossible to have such superior stock selection that the impact of the outsized beta is mitigated. The sides of the investment road are littered with numerous spectacular crashes of such funds. All too often a great number of investors in these efforts entered shortly before the failure, lured by the history of outsized returns without thinking of the potential risks.

A majority of long/short equity funds try to operate in an intermediate zone of beta between 20% and 70% and without any meaningful leverage. This is a "safe" area for managers, with a meaningful reduction in the volatility associated with the market, but with enough exposure so they will be able to benefit from the long-term upward trend in valuations. The tough question for investors is whether the skill from security selection and timing market exposure is large enough to justify the higher management fees, a performance fee, and the lockup associated with most hedge funds.

Testing whether these managers are worth the fees and relative illiquidity goes back to the discussion in Chapter 5. Great caution should be used not to rely exclusively on a time series of past returns. Instead, more detailed attribution analysis should be pursued to see if a particular manager makes sense in the overall portfolio.

9.7.2 130/30 Hedge Funds

A subset of the broad category of long/short equity hedge funds that appeared to be gathering a following before the financial crisis was known as 130/30 funds. These products were structured to be approximately 130% long and 30% short on a dollar basis as a statement of policy. This meant that being 100% net long, investors should have expected full equity market exposure, with all the return and volatility that comes from a beta of 1. The added attraction was supposed to be from the managers, applying either quantitative or fundamental techniques, identifying the superior stocks to buy and the inferior ones to sell.

These funds had a moment of considerable institutional interest, as investors looked for ways to enhance their long-only equity portfolios. In 2007, when there was approximately $50 billion allocated to US-focused 130/30 funds, the consulting firm The Tabb Group predicted there would be $2 trillion in the strategy by 2010.[35] This growth never materialized, as the anticipation of positive alpha was shattered by the financial crisis.

The primary culprit in the failures was that many of the 130/30 funds were highly quantitative, using similar techniques followed by the model-driven market neutral funds discussed in the preceding section. Many of these models were based on some variation of relative valuation based on popular factors. This meant that the 130/30 funds held a large percentage of the same trades as the more leveraged market neutral cousins. The heavy liquidations after the Lehman Brothers bankruptcy pressured stocks on both the long and short sides. Many 130/30 funds generated negative alpha across their holdings as a result.

Many 130/30 funds closed their doors after the crisis. Some still exist, though they are rarely referred to in those terms, as the label has become something of a damaged brand. Today one will hear about "enhanced alpha," "extended alpha," or "alpha extension" funds. Specific investment guidelines vary across products, but all have the ability to use modest gross leverage while targeting a beta of 1 at the fund level. Some of the highest-quality enhanced index funds still use this basic approach but distinguish themselves from the crowd through genuinely differentiated analytical processes.

The lesson of 130/30 funds is that investment fashion changes through time, but the key forces dictating fashion rarely do. The promise to investors was that they could achieve better-than-index returns while taking no more than average market risk. The motivation of the fund managers was that they could charge higher fees than any vanilla long-only equity manager could on the basis of that promise. When the managers' incentive to promote higher profit investment products is met by an almost insatiable desire to outperform by the consuming public, great hype can surround any approach. At least for a while.

In the case of 130/30 funds the big parade may have been stopped by the crisis before it really got going. Unlike many complicated and expensive credit structures

---

[35]Turner, G. (2011). The Rise and Fall of the 130/30 Fad. *Financial News*. (14 March).

that grew like weeds before the collapse, the aggregate damage done to investors in these products was not that great. But if the timing of the crisis had been a few years later and institutions had dedicated even a trillion dollars to the strategy rather than 1/20 of that amount, there would likely have been another major, and expensively learned, history lesson.

9.7.3　Convertible Bond Arbitrage and Other Relative Value Hedge Funds

The general category of long/short equity funds and the specific example of 130/30 funds are examples of hedge funds where the manager is picking long stocks believed to have superior performance and simultaneously trying to select underperformers with short stock sales. In most instances it is long stocks and short stocks, like Ford versus Toyota, or Hewlett Packard versus Dell. There is another category of hedge fund that is also trying to find relatively overpriced and underpriced assets, but the trades are done with different parts of the capital structure within the same company. Convertible bond arbitrage is perhaps the best known of these approaches, but the principle can be applied more generally.

As discussed in Section 9.5, convertible bonds are coupon-paying instruments with a finite life that also come with an option to convert the bond into equity at a given strike price. This means that it is a security in a company's capital structure that is related in value to both the equity of the company and its bonds. Using models to value the embedded option in terms of shares of the underlying stock, hedge fund managers set up spread trades to exploit relative value mismatches.

Anticipating the discussion on options in the next chapter, the key variable in such calculations is the *delta* of the embedded option. The delta of an option can be thought of similarly as the beta of a stock. It gives an expectation of how much the value of an option will move if the underlying stock price changes. Deltas of call options vary between zero, when the option is so far out-of-the-money that there is effectively no chance of it being exercised, to one, which happens when the option is *deep-in-the-money*, and will almost certainly be exercised.

A simple trade example for a convertible bond arbitrage manager would be to buy $2 of equity exposure in a convertible bond when the delta of the option is 0.5 and then sell $1 of the underlying stock short. This is a *delta neutral* position with respect to the underlying stock price movement, but still leaves the manager exposed to the risk of interest rate changes and default on the bonds. There are other techniques that can mitigate those risks if desired.

The manager would enter into such a trade whenever the value of the option embedded into the convertible bond was seen as cheap relative to the stock. This is also a way to take a long exposure to volatility as the value of any long option should be enhanced if volatility spikes. Most of the best convertible arbitrage managers came into the business with a background in options market making or trading, adding value through dynamic repositioning of their long and short books.

Consider the example of being long $2 of notional value in convertible bonds and short $1 of stock, starting with a net delta of zero, or market neutral. If the stock price rallies by any meaningful amount the bonds become closer to being exercisable and the embedded equity exposure gets bigger. As the delta of the long options position grows beyond the 0.5 starting point, and the net position of the combination shifts from neutral to slightly positive, there are profits on the long bonds that exceed the losses on the short stock. A highly conservative manager would sell off some of the convertible bond position to get back to neutral, but more trading-oriented managers often let the trend be their friend for at least a little while before tightening the arbitrage back up. Similar non-delta neutral trading can produce gains in down markets as well.

Convertible arbitrage began seriously in the 1980s and expanded quickly in the 1990s. As shown in Figure 9.13, it stumbled a bit in 1998, losing 4.4% for the year. This was the year that important relative value player, Long Term Capital Management (LTCM) imploded largely on the basis of highly leveraged fixed income spread trades. LTCM also had a large convertible arbitrage book and when they needed to liquidate their positions, the price of convertible bonds across a wide spectrum tumbled.

Managers who were not eliminated from the game in 1998 were able to buy cheap bonds and the strategy rebounded, earning more than 16% and 25% in the next two years. This began a cyclical pattern of returns that always seemed to have many investors adding money *after* a good trading period and then scrambling to redeem when they experienced disappointments.

The extreme of this cycle also happened in 2008 when convertible arbitrage managers on average lost over 30%. Like many assets after the Lehman Brothers collapse, convertible bonds became quite cheap. Investors who could maintain or expand their portfolios benefited greatly as the category earned 47% in 2009 and another 11% in 2010.

One might wonder why convertible bond arbitrage was able to bounce back and recover losses after the crisis while equity market neutral managers could not. The answer lies in the fact that one strategy trades on the relative values of securities of the same company (convertible arbitrage) while the other approach looks at values across different companies. In an important sense, it is much easier to identify convertible bonds that are incredibly cheap relative to a stock's equity value than it is to definitively say widget manufacturer A is cheap compared to widget manufacturer B. There are also more natural forces working to keep securities of the same company in line with one another than one finds across companies.

The dominant message about convertible arbitrage is that it is an analytically driven process that in most cases leads to reasonably predictable results. It is also, however, a strategy that has sometimes grown too large relative to the underlying asset base for it to behave reliably. In the period right before the financial crisis so many convertible bonds were being purchased by hedge fund managers that traditional bond managers virtually abandoned the asset class. Prices were bid up not because the bonds offered some appropriate risk-adjusted return to bond investors, but because there was an almost insatiable demand to put these bonds into arbitrage programs. When the collapse happened, the price of convertible bonds had to fall dramatically before the traditional buyers were attracted back to the market.

Convertible bond arbitrage is just one example of equity-based relative value strategies. Expanding the spectrum of instruments a bit leads to *capital structure arbitrage* where the manager looks up and down the cap structure of a company to find securities that they believe are mispriced within the firm. Note that these managers never take an absolute bet on whether a company's stock price is over- or undervalued relative to another company or the market as a whole. Instead, they look for inefficiencies that can be exploited by selling one bond versus another, or doing stock versus bond trades.

This does not say that these managers don't care about what happens to the value of a company's stock. Managers who establish these positions usually simulate returns in both up and down markets, looking for critical price points where the arbitrage nature of the trade might become challenged. This helps in risk management, and moreover it identifies ways the managers can position a trade to do better if the manager's beliefs about a company become true.

Like the convertible arbitrage example outlined above, capital structure arbitrage traders often benefit from having cash on hand to exploit opportunities that arise from periodic market disruptions. This approach runs contrary to some limited partners' wishes who believe a manager should be fully invested in a strategy at all times. But it is in fact the fully invested managers who suffered the greatest problems and had to liquidate positions in the middle of the credit crisis. Even the tightest of arbitrage relationships can suffer through periods of considerable disruption. Only if the LPs are fully committed to a strategy and are unfazed by short-term volatility does the fully invested strategy really work.

9.7.4 Event-oriented Hedge Funds

There are many approaches that fit under the big tent called event-oriented hedge funds. Merger arbitrage, event-themed equity strategies, and activist managers are just three examples. As is often the case, looking at the broad label doesn't tell you very much about how the manager makes money or what risks investors face.

At the most conservative end of the spectrum are merger arbitrage specialists. Also called *risk arbitrageurs,* these managers take long and short positions in the stocks of companies that have announced their intention to combine. A simple example will convey the approach.

Suppose Health Care Company A's stock is trading at $42 a share, and Health Care Company B's stock is at $15 a share. Company A announces its intention to acquire Company B by offering one share of its stock for every two shares of Company B's stock. The merger plan can be a friendly one negotiated between the boards of the company or it can be hostile. At the current value of A, Company B is being valued at $21, a 40% premium to its traded value.

This is where the arbitrage opportunity appears. A nimble investor could buy two shares of Company B (total price of $30) and then short one share of Company A at $42. Since at the point of the merger these two positions become exactly offsetting, the spread trader reaps a $12 profit. Of course, if this trade was available to all market participants, millions of shares would trade hands on both the long and the short sides and the prices would shift. B's shares would be bid up and A's shares would fall on the short sales until their ratio approached, but did not quite reach, 1:2.

The difference between the current price ratio and the target exchange rate gives an indication of the potential profit in the arbitrage. In the example above, the spread between the original traded prices and the target ratio was quite large. Any trades that could get done as the example described would be very lucrative.[36] A more likely

---

[36]The example assumed the arbitrageur paid for the long position in full, and that in turn could be used as collateral for the short position. In reality, many such trades are done with leverage obtained from the fund's prime broker. This can increase the profit potential from any trade, but also magnifies the risks should the merger not get completed for any reason.

outcome would be for the prices to adjust almost instantaneously, with the arbitrage transactions actually getting done at a competitively determined spread that reflects the risk that the merger plan might fall through.

If in the example above the price of Stock A trades down to $40, the implied value of Stock B would be $20 (the 2:1 announced ratio). Assume there was six months before the transaction was to close. If Stock B was instantaneously bid up to $19 on the news, there would be $1 per share of profit potential left. Earning a dollar on every share bought at $19 would earn 5.26% for the 6 months, or about 10.5% annualized. Notice that if the arbitrageur buys two shares of Stock B and sells one share of Stock A at these prices, the profit will be the same whether the 2:1 ratio is achieved by Stock B trading up to $20, or stock A trading down to $38. All that matters is that the prices eventually converge to the right ratio.

How close the price ratio gets to the announced exchange ratio is a function of several variables. The three most important are: 1) the likelihood the transaction will occur; 2) the time left before the transaction closes; and 3) the opportunity cost of money. High probability mergers with a short window of time left to completion will see prices converge toward the announced merger ratio, leaving little extra return available above the risk-free rate. That leaves open the question, "Why don't all such transactions converge?"

The more speculative the transaction, the farther the spread will remain away from the target ratio. If the target company doesn't want to merge, the plan will be seen as a hostile takeover, and the target company may convince shareholders to reject the suitor. There may be regulatory or anti-trust issues with any potential combination that would keep a deal from closing. A major disruption in the stock market as a whole might knock down the value of Company A's stock to the point where Company B shareholders no longer feel appropriately compensated to complete the transaction.

This last risk is less of an issue where the acquiring company offers cash for the target instead of its own stock. Here the perceived arbitrage does not involve any short at all, but instead involves buying shares of the target company as long as the market price is far enough below the takeover price to provide a return that compensates for the time value of the cash tied up in the deal and the risk that the deal never gets finalized.

The outcomes of an announced merger are often binary. The deal comes off as planned or it breaks for potentially a variety of economic or regulatory reasons. That implies that merger arbitrage is similar to writing options in that there is usually a maximum profit potential in the trade if everything goes as planned, but if things go wrong the losses can be much greater.

To demonstrate this, consider the previous example of health care companies merging. Before the announcement, the two stocks were trading at $42 and $15. Immediately after the announcement, they shifted to $40 and $19, respectively, and it was assumed this is where the arbitrageur entered the spread trades. As was shown previously, there was a profit potential of $1 for every share of Stock B purchased in the trade. But suppose a regulator steps in and says the merger should be blocked for anti-trust or any of a number of other reasons. If the deal gets killed, the best guess is that both stocks move back to where they were before the merger announcement. The arbitrageur would then lose $4 for every share of B purchased and $2 for every share of A sold short.

Occasionally you make more than the projected return. This can occur if a competing bidder enters the arena after the arbitrage spread is established, or if the target plays hard to get, causing the bidder to sweeten their own offer. While such events are always nice, they should not be expected and should never be the motivator for overpaying for the arbitrage spread.

Some hedge funds advertise themselves as event-driven merger arbitrage managers, but they then build portfolios based on their fundamental analysis of what companies might look attractive to potential acquirers. This is basically an exercise in trying to outguess investment bankers about where they will ply their merger craft and at what prices. While this may be a perfectly legitimate way to build a fundamental stock long/short hedge fund, it has nothing to do with arbitrage.

A little closer to the mark are managers who establish spread positions between companies that have been suggested to be discussing merging, but for whom no deal has been announced. This is sometimes called *rumortrage* and it is an attempt to jump the gun over more traditional arbitrage players by establishing a position before the existing spread compresses. This is a tricky business too, as it is not obvious what the right ratio of stocks on the long and short side is, or if there is going to even be a deal ultimately announced.

Mergers are not the only kind of events that attract hedge funds. Bankruptcies and other forms of capital restructurings offer opportunities as well. Distressed investors buy the equity or bonds of companies that have either declared bankruptcy or are likely too. The objective is to evaluate the underlying assets of the firm and identify how the various parts of the capital structure will be affected when the company is liquidated or restructured.

As previously discussed, corporations can have highly complex capital structures ranging from bank loans to secured bonds to unsecured debt and common equity. Under contract and bankruptcy law, each part of the structure has a different priority. Firms that go bankrupt will likely see their equity shareholders severely impaired if not wiped out. The trick in this kind of trading is to identify undervalued assets that get pressured in the heat of the event that will ultimately receive a much greater compensation in any restructuring.

The complexities of this kind of trading should not be underestimated. The legal structures can be multidimensional with different bonds issued over time having varying covenants and rights. Any hedge fund manager in this area needs to enjoy poring over the most detailed documents around the issuance of stock and bonds, and then have the economic skill set to evaluate the underlying assets in a real-time, dynamic market environment.

While the bankruptcy code in the United States is well-established and backed by decades of case law, differences of opinion still prevail especially when large sums of money are involved. The hedge fund manager may think certain bonds deserve full payment, but other creditors of the bankrupt company may disagree and be willing to litigate their claim. This introduces an additional uncertainty to this kind of event trading. There is always the risk that even the best designed position can be torpedoed by an adverse court ruling.

Event managers must constantly evaluate both the legal and market environment for their positions. The time it takes for any bankruptcy case to work its way through the court is a critical element in projecting the ultimate return on the investment. One might ultimately see an adverse court ruling overturned on appeal, but the additional time required to reach a good resolution certainly lowers the return on the investment. Careful event managers try to provide a large margin of error when determining a bid for these types of assets because they understand all the potential uncertainties involved.

This type of investing is done globally. Unfortunately, not all jurisdictions have as well developed bankruptcy codes as the United States, Canada, or Great Britain. The manager should demonstrate expertise in the laws of any jurisdiction of the relevant bonds. Managers should understand that in some countries it is more important whom you know rather than what is the state of the law. This is actually no different in principle than any other kind of investing in these countries, but given the critical role played by the courts in bankruptcy situations the impact in event investing is magnified many times.

Perhaps one of the clearest cases of this involves sovereign debt of Argentina, which selectively defaulted on its obligations in 2001. Several US-based hedge fund managers argued that Argentina had violated its own bond terms and sought out full repayment. These bonds were formally issued in the United States, presumably to give investors greater assurance that the rules of US bankruptcy code would apply. Despite this, for many years after the default Argentina argued that because it is a sovereign country it was not bound by judgments in a US court. More than a dozen years later, it took a change in administrations in Argentina before negotiations progressed and a settlement was reached.

A first cousin of the bankruptcy event managers is the general category of *activist* managers. The vast majority of investors are passive, which does not imply that they are index investors, but says that once a position is established no real attempt is made by the investor to try to influence the course of the company or the investment. This is almost always the default position of investors because they hold such small positions that they have no influence on the board or the senior management of the company they own.

Activist managers are much different. Their first step is to try to acquire a large enough position so that they can influence the selection of board members and the decision process of management. They try to do this as quietly and with as little market impact as possible, because the world is filled with other investors who would like to piggyback upon their good ideas. Once the position is established, the activist manager's behavior changes radically. Not only is the position disclosed but the rationale for it is often publicly discussed.

The manager wants to explain publicly the investment thesis. Why is the firm fundamentally undervalued? What steps should be taken to correct these flaws and "unlock shareholder value"? Sometimes this has to do with complicated issues like an inefficient capital structure for the corporation. Sometimes it is as basic as a belief that the board and senior management are pursuing a flawed strategy and need to be replaced. Whatever the reason, the activist manager seeks to create a public dialogue in order to persuade other shareholders that they should join the cause.

This is quite different from private equity investing. Private equity investors typically seek to make a large enough investment that there is no question that they control the decision process. Activist managers rarely want to control a majority of the voting shares outstanding. It may be practically impossible to acquire complete control and force change, or it may simply be a matter of style where the activist is trying to make a significant profit from a minority position over a shorter time horizon

Activist managers fall under the broad classification of event managers because in many ways they create their own events. It may be a shareholder resolution that gets presented to the annual board meeting. It may be a legal challenge to some corporate activity that the activist believes has hurt existing shareholders. Just like the bankruptcy-oriented event managers, activist managers must be expert in all the legal ins and outs of corporate governance.

Companies sometimes respond quickly and positively to the suggestions of activists. More often they do not. It is rare for a board of directors or CEO to have a sudden epiphany that they have been on the wrong track just because a large, vocal shareholder has decided to take a public position. Activist managers always say that they prefer an amicable resolution of their grievances, but they are not afraid of confrontations.

SEC regulations have evolved over the years to require more and quicker disclosures of positions by all investors that reach meaningful ownership levels. The spirit behind these disclosures is to prevent public investors from being significantly disadvantaged by the trading of people who want to take large long or short positions in a company's stock. These policies may ultimately make it more difficult for activist managers because they may have to reveal their position before they acquire enough stock to have the level of influence they would ultimately desire.

Activist managers have been agents for positive change at many corporations around the world, but this is still an uncertain investment process. Not all countries around the globe are equally friendly to minority shareholders. It is particularly difficult to be an effective activist in a country like Japan where there are both legal and cultural barriers to typical activist activity. It is also the case that not every investor wants to be associated with an aggressive activist manager. Not-for-profit organizations often prefer that their investment managers maintain much quieter public profiles.

The summary comment to conclude the discussion of event-driven hedge funds is that they all have the common theme of basing the investment decision in large part on discrete events as compared to the normal ebb and flow of business. Whether the events are financial, legal, or regulatory in nature, they all are anticipated to create a sudden change in the value of the company. Event managers can have both bullish and bearish opinions. They can run portfolios that have varying degrees of general market exposure.

Simply knowing that a manager is labeled an event hedge fund conveys little meaningful information about what is really going on inside the portfolio. The manager may try to eliminate most direct market exposure in the fund, or may consciously maintain a significant beta. These managers will usually argue that the events on which they base their decision are highly specific to the companies in question, implying that their ability to make money is less correlated to the general market than many other hedge fund approaches. This unfortunately means that there is no standard risk profile that investors can apply when comparing managers in the strategy. Each fund needs to be evaluated in terms of its historical behavior as well as the current portfolio. Lacking that information, a prospective investor is flying blind regarding both risks and opportunities in the fund.

9.7.5 Credit Hedge Funds

Another important fundamental hedge fund strategy includes credit-oriented funds. The easiest way to think about this category is to analogize it with equity long-short strategies. The manager does the same kind of fundamental research on the income statements and balance sheets of a company and then decides whether the bonds of that company are a good investment or not.

Just like with stocks, there are many long-only credit funds that lack the ability of expressing bearish sentiments in any other way than an underweight to a long position. The credit hedge fund manager has the ability to go short either specific credit instruments of those companies expected to do poorly, or credit indexes if the manager believes that the entire market is at risk of trading down.

Just as there are many previously discussed flavors of equity hedge funds, there are different styles within the credit hedge fund category. Some managers specialize in relative value trades much like the market neutral equity hedge fund manager. Bonds are purchased by companies where there is perceived hidden value and then other bonds are sold short where there are concerns about the borrower's ability or willingness to pay.

There is an adage in bond trading that says there are no bad bonds, but there are many bonds you can buy at poor prices. The long short credit hedge fund manager lives this adage every day from both the long and the short sides of the market. If the manager is pursuing a pure relative-value strategy, the longs and shorts come from companies of similar sizes and fundamental credit rating. Again, similar to the equity long short manager, this kind of credit hedge fund may deploy leverage to enhance targeted returns because there is little directional market risk in the basic offsetting long and short positions.

There are other approaches that on the surface look similar but in fact possess different risks. Suppose the long positions in the credit hedge fund are all in below investment grade bonds, but the short positions are in bonds of companies that are highly rated. Presumably this portfolio will create positive carry in the marketplace as the long bonds will have a higher yield than the bonds that are sold short. Through time it has been popular to use leverage on such positions in order to generate consistent cash flow. It is a strategy that appears low risk and dependable as long as not much is happening in the broader credit or equity markets.

Even if the dollar value of the long and short positions are identical, the mismatch in the credit rating creates market exposure. This position is basically wagering that the credit spread between investment grade and junk bonds will shrink, or at least will not expand so far that the interest rate carry will be lost. Like many carry trades this one is susceptible to sudden negative shocks to the equity market. Credit spreads between junk bonds and investment grade bonds invariably expand in market crashes potentially creating meaningful losses in this bond long/short portfolio.

It is incumbent upon the investor to determine how hedged such portfolios really are and what types of market risks remain. Even multiple years of steady returns are no guarantee against disaster. Too many investors flocked into credit relative value funds after they experienced great outcomes from 2003 into 2007. When the credit crisis began in the second half of 2007, the most leveraged examples of these funds quickly went out of business. A large number of even more conservative efforts fell by the wayside in late 2008.

Many of the managers who were involved in these blowups simply re-created themselves in late 2009 or 2010 with new versions of the old strategy. A potential red flag for investors is a credit fund that began in 2010 run by a manager claiming to have 20 or more years of experience. In such circumstances it is perfectly proper to ask for the track records of managers' previous funds. Nobody is required to highlight previous problems in current marketing material, but the manager's total history should never be ignored.

Given the extremely cheap prices and the genuinely benign environment that evolved in the credit markets after the crisis, new funds could post attractive returns without the use of much leverage. That does not mean that leverage won't be employed in the future in an attempt to boost returns. Prospective investors considering these funds should try to determine what limitations are specified in the PPM that might prevent the kind of disasters that were too typical in 2007 and 2008.

Other credit hedge funds are more directional in their orientation. For example, the manager may specialize in identifying particularly difficult to analyze high-yield bond situations. The fundamental research that is done on each company focuses on cash flow needs of the organization and the value of any assets that might be available to satisfy claims in a bankruptcy. Like capital structure arbitrage managers, these credit managers must be expert in the legal aspects of the company's capital structure. The manager wants to find bonds trading at a significant discount to par that either have sufficient projected cash flow to pay off the obligation or good enough asset coverage that there will still be a gain in the event of a default.

This is where understanding priority in the capital structure is vital. The worst mistake this kind of credit hedge fund manager can make is to discover after the fact that the assets they believed would cover their investment are actually being used to pay off lenders who are higher up in the priority scheme. In these cases 100% loss of capital is not unusual.

Since these managers take a net market exposure, they need to be sensitive to both the idiosyncratic features of the bonds they own as well as the general tone of the marketplace. At the beginning of 2009 in the depths of the crisis credit spreads were so wide for high-yield bonds that it was hard to imagine not making a profit on a diversified portfolio. The prices were so low, and the implied yield so high, that there was a great margin of safety against even the most extreme default assumptions. Most directional credit hedge fund managers at this time held very few hedges in their portfolio.

Figure 9.14 the pattern of credit spreads for high-yield bonds for five years before and after the worst of the crisis. It took many quarters for the credit markets to recover from the extremes in the crisis. But as high-yield spreads fell below their long term-average near 600 basis points, hedge fund managers needed to be more concerned about the possibility of reversals. Virtually all of the obvious, easy trades had been snapped up, making careful fundamental research and overall portfolio exposure essential to success.

As the spreads over Treasuries narrowed, the same credit hedge fund managers were more inclined to hedge, sometimes going short specific bonds that were felt to be overvalued, but often by going short OTC bond index derivatives or by purchasing credit default swaps on such indexes. These trades would create an effective short exposure and end up reducing the long directional bets in the fund.

Just as there are many variations on the theme of being an equity long/short hedge fund manager, the range of risks and potential rewards in the credit space is wide. The one common factor, however, is that the managers engage in fundamental analysis of the issuers of the bonds to make their investment decisions. Those that trade bonds from a "top-down" perspective generally fall into another hedge fund category, namely, macro hedge funds.

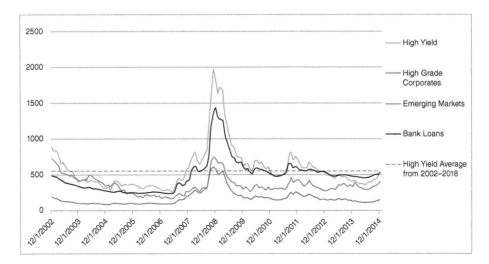

FIGURE 9.14 Credit Spreads 2003–2014
Source: Bloomberg

9.7.6 Macro Hedge Funds

Among the very first hedge fund managers were those that had opinions that ranged well beyond stocks and bonds. Taking a top-down view of the world, they often included currencies and commodities as arrows in their investment quiver. Literally, the world was their oyster, and the only way to categorize them was as *global macro hedge funds*.

Legendary managers like George Soros and Julian Robertson fall into this category. Investors in the Soros' Quantum Fund and Robertson's Tiger Fund trusted their managers to find opportunities across every possible arena, which were usually rewarding. What was completely unpredictable was where the risks would be concentrated, or from what source returns would be found. Currencies, stock indexes, and individual companies all played prominent roles in these macro portfolios at one time or another.

Macro funds can be thought of as the ultimate quest for alpha. Many of the trades in areas like currencies have no fundamental expected market return. Since one day the fund may be long a large amount of equities and then the next day hold nothing, there is no predictable beta that investors can identify beforehand and count on when imagining how such an investment might shift the exposures of their portfolio. The investors trust the general partner and then wait for the results.

If one believes that a manager has demonstrated great trading skill, that is only one ingredient in a successful mix. Is tomorrow's market environment going to be equally conducive to expressing that skill or is the manager in a less favorable spot? An analogy to sports may be effective here. Some tennis players excel on grass and others on clay. Only the truly great champions can adapt their games to all surfaces and prevail. The phrase "Past returns are not an indicator of future results" needs to be taken to heart with macro managers because you do not know what surface they will be playing on next year.

Size has often been a challenge to macro managers. Most will posit that their funds have no meaningful capacity constraints because they deal primarily with the biggest, most liquid markets in the world like currencies, sovereign interest rates, and equity market indexes. This assertion, however, has frequently proven to be wrong. Managers that have had great success managing a modest-sized fund sometimes stumble badly as their assets grow.

Vega was a prominent European-based macro fund that was known for its large directional bets in interest rates. It produced best in class returns for several years and attracted a great deal of LP interest. Started in 1996 with seed capital of $25 million, it grew steadily through 2002 when it was managing around $2 billion in assets. A year later, with an impressive five-year track record under its belt, its AUM had exploded to more than $12 billion from additions by new investors chasing the hot returns.[37]

2005 saw Vega's first ever negative year and 2006 brought on more returns problems. Investors in the Vega Select Opportunity Fund lost more than 25% from the start of 2005 through the third quarter of 2006.[38] Much of the hot money that had flooded into Vega in 2003 decided to leave. By late 2007, assets at the fund were reported to be down near $1 billion.[39] At this point the firm closed to new investors as it restructured, selling a majority interest in its hedge fund investment unit to Spanish Bank BBVA, which rebranded it Proxima Alfa Investments, and began emphasizing other strategies than macro.

History did not cooperate with the restructuring. The financial crisis put pressure on the underlying funds and BBVA. BBVA bought out Vega's ownership share in 2008, but then decided to close Proxima in early 2009 as the bank decided to exit the hedge fund business. The Vega funds continued in a considerably smaller format trying to exploit opportunities in European sovereign debt that arose from the financial crisis.[40]

It is impossible to conclude that Vega's problems were a direct result of its rapid growth and large size, but neither factor could have made its challenges easier. The faster a fund grows the more likely that the growth was due to fast money investors chasing great returns or from funds of funds that are attracted by the apparent lack of capacity constraints. Neither of these groups has a reputation for being patient, long-term investors. When Vega's returns faltered, redemption requests came in droves. Even before the financial crisis, Vega's liquidations had a market impact and hurt returns further, reinforcing the redemption cycle.

The lesson here is not that all large funds should be avoided. It is instead to assure oneself that any-size position is being realistically monitored with an eye on what might happen in a worst-case liquidation scenario. The manager who blithely proclaims that the fund only trades in the world's most liquid markets so there is no effective capacity constraint should be viewed with caution.

---

[37]Zuckerman, G. and MacDonald, A. (2006). Hedge Fund Empire Falters. *The Wall Street Journal.* (17 October).

[38]Patrick, M. and MacDonald, A. (2006). Vega's Funds Are All Losing Money. *The Wall Street Journal.* (6 October).

[39]Hamilton, D. (2007). Vega Hedge Fund Clawing Its Way Back from Losses. *Thomson Reuters.* (16 November).

[40]Spiegel, P., Mackintosh, J., and Kontogiannis, D. (2011). Fund Threatens to Sue over Greek Bond Losses. *Financial Times.* (21 December 21).

Investors should query macro managers about their use of derivatives and how those positions are managed. A typical derivatives position requires only a small percentage of the notional amount of the fund to be posted as a good faith performance bond. Where are the excess funds invested and who controls that money? Beginning in the summer of 2007 and through the crisis, investors learned the hard way that their supposedly safe collateral was an additional source of risk. They further discovered that not all derivatives are equally liquid when it comes to offsetting the exposure.

Macro managers are not always easily placed in a narrow activity box. Some take on large exposures. Others play close to the vest. Positions can be made in equity, currency, interest rate, and commodity markets. That makes it doubly important to receive thorough risk reports that describe the bets being made and the instruments used. When Julian Robertson's Tiger Fund hit big losses in its short positions in Japanese banks, Japanese equities generally and the yen in October 1998, investors should not have been surprised. The fund had clearly communicated its conviction that the Japanese economic story was a troubling one and that it had expressed that conviction in several places in the portfolio. Many investors simply had not been paying attention.

9.7.7 Multistrategy Hedge Funds

Another category of manager that can go anywhere and do almost anything is the *multi-strategy hedge fund*. These funds grew rapidly in popularity at the start of the century when many of them had included non-equity relative value strategies like convertible arbitrage discussed above. As the stock market dramatically sold off from its tech-induced 2000 highs, these multi-strategy funds made positive returns, enhancing their reputation as a solid contributor to portfolio diversification and performance.

The appeal of a multi-strategy fund is simplicity itself. A single general partner collects trading teams that specialize in specific strategies. Capital is allocated to the teams according to where the best opportunities reside. The limited partners of the fund get a diversified hedge fund program that is guided continuously by thoughtful professionals who have skin in the game. Performance fees are based on the total return of the fund, which means no fees are paid if losing strategies offset the winners. There is no double layer of fees that would come with a hedge funds of funds trying to do the same allocation process but with frictions arising from individual fund liquidity terms.

Sometimes the multi-strategy fund does not pretend to be expert in all hedge fund areas. There are multi-strategy credit funds that allocate across different substrategies in that area. There are event oriented and distressed funds that include many varieties of those strategies. Rarely will you see a multi-strategy fund that advertises itself as a complete jack-of-all-trades. It is difficult to imagine a general partner so accomplished in all areas that one multi-strategy fund could replace a broadly diversified portfolio of hedge funds.

Flexibility, lower fees, and opportunistic trading are powerful inducements for LPs to invest in multi-strategy funds. After their success in the early years of the century, their growth was among the best in the industry. This growth may have had something to do with the fact that there were many major stumbles from these firms in the 2008–2009 crisis period that have seriously tarnished the reputation of this group of hedge funds.

Two problems emerged as these funds grew. The larger multi-strategy funds began to recruit specialist teams to cover important sectors. Whether it was convertible arbitrage or event-driven strategies, these teams were attracted to the multi-strategy funds often on the promise of good profit sharing on a rapidly expanding pool of assets. This structure compromised one of the basic principles. If the trading opportunity in a particular strategy was fading, it became hard for the general partner to take capital away from specific teams to reallocate to more promising strategies. Instead the teams searched beyond the core for opportunities. This contributed to the second problem.

The crush of new assets were increasingly deployed in less liquid investments, as there were diminishing alpha opportunities in the liquid markets. This appeared acceptable in the general bull market of 2003–2006, but when stresses started opening up in the second half of 2007, many of these managers were in trouble. Redemption requests grew and quickly became greater than any new investments. General partners were faced with selling their liquid assets and greatly skewing the exposures of the overall portfolio or resorting to other measures.

The step many of them took was to set up side pockets or liquidating trusts. Some offered to distribute the illiquid assets in kind. This step avoided the suggestion that clients could not get their assets when they wanted them, but put most LPs in a horrible position of owning things about which they knew little and for which there were limited markets.

Some of the multi-strategy funds handled the side pocket issue better than others. Nearly everyone acknowledged that it would be completely irresponsible to have a fire sale of these assets at the height of the financial storm, but some tried harder than others to move the liquidation process along as the markets recovered.

These assets were sometimes held in active portfolios of the manager as well as the side pockets and liquidating trusts. This led GPs to place most of their energy and attention to managing the portfolios for the benefit of continuing LPs. Getting money back to departing LPs, many of whom would likely never invest with that manager again, was a much lower priority. The fact that most managers continued to collect management fees of up to 2% on these side pockets did not exactly present a strong incentive to liquidate.

Some managers went even further. In letters to LPs seeking to redeem, they expressed great sympathy for their plight and offered up the solution of buying back these side pocket investments – but at a meaningful discount. The manager was using cash that existed in the fund, or in some cases was trying to use cash raised for "distressed" or "opportunistic" funds after the crisis to support these offers. It is hard not to see these offers as rubbing salt into the wounds of the people who simply wanted their money back.

In most cases the GP of the funds with side pockets was highly unlikely to earn performance fees on these assets as losses had taken the funds well below the high water mark. By buying the assets back at a big discount and putting them in a new fund, not only does the high water mark problem go away, but the manager also has an automatic profit in these assets as he or she marks them not at the purchase price but at their *fair value*. The managers who created the problem with their choice of assets and then by invoking the side pocket provisions of the fund ultimately were trying to extract even more flesh from the departing LPs. It seems that without exception these offers were packaged as attempts to "help the LPs."

A much smaller number of managers really did try to do the right thing and help provide liquidity. One manager, Farallon, organized an auction of side pocket interests where LPs interested in liquidity could offer their shares to a competing group of potential buyers. The potential buyers indicated at what discount they would be willing to buy and the sellers specified the maximum discount they would accept. The auction was organized by a major investment banking firm that received a commission on all transactions, but otherwise did not participate. Farallon announced at the start of the process that they would not bid for any of the outstanding interests.

The bidders in the auction included other fund managers that specialized in buying illiquid investments at a discount to NAV. It is also believed that there were other existing LPs from the fund who had expressed an interest in adding to their holdings if the price was attractive enough. A good number of side-pocketed LPs sold their interest at a meaningful discount, but many others chose to hold onto their investment.

The big advantages of such a process were that it was entirely voluntary, competitive, and mostly free of internal conflicts. Farallon showed that they would spend resources to be responsive to LP calls for additional liquidity, while letting the market determine the clearing price. Many LPs got the liquidity they were seeking. Farallon got the ability to tell the remaining LPs, "You had your chance," while not having to radically change anything about how they were managing the underlying assets.

Ten years after the crisis, the surviving, large multi-strategy hedge funds seem to have largely recovered their assets and several have grown. The story of how these funds attract strong talent and have the ability to shift capital across strategies as market opportunities and risks suggest is no different than it was when they first began to gather assets 20 years earlier. Whether the managers have truly learned from the major blunders they made before the crisis or whether they have simply avoided repeating them in what have been generally benign markets since remains an open question. The size of several of the largest multi-strategy funds remains truly staggering, and it is hard to imagine that they can show the creativity and nimbleness they demonstrated many years ago when their reputations were forged.

9.7.8 Commodity Trading Advisors

Commodity Trading Advisors, or as they are more familiarly called CTAs, are a specialized subset of managers that grew up on "the other side of the fence" from traditional macro managers. CTAs, as their name suggests, first focused on building speculative portfolios of long and short commodity futures positions. CTAs often traded domestic agricultural products, which attracted all kinds of attention from farm interests and ultimately Congress and regulators. This set them apart from their macro hedge fund cousins who largely avoided comprehensive regulation until the Dodd-Frank Act.

Since the late 1970s the *Commodity Futures Trading Commission* (CFTC) has had authority over these traders, which has been largely delegated to the *National Futures Association* (NFA). Rules governing CTAs and the fund managers that organize the pools (*Commodity Pool Operators*, or CPOs) were initiated in 1979 and covered registration, reporting requirements, and a general prohibition against commingling of funds or stealing customer assets. While these are all good and commonsense rules, there is nothing in the regulations that either precisely defines what a CTA does or how much risk they may take to achieve their objectives. This leaves it squarely as the responsibility of the investor to understand the approach any given CTA is using.

Since futures markets expanded into currencies and interest rate products in the 1970s and broad stock index instruments starting in 1982 there is essentially no limit on the range of markets that CTAs now trade. There are some that have tried to remain true to their agricultural or industrial product roots, but given the inherent limited size of these markets, all of the biggest CTAs have embraced trading in the much bigger financial futures pool.

CTAs fall into two broad categories: fundamental and systematic. Fundamental traders attempt to apply the same kinds of supply and demand analyses that most macro hedge funds do in betting on interest rates or stocks and stock indexes. In this case the differences between the two groups are mostly cosmetic. CTAs trade futures and options on futures, while the macro hedge fund manager will trade bonds, stocks, currencies, and, more frequently over the last several years, swaps and other OTC derivatives.

One of the typical tailwinds for CTAs is the interest they collect on excess collateral. Futures contracts require a tiny percentage of the notional value to be posted daily at the clearinghouse as margin. CTAs calibrate their position size to target volatility, and rarely do they push their opportunity to leverage anywhere close to the theoretical maximum allowed. This results in considerable sums of excess collateral that are usually invested in highly conservative investments like short-dated T-bills. Historically this has been a solid source of returns for managers. Unfortunately, the post financial crisis period policy of near-zero interest rates pursued by the Fed has removed this easy source of return for most CTAs.

Systematic traders use analytical programs to try to predict future prices from past prices of the target market and any other prices that CTAs might believe to be relevant in helping to see into the future. Trend-following CTAs are perhaps the most traditional, but there are also reversion traders who try to guess when prices have gone too far in any one direction before turning around. Many of these CTAs take some pride in knowing virtually nothing about the underlying markets, preferring to keep their models "pure" and without any influence from efforts to forecast fundamental factors.[41]

Long gone are the days when a CTA would have a single model to guide them through the workings of many traded markets. More typical today is a battery of models that generate different trading signals. The trend-following models can have different histories and consequently different forecast horizons. The same is true for mean-reversion models. The CTA constantly evaluates which models are working or not in different market environments, bringing on new ones if they perform well in tests and retiring those that seem to have lost their predictive power.

Since CTAs are agnostic about whether they want to be long or short in any given market, it is difficult to conceptualize any kind of beta to the strategy. Money is made or lost entirely on the ability of the traders to profit from other participants in the market. In that sense, CTAs form the purest of alpha strategies.

---

[41]It has been suggested that most systematic CTAs could not distinguish between corn and soybeans as they drove through the Illinois countryside on a summer day. This is probably an exaggeration, at least for CTAs based in Chicago, though many of those might be challenged to distinguish among bulls, steers, and cows.

An additional benefit, which CTAs are quite quick to point out, is that by pursuing a largely alpha strategy, CTAs have among the lowest correlations to other managers across an investor's portfolio. We have seen the benefits of adding less correlated strategies in terms of improving risk-adjusted returns, but we should remember that an investor can only take actual returns to the bank. Any perfectly uncorrelated strategy that earns nothing above the risk-free rate is actually worse than owning T-bills as overall portfolio volatility is higher. CTAs have to demonstrate an alpha ability to justify their inclusion in any portfolio.

Like most investment areas, hope springs eternal. Young traders can establish track records on relatively small capital bases trading in futures. Investors never see the track records that show even mediocre returns. Trader apprenticeships are done in private and only the best results ever get revealed in efforts to raise funds. Evaluating CTAs is really no different than evaluating any other potential manager. If someone shows up at your door with a sparking track record built on a few million dollars and a claim of a superior set of models, ask yourself how this trader discovered something in the data that firms managing billions of dollars and employing scores of researchers missed. There is always the chance that insight and genius really found a different path, but there is always also the chance that the past was a result of pure luck that has a small chance of repeating in the future. Don't let optimism alone trump judgment.

9.7.9   Quantitative Strategies

Funds that employ pure quantitative strategies to dictate their trading decisions are quite similar in principle to systematic CTAs. Models are developed around a basic concept and then applied to historical databases to calibrate the key parameters. Long Term Capital Management (LTCM) generated most of their trading ideas from the principle that relative prices fluctuated around long-term averages with predictable distributions. The modeling driver was to get good estimates of each distribution and then place trades when the risk/reward ratio was skewed enough in their favor.

Stable and predictable distributions are often at the heart of quantitative strategies. The fund manager believes that the past price behavior, often observed for many years, is a genuine guide to the future. Given that assumption, meaningful deviations away from what the model would predict are viewed as trading opportunities. As long as the system operates at least somewhat consistently with the predicted model, the trading behavior is reinforced with profits.

Some managers in this area operate with a reasonable degree of transparency, offering regular risk exposure and performance attribution reports. But many others do not. It is not completely paranoid for such managers to fear reverse engineering of their intellectual property. After all, the barriers to entry to such trading are relatively low. One needs data, high-speed processors, and a facility with advanced mathematics and statistics. The human capital may not be commonplace, but most graduates from technical programs in math and sciences have all of the requisite skills needed to construct and test the models. At last glimpse, the pay scale for successful fund managers far exceeded that of NASA physicists, leading to a fairly large supply of potential workers willing to swap the hard sciences for the soft.

The desire for secrecy has led to a number of fund complexes that can be accurately called *black boxes*. The creators of the models are loath to describe even their basics, lest competitors discover their secret sauce and trade away their edge. This leaves potential investors with a considerable dilemma. While the historical track record is observable, there is no way to determine what risks were taken to establish it. Furthermore, there is no way to know whether the process that produced profits in the past is still in operation or is being used with the same leverage or underlying liquidity.

This is the ultimate "Trust me" situation. The successful quantitative manager almost always has impeccable credentials as a brilliant individual or team. Multiple advanced degrees go a long way toward giving credibility to a history of money making. But it doesn't always work out as planned.

LTCM is perhaps the starkest example of this. Started in 1994 by John Meriwether with a stellar team of partners including two Nobel Prize winners, the firm took quantitative models of arbitrage theory to the extreme. They identified mispriced securities, established positions to minimize general market risks, and then applied leverage to achieve their targeted returns. In the early years the fund averaged 40% returns annually, but it was never entirely revealed to investors what was inside the black box.

By 1998 their success had attracted all kinds of imitators, sometimes from the proprietary trading desks of the prime brokers that worked for LTCM. These organizations appeared not to be satisfied by the considerable revenues generated by the huge volumes of trading from LTCM. In many cases these firms piggybacked on the hedge fund's general approach if not the specific trades. The result was an environment where wide spreads were more difficult to find. Given the quantitative risk measures of the day signaled low volatility, leverage was added to reach target rates of return.

In retrospect the outcome was easy to anticipate. In a market of crowded trades, the first adverse price moves create demands for more collateral. If excess capital is not in ample supply, the only alternative is to try to liquidate positions.[42] In LTCM's case, many of the trades had become almost the exclusive domain of quantitative traders and their imitators. Similar to the discussion of bubble markets in Chapter 8, there were no logical traders willing to take these positions at any prices remotely close to the current marks. Small losses quickly grew to massive ones. LTCM was effectively out of business by the end of 1998.

While LTCM's models were built by some of the smartest people in the industry, they were ultimately faulty in that they had no meaningful provision for measuring limitations due to illiquidity. It turns out that such parameters are incredibly difficult to estimate, especially when all of the previous data are drawn from periods when liquidity caused no concerns. Like many financial market models, LTCMs worked until they did not. But unlike T.S. Eliot's world, this one ended with a bang and not a whimper.

This experience is not an indictment against all quantitative strategies. It is, however, a cautionary tale about what investors potentially face when they invest in a

---

[42]In LTCM's case they began to recognize that many of their trades were capital constrained a year or so before their crisis. Their solution was to largely return outside investor money after these investors had enjoyed a strong three-year run (and paid LTCM handsome fees). Many investors begged to be able to retain their investment, but they were rebuffed. Several months later when LTCM needed capital to support their positions, these same investors were contacted about reinvesting. Perhaps not surprisingly there were few new funds forthcoming from this group.

mechanical program that they have no ability to evaluate beforehand. Few investors in hedge funds have deep backgrounds in risk management or trading, but there are more than a few who might have disagreed with the LTCM approach if they had been given the opportunity to critique it.

Instead, these investors were given a choice. Take it or leave it based on the partners' reputations. In other words, "Trust us." Lots of investors trusted the partners and the lucky ones cashed out when LTCM generally returned outside capital. Others rejected the initial invitation and never joined the party. There were high fees. There was a long lockup. But most importantly LTCM was among the blackest of black boxes. Losing money when you know the risks you are taking is one thing. Losing it in the dark because you have blind faith is quite another.

It is true that fortunes have been made following highly quantitative approaches, but current investors don't profit from the histories of fund managers like David Shaw or James Simon. As discussed many times in this book, markets are dynamic, adjusting to how people trade in them. An algorithm that might have identified an inefficiency in stock index prices in 1985 no longer works because so many traders have found it and acted accordingly.

One of the genuine joys of financial markets is that there is so much data to analyze and no shortage of smart people and machines to do the work. Today's quantitative strategies, however, are often highly dependent upon receiving news or trading data milliseconds before competitors. In these instances quantitative trading is analogous to thermonuclear war. Coming in second means you have lost. Great sums of money, energy, and time can be spent pursuing models and trades that ultimately are inferior to those of the quant shop down the street.

This leaves investors in something of a quandary. There are more than a few high-profile success stories about quantitative strategies that proved highly profitable over many years. There have also been more than a handful of spectacular failures. The hundreds of mediocre to worse managers that have tried the space and failed never find their way into the limelight. Any investor trying to look forward must navigate in virtual darkness. There is no easy path.

It seems there will always be a ready group of investors poised to be sold the latest quantitative story. It is not clear how they set their expectations or gauge whether they are getting enough reward for the risks being assumed. Even if they experience some success, there is no assurance that any edge won't be discovered by other traders and be competed away. Since theory says that all risk-free trades should ultimately earn the risk-free rate, it is imperative to be associated with true and consistent innovators.

Since most investors are not given the tools or enough information to differentiate an innovator from an also-ran, any capital allocated to quantitative strategies comes from investments where there is much more transparency. Because of these challenges, some investors choose to avoid the area altogether. There is too much competition for ideas and capital in the space to expect outsized returns for acceptable levels of risk. And the costs of being wrong can be huge.

9.7.10 Insurance and Litigation Funds

In Section 9.2.10 of this chapter, Cat Bonds were described as a financial structure designed to expand the sources of reinsurance capital. Shortly after these instruments began to get traction in the marketplace, dedicated insurance hedge funds also appeared. The chart below shows how insurance oriented funds have grown from almost nothing in 2000 to a respectable subsector of the market.

Cat Bond funds have certainly benefited from the desire for uncorrelated assets. Figure 9.15 shows the growth of the industry since its infant days in 2000. Each color is a different fund. Many shade firms have entered the space. A few have already left. 2019 marked the first year of decline of AUM in two decades, partially from losses and partially from redemptions. Investors seeking diversifying assets have discovered that investments that should logically be uncorrelated may not in reality act independently. The other lesson is that less correlated does not mean adequate return for the risk.

The problem with Cat Bonds for most investors is that they lack the skills necessary to evaluate the myriad of insurance risks embedded in them and to answer the question whether the implicit premiums being paid for the reinsurance is sufficient given the actuarial risks. The solution has been the creation of dedicated insurance funds where the portfolio manager possesses this specific human capital, which is shared with LP investors for a price.

This segment of the industry is growing rapidly for two reasons. The first was the performance of most insurance funds through the Lehman Brothers bankruptcy triggered financial crisis. There were losses in many of these funds, but they were minor relative to equity funds or credit hedge funds that deployed meaningful leverage. The second reason was the appeal of adding hedge fund managers that should have limited correlation to most of the market factors that dominate modern portfolios. The fact that this diversification benefit seemed to be proven in the crisis reinforced the theoretical argument long advanced by the funds' advocates.

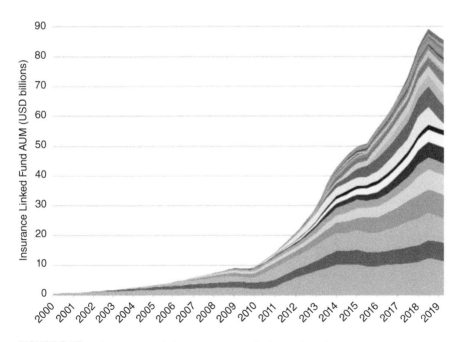

FIGURE 9.15 The Growth of the Insurance Linked Fund Market 2000–2019
Source: Adam Alvarez

The portfolios are not terribly complicated, looking much like any other fixed income hedge fund portfolio. Some funds are primarily long, but reserve the right to hedge out interest rate and other risks. Cat Bonds are not the easiest securities to borrow so it is more difficult to construct an active long/short portfolio than a regular equity or fixed income hedge fund. Leverage can be used, and when comparing different funds it is essential to understand gross and net positions.

The other key factor to be considered is the quality of the Cat Bonds the fund is buying. There are different loss expectations across Cat Bonds, with the higher loss bonds carrying higher yields. This is analogous to credit quality across corporate bonds. One manager may specialize in investment grade corporates in building their portfolio, while another manager may only own junk bonds. Similarly one may dial up or down the expected loss profiles for the underlying holdings in Cat Bonds.

The insurance funds are not constrained only to buying Cat Bonds. Some of them write fully collateralized reinsurance. This is effectively the same exposure and having the ability to place different structures within the fund allows the portfolio manager to maximize the opportunities available to it. The downside of not using Cat Bonds is that direct insurance contracts don't offer the same liquidity, posing additional challenges whenever redemptions are requested.

An $80 billion market is nothing to sneeze at, but in the grand scheme of investments, it is still fairly small potatoes. Financial disruptions in late 2008 and 2009, as well as concern about the Eurozone in 2012, had ripple effects into the Cat Bond market. If the insurance-linked fund market continues on its current path and reaches several hundred billion dollars, these linkages will only grow, diminishing somewhat the fundamental assertion that this type of investing is uncorrelated with stocks and bonds. It also remains to be seen how Hurricanes Harvey, Irma, and Maria in the devastating 2017 season will impact returns and investor expectations going forward. It is likely that future premiums received will be higher at least for a while because of these losses, but if large amounts of capital move into the space, reinsurance rates will compress again.

Another relatively recent type of hedge fund that claims uncorrelated status invests in litigation efforts. The funds finance, either in part or in total, legal suits in exchange for a percentage of any recovery awarded to the plaintiffs. This is a small segment of the hedge fund market but it is growing because people believe that tort claims, and awards, can produce large payoffs that have no connection to either the stock or bond markets.

Traditionally tort claims in the United States are pursued through a partnership between an attorney and an aggrieved party. The law firm finances its own expenses as it pursues the case, and the plaintiffs agree to compensate the attorney a meaningful percentage of the reward they receive through trial or settlement. If the plaintiff loses the case, the law firm typically eats the expenses.

Litigation funds were created to disperse this risk across a broader group. They are not dissimilar in spirit to venture capital partnerships in their bimodal payoff patterns. The general partner of the fund identifies promising areas of litigation and enters into partnerships with the attorneys and the plaintiffs. As the case develops, fund capital is used to pay for the ongoing expenses like depositions, expert witnesses, and investigations. If the case has merit in the eyes of the court, the fund investors benefit from a meaningful share of the total reward. If the plaintiffs lose, the LPs lose 100% of their investment devoted to that effort.

While it is easy to see how such activity should be basically uncorrelated with stocks and bonds, it is a challenging business to estimate what the expected returns or variances of those returns should be. This is not like a bond portfolio where you have a probability of default based on the credit worthiness of the issuers, and then you can work backward to determine the most you can pay to achieve a target yield. Instead there are only guesses about the likelihood of success in the case and the subsequent reward. The variance around any of these estimates is large.

One should also ask whether there are bigger issues at both the micro and macro levels. Given that the current system of torts has worked pretty well with lawyers financing their own efforts, what problem are these litigation hedge funds solving? One might guess that the best lawyers pursuing the most solid cases would have no need for outside capital. This might lead to the funds backing younger, less well-founded lawyers, who have a lower probability of success. This is the micro question.

The macro issue relates to what kind and how much litigation is actually useful. If lawyers are adept at self-funding the best cases, does the existence of capital from litigation funds encourage them to pursue weaker cases? After all, if the litigation produces no return to the plaintiff, the law firm has still been compensated, at least partially. Litigation fund resources may allow firms to keep extra lawyers on staff on an as-needed basis that would never be employed if all of the expenses were shouldered by the law firm.

This also raises the question whether such fund investments encourage litigation that would not otherwise be pursued. LPs in such hedge funds need to consider whether they want to encourage more activity in an area that might not be underserved from society's perspective. There is no way litigation financing can be viewed in the same light as other equity investing. Nothing new is being created here except possibly more lawyer jobs and a different division of an existing pie.

There are, however, some comparisons to venture capital that might apply. The size of the capital pool determines the quality of the marginal investment. If more and more assets are dedicated to litigation hedge funds, they will find something to do. This could mean funding less promising cases both in terms of probability of success and in terms of size of the ultimate reward. The end result may be a plus for the fraternity of tort lawyers, but not such a great return for the LPs of the funds.

The only serious defense against this kind of outcome comes from only participating with GPs that have fund terms that protect the LPs. A hurdle rate before any GP performance fee gets paid could offer some assurances. Demanding that the GP provide a meaningful percentage of the total investment corpus at the same terms as the LPs is another protection. Other terms could similarly be devised. Given the nature of the payouts from the underlying investments, aligning the interest of the GP with the LPs is as important here as it is anywhere in the investment world.

9.7.11 Risk Parity Funds

With some regularity the fund management industry reveals a new category of products that is hailed as a major innovation in portfolio management. History suggests that most of these innovations are not all that profound, with a few finding their way ultimately into the mainstream while many others fall by the wayside.

Risk parity funds are among the later entries on the list of innovations and they have attracted hundreds of billions of dollars in investments. Ray Dalio, founder of

Bridgewater Associates, is largely credited as the pioneer in this area, being one of the first institutional money managers to target risk at the portfolio level. Bridgewater has grown to more than $150 billion in AUM with products that work to separate alpha and beta, and then combine investments in ways that emphasize the long-term risk profile of the allocations.

Bridgewater's flagship fund is called Pure Alpha and it has been an important force in the relative value hedge fund arena for many years. In the middle part of the 1990s Bridgewater's team applied the principles that have become broadly known as risk parity to a portfolio of Mr. Dalio's personal trust assets. It was dubbed the All Weather Portfolio.[43]

The key feature of the risk parity approach is to identify how different assets behave in different economic and market environments. The primary variables are expectations about economic growth and inflation. Risk parity starts by sorting out which investments do well or poorly in each environment, rising or falling growth, and accelerating or declining inflation.

TIPS and other inflation-linked bonds, for example, do well historically either when inflation is rising above expectations and the inflation payout is growing or when the economy is slowing down and real interest rates are falling. So TIPS play a role in either an "inflation on" or "growth off" scenario. Traditional bonds work in "inflation off" and "growth off" worlds. Equities, commodities, and various types of credit are similarly sorted.

Anyone who had a crystal ball and knew before anyone else in the market where growth and inflation were going would concentrate their portfolio in the asset groups that do well and avoid those investments that do poorly. Of course, nobody has that crystal ball, so risk parity says you should own all of these assets to make sure part of your portfolio will be doing well no matter what the outcome. Since the average return of all the investments is expected to be greater than holding cash, you will make money over time with considerably less volatility than a traditional, equity-dominated portfolio.

The broad outline above still doesn't provide much guidance as to how much should be invested in each bucket. Putting equal dollars to work in every category would skew the risks badly. Since equities are typically more volatile than bonds, an equal dollar-weighted portfolio of investments would likely lose more in equity downturns than could be offset by investments that are expected to do well. The answer comes from risk weights.

Each of the four potential states of the world is allocated 25% of the risk budget. Hence the term, *risk parity*. This might mean that you need $4 of TIPS for every $1 in domestic equity in order to equalize the projected risks. The calculations behind the estimation of risk are quite complex, but are fundamentally grounded in the same kind of expected return, standard deviation and correlation analysis that lies at the heart of modern portfolio theory.

Bridgewater began broadly talking about this approach after the stock market decline in 2000–2002, signing up its first institutional investor in 2003. The field became more crowded as several other fund managers brought products forward in the middle

---

[43]Dalio, R. (2010). Engineering Targeted Returns and Risks. Bridgewater Associates web page, https://www.bwater.com/ViewDocument.aspx?f=40.

part of the decade. These managers often tinkered with the labels and composition of the risk buckets, but the principles were largely similar.[44] The managers often showed their simulated results against a 60/40 blend of S&P 500 and the Barclays Aggregate Bond Index to show how this traditional blend could be beaten with less volatility.

The timing was impeccable for the launch, but as is usually the case the adoption rate by investors was slow. By the end of 2008 there was less than $75 million invested in all risk parity mutual funds combined.[45] The risk parity funds did ok as the stock market moved steadily upward after 2002, but they underperformed indexes like the S&P 500. When the stock market peaked in October 2007, the sun really began to shine on the approach.

Throughout the turbulent months from late 2007 to early 2008, the fixed income assets and commodity exposures held by risk parity funds offered a major cushion to the eroding stock market. When commodities tumbled in the second half of 2018, followed by the collapse in most risk assets after the Lehman bankruptcy, it was the major allocation to traditional Treasury bonds and TIPS that saved the day. Risk parity funds, like hedge funds generally in 2001–2002, had delivered on their promise.

This performance was fueled in part by the fact that the bond allocations were all leveraged up so that their risk was equal to that of the unleveraged stock portfolio. This is one of the hallmark features of risk parity. Once again, financial engineers had dipped into modern portfolio theory and found no issue with applying leverage in what appeared to be a relatively safe set of assets.

By now, everyone should know the next lines of the story. After the investment outperformance came a big marketing push. The mystery of the ages had been solved. Major pension plans and sovereign funds flooded into the market and assets in risk parity products offered by a wide range of blue chip companies grew by leaps and bounds. According to some estimates, there was more than $15 billion in risk parity mutual funds, and almost $400 billion dedicated to the strategy by late 2015.[46] Since the definition of these funds is less precise than for mutual funds or ETFs, there is no central clearinghouse of information like the Investment Company Institute to monitor the sector consistently.

The money flowing into these funds did not come from cash but in part from traditional, equity-oriented portfolio allocations. As such, they represented more of a rearrangement of assets than a wholesale net inflow. On average, however, stocks were likely sold and both traditional bonds and inflation-linked bonds were purchased in size. Because of the leverage inside the fund, a billion dollars in capital meant buying a multiple of that in both traditional bonds and TIPS.

One of the hallmark features of risk parity funds is their belief in the long-term outperformance of all of the asset classes versus cash. History is squarely behind this

---

[44]AQR's Risk Parity Fund identifies four risk categories: equity risk, nominal interest rate risk, inflation risk, and credit/currency risk. These differ somewhat from Bridgewater's classifications, but like most of the risk parity offerings, they generally rhyme in terms of assets represented in the total portfolio. Source: AQR Risk Parity Fund Prospectus.

[45]Corkery, M., Cui, C., and Grind, K. (2013). Fashionable "Risk Parity" Funds Hit Hard. *The Wall Street Journal*. (27 June).

[46]Sender, H. and Wigglesworth, R. (2015). Investing: Whatever the Weather? *Financial Times*. (23 August).

belief, but history was also highly supportive of the popular notion of the 1990s that if you held stocks long enough they *always* were the superior investment option. Risk parity funds continued to load up on TIPS with explicit negative real interest rates and traditional bonds with implicit negative real interest rates because the models made allocations according to expected risk. Expected return is not a factor in the decision process.

When Ben Bernanke started talking in May 2013 about the eventual end of quantitative easing, the best days for risk parity seemed like a distant memory. Stock markets fell. Commodities tumbled. Both traditional bonds and TIPS suffered significant losses as real interest rates climbed without any real improvement in the underlying economy. Once again investors were reminded that correlations offer a glimpse at how assets usually behave together, but offer no assurance about how they will behave at any given point in time.

Instead of meaningfully outperforming a declining equity market, risk parity funds lost as much as equities, if not more. 2013 was a particularly tough year for the strategy, with some funds actually losing money as the S&P 500 climbed 32.4% and the 60/40 blend of S&P 500 and the Barclays Aggregate bond index rising 16.8%. In hindsight it was the leveraged bond and TIPS bets in an environment of rising real interest rates that did the most damage for the year. Since rates ended the year at low levels by any objective historical standard, questions remained whether Risk Parity was really an all-weather strategy or one that could do well only in a world of secularly declining interest rates.

As of this writing, Risk Parity is a strategy that is still collecting assets. To date it seems that Bridgewater's efforts have achieved long-term success against their stated objectives, but even that record is tarnished by the fact that the best years were at the beginning when there was either no or very little customer money in the fund. It remains to be seen whether actual performance catches up to the simulated history most of these funds used to build their portfolios. AQR, another major provider of Risk Parity funds, dropped the label from their main mutual fund product in January 2019, while also saying they were tweaking the models behind the portfolio.

If the struggles continue, you can expect the risk parity managers to begin emphasizing their Sharpe Ratios over their actual returns. "We didn't make as much money as the 60/40 benchmark, but we did it with better risk characteristics." Clients will only be patient with this approach for a while. Unless the investor is willing to add explicit leverage to an investment program that already uses a healthy dose of embedded leverage, a high Sharpe Ratio doesn't do that investor any good. Most institutional and individual investors will not leverage their portfolios, and will likely come to realize that if they want to reach their return objectives they will return to more traditionally structured portfolios and live with the extra short-term volatility. At the end of the day expected returns really do matter.

9.7.12 Replication Funds

Replication hedge funds arrived on the scene when academics studying primarily long/short equity hedge funds began decomposing the exposures inside the funds. They found that hedge fund returns are not often the result of pure genius of the managers, but are built up from various identifiable market betas with a bit of alpha added on top. For example, a simple long short fund that was on average100% gross long and 40% gross short large-cap US stocks might be replicated by S&P 500 stock index futures in a notional amount of 60% of the capital committed. The expenses associated with the basic replication should be a fraction of the typical fees charged by hedge funds.

The example above is simplistic and naive. The hedge funds that one might want to try to replicate may make nuanced bets on cap size, credit spreads, movements of interest rates and currencies. What the replicator does, therefore, is perform regression analysis to identify the significant market contributors to performance. The process then builds a synthetic portfolio of exposures, usually employing exchange and OTC derivatives backed by very safe collateral like T-bills. This replicated portfolio captures the average asset allocation exposures of the fund being copied and if the derivatives perform as expected, the return and risk experience should be comparable.

It is important to understand what can and cannot be accomplished through replication. If one replicates stock exposure through index derivatives, there is no possibility for an alpha from superior security selection. If the active hedge fund manager moves into new areas or makes adjustments to portfolios that are not reflective of the fund's history, the replication fund will not immediately be able to identify and size the appropriate exposures. Many of the things one pays an active manager to do cannot be replicated. But it is the basic premise of replication that the vast savings in fees will more than make up for any loss of alpha advantage the hedge fund manager creates.

Replication funds try to keep as current as the available hedge fund data allows. If there are big shifts in net exposures, or the allocation of stocks versus bonds, the replication funds may lag the active managers. Depending on how quickly the actual funds change their underlying holdings, this may be more or less of a problem for the replicator.

The experience with replication hedge funds has been mixed, at best. One might believe that there should be an inexpensive, liquid alternative available to the costly and illiquid hedge fund industry. After all, stock index funds showed how much of the active long-only stock picking world could be replicated with passive products. With a meaningful fee advantage, passive index investing often provides most of the net benefits of many active managers.

Hedge funds, it turns out, are a tougher nut to crack. Unlike a long equity fund that routinely holds little cash, even the simplest long/short equity funds have gross and net exposures that can move around quite a bit. Replicating the last reported beta and factor exposures is like driving a car along a curvy road while only looking in the rear view mirror. There's a very good chance that where you think you ought to steer takes you right off the road.

Attempts to replicate more complicated strategies like credit long/short funds get even more complicated. The estimated factors are sometimes implicit and less dependable. For example, it is logical that credit spreads should get wider in a declining stock market, but not every 5% move in equities has the same impact on spreads. This means there is more noise around the replicating factors, which increases the chance that the replication portfolio will miss the mark.

The most promising area of hedge fund replication is likely to be found in mimicking broad-based hedge fund indexes. As the indexes aggregate across managers and styles, one is less likely to see sudden shifts in exposures or key investment factors. This makes the replication process more dependable, but leaves one important question unanswered. Why do you want to make an investment copying an area that includes many mediocre or worse managers and strategies, and are never likely to be worth the fees they charge?

9.7.13 Volatility Funds

Volatility is a key parameter in sizing various positions in a risk parity fund but it is little more. Those funds typically have no opinion on whether markets are becoming more or less choppy, and volatility is not viewed as a source of return. The exact opposite is true for volatility-based hedge funds. These are trading vehicles that try to use the increasingly popular volatility measures like VIX to construct trades, just like an energy-oriented CTA uses the price of crude oil.

Traded volatility may be the common element across these funds but the way it is used can vary widely, leading to very different risk profiles. In general, these funds fall into one of three broad buckets: long vol funds to provide protection against market drops, volatility relative value strategies, and short vol funds to collect premiums from time decay.

All volatility-based funds share an evolutionary chain going back to the earliest option market makers. The principles of time decay were introduced in Chapter 3 and will be expanded on in Chapter 10, Derivatives, but for this discussion all that is required is the understanding that the buyer of an option pays a premium to the seller, and the time value of that premium goes down as the option approaches its expiration date.

Long vol funds generally consist of purchased options on stock indexes like the S&P 500 or long positions in VIX futures. Both experience time decay and an expected loss of value. The trade-off for this is the chance that there will be a big payoff if there is a severe market correction. These funds are often sold to investors that have already experienced a large run-up in the value of their equity holdings as a form of insurance.

The principle of insurance is sound but how much you pay for premiums matters. After long bull markets, insurance against pullbacks is rarely cheap and such funds in their simplest form may have an annual expected loss of 2–7%. Any manager that claims to offer insurance and also suggests they will have a positive return either is being selective as to when insurance is being purchased or is actually more of a trading fund that hopes to be in a positive insured posture if a bad market event happens. In either case, the premise of the fund being a reliable hedge should be questioned as nobody routinely gets paid to have insurance.

Relative value managers can specialize in volatility. Some sell options on individual stocks that display high volatility while buying options on indexes, which by virtue of their portfolio characteristics have lower implied volatilities. In theory, such trades should be profitable in both up and down markets. How profitable depends on how much capital is devoted to these trades in total. As more and more capital has been devoted to hedge funds in general, this group of managers has seen their AUMs grow, driving down returns for any fund not employing large amounts of leverage. When evaluating these managers, all of the usual questions about leverage and liquidity apply.

The last group of volatility managers, those that write options or sell volatility futures, thrive in periods when markets are relatively calm and measured volatility is falling. They have the mirror image return pattern of the first group. This was first discussed in Chapter 6 as one of several flawed approaches to adding alpha consistently. These funds may have long periods of steady returns as the options they write expire worthless. Such a pattern can fool potential investors into believing there is little risk in the strategy. When a market correction occurs, however, losses considerably greater than the aggregate stream of previous returns can happen. Being short volatility can be a valid strategy but only as long as the investor understands the likelihood of an outsized loss along the way. These funds are generally not appropriate for investors primarily trying to preserve capital.

9.7.14 Hedge Mutual Funds and Liquid Alternatives

Consider the following progression for the hedge fund industry:

1. Start a difficult and limited trading program designed to meet the needs of sophisticated investors, and charge a premium fee for it.
2. Perform spectacularly in a challenging equity environment like 2001–2002, laying the foundation for impressive comparative returns histories, which leads to the gathering of new investors and many more assets.
3. Perform well below expectations and past history with losses through a crisis like 2008–2009, but still beat equities by enough of a margin so that the average risk-adjusted returns can still be painted in a reasonable light.
4. Find a new market to sell the story to.

It was only logical that the industry should try to evolve in the direction of making hedge fund strategies available to the masses. The entire premise of hedge funds being only lightly regulated for decades was that they were complicated investments sold only to sophisticated investors without general advertising or solicitation. It took a long time and the history outlined above, but hedge funds grew from essentially a footnote to the investment industry in the 1980s to a $2 trillion industry before the 2008 crisis. After declining by more than a third, recovery was swift, with assets in the $3.0 trillion neighborhood less than a decade later. Still, hedge fund managers responsible for tens of billions of dollars were not satisfied and saw a tremendous, untapped market among less sophisticated investors. *Hedge fund mutual funds*, also known as *liquid alternatives,* were born.

The hedge fund managers looking to expand into mutual funds play on the emotional tug-of-war experienced by most investors that want the higher returns the stock market can provide while hating the volatility. After a couple of equity market drubbings in less than a decade, they respond positively to terms like *downside protection*. Throw in zero risk-free interest rates and even the most mediocre hedge fund performance can begin to look appealing by comparison.

The biggest problem in this business evolution is that the regulations surrounding '40 Act mutual funds are not always compatible with the trading strategies and instruments that distinguish the best hedge funds. There are liquidity and leverage restrictions that are designed to ensure that the funds will be able to strike a daily NAV and that investors will be able to easily invest in or redeem from open-ended funds. Both of these restrictions potentially affect what parts of any hedge fund can find their way into the hedge mutual fund product.

The portfolio managers attack this problem two ways. First, they modify the underlying portfolio holdings, moving to more liquid securities and employing less leverage. This eliminates many of the true arbitrage strategies that are designed to exploit small mispricings between pairs of investment options. It also has the effect of creating lower octane portfolios than the hedge funds that may have created the manager's attractive records.

The second approach is to use derivatives that have payoff patterns that implicitly create leverage. This is a great example of the technology of investments outpacing the regulations meant to set boundaries. In general a '40 Act mutual fund is prohibited from issuing bonds or other forms of debentures against the assets in the fund. They are, however, allowed to borrow from a bank to create leverage as long as there is at least $3 of collateral for every dollar of borrowing. This translates into a maximum leverage ratio of 1.33 times the equity assets of the fund. Most fund managers are loath to use maximum leverage since any market setback would induce forced selling to get back to the limit. Instead they might go to 1.2x to 1.25x, giving them some latitude within the limits.

But that is explicit leverage. Suppose the mutual fund invests exclusively across an array of 3x ETFs. That would be a strange business model, but it is certainly possible. By buying a dollar of ETFs for every dollar of capital, the fund could argue that it was unlevered, though the market octane of the investments would say otherwise. Leveraged ETFs are just one of literally an endless array of structures and derivatives that can create contractual leverage, yet the SEC regulations are largely silent on this topic.

It is not because the SEC is unaware of the issue. In April 2009, Andrew J. Donohue, Director of the SEC's Division of Investment Management, gave a speech before the Spring meeting of the American Bar Association entitled "Investment Company Act of 1940: Regulatory Gap between Paradigm and Reality?"[47] In it he outlined many of the concerns the SEC staff had about how the law governing '40 Act funds had not kept pace with investment reality. This talk was given in the direct aftermath of one of the worst financial crises in US history, a time when one might think a call to action would be heard. Years later, nothing fundamental has changed.

Most of the concerns Donohue expressed focused not on whether actual investment practice was consistent with the spirit of allowed leverage in the '40 Act. Instead, he acknowledged that there were gaps, and then spent most of the address questioning whether current disclosures were complete or clear enough for investors to make informed choices.

Hedge mutual funds are relatively young and because of the distinct lack of precise guidelines pose great challenges for the potential investor. What is the economic leverage? Are the underlying holdings liquid enough to comfortably fit into a daily liquidity vehicle? Is the portfolio positioning really similar to the manager's limited partnership hedge fund, if there is one? If there is a problem in the market, will trading across a manager's mutual fund and partnership holdings be done consistently and fairly? The best place to start looking for answers to these questions is the manager's mutual fund literature.

The SEC's concerns about disclosure are well placed as the quality of hedge fund mutual fund communications can vary quite a bit. The best companies not only give performance and some modest risk data, but list the strategy exposures and the

---

[47]Donohue, A.J. (2009). Investment Company Act of 1940: Regulatory Gap between Paradigm and Reality? Speech given before the Spring meeting of the American Bar Association in Vancouver, Canada (17 April 2009).

largest positions both long and short. There are multiple examples of good reports available, but one of the clearest is provided by the MainStay Marketfield Fund, a New York Life product.[48]

Using their 30 June 2013 semiannual report as an example, a potential investor would learn that the predominantly long/short global equity fund was positioned 79% long, 26% short, for a net exposure of 53%, which was slightly below its historical average of 58%. All of the securities held, both long and short, are listed with their weights in the portfolio. One also learned that there was a Chinese currency hedge covering approximately 14% of the portfolio's value executed with purchased options. In addition, part of the short strategy was being executed with purchased puts against individual securities and ETFs. They gave a detailed breakdown of the pricing of the book, showing that only the CNY/USD options are Level III securities, priced outside a liquid market. All other instruments in the portfolio are Level I, meaning that there are reliable market determined prices regularly available.

The manager went on to describe performance attribution over the reporting period and to explain what themes drove current portfolio positioning. This was all done in basic English that even non-lawyers or accountants could understand. It was only in the last 10 pages, which comprise the notes to the unaudited financial statements, that the lawyers take over, but even there one sensed a desire to communicate rather than just meet the letter of the disclosure requirements. It is a model of reporting that is all too rare.

Not all mutual funds, whether they advertise themselves or not as alternative funds, are anywhere near this candid. In fact, some of the world's largest mutual funds in traditional areas like fixed income seem to try hard to avoid mentioning in their public communications that they use leverage or the occasional short positions. If the investor really wants to know what is going on, the only complete source are the *SEC EDGAR filings*.[49] These reports, which are mandated by the SEC every six months, are a complete listing of the portfolio holdings. They do not need to be organized in a user-friendly fashion, nor are they annotated to describe why positions are in a portfolio or whether they work or not. If anyone thinks they are investing in a vanilla bond fund, they might be surprised to find themselves in what could be considered a low-octane fixed income hedge fund. Such managers have chosen to not emphasize these features of their approach, perhaps out of fear that investors might not want leverage and derivatives in their fund.

Yet there clearly is a market for this kind of product, even accurately labeled. The MainStay Marketfield Fund began in the summer of 2007, which was hardly the most auspicious starting point for any investment activity other than buying US Treasuries. By the end of 2013, it had grown to almost $20 billion in AUM, enjoying the benefits of a Morningstar five-star rating.[50] It managed to lose less than the market in its early history as the financial meltdown occurred, but underperformed the broad US stock market during the big rebounds after.

---

[48]MainStay Marketfield Fund Prospectus and Reports. https://www.nylinvestments.com/mainstay/products-and-performance/MainStay-Marketfield-Fund.

[49]http://www.sec.gov/edgar/searchedgar/mutualsearch.html is the link to begin searching the EDGAR database for mutual fund filings.

[50]MainStay Marketfield Fund Prospectus. (10 April 2017).

All this comes at a price. All share classes have a basic management fee of 1.4%. There are numerous other fees charged to the fund including dividend expenses and brokers fees on securities sold short. In total these miscellaneous expenses range from approximately 1.5% for the institutional share class to 2.4% for share classes aimed toward retail investors. There are 12b-1 (distribution and service fees) ranging from 0.25% to 1% for all but the institutional share class. In addition, retail share classes have a one-time maximum sales charge of up to 5.5%. This brings the total annual fund operating expense to a range of 2.34% to 3.37% depending on the share class.[51]

While steep by regular mutual fund standards, these kinds of fees are not unusual for alternative mutual funds. They may not be as lucrative as 20% performance fees for the most successful hedge fund managers, but they still provide a healthy income to any organization fortunate enough to count their AUM in the billions of dollars. What did investors get for these fees? In 2013, the fund's peak saw Class I institutional shareholders earn 16.6%, a respectable return in a strong equity bull market. The next three calendar years produced losses of 12.51%, 8.48%, and 3.58%, all the while the S&P 500 was regularly setting new highs. Over five years, ending December 2016, Class I investors earned an average annual return of 0.62%, while the S&P 500 was compounding at 14.66%. Not surprisingly, the Morningstar rating tumbled and assets fled, dropping below $500 million by mid-year 2017.[52]

The stated objective of this fund was to capture 70% of the upside during equity bull markets while preserving capital on the downside. This may have been achieved in the early years of the fund, but proved elusive later. From the investor's perspective the basic question remains whether one can achieve similar exposures and returns from a portfolio of other positions without incurring such charges.

Adding to the landscape are a number of '40 Act hedge funds of funds that have arrived on the scene after the financial crisis. This innovation was designed to appeal to the cautious investor who doesn't want to put all of his or her hedge fund eggs in a single basket. The problems with this approach, however, are not insignificant.

The first issue is finding a collection of underlying hedge funds that are consistent with the daily liquidity feature of these funds. This has created a natural demand for underlying '40 Act single manager hedge funds. While not easily tracked by available public data, it appears that a significant part of the growth in this space is from funds of funds that require daily liquidity themselves. This in turn creates a selectivity bias in the construction of the funds of funds. It may be lower quality funds that offer these liquidity terms in an attempt to raise assets.

The second problem is the issue of fees. The '40 Act funds of funds are no different than any partnership funds of funds in that they layer on another set of fees and expenses that get charged to the fund. At some point the burden of these multiple charges almost guarantees a mediocre result for the ultimate investor.

The jury is still out on this relatively young part of the industry. It is not hard to find liquid alternatives that have had a better recent track record than the Marketfield Fund, but it is difficult to find examples of superior returns and longevity. For many investors already dedicated to the idea of hedge funds for part of their portfolio, the somewhat lower fees linked with meaningfully improved liquidity can prove to

---

[51]MainStay Marketfield Fund Semi-annual Report, 30 June 2017.
[52]MainStay Marketfield Fund Prospectus, op. cit.

be a strong attractor. The challenge remains to thoroughly understand the holdings of the fund. Not only is this the only way to appreciate the investment profile you are buying into, but it will alert you if the holdings pose risk given the daily liquidity mandate of the fund.

9.8   PRIVATE EQUITY PARTNERSHIPS

Before the 1990s *private equity partnerships* could hardly have been called an example of a traditional investment. In total the industry was quite small and was only seriously employed by the most sophisticated individual and institutional investors. That all began to change in the bull market of the 1990s. Many think that it was purely a tech industry-driven model, but that would be incorrect. While some of the most dramatic venture-capital stories obviously arose out of the tech industry, there were important investments realized across all sectors

The important thing about the 1990s was that there were enough highly visible success stories to attract the attention of almost all institutional investors. Most individuals were shut out of this phenomenon because they fail wealth tests that would allow them to participate in these private partnerships. Foundations and endowments were some of the earliest innovators in this space, but they were quickly followed by insurance companies, pension plans, and other institutional investors.

Today private equity partnerships have graduated to become a standard bucket in most large institutional consultant portfolios. The argument is typically that the investor should be compensated for giving up liquidity versus publicly traded stocks and bonds, and therefore long-term investors should allocate at least part of their equity and credit exposures to these private partnerships. The size of the bucket is a function of the investor's need for liquidity. As the consultant community has embraced these products, they have grown considerably, with the largest institutional funds being measured in the tens of billions of dollars.

Investors should be as careful about this kind of approach as anything else in which they invest. Just as we have discussed for hedge funds, the structure of the investment does not define how it contributes to the overall portfolio. If one wants to be exposed to the equity market, there are multiple vehicles available to achieve that goal. The evaluation of those vehicles will of course include an analysis of their fees, liquidity, and tax efficiency. It is not obvious on an *a priori* basis that any one particular structure holds a permanent advantage over the others.

This section begins with a brief introduction to the common structures employed by most private equity partnerships. While the features of these partnerships share many common features, each program is individually constructed. It is the investor's ultimate responsibility to review all of the terms and conditions in the partnership and decide whether or not they are consistent with his or her goals. In this description we shall try to flag those terms that are more user-friendly to the limited partners in the modest hope that if LPs begin to critically shop among partnerships that the average terms and fees might begin to tilt back toward the advantage of the limited partners.

The most obvious feature of private equity partnerships is the extended term of the investment. To take advantage of what are perceived to be opportunities or inefficiencies in a company's capital structure, the private equity fund manager takes long-term investments that are completely inconsistent with the liquidity features of public mutual funds or even hedge funds with regular periodic liquidity. This means that the investments are made with an eye toward a long horizon, and no particular schedule of purchases or sales.

It is certainly wonderful when an investment thesis plays out immediately and a company can be purchased and sold for a quick profit, but this is rarely the case, and the fund manager needs latitude to manage any investment through time to maximize return. This necessitates a structure that puts liquidity events entirely in the hands of the manager. Once you make a commitment there is only a vague idea of when money will be invested or returned. Unless you have flexibility in other parts of your portfolio to provide liquidity when needed, private equity partnerships are not for you.

There are three phases to most private equity partnerships:

1. Fundraising and early investment
2. Core investment period
3. Harvesting period

The general partner will typically determine a target fund size that is a function of what they think the investment opportunity set is versus their capacity to invest. It is also heavily influenced by the very practical consideration of what they think is feasible in the current fundraising environment. Newer funds typically start small, not because the partners don't believe in their ability to manage a large pool of investments, but because they realize that many people choose not to invest in first-time funds. The time and energy spent trying to raise a lot of assets definitely can detract from the quality of the investment process.

The general progression for a successful organization is a modest-sized first fund with money raised from friends, family and those outside investors with the most familiarity with the capabilities of the general partners. Once that fund is largely invested and there is enough of a track record to sell more broadly, a slightly larger second fund is launched. If this process is successful, subsequent funds keep getting bigger until the general partners believe they have reached a logical capacity. The most successful partnerships then find themselves rationing out capacity as demand can greatly exceed supply.

The siren song to progress to ever larger funds is a highly tempting one. There never seems like there is a cap on opportunity in a bull market, and the lure of fees is strong. A 2% management fee on a $10 billion fund produces $200 million in revenue annually for many years whether that particular fund is particularly successful or not. Obviously, partnerships that want to create lasting franchises never want to seriously jeopardize performance by amassing too many assets in a single fund, but it is difficult to say no to potential limited partners who are anxious to invest. It is rare to find general partners who after the fact say that their previous fund was designed to be too small.

The fundraising phase has a number of sub-phases as well. There is an initial quiet phase where the general partner tries to identify potential LP interests as a help to establish the target fund size announced to the public and to prioritize resources to reach that goal. Established funds regularly reach out to existing LPs to gauge their appetites. This is especially important after events like the financial crisis of 2007–2008.

Many long-standing LP investors reassessed their liquidity needs after the crisis and either meaningfully scaled back their commitments or sat out new funds entirely.

Just as these funds don't offer regular redemptions, the process of making the investments is lumpy as well. GPs often have multiple *fund closes* that are days when the LPs that are ready to invest file their commitment letters. This may or may not actually involve a transfer of funds from the LPs to the GP. Closes that call some of the committed capital are known as *wet closes*. Not surprisingly, when no money is called, it is a *dry close*. The first close is scheduled when the GP believes there is enough LP interest to start the investment process. Fundraising may not be completed, but it is time to start investing.

There can be one or more closes after the initial close, depending on the pace of fundraising and investing. From the GP's perspective, the quicker the target fund size can be reached and LP commitments firmly established the better. Rapid commitments do not mean the pace of investing is also quickly paced. It just means that no further time and energy need to be spent on the fund raising process.

LPs can be notoriously slow in making up their minds, completing legal reviews and actually filing in their subscription documents. To nudge them along, fund terms are often set up that give some economic advantage to participants in the early closes. Sometimes LPs in later closes do not get to participate in the investments already in the portfolio at the time of their later commitment. Some funds are structured so they can join the main pool of assets, but at a higher price than the first investors. Without these types of incentives, a rational LP would procrastinate, let the early LPs take the initial risks, and then evaluate whether the developing portfolio of investments is likely to succeed. A well-structured partnership discourages this kind of free-loading behavior while being as fair as possible to all the participants in each close.

Once the GP has completed the final close, the potential investment pool is pretty much set, and the investment phase goes into full gear knowing how much capital will be available in the fund. The amount is not completely determined because many funds reserve the right to take the proceeds of early realizations and reinvest them into the fund. This *reinvestment period* can be a small number of years in a typical multiyear partnership structure.

As the GP identifies and negotiates transactions that will become part of the fund, capital is called from the LPs. Usually once an LP makes a commitment, their fondest desire is to get the money to work quickly and profitably. It rarely works ideally. This process can be a source of frustration because capital calls can be small and made on an irregular schedule. The partnership agreement typically specifies the length of the investment period (in years!) but it is not unusual for the documents to allow one or two year extensions, at the GP's option, if the investment environment was insufficiently fruitful in the initially determined era.

Why doesn't the GP just ask for all the money at once, put it into ultrasafe T-bill investments and then dip into those funds as investment opportunities arise? Wouldn't that be easier for all parties involved? The answer to these questions lies in how returns are calculated. Private equity partnerships typically report two numbers to their LPs, first discussed in Chapter 5.3.3. The first is the *multiple of invested capital* or MOIC. This is a simple figure that says if you invested $1 in total in the partnership and received $2.50 back in total when the partnership wound down, your MOIC was 2.5. This is certainly the easiest way to answer the question, "Did I make or lose money and how much?"

Unfortunately the important dimension of time is missing from the MOIC calculation. If you got your $2.50 back in a year that would be nothing short of astonishing. If it took you 15 years for that return to realize, the result is considerably less exciting. To incorporate the time element in the comparison, private equity funds calculate what is known as the *internal rate of return* or IRR. The IRR of the fund is calculated by carefully accounting for all the investments made each period and similarly all of the realizations, and then determining what interest rate would make the *net present value* (NPV) equal to zero.

NPV is a bit technical, but a simple example can demonstrate the concept. Suppose a partnership calls $1 from investors at the start of year one and then another $1 at the start of year two. At the end of five years, the fund is liquidated and investors receive $4. The MOIC is 2x. What is the IRR? There are numerous software programs available to do this calculation, and the answer is 16.6%.[53]

As a rule, the shorter the time to produce a given profit on an investment, the higher is the calculated IRR. For example, if the GP had managed to create $4 of return in four years rather than five, the IRR would jump to 21.7%. IRR is most helpful to compare funds that called capital over a similar period of time.

Consider another case where the GP had asked for $2 on day one and still returns $4 at the end of the fifth year. The MOIC on all of these examples is 2x, but now the calculated IRR falls to 14.9%. Has the investor been hurt by the decision to call all of the committee capital at once? The answer is, "It depends."

What it depends on is how the LP invests the uncalled dollar for that first year. If the LP invests it carefully in T-bills, the same way a cautious GP would, there is absolutely no difference in the economic outcome for the LP. If the LP puts the money anywhere else, it could do better or worse.

The main conclusion is that from the perspective of the GP, he or she just does not care what the LP chooses to do. Managing the committed but uncalled capital is the LP's problem. The GP understands that anytime a dollar is called and not immediately put to work the calculated IRR falls from the value that would come about from having no idle cash reserves. In the world of competitive private partnerships, calling money before the GP has a profitable project to use it on is simply bad marketing.

This sensitivity to not calling money before it is needed can produce the annoying (to the LP at least) behavior of many small capital calls, perhaps only separated by a few weeks. There is no consideration that there are transaction costs associated with each capital call including the time of the LP as they juggle the cash flows. Some GPs seem to understand this better than others. They have a pretty good idea of when different transactions will close and they are willing to sacrifice a bit of advertised IRR in order to group together several small calls into more reasonably sized calls spread out over the investment period.

Another approach to the capital call issue that has become more popular in the post-crisis zero interest rate environment is for the GP to acquire an outside line of credit that can be drawn on prior to making the capital call. These lines are usually a minority of the committed fund size and the collateral for the loan is the aggregate

---

[53]IRR comes from solving for the interest rate, r, that equates the present value of payments and receipts:

$$\sum\nolimits_0^t \frac{P_t}{(1+r)^t} = \sum\nolimits_0^t \frac{R_t}{(1+r)^t}$$

LP commitments. This is very secure lending from the perspective of the bank, and the spread above the risk-free rate is typically quite small.

Instead of making capital calls to LPs when a particular transaction in the portfolio closes early in the fund life, the GP will draw on the line of credit. When enough activity has been lined up, the GP will then make a large capital call and replenish the line. Assuming the investments being funded are profitable projects, this has the effect of increasing the calculated IRR as capital for any given investment is called later than it normally would be.

Any LP in this kind of fund needs to appreciate what is actually going on. It may appear the GP is sipping piña coladas on the beach as no money is being called, when in fact investment activity may be proceeding at a brisk pace. Once again, it is the LP's job to understand the process and plan their own cash flow accordingly. Also when doing due diligence on an apparently successful GP, the investor should ask if there were credit lines used in previous funds that would have the effect of boosting apparent IRRs without fundamentally changing the MOIC.

By the time a partnership is 70–80% invested, the GP will likely be thinking about the fund raising effort for the next partnership in the series. Successful GPs are well organized in this area, but before they focus too much on future efforts they need to button up the present.

The investment phase is followed by the liquidation or harvesting phase. Depending on the investment, the portfolio companies might be exited through an initial public offering (IPO) or a private sale to a strategic or financial buyer. Depending on the specialty of the GP, an early-stage private investment might be sold to a different general partner that specializes in later stage investments. There are many potential exit doors, but the key is for realizations to occur during the stated life of the fund plus any extensions.

Just as the GP doesn't want idle cash called before a portfolio investment is made because it will lower the calculated IRR, there is an equal incentive to distribute the proceeds of realizations as soon as they are made. This leads to a pattern of variable cash flows that might span many years if the opportunities to sell are not attractive, or the LP may get money back quickly if the exit market is hot. When an LP signs up for a private partnership there will only be a general sense of when the investment will be returned.

While there is usually a contractual end to the investment period, it is not unusual for there to be provisions to extend the investment window by one or two years, at the option of the GP. This is a safety valve to give the GP latitude for exits should the environment be particularly poor. Imagine a private partnership begun in 2000 that was scheduled to liquidate at the end of 2008. Nobody could have envisioned the specifics of the market meltdown that unfolded after the Lehman Brothers bankruptcy in Q4 2008. Any GP looking to contractually liquidate their fund then would have benefited greatly by using available extensions and pushing that window out to 2010.

The structure of how the GP gets paid is a big driver of this process. Most private partnerships have a management fee plus a participation fee based on the profitability of the fund. Unlike hedge funds where there are assets potentially flowing in and out at monthly or quarterly calculated NAVs, private equity partnerships don't have to worry about LP transactions subsequent to the final close. This then allows the performance fees essentially to be deferred until one knows whether a profit has been realized or not.

In the old days private equity partnerships often held every investment at historical cost until it was liquidated. After all, interim marks would be just a guess anyway that made no difference to the LP's final return or the GP's compensation. More recently there has been pressure from institutional investors and the accounting profession to get more precise indicators so they can compare their partnerships' performance to the other more liquid holdings in their portfolios. Such marks still don't really define anything, but they can act as an indicator.

If a fund is marked up 2x after a few years, but there have been no realizations, the LP may feel good, but nobody should be sanguine about the investment. The GP knows they will not get paid until the investment is liquidated profitably. In fact, it is often a bit more complicated than that. In many funds the GP is not allowed to start taking a performance fee until the LPs' entire original capital has been returned. This is an important safeguard against unscrupulous GPs who might rush profitable investments into early realizations just to collect fees while keeping losing investments hidden and unrealized in the portfolio.

There are a couple more wrinkles in fee structures that deserve note. The first is the concept of a *preferred return*. Funds might be structured so that the GP will not begin receiving performance fees until the LPs not only receive all their capital back but also meet a certain return. Historically preferred returns have clustered around 8% or 9%, though there is absolutely nothing magical about these numbers. Preferred returns are a nice way for the GP to communicate in a most tangible way what the expectations for the fund are.

Investors should be clear on how preferred returns typically work. A partnership that receives a 20% performance fee with a preferred return of 8% is not the same as a fund that only collects a performance fee above 8%. The LPs in such a fund get 100% of the return all the way up to 8%, but after that mark has been reached the split between the LP and GP is set by formula so that the GP eventually receives 20% of *all* profits. An example based on the outline above will show how this works.

A simple split formula could work this way:

1. From zero profit to 8%, the LPs receive all the gains.
2. From 8% to 10%, the GP receives all the gains.
3. Above 10%, the split between LPs and the GP is 80/20.

With any profitability at the fund level above the 10% mark, neither the GP nor LP shares are different than if the fund had no preferred rate. It is only when returns are under 10%, but especially when they are under 8%, that the concept of the preferred returns helps the LP. Having said this, one shouldn't forget that the GP still collects management fees whether the fund makes money or not.

Management fees for private partnerships may seem direct enough, but there are important nuances at work here as well. The common practice for many years was to charge a management fee based on *committed capital* that commenced with the subscription closing. This means the LPs begin paying fees potentially long before any capital is called or investments made.

This seems quite strange to investors used to mutual funds or hedge funds. Why should a manager get paid before there are investments working in the portfolio? The answer lies in the fact that adding an investment in a private equity partnership is considerably more complicated than calling a broker and buying some shares or bonds.

Many liquid market portfolio managers claim they evaluate a company as if they were buying the whole thing. Then they turn around and purchase a tiny fraction of it. Private equity GPs typically really do buy the whole company, or at least a controlling stake. Given that these are illiquid investments, mistakes cannot be easily reversed. Consequently a tremendous amount of work needs to be done before a private equity transaction gets across the finish line.

All of this requires money. Salaries need to be paid. Telephones need to be answered. It is these types of expenses that are usually funded by the management fee that starts once the subscription documents are filed. Given the lengthy due diligence and effort behind most private equity investments, one can begin to understand the genesis of this practice.

Another feature that can drive a wedge between gross returns on a transaction and the net returns received by the LPs is the practice of charging certain investment expenses directly to the fund. These expenses might include travel to a target company's locations to do due diligence, the legal fees associated with reviewing corporate documents, and the expense for outside experts to evaluate the competitive landscape.

While there are general guidelines as to what constitutes accepted practice, there are no hard and fast rules. LPs need to review the documents carefully before investing, and they shouldn't be shy about asking for information on past accounting practices. If you discover that salaries for temporary office workers, the canteen's espresso machine and the upkeep of the in-house gymnasium are all being classified as investment expenses charged to the fund, you can safely assume that much of the management fee translates to profit for the GP.

Recently there has been some disturbance in this pattern of fees and happily in a direction favorable to LPs. Some large, well-funded GPs have created new partnerships that charge management fees only on *called capital*. This means the GP is incented to identify potential targets quickly and close deals. This change, which can make a big difference in net returns to LPs, is likely thought of as a sweetener by GPs who were faced with a tougher fundraising environment in the years immediately after the financial crisis.

Charging on called and not committed capital is a feature the largest and best-established GPs can afford to offer. After all, they likely have a string of fully committed funds still paying the regular bills and they are likely charging any direct investment expenses to the fund anyway. Newer GPs working on a tighter budget may not be able to match these terms without sacrificing investment quality. An LP should never be seduced by saving a relatively small number of basis points in fees if it means that there will be investments rushed into the portfolio just to start the fee clock.

Private equity partnerships typically report to investors on a quarterly basis to let them know where the capital calls stand versus the commitments, what investments have been put into the portfolio, and whether there have been any dispositions and distributions. These reports are designed to keep the LPs aware of activity in the fund, though there really isn't much the LPs can do if they don't like the picture.

In the early days of private equity little attempt was made to value the portfolio companies in real time. As the portfolio holdings are completely private, there is no readily acceptable value available like you would have with closing market prices for stocks in a mutual fund. GPs tended to hold investments at cost unless there was a material event that would force them to take a write down. Only when the company was sold would the investment be marked up and the proceeds distributed.

This has changed dramatically over time at the insistence of institutional LPs. *Financial Accounting Standards Board Bulletin 157* (FAS 157) prescribes fair market accounting standards for investment portfolios. Foundations, endowments, and pension plans need to try to estimate the value of their investment portfolios, including their private investments. It is no longer good enough to hold them at cost until a realization occurs. GPs are now expected to assess their portfolios on a continuing basis relative to the market.

This is an almost impossible task to do with accuracy, but GPs have responded with quarterly reports that show their best guess about what is going on in the portfolio. They dutifully put a value on each investment and then report gross and net IRRs as if all fees have been paid. Because of the complexity of estimating the value of the holdings, these reports usually appear quarterly but with lags that can be up to several months. LPs in turn plug these reports into their accounting frameworks and come up with total return estimates that reflect mostly unrealized gains and losses. As long as the process for coming up with valuations is consistent and well documented, the accountants are happy.

Because fees and expenses begin in most cases before portfolio companies are purchased, let alone profits realized by dispositions, the industry talks about a phenomenon they call the *J Curve*. GPs warn LPs that the early quarters of a fund can show actual losses (negative IRRs and MOICs less than 1.0) until the investment program gets fully built out. Once companies are purchased and improved, there will be more than enough profits for portfolio sales to replace those losses and move the fund to a rising level of returns.

If there were no quarterly reports, there would only be a final accounting as each company was sold showing the profitability, or not. GPs don't want to scare less experienced LPs with the reality of front loaded fees and expenses, so they are careful to explain how in successful programs the returns through time will appear like the letter J. Of course, if the fund is unsuccessful, the returns will be fortunate to trace out the letter U. Nobody likes a mirror image J.

While there are certainly parallel structural features in virtually all private equity partnerships, the specific elements can vary widely by fund. Private equity due diligence requires intense examination of the fund structure, a task that only the most detail-oriented investor could ever truly enjoy. Still, such a deep dive is absolutely required because seemingly small differences in terms can translate into big differences in net returns. One should assume that fund terms written by the GP's lawyer will tilt toward them. It is an altogether different story if they are so skewed that the risk-reward equation for the LP is unacceptable. Once the LP signs the subscription documents, the relationship will last for several years, for better or worse. It pays for the LP to be critical in the dating phase.

While the general characteristics discussed above are common to all types of private equity partnerships, the investment focus and risk profiles of the funds can vary widely. In the subsequent parts of this section we shall discuss the investment focus of venture capital, growth equity, buy-out, and credit-equity hybrid funds.

9.8.1 Venture Capital

To many investors *venture capital partnerships* make up their foundation for entrepreneurism. It offers them an opportunity to get into investment ideas on the ground floor, with the promise of great returns if the idea and the environment come together. Of course, there is always the possibility of backing the wrong horse in an ill-defined race and ending up with a complete loss. That is where the skill of the venture capitalist comes into play and why the best of them have become fabulously wealthy putting other people's money to work.

Some venture capital funds are billed as *early-stage* investors, while others focus more on late-stage investments, referring to the point in the target firm's evolutionary cycle. In early stage investing the entrepreneurial team has an idea and the outline of a business plan, but lacks the capital to execute on it. The team often lacks any meaningful collateral that would make more traditional sources of capital like bank loans feasible.

Most entrepreneurs don't start out literally at square one with a venture capital partner. Instead they cobble together the savings of the partners and contributions by friends and family to get enough working capital to finance the idea's launch. Once there is some positive momentum, the decision can be made whether selling part of the company to a venture capital firm makes sense to reach for the next level.

The evolutionary path of Facebook is illustrative of the process. Begun as a collaborative effort among a handful of Harvard undergraduates, Facebook was incorporated early in 2004 initially without any outside investors. That same year Peter Theil, a veteran of the website PayPal, was introduced to Mark Zuckerberg. For a $500,000 cash investment Theil purchased 10.2% of the young company and joined its board of directors.[54] In industry parlance, Theil was known as an *angel investor*, which means he committed his own funds at a critical early juncture of the enterprise's life that kept it going while the concept was being tested. One hears the term angel investor applied to early backers of Broadway plays as well. There is nothing necessarily divine about the investor's insight, but in the case of Peter Theil, things worked out pretty well.

After this initial outside investment Facebook's trajectory was swift. The "B" round of financing was led by the early-stage venture capital firm Accel Partners in 2005, who invested $12.7 million to acquire just under 13% of the company's equity. Between the A and B rounds the implicit value of Facebook grew from $5 million to almost $100 million. A year later there was a "C" round of equity financing with two more venture capital firms joining Thiel and Accel in providing an additional $27.5 million, with the company valued at $500 million.

There were subsequent private transactions after this leading up to Facebook's initial public offering in May of 2012, but throughout this period Facebook continued to add users and revenue. When the company went public it was at a valuation of more than $100 billion. After the dilution stemming from the various capital raises, Mark Zuckerberg ended up owning 22% of the equity in Facebook and 57% of the voting shares.

Peter Thiel and the various early and later stage venture capitalists that participated in the process reaped extraordinary returns. It is this kind of story that every venture capital investor dreams about, and they really do happen. But the headlines

---

[54]The initial investment was structured as a loan, with the option for Facebook to convert it to equity if it met certain performance metrics. While those metrics were not met in the time specified, Theil saw progress in the company and allowed the bond to convert. Theil, P. (2011). Life after Facebook. *Forbes*. (26 January).

are almost always about the winners. The many companies that are funded every year by angel investors and early-stage venture capitalists that fall by the wayside and produce 100% losses for their investors are rarely given much attention. But it is the whole story that warrants discussion.

The returns to the average early-stage venture capital investor in the decade ending 30 September 2013 was 7.63% virtually identical to the 7.57% earned by the S&P 500 Index over the same period.[55] Perhaps a better liquid market comparison would be with the Russell 2000 that is composed of small cap stocks. That index had an average return of 9.64% over the same period. The public is slowly becoming aware of the fact that the eye-popping gains of many of the first generation of venture capital funds have not been easy to replicate.[56]

The reason for this may not be hard to find. In 1991, the entire private equity industry (venture capital, buy-out funds, energy, and credit), invested $16 billion. By 1996 there was $14 billion going into venture capital funds alone. At the peak of the dot.com frenzy in 2000 new venture investments had swelled to $105 billion. The best firms routinely turned away potential LPs as institution after institution scrambled to emulate those investors who had shown foresight and courage in the first part of the 1990s and had been handsomely rewarded.

While venture capital investments were growing 25-fold over that decade ending in 2000, the total US stock market capitalization had only tripled from $4.1 trillion to $15.1 trillion.[57] There may have been a shortage of venture capital at the start of the 1990s, but by the end of the decade there was perhaps too much money chasing too few quality ideas.

It is often said that the key to investing successfully in venture capital is to only associate oneself with the best venture capitalists. Riding along with the brightest people in the business makes a lot of sense intuitively, yet even smart people can stumble. Peter Thiel, for example, started a macro hedge fund in 2002 called Clarium that traded currencies, interest rates, and commodities. It was not the source of the funds for Facebook, which were his personal funds. After a positive beginning assets quickly grew to more than $6 billion dollars in the middle of 2008. Then oil prices collapsed. Clarium's full year returns for 2008, 2009, and 2010 were −4.5%, −25%, and −23%.[58] By the start of 2011 assets at Clarium had fallen from poor performance and redemptions to under $500 million. Later that year he announced he was changing the investment mandate of the hedge fund so that it could invest in tech startups.[59] The following year he began two new venture capital funds focusing on early and growth stage investments in tech companies. It remains to be seen if investors trying to tag along with Peter Thiel will experience the kind of success he has achieved for himself.

---

[55]Cambridge Associates LLC, US Venture Capital Index® and Selected Benchmark Statistics, 30 September 2013.

[56]Garland, R. (2013). Venture Capital Returns Rebound, but Beating Public Markets Remains a Challenge. *The Wall Street Journal.* (31 October).

[57]Sources: World Federation of Exchanges and Dow Jones Private Equity Analyst.

[58]Caulfield, B. and Perlroth, N. (2011). Life after Facebook. *Forbes.* (26 January).

[59]Weiss, M. (2011). Thiel's Clarium Hedge Fund to Make Tech Investments After Losses. Bloomberg. (15 August).

In 2012 the Ewing Marion Kauffman Foundation published an analysis of its 20 year experience of investing in more than 100 venture capital funds.[60] This was not some late comer to the party, but a major foundation with a seasoned investment staff and trustees on its investment committee. Their objective was to objectively assess the wisdom of their venture capital program. They scrubbed all the data and were remarkably candid in their appraisals. The fact that they chose to share their findings with the broader investment community is even more remarkable, but quite laudable.

Because of standard confidentiality provisions that exist in virtually all private partnership agreements, Kauffman was unable to publicly identify specific fund performance or GPs, but their experience was so broad and over so many years that the summary data they share in the report is still quite illuminating. A snapshot of key findings includes:

1. Only 20 of 100 venture funds generated returns that beat a public-market benchmark by more than 3% annually. Ten of those 20 began investing before 1995.
2. After fees and carry, 62 of the 100 funds failed to match the returns available in the public market.
3. Their average VC fund failed to return investor capital after fees.
4. Many VC funds last longer than 10 years. The foundation has eight VC funds in their portfolio that are older than 15 years.

It is certainly true that the last half of the Kauffman experience corresponded with one of the worst periods in US equity markets generally, but it is equally true that the first half was one of the best. Since Kauffman's program grew through time similar to almost all institutional investors, they had a lot more money at work in the weaker times. Still, their analysis shows clearly that the results were not all environmentally driven.

It might have been easy for the authors to conclude the GPs were entirely at fault. Many disappointed investors regularly blame others for their anguish. Instead, the Kauffman investors were first introspective and then reached out to others in the LP community to see how their expectations, approach, and execution compared. They concluded that the VC model was broken, with the economics tilted too far toward the GPs. This in turn created tremendous hurdles to the LPs making any meaningful performance edge over what the public markets offered. And it was largely the community of LPs that allowed this situation to persist.

The features of the model most in need of repair are fees, expenses, and the amount of capital the GP has at risk alongside the LPs. They note that LPs regularly participate in venture funds without fully understanding GP compensation, the carry structure, details about the ownership of the firm or its income, expenses or profits.

The typical GP in their funds committed around 1% of the risk capital of a new fund. This feature along with a 2% management fee and 20% profit sharing pushed GPs to raise large funds that lock in high levels of fee-based personal income for many years whether the LPs are making money or not.

---

[60]Mulcahy, D., Weeks, B., and Bradley, H. S. (2012). *We Have Met the Enemy ... and He Is Us.* Ewing Marion Kauffman Foundation.

Kauffman found that to support the launch of new funds after a few years, GPs are incented to flip early winners in the current portfolio so they have attractive tangible results when they go to raise the next round of funds. This can mean that some companies are sold for their early headline value rather than sold at a time that maximizes the returns to the existing LPs. This finding was discovered by noting that the best reported IRRs of the funds tended to be in the first few years of a fund's life. This is in direct contradiction to the expectation one would have from the J Curve theory that suggests IRRs should rise through time as good realizations increase and front-end expenses become less and less important.

The big conclusions that Kauffman drew about VC investing is that the model is designed to heavily favor the GP community and that LPs collectively allow that to happen. Many are afraid to rock the boat, fearing that they will lose access to perceived star players. But if the chance of success is so low, what is there really to fear?

Maybe the right approach is to largely ignore a dedicated allocation to venture capital funds and be much more tactical in one's approach. That would include focusing on the smaller venture funds where the GP represents a more meaningful share of the capital at risk and thereby creating a better alignment of interests. It might also include investing directly in small companies or co-investing in later round financings with seasoned investors. Finally, Kauffman suggests moving at least a portion of funds invested in VC to the public markets where there are much lower costs and complete liquidity.

9.8.2 Growth Equity

One of the Kauffman Foundation's suggestions was to shift away from early venture capital investing toward investments in companies that have well-established business structures, but require additional capital to execute on their growth plan. This type of investing is sometimes referred to as late-stage venture capital or *growth equity*. Readers will quickly realize that there are no bright line divisions between many of these types of investing, but the labels are helpful in establishing a sense of the risk profile of the activity.

Early-stage venture capital is mostly a binary activity. There will always be stories like Facebook that will feed investors' imaginations, but for every Facebook there may be scores of companies started by smart, honest, and hardworking people that never quite work out. In these cases the companies either fail completely or they require so much more subsequent financing that the earliest investors see their equity stakes considerably diluted. Either of these outcomes can produce a total or near total loss on the early-stage venture gamble.

This risk profile isn't for everyone. While a venture capitalist has more control over outcomes than someone picking numbers for the lottery the payoffs are similarly skewed. Many investors don't like lottery-style opportunities, preferring less chance of complete failure. For these people, investing in an established business that still has unrealized growth potential has a lot of the allure of venture capital but with considerably less chance of a total loss.

The activities of the GP of a venture capital or growth equity fund can be quite similar once they invest in a company. Not only do the funds provide needed capital, the GP usually participates actively in the governance of the company. Venture capitalists and growth equity GPs often fund brilliant people with potentially game changing ideas, but that doesn't mean they know anything about how to run or finance a company. Building a business and building a profitable business are two different things.

The best GPs in these funds typically have deep operating experience themselves plus a network of individuals who can fill key roles in production and finance. Many times the GPs look more like employment search firms than investors, though the payoff for finding the right personnel is considerably greater in the VC and growth equity world.

This all needs to be done with a great deal of finesse to be effective. In the Facebook example, after all the rounds of private funding and the IPO, Mark Zuckerberg still retained absolute majority control of the voting shares. While Peter Thiel and the GPs of the later round venture capitalists can suggest changes in corporate direction or personnel, ultimately it is Mark Zuckerberg's company to control. If the minority owners fundamentally disagree with his direction, their only effective action is to sell their shares and move on.

One sometimes hears stories of how the minority fund investors lean on management, which is often the majority owner and controller of the governance, to accept a buy-out or participate in another liquidity event. This advice may reflect the ultimate best course for the company, but given the restrictions arising from the private equity fund structures, the GPs may be pushing for what is best for them and not all of the shareholders in the long run.

The GPs may want an early realization at a good price to help promote their next fund when patience and more business development could produce an even better realization later. A worse problem exists when the company finds itself as one of the last portfolio holdings in a partnership that is nearing the end of its listed life. In these cases the GP needs a liquidity event and may be willing to take suboptimal terms just to wrap things up. Or they may extend the life of the partnership using one of several built-in options that all subscription documents contain. In that case the LPs bear most of the pain as the fee clock never stops ticking.

Minority owner issues should not be downplayed. We'd all like to think that every venture and growth equity-backed private company will be purchased by a strategic investor at a nice multiple or will IPO into a supportive bull market, but this is not the case. Market downturns after 2000 and again after 2008 were destructive for private equity exits on multiple fronts. Companies that see their own share prices tumble have less of what is often used as currency to acquire logical targets and the IPO market effectively closes down. In those circumstances GPs in venture capital and growth equity funds have to hunker down, manage expectations, and do what they can to keep their underlying companies on the right path.

Some of the issues that arise from being a minority shareholder often disappear with another style of private equity investing called buy-out funds. As the name implies, the GPs of these funds often take control over entire firms. While the structure of the partnerships is similar to what we have already seen, the philosophy of the investments takes on a different orientation.

9.8.3 Buy-out Funds

Venture capital and growth equity investors are looking to catch companies at an early, sometimes embryonic, stage of their life cycle. The motivation for *buy-out* investors is often quite different. Sometimes there are ownership issues in mature public companies. Sometimes there is hidden value in a company that might be unlocked if there could be a major overhaul of management and the board. Sometimes there is the chance to acquire a significantly undervalued asset that the market has overlooked. In each case the answer might be a private purchase of the entire company, or at least a large enough percentage of the voting shares so it can be operated as if the new shareholders owned the entire enterprise.

Like venture capital and growth equity fund GPs, the best buy-out fund professionals bring a combination of skills to their activity. They are experts in evaluating businesses from both operational and financial perspectives. They think strategically about the future of an industry and whether revenue and profits are likely to grow or be under pressure from domestic or foreign competition. They have extensive contacts of professionals who can be called on to fill key management and board seats. They think like owners, which they are.

A private equity transaction is often the best solution to the challenges caused by an aging ownership. Imagine a company started and successfully run for many decades by an entrepreneur nearing 80 years of age. The leader is vibrant and in total command of all elements of the business. Despite advances in modern medicine, everyone, including the owner, knows the clock is ticking. To make the example easier, assume that there is no second- or third-generation family members who have shown any interest or aptitude in the business. They like the idea of the wealth embedded in the company, but have no intention of participating first hand.

Presume, though, that there is a next generation of capable managers. These individuals have received modest stock grants over the years in recognition of their contributions but together own less than 15% of the company. The company grew through the years with modest bank loans when expansion was attractive. There is no debt currently and the company has never issued stock to outsiders.

If nothing is done the bulk of the ownership and control will move to the founder's heirs when he passes through the labyrinth of estate law. Everyone in the company understands the risks of this and they want to avoid it. The logical owners of the company are the next generation of management, but they don't have the immediate resources to buy out the founder, and their existing collateral in the company is too small to support financing of a buy-out. This is where a private equity owner can help.

An easy transaction would be for the private equity fund to buy out the founder and take over the running of the firm. This, however, risks alienating the senior management that are the logical heirs of the founder. Unless the private equity investors are supremely confident in their abilities to run the company themselves, they will be wary of this most direct path.

A more creative way to do the transaction would be to buy out the founder but then use a meaningful part of the ownership as an incentive tool to keep the senior management intact and motivated. This can be done with stock grants, discounted sales, or incentive-based options programs. The private equity fund may retain majority control in such a transaction, but by spreading ownership more broadly the likelihood of business continuity and ultimately success is enhanced.

Since the company currently has no debt, the private equity fund would probably tap into its many credit options to secure bank loans to finance at least part of the transaction. This kind of financial engineering is typical in the buy-out world and is often an important part of the total return to the fund. To make the example more concrete, assume the total value of the company is $100 million, with the founder's ownership at $86 million and the rest of the management owning shares worth $14 million. The private equity fund might put up $40 million in cash equity and then have the company acquire financing through senior secured bank loans of $46 million to buy out the founder. This would leave the company with a debt to equity ratio of 46%, which is not considered extreme at all if the firm has good cash flow or underlying assets as collateral.

The use of leverage is a powerful tool in the private equity fund's arsenal. It allows the capital that is raised in each new partnership to be spread over more deals, which, if successful, can create strong levered returns. All debt, of course, increases the chance of a firm's failure, and the bankruptcy courts are full of cases of firms that acquired too much leverage in a private equity transaction.

The normal evolutionary path of most companies is to start life privately and then go public with an *initial public offering* (IPO). In recent years there have been some notable cases where public companies have decided that their structure isn't worth the bother and they have reversed the usual flow. Private equity funds often facilitate these actions, structuring the financing of the buy-back and then ending up with a meaningful piece of the ownership.

The motivations for these "public to private" transactions can vary widely. Some such companies want to avoid the costs associated with public company governance. The Sarbanes-Oxley Act of 2002 (formally titled "Public Company Accounting Reform and Investor Protection Act") added many responsibilities to public company managers and boards. There is a debate over whether Sarbanes-Oxley fundamentally reduces American corporations' competitiveness. But few dispute that it raises the costs of running a public corporation by adding extra obligations to and regulatory oversight over the corporation. Some public companies have said that it just is not worth it anymore, and have gone private.

Perhaps a more frequent reason to move from public to private status is a perceived misevaluation of the company by the stock market. After the credit crisis of 2008–2009 many equities were badly beaten up for sound fundamental reasons. As the economy started recovering from this shock, the profitability of many of these companies began to turn around as well. This was not always quickly recognized in a company's stock price.

Savvy insiders, who might already be large shareholders, might see the pipeline of new business much clearer than stock analysts or the public at large. If they think the share price is trading at a meaningful discount to intrinsic value, they might try to purchase more stock on the open market. Because of disclosure laws, this would quickly signal their views. Another approach would be to team up with a private equity fund and take the whole company private.

For small and micro-cap companies this can be done pretty quickly. Shareholders are informed that there is a takeover bid, almost always at a meaningful premium to the current share price, and that there will be a shareholder vote on the transaction. The board of the company, that often includes several of the insiders, recommends that the company be sold. The vote is taken and, poof, the public company is gone!

Because the transaction occurs at a premium to the market stock price, the sale is a profitable one for the outside shareholders, but is it a good deal? A stock that has languished for a long time at $4 a share with very low multiples can be taken out at $5. That quick 25% gain may feel like a windfall, but if the stock was poised to double or triple in value because of greatly improving fundamentals, taking the company private actually stole value from the public shareholders.

In theory the board of directors is supposed to protect those shareholders and reject any bids that don't maximize the return to shareholders. In practice, insiders can tilt transactions in their favor. Unless there are strong independent directors or knowledgeable shareholders to challenge the valuation, this kind of private equity transaction will produce much better ultimate returns for the buyers than the sellers.

In one sense, that is what private equity buy-outs are all about. Identify undervalued companies and deploy enough equity and debt to take over the situation before other market participants correct it.

Buy-out fund GPs often need the same skill set as venture capital and growth equity managers. If management needs changing, they require access to the right talent. If the financing of the company can be improved, their contacts and experience make putting together the right deal more likely. Their goal is to improve the value of the company in any way they can in order to maximize the return on their investment. Unlike VC, growth equity, and activist equity managers, however, buy-out specialists usually have the advantage of being in control and able to affect the changes they want.

Most buy-out GPs will claim that their value added comes from identifying and buying undervalued assets and then working intensely at the operating level to bring out and enhance that value. While this is often true many buy-out deals are more exercises in *financial engineering*. Considerable leverage is put on the balance sheet to finance the transaction and if the economy and the stock market remain supportive the rising tide lifts the leveraged boat. Potential LPs should try to discern the typical methods of operation of the private equity GPs and align themselves only with ones that operate consistently with their own expectations and risk profiles. GPs that build companies fundamentally can often weather cyclical downturns better than those that simply apply leverage to make a profit.

Buy-out partnership funds operate with the same constraints as all other private partnerships do. There is an investment period where the capital is put to work, a multiyear period when value is supposed to be added to the company, and then a harvesting period that is capped at the life of the fund plus any extensions that are allowed and agreed to. Buying and building a company is just the first part of the equation. To be successful, the buy-out fund needs good realizations.

Realizations come from multiple potential exit opportunities. Private companies often go public with an IPO much the way successful venture backed companies do. Sometimes they are sold to a *strategic buyer*, meaning a company that wants to acquire or merge with the target to further their own business purposes.

Charles Schwab and Company was originally a private firm that sold itself to Bank of America in 1983. Charles Schwab and other investors bought the firm back from B of A four years later and then shortly thereafter IPO'd Charles Schwab Corporation. While not a high profile buy-out fund transaction, this sequence shows the myriad of paths available to the private firm.

Another exit option is to sell the private company to a *financial buyer,* which means in most instances another private equity fund or other financial institution. Buy-out funds that specialize in small and medium-sized companies often find buyers among the mega buy-out firms after they have grown the business as much as their resources will allow.

All of these exit paths are legitimate, but LPs should be a bit wary of sales to other buy-out funds. In these situations highly informed and seasoned professionals are facing each other at the negotiating table. Neither side will get a highly advantaged price, which is exactly what each fund's LPs are looking for. If you note that a large percentage of realization transactions are between funds, it is also a sign that the other exit options are probably too weak to support all the private equity assets that are pouring into the space.

Academics have studied the buy-out space for some time. In general they can identify a value that is being added through the organizational improvements and the financial engineering. But the effect is not large, in many cases being less than the fees charged by the GPs. Like the Kauffman Foundation study of venture capital investments, the best returns were realized in the 1980s when there were fewer and smaller funds operating in the space.[61]

LPs looking to invest in the buy-out space should pick their funds carefully. There has been a massive commitment of new money to the area and unless you are convinced that the GP can add value meaningfully above what the public markets can deliver, there may be no reason to sign up for a multiyear program with the only thing guaranteed being higher fees.

As suggested earlier in this section, venture, growth equity and buy-out funds have become a major force across the investment landscape. While this growth has expanded access to these strategies for a large number of investors, it has not come without challenges.

Take, for example, the sheer number of partnerships being offered. According to a Bain & Company report, there were under 200 private equity firms in 1990. Less than 30 years later the number had swelled to over 7,700.[62] The only explanation is that the potential financial rewards to GPs during a sequence of bull markets, punctuated by a couple of severe market plunges, has proven irresistible to entrepreneurial managers eager to participate.

This growth of funds has translated directly into a growth of assets raised and looking for deals. Figure 9.16 gives the growth in private equity commitments since 2000. The incredible thing about this chart is that the financial crisis barely made a dent in the growth path. The other part of this chart identifies the amount of committed, but uncalled, capital each year. By the end of 2018, there was more than a trillion dollars in "dry powder" waiting to be deployed. Given the apparent demand for these types of funds, this overhang of unused capital has done little to discourage existing GPs from raising new funds or from new funds entering the market.

This unbridled growth has come with a price. Every fund that solicits you will tell a persuasive story why outsized returns will likely be realized. Some will be more credible than others. A McKinsey & Company report shows how unpredictable recent returns have been.[63]

---

[61]Kaplan, S.N. and Strömberg, P. (2008). Leveraged Buyouts and Private Equity. Working Paper 14207. National Bureau of Economic Research, Cambridge, MA 02138.

[62]Bain & Company. Global Private Equity Report, 2018. p. 6.

[63]McKinsey & Company. (2019). Private Markets Come of Age. p. 11.

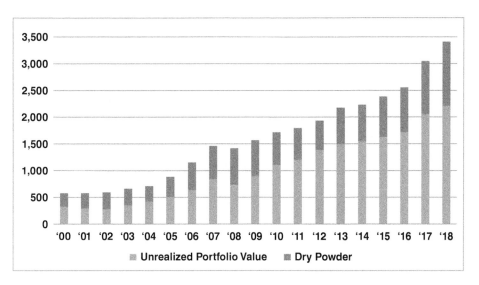

FIGURE 9.16   Private Equity Assets Under Management ($BN, 2000–2018)
Source: Strategas

A great deal of time and analytical power is devoted to trying to understand why active equity manager performance varies. Figure 9.17, based on the McKinsey report, should make you ask whether all that effort is necessary. It examines returns for traditional equity managers and private equity managers for the period 2013–2018. The comparison of the two groups is striking.

The range for equity mutual funds is roughly 5–15%. The midpoint is very near 8%. This is a reasonable dispersion and if you were participating with the annual 5% manager, you might be looking to change. Compared to the PE fund return dispersion, however, it is almost negligible. The top of the chart earned about 50% annually while the bottom showed 30% annual losses. How does one make 50% a year? Target a few companies that all become successful. How does one lose 30%? Follow the same strategy, but not be as good in selection, or as lucky, as the top funds.

One might think that losing this much money every year in the middle of a massive bull market for stocks would be hard. Given the explosion in the number of funds coming to market, you could argue that this is almost to be expected. The fourth quartile funds in this example will likely never raise another pool of capital, but that will not stop the GPs and a small army of new entrants from forming new partnerships, all marketed with convincing stories.

This is the kind of result that pushes large institutional investors into the arms of established firms. Blackstone's main buy-out fund raised in 2019 was capped at $25 billion in commitments, mostly from LPs participating in earlier funds. CIOs get fired for investing in funds that lose 30% a year. They do not get fired for allocating to the blue bloods of the PE world.

But what are realistic return expectations in this environment? Another look at Figure 9.17 suggests the average PE experience only yielded 2–3% more per year than the average equity mutual fund (that likely trailed an index). Is that enough

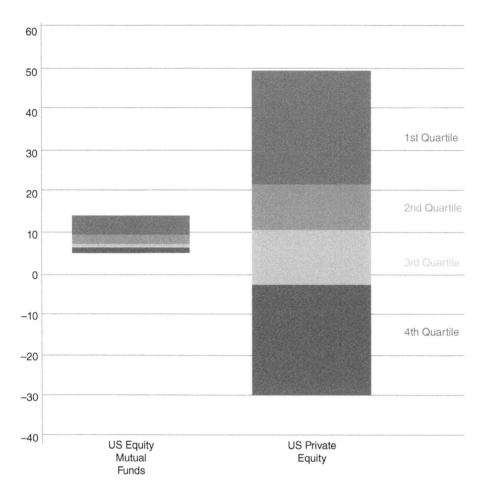

FIGURE 9.17   5-year annual returns from US private equity funds and US mutual funds by performance percentile, 2013–18
Source: McKinsey and Company

compensation for entering into an inherently leveraged strategy and giving up liquidity? It may appear worthwhile in the bull market that included 2013–2018, but you might get a very different answer if the investment period includes anything like 2000–2002, or 2017–2019. There may be a new generation of Kauffman Foundation reports somewhere on the horizon.

9.8.4   Credit-Oriented Private Funds

The previous sections have focused on partnerships that specialize in equity ownership of companies. The capital structure is much richer than just equity. Investors are increasingly embracing *credit oriented partnerships*. Some approaches, like mezzanine debt, have been around for some time. Others, like direct lending funds, have been rising in popularity since the disruptions caused by the 2008–2009 credit crisis.

Like the equity-oriented funds discussed above, credit partnerships have an investment period, a maturation phase, and then liquidation. In general, these funds tend to be a little shorter in duration than the equity funds simply because the loans that get made are of an intermediate term and have the characteristic of being generally self-liquidating. Since the investments happen at a more senior point in the capital structure, the investors in these funds should expect to earn less than the equity partnerships, but also experience less risk. Having said that, after the disruptions to the credit space in 2008–2009, the target returns for many of these funds were realistically higher than the historical returns to public market equity investments.

Mezzanine debt funds fill a specialty role in capital market transactions. In the section above on buy-out funds there was an example of a transaction that had debt to total equity ratio of 46%, which was advertised as a conservative structure. Many buy-out funds try to be more aggressive. In the example the PE fund wanted to buy 86% of the $100 million firm. Suppose instead of putting up $40 million in cash, the GP wanted to increase leverage and only put up $6 million, borrowing the remaining $80 million. In most environments banks would be very nervous to lend 80% of the value of the company, so they may tell the GP that they will supply $50 million of senior secured debt. Where does the GP get the additional 30%?

Enter the mezzanine fund. These funds specialize in providing financing that is subordinated to the senior bank debt. In some cases it is unsecured. In return the mezzanine GP extracts certain advantages as compensation. Mezzanine debt is often relatively short term in nature, but with meaningful call protection. These are much shorter than typical corporate bonds in maturity. The interest paid is at a large spread to the rate the company is paying the banks for the first lien loans. The mezzanine fund often gets *origination fees* for establishing these loans just like an investment bank would. And finally the transaction may include the granting of stock options to the mezzanine fund. All of these together are designed to compensate the mezzanine investors for the considerably higher risk profile of the debt they are holding.

Without getting into specific examples, the reader should get the idea that this is expensive debt the company is taking on. If they had other financing opportunities either from more bank loans or access to the corporate bond market, they wouldn't give the mezzanine fund GPs the time of day. But the world isn't always neat and tidy. If the choice is to pay dearly for mezzanine financing or see a deal fall through, with all the costs associated with that outcome, the owners will often reach out to the mezzanine fund.

All of these features are a plus for the LP investors in the mezzanine fund. The company is motivated to pay off this debt as soon as they can, but the call protection in the loans assures that the money doesn't get repaid too quickly. In the best cases the mezzanine investors see their underlying deals mature in a timely fashion and their capital distributed back to them.

In the worst cases the company fails. While the mezzanine lenders are in a superior position to the equity owners, they are well down the list behind the bank loans and any other secured lenders. The mezzanine GP must be prepared to participate in any bankruptcy reorganization and try to maximize the recovery for the fund's investors.

Some investors avoid mezzanine funds with the simple logic that because they are not equity holders there is no possibility of an outsized gain, but there is much more risk from this type of lending than the banks or other secured loans face. The theory is if you like the company, own the equity, and if you don't, own the senior bonds so you can take over the assets if there is a problem.

While correct at a general level, this philosophy leaves out an important factor. How much is the mezzanine lender getting paid for these risks? Just like in all markets there are times when the expected gain falls short of adequate compensation for the risks, but there are times when it provides a comfortable cushion. It is the LPs' job to assess the GP and the environment and make a judgment call. Once again, past results are a woefully poor indicator of what the future might bring.

Another class of credit-oriented private partnerships encompasses *distressed* investing. These funds are first cousins to high-yield bond funds, but with the critical difference that the bonds have fallen from being merely risky to either having already defaulted or are sitting at the precipice. The question is no longer, "How much will I be paid and for how long?" It has become, "What kind of recovery will I get if this company reorganizes or liquidates?"

Once a bond or loan has become stressed or it defaults almost everything about it changes. Entire groups of investors are prohibited from owning it by their own guidelines. The number of dealers who will make markets in the bonds shrinks. Not only do prices go down but the liquidity of the marketplace materially deteriorates.

If you own a performing bond, you care primarily about the cash flow of the borrower and the ability to pay timely interest payments. As soon as the bond defaults, you care a lot about the company's entire capital structure and how it might be reformulated. If you are sufficiently senior, you might get paid back near par. Under other circumstances you could see no return of your capital, but instead you become the owner of the equity. In a liquidation scenario, what the assets are worth and where you stand in the priority line are all that matter.

This is complicated stuff, worthy of the best investment and legal minds. Not only does the distressed credit GP have to understand the business like a private equity fund GP, he or she needs to understand the bankruptcy code sufficiently well to assess likely legal outcomes. Everybody wants a piece of a bankrupt company and the allocations ultimately can be determined by the courts and not the market.

The complexity of the transactions and the illiquidity of the underlying instruments virtually mandate a private partnership structure. These are not investments that follow a carefully constructed time line, nor can they be quickly traded in the market. The best distressed credit GPs know that they need to be able to quickly evaluate the state of a bankrupt company and then buy the bonds at prices that promise good upside as the company navigates its next evolutionary steps. In an ideal world, those bonds are purchased at low enough prices to minimize further downside risk, but the reality is often different. The world can change suddenly. Just when you think those bonds you bought for 30 cents on the dollar are pretty well protected by the firm's assets, a competitor announces a new technology that makes your plants obsolete, and the bonds tumble to 10.

Most high-caliber distressed debt GPs don't go out looking to own the equity of the companies of the bonds they hold, but they are quite capable of managing equity positions if that is the ultimate outcome. This means that the GPs need to have virtually the same skill set as private equity GPs, with one big exception. They acquire equity through corporate restructurings and not by bidding for it against other potential buyers. While both of these paths involve extensive negotiations, the psychology and the execution of the two processes can be quite different.

Direct lending funds have been around forever, but the credit crisis so disrupted traditional lines of finance that they have taken on new importance in the years since. Sometimes known as *shadow banking*, this activity frequently fills holes left when banks won't lend and the borrowers are too small to tap the public equity or bond markets.

In the simplest form, these funds identify borrowers who have limited access to or have exhausted traditional bank loans. These are typically small and micro-cap companies, often private in their equity structure. The borrowing can be secured by a wide range of potential assets, including trade claims or other receivables, royalties, or physical plant and equipment. Given the circumstances of the borrowers, interest rates are often meaningfully higher than those from traditional banking sources.

Business owners who go down this financing path often hate it. They believe in their businesses and also are frustrated by investment and commercial bankers who don't share their vision and won't work with them. But they also know that there are times when it is better to build your business with expensive financing than it is to sit on the sidelines.

Because of the nature of the underlying assets, a private equity structure is the best fund form. These are highly illiquid, privately negotiated loans that have no reliable market prices through time. Borrowers either meet their interest payment obligations or they don't. In the latter case, the GP of the fund must be prepared to do everything a distressed debt manager does to recover as much of the loan as possible.

In addition to PE structures for direct lending there has been an increase in this activity in a hedge fund format. Managers of these funds often show multiyear track records with steady monthly returns and no losses, which they would argue is the result of careful credit evaluation and the steady payment of the interest due. These track records are also the result of always pricing the underlying loans at par unless there is a default event that impairs them. While not entirely a falsehood, such records are largely useless in comparisons to other funds where the underlying assets trade and are regularly marked to market more accurately.

During the credit crisis, not only did defaults tick up for these funds, but LP redemption requests could simply not be honored. There was no bid for such customized assets and the GPs of these hedge funds had no choice but to set up liquidating trusts and side pockets. The appearance of liquidity in the fund document terms was in fact an illusion, and investors discovered that they owned a partnership that functioned much more like private equity than a hedge fund. It is better, perhaps, to start the investment process in a private equity-like structure to avoid the charade.

One area of due diligence that is mandatory, but quite difficult, with these funds is evaluating the abilities of the investment team to do the requisite credit work and to get paid appropriately for the risk. LPs will rarely be in a position to say which loans are good and which are suspect. Looking at a manager's track record is only relevant if it spans both bull and bear credit markets. Too many investors sign up with managers who show three or four year track records with no losses that were achieved in periods of little stress like 2003–2006 or 2010–2013. Managers who claim multi-decade experience in the field but only show results since 2009 should receive particular scrutiny.

Easier, but no less important, is an analysis of expenses inherent in the lending process. It is not unusual for the GP to perform, and get paid for, many services. If they don't do these steps directly, they might own an affiliated company that does.

These charges can include *loan origination fees* and ongoing *loan servicing charges.* The LP needs to determine whether these fees are necessary and proper, since they will likely be subtracted from the fund. All of these fees are additive to the management and performance fees collected by the GP and they can be substantial. In some abstract world, LPs might be happy to receive a steady 0.66% a month (8% per year) from such a fund. If the underlying loans are paying 1.5% per month because they are fundamentally that risky, but the majority of the return to LPs is being consumed by fees, that abstract return isn't close to being enough compensation given the risk.

Business Development Corporations (BDCs) are a specialized class of direct lending funds. They collect an initial pool of capital from investors, which they can augment with secondary fund raising if opportunities allow. They then compete with other direct lenders to build a pool of loans. BDCs often start off as private corporations with limited liquidity for investors. The logical evolutionary step is for the private corporations to eventually IPO, making their shares publicly tradable. While the BDC is private the NAV of the pool of loans is the best indicator of the value. After the BDC goes public its stock price can trade at a discount or premium to NAV, just like a closed-end mutual fund. Some of the most capable and experienced lenders on the street run BDCs, which gives many investors added confidence in this area of investing.

Direct lending funds come in all sizes, complexities, and geographies. As portfolios become more concentrated and involve loans of smaller, less-developed companies, investors should demand higher projected returns. Just like with traditional mezzanine funds, there is limited opportunity to achieve an equity-like return, but in many cases there is the equity-like risk of a complete washout. Unless LPs have particular skills in evaluating the underlying loan portfolios they should probably restrict their investments to the most reputable firms with reasonable fees and the clearest reports on how they made their money in the past.

9.8.5 Secondary Funds

The long lockups of private equity funds are absolutely essential given the underlying investments, but some of the partnerships seem to go on forever. In a portfolio of 20 underlying investments, 18 of them may be initiated, developed, and liquidated within the target investment period. The other two may not be sold in such a timely fashion for a variety of reasons. The general market environment is unfavorable. There's been a critical change in the company's sector that has depressed valuations, hopefully temporarily. The structure of the company may not be quite right yet. Whatever the reason, the result is the same. The private equity partnership that owns the company goes on and on.

Most LPs understand this well and live with the consequences. But sometimes circumstances change and the LP wants to move on before the natural end of the partnership's life. Since these are not marketable securities, there is no easy way to get out. Enter *secondary partnerships.*

These partnerships specialize in buying up existing LP holdings representing a variety of underlying funds and then managing them like a fund of funds. While secondary funds can vary considerably in their orientation and structure, there are a few common factors most try to possess:

Purchase funds that have a considerable majority of commitments to underlying investments already made. This allows the secondary GP the opportunity to look through to the underlying investments and make an independent assessment of the existing value of the holdings. Buying early-stage funds where most of the commitments are in the future exposes the secondary fund to the risk that new investments might not be as fundamentally attractive as they would like.

Purchase funds at a discount to current net asset value. If LPs want to get out of a fund early, they should be willing to pay for the privilege. Secondary funds compete for these assets, but they all try to buy at some discount to NAV. This provides a margin of safety in the investments and helps cover the extra layer of fees that the secondary fund charges.

Try to own a diversified range of underlying funds some of which are already in the distribution phase. The diversification allows the secondary fund to avoid concentrating in any sector or type of fund (venture, buy-out, etc.) that could be subject to a surprise shock. This reduces the overall risk of the portfolio, a feature many LPs desire. Buying funds that are already in the distribution phase is attractive for those who are looking for quicker cash flow and shorter investment periods. This has the effect of increasing the IRRs of the investment, but reducing the multiple on invested capital (MOIC). It also has the effect of greatly mitigating any J curve effect in the underlying investments.

The sources of supply for secondary funds have varied through time. Initially sellers were institutions or individuals that wanted to clean up their portfolios of partnerships that had largely run their course. It should not be a surprise to anyone that dealing with K-1s for many minor investments is annoying and costly. Secondary funds often have holdings in a broad array of funds and adding a bit more exposure to an existing name adds nothing to the complexity or expense of their portfolio.

The market changed abruptly after the bear market of 2000–2002 as some institutions that had been late entrants to the private partnership market found their marketable equity holdings had shrunk dramatically while their commitments to the private partnerships remained constant. This sudden skew toward illiquidity caused LPs to try to sell some of the partnerships and the secondary funds were the primary buyers.

While the first bear market of the twenty-first century might have been a catalyst to the secondary market's growth, the credit crisis that began in 2007 was a watershed event. The 2000–2002 bear market was marked with massive equity market losses, but hedge fund holdings by and large did their job and made money. Sophisticated investors who were in private partnerships at that time often had meaningful hedge funds that acted as a buffer, reducing the urgency to adjust the portfolios. This was not the case in the credit crisis.

Starting in the fall of 2007 and accelerating rapidly after the Lehman bankruptcy in September 2008, virtually every investment except treasuries tumbled. Liquid stocks fell by more than 40% in many markets around the globe. Hedge funds did better but in many cases still lost more than 20%. With credit spreads exploding, all but the safest fixed income investments also saw losses. Many investors who had previously thought of themselves as highly sophisticated quickly found themselves to be underwater in terms of liquidity. By the beginning of March 2009 it was not unusual to find investors who had more in uncalled commitments in their private equity portfolios than the total value of their marketable holdings.

Many of these investors decided to try to reduce their commitments by selling at least part of their partnership holdings, but it was not the best time to do so. Supply exceeded demand and with the depressed equity markets, what bids were in the market were based on low valuations for the underlying holdings. Discounts to NAV for the transactions that did take place were wide, much to the benefit of the LPs in the secondary funds.

In the immediate wake of the crisis, the bid/ask spread for secondary holdings was wide and the number of transactions perhaps less than one might have expected. Investors who had access to the credit markets sometimes chose to borrow, even at high spreads over treasuries, rather than sell their partnerships at fire sale prices. Some of the largest, most prestigious universities in the country borrowed billions of dollars during this period in order to meet their immediate liquidity needs. Not every investor had this option.

In the rosy days leading up to the crisis major banks around the world often added private equity funds to their assets. As the market crisis evolved into a full blown global recession these banks had massive nonperforming loans, questionable sovereign debt in many European countries, and private partnerships that no longer seemed like such a great idea taking up precious space on their balance sheets.

Regulators had to reorganize or shut down the worst banks in the system, but there were Herculean efforts to do whatever necessary to keep the biggest banks solvent. This sometimes involved creative interpretations of what constituted a performing loan. It also sometimes involved allowing banks to value their partnership assets higher than any market bid they might receive.

Under such circumstances the banks were not forced sellers, but the patience of regulators is finite. As economies rebounded and bank profit margins began to improve, the wink and a nod school of bank regulation was increasingly replaced with more traditional, and conservative, standards. In the United States the passage of the Volcker Rule greatly restricted the ability of banks to own private equity or hedge funds in their proprietary accounts. While the regulators did not want to create another round of market distress by forcing sales, the message became clear that banks needed to get these assets off their balance sheets.

All of these assets, of course, had to find a home and there were two major sources of demand. Some institutional investors who were not hamstrung with too little liquidity saw this as an opportunity to augment their holdings at a discount to NAV. The other logical set of buyers were the secondary funds. The existence of these competitive pools of capital allowed for a relatively smooth reallocation of billions of dollars in assets that might otherwise be subject to fire sale prices.

One feature of secondary transactions that is sometimes overlooked is the fact that an LP wanting to sell their interests cannot do so freely. They need the permission of the GP to transfer their ownership and there are many examples where this permission is withheld because the GP viewed the potential buyer as a competitor. This has disadvantaged several secondary funds run by some of the largest PE partnerships, and provided a competitive advantage to the truly independent secondary operators.

A relatively recent development is the appearance of *staples*. GPs being asked permission to allow the sale of an LP interest might be agreeable only if the potential buyer makes a commitment to the GP's current or next fund. The GPs know their assets are valuable and they are seeking to get compensated by demanding these staples. While economically justified in a competitive landscape, it puts the secondary fund GP in a spot. They have to commit to making blind pool investments inside their normally well-defined secondary funds. If the staples are a small part of the pool, they may not dilute the fund materially, but they can be counted on to add uncertainty, a small J curve and a longer expected life for the fund. When secondary fund LPs do their due diligence, these nuances need to be considered.

Potential buyers of secondary funds include any investors who might naturally be inclined toward a PE fund of funds to achieve diversification across the space or opportunistic PE investors attracted to the potential of additional alpha stemming from the discount at which the underlying assets are typically purchased.

The end result for investors in well-executed secondary funds is an index-like PE investment with somewhat better returns, because of the discounts, and a more rapid return of capital since the assets are purchased at a more mature state. This makes them particularly attractive to smaller investors who might otherwise be unable to develop an appropriately diversified portfolio of individual partnerships or for any investor with a shorter investment horizon.

Secondary funds are not immune to competitive pressures. As more and more capital is committed to new secondary funds, the industry may be more challenged to find great funds to buy. Like all sectors there is a natural ebb and flow, improving or diminishing the investment opportunity set. It is clear, however, that secondary funds follow the same cycle as direct private equity investing. Any time that new venture and private equity funds are operating in a crowded market, secondary funds will be experiencing similar pressures. The advantage of the secondary funds is that they are already diversified, they won't have the same J curve and the discount to NAV on their purchases will likely offer a measure of protection versus the brand new private funds in the market.

9.8.6 Co-Investments

Investing new capital side-by-side with a venture capital, growth equity, or buy-out fund has evolved from being a specialty of the largest pools of institutional capital to being a tool available to any qualified investor. This change through time has altered the menu of opportunities for private investors and has become an important source of capital for GPs to pursue their deals.

The structure of a *co-investment* is fairly basic. GPs identify a transaction that they want to make, but discover that the size is too large to fit well into the risk profile of their fund currently being invested. GPs generally love their deals but they are also respectful of the risks if their funds become too concentrated. In these cases they will seek other sources of capital to join their risk-appropriate fund allocation, and get the deal done.

One way to do this is to invite other GPs to allocate their fund capital in what is commonly referred to as a *club deal*. In such an arrangement there is a committee of highly qualified investors contributing capital and expertise to the investment process. Like all committees, there can sometimes be too many voices present. Each of the GP participants will have an opinion about valuation and ideal strategic and organizational direction. There probably has never been a club deal where afterward at least one of the GP participants didn't wish that they were flying the plane without a group of co-pilots. This is particularly true when deals fail to meet expectations, as the suggested mid-course corrections may pull the company in different directions.

To avoid these problems, GPs began to offer their largest institutional fund investors the opportunity to commit additional capital on a side-by-side basis to the GP. The sweetener in these deals was that the co-investments would not be charged either a management or a performance fee. The objective was to create partnerships with serious sources of capital that would let the GP remain completely in control of the management of each transaction.

There are many advantages to co-investments for these institutional clients. Typically they have allocation budgets that are not trivial to fill each year. By adding to existing positions with known GPs, more capital can be put to work without new major due diligence. The further advantage of no management or performance fees is a useful message to boards who are appropriately concerned about the area where most manager fees currently flow. If the typical fund in the portfolio charges 2% management fee and 20% of the profits, a large commitment to co-investments can average those numbers down meaningfully across the whole allocation.

There are disadvantages as well. The first is that most of these institutional investors do not have the skill or time to effectively due diligence each deal to see if it is worth an additional allocation or not. More often than not, the attitude is that if a respected GP thinks it is worth the investment, it probably is. Not surprisingly, GPs like this attitude among their co-investing LPs. The other major disadvantage is concentration of risk. If you already have exposure to a company through the main fund, adding a co-investment by definition puts more risk in play. This concentration risk should be compared to what you would have if you added another new GP fund with a completely different set of portfolio companies.

As the co-investment trend has progressed, some fund companies have viewed this as an opportunity to gather assets by packaging up a group of co-investments and selling them as a bundle. These funds are structured just like any other single PE fund or fund of funds, with an investment period where commitments will be drawn down, followed by a harvesting period where the underlying investments are sold. Like the direct co-investment activity described above, the GP creating the package usually also benefits from zero or minimal expenses. The LP in the co-investment fund, however, should expect a management and performance fee at that level.

It is pretty obvious why GPs offer co-investment opportunities to their best institutional LPs. It is a deep source of potential capital and the fee savings helps cement the notion in the LPs mind that their relationship is special. Why would GPs offer deals to co-investment fund managers? Most of these managers are also large traditional fund of funds operators, so they too are often major participants in the GP's core activities. They recognize their importance and ask for their share of the action in order to feed another revenue source. The LPs in these co-investment funds would never be on the call list from any GP to add capital to specific deals, so these funds give them access to otherwise impossible opportunities.

The differences between co-investment funds and traditional funds of funds need to be carefully considered. The biggest plus is the underlying fee savings, which eliminates one of the big downsides of fund of funds. The drawback is that co-investment funds can never be as diversified as a fund of fund or a collection of individual PE partnerships. These risk elements need to be considered in the context of the overall portfolio, where concentration in one area may or may not be a valid concern.

Doing due diligence on these funds is similar to evaluating either individual partnerships, secondary funds or fund of funds. One wants to know the investment team well to verify their skills in evaluating each co-investment opportunity. How many deals are looked at? How many are rejected and for what reason? If the fund manager basically adds every co-investment deal being offered, one should be concerned that this is an asset gathering exercise with little independent evaluation. The manager may be more concerned with keeping the GPs happy by being a reliable source of capital than they are concerned about LP returns.

There is also a concern about the quality of the deals being put into the fund. By definition, the best deals of an appropriate size never are put anywhere except the main fund of the original GP. Only the ones of a certain size get offered up as co-investments. Unlike allocating stock buys and sells across accounts, a practice that is governed by fairness rules monitored by the SEC, there are no such rules in allocating private transactions. The best deals get offered to the largest, most important LPs first. If all the capacity is used up with that group, the next tiers of investors never see those transactions. If the GP has seriously overpaid for a company, creating a large need for capital, everybody gets a look at those deals. It is fair to ask a co-investment fund manager for evidence that they are close to the center of the allocation universe and not just being shown the lesser opportunities.

All of these approaches can look like winners in a bull market. Private equity partnerships are by definition either bets on high beta companies or leveraged bets on regular companies. Sometimes they are both. In either case they look great until the bull market stops. Investors enthusiastic for the returns of the 1990s discovered another reality in the first decade of the twenty-first century, as documented by the Kauffman Foundation study.

Ten years after the financial crisis, the bull market continues to chug along, and may continue for several more years. But revisiting Figure 9.16, a great deal of money has entered this space in total since the crisis and there are legitimate questions about the industry's ability to deploy it effectively. When there is a trillion dollars of committed, but uncalled capital in the system, and GPs continue to raise new funds, there is a suspicion that not all of the LPs will meet their expectations.

9.9 REAL ESTATE

Some of the great fortunes the world has known are based in *real estate*. These are often heavily concentrated portfolios that are held for generations. This book isn't about that kind of investing any more than it is about how to start the next Ford Motor Company or Microsoft. Instead, we shall discuss how various types of real estate investments work and can contribute to portfolio performance.

Real estate may not be the least liquid of all possible investment assets, but it is far from the most. In fact, much of the innovation in real estate investments over the past decades has been an attempt to provide more liquid real estate options in order to expand the number of investors willing to participate in the space. Each form of real estate has its advantages and challenges.

9.9.1 Direct Ownership of Real Estate

The most prominent form of real estate investment for the majority of people is direct ownership, often in the form of their primary residence. While many think of this major investment more as a flow of highly personal services than as an impersonal asset, you should never lose sight of the fact that the risks and opportunities of your home can dominate the wealth outcome of your family.

Few investment discussions spend any time on the family home, but the lessons of home ownership are well understood by the majority of the population and are remarkably transferrable to the broader discussion of direct real estate ownership.

Acknowledging that the main objective is to secure basic housing services, the first question is whether to rent or purchase. For many people this boils down to what they can afford, but once a minimum qualifying threshold is met, the decision should be considered from an investment perspective. No matter what market you are considering, either buying a home or renting something closely equivalent will be a possibility. It is always possible to identify the cheaper option at the time of the immediate decision. It is far from obvious that the cheaper option is always the right choice.

On the rental side of the ledger, one must project over the life of the expected tenure the trajectory of future rent payments. Will general inflation be quick or subdued? Are there special factors that would cause the local real estate market's inflation to vary meaningfully from general inflation?

Of equal importance are the alternative opportunities for one's capital that are available to renters if they choose not to tie up assets in the form of a house. One of the best arguments for not buying real estate coming out of the financial crisis was the opportunities in stocks and higher yielding bonds that in retrospect recovered much more quickly than residential real estate.

Buyers of a home may think of themselves as living the American dream, but as was seen in the crisis, there can be nightmare scenarios. Buyers need to consider the direct costs of ownership, which usually include a large financing component, as well as all the associated costs of maintenance. Owner-occupied homes essentially combine the activities of landlord and tenant. Some individuals are more suited to one role over the other.

The same expectations about general and real estate inflation are critical in evaluating the attractiveness of home ownership. People often think of Manhattan luxury condos and San Francisco residences as being obvious situations where real estate inflation will outpace general inflation, but the relationship can work the other way as well. Homes in Detroit and many other once strong industrial cities in the northern United States have seen home values fail to keep up with general inflation for years. Fiscally challenged states like Connecticut also create a headwind to the economics of home ownership.

The returns to buying a home are implicit rent and price appreciation. The best part of the implicit rent is that no matter how grandiose the stream of housing services is to the homeowner, there is no actual cash flow or consequential tax obligation due. This fact, along with the long-standing deductibility of home mortgage interest payments for most taxpayers, adds incentives that advantage home ownership.

The biggest wild cards in the investment deck are interest rates and the costs associated with maintaining the property. For anyone buying a house with a variable rate mortgage, there is the obvious link between higher rates and lower value as an investment. But even if one has a fixed rate mortgage or no mortgage at all, rising rates reduce the value of the property as the discounted value of future service streams falls. Maintenance costs are almost always a negative surprise, which experienced real estate practitioners understand well. There are a score of additional considerations including the probability the property will be vacant, the tenants may not pay in a timely way, or you may just not like dealing with them.

From a portfolio perspective the risk factors that are important to consider are: real interest rates, inflation rates, costs of maintenance, and changes in real estate related tax codes. Note that nominal interest rates are broken into their two components because it really matters why nominal interest rates are increasing. If they are rising because the Fed is raising real rates in an attempt to dampen an overheating economy, this is bad. If they are increasing to reflect a higher expected level of inflation, the net impact on housing investments is less obvious.

The reason changes in tax policy are important, and not the policy itself, is that tax rules are quickly reflected in home prices. Politicians like to say the interest rate deduction for home mortgages makes owning a home more affordable. What they miss is that everyone already understands the impact of the deduction, and bids up the price of the house to reflect it. Given that the current rules are already fully capitalized into home prices, the interest rate deduction just offsets the added expense associated with the higher purchase price. Ironically, the benefit of the interest rate deduction accrued primarily to those homeowners who owned their properties before the rule went into place and not the pool of first time buyers the rule was advertised to help.

This also explains why any proposed tax reform will struggle with eliminating the deduction for home mortgage interest payments. If that benefit was eliminated, potential home buyers would scale back their bids and the value of the entire housing stock would fall. Even though the stream of housing services would not change, no politician wants to be blamed for destroying wealth because of a change in the tax rules.

Now we can extend the story beyond the owner-occupied home. Assume you are considering whether to buy a second home for rental purposes. Everything is essentially the same except for two critical factors. First, taking as a given you are an honest taxpayer and report accurately both income and expenses relating to the rental property, the income from the rent is subject to tax. The stream of housing services that your tenant clearly values at more than the rent he or she pays will net down to a smaller sum to you after taxes. The second big difference is that your tenant may be less patient than you yourself might be in getting the broken window screen repaired.

Like any other portfolio allocation, deciding whether to add a rental home to the investment mix depends on a wide range of expectations on the property itself as well as a broader array of things to consider. Such an investment will be expected to provide a regular stream of income that needs to be compared to other dividend and interest-producing assets. It also should offer protection against increases in inflation, which makes it different from the traditional bonds in your portfolio.

There are many more varieties of real estate than personal residences. Office buildings, shopping centers, apartment complexes, medical facilities, warehouses, and industrial properties are all examples of commercial real estate that can be purchased for investment purposes. While direct ownership of these kinds of properties is usually the domain of the ultra-wealthy, the basic principles are no different than an individual owning a residential property. One needs to attract renters, serve them properly, and maintain the facility. In return the owner gets a rental revenue stream and the chance for capital appreciation.

Evaluating commercial properties requires a deep set of skills. Assessing the physical condition of the property, and what expenditures are likely to be needed to bring the property into marketable shape, is just the beginning. One also needs to gauge the market demand for the space and guess where any likely competition will arise. Someone buying a warehouse outside of Columbus, Ohio, or Indianapolis,

Indiana must recognize that there is a great deal of nearby farmland waiting to be converted if the return on commercial real estate starts looking attractive. There are fewer such problems in more space constrained locations like San Francisco or Seattle, but the value of any property is always limited by the existence of alternatives that involve less convenient transportation.

Many readers are at this point thinking, "Stop. There has to be an easier way to get real estate exposure." While there are some people who are actually quite good at all the tasks required to run a portfolio of properties – or they have the resources to hire those who do – the vast majority of investors have no particular skills or perhaps even an inclination to the area. If real estate investments are going to be part of their portfolio, they can be in a much less labor intensive structure.

This section was structured starting with direct ownership to emphasize what should be an obvious point. Real estate is a massive asset in any economy and *somebody* has to own and operate it. If you do not want to spend the time and energy required to own a property directly, you have to be prepared to pay someone else to get their hands dirty. Given that these tasks are more complicated than clipping coupons from bonds in a mutual fund, you should not be surprised to have to pay a reasonable charge for those services. But there are alternative paths to owning real estate exposure and the following sections describe them.

9.9.2 Real Estate Partnerships

The illiquid nature of underlying real estate investments makes partnerships a logical vehicle for pooling a group of investors' assets. At a high level they look like private equity partnerships previously discussed. Capital is committed and drawn down as properties are purchased. There is a distinct investment period and a liquidation phase. The general partner of the fund may or may not be the manager of the properties, but without question those services will be paid for by the investors before any income or capital gains are distributed back.

Real estate partnerships often specialize by type of property. There are dedicated funds for office space, multi-family housing, retail space, and industrial complexes. Just as certain equity portfolio managers specialize in a particular sector, the general partners of real estate partnerships often believe they have superior skills in one type of property versus others.

Like private equity partnerships, there are different types of partnerships that work along the real estate risk spectrum. At the riskiest extreme are development funds that start with raw land and then build specific structures to rent out or to sell to another operator. These are sometimes labeled *opportunistic funds*. The riskiness of this approach becomes evident in a crisis environment like late 2008. The project of raw land 15 miles outside of Phoenix that looked so promising for development just a few months before the financial crisis suddenly finds itself without construction funding, without likely tenants for the new building, and with no bids for the land itself. Because of taxes and other expenses, these funds can experience serious negative cash flows on top of the mark-to-market losses from repricing the asset.

Next along the spectrum are *rehabilitation funds*. Here the GP buys existing buildings that may need significant capital investment to upgrade the facilities. Some funds have an investment thesis to buy "B" class buildings in prime locations and then bring them up to "A" building standards. While not as demanding of capital as a pure opportunistic fund, there is still a meaningful commitment of resources beyond the original purchase price. An important piece of this process is managing the rent rolls. In some cases it is preferable to buy a building that has a high vacancy rate so that after the reconstruction new tenants can be identified that will pay more attractive rents.

The exits from these kinds of real estate transactions are often sales to insurance companies, pension plans, or other institutional investors that are looking for long-term flows of rental incomes. Another source of demand for these buildings comes from *core real estate funds* that specialize in building portfolios of fully developed, income-producing properties. While there is an ability to profit from real estate appreciation in these funds, the primary motivation for being an LP in such a partnership is the regular flow of income from rents.

As one moves from opportunistic funds to core funds there is an increasing sensitivity to rising interest rates. If interest rates rise because of Fed policy or another reason that is unrelated to a landlord's ability to raise rents in a timely fashion, the value of these properties falls. This is exactly analogous to how fixed coupon bonds are priced. Once the rent or coupon is established, future increases in interest rates mean the discounted value of the cash flow falls and with it the price of the asset. This concept is captured analytically in the *cap rate* of the property.

The cap rate, which is a shorthand version of capitalization rate, is the ratio of the net rental cash flow to the value of the property. It is like the P/E ratio of an equity, except the ratio is upside down. If a property has a net income of $100,000 per year and its current value is $2 million, its cap rate is 5%. If the market value of the property doubles but the rent has not changed, the cap rate falls to 2.5%. Investors want to buy properties with as high a cap rate as possible and sell at lower cap rates. If interest rates on safe bonds are quite low, investors in core real estate will bid up properties that have perceived safe rental income as an alternative source of revenue, lowering the cap rates of the property. Conversely, if interest rates rise the rental income from a property no longer looks as relatively attractive and the cap rate will rise as well.

Most large real estate private partnerships are structured to include a portfolio of properties, even if they are of the same type (offices, hotels, shopping centers, etc.). This means that the LPs are often agreeing to participate in a blind pool of future deals. Great trust in the GP is required in such instances. One needs to be convinced that a favorable investing environment will exist over the life of the fund and that when opportunities arise the GP will be able to execute effectively.

An approach that requires somewhat less of a leap of faith attitude is the creation of partnerships around each project. In these cases the GP is often the developer who sources potential projects and then goes out and collects subscriptions against this single property. Successful practitioners of this craft have large contact files of potential investors. Over time, there develops almost a club atmosphere, where the same LPs get together when called by the GP. Of course, the main advantage of this approach to LPs is that they form their own opinions about whether a specific real estate project is likely to be a strong investment or not. They are not nearly as reliant on simply trusting the judgment of the GP.

It is rare that real estate is purchased without some form of financing and this translates into leverage at the fund level. An opportunistic development fund might buy land outright and then use that asset as collateral against a construction loan. Once the building is built and leased out, it is seen as a safer asset and the GP might replace the construction loan with a more traditional mortgage at a higher loan to value. When this happens there may be excess capital taken out and returned to LPs, which effectively translates the higher leverage in the project back to the investors.

The other main consideration in evaluating real estate private partnerships is whether the portfolio of properties is geographically diversified or concentrated. There is an old adage that the three most important things in real estate are: location, location, and location. This is a knife that can cut both ways. If one invests in a geographically concentrated portfolio of properties at the right time, the rewards can be impressive. Of course, buying into a hot market right before a correction can be a recipe for disaster. Many concentrated, leveraged opportunistic partnerships went to zero during the financial crisis that began in 2008. No amount of subsequent recovery in the property value could save the LPs that were wiped out. Others market participants got the benefits of the rebound.

9.9.3 Liquid Real Estate; REITs, Mutual Funds, and ETFs

Real estate partnerships were a major improvement for those investors looking to step away from direct ownership while still receiving the lion's share of exposure to the sector. Still, they were highly illiquid, leaving an unmet demand for real estate exposure that could be bought and sold on a more continuous basis. *Real Estate Investment Trusts*, or REITs, were created to meet that demand.

The basic idea behind REITs is that the REIT general partner would assemble a collection of properties and then issue shares against them. If it was a public REIT, the shares would trade on a stock exchange or in the open market. Private or nontraded REITs would have a similar structure but not trade on a listed exchange. Over the years regulators have carefully examined nontraded REITs because they have been sometimes aggressively marketed by commission sales people without adequate disclosure about the risks of the underlying holdings.[64]

Any such structure would fail competitively if the REIT had to pay income tax at the corporate level and then the REIT shareholder would also be taxed again on any distributions. While this type of double taxation is commonplace for US corporations, there are too many real estate partnerships out there that don't face this issue for any smart investor to pick the high tax option when acquiring real estate exposure.

When REITs received their preferred tax treatment, there were a few restrictions placed on them. First, there had to be at least 100 shareholders and there were limits on how much concentration there could be among the largest shareholders. The lawmakers did not want to pretend to create a vehicle for broad public ownership of real estate only to discover that they had built a clever tax structure for a handful of owners of some properties.

More importantly, the rules require REITs to distribute at least 90% of the net income from the properties back to shareholders in the form of dividends. These are non-qualifying dividends from the IRS perspective, which means they are taxed as ordinary income and not at some preferential rate that many corporate dividends enjoy.

REITs come in many flavors. Often the underlying portfolio of properties share a common theme: apartments, shopping centers, health care facilities, and urban office

---

[64]Whelan, R. (2014). Nontraded REITs Are Hot, But Have Plenty of Critics. *The Wall Street Journal.* (15 June).

buildings are all examples of actively traded REITs. A specialty area called mortgage REITs hold commercial and residential mortgages in their portfolios instead of the properties themselves. Mortgage REITs share the structure and many of the rules followed by property REITs, but they are much closer to fixed income funds than they are something you would buy to get real estate equity exposure.

The moment-to-moment price of a public property REIT is solely a function of immediate supply and demand. Just as a closed-end stock fund has an underlying portfolio and an implicit net asset value, there is at any given time a value of the underlying properties of a REIT. The fact that it is virtually impossible to observe this value accurately in real time only adds to the challenge of deciding where you might want to place your bids of offers.

The underlying properties are typically leveraged somewhat within the REIT structure, much like a private partnership adds leverage to its property holdings. This leverage feature added considerable uncertainty during the financial crisis as it was rarely clear which REITs would be able to service their debt obligations. At the depth of the crisis it was also questionable whether ongoing financing would be available for REITs approaching the maturity of their debt structure. In retrospect, many public REITs traded well below net asset value at the time, but that was far from an easy valuation decision in real time.

Nontraded REITs are sometimes marketed as a "safer" alternative to publicly traded REITs on the theory that they exhibit less volatility. Like real estate in general, not seeing prices move on a regular basis is not the same as a lack of volatility. No news is simply no news, and owners of nontraded REITs should not delude themselves into believing that they own a safe asset simply because there is no daily price to watch.

Public REITs may buy and sell properties within their structure, but the idea is that shareholders are buying into an actively managed and permanent pool of assets. Nontraded REITs have a slightly different model. Assets are raised and properties are purchased. Regular dividends are paid from the income generated. After a few years the sponsors of the funds liquidate the portfolio holdings and then distribute the cash back to shareholders. One might question why this approach is taken, and the answer may come from the other major knock on the industry.

Most nontraded REITs have massive up-front sales charges, not uncommonly ranging from 12% to 15%. There may be ongoing fees charged as well. By liquidating old funds and encouraging investors to invest the proceeds in new ones, the sponsors are able to repeat the up-front fee process. Proponents of the product say they give investors much needed, safe revenue at a time of historically low interest rates. Critics note that these investors would have done much better over the same holding period with any of the popular traded index REIT products.

Given the importance of real estate as a sector of the economy, it is no surprise that there are mutual funds and ETFs that cover the REIT space. Mutual funds can specialize by sector or cover a wide variety of REIT holdings. They are mostly actively managed portfolios, but there are numerous index funds available that take a passive approach. The differences between the mutual fund and ETF offerings are similar to any other comparison between the two fund structures. The fact that the underlying holdings are publicly traded REITs is insignificant.

The major advantage of owning a mutual fund or an ETF is the broader diversification available. One can get meaningful exposure to the sector without taking on specific REIT risk. This advantage comes at the costs normally associated with running a mutual fund or ETF, but for many investors unwilling or unable to construct their own REIT portfolio, these popular vehicles offer an attractive option.

9.10   OTHER REAL ASSETS AND COMMODITIES

Real estate is perhaps the biggest and most traditional way to own real assets in an investment portfolio, but it is far from the only way. For as long as there has been commerce in metals, energy *commodities*, food stuffs, and building materials, there have been individuals building wealth in this area.[65]

If one thinks being a landlord for an apartment building is complicated, imagine what is involved in running a cattle feedlot, or a natural gas processing facility. The basic investment idea behind owning commodities is similar to the real estate story. One wants to own assets that protect against a general increase in inflation. But there is one major difference. Commodities do not produce rents. The cash flow to holding commodities is negative, arising from storage costs, insurance and the opportunity cost of tying up your money. To make money in commodities requires market conditions and superior skills that can overcome these headwinds.

This section's discussion will parallel the last. We'll start with direct ownership and explain the benefits and sometimes considerable costs associated with this approach. Then we'll explore less direct methods of getting exposure to commodities. Just like with real estate, there has been a push in the last several decades to broaden the number of investors who can get this exposure conveniently. While undoubtedly broadening the investor base, the experience with these more liquid forms of commodity investing has been mixed. In commodities like much of life, you cannot have your cake and eat it too.

9.10.1   Direct Ownership of Commodities

It is possible, but not always practical, to build one's commodity investments with direct purchases. You could buy warehouse receipts for bags of cocoa in storage facilities along the US east coast. John Denver reportedly installed large gasoline tanks on his Colorado property at the height of the 1970s gas crisis. You could keep bales of crushed aluminum cans in your garage. You may think of the greatly loved but long dead sedan in your driveway as your trade on rising scrap steel prices, but your neighbor probably just sees it as an eyesore. As this list suggests, there may be easier ways to build out your commodity investments.

As a practical matter the physical possession of assets like these is usually best left to specialists who know the respective markets well and are the most efficient in minimizing all the costs associated with holding these products. It may be surprising to anyone not in the business, but these professionals typically succeed by avoiding as much as possible the risks of fluctuating prices. If you own a grain elevator, it is rarely because you think the wheat stored inside will make a great investment.

---

[65]Readers may note that in much of the Old Testament, there are accounts of wealth specified in quantities of gold and silver, spices, oils and livestock, and cedar trees. It is fair to conclude that real asset investing predates the public markets by centuries.

Still, there are a few areas where direct investment ownership is widely practiced. Jewels and precious metals like gold and silver share a characteristic that they do not physically degrade through time, and their high value-to-weight ratio makes them relatively easy to store. For these reasons many investors hold their own inventories of these commodities as their primary means of investment exposure.

The other desirable characteristic that these items possess is a grading standard that is widely recognized and relatively easy to confirm. Gold and silver can be assayed by reputable testing facilities. Diamonds conform to a color, cut, and clarity matrix that is also widely accepted. While none of these commodities could be considered perfectly homogeneous, the challenges they pose are considerably easier to deal with than, say, the variation in quality across bags of coffee.

Investors who decide on direct ownership of these commodities either have to invest in secure storage facilities and pay insurance premium against theft themselves, or hire out those services from a specialized storage facility. In either event, there are direct costs that eat away from the total return from holding these items as an investment. These are only partially offset by any potential consumption benefit arising from wearing your jewels in public or privately handling your gold coins with glee like Scrooge McDuck.

Whenever you buy anything, commodities, real estate, or shares of a company, there is the indirect cost of foregone interest not earned from this money had you purchased T-bills instead. This indirect expense should not be deducted from your return calculation like you would storage costs, but you should never lose sight of it. If real interest rates rise, some investors will see the rising opportunity cost as a reason to sell their gold or diamonds and deploy that money into an earning asset. In times of steady prices, but rising interest rates, it is not surprising to see the prices of precious metals and jewels come under pressure.

One argument for the personal physical possession of commodities like gold, silver and jewels versus entrusting that service to a specialist licensed warehouse is accessibility in times of crisis. Imagine a terrorist attack in central Manhattan that prevented access to your gold stored in one of the world's biggest facilities near the New York Public Library.[66] To prevent this chance occurrence, you could decide to store your gold at home.

Now envision your worst nightmare. There is a collapse in paper currency and civil order. You are in theory prepared in that you are holding a store of value that people trust. Or are you? Imagine trying to buy milk and eggs in Greenwich, Connecticut, with your one ounce gold coins. Why should the merchant trust you and your possibly counterfeit coins? What would be the exchange rate in this form of barter? In a wide collapse of society, many expected normal relationships could fail.

9.10.2 Equity Ownership in Commodities-Based Businesses

If direct ownership of physical commodities is too challenging, an alternative is to own companies that are natural resource based. Mines, energy producers, companies that own farm land or stands of timber are all ways to be exposed to commodity

---

[66]Worse yet, your gold could be made radioactive for decades, à la the 1963 classic James Bond movie, *Goldfinger*.

prices. The challenges here are that owning a lot of gold or oil in the ground does not necessarily translate into a profitable company and a strong stock price. Another challenge is that the management of these companies may choose to hedge away some or all of the commodity price risk. Your motivation for wanting to own the company may not be in alignment with the goals of decision makers who are trying to manage profits in the firm and not necessarily run the company as a conduit for rising commodity prices.

There are lots of natural resources companies you can buy in the public market. If your primary motivation behind this investment is to get exposure to rising commodity prices, you will want to focus on firms at the earliest stages of exploration and production and not so-called *midstream companies* like a refinery or pipeline. You will also want to examine company annual reports and accounting filings to see if the company hedges out some or all of the commodity price risk. Even a producing mine, which is often thought of as a great commodity play, fails in this role if the next several years' anticipated production is already sold in the futures or forward market.

Perhaps the biggest challenge to using natural resource equities to obtain commodity exposure is that these stocks move for many reasons independent of the underlying commodity price. There is individual stock risk stemming from how well company management executes on their plan. There is also sector and total market risk. It is entirely possible that some geopolitical event could spook the entire stock market even as commodity prices are relatively unaffected.

An example of how this affected investors was seen with the run-up in gold prices from 2009 to 2011. The normal intuition says that owning a gold mine should be a levered approach to owning gold. To see this, consider the following example. Suppose the spot price of gold is $1,000 per ounce, and the mine's cost to produce that gold is $900 per ounce. The mine's profits should be what the stock price is based on. If the spot price goes up 10% to $1,100 per ounce and the costs of production don't change, the profit per ounce of gold doubles to $200. This is why many investors who become bullish buy miners that do not hedge the gold price risk. This is a simple thesis that doesn't always play out as planned.

Figure 9.18 the path of gold prices and an index of gold miners' stocks for a three-year period, both scaled to start the period at 100. There was a strong advance for both series over this period but gold bullion advanced by about 70% while the miners increased by closer to 50%. This is not how this relationship is supposed to work.

What happened over this history was that as the price of gold increased, the price of mining stocks initially increased faster, just as the theory would predict. Then the dynamic of the mine industry changed. Decision makers at many mines decided on the basis of rising prices and low interest rates that this was the ideal time to expand their operations. Large portions of the profits being generated were used to start new mines or expand operations at existing mines. The hope was that these investments would eventually benefit shareholders more than they would if the profits were distributed. Instead, the total effect for the industry was a faster increase in the supply of gold than demand was growing, which led to an eventual severe drop in gold prices and profits. Collectively the management of the world's mines were not good stewards of shareholder capital in this episode. Beginning in

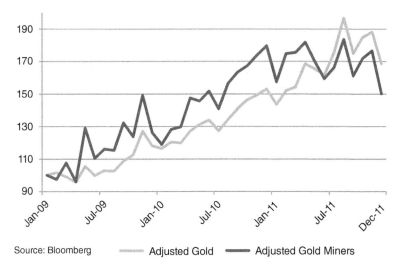

FIGURE 9.18   Gold vs. Gold Miners, 2009–2011
Source: Bloomberg

2011 stock market investors figured this out and the share price of the miners fell behind the path of gold prices. Years later the mining industry still struggled with value creation.[67]

It can, and sometimes does, work. Superior management at a natural resources company might be able to grow earnings even if commodity prices are moving south. Energy companies with great properties and technology and secure balance sheets remained profitable even as the price of oil fell from over $100 per barrel to under $50. The share prices of commodity-based businesses are often negatively impacted by the movement of the underlying commodity prices, but that in itself is not necessarily a solid predictor of corporate profitability.

Investors should also be sensitive to the fact that since many emerging market economies are heavily influenced by their commodity sectors, there is likely to be a reasonably high correlation across commodity prices, commodity-based company equities and EM equities. Placing money in each of these correlated areas may not achieve, many benefits from diversification.

9.10.3   Synthetic Ownership of Commodities: Commodity Index Products

The vehicle most often used by investors in commodities is a fund that rarely actually owns the physical product, but instead establishes long positions synthetically through the use of futures or other derivatives. The first products in this universe date from the early 1990s and were based on the *Goldman Sachs Commodity Index (GSCI)*. In the years since there has been a proliferation of competing indexes and products. All attempt to make owning commodity exposure as easy as owning a stock

---

[67]Nathan, V. (2013). How Gold Miners Became a Terrible Investment. *Forbes*. (1 July).

or bond mutual fund. While the mechanics of commodity index products look quite similar to those of a mutual fund, we shall see below that there ends up being some important difference that can impact performance.

Most of us are quite comfortable with the way our stock and bond funds work. In general, we give the manager a dollar and he or she buys a dollar's worth of securities. These securities are placed into a custody account for a nominal fee and we benefit to the extent that price appreciation plus dividends or interest exceed the costs of custody for the securities plus the management fees. We hardly ever think about the cost of storing stocks because it is so very low.

Commodities are different. Almost without exception, physical commodities are a pain in the neck to store properly. They can be bulky and difficult to transport. Grains and products like cocoa and sugar change in quality through time. In the extreme, some commodities are actually alive (cattle and hogs). All in all, most people who are interested in speculating in commodities do so using futures contracts because those instruments allow them to participate in price changes (up or down) without having to actually deal with the physical products if they choose not to.

Investors in commodity funds might think they have something akin to their stock and bond funds, but the difference is striking and it is all about storage. Very few commodity fund managers have any experience in the complicated business of physical commodity management. So what they do is construct unlevered synthetic collections of commodities using a combination of Treasury bills and long commodities futures contracts. Consider a simple example.

An investor wants to be long crude oil as part of their portfolio. Each NYMEX crude oil futures contract calls for delivery of 1,000 barrels of West Texas Intermediate crude oil. With the current front month contract trading at $50 a barrel, each contract is worth $50,000. For simplicity, let's assume the investor wants to invest $1,00,000, or 20 contracts worth of oil.

The typical commodity fund will first take the $1,000,000 and buy T-bills, or some other very secure interest bearing collateral. It will then go out and go *long* 20 of the front month futures contracts, which is the position that most closely corresponds to the spot price of oil. Note that when this trade is done, the end result is almost the same as if the investor had bought $1,000,000 worth of oil and hired some storage facility to hold the goods for him or her.

The key word, though, is *almost*. The commodity fund investor doesn't have to pay storage or insurance and the fund investor doesn't give up the interest on $1,000,000 by actually buying the product. This synthetic futures business sounds like a pretty good deal, but as you might suspect it's not as easy as it might seem. Let's break the source of the fund's returns down.

There are three components. The first is the interest earned on the collateral. It is your money and you are entitled to the interest. Small retail investors sometimes give this up to their brokers, but any commodity fund worth its salt captures this for the investor. The second component of the return is the price change of the commodity. If when you sell, the futures price is, say, $55, you will have a $5 per barrel, or 10%, profit. Of course, if you sell at $45, there will be a $5 per barrel, or 10% loss. Note that since you have committed the full value of the contracts as collateral, there is no leverage effect on the return. If the price moves a dollar, you make or lose a dollar.

Life would be pretty simple if that was all there was to it, but commodity fund investors tend to want to be long commodities for longer than a few weeks. When the front month contract approaches delivery, to stay long one has to sell the current contract and buy the next one in the string. Let's go back to the simple example. The only thing to keep in mind is that futures prices can always be expected to converge to the *spot price* as they move toward delivery.

Suppose the spot price is $51 and the market is *inverted* because inventories are relatively low. This means the first futures price might be at $50 and the next contract at $49. You go long the front contract as described above. Now suppose a few weeks pass and *nothing* happens to the spot price. The futures contract you own moves toward the spot price as delivery approaches, and we can assume the spread between the futures stays at a dollar. You sell your maturing futures near the $51 spot price and buy the next future for around $50. Note that in an inverted market you make money from what is called the *roll yield* even if commodity prices remain unchanged.

This leads us to see how the total return of a commodity fund consists of interest returns on collateral, price appreciation of the commodity, and roll yield. In a bull market that is inverted, this is like the trifecta of investing: you earn interest, a positive roll yield, and any price appreciation. But it doesn't always work that way.

In physical commodity markets that have ample inventories, the futures markets are usually in a *carry* relationship. That is, deferred contracts are more expensive than spot. In our simple example, the spot price might be $49, while the first and second futures contracts are $50 and $51. Going long the front futures contract and holding it a month in the example now produces a loss of $1 per barrel as the futures market converges to spot. And as long as the market is in a carry, this loss will happen continuously over the life of the investment. This is known as *negative roll yield* and it can be significant.

Whether a commodity market is in a carry relationship or an inverted one is not a random event. Futures markets exist not to provide a convenience to investors wishing to avoid the hassles of storing oil, but to allocate the product through time. How oil gets allocated and priced through time is largely a function of inventory levels. When inventories are quite low the value of having immediate access is high and the front month contracts are priced higher than deferred months. These markets are said to have *inverted forward curves.*

If inventories are ample, few will be willing to pay a premium for immediate access. In fact, if supplies are great enough you will need to provide a price incentive to have storers keep the excess supplies out of the immediate market. This is done by pricing the deferred contracts higher than the nearby, which encourages current inventory holders to look down the road before they sell. At the extreme, the forward price will be above the spot price by an amount that covers the total costs of storage, financing, and insurance. This condition is known as *full carry.*

Start with the important premise that every time someone goes long a futures contract there has to be an opposite *short*. As more and more investors get long commodity exposure through these futures-based vehicles it is logical to ask, who is taking the other side of all these trades? There can be only two answers. There could be speculators who simply believe prices will be falling and not rising. Or the shorts could come from the commercial side of the business, including people who already own the physical product and sell it short in the futures market at a price that locks in a profit.

Futures exchanges might like you to believe that their community of traders are broad-shouldered, risk-assuming individuals and firms that will take on the opposite risk as a public service. While there are no doubt speculators on both sides of a market that enjoy participating in this fashion, history shows that major shifts in supply and demand come from the commercial side of the ledger. As synthetic commodity index investors grew in importance in the market, they were increasingly facing commercial shorts that had the ability and the willingness to make delivery if necessary.

Over the years as more investors allocated to synthetic commodities strategies through these index funds they began to change the normal storage patterns. Crude oil is a great example of how this played out for a while. Traditionally, the most cost-effective storage of crude oil was done by Mother Nature. That is, it made more sense to keep oil in the ground and pump it up on demand rather than construct large numbers of massive, expensive storage facilities. This led to relatively small formal inventories above ground and futures markets that were inverted.

As more and more investors entered the market on the long side using futures-based investments, the shorts could not risk relying on oil in the ground to meet their obligations. Such a situation could lead to a short-term *squeeze* and considerable financial harm. The solution was a rapidly expanding storage complex. People bought physical oil in the spot market and placed it into storage whenever there was enough synthetic demand to push the forward price beyond full carry.

As the futures contracts approach maturity, the shorts are in complete control. The synthetic commodity investors never really wanted the physical product. They just wanted exposure to the price. At expiration the longs typically rolled their futures position out of the front month and into a more deferred contract month. Unfortunately for them, the shorts could command a big premium to do their side of the roll because they threatened the longs with actual delivery. After repeated expiration after expiration these *negative roll yields* add up, reducing the total return to the paper commodity strategy.

What these synthetic commodity investors should expect is that once all of the futures prices are priced efficiently, there will be no free lunch. The investor can either buy the physical commodities and incur all of the hassles and expenses of that activity, or they can try to replicate that exposure implicitly with a futures-based product in which case they will also implicitly pay the equivalent of those expenses to someone else through the pricing of the futures.

The shape of futures market prices through time is dictated by supply and demand, but in the first decade of the twenty-first century the demand from commodity index investors grew so large at a time when there were few shortages of physical products that most markets captured by the indexes were in a positive carry and significant negative roll yields were the norm. Investors who had high hopes of owning a cheap investment vehicle that would provide diversification and an inflation hedge found they owned something that lost money even as commodity prices stagnated.

This discussion has focused primarily on whether commodity index products are the best way to get exposure, but for many people there is a much bigger issue to be addressed. Because commodity investors are trading in important products like oil and grains, they sometimes become the lightning rod for complaints about high prices that periodically appear. Congressmen never want to hear from constituents that the government is turning a blind eye to the problem of greedy speculators making it difficult for Grandma to heat her home in the winter or put enough food on the table. For these reasons, commodity index products have periodically been raked over the coals in Washington, with some groups calling for extremely tight limits on what such funds can own. They see no reason to allow investors to buy products that they have no intention of actually consuming.

The debate can be quite intense and emotional. The language of the discussion has often been unhelpful, as some commentators use the terms investor, speculator, and manipulator with almost no distinction. As opponents of these products get increasingly loud, complaining about the high prices the fund buyers have supposedly created, the other side pushes back forcefully, trying to protect what has become a large and highly profitable segment of the fund industry. These discussions always seem to gain prominence after major market moves like the one that saw crude oil approach $150 a barrel in the second quarter of 2008.

The proponents of commodity index investing actually paint the activity as providing benefits to the commodity markets. Academic studies have been commissioned that conclude that commodity index investors are primarily liquidity providers and that they have no impact on the price of the underlying commodities. These assertions come in the following three varieties and they strain our intuition about how markets work:

Commodity index owners are always buying and then selling, never taking delivery. Therefore it is not real demand. The act of selling the soon-to-expire futures contract when the more deferred contract is purchased is a neutral act.

Commodity index owners rebalance their exposures to maintain target portfolio weights, just as they do their bond and stock exposures. Rebalancing involves selling after markets appreciate and buying after declines, so commodity index owners add stability to the market.

Examining the general increase in commodity prices that occurred in 2007 and the first half of 2008, it was argued that commodity index buyers clearly had no impact on their markets as evidenced by the fact that prices for commodities that had futures and those that did not both went up. If index buyers had an impact, the futures-based commodities would have gone up while those without futures would have not.

Each of these points is made with great conviction, backed with data where selectively appropriate, and each contains a grain of truth. But the broader assertions are false for the following reasons:

Any neutrality of rolling futures positions is true only *after* the initial positions are established. Every time a new long-only index futures client appears, they represent a new long position that has to be met by a short. Tens of billions of dollars of new money entered the index space in 2007 and early 2008, competing with other longs. Higher prices were required to encourage new shorts to be counterparties. This is exactly how markets always work, and these index buyers did not magically appear on the open interest records to assume their price neutral rolling activity. Additionally, the act of rolling futures contracts may be neutral with respect to price levels, but it is not neutral with respect to the spreads. Selling the front month and buying the deferred tends to create and widen the carry in any market. Many market participants believe commodity index buyers have had a meaningful impact on both price levels and spreads.

The rebalancing comment is quite accurate *if the number and size of commodity index participants is static.* The problem in 2007 and 2008 was that for every investor who was trimming an outsized commodity exposure because of price appreciation, there were probably 10 new participants who were being attracted to the space by recent strong returns. The net effect was still a major net addition to the long side as prices rallied.

The correlation argument is made only by those people who fail to understand or acknowledge that physical commodity markets are linked in many ways. Coal and rice are two commodities for which futures markets have never achieved serious liquidity. And yet, their prices increased in 2007 and 2008 without futures buyers. The flaw in the original argument stems from the fact that many end users of natural gas and heating oil on the energy side and wheat and corn on the food side have the ability and incentive to shift to coal and rice when the prices of the futures commodities go up. If futures buyers raised the price of natural gas, heating oil, wheat and corn by their buying, other market participants would transfer that impact to the non-futures markets. In economics this is called a *cross elasticity of demand*.

While it is certainly true that China, India, and many other parts of the developed and developing world were rapidly expanding their demand for all commodities in 2007 and early 2008, it is also true that tens of billions of dollars of demand was entering the market via commodity index investing. Ascribing how much of a price increase is attributable to each activity is probably beyond the powers of existing econometric tools. Saying one is responsible and the other is not is roughly the equivalent of trying to say which blade of the scissors is doing the cutting. Most sensible people believe that both activities had a role. Having noted all of the above, however, does not immediately hand an intellectual victory to those who would limit or ban commodity index investing.

The arguments on the other side include those who believe all institutional investors like pension plans, insurance companies, and endowments should be prohibited from investing in these unleveraged, futures-based products, not because they are manipulating the market, but simply because they have too great an impact. The theory goes that in the short run, the supplies of any physical commodity are relatively constrained and that when large sums of money appear on the long side, the result is unnecessary price volatility. Like the arguments on the opposite side of the debate, there is some intuition that has appeal, but the ultimate argument here is equally flawed.

The basic error comes from the assumption that such investors will either invest in futures based products or they will do nothing at all. While the futures-based instruments are perhaps the most convenient and cost effective, there are many other ways to gain exposure. As previously discussed, you can buy physical gold, a gold ETF, or a synthetic position using unleveraged gold futures. Banning the index futures activity would simply move demand to the other forms. Many of the same dealers who today provide futures-based structures will simply create private facilities for holding inventories of commodities, which they could unitize and assign to the investors. Sophisticated investors would decide whether the service was worth the fees, and might elect to manage the inventories directly. In either case, the institutional investor will secure access to physical commodities, which as we all know, will translate right back to the futures market through the arbitrage process.

An intermediate proposal would be to simply ban the activities of those investors who are deemed too big for the markets. Presumably at the top of the list would be state and national pension plans measured in the tens of billions of dollars. But under what rules does one draw the line? Is a $50 million endowment small enough to participate? Should small state pension plans be allowed access to efficient tools, but California and New York be kept out? The issue of equity is an important one, and discriminating across classes or sizes of investors is a very bad idea. Add that to the fact that any such scheme won't work for the reasons cited above, and this discussion should be given no attention.

Careful thinkers ask the question, "Don't these large flows of money matter?" and the answer is, of course, yes. They matter in the same ways that flows into tech stocks and emerging market equities in the 1990s mattered, and the path of prices as a result is not always pretty. But those price signals are not noise, and they do illicit a response from people who can modify their own supply and demand. There are people who believe they know better than the market what is a fair value, but anyone who has had experience with market control programs like gas rationing in the 1970s should be particularly cautious about such claims.

Seasoned observers of commodity markets know that as noncommercial participants enter a market, the opposite side is usually taken by a short-term liquidity provider, but the ultimate counterparty is likely to be someone active in the commercial market. In the case of commodity index buyers, evidence suggests that the sellers are not typically other investors or leveraged speculators. Instead, they are owners of the physical commodity who are willing to sell into the futures market and either deliver at expiration or roll their hedge forward if the spread allows them to profit from continued storage. This activity is effectively creating synthetic long positions in the commodity for the index investor, matched against real inventories held by the shorts. This can produce both high spot prices in the short run simultaneously with large inventories and strong positive carry relationships.

While some complain about the immediate resulting price moves, over a longer horizon two things likely occur. First, the buildup of inventories beyond historical norms will have a moderating effect on supply disruptions. The second effect is a natural decline in the attractiveness of the commodity index strategy. The large inventories and the prevailing positive carry in the market create a negative roll yield for the investor. This is not a random event, but a direct result of the size of the commodity index activity. As more people become aware of these features, the allure of commodity index investing may wane without any outside intervention. This is an accurate characterization of how this environment evolved after oil prices fell by more than half from above $100 a barrel in 2014.

Finally, it needs to be emphasized that if synthetic vehicles to acquire long commodity exposure are limited or made prohibitively expensive, investors will find other ways to achieve their ends. If we think such investors are disruptive to the futures markets, imagine how much more disruption would result from institutional investors taking over grain elevators or oil bunkers. Attempts to keep these investors out of the market will only succeed in moving them into storage activities where they have little skill and no advantage. It is much better to let them be met by professionals in the handling of the commodities, and keep them on the exchange, adding to both liquidity and transparency.

A final comment on synthetic commodity products is in order. As the market grew dramatically up to 2008, many of the price effects discussed above came to dominate the underlying markets. Returns to the original index products struggled, prompting researchers to run back to their computers and see where their models stumbled. What resulted were supposedly new and improved indexes that were less dependent upon rolling the front month futures contracts or that placed less weight on commodities that experienced the most pronounced negative roll yield.

The problem with these efforts is that when the original research was being done, there was nothing obviously wrong with the models that created the first indexes. It was the weight of the new investment funds following the models that caused them to falter. *There is absolutely nothing to suggest the same phenomenon won't be repeated if sizable funds flow into funds based on new models.* Investors should see this as just one more example of how the science of investing is often a back-testing exercise that has little chance of being successful once it moves from the lab to the real markets in any meaningful way.

The difficulties associated with investing in commodities in their various respective forms make them somewhat of a challenge for traditional investors. Owning physical commodities puts you toe to toe with people who are genuinely expert in the production, storage and trade of the products. Trying to achieve exposure synthetically has great intuitive appeal, but as history has shown, this approach has its own set of problems. The middle ground of equities of natural resources companies gives a diluted form of exposure that can be heavily influenced by general movements in the equity markets. There obviously is no perfect solution for investors seeking commodity exposure in their portfolios. The final decision must ultimately be whether the case for commodities at any point in time is compelling enough to accept the warts that come with the various options.

9.10.4 Esoteric Real Assets: Shipping, Power, Water Rights

The preceding section covered what could be considered traditional commodities, or those with large enough markets that futures markets had evolved over the years for them. While the range of products is vast (metals, energy, grains, livestock) and may seem esoteric to most investors, they are in fact quite mainstream as real assets go. There are many more niche areas that are sometimes presented to investors as attractive additions to their portfolios.

It is not unusual to pick up *The Wall Street Journal* and see a story discussing an imminent global shortage of phosphate fertilizer or peppercorns, or some other product. There are thousands of commodities in global trade, representing collectively hundreds of billions of dollars of production annually, and if you look hard enough there will always be one or two with supply or demand disruptions severe enough to be newsworthy. It is like turning on the Weather Channel during the spring and seeing a story of catastrophic flooding. The probabilities are high that *someplace* in America is experiencing a 100-year flood on any given spring day. These stories seem important, and for those directly affected by the event, they are. But in the case of commodities disruptions, this does not imply that there is a viable investment that results for most of us.

A good starting point to this discussion asks the question, "Why do certain commodities enjoy liquid futures markets while others do not?" Futures are not created as an accommodation to the general investing public. Instead they exist to facilitate transactions across a wide range of professional participants in that market. The fact that the public is afforded easy access to the space through futures is a beneficial, but unplanned, byproduct.

When considering physical assets like scrap steel, cement, or less common food stuffs that have never developed futures markets, one must conclude that they lack one or more critical features. They may not be big enough or volatile enough to represent a large amount of risk. They may not be democratic enough in that they are tightly controlled by a production cartel. Oil and gasoline futures markets struggled in the early years because of resistance by global integrated oil companies that did not want to see any of their considerable market advantages eroded. These commodities may not have a dealer community that can operate easily across both the cash and the futures markets, ensuring that the prices in one area are reflective of the other. Whatever the reason, one should conclude that anyone participating in such markets is a highly trained professional who learned his or her skills in the school of hard knocks.

If an average investor reads a story about how striking phosphate miners in Tunisia and Jordan have created a global shortage of this vital fertilizer ingredient, there may be an inclination to wonder where a profit might be found. Worse yet, that investor may be solicited by a fund manager who proclaims that he or she can exploit a great opportunity arising from the disruption. It is usually easier to dismiss one's own half-formed opinions than a polished argument from someone who is clearly an expert.

The first question that should be asked whenever there is a hot idea investment pitch is, "Why am I being let in on this?" That sounds cynical, but the reality is that if the fund manager has gotten down to you: 1) he or she doesn't have enough of his or her own capital to exploit what is likely a limited opportunity, and 2) many people before you were offered the opportunity and passed. The second question then becomes, "What is the chance of success in a world dominated by the most experienced of professional traders?"

That is the main message for anyone tempted to trade non-mainstream commodities. Commodity markets are highly complicated systems of global supply and demand. The likelihood of a part-time participant having an edge over a full-time pro is quite slim. This is, in fact, not an inappropriate caution for mainstream investors who are tempted to dabble in commodity futures. The other side of your order is also likely to be a commercial trader, but in the case of futures there is always a small population of amateurs who may be even less informed than you are giving you a slightly better chance of success. The following riddle is well founded in experience:

Q: What is the best way to make a small fortune?
A: Start with a large fortune and trade futures.

There are private equity funds that specialize in what can be best thought of as esoteric commodities. *Shipping* is a global activity that behaves much like a physical commodity in terms of cycles of supply and demand. There are times when economic activity is booming and the demand for charters is high. This raises the daily lease rates and improves the profitability of the ship owners. The natural response to this is to build more ships and increase capacity for the system. Since it takes a long time to complete new ocean-going vessels, the cycle in shipping can be quite long. Ships are comparable to real estate in terms of their lack of liquidity, making it highly desirable to invest via a private equity style partnership.

There are reasonably distinct markets for different classes of ships. Tankers cannot be used to haul bulk cargoes like coal and steel. Dry bulk carriers are not good substitutes for container ships. While all of these types of vessels can be similarly affected by the global economic cycle, how each sector responds on the supply side determines the near and intermediate term profitability of an investment in the ships.

A few private equity funds have made dedicated investments in owning ships as part of their total portfolios. A smaller number of specialty funds are dedicated entirely to shipping investments. The general partners in these funds must be expert in both maritime economics but also the operational and logistics side of shipping. Lacking those skills requires partnering with a shipping management company to minimize revenue losses arising from the inevitable challenges associated with chartering and operating a fleet of vessels.

Investors should think of shipping private equity as a pro-cyclical investment. When the world fell into recession after the 2008 financial crisis, chartering activity fell dramatically and with it went day rates for leasing vessels. There was considerable current excess supply of ships, and the pipeline of new ships due to be completed in the next year was full. Add to this mix a financing environment where it was difficult to refinance marine loans and one had a market of opportunity for investors with fresh capital and the knowledge to deploy it.

There is a lower bound on the value of an ocean-going vessel. If the charter rates fall below the operating costs, the ship will be idled. If the carrying costs associated with an idle ship are too high, the ship can be sold for scrap. In major cyclical downturns, older, less fuel efficient vessels are taken out of the fleet and scrapped, which is an important natural correcting force working to eliminate the excess supply.

Private equity investments in shipping do best at these moments. Ships can be purchased from sometimes distressed sellers or banks that have seized them as collateral for defaulted loans. The purchase price is somewhere near the scrap value of the ship, which is usually much less than what it costs to bring a new ship on line. If the shipping cycle recovers, charter rates increase as does the value of the ships. If the cycle remains depressed, the downside for these investments is limited.

Investors should try to demonstrate discipline in their shipping investments. A private equity manager may try to use the great record of a fund that commenced at the trough of a cycle to market a new fund that would be buying ships at the peak. This should be avoided at all costs because the return pattern is skewed the wrong way. Even if the world stays a nice place and economic traffic stays high, elevated charter rates will encourage more ships to be built, which inevitably will lead to lower rates and returns on invested capital. If the world economy goes into a tailspin, charter rates and the price of ships will fall more quickly. Investing in ships at the top of the cycle has limited return potential but large downside risks.

Electric power used to be the exclusive domain of government monopolies or highly regulated private utilities. Rates were set by commissions based on the costs of generation and transmission. Chile was an innovator in creating competitive private markets, with several other Latin American nations close behind. North America and parts of Europe followed in allowing more market competition and where that has happened a broader trading community has developed.

Enron was famously into energy trading and when interstate electricity markets appeared they quickly became an active player, brokering deals for both short- and long-term supplies of power. There were many other electricity trading pioneers, and there are scores of firms active in the business today. Of more recent vintage has been the arrival of dedicated hedge funds that trade electricity. The GPs of these funds typically are graduates of a desk of one of the private energy trading companies.

Unlike oil and natural gas, electricity is not an easily storable commodity. This in itself is not an insurmountable problem. Live cattle and hogs are not easy to store either and there are major futures contracts on both of those commodities. The challenge of little or no storage translates into differences in supply and demand having to be worked out quickly, usually through meaningful price adjustments.

Very few, if any, of these electricity hedge funds should be thought of as a pure play on the commodity. There is no buying and holding to take advantage of inflation or any other long-term trends. These are funds that try to profit from disruptions in price that occur across space and through time. The gains of the funds are entirely dependent upon the skills of the traders. In this way the funds may be more accurately be compared to Commodity Trading advisors (CTAs) than to a commodity index fund or an electricity themed collection of equities.

A final area to be mentioned that fits squarely into the mold of long-term commodity investing is water. Fresh, potable water is one of the major limiting factors in human growth. While there may be massive quantities of it available in the aggregate, it is not evenly distributed, or easy to move around. According to the US Environmental Protection Agency, 84% of all of North America's surface fresh water rests in the five Great Lakes. This resource also represents 21% of the world's total. Only the polar ice caps contain more fresh water.[68]

Given the maldistribution of fresh surface water across the planet, we are fortunate that groundwater is distributed in a much more uniform way. When rain or snow falls, some of the resulting water runs off to streams and rivers, some is used by plants, and some evaporates back into the atmosphere. This is what we see on a regular basis. What are less obvious are the massive quantities of water that percolate through the soil and eventually become groundwater. This water forms in spaces between soil, sand, and rocks, and is found in varying quantities almost everywhere in formations called aquifers.

Groundwater is typically tapped using wells ranging from tens to several hundred feet in depth. It supplies over half of the drinking water in the United States and over 90% of that water for rural America. The predominant use of groundwater (over 60%) in the United States is for irrigation of agriculture.[69]

Aquifers are not usually static, underground lakes. Instead there is a complex hydrology constantly at work with water flowing through the soil, sometimes for hundreds of miles. The underground water is eventually discharged back to the surface through springs or by bleeding into lakes, rivers, and oceans. Engineers and geologists have mapped the system of aquifers and can monitor whether the rate at which groundwater is being used exceeds nature's capacity to replenish it. If too much water is being pumped out, the water table falls and more expensive methods to retrieve it are required.

Rights to this water have been subject to law almost since the founding of the nation. In the western half of the country where all water is relatively scarcer, the law around water rights is highly defined and closely followed. State law generally prevails, but since the flow of water in aquifers rarely respects political jurisdictions, interstate and international case law has developed over the decades.

Australia and Chile are two other nations where defined *water rights* distinct from surface property rights are highly developed. Both nations have had active market mechanisms to help allocate water among competing parties. It is perhaps not surprising that it is in geographies of relative water scarcity that the law behind buying and selling of rights is well defined and respected.

Water-themed investments are of a relatively newer vintage. There are equity funds that hold only water-related companies, but the limited universe of stocks

---

[68]http://www.epa.gov/greatlakes/basicinfo.html.
[69]Ibid.

makes for some incongruities for the investor looking for a pure water play. Owning a company that makes water meters alongside local utility providers is not a portfolio that will precisely capture the theme of water as a scarce and valuable resource.

Better approaches can be found in hedge funds and private equity structures. One way to express a long-term opinion on the theme is to acquire agricultural land that comes with well-defined water rights from an ample aquifer or surface water like a river. Preferably this land is at least theoretically close to a growing metropolitan area that is projected to need more water through time. The water theme is developed over time as the agricultural land produces a regular income.

If such land can be bought at a relatively small premium to similar agricultural property that is not as well situated in terms of water, one has essentially created a call option on the value of the water. The agricultural land should ebb and flow like all such real estate on its own merits, but if the demand for the water can be tapped, there is a chance for an outsized upside return.

The risks of investing in water rights like this are many, but experts should be able to manage them. There are all the risks associated with running an agricultural operation but there are also risks associated with realizing the water's potential value. Hydrology, engineering, infrastructure spending on water transmission and storage, politics, and law are necessary areas of expertise. But for investors looking to participate in long-term water appreciation this may be the best available path.

The next section focuses on a narrow, highly specialized investment area: collectibles. These are certainly real assets, but their supply and demand characteristics set them apart from the ones we have just discussed.

9.11   COLLECTIBLES

Paintings, sculptures, ceramics, furniture, antiques, coins, stamps, fine wines, books (hardcover and comic), sports memorabilia, exotic cars, antique flags, and beanie babies all have one thing in common. Some people believe that they have value well above their cost of production simply because of their inherent qualities and their scarcity. They are *collectibles*.

The economics of collectibles is unlike almost anything else discussed in this book. Monet is no longer with us to produce another painting in the *Water Lilies* series. If you happen to have one, it can be lost, stolen, or destroyed, but there can never be another. Supply of the original can only go down, and never up no matter what the price. Demand alone determines the current worth of any collectible. As more people of means become interested in an object, the price goes up. If there is a disruption in demand because of change of fashion, economic depression, or act of war, prices can tumble.

Putting collectibles into an investment mix is something of a challenge. The best of them tend to be objects that appeal to wealthy individuals, which means that their prices should increase in a pro-cyclical manner. How much they increase relative to other cyclical investments like common stocks is a function of many variables that have little to do with other investment factors like the level of interest rates or credit spreads. This means that while you may believe owning a dead painter's masterpiece may appreciate through time, it is difficult to assess whether that purchase will do better than available alternative investments.

Many major areas of collectibles have seen databases of transactions evolve. This has two key advantages. First, it gives a history of prices so that potential collectors can see how specific pieces have performed over time. The second benefit comes from establishing the provenance of the piece. Assuring the authenticity of an item is critical in maintaining or enhancing value. Anyone who watches episodes of *Antiques Roadshow* knows well how often supposedly old, scarce items are in fact copies made to deceive and defraud.

Taste and fashion is the ultimate arbiter of a collectible's worth. If the interest in an item is narrowly shared by two individuals, the seller and a potential buyer, the outcome is a negotiation that tests the skills and patience of both. If there is one more interested buyer, things get more interesting and if an item suddenly becomes in vogue you have a real auction.

Nobody should assume that just because prices of an item have increased in the past that they will continue in the future. Autographs of the Beatles may appear to be sure things as Baby Boomers age, see their disposable incomes rise, and their demand for nostalgia grow. Those Baby Boomers should remember that their children think of the Beatles as Paul McCartney's first band and most of their as yet unborn great grandchildren will not recognize either the individual or the group.

One might expect that like all real assets, collectibles should at least keep up with inflation. This is likely true over relatively short time horizons, but over many decades the shifts in tastes and fashions will be much more important. Since collectibles by definition are not being created anew, the price does not influence future availability. This means at any given point in time the price is simply an indicator of interest and ability to pay. If either of those factors change, there is nothing about inflation that will prevent prices from moving on their own.

Museums (and basements of museums) are full of collectibles once owned by people who bought them primarily for investments. Sometimes they got to the museums via a purchase by a curator who decided that the museum's collection would be greatly enhanced by the addition. Those were likely the most successful investments. The items that were donated by the collectors might have been a good investment, or they may have been a disappointment where a tax write off was a preferred outcome to a disappointing potential sale.

Collectibles can be an important part of any individual's wealth profile, but like commodities in general, without specific expertise the buyer is likely to be disadvantaged relative to the professional dealing community. Collect what pleases you and spend only what you can easily afford. If it turns out to have been a great investment, that is a bonus. Making collectibles a centerpiece in a long-term investment portfolio is likely an activity best left to specialists.

9.12 THE QUESTION OF CURRENCIES IN A GLOBAL PORTFOLIO PERSPECTIVE ONCE AGAIN

Whenever an investor places assets from outside their home country into their portfolio the question of currency risk arises. A US investor understands that owning the equity of a Swiss or Korean company involves all of the market, sector and company specific risks that buying a US equity entails, but there is also volatility that stems from changing exchange rates. On the surface it would seem that this should make global portfolios riskier than domestic ones, but the reality is considerably more com-plicated than that.

As was discussed in Chapter 3, it is the interaction of asset prices that determines portfolio risk. Correlations matter and the links between currency exchange rates and equity valuations can be quite nuanced. Consider the example of a Brazilian commodity export company from the perspective of a US investor. If the Brazilian currency declines against the dollar, the initial impact will be a decline in the dollar price of the stock. Fewer dollars are required to buy any quantity of Brazilian real, so if nothing happens to the stock price on the local market, the dollar price declines.

There are likely to be secondary effects, however. Everything that the Brazilian company exports has also gotten cheaper with the currency devaluation, which in most instances should be a plus for business. Revenues of the company could be expected to rise, raising their earnings. Depending on a number of factors, the local stock price could rise by more than the currency devaluation. Instead of losing value in dollar terms, the investor could in some cases profit from a currency devaluation.

Exporters are typically favored by a currency devaluation and importers disad-vantaged. In theory, purely domestic business should be little affected, but everyone should understand that the dimensions of complexity in any macro economy are great. Depending on what industries dominate the composition of a country's stock index, the overall equity market can be expected to move up or down with a change in currency valuation.

While that analysis is complicated enough, there is the further question of how these assets interact with everything else the investor owns in his or her portfolio. If non-dollar assets are a small part of a US-based portfolio, it could be that the varia-tions stemming from currency changes can actually be a beneficial diversifier at the portfolio level.

There is simply no universally right or wrong answer on this topic, but there are a few guidelines that can help protect against extreme risks:

If an investor's liabilities are completely in one currency, it is probably not a great idea to have massive investment exposure to another currency. Canadian pensions discovered this lesson the hard way. After many years of benefitting from large hold-ings of US stocks as the Canadian dollar fell during the 1990s, these assets struggled mightily as the exchange rate went from $0.62 US to CAD $1 in 2003 to over parity just five years later.

If there are specific asset/liability mismatches, a currency hedge can help. The US citizen who gets a large part of their compensation paid as a deferred bonus denominated in another currency may want to consider multiyear currency hedges using either forwards or options to minimize the chance that the ultimate realized dollar returns fall short of expectations or goals.

Most wealthy individuals and institutions are citizens of the world in an eco-nomic sense. If the dollar fluctuates against the Euro, the Yen, and a whole array of developing country currencies, the prices of high-end real estate in New York, Miami, and Los Angeles are also affected. Trying to isolate and analyze currency risk in a narrow part of one's investment portfolio is likely to be ineffective and perhaps destructive to total wealth.

Investors are constantly being challenged as to how they should invest interna-tionally. Given that there are often similar investment funds offered in both currency hedged and unhedged versions, which should an investor choose? When you speak with veteran international equity managers, their candid answer is that it makes very little difference over long periods of time. Over any three- or five-year period there will definitely be a difference in return, but just because the hedged version of a fund did better (or worse) over the last few years suggests very little about which will win the race going forward.

The more important consideration is to be sensitive to the types of extremes listed above. In those cases there should be an active and careful discussion of how to deal with currency risk. For most investors, however, even investing half of their portfolios outside of their home country does not create a massive long-run exposure simply because markets adjust over many dimensions, including currencies. Any time and energy spent somehow trying to optimize one's investment currency exposure is likely much more profitably spent in other pursuits.

9.13 CRYPTOCURRENCIES

No discussion of investing in the twenty-first century would be complete without cryptocurrencies. Bitcoin was created in 2009 as an alternative to government issued fiat currencies. Its founders claimed it solved multiple problems with the traditional model. More than 2,000 alternative cryptocurrencies have been introduced since, having a collective value in the hundreds of billions of dollars. The future of cryptocurrencies may still be uncertain, but many investors are asking whether they should be part of their portfolios.

Bitcoin and its many followers were not included in either of this chapter's sections on currencies because it is far from clear that they actually fulfill that role. If they will eventually compete with government currencies then the previous discussions will apply. If they do not end up serving that role, they still must be considered from an investment perspective if for no other reason than their sheer size. But the starting point has to be, are they really currency? We shall use Bitcoin as an example below, but the principles apply more broadly.

Bitcoins are simply entries in a master computer file that keeps track of their existence. They have no physical attributes. New Bitcoins are created according to a computer program that awards them to "miners." Miners are actually programmers who have contributed to the development of the Bitcoin transaction network or have solved complicated mathematical puzzles. It is an open architecture protocol and software so anyone with the skills and sophisticated hardware needed can become a miner. Bitcoin was designed so that it becomes harder to mine new Bitcoins over time and once the number of Bitcoins gets to 21 million (an entirely arbitrary number) the creation of new Bitcoins stops. The current supply of Bitcoins is known to everyone and the market is left to decide what each is worth. Bitcoins can be used as a medium of exchange between any consenting parties.

Any introductory economics text will tell you that a currency has two features: 1) it is a convenient medium of exchange, and 2) it is a store of value. Many years ago there were "hard currencies" that were usually gold or silver, or if they were paper, they were convertible into gold or silver. For almost a hundred years sovereign currencies have been "fiat currencies," which says that they have no hard backing. If you present one to the issuing central bank, all they promise is to replace it with another of the same. People hold fiat currencies not because they know it can be turned into a certain quantity of gold or silver, but because it is easier to transact with currencies than to trade using barter. Bitcoin is just another fiat currency in electronic form.

The value of any currency is a function of its acceptability. People want to hold widely acceptable currencies that maintain their value. Gresham's Law says that "Bad currencies drive out good." This means if one currency is perceived to be more valuable than another, people will hold onto the good currency and try to spend the bad. This is why many people in Argentina today want to be paid in US dollars while they try to pay others in Argentine pesos.

Some currencies meet these functions better than others. Bitcoin supporters argue that their cryptocurrency is actually superior to traditional currencies because, with the proper security encryption, safe, nonreversible transactions can occur 24/7 without the intervention and expense of third parties like banks and credit card companies.

Unfortunately, it is the store of value part of the definition that Bitcoin and many other currencies struggle with. The Bitcoin community notes that most fiat currencies that fail do so because their governments create too many of them leading to hyperinflation. The value of the currency tumbles until it is essentially worthless and is replaced with something that better preserves value. Bitcoin's solution to this is the absolute cap on the number of coins that can ever be created. This feature is probably essential to anyone accepting Bitcoin. After all, if a computer program could create limitless Bitcoin supplies, why would anyone pay for one now with the risk that it will be greatly diluted in the future? This, however, may be its Achilles heel when it comes to ultimate usefulness as a currency.

Truly successful currencies expand with the real level of economic activity because that pace keeps prices relatively stable. Currency growing faster than an economy creates inflation. Currency failing to keep up with economic growth creates deflation. The Bitcoin model of an absolutely fixed quantity of currency in circulation is a recipe for extreme deflation and all the problems that come with it. But it is not just long-term valuation that is an issue.

The big problem with Bitcoin is volatility. In one extreme example, data from Mt. Gox, a once popular cryptocurrency market that failed in 2014, showed that on 1 December 2013 the low value of Bitcoin traded was $850 and the high value was just over $1,200. That is a variation of more than 40% from the low in a single day. What merchant can price their products in Bitcoin and have any assurance that the value they choose won't be wildly too high or too low? Not surprisingly, multiple services have arisen that a merchant can use to quickly translate Bitcoin into a traditional currency. These services come at a fee, of course, obviating some of the benefits originally advertised by the cryptocurrency.

There is little doubt that much of modern banking is too costly and too slow relative to the abilities of modern technology. If Bitcoin pushes banking into the twenty-first century all consumers and merchants will benefit, but it will not take an overthrow of the entire system of global currencies to achieve that end.

Saying that a currency is a store of value implies that it is a relatively stable value. Without that stability the costs of normal commerce far outstrip any credit card or bank transactions fees. Bitcoin and other cryptocurrencies so far fail miserably on this important measure.

Neither Bitcoin nor any other cryptocurrency is being actively used as a medium of exchange. While there are some merchants that claim to accept Bitcoin, this is mostly a publicity stunt with the received crypto immediately changed back into dollars or other traditional currency. The variability in moment-to-moment value makes it virtually impossible to actually price any goods or services in terms of cryptocurrencies. People betting for or against the future value are doing the overwhelming majority of transactions in the space. This makes Bitcoin and cryptos a trade and not currency.

Even if cryptos fail the strict currency question, there are many that advocate for their inclusion into a portfolio. They support that advice with the following assertions:

There are trillions of dollars of fiat money-denominated assets in the world held by people who are afraid their governments cannot be trusted. A popular statement by proponents is something like, "If only X% of these assets go into the fixed supply of Bitcoin, this would lead to a price of Y." Other assertions include:

- Transactions along the blockchain are both secure and anonymous. Anyone trying to avoid an overly prying government will find a haven here.
- Transactions are fundamentally cheaper using cryptocurrencies than traditional banking networks.
- The introduction of futures on Bitcoin in a regulated environment proves the legitimacy of the space.
- Investors should want to own them because they are uncorrelated to traditional investments.
- More than 95% of cryptocurrency transactions are done by individuals making them highly inefficient markets and creating opportunities for more sophisticated institutional traders.

To address these assertions it is best to start back a few steps. The blockchain is the backbone of all cryptocurrencies and it is an important innovation. As multiple people do transactions in the relevant market, they are grouped in small time intervals. The "block" is then announced to the community of independent, competitive miners who then try to solve complicated mathematical puzzles. The first one that arrives at the answer is awarded some quantity of the cryptocurrency; the block is officially closed, made public and added as the last link in the ever-growing chain. All of this information is simultaneously available to anyone who chooses to participate in the system.

What results is a decentralized registry of transactions that is both completely public and cannot be modified without affecting all subsequent transactions on the chain. This is what makes the ultimate trades in cryptocurrencies secure. Anonymity is an added feature that enhances the allure. Because any user can transparently consult all encoded transactions in real time, all of the traditional issues of fraud and deception are eliminated. Many traders, however, have learned there are other vulnerabilities in the ecosystem that attaches to and feeds the blockchain.

Think of blockchain as a disruptive technology for transactions and cryptocurrencies as one application arising from it. An analogy could be with light emitting diodes (LEDs) that have found their way into automobiles, holiday lights, powerful flashlights and a thousand other uses. IBM, Microsoft, and many other corporations are spending tens of billions of dollars to try to discover the most powerful uses for blockchain. This creates a classic challenge for equity analysts. How disruptive is this technology? How expensive is it to develop? How profitable will it be in the future? There will no doubt be winners and losers along the way and investors will try their best to identify them before everyone else in the market.

Cryptocurrencies cannot exist without a blockchain, but the reverse is not true. The advantages of blockchains, including lowered transaction costs, may revolutionize the financial industry without ever requiring any cryptocurrencies to exist. That leaves a big open question for investors. Should any cryptocurrencies directly find their way into a portfolio, and if so, which ones?

Traditional stock analysts like companies that have good profit margins and natural barriers to entry like patents or brand value to maintain those margins. This is what gives these companies earning power and ultimate value. While each cryptocurrency claims scarcity value because of the cap on issuance, there are essentially no barriers to entry. While the capitalization of Bitcoin might exceed $180 billion, one must ask why it is fundamentally superior to Ethereum's product, in second place at $20 billion, or Ripple, a rising star in third place at $11 billion.[70] At the other end of the spectrum there are almost a thousand entries out there with total capitalizations less than $100,000.

A fundamental analyst for cryptocurrencies would want to ask why any single effort should stand out versus the others, and to most observers the distinctions are nuanced and hardly worthy of valuations that differ by a thousand times or more. As new cryptocurrencies arrive almost daily there is no total fixed supply and no defendable profit margin in the industry. So why do people keep buying these things? The truth is if people think something is scarce and going up in value, they want to own it. It doesn't matter what it is.

The explosion in offerings and the large price volatility has led some to suggest that the entire cryptocurrency phenomenon is nothing more than the latest Ponzi scheme to exploit gullible investors. Ponzi schemes are centralized efforts where someone promises an attractive return to investors. The fraudster has no true means of earning the target return and instead pays off early investors with funds provided by subsequent investors. The scheme has to keep attracting increasing numbers of participants through time to persist. Bitcoin and other crypto are not a classic Ponzi scheme.

Cryptocurrencies are, however, markets where if early buyers can convince others that there is greater value to be realized, continuously rising prices can create a bubble market. In this fashion, Bitcoin may be no different than Dutch tulip bulbs in the seventeenth century or Beanie Baby toys in the 1990s.

Investing in companies developing blockchain applications is a very different business than buying cryptocurrencies. The first is a classic stock analysis problem no different than asking whether Tesla's electric car technology will give it a permanent edge in the automobile industry. There is considerable experience among the analyst community for those kinds of questions. Trading in cryptocurrency has a much looser link to fundamental value and any investor should acknowledge this.

Earlier in this section it was suggested that cryptocurrencies were not really functioning as a real currency, but they were active as a trade. They are the type of trade that drives traditional portfolio analysts crazy. What is the expected return? What about the volatility and the correlation with other portfolio holdings?

In the section on collectibles above, there were several investment challenges described. There was no good way to comfortably frame an allocation in any portfolio.

---

[70]All capitalization references are from coinmarketcap.com.

The suggestion was to buy only that which pleased you and in amounts that were well within your budget. Cryptocurrencies are very much the same except that the aesthetics question is perhaps more challenging and people have centuries worth of experience dealing with collectibles. Investors contemplating cryptocurrencies as part of their portfolio need to shape their decisions similarly and ultimately ask themselves why they believe they have an informational advantage over the cryptocurrency's creators or the person trying to sell you theirs.

9.14 SPECIAL PURPOSE ACQUISITION COMPANIES (SPACs)

A relatively recent phenomenon in the investment landscape is the special purpose acquisition company (SPAC). Sometimes called "blank check companies," SPACs have been the primary force responsible for reversing the decades-long decline in the number of public companies. They give private companies a shortcut to the initial public offering (IPO), but the real appeal may be how lucrative they are for the sponsors of the SPAC. Whether they fit well into one's investment portfolio is another question.

A SPAC is a public company with a single mission. It collects capital from investors with the goal of identifying a private company with which to merge. When it raises its capital, typically in an IPO, the SPAC has no revenues or accounting history, which makes its required IPO disclosures to the public pretty simple. The sponsor explains what kind of company it might seek to acquire and the desired fund size. Investors tend to be attracted to established investment professionals, though there have been several celebrity sponsors lending their names to a SPAC. The SPAC fundraising IPO either succeeds or fails based on the sizzle of the story. At this early stage there is no steak.

The SPAC places the proceeds of the fundraising into a secure escrow account, typically invested in short-term Treasuries. They also promise that within a certain time period, often two years, they will identify a private company with which to merge. Any proposed merger is subject to approval by the SPAC shareholders. If approved, the funds in escrow are used to acquire the target company. Once the merger is complete the private company has become a public one, but without the complications of working with investment bankers and regulators to float their own IPO.

There is no uniform SPAC model, but they often have several common features. Investors in the SPACs receive an equity share of the company and sometimes they receive separable warrants on their shares. This allows an extra reward if the post-merger price rises above certain thresholds. If the SPAC is unsuccessful in finding an appropriate target in the investment window, the capital in the escrow account is returned to the SPAC investors with whatever interest has been earned.

Another important option the SPAC shareholder has is the choice between owning shares in the merged company or declining to participate in any approved deal. In the latter event, the SPAC shareholder gets back their initial capital plus interest, but they typically keep any separate warrants. The SPAC sponsor then must replace that capital from other sources to complete the transaction.

The SPAC sponsor is responsible for the funding of the administration costs during the period between when a merger candidate is identified and a deal negotiated. These funds, known as risk capital, are specified at the SPAC IPO and will vary with the size of the fund. There is no standard formula but a typical pool of risk capital might be $2 million plus 2% of the fund size. This would mean the SPAC sponsor would contribute $6 million in risk capital for a $200 million SPAC. This risk capital is the first source to be tapped in event of losses, giving SPAC shareholders some protection against immediate dilution of their equity.

It would appear that the owners of SPAC have a wonderful payout pattern. The worst thing that can happen is they get their capital back. They sometimes get warrants in the new company and the sponsor's risk capital provides another layer of financial protection.

These attractive features do not come without costs. In return for putting up this risk capital, the sponsor is rewarded with a "promote" upon closing, typically 20% of grossed up proceeds from the SPAC IPO capital raise. For example, a $200 million SPAC will generate $50 million of promote, resulting in a grossed-up SPAC of $250 million (the initial $200 million raised from investors represents 80% of this total). What this means is the sponsor receives 20% of the ultimate SPAC ownership stake in the merged company. In the example, for $6 million in risk capital the sponsor has received equity that at the merger is valued at $50 million. That is quite the incentive for the SPAC sponsor to find a deal, but it leads to immediate dilution for any SPAC shareholder that holds their shares through the merger.

This raises questions about how likely SPAC shareholders are to receive good returns from their investment. Most stories touting SPACs mention companies like Virgin Galactic and DraftKings that were made public through a SPAC transaction and quickly saw their share prices rise. This, however, is not the typical SPAC experience.

Michael Klausner, Michael Ohlrogge, and Emily Ruan analyzed 47 SPAC mergers that happened between January 2019 and June 2020.[71] What they found was the dilution was extreme and the average SPAC shares tended to drop in price by about a third in the year following the merger. They also identified an important dynamic among the SPAC owners. Investors in SPAC IPOs tend to be sophisticated institutional investors, including hedge funds, apparently attracted to the safety of being able to get their capital back if they do not like the announced merger. But those investors understand the dilution features of a SPAC and almost always dispose of their SPAC shares in the window between when a merger is proposed and when it is completed.

The initial investors either redeem their shares from the SPAC as described above or sell them in the public market. Klausner et al. found that between the announcement of the merger and the transaction the vast majority of the institutional investors exit and are replaced with more retail-oriented shareholders. It is this group that suffers the dilution from the sponsor's promote.

The SPAC sponsor promote of 20% appears comparable to performance fees earned by hedge and private equity funds, but there is a big difference. Performance fees are paid if the hedge fund makes money or returns exceed a stated hurdle. SPAC sponsors earn their promote just by completing a deal, whether it makes money ultimately or not. In the example of a $200 million SPAC, if the new public company shares fall in

---

[71]Klausner, M., Ohlrogge, M., and Ruan, E. (2021). A Sober Look at SPACs, *Stanford Law and Economics Olin Working Paper No. 559, NYU Law and Economics Research Paper No. 20–48.*

half, the sponsor still owns a promote worth $25 million. The misalignment of interests between the sponsor and the SPAC shareholders is well understood by the sophisticated investors that initially fund the SPAC, but apparently is less well understood by retail investors clamoring for the chance to participate in a new public company.

The entrepreneurs that control the private companies targeted by SPACs may be attracted to the process by the less rigorous regulatory process than that described in Chapter 13 for IPOs. They may also like the certainty of knowing how much they will get from a SPAC merger versus the inherent uncertainty of valuations that arise from an IPO. Finally, with tens of billions of dollars being raised for SPACs, each of which has a deadline to find a deal or return the original capital, private business owners are in a good bargaining position to extract top value for their company when merging with a SPAC.

The growth of SPACs is another example of products that are sold with great fanfare and promise, but by their structure are likely to be far more rewarding to the sponsors than the ultimate participants. If you want to own shares in a company created in a SPAC merger, rather than buy the shares of the SPAC after the announcement, wait until the new company begins trading. The price you buy at may be higher or lower than the initial prices, just like an IPO, but you will avoid the immediate dilution from the promote that puts one in a hole before the real investment process begins.

This lengthy chapter has attempted to give an introduction to the vast array of opportunities available for direct investment. Several of the discussions alluded to the use of futures and options by fund managers in order to acquire exposures and to shape their risk profile. The next chapter describes these derivative instruments in more detail, hopefully removing some of the mystery that surrounds them for many investors.

CHAPTER 10

Derivatives

Can investors live without *derivatives*? Yes. Should they want to? No.

Derivatives are not an asset class. No one should ever plan an allocation between derivatives and cash securities. Derivatives are tools that have evolved over decades to improve the efficiency of trading. Like all tools, they can be dangerous in the wrong hands. They require training. They should be respected. Fund managers should be evaluated in how they use or abuse derivatives in trying to meet their goals. Realistically, no thoughtful investor in the twenty-first century should strive to build a portfolio without derivatives any more than a home builder would want to only use hand tools. The goal of this chapter is to provide enough background on the subject to allow investors to ask the right questions of managers and brokers.

Derivatives have been a part of the investment landscape for as long as futures traders have traded grains in Chicago. In the beginning there were only futures on storable commodities like wheat, corn, and metals. This activity was considered fringe investing then, fit only for the most skilled or most risk loving. Over the last 40 years exchange-traded and OTC derivatives have been built around interest rates, currencies, stock indexes and credit spreads. As the product array has expanded to cover more traditional asset classes, derivatives have become almost commonplace in modern portfolios.

Despite their wide use, derivatives remain a little-understood and sometimes widely maligned investment tool. After the prominent losses in interest rate swaps by Procter & Gamble and Gibson Greetings Cards in 1994, many investment guidelines were rewritten to include "no derivatives" clauses. Such attempts to broadly insure the safety of portfolios invariably managed to throw the baby out with the bath water.

Today the exchange-traded derivatives market can be measured in the trillions of dollars of activity. Privately negotiated, or OTC, derivatives are many times larger. The reason for this spectacular growth is that hedgers and speculators alike have found derivatives to be in many cases more efficient tools to express a market opinion than are available in standard cash market vehicles.

The regulation and industrial organization of derivatives were subject to considerable change in the wake of the financial crisis of 2007–2009. How these products trade, clear, and settle are still evolving, but this is less important for this discussion than the ways they shape investment portfolios. No matter what regulator oversees the activity, if derivatives are not priced out of the market through foolish taxes, margins or capital requirements, one can expect them to be an important part of the financial landscape for the foreseeable future.

The type of the derivative used should be quite important to an investor, because it shapes the risk profile, liquidity, and transparency of the investment. Exchange-traded futures and options are perhaps the most easily understood form of derivatives, but they represent a minority of activity across all of the market. Much larger pools of activity can be found in interest rate, equity, and currency swaps and credit default swaps. These OTC markets offer investors a much higher degree of customization, but at the cost of less pricing transparency and liquidity.

10.1 FUTURES CONTRACTS

Futures contracts have been traded in the United States since the nineteenth century. Originally focusing on storable agricultural products, they were developed to assist farmers and grain merchants market the commodity over a growing season. The easiest way to define a futures contract is to compare it to its intellectual predecessors the cash and forward contracts. While hardly a mainstream component of most investment portfolios, agricultural futures easily demonstrate the principles behind the model that has been extended to stocks, bonds, currencies and credit.

A *cash contract* is simplicity itself. A seller offers a specific product like a wagon full of corn. He negotiates with one or more potential buyers to arrive at a price for prompt, or *spot delivery*. The world is filled with cash markets covering every imaginable commodity or service.

In contrast, a *forward contract* introduces a time dimension to the situation. A farmer anticipates that he will have a wagonload of corn after the harvest three months away. A lot can happen in three months, so the farmer may want to sell that wagon of corn forward, to be delivered when harvest takes place. Cereal or tortilla manufacturers may also find it advantageous to secure their input for a future date. Buyers and sellers come together and agree for future delivery with a forward contract.

Unlike a cash contract where the merchandise is available for inspection and delivery on the spot, forward contracts need to be precisely defined in terms of quantities, timing, and the quality of the product. If the harvest produces the right amount of good quality corn, the farmer fulfills the contract as specified.

It is easy to imagine a range of potential failures to the plan. The crop could be damaged by hail, reducing the quantity and quality of the farmer's corn. It could be a cold growing season or a wet harvest period, either event delaying the timing of delivery. The buyers could have problems as well. Business could have fallen off after the forward contract was signed. Or possibly, the cash price of corn could have tumbled because of a bumper crop, leading the buyer to regret the earlier contract and tempting him to back away.

Enforcing forward contracts can often be a challenge, and futures contracts were developed to provide more certainty in the contracting process. But this greater structure and certainty comes with a price. With exchange-traded futures contracts, participants lose the ability to customize their transactions.

Futures contracts can be thought of as standardized forward contracts that are traded on an exchange and guaranteed by members of the clearing organization of that exchange. Instead of 4,550 bushels of No.1 corn delivered at a corn miller's doorstep on the first Tuesday of next month in a forward contract, the futures contract would specify 5,000 bushels of No. 2 Yellow Corn to be delivered in any one of a number of approved warehouses or shipping stations at the seller's option during the month of December.

For the corn miller, it would appear to be a terrible proposition. The futures contract is for the wrong quantity, quality, and location. But it is hardly perfect for the farmer either. So why would anyone use a futures market? There are two answers: liquidity and security.

Futures markets are constantly trying to strike a balance between a wide array of potential buyers and sellers. The contract specifications will likely be perfect for neither, but hopefully they are close enough. The idea is that there will be many more potential buyers and sellers negotiating over a general product than there ever will be for a highly specific forward contract. The farmer or the miller can enter into a futures contract easily and quickly, with the idea that before the futures contract comes due the desired specific spot transaction can be established and the futures contract traded out of.

Trading out of a futures contract is possible because of the unique system of clearing and settlement used with futures contracts. When one buys a futures contract from a seller, the positions are posted to a *clearinghouse*. The clearinghouse, in turn, breaks the futures apart and becomes the buyer to every seller, and the seller to every buyer. *Once the futures contract is cleared, neither original buyer nor seller cares what the other ultimately does.* The farmer could buy back his short futures position tomorrow from some other seller, while the miller could hold his long position to delivery. Once the trade is cleared the two parties are completely independent of each other.

10.1.1   Original and Variation Margins

The elimination of the counterparty relationship requires a strong system of *collateral* to back the contracts. The clearinghouse demands that both buyers and sellers post good faith performance bonds, called *original margin*, to secure their positions. These are not down payments to buy a security like stock margins. Both the buyer and the seller post original margin, but the system goes further. These margin balances are adjusted at least every day to reflect gains and losses. Losers will pay daily *variation margin*, while the winning side of the trade will collect an equal amount. If the margin accounts of the traders fall below minimums set by the clearinghouse, more collateral must be posted or the positions will be liquidated.

The corn miller in the forward contract example above saw prices tumble after the contract was made. Unless he was entirely true to his word to the farmer, he might be tempted to default on his forward contract and purchase from another supplier in the subsequently cheaper spot market. Futures markets have seen that behavior before and demand more collateral from the miller as prices decline. He may want to change his mind at some point about the attractiveness of his long position, but he will be paying for his losses in real time, which provides security to the clearing members and ultimately to the original seller.

This *mark-to-market* system is the foundation of any well-structured futures markets. Original collateral requirements are set high enough to provide a margin of safety and extra money is called continuously from traders holding losing positions. While the terms of a futures contract may not be ideal for any specific participant, the combination of liquidity provided by many buyers and sellers along with the financial security of margin has made the futures model a winning one.

10.1.2 The Price Basis

The effectiveness of any futures contract depends critically on the behavior of the *price basis*. This is the difference between the futures price and the relevant cash price for the commercial participant in the market. Suppose the corn miller is located in Battle Creek, Michigan, an important manufacturing point for corn-based cereals, but not a delivery point on the corn futures contract. The price of the futures contract may vary somewhat from cash prices, which creates *basis risk*. The worst outcome for the miller would be to go long corn futures and see that price decline, while simultaneously seeing prices in the Battle Creek, Michigan, market rise.

In a well-functioning futures market, the price basis shows some degree of predictability. Prices may not move exactly parallel between cash and futures, but the variance of the basis is not so large as to make hedging with futures an additional source of risk.

2020 provided a prime example of futures markets that do not always work as planned. The NYMEX crude oil futures contract calling for delivery in May was scheduled to expire on April 21. Because of the steep drop in demand due to the COVID-19 pandemic rapidly shutting down more economic activity, inventories of crude oil, distillates, and gasoline were well above normal. Not surprisingly, prices fell continuously in March and April, reaching multiyear lows approaching $20 per barrel.

Such extreme movements seem to attract risk-loving speculators. Some go short playing the downtrend. Others make a judgment that the decline has produced prices too low to be sustained, and they go long expecting to profit from a market reversal. There was no doubt both kinds of traders in the market as the May contract approached expiration. What was not so obvious was the role that commercial owners of crude oil at the delivery point of Cushing, Oklahoma, were going to play.

To understand what happened in this contract requires some understanding of how oil is delivered on the NYMEX crude oil contract. Delivery contracts are always more complicated than vanilla stock index futures contracts that expire with what is called cash settlement. With cash settlement there is a final index value at expiration. The losers pay the winners and the contracts disappear. It was the specific delivery terms at Cushing that the speculative longs apparently did not understand.

There are designated storage bunkers in and around Cushing that are approved delivery terminals. Sellers who intend to make delivery must have product in one of those storage facilities. The longs, or buyers, taking delivery must have their own storage facilities or access to pipelines to carry the product to alternate storage away from Cushing, an export facility or a refinery. In normal times there is a reasonable balance between commercial buyers and sellers, the futures price reflects this supply and demand and the basis is well behaved. April 2020 was anything but normal.

Buyers of commodities like gold, coffee, and cocoa are used to receiving a warehouse receipt conveying ownership when they take delivery on a futures contract. The buyer pays the full settlement price and receives ownership title. Food commodities like coffee and cocoa eventually leave the warehouse and get consumed, but perhaps not for several months. Physical gold rarely moves from its storage vaults.

Crude oil is completely different. There is no warehouse receipt and the long should expect to take the oil away from where the short stores it.

The seller could allow the long to assume their space in the bunkers, but they are not obligated to do so. If they deny the longs that option, the longs must physically remove the oil. The problem in April 2020 was all the Cushing tanks were full, the pipelines leading away from Cushing were booked, and the logical buyers of super cheap oil, the refiners, were already overloaded with inventory. The speculative longs were proverbially over a barrel and they had no choice but try to offset their positions by selling before the contract expired. The logical buyer would be the short getting ready to deliver, but willing to offset their position at the right price.

It was not pretty. On 20 April 2020, the day before expiration, prices fell from the opening bell. TV reports sounded the alarm at $15, then $10, and then $5 per barrel. Some foolish speculators, believing prices could not go negative bought contracts believing there would be a floor at zero. No such floor exists. The Chicago Mercantile Exchange (CME), owner of the NYMEX, had some time earlier anticipated the possibility that any market could go into negative territory and had their systems programmed accordingly. They may not have expected crude oil to be the first experiment in negative prices, but when it happened the electronic trading systems were up to the task.

Prices broke through zero and kept plummeting. As the trading day was drawing to a close, the price dropped below −$40, finally settling for the day when the closing bell rang at −$37.63. Most observers were completely befuddled. Commentators, scrambling for a story line, said that crude oil traders were signaling a massive and prolonged depression. The actual story was less cataclysmic.

It was instead an example of a large number of noncommercial longs that stayed in their front-month futures positions too long with no appreciation of the delivery rules or the actual inventory situation in Cushing. The commercials knew both the rules and the true storage picture and simply took advantage to the extreme. The next day, the last day of trading on the May contract, prices inched back up into positive territory and settled just above $10.

Not surprisingly the longs that suffered massive losses decided to sue, stating that a negative price was prima facie evidence of manipulation. It will take years to sort out the litigation, but the commercial participants in the market will no doubt argue that they were simply using the short positions to hedge the price risk of their inventories at Cushing. The fact that there were so many longs in the market who did not want physical oil, and ended up climbing all over each other trying to avoid delivery, was not the shorts' problem.

There are no real angels in this story, however. Lacking emails, texts, or phone records showing collusive activity of the shorts refusing to buy back their positions and allowing the price to tumble, manipulation may be hard to prove. But the shorts used their temporary market power aggressively on 20 April and the futures contract most used as a benchmark for crude oil was briefly way off the mark in reflecting true supply and demand.

This is basis risk in the extreme. There is no evidence that crude oil transactions occurred anywhere else in the world that day where a buyer paid the seller not to accept crude oil. Anyone in Europe, Asia, or Latin America who was long the May NYMEX crude oil futures as a hedge against physical oil purchases saw a complete and expensive breakdown of the normally well-behaved relationship between spot and futures prices.

The CME should feel good about their technological foresight. Unlike the NYSE in October 1987, when order volume on the exchange exceeded the exchange's computer capacity to receive and match orders, the CME trading system worked without fail. This is far, however, from a total victory as exchanges have traditionally been more than mechanical arenas. A long-term successful futures contract can be relied on by a wide range of commercial users beyond those immediately involved in ultimate delivery.

That reliance is earned by regular expirations where the basis is well behaved. The futures price converges to the true physical market at expiration. Variations like those seen in April 2020 are the kinds of expensive episodes that can drive core commercial users away.

Futures contracts, like all financial instruments, are based on basic trust. Nobody is conscripted to trade futures, and if the basis between the futures and physical markets regularly gets distorted either by manipulation or massive supply and demand imbalances, the contract will die.

On its web page in late 2020 the CME called the NYMEX contract "a global crude oil benchmark." Most days and weeks it is. In late April 2020, it was far from that. The exchange and the federal regulator for commodities exchanges, the CFTC, have decades of experience with imbalanced deliveries in grains, livestock, and food products like orange juice, coffee, cocoa, and sugar. They monitor all the position holders, and if a disorderly expiration is likely, they work with both longs and shorts to identify and avoid trouble spots. They try hard to prevent a Dan Aykroyd/Eddie Murphy moment seen in the movie *Trading Places*.

Why this did not happen for NYMEX crude oil in April 2020 is something of a mystery. But to veteran observers of commodity markets it was a failure producing unprecedented basis risk. The circumstances leading up to this event eased as the economy began to turn around from the COVID-19 trough. Expirations after the May contract in 2020 were less eventful, perhaps because the delivery choke points were naturally removed, or perhaps the exchange and the CFTF were more mindful to eliminate position congestion late in the contract.

This section began with a simple description of the price basis, which most of the time is of interest only to the trade professionals. April 2020 reminded us, however, that noncommercial amateurs who choose to speculate in any futures contracts involving delivery should be out of those positions well before the days immediately before final expiration. The lessons that were learned then by those traders came with a very steep tuition.

10.1.3 The Dealer Community

The example of the farmer and the miller describes the basic futures transaction, but the real world almost never works that way. Farmers are busy farming and millers spend their time milling. Transacting in their goods is a small part of their lives. Enter the most important participant in the futures market: the *dealer-speculator*. These people make a living trading futures and the cash product. Think of them as the great facilitators.

These dealer-speculators dedicate capital to make bids or offers whenever the farmer comes to sell or the miller arrives to buy. They risk their capital trying to buy a few cents below where they will ultimately sell. The dealer function in organized futures markets is both risky and highly competitive, a fact that will help explain the greater attractiveness of over-the-counter derivatives for many dealers.

The great myth that futures markets try to perpetuate is that the world is composed of two types of participants: risk-averse farmers and millers and risk-absorbing dealers. Through their trades, the poor, frightened end users place the vast price risk of their enterprises onto the broad, risk-loving shoulders of the dealer-speculators. This view of the world places futures markets among the greatest public service organizations known to man.

Futures markets clearly perform an important function, but public charity is not one of them. The best dealer-speculators have no more appetite for risk than anyone else. What they do have, however, is a great ability to scan across markets and evaluate the many price basis relationships. Chances are excellent that if a dealer quotes the farmer $4.90 bid for a December corn futures contract, it is because he believes he can sell it for $4.92 to a miller or ethanol producer. In fact, his $4.90 bid is often predicated on the knowledge of that sale opportunity.

Basis uncertainty is the biggest business risk dealers typically face. The most experienced dealers in a market rarely take directional market positions, preferring instead to always have offsetting long and short positions. If the basis moves against the dealer, losses can be significant, but it is rare that the volatility of the basis is remotely close to the fundamental price risk routinely taken by both producers and consumers.

Because of the highly competitive nature of futures trading, dealer profits are slim in the most liquid markets. There is no persistent *risk premia* paid to the dealers. Decades of research show that there are no dependable biases that come from hedgers paying to shed risk to dealer-speculators. Dealers make their money by having superior information networks and the ability to position their trades favorably versus the basis.

10.2 EXCHANGE-TRADED OPTIONS

Futures contracts *require* the buyer and seller to perform their duties if they do not offset their contracts before maturity. Options, as their name suggests, give the owner the *right* but not the *obligation* to perform. Buyers of *call options* have the right to buy the underlying stock, bond, or commodity at an agreed-upon price. *Put options* give the buyer the right to sell the underlying at an agreed-upon price. Calls and puts all have finite maturities that can span from days to years.

While the owner of an option has rights, the seller, or *option writer*, has a strict obligation. *If* the call owner elects to exercise his or her option to buy, the writer of that call *must* sell at the designated price. Similarly, the writer of puts must buy whenever the put owner elects to sell. This asymmetry of rights and obligations leads to an asymmetry of risks and payouts, which will be discussed in more detail below.

An exchange-traded option has a number of standardized features:

- The underlying security, index, or commodity.
- The expiration date of the option.
- The exercise price of the option, often referred to as the *strike price*.
- The size of the option.

OTC options have each of the above features specified on a negotiated basis between the buyer and writer.

Options that trade on exchanges usually have a clearinghouse where, like futures, collateral is maintained in both the buyer's and seller's accounts and regularly marked to market. Given the highly asymmetric payouts of options, the margin calculations for options are necessarily more complex than those used for futures. But the basic principle is the same. The clearinghouse allows the two sides of the initial transaction to operate independently with a high degree of financial security.

10.2.1 Call Basics

The buyer of a call thinks the price of the underlying is going to increase sometime during the life of the option. The maturity and the strike price are chosen to match that expectation. In general, the longer the maturity of the option, the more expensive it will be. There are two other main factors that influence a call's price: 1) the strike price relative to the current market price and 2) the expected volatility of the underlying instrument. An example will demonstrate these effects.

Suppose the S&P 500 Index is near 3000. Someone who thought there was a strong chance of the stock market moving up in the next six months could buy a basket of stocks that replicated the index in a mutual fund or ETF. The biggest risk with that approach is that if the market suddenly declined, the losses would be virtually unlimited. By buying calls, an investor constructs an asymmetric payout, where the upside is unlimited but the downside is capped at the cost of the calls. Popular and liquid options based on this index are traded at the Chicago Board Options Exchange (CBOE).

Table 10.1 gives an array of prices for S&P 500 Index calls covering different strike prices and maturities. This is just a sampling of the hundreds of index calls available for the option investor.

The table demonstrates a number of key elements of call option pricing. At the time the table was constructed, the December options had about six months until they expired. The March contracts expired in nine months and the June calls expired in about a year. The reader can easily see that the longer the option, the higher its cost. Choosing the option month is largely dependent upon the forcefulness of one's opinion. If one were absolutely convinced the stock market is going to rally significantly

TABLE 10.1 Premiums of Representative S&P 500 Index Calls 30 June 2019 Index and Option Values Underlying Price = 2942

Strike Price	Dec '19	March '20	June '20
2875	166.0	195.4	220.7
2900	148.6	178.6	204.2
2925	132.0	162.2	188.2
2950	116.0	146.4	172.6
2975	101.0	131.2	157.6
3000	86.8	116.7	143.0

Source: Bloomberg

within days, one would buy even shorter options than those listed above. There's no reason to pay more for a longer option if one's confidence is high. If, however, the market opinion is bullish but less certain whether the rally would start next week or the beginning of next year, the additional expense of the March or June options may be worth it.

The strike price relative to the current price also plays a role. The 2875 strike calls allow the owner of the option to buy the index below the current index value of 2942. These options are said to be *in-the-money*. The amount that the option is in the money is called today's *intrinsic value,* which in this case is 67 index points. The difference between the option's market price and its intrinsic value is called the *time value*. In the first line of Table 10.2, the reader can confirm that the time value of each option goes up as the maturity extends.

Table 10.2 is derived from the call price data in the previous chart. It shows only the time value of each option. The key point here is that for options that are deep in-the-money or deep out-of-the-money the time values are smaller. Options that are stuck very near to the current price have the greatest time value for any given maturity.

Not surprisingly, time value increases as the length of an option extends. Less intuitive, however, is the fact that the cost of time is not linear. A four-month option is not four times as expensive as a one-month option. It is typically closer to twice as expensive. The basic rule of thumb is that an option's price expands with the square root of time.[1]

Interest rates also play a role in the value of options, as the premiums received by the seller can collect a return over the life of the option. Generally this is a minor influence in the pricing of options, important mostly to professional market makers and arbitrageurs.

Once the maturity and strike price of the option are established, market supply and demand determine the trading price. Unlike the market for stocks where the

TABLE 10.2   Time Value of Representative S&P 500 Index Calls Time Value of Representative S&P 500 Index Calls 6/30/2019 Index and Option Values Underlying Price = 2942

Strike Price	Dec '19	March '20	June '20
2875	99.2	128.6	153.9
2900	106.9	136.8	162.5
2925	115.2	145.4	171.4
2950	116.0	146.4	172.6
2975	101.0	131.2	157.6
3000	86.8	116.7	143.0

Source: Bloomberg

---

[1]The specifics of option pricing models are not needed for this discussion. The two main option-pricing models are called Black-Scholes and the Cox-Ross-Rubinstein Binomial model. The interested reader can learn more by reading Petzel, T. (1989). *Financial Futures and Options*, or Natenberg, S. (1988). *Option Volatility & Pricing: Advanced Trading Strategies and Techniques.*

prime point of negotiation is the expected price of the shares, option participants are mostly concerned with future volatility. If there is a great deal of price variability expected in the future, calls and puts will go up in value. If one could imagine a world where a government agency declared that prices could not change in the next year, option prices would collapse to their intrinsic values. Nobody should be willing to pay for any time value since out of the money options with less than a year to go cannot legally become in the money.

The maturity, strike price, and interest rate for the term in the option are all known with certainty. Once the market determines a price for an option, the *implied volatility* may be calculated from any of the standard option pricing models. Different models will almost certainly give slightly different answers, but what is important are the relative values of implied volatility across different maturities and strike prices.

It is not unusual for calculated implied volatilities to exhibit a shape that looks like a smile as shown in Figure 10.1.

As an option's strike price moves increasingly away from the current price, implied volatilities often increase because buyers are willing to pay higher time value per unit of potential gain because of the lottery-like feature of deep out-of-the-money options. Sellers, on the other side of the asymmetric risk profile, demand higher premiums to protect themselves against extreme tail events. Hedging deep out-of-the-money short options is a very risky business, and sellers often demand greater premiums as an extra measure of protection. This helps create a volatility smile.

Implied volatilities also vary through time. Commodity options have different implied volatilities depending on whether the option's life spans a volatile part of the growing season or whether it covers the relatively quiet storage period between seasons. Natural gas options are not affected by anything akin to growing season issues, but production can be rapidly impacted during hurricane season, and demand can fluctuate dramatically with the cold weather in winter or hot spells in the summer. The market is well versed in these risks and natural gas option prices reflect different implied volatilities depending on the season.

Time decay is the one constant force when it comes to calls. From the moment the call is purchased or sold, the clock is ticking. If you are absolutely certain of your market opinion (or perhaps you are trading on inside information), you might feel quite comfortable in buying the shortest-dated options and saving a lot of premium.

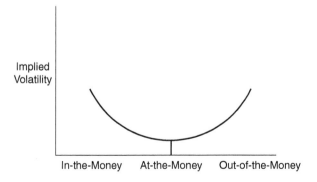

FIGURE 10.1 A Volatility "Smile"

If, however, your investment thesis may take some time to be realized, you will want to pay the extra money to buy longer dated options.

Since longer dated options are more expensive than short maturity options, why isn't it a good strategy to plan to buy a series of short-dated options over the investment horizon? For example, instead of buying a call with a week until expiration, start off by buying a Monday-only option with the plan of buying a Tuesday-only option if the first call doesn't go into the money. You might get lucky on any of the first few days and avoid having to pay for the time value for the days you did not need.

This would work if each one-day call were priced around 20% of the (five-day) week call. Unfortunately for this simple scheme they are not. The market makes buyers of short-dated calls pay more per unit of time in part to encourage them to match the maturity of their investment horizon with the life of the option. As stated earlier, in general, the price of an option will expand with the square root of time. So a five-day option on Monday morning should be about 2.24 ($= \sqrt{5}$) times the price of the Monday-only option.

The reverse side of this coin explains the basic feature of time decay. Every one-year call eventually becomes a one-month, a one-week, and then a one-day call right before expiration. The price changes along that time line are far from linear. If one buys a one-year call and a day passes, it has lost $1/365^{th}$ of its existence. But just as importantly, that lost day is not one of the expensive days right before expiration. If nothing else happens to the underlying price or the expectation of volatility, that option should lose less than $1/365^{th}$ of its value.

Eventually, though, time takes its toll. Each passing day represents a greater percentage of the time remaining and the days become increasingly valuable. As the clock ticks, the path of a call's time value begins to resemble the flight path of a tossed manhole cover. Once the decline begins in earnest, it is quite swift as shown in Figure 10.2.

Understanding time decay allows the investor to match the right call maturity to the investment time horizon. Buyers will want to make sure they are buying long

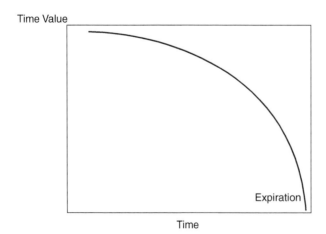

FIGURE 10.2 Time Decay of an Option

enough dated calls to cover their expectations so they don't overpay for a series of shorter dated calls. Sellers of calls will typically want to emphasize the steep part of the time decay curve.

10.2.2 Simple Call Strategies

Buying a call is a bull market strategy, with the buyer hoping that the underlying price will increase to beyond the strike price during the life of the option. While the preceding sentence captures the essence of buying calls, there are so many strike prices, maturities, and option combinations to choose from, that this section will describe some of the most basic approaches using calls.

The advanced student of options and any option professional will fine-tune these descriptions with a serious application of algebra. But for the purposes of understanding the intuition behind each approach, all that is really required is a basic profit–loss diagram. This will be used repeatedly throughout the balance of the options discussion. It graphs the profit or loss of any position as the price of the underlying security, index or other asset being traded changes. E in the chart is the existing price when the position is established.

Figure 10.3 shows how the chart works for the two most basic trades that one would take without options: an unleveraged long and an unleveraged short in the asset being traded.

The horizontal axis gives the price of the underlying asset. The vertical axis gives the profit or loss of the trade. When a trade is established at the existing underlying price, E, either long or short, there is no profit or loss as it is assumed one could reverse the trade at no cost. To be concrete, assume the example is talking about IBM stock, and the current price is $150/share.

The buyer of IBM shares is said to be *long*, and if the purchases are made for cash, it is an unleveraged position. This is shown in the chart as the solid line sloping upward at 45°. If IBM stock goes up $10, there is a $10 profit. Conversely, if IBM falls to $140 a share, there is a $10 loss. The trade is completely symmetric and today's profit or loss is only a function of IBM's share price. When the examples move into options strategies, we will need to introduce the dimensions of time and volatility.

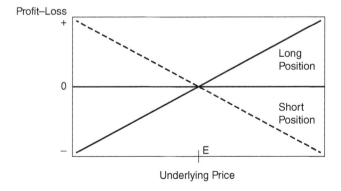

FIGURE 10.3 Basic Profit–Loss Diagram

A person selling IBM stock short has the opposite exposure, as shown by the dashed line sloping downward at 45°. Here if IBM stock falls to $140, a $10 profit is generated for the trade. Of interest in this position is the fact that the maximum gain from the short is today's price. IBM stock won't trade below zero, so profit from this short position is capped at $150, which happens when IBM fails as a company. *Loss from a short position is not capped.* It is not hard to believe IBM shares could grow to $200, $300, or more per share. We shall see later that this can be an important factor, especially with low-priced stocks, that influences some stock traders to use options instead of short positions.

10.2.2.1 Long at-the-Money Calls

The most basic long call strategy is buying a call that has a strike price that is equal to today's underlying price. The buyer of that call believes that the price of the underlying is going up and that increase will be large enough to cover the cost of the option. The buyer also receives assurance that if the underlying price declines, the most that can be lost is the premium paid.

Because of the time dimension of the call, the simple profit–loss diagram used to portray basic long or short positions in Figure 10.3 is no longer adequate. For each option strategy, different expected profit–loss curves can be estimated for the day the strategy was established, the day the strategy expires, and every point of time in between. Figure 10.4 shows an at-the-money call at the moment of purchase (dotted line) and at expiration (solid line). In all of the option valuation slides that follow, we will follow the convention of using the dotted line to indicate the time of purchase price sensitivity and the solid line to show profit and loss at the expiration of the option. As time passes to expiration, the dotted line will converge to the solid one.

At the time the call is purchased, it could theoretically be sold back at the same price (ignoring commissions and bid/ask spreads), which explains why the dotted line goes through the zero point of the P/L axis at the current underlying price. If the underlying price increases, the call goes up in value, but not dollar for dollar. This is due to the fact that there is still time value left in the option and time could

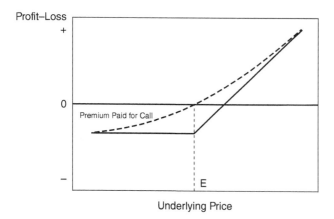

FIGURE 10.4 Long at-the-Money call

see the underlying price falling back as easily as it increased. The same is true for price declines.

The rate at which the call changes value for every unit change in the underlying price is called the *delta*. For investors, it is the most important of the "Greeks," which are a collection of measures used to describe an option's sensitivity to a variety of factors. The other Greeks capture how an option changes with respect to volatility (*vega*), time (*theta*), interest rates *(rho)*, and delta *(gamma)*.

A good rule of thumb is that the delta of an at-the-money call is about 0.5, which is the slope of the dotted line at the origin in Figure 10.4. As the underlying price falls, the call loses value and the delta moves toward zero (the dotted line gets flatter). If the buyer of the call is correct and the underlying price moves up, the slope of the dotted line approaches one.

To see the intuition behind this, go back to the IBM stock example. If you buy an at-the-money $150 strike price call and the price falls suddenly to $50, the call doesn't look so inviting any more. A price move from $50 to $51 still leaves your call deep out-of-the-money, and its current market price won't change much. The delta at that point will be close to zero.

If, on the other hand, Japanese computer giant NEC announces it wants to buy IBM for $225 a share, your call struck at $150 is now in the money by $75. This produces a call with a delta that is quite close to 1. The call behaves a lot like the underlying stock at that point, and there would be little of the limited downside benefit that calls traditionally provide. If NEC decided to cancel its offer, the price of both the stock and the call would tumble together.

The other Greeks that have relevance to most investors can also be discussed in terms of the previous charts. Theta, or the sensitivity to time decay, is best seen in Figure 10.2. For long-dated options the slope of the time decay curve is relatively flat and theta is low. As a call approaches expiration, the decay curve gets steeper and theta grows.

As time passes, and everything else stays the same, the dotted line in Figure 10.4 begins shifting down toward the solid line showing profits or losses at expiration. The rate at which the whole curve moves is theta.

Investors owning long calls in their portfolio could ask their manager what their theta is, but the answer won't have much intuitive meaning. A better question to ask is, "What are the maturities of the calls and if nothing changes in the underlying prices over their life, what will it cost the portfolio?" If the answers are "Two weeks and 40%," the investor should be prepared for a big move in portfolio valuation.

Vega, which only sounds like it should be a Greek letter, measures the sensitivity of a call to changes in volatility. A high vega call will fluctuate widely as the market's perception of future volatility changes. Interestingly, if the market suddenly believes future volatility has fallen in half, the effect on the call will be as if time has speeded up. The market premium will fall just like it does when time passes. Conversely, a belief that future volatility will be high has the same impact as reversing the calendar!

In general, once an investor has bought a call, the position is helped by increases in expected volatility. It is even possible that a drop in the underlying price can help the owner of a call if the implied volatility jumps enough to offset the directional disappointment. While call buyers should never count on such an outcome, it highlights the power of having positive vega in a portfolio.

Gamma is one of the more esoteric of the Greeks, but it is increasingly popping up in investor conversations. Gamma captures how quickly delta, the slope of the option profit–loss line, can change. Owning a lot of gamma is a two-edged sword. Favorable price changes generate gains at an increasing rate. Contrasting that on the downside, high gamma call portfolios can melt away quickly if underlying prices drop.

Time to expiration is an important factor in determining gamma. As the dotted line in Figure 10.4 drifts toward expiration, the gamma of near-the-money calls grows. In the IBM call example, if a $150 call has two days before expiration, it will likely not be worth much if the stock is trading at $146. However, if some positive news occurs in those last two days, the stock could run up to $152, putting the call into the money. The delta in that case would quickly shift from a very low number to being near 1, which is what having a large gamma means.

Options close to expiration that are not near the money will have very low gammas. IBM could go from $50 to $70 in a wink the day before expiration and the delta of the $150 call would barely budge.

Buyers of calls should be thought to be bullish in terms of price direction, though less bullish than the direct buyer of the underlying stock. That conclusion comes from the fact that the call buyer is willing to pay a premium, *which is a wasting asset,* in order to reduce downside risk. People who buy the shares outright must be confident enough that prices will rise that such an expense on option premiums is viewed as a waste of money.

Call buyers are also bullish on volatility, though there is a decided preference for upside volatility. It will be shown below how strategies that combine calls and puts can be used to express bullish or bearish volatility opinions without any underlying opinion on the direction of price.

10.2.2.2 Long out-of-the-Money Calls

Buyers are not restricted to calls with strike prices equal to today's market price. Buying out-of-the-money calls allows the bullish investor to express an opinion with even less downside risk. The trade-off is a higher likelihood that the call will expire out of the money and the entire premium will be lost. Figure 10.5 shows the profit–loss

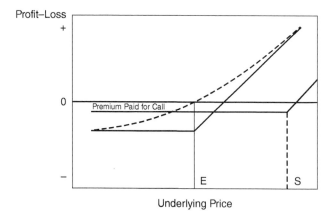

FIGURE 10.5 Out-of-the-Money Call

picture for an out-of-the-money call struck at S compared to the original at-the-money call struck at E.

The figure shows that the premium paid for an out-of-the money call will be less than a similar-duration at-the-money call. This means that the maximum loss is less, but it also means that profits don't begin until the underlying price has moved up past the strike price, S.

As one considers calls with higher strike prices that are increasingly out of the money, everything about the option becomes more muted. The delta moves toward zero, meaning changes in the underlying price have little impact until they accumulate enough in the right direction to bring the call closer to the money. The impact of volatility and time decay are also less than with at-the-money options.

Choosing the right strike price is a big challenge for the call buyer. If IBM is trading at $150, any move up will start generating profits for the at-the-money call buyer, but that is not the case for the out-of-the-money call owner. In the extreme, buying a three-month option with a strike price of $200 is akin to buying a lottery ticket. Of course there is *some* chance that IBM stock could go up 33% in that time period, but it is certainly not a big one. Buyers of such options should either have a lottery player's mentality or possess information about the company that is not widely known.[2]

If one is going to buy an out-of-the-money call, the maturity chosen should match the time horizon of the investment. If one thinks that IBM should increase by at least 10% within the next six months, with very little downside risk, the best strategy might be to simply buy the stock. If, however, there is a concern over potential losses over the period, an out-of-the money call might be appropriate, but there are no obvious or easy guides.

An option that expires in a month is probably not a good fit with that investment thesis. An option with a strike price of $200 is not consistent with the market view either. It may seem obvious that a good choice might be a six-month, $165 strike option, but just because an option matches one's expectations does not make it a perfect choice.

If the market price for such an option were $0.05 per share, the bullish investor would probably load up. If, however, the option was trading at $7 per share, one might wonder whether the chance to profit was worth the risk. The challenge with options is always contrasting one's views on direction and volatility with what the market is reflecting. The two dimensions transform a simple stock purchase decision into something more complex and nuanced.

10.2.2.3 *Simple Short Calls*

Selling a call is operationally the reverse of buying one, but the return and risk implications are quite different. Instead of owning an option to buy at the strike price, where the maximum downside is known with complete certainty, the seller of a call has an *obligation* to take the other side. The call seller must agree to sell the underlying at the strike price if the option is exercised. The risk profile of the short call is very

---

[2]The author is not advocating trading on inside information with this comment. In fact, the reader should be aware that the SEC and the options exchanges routinely monitor transactions in deep out-of-the-money options in an effort to detect such activity.

different as well. Here the maximum upside is known in advance, and the potential loss is not bounded.

Figure 10.6 shows the profit–loss diagram of a short at-the-money call. It is the mirror image of the long call diagram Figure 10.4. The dotted line is the profile when the call is written, which converges to the expiration solid line as time passes. Here time decay is an asset.

Changing the strike price to writing out-of-the-money calls is less risky, but also less rewarding. There is a higher probability that the options will expire worthless when the call is struck out-of-the-money, but in the rare moments when the call writer is wrong, the losses can be many times the small expected gain.

A comparison to big prize lottery tickets is appropriate here. The state gets away with selling a few winning tickets every year because they sell millions and millions of losers as well. Writing deep out-of-the-money calls may have a similar payoff profile as selling lottery tickets, but there is an important difference. Writing options is not an actuarial fair game governed by the laws of probability. It is an economic contract affected by market forces over which the call buyer and writer have little influence. If the underlying price shoots up like a Roman candle, saying that the price move was a six standard deviation Black Swan rarity offers no protection to the call writer. Selling a diverse portfolio of out-of-the-money calls also won't help if the rally occurs at the level of the overall market.

The Greeks for short calls are the same as for long calls with the signs reversed. An at-the-money short call has a delta near -0.5. As the call moves into the money delta approaches -1, and begins to act like a straight short position. Time decay helps the option writer as do declines in implied volatility.

Managing basic short call positions through time should be an active process. If a position quickly moves against the call writer, the absolute value of the delta grows, as does the fundamental risk. The option writer needs to assess whether the increased risk profile is consistent with their overall investment thesis, keeping in mind that there is no limit to the downside for the call writer.

Positions that move in favor of the option writer ironically can pose even a greater challenge. Few investors need to have their attention focused as they are

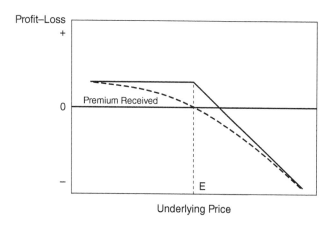

FIGURE 10.6   Short at-the-Money Call

losing money. Winning is another story, especially when winning comes from something as passive as time decay.

Imagine writing an out-of-the-money call that expires in two months, where you collect $1,000 in premium on an underlying position that is worth $50,000. Six weeks pass, and the underlying price has drifted down a bit. The call's market price is $75. On a mark-to-market basis you have made 92.5% of the original maximum gain in the trade. Time decay is working in your favor, and as shown in Figure 10.2, the rate of decline is getting faster as expiration approaches. What do you do?

An inattentive seller might let nature take its course. After all, there is a much lower chance today of the option going into the money. An easy non-decision is to simply wait, and let the option slide into worthlessness. But what if you are wrong? If good news comes out about the company or the sector, the option couldquickly move to be in the money. The chance to make an extra $75 from the remaining time decay could end up costing hundreds or thousands of dollars.

Dealing with short-dated options is a highly specialized activity often best left to professionals. Investors would do well to declare victory, buy back the very cheap option, and let someone else worry about the tail risk that can sink such a position. Most people, however, let inertia take over. The vast majority of the time, inertia will not hurt you. After it has, however, the next position in short calls will receive more attention. Remember the adage, "Bulls can make money. Bears can make money. Pigs get slaughtered."

10.2.2.4 Simple Call Spreads

To help further refine the fit between an investment thesis and the strategy, the investor can consider call spreads, which involve both long and short call positions. The easiest conceptually is the bull call spread where the investor buys a certain maturity call at one strike price and sells another call with the same maturity but with a higher strike price. An example will demonstrate the advantages.

Consider the person who believes IBM stock, currently at $150, will rise at least 10% in the next six months, *but that the probability of it going above $200 is quite low*. We have seen how this investor can buy the six-month 165-strike call to express the basic bullish view, but a single long call doesn't quite match the total perspective. This investor could also sell a six-month 200 call to complete the picture. The investor is saying that he wants a long position, but is willing to sell away the upside over $200 because in his opinion the current price of that option is higher than the likelihood of additional profit.

Figure 10.7 shows the expiration profit–loss charts for the individual long and short calls, as well as the payoff diagram for the combination. The dotted line is the profit–loss pattern when the spread is established for a combination known as a *bull call spread*. The main advantage of the spread in this example is that the investor can express the bullish view with a smaller net premium, as the small amount received from the out-of-the-money short call partially subsidizes the cost of the purchased call. The trade-off, of course, is that the chance to metaphorically win the lottery if IBM stock really takes off has been sold to another investor.

The opposite side of this position is a bear call spread. The investor selling the lower strike price call and buying the higher priced option is *receiving a net* premium,

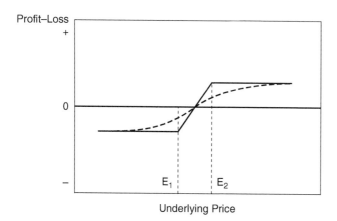

FIGURE 10.7   Bull Spread

which represents the maximum gain on the combination. This gain will occur any time IBM's price ends up less than $165, so this side of the trade is arguing that IBM's price will not rally by at least 10% in the six-month window. The other leg of the spread, the purchased call at 200, can be thought of as insurance for the writing of the first call. If the investment thesis is really wrong and IBM's price goes well beyond $200, the long call truncates the loss. The profit–loss diagram for the bear spread at initiation and expiration is given in Figure 10.8.

In both the bull and bear call spreads above the options were balanced in terms of underlying value. If you bought a call giving the right to purchase 100 shares, the call you sold was also for 100 shares. This is the only way to assure balance in the spread position no matter what the underlying price ultimately becomes.

There are more complicated spreads that try to refine the process further. A common approach is to try to match the deltas of the options. For example, in the IBM bull spread example, assume the 165 call has a delta of 0.4 and the 200 call has a delta

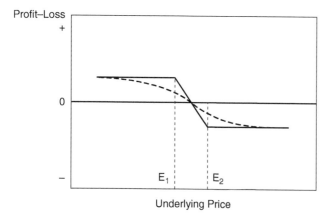

FIGURE 10.8   Bear Spread

of 0.1. Buying the 165 and selling the 200 produces a net delta of 0.3. This says that the value of the *spread* will move up 3 cents for every 10-cent move in the underlying price. Since owning the 165 call outright has a 0.4 delta, one can see that while the spread is still bullish, it is somewhat less bullish than the long call alone.

Someone with an incredibly strong view that IBM stock will not exceed 200 might try to cut the cost of owning the 165 call even more by selling four 200 calls to create a spread that is, for the moment, *delta neutral*. The 0.4 positive delta of the 165 call is completely offset by the four 0.1 deltas of the 200 calls on the short side. The obvious advantage is the much greater premium one receives from selling four options. This is known as a *ratio spread*.

The downside, however, is no longer capped. If IBM stock rallied suddenly, the deltas on all of the options would expand quickly, producing a net delta that was negative. A position that started with the premise that IBM stock would increase to above $165 would begin to behave like a short position as prices increased further. Figure 10.9 shows at expiration just how badly the ratio spread can behave if prices rise well above the second strike price.

A delta neutral spread trader needs to monitor and adjust the spread ratio in virtually real time to keep the risks shown in Figure 10.9 contained. As the underlying price moves up, the spread trader buys back some of the short 200 strike options, potentially getting back to 1:1 if the price goes high enough. All of this adjustment comes at a cost as the purchases are made at higher and higher premium values.

The bigger risks come when the market gaps. In those instances the spread moves out of delta neutrality before the trader can rebalance. Losses can accumulate quickly. In general, ratio spread trading should be left to option professionals. One even needs caution when dealing with professionals. Regular investors should be wary of anyone

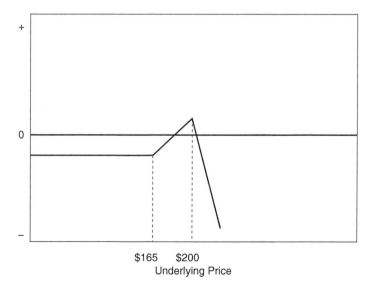

$165 $200
Underlying Price

FIGURE 10.9   Static Bull Ratio Call Spread

who claims to be able to always adjust their positions before losses occur. That is not possible and hubris or dishonesty, or both, affect anyone making such claims.

10.2.2.5 Call Calendar Spreads

The spreads discussed above combine options of the same maturity but with different strike prices. One can also spread calls with the same strike prices but different maturities, which are known as *calendar spreads*. Usually such a trade is done to exploit the shape of the time decay curve.

Using the IBM example again, with the current price being $150, one could buy a four-month 165 strike call for a premium of say $4 and sell the one-month 165 call for $2. This is mostly a wager on the decay of time. If nothing happens to the underlying price in the first month, the short option expires worthless, and the longer dated option will likely have fallen, but not by as much. This is shown in Figure 10.10 with S_1 being the expected decline in time value for the long option and S_2 being the larger decline from the shorter dated short option.

The ideal outcome in the example where the short one-month option expires worthless would be to sell the now three-month option and reap the gain. If the trader's views on the underlying had become more bullish, he or she could keep the outright long position, but this would mean risking the $2 net premium paid for the original spread.

The risks of a calendar spread are from rapidly increasing or decreasing prices. If, for example, NEC announced a takeover bid for IBM the day after the spread was put on, the underlying price would shoot well above the 165 strike price and both calls would increase rapidly. That sounds neutral, but if the price increase were large enough, both calls would begin trading at their intrinsic value, losing all of the time value that was present when the spread was put on. The spread trader in the example would see all of the $4 of time value in the long call evaporate, while benefiting only from a decline of $2 in time value in the short one-month option. Similarly, if there was an accounting fraud scandal at IBM and the stock price was cut in half, both the long and the short calls in the calendar spread would tumble toward zero.

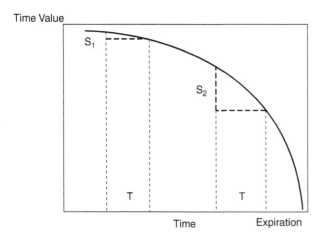

FIGURE 10.10   Time Decay and Calendar Spreads

In both of the examples above the underlying price moved so far away from the money that the time value of the calls evaporated. Since the spread trader was long the call with more time, the trade loses money. But the maximum loss in this case is the difference in the premiums. This is an important example of how even apparently market neutral spread trades can be affected by volatility. In this case, the spread trader is short volatility, hoping for a decline that would effectively accelerate the effects of time decay.

It is possible to do the reverse trade, but this is much less common. Owning the one-month option and selling the four-month one is a bet that is pushing back against the tide of time decay. The owner is hoping for some large market event (and soon!) in a hope to capture the extra $2 premium that he has collected. If that increase in volatility is not forthcoming, the position erodes quickly for the short dated option. At expiration, the trader would need to buy back the remaining three-month option, for a loss on the overall position, or face a completely different risk profile of a naked call writer for the remainder of that call's life. There are easier ways to bet volatility will increase.

Even more complex spreads are always available to the call trader. Combinations of different months and different strikes can always be constructed. Analyzing the profit–loss and risk profiles of such combinations pretty quickly strains simple diagrams, but the arithmetic of combining the various Greeks is direct and fairly reliable. As a general rule, unless there is a very well-defined investment thesis that requires a complex spread of calls, the trading of such instruments should be left to the option professionals that are accustomed to managing multifaceted portfolios.

10.2.3 Basics of Puts

A *put* is structured exactly like a call except the buyer has the *right to sell* the underlying asset or index at the agreed-upon strike price during the life of the option. Similarly, the put seller or writer has the *obligation to buy* the asset or the value of the index if the put buyer chooses to exercise. The profit–loss payoff of a long put, as shown in Figure 10.11, shows a maximum loss of the premium paid, with gains occurring

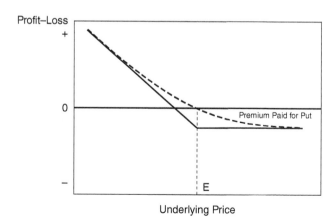

FIGURE 10.11 Long at-the-Money Put

anytime the price falls below the strike price by more than the premium. Unlike a call where the maximum gain is unlimited, the most a put can make is the strike price, less the premium, as the price of the underlying asset cannot go below zero.

The discussion of at-the-money versus out-of-the-money puts is completely parallel to that of calls, except the out-of-the-money puts all have lower strike prices than the current price. The calculation of all the Greeks is virtually identical, with only the signs reversed. Someone being long puts is in a negative delta situation and that delta gets more negative (to a limit of −1) as the underlying price drops.

The seller of puts has a mirror image profit–loss profile, as shown in Figure 10.12. Like the seller of calls, the maximum gain is limited to the premium collected, while the loss is essentially unbounded until the underlying price goes to zero. A long put position is a bearish bet on the underlying asset or index, though it is less bearish than selling the asset short. The buyer of the put is willing to risk no more than the premium to achieve a profit, which will always be less than the straight short bet by the size of that premium.

Selling puts in isolation is a fairly risky proposition, as crashes can hit individual securities or the market as a whole. But as was shown in Chapter 6, writing fully collateralized, out-of-the-money puts on high-volatility stocks may be a useful strategy to lower the purchase price of portfolio holdings.

10.2.3.1 Put Spreads

Puts can be combined in much the same way as calls, and the profit–loss diagrams are virtually identical and will not be repeated. Buying an at-the-money put and selling an out-of-the money put can similarly create the bear spread in Figure 10.8. One would do this trade, for example, if the market view were that IBM would fall from its current price of $150, but would likely not go below $100 during the life of the option.

Spreads like the above can be constructed between strike prices of the same maturity, between different months of the same strike to capture time decay, or any combination of the above. As long as the notional values of the two legs are the same, the risk at expiration is well defined in advance. If the put spread is done on

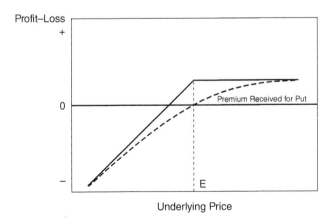

FIGURE 10.12   Short at-the-Money Put

some kind of a delta ratio basis, the risk profile needs to be monitored and managed dynamically as the exposures will change with the underlying price.

10.2.4 Combinations of Calls and Puts

Combining puts and calls increases the range of trading options considerably. Some of the combinations are primarily of interest to option professionals, but many others have relevant applications for all investors.

The most basic combinations create *synthetic long or short positions*. For example, buying a call and then selling the same month, the same strike price put creates a position in aggregate that behaves exactly like a simple long position in the underlying security, index, or asset. One might logically ask why anyone would want to jump through two hoops to create something as simple as an unleveraged long position. The answer is that most investors would not, but option professionals use the synthetic relationships as a guide to whether a specific option is trading at too high or too low a price. If it is, a synthetic position can be created against an offsetting position in the cash market to create a true arbitrage.

Table 10.3 all the synthetic relationships from simple combinations of calls, puts, and cash positions. Figure 10.13 shows the profit–loss diagram for a synthetic long cash position.

TABLE 10.3 Synthetic Equivalents

Direct Trades	Synthetic Equivalent
Long Call + Short Put	Long Cash
Short Call + Long Put	Short Cash
Long Cash + Short Call	Short Put
Long Cash + Long Put	Long Call
Short Cash + Long Call	Long Put
Short Cash + Short Put	Short Call

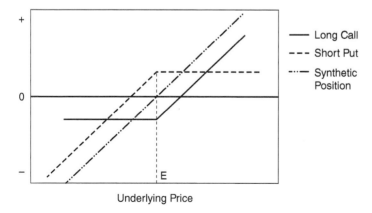

FIGURE 10.13 Long Call + Short Put = Synthetic Long Futures

This may appear arcane to many readers, but the principles are quite important. It was shown in Chapter 6 that one could try to enhance returns by pursuing a covered call strategy, that is, owning a security and then selling a call against it to collect the time premium. The table shows that this strategy is the exact equivalent to selling a put at the same strike price.

Once again the question becomes, "Why jump through two hoops?" The answer is that many people have long-term stock portfolios around which they wish to adjust exposures. One owns stock because of a bullish opinion. Subsequently, either because the bullishness fades a bit, or because of a strong volatility opinion that calls are rich, one could modify the stock position by selling some calls against it. This creates a portfolio that looks like a short put, but it is easier to add short calls to the existing position than it is to sell all the stocks and then sell puts. In this case the dynamics of managing a synthetic position are easier than doing everything directly.

Taxes can also make a difference. In the covered call example above, by selling calls against the stock portfolio one has adjusted the risk of the position without selling any stocks and creating an immediate taxable event. Every taxpaying investor should be aware of the synthetic opportunities to manage portfolios to minimize the tax impact of transactions.

While the IRS allows everyone to minimize their tax obligations using the current rules, tax avoidance is another thing altogether. The last few decades are filled with examples of people who attempted to avoid taxes using synthetic positions. Creating *boxes* of offsetting synthetic longs and short positions, and then trading out of losing individual options to create investment losses may have looked clever at one time, but the IRS is onto those operations. The basic rules say that if there is a legitimate economic purpose for a trade, it is allowed. If, however, the transaction carries little or no economic risk and appears designed only to avoid paying taxes, it will be disallowed. Investors should be aware of the synthetic positions table (Table 10.3) if for no other reason than to help them identify schemers who have plans to help minimize taxes.

Of much great importance to individual traders are combinations of puts and calls that are directionally neutral, but allow opinions about volatility to be expressed. We have already seen bull and bear directional spreads. It is now time to expand the menagerie.

10.2.4.1 *Straddles and Strangles*

Combining pairs of calls and puts from the same side of the market allows the creation of directionally neutral positions, but with a definite opinion on volatility. If one buys a call and a put at the same strike price, one is indifferent in what direction the underlying instrument security moves, but there is a strong preference for some really active market moves, and soon! A long *option straddle* struck at-the-money is shown in Figure 10.14, demonstrating that there is a profit to the position only after the underlying price moves up or down by more than the sum of premiums paid for the options.

This expresses much more than an opinion that the underlying will move through time. Every market moves through time. This is an opinion that the actual movement will be more than the market expects as revealed by the premiums paid for the options. It is a little bit like betting on the over/under in football games. You

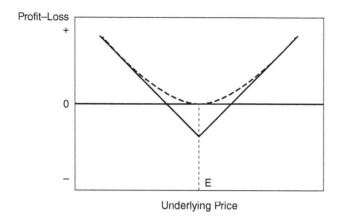

Underlying Price

FIGURE 10.14 Long Straddle

don't care whether the underlying price goes up or down any more than you do which team scores the points. You only care whether the price movement, or the sum of the points, is bigger or smaller than the market expected.

The buyer of an option straddle has limited downside and unlimited upside. It is among the purest expressions of a long volatility opinion. It is best put on whenever the market is in a period of calm, perhaps even complacent. It can be an expensive strategy if executed when volatility is already elevated and you are banking on further excitement.

For every long there is a short, and the short straddle strategy is a bet against volatility. Ideally after writing an at-the-money call and put, the market just stops dead in its tracks. The underlying price stays exactly where it started, and both options expire worthless. This is the point of maximum profits for the straddle writer. *Any* deviation makes either the put or the call go into the money and begins eating away at the collected premium (Figure 10.15).

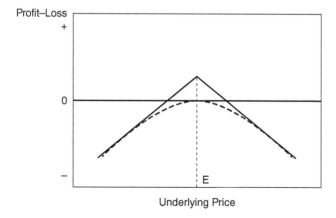

Underlying Price

FIGURE 10.15 Short Straddle

Using Ford stock as an example, let the stock be trading at $13 per share. $13 strike price puts and calls that expire in two weeks could be sold for $0.25 per share each. If Ford stock trades right at $13 when the options expire, the maximum profit of $0.50 per share will be realized. There would be some profit as long as Ford stock stayed within the range $12.50–$13.50, a range of plus or minus 3.8%. Deciding whether you believe that range to be too big or too small determines what side of the trade you want to be on.

One can use different strike prices to alter the size and risk of the bet for or against volatility. If one buys an out-of-the-money call and an out-of-the-money put, both options are cheaper than the at-the-money options purchased in a straddle. This combination is known as an *option strangle*, a colorful name that is more easily understood from the short side. The buyer of a strangle, like the buyer of a straddle, is making a directionless bet. But that bet is now that the underlying price will move more than the two premiums plus the out-of-the-money amount. If the option strikes are well away from today's price it is almost like buying a bull lottery ticket and a bear lottery ticket. The total outlay may be modest, but the potential rewards can be great for the few times it works.

Writers of strangles typically are trying to exploit short-term spikes in volatility that have temporarily raised option premiums or the most extreme moments of time decay. Using Ford again as the example with the stock trading at $13 per share, the two-week $14 call can be sold for $0.05 per share. This is the same price as the same maturity $12 put. The strangle writer collects $0.10 per share and then holds his breath for two weeks hoping the stock stays within the bands $11.90 and $14.10 (with the maximum profit earned when the price stays anywhere between the strikes). While there is a wider range of profitability for the strangle writer, the maximum gain is less ($0.10 versus $0.50 with the straddle). Everywhere there are trade-offs to be considered.

In this stylized example, imagine what would happen if in the first week Ford announced better than expected earnings, and the stock rallied to $15. With *American-style options*, which can be exercised at any time before expiration, the owner of the $14 call might exercise his rights and the strangle writer would have to deliver stock at that price. Usually when such events happen, the strangle writer won't want to carry the resulting outright stock position, so he will buy the stock in the market at $15 and absorb the $1 per share loss.

Then imagine the following week the Federal Highway Safety Commission issues a major action against Ford, which results in a safety recall of millions of cars. The stock price could fall to $10 in a wink and the written put could be exercised forcing another losing transaction. The strangle writer would buy in Ford at the $12 strike and then sell it at the $10 market price. This kind of example is rare, but it has happened frequently enough to have the option writer feel strangled from both sides, and hence the name.

Writing straddles and strangles without any other offsetting positions are speculative activities that should be largely left to market professionals who have the capital, temperament, and discipline to manage what can be highly dynamic portfolios. Risk can change rapidly and losses mount. Unless one can readily absorb those losses and be willing to trade quickly out of exposures, short straddles and strangles are inappropriate strategies.

The easiest way to mitigate the risks of short straddles and strangles is to take some of the collected premium and buy protection against extreme events. This leads to two new strategies known as *option butterflies* and *condors*. These strategies are simply combinations of bull and bear option spreads. The Ford example can be extended to show how they work.

The straddle writer collected $0.50 per share in premiums when he wrote the $13 strike ($E_2$ in the chart) put and call. To limit the downside risk he could actually purchase the strangle discussed above, buying the $14 ($E_3$) call and the $12 ($E_1$) put. This would cost in total $0.10 per share, capping the maximum profit of the trade at $0.40 per share, but if something really crazy happened either up or down, there would be an insurance policy in place. The profit and loss from an option butterfly is shown in Figure 10.16 and can be thought of as volatility speculation for the highly cautious.

Limiting the risk of the short strangle is done similarly. After writing the $14 ($E_3$ in the chart) call and the $12 ($E_2$) put to collect $0.10 per share, the trader buys a $15 ($E_4$) call and an $11 ($E_1$) put for $0.01 per share each. This puts wings on the strangle, as shown in Figure 10.17. The maximum profit is only $0.08 per share, but there is

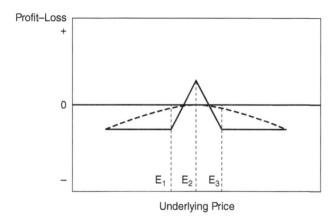

FIGURE 10.16   Long Butterfly

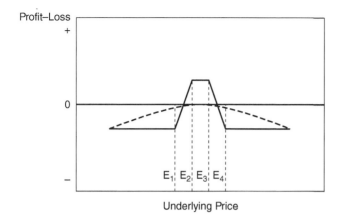

FIGURE 10.17   Long Condor

now a limit to the loss as well. This strategy has a wider "body" to the trade than a butterfly and is known as a *condor*.

Seeing the metaphorical shape of butterflies and condors in the profit and loss charts above requires a bit of imagination. Perhaps the earliest option traders were like ancient shepherds tending their flocks on cloudless nights. Staring at computer screens with shifting graphics may be the twenty-first-century equivalent. With enough quiet time, shapes of rams, fish, and swans appear from groups of stars. Millennia later, birds and insects fly from options data. Both activities have helped those of us with less focused minds remember difficult combinations.

10.3 SWAPS

Exchange-traded futures and options for financial markets are widely considered the single most important financial innovation in the last 30 years of the twentieth century. Privately negotiated *swaps* and options on swaps, commonly known as *swaptions,* are close behind. These instruments were initially conceived as filling in all the gaps not covered by exchange-traded futures and options. In many cases today they have become the first choice of investors and financial professionals to acquire or shape investment risk.

The basic structure of a swap involves a customized, legal agreement between two counterparties to exchange two payment streams. An example of a classic *fixed for floating* interest rate swap will have Party A obligated to pay Party B 4% annual interest on a million dollars, payable quarterly, for the next five years. Party B, in return, is obligated to pay Party A 90-day LIBOR + 50 basis points, quarterly, on the same $1 million. Party A knows they will owe Part B $10,000 each quarter (the fixed payment of 1% of the notional), but Party B's obligations are not known until the payment dates, at which point the LIBOR rate relative to that payment will be set. For convenience, cash does not flow in both directions on the swap. If 90-day LIBOR + 50 is less than 4%, Party A will send the difference to B. Conversely, if LIBOR + 50 is greater than 4%, B will make a net payment. On the odd chance that the two rates are equal, no cash moves.

In the above example, if the swap is the only interest rate sensitive part of the two parties' portfolios, the market opinions are obvious. A believes interest rates are going up and they will benefit from rising rates as B's obligation grows through time. B is betting on falling rates. Oftentimes this surface appearance is only part of a bigger picture that can involve speculation or hedging on interest rates.

Starting primarily with interest rate swaps in the 1970s, the industry quickly expanded to include foreign currency swaps, and equity index swaps. Since the model is completely customizable, one could feasibly construct a swap where Party A pays Party B the US dollar return on gold bullion and in return receives a floating, short-term Brazilian interest rate paid in Argentine pesos. There may be no obvious investment logic to such a swap, but the only limitations are the counterparty's willingness to transact.

The market is huge. In 1985 the trade had progressed to the point where 10 major dealers formed ISDA in order to promote best practices, try to achieve efficiencies through documentation standardization, and to represent the industry in regulatory matters. Initially ISDA stood for the International Swap Dealers Association. In 1993 the expanded range of activity into OTC derivatives prompted the organization to change its name to the International Swaps and Derivatives Association, conveniently keeping the by then widely recognized anagram ISDA.

ISDA did its first industry survey of activity at year-end 1987 and found that there was over $800 billion in interest rate and currency swaps and options outstanding. By 1998 the figure stood at more than $50 trillion. At the end of 2009, ISDA's original membership of 10 had grown to more than 800, and the notional value of all swaps outstanding exceeded $450 trillion. Given that the world's GDP in 2009 was only estimated to be $58 trillion, ISDA has had a fairly active first 25 years of life.[3] By year-end 2018, the total grew to $544 trillion according to BIS statistics.

The more important part of the puzzle is how the $500 trillion number is almost irrelevant. Unlike exchange-traded futures and options there is no offset of positions. This means I can enter into a $100 million, five-year, fixed for floating interest rate swap where I pay fixed today, and then enter the exact same term swap next week where I pay floating, and it results in $200 million in gross exposure on the books that the BIS examines for its data. There is no economic risk, and the quarterly payments in each direction will offset, resulting in no flow of funds, but both swaps will be counted as outstanding until they naturally roll off in five years.

What the $500 trillion number does tell us is that an awful lot of large transactions take place every year. It tells us little about the risks that activity creates. The CFTC, which was given regulatory responsibility for swaps in the Dodd-Frank bill after the financial crisis has begun exploring more relevant measures of the activity, focusing on net exposures between independent counterparties. As more and more swap activity moves to specialized execution facilities and clearing houses, a more useful picture of the industry will eventually emerge.

The basic model of a swap transaction is shown in Figure 10.18. There are two counterparties that agree at the inception of the swap that they will exchange periodic

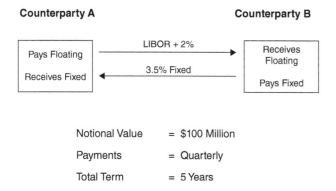

FIGURE 10.18 Structure of a Basic Interest Rate Swap

---

[3]Source of ISDA data is ISDA.org. World GDP estimates come from the International Monetary Fund and the World Bank.

payments. There is a fixed term to the swap. The frequency of payments is agreed to. A *notional amount* is agreed to as the foundation for the calculation of the payment streams, which forms the meat of the agreement. One or both of the payments will be variable depending on market events.

A swap can be as simple as the fixed-for-floating rate swap described above, or as complex as one desires. One party could agree to pay what $1 million would return on the S&P 500 Index and agree to receive the value of $1 million invested in coffee futures denominated in Brazilian real. The biggest advantage of swaps is the limitless customization available as long as the parties agree.

The notional value is hardly an indicator of risk. Just like owning $1 million of T-bills is not the same risk as $1 million in equities or a $1 million position in cattle, looking at two swaps with the same notional amounts tells you nothing about exposures. The data above showing eight times world GDP outstanding in swap notional value also says very little about the amount of risk in the system, but it does confirm the sustained growth of the industry.

The other major unknown in the above statistics on outstanding notional amounts is the difference between gross and net exposures. As mentioned above, swaps are frequently not offset against the same counterparty. Party A will transact with Party B, who then decides to get rid of the exposure. B could go back to A and ask to get out of the swap, but A would probably extract a good toll for the exit. Instead B will do an offsetting trade with Party C. If each swap were for $1 million of notional value, the ISDA statistics would show $2 million of swaps outstanding. From a market risk standpoint, however, there is only $1 million in exposure, as counterparty B has netted their exposure to zero and left the risk picture.

Given the current reporting system for swaps, there is no easy way of sorting out gross and net exposures from the ISDA data. Strides have been made post crisis with the mandatory clearing of the most basic types of swaps, but coverage is not universal. Until there is a centralized repository for all swap positions, regulators and market users alike will be operating with incomplete data.

Leverage can be added to the payment terms of swaps to magnify their impact. In 1994 Procter & Gamble had a $200 million notional interest rate swap against Bankers Trust. P&G would receive a fixed rate of interest and pay floating. In a simple fixed-for-floating world, it would be hard to imagine losing more than a few million dollars on such a transaction. But P&G's swap was far from simple. The payment terms were nonlinear and leveraged. When the Federal Reserve began raising interest rates in early 1994, P&G's losses quickly exceeded $100 million.

Breaking down the P&G transaction, one finds that this $200 million notional swap was the equivalent of writing naked puts on more than $2 billion in five-year and 30-year Treasury securities. When the position turned against them, P&G sued Bankers Trust claiming that they had been misled about the potential risks of the position. Reasonable people can disagree about whether the Treasurer's office at P&G was duped or not, but it seems likely that the P&G Board had no clue about the risks. A $200 million Treasury transaction at a company the size of P&G might not even be a reportable event. Speculating on $2 billion in Treasury bond options probably would have been of interest to directors of even a soap company.

The P&G story also points out another big difference between swaps and exchange-traded futures and options. In virtually every swap, one of the counterparties is a dealer. For exchange transactions, one does not know, or care, who the counterparty to your trade is. All that is important is that the trade clears. For exchange-traded futures and options, the clearinghouse becomes the buyer to every seller and the seller to every buyer. For swaps, one is typically married to one's counterparty for the life of the swap.

Dealer-dominated networks tend to be much less transparent than exchange transactions. The dealers have much better access to pricing and liquidity information of the underlying markets relative to their counterparties. Thoughtful counterparties know this and they make sure to canvass multiple dealers before executing a swap. The simpler the swap, the better is the competition among dealers and the tighter the pricing. When contemplating complex swaps, a counterparty should expect to be at something of a disadvantage to the dealer.

There are important regulatory and market trends that may be changing the landscape. The Dodd-Frank legislation in 2010 mandated widespread clearing and price reporting of standardized OTC derivatives. The regulators and the participants are still working out the actual mechanics of what derivatives would be included in this, and how it might work.

The challenges of turning a dealer network completely into an exchange/clearinghouse model should not be downplayed. Complex vehicles are by their nature illiquid, and trying to capture the salient terms in a simple public price feed is virtually impossible. Still, the spirit behind Dodd-Frank is to gather all of the major market risks into one pool that can be analyzed by government and self-regulators. Avoiding systemic risk issues can only be done effectively if the right information on transactions can be gathered and analyzed.

Perhaps the biggest difference between exchange-traded futures and options and swaps is in the treatment of collateral. As appropriate to any bilateral credit relationship, the existence and management of collateral is subject to negotiation. There may or may not be any posting of collateral to initiate a swap, though again Dodd-Frank has pushed more instruments to an initial margin model similar to what has always been standard practice in futures. Some dealers will ask for the right to receive unscheduled interim payments if a swap moves sufficiently against the counterparty. These catch up payments help ensure that the counterparty won't default on their obligations by collecting small losses on a regular basis, rather than have them build up to one of the scheduled payment dates.

Increasingly, counterparties are asking for symmetric treatment. In the early days of the swaps industry it was universally assumed the swap dealer would be good for their losses. After the credit crisis of 2008, that assumption could no longer be made. By having the swap dealer also make interim payments whenever the swap moves against them, the counterparty minimizes the risk that their profits could be held captive in the event of a bankruptcy. The safest policy is to receive the profits and then remove them from the broker/dealer to the relative safety of a custodian account.

No swap dealer is too big to fail. That is why the question of collateral at futures and options exchanges is never negotiated. Everyone, whether they are an individual speculator or a well-capitalized swap dealer hedging a proprietary book, is subject to the margin rules. Losers pay variation margin daily or they have their positions closed out. Winners receive their cash on the same time line.

This is perhaps the clearest differentiator between the swaps and the exchange-traded derivatives worlds. Swaps have always been negotiated and they rely on careful analysis of each counterparty. As regulators try to force the worlds together, there should be a realization that many transactions need to be customized and there should be a return to assuming counterparty risk. It is not desirable, nor will it be possible, to force all swap activity into the exchange-traded mold.

Who uses swaps and why? ISDA surveys the universe, and the answer to who uses swaps is, "almost everyone." More than 90% of global Fortune 500 companies report using derivatives, and the vast majority of them use swaps as part of their active treasury functions. Long-term investors have not been big users of swaps, but as hedge funds and other active investors expand their use this could change.

Perhaps the biggest source of potential growth of swap usage for investments is indirectly as support for retail structured products. Clients have increasingly been sold structured products for their investment portfolios as brokers and bankers have discovered their lucrative profit margins. Discussed in greater detail in the next chapter, retail structured products are often supported by swaps that allow a high degree of customization.

The "why" of swaps usage depends greatly on the product and the user. By far the biggest use of interest rate and currency swaps comes from both treasurers of financial and nonfinancial firms who are trying to manage basic financing and cash flow needs of their companies.

The best example comes from a firm with floating rate debt already issued. The company may be concerned with the risk of rising interest rates. One option would be to issue new fixed rate debt and then use those proceeds to retire the floating rate debt. That option, however, like many transactions in the cash market, involves significant underwriting and placement fees. The company can accomplish the same economic end by entering into a fixed for floating rate swap. They would pay the swap dealer a fixed rate and agree to receive a floating one that was closely tied to their own floating rate obligations.

As interest rates fluctuate through time, the revenue from the swap would rise and fall with the obligations on the initial floating rate debt. By entering into the swap, the firm has synthetically issued fixed rate debt.

Financial engineers are always trying to identify ways the use of a swap might improve the financing options for a borrower. Since fixed and floating rate markets are influenced by somewhat different forces, one might be able to lower total borrowing costs by creating either synthetic fixed or floating rate debt relative to the options available in the market at any given time. But the synthetic debt issuer should always be aware of that because of collateral management adding a derivative to the mix can complicate cash flows in the short run.

Imagine a town or corporation that borrows at a floating rate and then enters into a fixed-for-floating-rate swap where the borrower agrees to pay a fixed rate and receive floating. This would create a synthetic fixed rate debt, which protects the borrower from a rising interest rate environment. Now suppose rates tumble. The borrower is completely hedged at the fixed rate they are paying on the swap, but the swap taken in isolation is moving against the borrower. The swap dealer may be concerned that their counterparty won't perform and will invoke their collateral clause.

This has the effect of making the borrower today come up with cash representing the value of the new expected cash flow for the life of the swap. If rates have fallen dramatically, this can be real money. One might think that if rates were falling, financing the collateral call would not be much of an issue, but the credit crisis of 2008 showed the danger of that assumption.

Harvard made the news after the market turmoil of 2008 because in 2004 it had entered into forward interest rate swaps to protect it against rising rates on borrowing it *expected* to use to develop several parts of the campus neighborhood beginning several years later. It agreed to pay a fixed rate of interest over the life of the swap and receive floating. If its worries about higher rates came about, the higher cash flow from the floating ratepayer would hedge its future borrowing and effectively protect the cost of the project.

At the level of being an effective hedge to fix rates, the swap worked. Unfortunately for Harvard, when things started falling apart in September 2008, Treasury interest rates and LIBOR both tumbled, and Harvard's counterparties' future obligations to pay Harvard fell dramatically. The school had a few bad options open to it. One of them was that it could post new collateral on the swap that was moving against it and keep the anticipatory hedge in place. It chose instead to buy back much of the position, locking in the loss.

With perfect foresight, it would have made sense to post the new collateral. The credit market stabilized over the next months and the losses on the swap would have been pared back. Much of that extra collateral would have been returned to the school. But Harvard did not have the luxury of waiting things out and hoping rates would bounce back. First of all, where was it going to get the money to post the collateral? Interest rates were falling because investors were scrambling to buy T-bills for safety. Credit *spreads*, in contrast, were exploding in the crisis. Everyone except the US Treasury was having trouble finding funds.

Furthering the difficulties were the market losses in other parts of Harvard's assets. Its endowment fell by more than $10 billion during the crisis and its liquidity funds, many of which were invested side by side with the endowment, lost $1.8 billion.[4] Harvard resorted to borrowing $2.5 billion in an expensive fixed rate market to cover all of its immediate obligations. At least $500 million of that was used as a one-time payment to terminate a portion of its outstanding swap exposure.

Harvard's story points out a number of features of the swap market that counterparties find easy to ignore when times are good. The most important of which is planning for collateral management. Like many people's experience with futures contracts, counterparties to swap trades either believe the derivatives will never move against them or they simply don't have adequate plans for the negative cash flow when they do. Every advantage swaps provide needs to be weighed against the risk of collateral calls before the position is established.

The other feature worth noting is the seductive nature of how easy it is to put on a swap. In 2004 Harvard had multibillion-dollar development plans that were not going to be ready for construction for many years. What would a concerned Harvard have done if swaps or derivatives were not available? It would have had only two choices. It could borrow before the start of the project in order to fix the rate or it could have worried a great deal while waiting to begin construction.

Because swaps were available that allowed the borrower to know exactly what their interest rate payments would be multiple years in the future, the managers at Harvard could feel confident that they were lowering the risk of their development

---

[4]Harvard Swaps Are So Toxic Even Summers Won't Explain. (2009). Bloomberg. (19 December).

projects. While they were successful in avoiding the risk of higher rates, they perhaps unwittingly took on many other risks that would cost the institution dearly.

Equity swaps and credit default swaps (CDS) tend to be used differently than interest rate and currency swaps. There are no doubt holders of corporate bonds that use CDS for protection against default, but the vast majority of CDS are simply trading instruments allowing hedge funds and other traders the opportunity to express an opinion on an individual name or an index of credits. Section 10.5 discusses the properties and uses of CDS in greater detail.

Equity swaps are also used in investment portfolios, but with the rise of ETFs they are less often used to take outright long or short positions than they are to overlay equity exposures onto a portfolio. In a technique called *portable alpha*, first mentioned in Chapter 6, a manager can take an investment portfolio that is completely devoid of equities, add a total return swap to it, and create an enhanced index fund.

Portable alpha programs are often created around a hedge fund as the source of basic return. For example, a hedge fund manager may claim that he or she has identified a way to do fixed income arbitrage that can add 3% over the risk-free rate with very little volatility. From a Sharpe Ratio standpoint, this may seem like an exciting trade opportunity, but from an absolute return perspective it is a snore. The manager could apply more leverage to the hedge fund in an attempt to boost the absolute returns, but this flirts with tail risk disaster in the event of a credit or liquidity crisis like 2008.

To package this great trading idea more attractively, the manager creates a new fund advertising steady outperformance against the S&P 500. Without trading a single stock, this fund can deliver on its promise by using a total return swap. "Arbitrage Fund" is designed to create a return above T-bills. The manager then enters into a swap where he or she pays T-bills plus, say, 15 basis points, and in return receives back from the swap dealer the total return of the S&P 500. Figure 10.19 shows how the cash flows work.

One of the first questions people often ask about these swaps is why any swap dealer in his or her right mind would be willing to pay out the total return of stocks in exchange for a small increase over the risk-free rate. A hint to the answer lies in the 15 basis point spread above T-bills that they are receiving. The swap dealer agrees to pay out the S&P total return only after they put on some kind of hedge in the equity market. They often use index futures to do this but there are many good hedges available. The swap dealer is extremely efficient in funding these activities, often having access to capital at or near T-bills themselves. If they hedge by effectively paying out T-bills and receiving the S&P total return, that trade completes the box with a 15 basis point return to them *no matter what T-bill yields and the total return to the S&P 500 turns out to be.* It is this kind of arbitrage that swap dealers live for.

One might imagine that if the hedge fund alpha engine was strong and dependable enough, a great case could be made for all of one's equity exposures to be done synthetically using derivatives. There are, as discussed in Chapter 6, reasons why this approach is not 100% dependable.

Using swaps as a convenience in an investment portfolio or to manage interest rate or financing risks can be quite compelling. But the user should always ask what can go wrong, and what the consequences are when they do. Having to adjust one's swap book in the heart of a crisis is something to avoid.

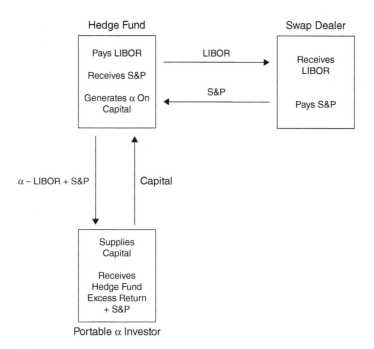

FIGURE 10.19 Equity Total Return Swap to Create Portable Alpha Program

10.4 SWAPTIONS

It was not long after the introduction of fixed-for-floating interest rate swaps that dealers and their customers discovered the advantages of adding option features. Instead of having two precisely defined, linear payment streams like a swap, a *swaption* has payment streams that are contingent on market outcomes. For example, Party A will pay a fixed amount each quarter, while Party B pays a floating amount *if interest rates exceed a defined strike price.*

The swaption just described has similar ISDA documentation as a basic swap and the same legal foundation. The fixed payment works out to be the equivalent of an option premium, except it is paid in installments. The floating payout corresponds to the profit profiles discussed for exchange-traded options in Section 10.2.

Recall Harvard's risk management problem. In 2004 it was worried about higher interest rates that might impact construction financing several years down the line. To address that concern it entered into forward swaps, which turned out to cause collateral calls and market losses when the credit crisis occurred and the planned projects were put on hold.

Harvard could have used swaptions instead of forward swaps. Such a trade would have been structured to cover the period up to the expected date of project financing. Harvard would agree to pay a fixed amount each quarter. If at expiration the reference interest rate were below some level, Harvard would receive nothing. If the actual interest rate were higher than that level, it would receive a payment. The higher the ultimate rate, the higher would be the payment to Harvard. In this way Harvard would have been protected from rates rising in the future beyond a level that would damage the economics of its project.

The other key advantage of a swaption is that the fixed costs to the buyer are completely known in advance. Just like an exchange-traded option's premium, the fixed payments of a swaption precisely limit the maximum expense to the buyer. Had Harvard owned a swaption rather than a forward swap, it would have simply written off its known fixed payments and would not have been faced with any possibility of collateral calls. It would have been the equivalent of the person who pays for life insurance each year but doesn't die. One can complain a bit about wasting the premiums that were paid, but the complaints should not be too loud.

Why didn't Harvard take the swaption approach and fix its costs of interest rate protection? One plausible reason is that the decision makers were so confident that rates would rise, that they did not believe they could lose. Or they may have looked at Harvard's vast wealth and liquidity and assumed that if rates fell, the forward swap would not cause any serious disruption to the university.

The most likely explanation is a combination of the above plus a belief that the cost of the swaption was an unnecessary expense. Why pay for insurance when the position can be managed dynamically to achieve the same outcome? If this was Harvard's motivation, they would not be the first, or last, group to have a blind spot about how bad things can get when one combines a dynamic trading strategy with extreme market outcomes.

A simple truth cannot be repeated often enough. The worst time to buy insurance is when the storm has already started. The best time is when there is not a cloud in the sky. Long-term successful individuals and firms are methodical in evaluating necessary options or insurance, they buy only those that make sense to their financial plans, and then they build the associated premiums into their expense budgets without regret.

Given that swaptions are traded OTC in customized form, one always needs to be diligent in evaluating the terms. The more vanilla the swaption, the more likely the embedded options will be priced competitively. Anyone contemplating buying a swaption should secure quotes from multiple dealers. They should also try to secure terms so that if the swap moves dramatically in their favor, the dealer posts extra collateral to secure the trade. The swaption writer is just like the writer of exchange-traded options in that the potential loss is not limited. The buyer always needs to keep counterparty risk in mind.

10.5   CREDIT DEFAULT SWAPS (CDS)

In the array of OTC derivatives, credit default swaps, or CDS, are among the youngest innovations. Through the credit crisis of 2008, they became among the most discussed and vilified. The crisis caused the total notional value of CDS to drop severely, but the long-term applications of this derivative suggest that it should continue to grow in popularity. Refining risk management of the CDS market is a work in progress at both the micro and the systemic level.

The principle behind CDS is simplicity itself. The buyer of a CDS contract pays a fixed rate, usually quoted in basis points per year, to the seller for insurance. In the event of an underlying bond default, the seller guarantees par value on the bond. Some CDS involve delivery of bonds, but most are cash settled, meaning that the seller simply pays the buyer the difference between the market price of the defaulted bond and par.

CDS are quite complicated from a legal perspective. For example, when have the default terms been triggered? Some restructurings are unambiguously a default event while others may not qualify on technical grounds. When the subject is sovereign debt, the waters are even murkier, as governments routinely change the rules surrounding their debt payments. As an example, there is an active market for CDS on US Treasury securities, but it is difficult to imagine a scenario where the United States, which has limitless ability to print money to cover its obligations, actually defaults. Users of CDS must be quite focused on the details in order not to be disappointed to discover their insurance was not as protective as they expected.

The CDS market has grown from virtually nothing at the start of the century to a major industry passing tens of trillions of dollars in notional value. A sudden and previously unmet demand for insurance by the bondholders cannot explain this growth. In general, the same people and institutions hold the cash bonds today as they did in the twentieth century. They are no more or less risk loving. Some may be using CDS for hedging purposes, but people who do not own the bonds, but simply want to express an opinion on either macro or firm-specific events, purchase the vast majority of CDS.

In theory, there should be a close connection between the price of a CDS and the probability of default for the underlying bond. One should be able to buy insurance against the default of a strong credit at a lower premium than for a firm or country that is having trouble paying its bills. As an example, Figure 10.20 shows the history of Greek and German Sovereign five-year CDS for the years 2007 through 2013. CDS are quoted in basis points, so a value of 200 means that the buyer pays the seller 2% annually for the life of the contract for protection against default.

Before the credit crisis, Greece was perceived to be a weaker credit than Germany, but the difference was subtle. In July 2007, one could buy five-year CDS on German debt for less than two basis points. Similar Greek CDS went for five basis

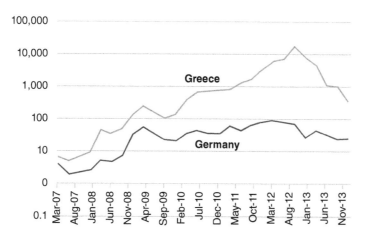

FIGURE 10.20 Greek and German Sovereign Five-year CDS 2007–2013

points. From these quotes, Greece might have been inferred to be two and a half times more likely to default than Germany, but for both countries the chances were viewed as essentially zero. In Q1 2009, which was the trough in global equities markets, German CDS was out to 90 basis points and Greece traded at more than 250. At the end of Q1 2012 when fears about sovereign default in Southern Europe made daily headlines, Greek 10-year bonds were priced to yield 44% and the five-year CDS traded above 25,000, but German CDS stayed below 75.

The pattern of CDS prices matches reasonably with broad perceptions of risk, but it is hardly a precise relationship. One can reasonably ask who in their right mind sells insurance on anything for two basis points. The answer in the first half of 2007 was obviously financial organizations that had models that said there was absolutely no chance of default, which in retrospect should have been reason to question their assumptions and maybe their sanity. The notional quantity of this model-driven CDS writing, picking up supposedly risk-free premiums, was in the hundreds of billions of dollars, contributing greatly to the depth of the financial and credit panics the following year.

As the German CDS moved from under two basis points to 90 in less than a year, was Germany 45 times more likely to default? These kinds of questions highlight the fundamental imprecision of the process. Default is not a continuous process, but a highly discrete one. Evidence that default is more likely should push credit spreads wider and raise the price of CDS, but it is virtually impossible to look at a company or country and say with any confidence that the probability of default has moved exactly from, say, 2% to 3%.

CDS has grown in popularity because it offers traders a vehicle to express their opinion in a very efficient form. In this way the CDS story is not terribly different from any other popular exchange or off-exchange derivative. If a trader thinks Greece is going to have trouble paying its sovereign debts in a timely way, one buys Greek CDS from someone who believes 9% (900 basis points) a year premium is adequate compensation for the risk.

The buyer of CDS in this trade is not acting like a traditional insured party. One doesn't buy fire insurance on one's house because of a belief that a fire is imminent. CDS buyers either own bonds that they fear will lose value or they are simply taking a negative bet on the bond. The CDS market has become more liquid than many cash bond markets and buying CDS is in many instances more cost effective than trying to short the bonds.

Sellers of CDS do look a bit more like an insurance company, assessing the risk of default and then deciding whether the premium collected is sufficient to compensate for that risk. But big mistakes have happened. In early 2007, the premiums for all CDS, but especially for sovereign debt CDS, were so low that it was like an insurance company writing hurricane insurance without knowing where the properties were located. Then one day they awoke to discover it was July and all the insured properties were in the Caribbean and along the Gulf Coast of the United States.

When CDS contracts move from five basis points to 1,000 basis points and more, as they did in the case of Greece, even small bets can produce staggering gains for the buyers. Investors like John Paulson didn't make small bets, but instead made the purchase of CDS contracts a core theme of their investment funds. If they had been wrong, they would have lost their premiums, creating a drag on their overall performance. As it turned out, their cheap insurance policies became much more valuable as the crisis evolved. They were able to reap returns that were probably once in a lifetime events.

After the crisis, many fund managers came forward offering tail risk funds that were discussed in detail in Chapter 7. They were designed to buy CDS or other options and then profit whenever a crisis event occurred. These funds are structured similarly to those of Paulson and other successful investors during the crisis, but there are two big differences. First, a crisis, almost by definition, doesn't happen every few quarters. Missing the first event may have meant you missed the whole show. Second, the market has gotten a lot smarter about pricing risk. Greek CDS that could be bought for five basis points in early 2007 sold for 900 at the end of 2010 and north of 20,000 in 2012. If you want to buy insurance in the post-crisis world, be prepared to pay a meaningful premium.

Long CDS can still be an effective tool to express a negative opinion. One just has to recognize that the cost of being wrong is now much higher and the payoff from being right will probably never replicate the extraordinary returns achieved by the early purchasers in 2007. Investors should be wary of managers who claim they can always find cheap insurance right before a catastrophic event.

There is an active public policy debate about whether CDS serve a social purpose. Few argue that owners of bonds seeking protection against default should be denied a hedging tool like CDS. The issue arises for some, however, because people who do not own, and will probably never own, the underlying bonds, purchase the vast majority of CDS. For the critics, this is like buying life insurance on someone else. Life insurers figured out that there was a moral hazard issue from allowing people to bet on others' lives. Doesn't buying CDS without owning the bonds create similar issues?

Such reasoning probably pushes the insurance analogy past its useful point. Life insurance is written on what are essentially actuarial events. So many people will die each year from car accidents, colon cancer, and cardiac arrest. The insurer knows these probabilities with a high degree of confidence and prices the policies accordingly. Given the actuarial odds favor the underwriter, it is highly suspicious if someone comes in to buy insurance on a stranger's life.

Default on a bond is not a well-behaved probability process no matter how earnestly financial engineers once believed it was. There may be a certain percentage of firms or even countries that default each year, but that percentage is highly dependent upon the macroeconomy and a host of other interconnected factors including market liquidity. One can persuasively argue that many CDS writers in 2006 and early 2007 erred badly by thinking they were engaged in an actuarial science rather than a market activity.

The great thing about market errors of the magnitude experienced in 2007 and 2008 is that the people paying the greatest tuition tend to remember the lessons for a long time. As regulators and Congress have been working to avoid the financial stresses created by CDS writers having inadequate capital, the market has responded by making CDS premiums much more reflective of true risk. There are good evolutionary steps like moving standardized CDS into a clearinghouse framework, but these are unlikely to be any more important than a market disciple between the buyers and sellers of CDS and other OTC derivatives.

Cries to ban "naked" CDS are reminiscent of similar ill-informed protests throughout history against every kind of short selling in cash and derivatives markets.

There is an important function played by investors who see the darker side of any story and seek to benefit from it. The world is not always a cheerful place, and legislating against shorting in a market does not eliminate the bad news, it only makes it more expensive to express.

If CDS were banned, there would still be good reason at times to short bonds, but the vehicles used would be more expensive, making the entire market less efficient. No regulator or legislator should ever believe that erasing one activity would ever eliminate the motivation for it or the ingenuity of individuals to do it in an alternative form. It is far better to have an open, liquid CDS market to complement cash bonds than to force investors into other venues and trades.

CHAPTER 11

Investment Structures and Packages

In the preceding chapters a great many investment instruments were described. To most investors, having a working knowledge of just a handful of the choices is a noble ambition. Many people feel intimidated by anything beyond simple stocks and bonds, and even there the mastery of the subject is elusive. In such a complicated world it is perhaps not surprising that the financial services industry tries to fill the knowledge gaps by structuring basic investments into packages designed to meet specific objectives. It should also not be surprising that these structures are among the most lucrative activities these institutions pursue.

At the noblest level, *structured products* are like many derivatives that were created to shape risks for institutional investors in ways that are difficult to create with basic investment tools. At a baser lever, structures are created in a slick marketing fashion to appeal to investor emotions, while generating large and often disguised fees. This chapter will describe some of each type, hopefully highlighting both the perils and opportunities investors face.

11.1 ASSET-BACKED SECURITIES

In the 1970s banks and savings and loan companies were struggling to deal with the size of their mortgage loan portfolios. The book of loans was often geographically concentrated and posed interest rate risks that were quite difficult to manage in that volatile, inflation-prone decade. The solution was to create securities that were backed by pools of mortgages and then sell those securities to investors who sought particular cash flows. These instruments, described in Chapter 9.2.8, were the first *asset-backed securities* and they allowed the issuing financial institutions to diversify their risks and free up capital for new lending activity. In many ways mortgage-backed securities (MBS) addressed many of the same type of problems that insurance companies had before the widespread use of reinsurance and Cat Bonds.

While the motivation behind the creation of MBS may have been driven primarily by the needs of the issuing banks, it wasn't long before the sellers of those securities were listening to the buyers and customizing the instruments to meet specific demands. What began as simple pass-through vehicles evolved into more complicated structures. The first evolutionary steps separated interest and principal payments into different vehicles. Next came the creation of sequential tranches of the payments. The first interest payments could go to one group of investors while the principal payments from years 8 to 10 could go to another. Some securities were created that had fixed payments, while others floated. Some could move inversely with the level of interest rates. As long as there was a priority of payments established and the pieces added together to make up the whole pool, there was almost no limit to the imagination of the financial engineers.

One might logically ask why all of this complexity was required. The answer lies in the specific desires of the large institutional pools of capital that are the potential buyers of these securities. A life insurance company, for example, might have very long-dated liabilities against which they want to hold long-duration assets. This makes securities that begin paying back in 10 years or more quite attractive. Consequently, creators of these securities make sure there are tranches that are highly desirable, and therefore easy to sell at a good price.

If there are wonderfully attractive tranches created, there is a good chance that at least some of what is left will be less attractive and more difficult to sell. It is not unlike butchering an entire steer. It is a big animal but there are only so many steaks and roasts to be sold. Just like butchering, there will usually be the equivalent of hamburger, shinbones, and viscera in any complex asset-backed security. The good news is that at the right price the entire animal gets consumed and all the tranches get sold.

Mortgages were the early foundation for asset-backed securities, but the industry has evolved into many different areas. Pools of credit card receivables, auto loans, aircraft leases, and royalty payments have all been used to create asset-backed securities. While the underlying collateral varies, the basic analysis of these securities has many commonalities.

There are two elements important in judging whether an asset-backed security is a good investment:

- What is the value of the underlying collateral?
- Where do my security interests sit in the legal priority of payments?

Assessing the underlying collateral is often an arduous exercise in credit research. Depending on the type of security, there may be hundreds or thousands of individual assets in the collateral pool. In an auto loan security one needs to be concerned with the risk that an individual may default and the value of the car that is repossessed is less than the value of the outstanding loan. Average FICO scores may be a useful indicator of initial credit quality, but there is always the risk of a macroeconomic shock quickly pushing the unemployment rate from 5% to 10%. In those instances even people with previously solid credit scores might find it hard to keep current on their payments.

Defaults are a fact of life in credit securities, and the main question becomes whether their likelihood is accurately priced into each security. One way to assess this is to estimate *coverage* for your security. Suppose you bought a security with a face value of 100 at a price of 90. Your security is neither at the top nor the bottom of the priority ladder. The first step is to evaluate the collateral and then subtract from it all the potential claims on it that are superior to yours. Let's say at the end you find 120 worth of collateral supporting your tranche. The estimate for coverage would be 120/90, or 133%. This might give you comfort that even in a tough economic environment your capital is reasonably secure.

If the coverage ratio were under 100% you would be betting that there would have to be a material improvement in the underlying collateral market in order to secure your capital. While there may be scenarios where that is plausible, there is also a chance that you've paid too much for the security, leaving little or no margin for error over the life of the security.

Your position in the payment priority structure dictates the likelihood of repayment and hence the riskiness of the investment. The first to be paid are the most senior tranches, and as long as there is good coverage these instruments will be seen as highly safe and should yield only slightly more than high-quality government and corporate bonds. As you move down the priority structure, uncertainty and risk grow, and with them yield spreads increase.

At the bottom of the structure there is the *equity tranche* that has no contractual or targeted yield, but instead receives whatever is left over after all of the other obligations of the pool have been met. Just as the most senior tranche received the first principal payments, the equity tranche is hit with the first losses any time an underlying security defaults. If losses ultimately exceed the value of the equity tranche, it is wiped out and subsequent losses are taken from the most junior bond tranches in reverse order of seniority.

As the name implies, the equity tranche is the riskiest, with there being a meaningful probability of an outsized return or a total loss. At the right price, the equity tranche can be one of the most attractive elements of an asset-backed security. History shows, however, that at times of low volatility and considerable optimism, all tranches of asset-backed securities can be overpriced, leading to great disappointment at the equity end of the spectrum whenever a shock ultimately hits the system.

To anyone unfamiliar with the asset-backed world, it would seem that the complications of evaluating the underlying collateral and the priority structure of the securities would preclude most investors from participating. Indeed, this was a major stumbling block in the early days, but as the market expanded, steps were taken to assure investors. These included both internal and external *credit enhancements* as well as investment-grade credit ratings for the highest-quality tranches.

Internal credit enhancements can come in the form of the basic seniority structure, the establishment of excess spread or over-collateralization. Excess spread occurs when the interest paid on a tranche is less than the coupon paid by the underlying securities. Over-collateralization means that the face value of the underlying securities exceeds the face value of the structure. Both of these features enhance the likelihood that a given bond tranche of an asset-backed security will be paid off.

Sometimes the security issuer will add external credit enhancements. These come in the form of insurance purchased against losses in a specific tranche or from actual dedicated cash collateral accounts. These latter vehicles are created when the issuer borrows funds sufficient to cover any credit enhancement and then places cash in a bankruptcy remote account. Unlike insurance, in these instances there is no doubt that the credit enhancement will be there if needed.

Credit enhancements are an important piece of the puzzle when appealing to institutional investors but it was not until the ratings agencies entered the picture that the market really took off. Given the bond-like payment structures of the most senior securities it was a natural business extension for S&P, Moody's, and other ratings agencies to begin evaluating these structures. Unlike corporate or municipal bonds, however, there was no extensive history of performance for these structures on which to base the ratings. Instead, models were constructed to simulate their performance under various scenarios.

Models can be a powerful tool of analysis, but only if the underlying assumptions are reflective of what might actually occur. In the case of ratings for many asset-backed securities the assumptions were drawn from a very benign history. Housing prices only went up. Credit spreads stayed within historical norms. Defaults occurred when there was a family-specific event like a loss of job or sickness, but there were no macroeconomic shocks like a massive recession considered because they had never happened over the life of these structures.

The other major feature of these models was a strong credit boost from diversification. Since the implicit assumption was that defaults were family-specific and not a system-wide phenomenon, the act of pooling a great many assets into the collateral of an asset-backed security lowered the risk. This allowed AAA and AA tranches to be created out of underlying assets that had considerably lower fundamental risk levels.

This all came unglued during the credit crisis when none of the underlying model assumptions came close to capturing the range of events experienced. Institutional investors who thought they were purchasing highly rated securities quickly discovered they were holding assets where the full value of their principal was in question.

In hindsight there were two big problems. The first was the overreliance on quantitative models that had virtually no foundation in the risks that were ultimately the most relevant. This problem was not unique to this specific story, but has repeated itself multiple times through history. The second problem came from the investor side of the fence and it was the uncritical eye used to evaluate these securities. Some very large investors looked at AAA or AA labeled securities that were yielding better than similarly rated corporate bonds and decided to gobble them up. Instead of asking why there was a yield premium and questioning the fundamental credit, they assumed the best and thought they were getting a windfall in the form of higher yields.

The ratings agencies have been criticized in this affair for lacking expertise, but they were probably no more culpable in this regard than many of the financial firms creating the securities. A more serious allegation was that because the agencies received more compensation for evaluating these asset-backed securities than they received for rating bonds they were inclined to be less critical in their final grades. Absent knowledge about conversations inside the senior suites at those firms, this allegation may remain no more than a nasty conjecture that is plausibly consistent with a very sad history.

Asset-backed securities have made a reasonable return after the financial crisis because the packaging benefits available to the institutions that create the underlying collateral are considerable. Thoughtful institutional investors also get considerable advantages from buying the right structures. The biggest difference between the pre- and post-crisis environments is that investors are much more discriminating in their choice of structures and demanding about getting paid for the risks they are assuming. In that regard, the market seems to have learned some important lessons.

In an attempt to make sure those lessons are not lost, the SEC instituted new rules covering asset-backed securities in August 2014.[1] These rules toughened

---

[1]SEC Adopts Asset-Backed Security Reform Rules. https://www.sec.gov/news/press-release/2014-177. (27 August 2014).

disclosures about the underlying collateral inside asset-backed securities and added extra obligations on the ratings agencies. It took the SEC almost six years after the crisis to come up with solutions that had largely been addressed by the market in a much shorter time, but these rules should minimize the chance of backsliding as the markets improve and a new generation of investors comes to discover these securities.

11.2   CDOs AND CLOs

Collateralized Debt Obligations (CDOs) and *Collateralized Loan Obligations (CLOs)* are special cases of the broader category of asset-backed securities discussed above. The common feature is the creation of a special purpose vehicle to hold the collateral, within which all manner of interesting things can take place.

Using the earlier butchering analogy, suppose you slaughtered 100 head of cattle and quickly sold off all of the steaks and roasts, but there was little demand for the rest of the carcasses. The harsh reality would be that your creative butcher would grind up into hamburger what he could and mark down everything that was left until buyers could be found. In the first part of the decade beginning in 2000, financial engineering tricks were devised that got around the butchering problem for CDOs.

The simplest CDOs were constructed using corporate bonds or mortgages exactly as described in the section above. The most attractive pieces were sold off, leaving the financial engineers with the much less desirable securities. This is where the engineers really became creative. They took all of the less attractive pieces and combined them into a new CDO. There were new senior, junior, and equity tranches created simply by ordering the priority of payments in the underlying pool of securities.

This meant that pools made up entirely of the lowest-rated elements of a bunch of CDOs were repackaged in a way that the majority of the new securities could be sold as highly rated, and presumably safe.

In this practice the financial engineers, and ultimately the ratings agencies, relied on elaborate models of the cash flows that were based on a relatively short time series of history that had contained no genuinely bad events. House prices only went up. Defaults only happened due to illness or loss of employment, which were thought of as actuarial and diversifiable events. Systematic risk seemingly never entered into any of the models. So much money was being made in almost every part of this activity that nobody seemed to think about what could really go wrong.

Financial institutions structured some CDOs and CLOs to include leverage. If the cash flow from the underlying securities were insufficient to create an attractive target rate of return, banks would lend against the underlying collateral, allowing the structure to sometimes own multiples of the capital dedicated to the structure. Similar leveraged products have been created with presumed low-volatility hedge funds or funds of funds as the underlying asset base.

The financial sponsors of these products generally argued that they had great risk management programs in place to monitor the underlying investments and if anything started to go wrong they would lower the gross exposures dynamically in order to minimize that chance of loss. This is the same philosophy that was pushed by providers of portfolio insurance before the 1987 crash and by the portfolio managers at LTCM before they imploded in 1998.

All of these investment processes are *short volatility*. That is, they typically do quite well in stable market environments when market volatility is low and trading liquidity plentiful. It is when surprises happen that the structures really get tested. Beginning in 2007 many things started to go wrong. The values of the underlying assets tumbled, portfolio managers trying to rein in risk found little liquidity in the markets, and providers of leverage began to pull the credit lines that were supporting the structures.

In almost all cases, the banks making the loans to the leveraged structures were senior to the public investors. This meant that the banks got to protect their assets first when possible, leaving the investors' equity as the shock absorber on what turned out to be a very bumpy ride.

Many financial institutions that created the mountain of CDO and related products from 2000 on ended up taking huge losses on this business. But the reader should understand that these losses did not come from assets that the banks and brokers wanted to have on their balance sheets. Going back to the butchering analogy, the big financial firms cranked up their CDO creation and sales businesses to a huge scale before the crisis. At any point in time they had large, unsold inventories on their books. When the crisis began to unfold, sales stopped almost immediately leaving these firms holding lots of ears, tails, and hooves, but very few steaks and roasts.

The conclusions from this experience for investors now seem obvious. Nothing should be added to a portfolio unless it is well understood in terms how it can earn the expected return and, just as importantly, how it can lose. Labels and ratings mean very little. There are many well-structured CDOs and CLOs available in the market that earn appropriate returns and could play a role in sophisticated opportunistic fixed income portfolios. But there are also many more that stretch boundaries to make them appear more attractive, while generating handsome fees for the firms structuring, financing, and selling them. Chances are good that the most sophisticated investors and traders will be able to differentiate between them. Investors who try to take shortcuts and rely on the promises of salespeople will likely not.

11.3 INSURANCE WRAPPERS

Individual investors face one big investment challenge that many institutional investors do not: taxes. An endowment can make every buy or sell decision in its portfolio thinking only of the investment merits. An individual starts there but must always ask, "What is the net benefit of this decision after I pay the tax man?"

This is a particularly acute problem when it comes to hedge fund investing. An individual can buy and hold a portfolio of individual equities or an index mutual fund and have reasonable control of the tax implications of their choices. Once you send money to a hedge fund manager, the game is out of your control.

There are some hedge fund managers who attempt to be somewhat tax efficient, but they may be the minority. Either because their strategy doesn't lend itself to it or because the majority of their LPs don't pay taxes, most hedge funds end up having the vast majority of their returns treated as ordinary income for tax computational purposes. This can drive a huge wedge between the opinions of individuals and those institutions concerning what constitutes an attractive investment.

Enter the insurance industry to offer a solution. One long-standing feature of the US tax code is that investment gains that build up inside a whole life insurance policy are not taxable on an ongoing basis. This means that like a retirement account the investments supporting the insurance policy can be bought and sold without an immediate tax consequence. Not surprisingly perhaps, this feature has attracted the attention of taxpaying investors.

Traditional whole life policies have fixed payout values and premiums and therefore cannot realize many of the tax benefits discussed already. Variable life policies are different, however, in that their cash value fluctuates with the performance of the investment accounts within the policy. Some state regulated insurance companies have seized upon this feature to create hedge-fund-based policies that allow the policy owners to have an investment portfolio (hopefully) growing tax-free inside a variable life insurance wrapper.

Introduced in the 1990s, insurance regulators and the Treasury Department have shown interest in these products. The first group is primarily interested in the quality and diversification of the assets inside the product. The Treasury Department wants to make sure the resulting structure is not a naked tax avoidance scheme. When the IRS issued guidance in 2003 laying out parameters they would view as acceptable, the products began to gain traction with investors.

Insurance products that could be sold to the public tended to be more conservative in their investment orientation than many high-net-worth individuals were seeking. The industry responded to this by offering private placement insurance policies that were highly customized to the desires of those customers. By definition, the target audience consists of ultra-high-net-worth individuals. The minimum annual premium can be $1 million with the average policy size being around $5 million.[2]

These programs make the most sense for investors who would normally want to hold these types of hedge fund assets. The downside is that any gains in the portfolio are taxed as ordinary income upon withdrawal, but for highly tax-inefficient investments this is not too great of a burden. The return and risk profiles are generally enhanced by the tax deferral advantages of the insurance wrapper. It is questionable whether anyone should start at the end of the logic chain, which is saving taxes, and then work backward to justify the underlying portfolio that may or may not make sense from risk, return, and liquidity perspectives.

Like many strategies to minimize taxes, some have pushed insurance wrappers into areas that may fail the Treasury Department's scrutiny. There have been large and highly successful hedge fund managers who have purchased or created offshore reinsurance companies in low tax jurisdictions as an adjunct to their trading operations. The assets of these insurance companies were in some cases the holdings of the hedge funds, and there was precious little actual insurance business being done.

Hedge funds report all of their income annually on K-1s and the limited partners incorporate this data into their annual tax filings. By placing the hedge fund assets into an insurance company in a low tax jurisdiction, the immediate liability from the K-1 income is mitigated. The owners of these companies argue that their tax liability should be based only on the distributed income of the corporations. If there are no dividends, the value of the company can compound with minimal tax friction. If the

---

[2]Abrahms, A. (2014). Tax Efficient Investing Through Private Placement Annuity and Life Insurance Investment Accounts. www.wealthmanagement.com. (6 May).

company were sold after a period of years, the majority of the capital gain would be longterm in nature.

This activity is of relatively recent vintage. Press reports suggest that Louis Bacon's Moore Capital was the first prominent hedge fund manager to set up a large Bermuda-based reinsurance company in 1999.[3] Once the model appeared to be viable, others followed. The Senate Joint Committee on Taxation gave the topic close scrutiny in 2014 as publicity built around the number of billionaire hedge fund managers who were apparently escaping the tax obligations that most investors paid. In 2015, Senator Wyden introduced Senate Bill 1687, Offshore Reinsurance Tax Fairness Act, to eliminate the tax advantage. The bill was referred to the Senate Committee on Finance, but it was not reported out of committee. To date there have been no adjustments to the law.

This specific topic may appear to be irrelevant to the vast majority of investors, but such stories often follow an evolutionary path that eventually involves a much broader audience. The early adaptors to these kinds of tax management strategies are almost always incredibly wealthy individuals or corporations that have the biggest incentive to find these solutions. They can afford the best and most creative legal talent and the returns to everyone involved – except Uncle Sam – can be staggering.

The ideas pursued are not exclusive or patentable. Once the solutions are in place, lawyers and accountants try to get additional return from their considerable investment of time and energy by reaching out to others who might benefit. Often the eventual end point is the creation of structures targeting less wealthy individuals. In this case, the target audience would be investors who neither run hedge funds nor have any real interest in reinsurance, but who are looking to save a lot on their K-1 origin taxes.

Similarly spirited schemes have appeared regularly for as long as there have been complicated tax codes and high rates. In the 1970s ordinary investors were sold commodity spread strategies that were supposed to defer taxes from one year to the next and convert ordinary income into long-term capital gains. There were aggressive oil and gas drilling programs to create large depreciation deductions. The list goes on and on.

The usual denouement is that as long as only a few (usually rich and well-connected) people are taking advantage of the rules, it is not a priority for the Treasury. When it becomes an active industry to add participants and the Treasury sees real estate developers offsetting all of their short-term gains with losses generated from commodity spread trades, it gets their attention. In some cases the aggressive tax behavior is challenged in court and is found to be abusive because its core motivation is tax avoidance. If that remedy does not work for the Treasury, Congress can change the law.

The conclusion for most investors is pretty clear. When considering any investment, the full tax implications need to be understood. If the investment involves a structure designed to defer or avoid taxes, try to determine how thoroughly it has been tested in tax court. No salesperson will ever suggest anything less than confidence that the structure is solid. Check with your own tax professional. And then consider how difficult or expensive it would be to reverse course should you lose a challenge from the IRS or the rules someday change.

---

[3] Zachary, M. (2013). Paulson Leads Funds to Bermuda Tax Dodge Aiding Billionaires. *Bloomberg News*. (19 February).

11.4 ANNUITIES

Annuities are contracts that agree to pay the holder a stream of future income. The basic structure is the owner makes a lump sum payment or a series of periodic payments in exchange for the promise of future cash flow. There is a defined investment period followed by a specified payout period. The payout period can be a fixed number of years, a variable number depending on the life of the owner, or in some cases a variable period covering the owner's life and that of a spouse. They come in various flavors that are discussed in more detail below, but all are designed to appeal to people seeking more stability in their future income. Annuities have been a big part of private retirement planning for decades.

There are three broad categories of annuities:

- Fixed
- Indexed
- Variable

Fixed annuities are the simplest structure, promising to pay no less than a stated rate of interest during the investment period. This translates into a promise to pay a certain amount of dollars on each of the periodic payment dates. Sometimes there is indexing applied to the payment schedule. The underlying investments behind a fixed annuity are almost always bonds designed to safely cover the obligation of the annuity.

Indexed annuities are typically based on popular stock indexes. The benefit stream to the owner is not precisely known in advance, but fluctuates with the underlying investments. The feature that makes this investment an annuity is a guaranteed minimum payout independent of the index performance. People sometimes choose indexed over fixed annuities during times of low interest rates with the expectation that stock performance over the investment window will exceed that of bonds.

Variable annuities are much more flexible in their underlying investment holdings. Typically the owner can pick from a menu of mutual funds and the ultimate payout can be completely dependent on investment performance. Providers of variable annuities sometimes include minimum guarantees and insurance benefits, but all of these features are additional services that come with their own fees priced into the product beyond the basic cost of the funds.

The variability feature in its simplest form seems to defeat one of the greatest advantages of an annuity, which is certainty of income through time. Variable annuities certainly enjoy tax deferred compounding like the insurance products discussed in the preceding section, but without some measure of payout certainty much of the appeal to risk averse, older investors is lost.

To answer this concern the institutions offering these products began offering variable annuities with some measure of lifetime income guarantee. In essence, the underlying mutual fund portfolio was supported with put options that were invisible to the annuity buyer. The buyer knew that there was a level, below which the value of the portfolio was not going to fall.

It is one thing to promise a floor on a portfolio's value and another to deliver on that promise. After the market peaked in the third quarter of 2007 there was an 18-month period with one nasty surprise after another. Insurance companies that had offered variable annuities with too generous protections found themselves scrambling to cover deteriorating positions. In many cases, standing behind their guarantees cost them billions of dollars in reserve capital, which might have been used much more profitably in acquiring distressed assets at the scariest part of the cycle.

The crisis was also a reminder that an annuity plan is only as safe as the firm that stands behind it. Billions of dollars were at risk during the crisis. The fact that there were as few failures as there were is a testament to prudential insurance regulation, helped out with some judicious government guarantees. Annuity buyers should never assume things will automatically work out in the next crisis.

The biggest complaint about annuities in general, and variable annuities in particular, is that they are absolutely loaded with high fees, sales commissions, and expenses that make it likely for the annuity buyer to perform much worse than a comparable portfolio of investments held outside an annuity structure. To highlight this issue, one only needs to note that the Financial Industry Regulatory Authority (FINRA) feels it is necessary to have on their website a brief piece entitled "Variable Annuities: Beyond the Hard Sell."[4]

In this way, variable annuities are similar to whole life insurance policies. Because of the layers of fees and expenses in whole life policies, most people would be better off buying term insurance and then funding a low-cost index mutual fund stock portfolio with the premiums they save from not buying whole life. This simple advice has been known for decades, yet the whole life insurance industry continues to thrive. Motivated agents, sometimes also carrying the title of advisor, similarly sell variable annuity programs.

If there is a case for buying variable annuities, it must be made on an individual basis. Variable annuities might make sense if:

- The buyer is extraordinarily risk-averse, valuing highly any income guarantee offered by an annuity as compared to the totally risk-exposed mutual fund portfolio.
- The buyer is concerned with *sequence-of-returns risk*, which is the chance of sharply negative investment returns early in one's retirement.
- The buyer expects to live a lot longer than the insurance company writing the annuity is assuming.

It is perhaps not a surprise that few investors advised by independent RIAs have annuities in their portfolio mix. In side-by-side comparisons it is easy to find superior outcomes on an after-tax, net-of-fee basis. Still, the variable annuity business thrives, commanding more than $1.6 trillion in assets at the end of 2015.[5] This is just another example of a popular product falling well short of being a superior one.

11.5   RETAIL STRUCTURED PRODUCTS

Almost everyone likes convenience. The popularity of drive-through fast foods is a testament to this. The quality may not be the best. The food might not be the hottest

---

[4]FINRA. Variable Annuities: Beyond the Hard Sell. https://www.finra.org/investors/alerts/variable-annuities-beyond-hard-sell.

[5]The Investment Company Institute. (2016). The Investment Company Factbook, p. 229. http://www.icifactbook.org.

or most nutritious. But every day tens of millions of Americans opt for these meals because it makes their lives easier.

Anywhere you look in modern life, entrepreneurs are trying to sell convenience. This is especially true in investments. Find picking individual stocks and bonds hard? Try an index fund or an exchange-traded fund (ETF). Want to save while insuring against the loss of your life? Whole life insurance policies cover both bases in one package.

Competition between index fund and ETF providers has generally produced well-constructed, reasonably priced products for investors, though there are some notable exceptions. We have already noted that whole life insurance is a product that is generally inferior to two separate transactions consisting of buying term life insurance coupled with an independent savings strategy. Yet these policies continue to be sold by commissioned agents to people who either value convenience highly or who lack the discipline necessary to execute two independent plans.

Today the world of investments is marked by a rapid increase in the merchandising of *retail structured products* for client portfolios. These products include principal protected notes, customized options to provide portfolio insurance, and a wide range of swaps to create exposures to commodities, interest rates, equities, and currencies.

The creators of structured products cite the following advantages:

- Structured products can be highly customized to meet the needs of the investor.
- They can combine investment and insurance/option features in one product.
- They distill complicated portfolios that are probably beyond the understanding of most investors into simple products accessible to everyone.

They often fail to mention the less attractive features:

They are illiquid. The client is usually restricted to dealing with one counterparty for the life of the structure, which can extend for years.

- Like whole life insurance, they are typically much more expensive than a marketable portfolio of instruments that replicates the product.
- Their pricing is so opaque that identifying these cost factors is almost impossible for the average investor.

To see how structures can be analyzed and the importance of the above factors, consider a real-life example. A major investment bank offered its clients a "buffered" equity-linked note, which is non-interest bearing. Not dissimilar from many structured products offered to investors, this product was built with as many twists and somersaults as an Olympic dive. The note had two times leverage on the upside, a cap on total return, no downside leverage, but full exposure to price declines beyond 10%. The note's specific terms were:

It pays twice the percentage change in the S&P 500 Index over two years, up to a maximum index return of 10%, *which is less than 5% per year*. This caps the total return on the structure at 20% over the two years. The investor is giving away all upside beyond this level.

- If the index falls by no more than 10% over two years, the investor's capital is guaranteed. This is the only buffer in the structure.

- If the index falls by more than 10% over two years, the investor loses the amount in excess of −10%. Losses are effectively not limited. *The investor is exposed to 100% of the losses beyond 10%.*
- The note produces an asymmetric pattern or returns with limited upside participation and much less limited downside protection.

This looks pretty complicated, but in fact can be unpacked into its component parts. The investor should try to identify each of the building blocks needed to produce that return pattern, because that is what the investment bank selling the product is doing. They will sell such a note only if they can hedge out the various risks at prices that guarantee them a profit no matter what the stock market does.

The investment bank looking to hedge its exposure when writing such a note would combine a leveraged index stock portfolio with different puts and calls. The specifics of such a portfolio are given in Figure 11.1. *It should be emphasized that any investor can construct this portfolio, but they may face higher transactions and margin costs than the bank or dealer.*

Description of a Two-Year "Buffered" S&P 500 Structured Note

Terms of the Note

- 2-year maturity, issued at 100.
- If S&P Index goes up, note pays 2X percentage change in index up to a maximum of 120 (This happens when the index goes up a total of 10% over the two-year term).
- If S&P Index falls from 0 to −10%, note pays 100.
- If S&P Index falls beyond −10%, note pays 100 minus 1X percentage change in index beyond −10%. Investor could lose 90% of capital if the market lost all its value.

Key Market Prices and Factors

- Annual dividend yield on S&P 500 is 1.9%.
- Current value of S&P Index is 2000.
- 2-year 2000 Puts are trading at 220 (11% of index).
- 2-year 1800 Puts (apprx. 10% out of money) are trading at 144 (7.2% of index).
- 2-year 2200 Calls (apprx 10% out of money) are trading at 98 (4.9% of index).

Investment Bank Creates Following Portfolio to Replicate $1m Note Exposures

- Go long $2m in S&P ETF using broker/dealer allowed leverage
- Sell $2m 2-year 2200 Calls
- Buy $2m 2-year 2000 Puts
- Sell $1m 2-year 1800 Puts

FIGURE 11.1

Since the bank charges no direct fees on a transaction like this, where are they making their money? First, they are receiving, *but not passing on*, the dividends of the stock portfolio. In today's market, even the 1.9% current yield on the S&P is meaningful against the zero interest rate implied in the note. Second, they receive any net proceeds of the purchased and sold options. In this example there is a small net option expense, but it is more than covered by the dividend yield. Under every market outcome, the creator of the note receives 2.6% *more* from their hedged portfolio than they ever pay out to their client. This is the hidden fee on the structured note. In addition, there sometimes are sales commission charges independent of the implicit fees inside the structure.

For a $1 million note investment that turns out to be $26,000. This may not seem like a large spread, but these notes can be constructed literally in minutes using readily available, liquid market instruments. Since a bank can sell hundreds of millions of dollars of this note and others like it, the attraction of these structures to the sellers is clear.

Is this a reasonable price for the investor to pay for the convenience of the structure? People will disagree on this. These charges seem steep when compared to active fund management fees, especially since there is very little to manage once the structure is in place. But they are not out of line compared to mutual funds with sales loads and distribution fees, another historically suspect investment product.

In general, structured products should be seen as expensive conveniences that are bound to eat away at investment returns. Serious individual and institutional investors can do better with minimal amounts of understanding and effort. Building one's own structures also has the major advantages of complete liquidity and the power of clearinghouses as counterparties.

Several opposing views can be raised against the comments above. The biggest criticism is that exchange-traded products cannot be fine-tuned enough to match the precise customization of the structure. This is true, but $26,000 per $1 million is a steep price for exactitude. This kind of investing is a bit like a game of horseshoes. Being close enough can make you a winner.

A second comment would note that a taxpaying client has an advantage that the structure's returns are treated as capital gains. In the unpackaged version of the note, the client has long-term gains and losses on the passive portfolio and the two-year options. The client also receives the dividend tax rate on those payments. There does not seem to be a large tax advantage to the structures for taxpayers. And for not-for-profit institutions, there is none at all.

The banks and dealers writing the structures will also say that they only produce what clients demand, and few of their clients have the ability to create replicating portfolios. The reader may agree that they might struggle to build complex securities and options portfolios, but it remains questionable whether any client actually came to the investment bank and asked for the convoluted structure described above.

Structured products are created in every area that has a "buzz" factor. Is stock market volatility concerning you? Banks will offer principal protection in an equity-linked note. Has the recent run-up in wheat prices caught your eye? Expect to see new structures linked to indexes of agriculture prices. Investors get an idea that they would like to be exposed to an area, and the financial engineers come up with something that scratches that itch.

The SEC has discussed disclosures around structured products, but to date there has been nothing but some rumblings. For many years, structures were largely the domain of more sophisticated investors who should have had the ability to analyze prices and seriously negotiate the form of the structure and its costs. That is rapidly changing. With brokerage commissions and interest rate margins shrinking away, banks and brokerage houses are scrambling to find revenue anywhere they can. Selling retail and near-retail investors expensive portfolio structures is too tempting to resist.

Americans have enough experience with burgers and fries to understand whether they are getting their money's worth at the drive-thru window. That cannot be said for structured products. One can debate forever whether a Happy Meal is a good menu choice for a busy parent, or whether the risk profile of a principal-protected note makes sense in a portfolio. But what is not debatable is that there are almost always superior options available if the parent or the investor is willing to look past the convenience factor.

Governance, Regulation, and a Look into the Future

12

Investment Decision-Making and Governance

The entire contents of this book to this point focus on the factors relevant to creating effective portfolios. Knowledge, clear objectives, and an ability to evaluate investments and managers are essential pieces of the portfolio construction process, but a bad decision-making process and *governance* can be undermining. The needs in this area differ with the type of organization involved, making it impossible to set up a universal program, but there are useful guidelines that can be outlined for families, not-for-profit organizations, corporations, and pension plans.

The process starts with defining objectives and articulating risk concerns. Once everyone agrees with the broad parameters of what everyone is trying to achieve, the bigger challenge of execution and monitoring begins. Establishing a solid foundation for decision-making before this journey begins greatly enhances the probability of success.

12.1 THE FAMILY

Perhaps the discussion should start with individual decision-making, but if a person investing only on his or her own behalf has trouble with decision-making, a book on psychology may be a better place to look for answers than one on investments.

The most frequently followed model within a family can be described as either active or passive delegation of responsibility. One person in the group either actively assumes all of the responsibilities involving investments, or someone gets the job because nobody else wants it. This model works great as long as the individual is capable, focused, and dedicated to the welfare of the family unit.

Problems begin when the decision maker either loses interest in this authority or, more likely, dies before adequate provisions have been made to transition decision-making. Where there is considerable wealth involved, the family often enjoys the benefit of a family advisor or trustee, but these individuals can only supplement the family decision-making process and they do not replace it.

If the individuals responsible for the wealth creation are still in the picture the dynamic can be much different, and in many ways more challenging, than if all the family members are recipients of inherited wealth. The energy, intelligence, and entrepreneurial spirit of the wealth creators may not be as prominent in subsequent generations. Even if they are, the founding generation may not recognize it or be interested in sharing responsibility. This often leads to a situation where the people who rightly think that it is their money and that they are the logical stewards for all family members (including unborn generations) are exclusively making the investment decisions.

At best, these situations work wonderfully, with good allocation decisions being made and the entire family benefitting. Unfortunately all good things must come to an end. Unless there has been solid planning on how the decision-making will transition, there will likely be a rough patch until a new model gets implemented. One of the key responsibilities of the first generation is to plan for that succession, with the best designs taking advantage of that first generation's skills while they are still capable of shaping the outcome into something they want.

When there are multiple members involved in shepherding the family's wealth, all of the dynamics of any decision-making process will be in play. Siblings interact differently than parents and children (and grandchildren). Investment decisions are not fundamentally different from deciding the question where everyone will eat their next Thanksgiving dinner, but they occur regularly enough that there are a few things that can facilitate the process.

The first step is to agree on investment objectives and limitations. An investment policy statement is standard operating procedure for any institutional investor, and it is an excellent idea for families as well. This document does not have to be long, complicated, or overly legalistic. Its primary objectives are to articulate what the return goal is, what investments are allowed or not allowed in the portfolio, and to specify risk guidelines.

The family should agree whether the long-term plan is to try to grow the wealth through investments, maintain its real value, or spend it down through time. There are many entrepreneurial families that have amassed fortunes well beyond their needs to support a very comfortable lifestyle. Some of them make the conscious decision to further their charitable activities by donating a large percentage of that wealth rather than create dynasties for unborn generations. If this is a key objective, it should be clearly articulated in the investment policy statement. That in turn will help shape the investment guidelines for the portfolio.

Risk tolerance is a key element in any such exercise. What may be appropriate risk for the first generation in their 70s may be all wrong for the third generation that are all still pre-college age. If the portfolio management process is sophisticated enough to segregate assets by family unit, such distinctions are important enough to identify explicitly.

The investment policy statement should be viewed as a long-term document, but it is not written in stone. Innovations happen continuously in the world of investing and new instruments may appear that were never contemplated even a few years earlier. A simple review of the statement annually is useful to catch any minor misalignments before they become problematic. A thorough reevaluation of the document and the needs of the family might be done every five years.

If different branches of the family are represented around the table, they will want to decide how formal they want the decision-making process to be. Most families believe that harmony is best preserved through informal, consensus decision-making, but this is not always possible. Rarely do families opt for a rigid investment committee structure, but in some instances this can be a very constructive idea. It is far preferable to have more structure and an ability to make timely decisions than it is to allow the process to lumber along in a state of inactivity.

Wealthy families can turn to an outside advisor to play the role of organizer and facilitator. This advisor could be a formal trustee, an accountant, a lawyer, or an investment advisor. The specialty is less important than the fact that the individual has access to all the types of service providers the family needs and that he or she holds the trust of all the family members. Having this person own the organizational aspects of the process is vital. Failure to establish clear agendas or collect and present the relevant data efficiently has scuttled many family decision-making efforts.

12.2   NOT-FOR-PROFIT BOARDS AND COMMITTEES

Millions of people express their generosity and commitment to improving their communities by serving on a board of a not-for-profit organization. For some, this activity is as important as the work they do on their day job. Many such organizations live a hand-to-mouth existence. Their primary challenge is to meet the annual goals while staying within a limited budget. For other organizations, however, an endowment exists that provides either partial or full support to the program. In these cases there is usually a formal investment committee to oversee these funds.

The committee's first job should be to establish an investment policy statement. Like a family's policy statement discussed above, this document should describe the investment goals and risk parameters that will be followed. One of the primary objectives of such a statement is to provide continuity of approach and execution. Board and committee members come and go. The organization's investment behavior should not shift around dramatically as personalities change.

There is a relatively small fraction of not-for-profit organizations that have one or more dedicated investment professionals on staff. This is a result of simple economics. Unless the organization has several hundred million dollars of assets to oversee, it is difficult to justify the relatively large expense associated with high-quality investment professionals. A cheap but low quality dedicated investment professional just might be the worst expenditure a not-for-profit can make. The more typical model has a vice president of finance in charge of budgets, operations, safety, personnel, and a roster of other duties. Oversight of the investment portfolio is just one more item on a long list of responsibilities.

It is not unusual for the VP of Finance to have an accounting background, and investing is more of an avocation than a vocation. In such instances the investment committee of the board might take a more active role in specific decisions. Each organization needs to candidly assess the human capital of its staff and its board members to assure investment decisions are done prudently and in a timely manner.

Decades ago a typical endowment held mostly bonds, and the job of the investment staff and committee was to monitor the interest payments and make sure proceeds from maturing bonds were reinvested. Sometimes there were also individual equity holdings among the assets and the committee would act as a portfolio manager. While this approach may live on in a few organizations, access to mutual funds and more sophisticated investment products has allowed most not-for-profits to delegate specific security selection to dedicated outside professionals.

Since boards and committees meet only a few times a year, this delegation makes a great deal of sense. Most board and committee volunteers have day jobs that prevent them from monitoring any portfolio in real time. It is much more realistic for the committee to focus on periodic reviews of manager performance, having assigned the moment-to-moment oversight to those managers.

Even with this delegation, it is not unusual for these organizations to also engage an outside consultant or advisor. These professionals are tasked with giving advice on the market environment, suggesting an asset allocation consistent with the group's goals and risk appetite, and sourcing ideas for specific investment options. They also typically evaluate the ongoing performance of the managers and funds engaged by the endowment, suggesting changes when they believe it to be appropriate. There are various models of advisory services present in the market, which were discussed in Chapter 5.10.

Board and committee members must be constantly aware of their fiduciary responsibilities. Too often participation with these organizations is viewed as a social event or as a means to demonstrate status. Most board members are highly dedicated to the cause of the organization, but they may find themselves serving on committees where their skills and expertise are weak. It is critical that the chair of the board and the CEO of the organization strive to match the talents of their board members with the needs of the specific committees. If there are key skills missing, the board nominating committee should prioritize trying to fill those gaps.

Investment committees sometimes attract members for the wrong reason. Having responsibility over a large endowment is certainly a position of status, but nobody should seek to join an investment committee if that is their primary motivation. Other members sometimes want to join primarily to get stock tips or other specific investment suggestions. If a committee member isn't giving much more to the process than they receive, another person should probably be filling that seat.

Investment committees come in all sizes, though large numbers make effective decision-making more difficult. It is certainly understandable that not-for-profits invite major donors to become board members, but the temptation to liberally populate the investment committee with such individuals should be resisted if that is all they bring to the group. Like the executive committee of the board, the investment committee needs people who have the energy and expertise to guide the endowment as well as enough time to make good on the commitment.

Not-for-profit committee meetings are sometimes scheduled quarterly or even less regularly to match the meeting of the bigger board. This is usually done as an appropriate convenience to the volunteers in an attempt to minimize the disruption to their schedules. The market crisis that started in 2007 and didn't really end until the second quarter of 2009, called such an approach to scheduling into question. As market volatility reached heightened levels, many committees called impromptu meetings in an attempt to stay abreast of rapidly changing market conditions.

The best functioning committees used these meetings more as monitoring events than as opportunities for snap decision-making. If the original investment game plan was a sound one, the action items could focus on valuations, some opportunistic investments and possible rebalancing decisions. Sadly, many not-for-profits discovered in the heat of the crisis that their basic plan suffered serious flaws. This forced the conversation into a reactive mode.

The most challenging situations arose when institutions discovered that their allocation had put too many resources to work in private partnerships that were either illiquid by design (real estate, private equity, venture capital) or by circumstances (hedge funds that suspended or limited liquidations). Some very prominent institutions found themselves "upside down" in their portfolios in that the liquid part of their assets fell to a point where they were smaller than the unfunded private investment commitments to which they committed before the crisis.

At that point the decision-making was almost entirely in response to the crisis. Some institutions sold much of their remaining liquid equity portfolios to meet their liquidity needs. This turned out to be selling near the bottom of the cycle, eliminating any opportunity for a recovery. Other institutions with better credit ratings increased their debt. The roster of universities that issued new bonds for more than a billion dollars reads like a who's who of American higher education.

These are among the trickiest of meetings. If the committee is large, there is an excellent chance that there will be a broad range of firmly held opinions. The Chair will have to navigate through emotionally charged waters as some members try to spend more time assigning blame for past decisions than looking forward. As difficult as it can be, the committee needs to focus on the tasks at hand, assessing the current state of the investment pool in the context of the needs of, and risks facing, the institution.

Sometimes difficult decisions are unavoidable. If an institution finds itself with a tremendous mismatch between the liquid resources of the endowment and the cash needs of the organization there may be no prudent choice but to sell risk assets. The question shifts from, "How did we get to where we could be down 30%?" to "What happens to our institution if we suffer another 20% drop in the market?"

Keep good records of the decisions. People sometimes forget after the fact why they made the choices they did. Not only do committees lack perfect foresight, they sometimes have selective memories. Many people remember that the S&P 500 was down around 37% for the calendar year 2008. What they sometimes forget is that it kept falling at the start of 2009, tumbling another 18.5% in January and February before beginning its ultimate rebound in March.

Committees that had to make very tough decisions in the middle of the turmoil were sometimes later criticized because they should have known that the market would turn around. This sort of criticism is completely unfair to the committees and the professional staff of these organizations that never had the benefit of perfect foresight. Most people started 2009 with an expectation that the worst was behind them. Once they absorbed the surprising body blows of January and February, everyone had to consider the risks of further declines.

The biggest lesson from this experience was to structure portfolios in such a way so that even if there is a crisis event there are ample, and liquid, resources available to give the organization staying in power through the worst days and months. This is the organizational equivalent of the sleep-well-at-night pillow for a family discussed in the very start of this book. Those organizations that were so positioned before 2008 gave their committees the chance to ride out the market volatility and perhaps even seize temporary opportunities.

The other major takeaway from this experience is that institutional lethargy that often marks committee decision-making can be particularly dangerous. Consensus can be difficult to build, especially in large committees, and there is a temptation to put off potentially tough decisions until the next meeting. As this inertia builds, the institution's problems can build. Here the question becomes whether failure to make a tough choice today potentially sets the organization up for much worse scenarios in the near future. Tough choices are rarely universally popular when they are made, but they can prove to be institutional lifesavers.

12.3   PENSION PLANS

Among the largest and most influential institutional investors around the world are private and public pension plans. Their decision-making challenges differ from those of families and not-for-profit organizations primarily from the nature of the liability side of their responsibilities. While there is growing emphasis on defined contribution style retirement plans, there are still trillions of dollars dedicated to defined benefit plans that have reasonably well-known liability obligations. This should narrow the range of investment decision-making, but challenges still remain.

12.3.1   Defined Contribution Plans

For the decision makers responsible for defined contribution (DC) plans, the focus should primarily be on two areas: (1) the range and effectiveness of the investment options offered and (2) costs. There are almost countless options available for the execution and administration of such DC plans. The trustees of these plans must decide how paternalistic the organization wants to be to its active and retired employees. That decision alone will shape the scope of investment decisions to follow.

One school of thought says that most employees are not well schooled on either investment themes or specific funds to execute on those themes. Followers of this belief will likely want to offer a narrow range of options across traditional investment assets ranging from cash to long-only fixed-income and equity funds. They may have prepackaged portfolios designed to be generally age appropriate. By staying away from narrow investments and alternatives, the employer cannot be accused of straying into challenging or possibly inappropriate investments.

At the other end of the spectrum is the laissez-faire approach. The employer establishes a relationship with a major mutual fund company or another sponsor with broad access to a wide range of investment options. It is the employee's responsibility to pick from this sometimes-dizzying array of options to construct their portfolio. It is also the employee's responsibility to monitor this pool through time and make adjustments as necessary.

Notice how the DC approach removes most of the highly challenging decision-making that individuals and non-for-profit decision makers routinely face. The allocation between stocks and bonds is either already made in the packages offered or it is entirely the responsibility of the employee. If the company provides a program of generally high-quality, reasonably priced options, its job is virtually complete.

Understanding that many employees are not well suited to these kinds of decisions, some companies associate themselves with firms that can offer education on retirement planning. Such efforts are pretty basic, but they try to encourage the right choices. Young employees, for example, should not be completely insensitive to stock market valuations when establishing their game plan, but they have many more decades to work through rough spots in the market than their colleagues that are counting the days to retirement. Some plan sponsors try to educate the participants about specific funds by using public ratings systems like Morningstar. We have already discussed how such ratings have virtually no predictive ability, but they appear to give the employees a sense of fund quality that they would otherwise lack.

Because plan sponsors want to avoid the disruption of changing managers among the fund offerings there is a tendency to hire active managers that are highly diversified and that don't take large over weights or underweights versus their benchmarks. That is, they have a low active share in their portfolios. We have argued this is often a recipe for subindex performance as it is very hard to make more than the active management fees by taking modest bets against the index.

Trustees of DC plans might have strong philosophical opinions about active versus passive management and may want to shape the programs to reflect their philosophy. This should probably be avoided. History has shown that there are irregular cycles of out- and underperformance by active managers. By offering only one philosophical option, plans' sponsors can be open to criticism whenever that style is out of phase. A better approach is to give both passive and active options while providing as much education as possible on those choices.[1]

Plan trustees should also focus on expenses and the quality of the administration. A poorly managed plan with late or inaccurate reports to employees should not be tolerated. The negative impact on a firm's employees will go well beyond any gaps in investment performance. Expenses need to be evaluated on a broad basis, looking well beyond the basic fund management fees. Some companies that administer DC plans add on annual oversight fees or portfolio change fees that can add up. These fees are almost never incorporated into the reported performance figures, so it is up to the plan's trustees to monitor them for fairness. Another reason for trustees to be mindful of fees is the increased activity of the tort bar filing suits on behalf of plan participants arguing that higher fee investment choices are evidence of a failure of fiduciary duty.

12.3.2 Defined Benefit Plans

Defined benefit (DB) *plans* are structured to promise a stream of payments to retirees. In this way they are similar to annuity contracts, but they differ in how they are funded. Depending on the terms of the plan the employer can be responsible for 100%, a majority or a small amount of the contributions used to fund the plan. The actual terms are often the subject of negotiations and any effort to shift the funding burden from the employer to the employees is rightfully viewed as an attempt to cut compensation.

The trustees of a DB plan usually view the funding side of the equation as beyond their control. Their main responsibilities involve finding an asset mix that is likely to meet or exceed the projected liabilities arising from promises to pay future benefits. In this sense their deliberations are similar to those of family and not-for-profit investors. All of this chapter's discussion so far concerning timely and effective decision-making applies here as well.

But there is one major difference. Most DB plans have fairly well-defined liability streams that they are trying to match. This should make the construction of

---

[1]See Chapter 5.2 for a discussion of active versus passive investing.

the investment policy statement a more precise exercise than that experienced by families and not-for-profits. Exceed the return objectives and the plan becomes overfunded. Lag the objectives and the gap between future liabilities and a plan's assets to meet them grows.

Trustees of DB plans should remember what their objective is and stick to it. Starting in 1982 and continuing to beyond 2000 the US stock market was on an unprecedented bull market path. Relatively few DB plans at the start of this era had large exposure to equities, but some innovators were watching the evolution of endowment portfolio management into both marketable and private equity investments. These plans quickly were identified as being in the vanguard by peer group publications like *Pensions and Investments*, attracting many imitators.

By the second half of the 1990s many corporate pension plans were meaningfully overfunded because of the unexpected largess from the stock market run. Trustees had the opportunity to do something quite radical. They could have abandoned the portfolio allocation that had served them admirably over the last several years and placed all of the assets into matched maturity Treasury securities. In this way all of the future liabilities would have been covered with as much certainty as is possible in investing. However, few plans went down this path.

Instead it seems that plan trustees and administrators had become more attached to the idea of relative performance across their peer group. If they cut equity exposure and the bull market continued they would no doubt fall to the bottom of the peer group rankings. Corporate plans also sometimes looked at the excess funding that was created by the bull market as an asset allowing the corporation to reduce future pension contributions. These factors led to decisions that ultimately cost the community hundreds of billions of dollars as the bull market turned into a bear and large-cap US stocks were essentially flat for a decade.

There are other challenges for DB plan trustees. While the plan may have a pretty good idea of how many retirees there will be at any point in time and how many dollars will be owed to them, what nobody knows with precision is how interest rates are going to evolve. Our best guess on the size of the future liabilities comes from an accounting exercise calculating the discounted value of those cash payments. This is based on the current term structure of interest rates. While family and endowment investors welcome falling interest rates because they raise the market value of their fixed-income investments, those same falling interest rates are the bane of DB plan trustees as future liabilities grow in importance.

This can lead to some anti-intuitive lines of thinking for the trustee accustomed to the endowment approach to institutional investing. For any DB plan that is not fully *immunized*, that is having fixed-income assets exactly matched to the timing of liabilities, rising interest rates are a good thing. As long as equity prices do not fall in lock step along with bond prices, rising rates likely lead to the discounted value of future liabilities falling faster than the value of the portfolio. While it is true the plan assets are smaller, the future need for those assets to cover liabilities has fallen by a greater amount. The net position of the fund is improved.

It is possible to think of a life cycle for a DB plan. At the beginning there is a good chance that it will be underfunded as the sponsor anticipates making many years of contributions to back the portfolio. If a plan becomes fully funded, the decision makers behind that DB plan need to think long and hard about any asset allocation that strays from being completely immunized. But before that happens many strategic decisions need to be made. What are the appropriate allocations as the plan tries to return more than the long-term target amount and close any funding gap? If the plan is successful in narrowing any funding gap, should the risk profile of the portfolio shrink to lower the chance of the gap suddenly widening? All of these decisions have important strategic implications to the shareholders behind corporate plans or taxpayers supporting public DB plans.

For many corporate DB plans the key decision makers are a professional staff that reports up the finance ladder of the corporation. There may or may not be an autonomous investment committee. Ultimately the board of the corporation is the one responsible for the major policy decisions surrounding the plan, but it is rare that they participate in manager or security selection or detailed asset allocation decisions. In this regard the staff member head of a corporate DB plan is one of the more independent decision makers in the investment world.

Public DB plans almost always have a professional staff as well, but they also have important governing boards that can vary in how actively they participate in the decision process. The biggest wildcard in this process concerns those who sit on these boards and how they are selected. Pension plans for retired firefighters and police officers often have senior representatives of those communities serving on the investment committees. This makes sense when discussing big picture funding challenges, but strains the imagination when describing asset allocation and manager evaluation questions.

Any gap in market knowledge can be closed at least somewhat with consultants and advisors, but history has shown an unfortunate pattern of also including politically connected placement agents that "educate" at times by strongly recommending funds and managers with whom they have major economic ties. Conflicts of interest can be as small as the friendly broker who arranges for a sporting event for the bond desk of the DB plan ("If this bond can't be sold with a pair of hockey tickets, it can't be sold") to outright (and highly illegal) kickbacks to staff or board members of the plan.

The asymmetry of incentives in these situations is staggering. Start with some of the largest pools of investable capital being run by staff paid like civil servants and overseen by political appointees. The fees paid to active fund managers and the general partners of private partnerships are potentially in the billions of dollars over a number of years. It is not surprising that highly mercenary market participants will offer improper incentives to get hired. Extraordinary ethics are required on the plan side to resist. The only real defenses against bad behavior are disclosures and as much transparency as possible. It is not a hopeless quest to run an honest public DB fund, but it is a never-ending gauntlet of temptations that needs to be navigated.

12.4 CORPORATE INVESTMENTS

The span of activities that falls under the umbrella of corporate investments can be quite broad. It ranges from the relatively mundane activity of investing excess cash to the potentially highly-complicated management of hedging and trading programs. Almost all of the activity falls under the responsibility of the treasurer or the chief financial officer, with the board of directors overseeing at the highest levels of execution and risk management. In many ways these activities pose no different questions of decision-making than any other activity in the corporation, but there are so many examples of errors and malfeasance when it comes to corporate investments that at least some comment is warranted.

Entire books have been written on corporate governance and the challenges of aligning incentives across management, the board, and shareholders.[2] At a high level, the problem is not that complicated, nor are the solutions terribly profound. You first have to have a clear understanding of the objectives of any investment program, which includes return expectations as well as the level of risk that the firm is willing to assume. Then you need programs of execution, oversight, and evaluation in real time.

Start with an example of a firm that generates excess free cash flow in general, but those flows are lumpy over the course of a year (e.g. a Christmas tree farm). During the season where cash is building, decisions have to be made to invest that cash until it is needed. Most readers might quickly conclude that there are no investment decisions at all to be made, as the prudent act is to keep the money in the bank and insure that the capital is preserved until it is needed later in the year. That is probably the correct decision in many cases of this type, but it is important to acknowledge that this in itself is an investment decision.

Good governance would establish that approach in a simple investment policy statement, which would then be followed by periodic reviews to confirm compliance. That investment policy statement would list the allowable banks where the money could be placed. It would say whether high-quality money market funds might do as well. It would specify whether the assets could be concentrated with one institution or whether operational diversity was required. There should be no ambiguity as to the expectations of the firm or how actual behavior is matching those expectations.

Consider the case of the same seasonal firm, but with the wrinkle that everyone involved is completely frustrated by earning nothing on their bank accounts or money market funds. The decision makers conclude that there should be some risk taking with these cash assets. This requires a more interesting and complete investment policy statement. What form of risk is allowable? Credit? Duration? Equity? Commodity? How much of the proceeds should be exposed to these risks? Again, the investment policy statement should be well defined and get all of the decision makers and the staff that will execute the program on the same page.

As the investment problem gets more complicated, the challenges only change by degree. Suppose you are in the treasurer's office of a major airline. One of the greatest uncertainties comes from the price of jet fuel. Should your airline hedge those risks by trying to lock in the price of fuel? If so, at what price and for how long? Each of these decisions is made in a competitive environment. If your airline locks in the price of fuel and the competition does not, only one of you is going to look smart after the fact.

Setting the strategy may be the first step, but the subsequent steps of execution and monitoring quickly follow it. Firms that were in theory "hedging" their currency, commodity, or interest rate exposures have lost hundreds of millions of dollars, and in some cases billions. The reality in many of these unfortunate cases is that the basic function morphed into a trading and risk-taking activity that went bad.

---

[2]A fine example can be found in Munk, B.E. (2013). *Disorganized Crimes: Why Corporate Governance and Government Intervention Failed, and What We Can Do About It*, Palgrave Macmillan.

Incentives matter in these examples. In the early 1990s Procter & Gamble became a corporate innovator by using interest rate swaps to manage the financing costs of the company. Their counterparty for much of this activity was Bankers Trust, and the swaps were structured to generate incremental revenue if rates were steady or falling, as they had been for some time at the start of the decade.

Things turned ugly very quickly when the Fed started to raise interest rates in February 1994.[3] To generate incremental income, P&G's swap position was implicitly writing put options on US Treasury securities in a highly leveraged way. As interest rates increased, bond prices tumbled and P&G's expected positive cash flow turned into tens of millions of dollars of losses. Accusations flew back and forth, followed by litigation.

It is irrelevant to this discussion whether P&G understood the risks they were taking, or whether Bankers Trust had led them down the garden path. What is relevant is the environment in which P&G was making decisions, which was revealed after the fact. Following the management practice of trying to incent good performance, it seemed that P&G used the cost of borrowing as one factor determining compensation for its treasurer's office. If they could lower the cost of the short-term borrowed funds that almost every major corporation uses to finance its ongoing activities, the team would be rewarded.

This program went on for some time, and after every period that the office met its goals, the incentive bar would be raised. How nobody involved with this plan failed to immediately see that they were incenting the treasurer's office to add increasing levels of risk to their portfolio through time is beyond imagination. The program of implicitly writing puts through the interest rate swaps worked very well initially as interest rates were steady or declining, but it had to be continuously geared up to reach ever more ambitious goals. The last interest rate swap established with Bankers Trust had an explicit goal of allowing P&G to borrow at least 40 basis points *below* the then prevailing commercial paper rate.[4] When the swap stopped working favorably the results were a disaster.

The most obvious lesson from this example is that corporations might not want to try to turn their basic corporate finance function into a profit center. If your firm can borrow in the basic credit market for the prevailing commercial paper (CP) rate, asking the Treasurer to borrow at CP minus a spread should be a red flag that there will be meaningful risks taken along the way. The second lesson that became clear after the fact is that almost nobody among the board of P&G or the most senior management understood what the Treasurer's office was doing while it was in theory succeeding against its goals. As long as the bottom line results were positive, everyone thought it was a great program. It was only after the fact that the swap was labeled a complete violation of their guidelines.

P&G sued Bankers Trust and eventually secured a large settlement that reduced its losses to Bankers by more than $100 million, but the episode could have been avoided completely if there had been a clear vision about the objectives of any investment program and meaningful guidelines defining the allowable instruments and risks.

---

[3]Malkin, L. (1994). Procter & Gamble's Tale of Derivatives Woe. *New York Times.* (14 April).
[4]Khatkale, S. (n.d.). A Case Study on Bankers Trust: How They Lost Trust. ICFAI Business School.

Similar corporate challenges have arisen through commodities trading (Sumitomo lost $2.6 billion in 1996 in copper trades),[5] currencies (Austrian bank Bawag lost $1.3 billion in currency speculation in 1998 and then tried to disguise the loss),[6] and credit (JPMorgan lost more than $6 billion in credit derivatives in 2012).[7] Each of these episodes and many more has its own particular tale, but there are too many similarities to believe that there are not important general lessons to be learned.

In every case the people creating the losses were initially assigned an activity completely consistent with the broader mission of the corporation. Hedging exposures is a frequent starting point, which sounds about as virtuous as one can imagine. Then there is a measure of success against the initial objectives. Perhaps there is a little too much success given the mandate, but it is easy for corporate overseers to become less diligent if the news is good. One of the truisms of these stories seems to be that you can't be in a position to suffer a truly massive loss until you have gathered the confidence of your superiors through a series of smaller gains.

The second frequent common point is that small losses are allowed to become big and then eventually too big. This is not to say that digging the hole deeper is a conscious strategy. Instead, after an initial loss the successful individual or team believes that the loss is an aberration and it will likely be fixed with time and a more rational market. Terms like "doubling down" are never used because of their negative connotations, but the behavior after the initial loss can look a lot like that. There is always confidence, at least at first, that profits from more trading will erase the loss.

If risk management while the loss was evolving failed to catch the problem, there's a chance it will also miss the efforts to correct it. There are examples of risk models being modified in real time to effectively turn off their alarms. Once the decision-making goes up the management chain, the activity is either quickly shut down or senior management actually adds to the risk taking. We shall never know how often near disasters have been avoided by big risk positions and a fortuitous turn in the market. It is only the examples of crashing and burning that make the shareholders' reports and the newspapers.

The basic problem in all of these stories is the misalignment of incentives between the traders and management on one hand and the shareholders on the other. Compensation is often set on a performance basis, but it is incredibly hard to adjust those metrics for the risks being taken. The employee goes to management at year-end and points to all of the profits he or she created, explains how the compensation is woefully inadequate, and then threatens to take the human capital elsewhere if the company fails to respond adequately.

That's the story if there are profits. If there is a big loss the employee apologizes and hopes to hold onto his or her job. The trader gets a meaningful share of any upside. Shareholders eat the vast majority of the downside. This explains the basic challenge hindering good investment decision-making at corporations.

---

[5]Humber, Y. (2014). Sumitomo Losses Prompt Biggest Drop Since '96 Copper Scandal. Bloomberg. (30 September).

[6]Pekarek, E. (2007). The BAWAG Banking Scandal: How over a Billion in Concealed Currency Trading Losses Caught Up with an Austrian Bank Almost a Decade Later. Pace Law School. (25 July).

[7]Protess, B. and Silver-Greenberg, J. (2013). JPMorgan Expected to Admit Fault in "London Whale" Trading Loss. *New York Times*. (15 October).

The only remedy to these corporate investment decision-making challenges is a culture of risk management that is in place well before any activity grows to a point where it could do meaningful harm to the firm's bottom line or ultimate existence. The board of directors must hire senior management with this orientation and then continually evaluate them accordingly. Investment decision-making for corporations is not fundamentally more challenging than it is for families, not-for-profits, or pension plans, but without appropriate structures and aligned incentives the opportunity for mischief or worse is high.

12.5   SOCIALLY RESPONSIBLE INVESTING

For many decades people have discussed the idea of *Socially Responsible Investing* (SRI) as an active program to combine the aims of good investment returns and the advancement of an agenda of improving parts of society. Discussions about SRI come with many different labels, with the anagram SRI being modified by some to stand for the more descriptive *Sustainable, Responsible, and Impact Investing*. Others refer to investing according to Environmental, Social, and Governance (ESG) issues. Any way the alphabet is sorted out, most of the broad topics are similar.

All of the managers and advisors discussed above confront these issues on a regular basis. The biggest challenge is to identify the topics of greatest concern to the family or organization and then decide the best way to shape investment decisions accordingly. This is a reasonably straightforward discussion at a high level. The devil is in the implementation details. Usually someone along the line asks the question, "What will these changes in the portfolio cost us in terms of return?"

One of the first well-organized SRI efforts took root in the 1980s when many not-for-profit institutions pursued South Africa-free equity funds to express their condemnation of the apartheid government. Public companies that were based in South Africa or that derived a meaningful part of their business from trade with South Africa were put on a disapproved list and excluded from portfolios. When apartheid came to an end, many of those same institutions actively sought out South African stocks in a show of support for the new regime. In this example the SRI effort started with a *negative screen* (no companies that were based or got much of their business from South Africa) and then transformed to a *positive screen* (actively embracing South African stocks).

The biggest area of discussion 20 years later concerns energy. Some investors say no to owning carbon energy companies while actively trying to invest in solar, hydro, or wind power projects. Again there can be negative and positive screens. There are nearly endless variations on these themes.

The theory behind SRI seems direct enough. The execution is much trickier. When South Africa-free funds were dissolved because that specific problem had been dealt with, institutions sometimes asked for products that addressed other issues of concern. The challenge was agreeing on the screens. Many investors wanted to avoid tobacco stocks, while a smaller number had issues with alcohol. Some Catholic institutions had strong feelings that were not shared by others about reproductive rights. Some people wanted to avoid arms manufacturers and defense contractors. The list went on and on, with precious little common ground around which to build portfolios.

This means the first step in the process for any investor is deciding on what the family's or institution's values would dictate. Not-for-profit communities like colleges and universities have divergent and respected opinions, so this is not as easy an exercise as one might first think. Majority rule is probably not the best criterion, as that sometimes boils down to "loudest voice." But assume for the moment that one can identify an articulated list of activities to be avoided and another to be encouraged.

Executing against those specific criteria is where the challenges really begin. Most listed funds will not change their mandates simply because a potential or current investor wants certain stocks excluded or included. Even if a fund met all the criteria on any given date, without continuous monitoring of the holdings it would be impossible to determine at any other point in time whether the fund was consistent with the objectives or not. This is a major challenge with any actively managed fund in which one may invest. Unless the fund's guidelines are specific enough to be in concert with an investor's objectives, there can be little confidence that the actual holdings will mesh continuously with the investor's objectives.

An alternative would be to set up a separately managed account with a manager and give them explicit negative and positive screens. Some institutions and families do this, but this requires some meaningful scale to be economically viable. An investor may have to terminate many of its existing diversified manager relations to reach the size necessary for such a separately managed account. The resulting portfolio could be appropriately diversified by name, but the investor would still be left with single manager operations risk. Some costs and risks associated with this approach would have to be weighed.

Many investors today have a meaningful part of their assets allocated to extremely low fee equity index funds and ETFs. The problem here is that there may be no large, cheap index funds based on particular SRI principles that the investor may want to pursue. No investor will ever influence the S&P Corporation to change their index of the top 500 US stocks to reflect SRI preferences. Instead the investors would have to decide if they would be willing to eliminate this tool from their portfolio management approach. Some institutions where the trustees said they do not want to own oil or coal companies in the school's portfolio decide to make exceptions if those companies reside in an index fund. This seems at least somewhat hypocritical. Most people might see an inconsistency with an institution telling the world that it was shunning certain groups of stock, when in fact it had meaningful exposures through an index.

Because of these many practical challenges some trustees and decision makers have historically said that their job is to achieve investment goals within appropriate risk parameters, but with no specific restrictions on managers in the SRI area. The feeling is that by maximizing the return from a pool of investments and then directing the fruits of that labor to the appropriate cause, the total impact is greater than anything positive or negative investment screens could produce.

Another challenge some people raise about negative screens is that if one investor chooses not to invest in a company, that company's stock does not disappear. Somebody else holds it and gets the benefits of ownership. Furthermore, it is that other investor who controls the proxy guiding the company's decisions that appear before shareholders. By pursuing negative screens, an investor forgoes any influence they may have on the behavior of the company beyond any moral suasion that might arise from their stance. From a practical perspective, negative screens should be viewed as expressing a moral preference rather than a means to changing behaviors of the company.

It would be a mistake, however, to draw too bright a line between SRI and non-SRI investment approaches. Whether there is a formal SRI policy or not, chances are good that the portfolio investors pursue generally reflect their values. A couple of examples will demonstrate this point.

In the wake of the financial crisis, private equity funds appeared and purchased repossessed homes from banks, invested to improve them, and then rented them out at competitive rates. There are higher and lower quality ways to pursue this activity. The press highlighted some operators that were exploiting the housing crisis to buy properties on the cheap and then perform little or no maintenance for their renters. Some fund investors were essentially financing slum landlords. By performing thorough due diligence, visiting properties and meeting with people responsible for the rehabilitation of the homes, an investor could determine whether the firm was actively improving the neighborhoods in which they operated. Many of these funds were the complete opposite of slum landlords. They were not only potentially good investments, but they were investments that did good things. Only after such due diligence can one determine whether any investment is consistent with the core values of the family or institution.

Of course, some people would not mind financing a slum landlord or other dubious activities if the return was high enough. There were many investors who sent vast sums of money to hedge fund managers who were engaged in insider trading. Even in the face of rumor and strong suggestions that not everything is on the up and up, there are often people who take the attitude that anything a fund manager does is ok as long as they don't steal from their investors or get caught in illegal activity. One way or another, a portfolio usually reflects the values of its managers and investors, whether good or bad.

There are many alternative investments that should be viewed through the same value lens. Consider the following three examples:

- Many funds now exist that are dedicated to businesses associated with the increasingly legalized marijuana industry in the United States.
- There are life settlement funds that purchase life insurance policies from elderly people for a lump sum. The profit upside occurs if the insured die earlier than the actuarial tables suggest they might.
- There are litigation financing funds that go around and find all types of cases that they pay the discovery and trial expenses for in exchange for a large percentage of any reward.

Investors in these funds have to decide if they are comfortable with (1) supporting an industry that is still largely illegal and shown to be highly detrimental to the development of young people; (2) hoping anyone dies quickly; or (3) encouraging litigation not to benefit those harmed but to earn a high rate of return. While it may be difficult to think of specific SRI screens that address these issues, it is not hard to imagine that an investor's core values would play an important role in any decision in these areas.

For as long as there have been these discussions there have been questions about whether SRI investments detract from overall investment performance. Like much of finance, a Google search on the topic will produce many studies. Some find definitely that SRI funds underperform while others find little or no effect. For a short while in the 1990s there was a body of research that argued that tobacco- and alcohol-free portfolios were superior performers. This was, of course, when those sinful allocations were reallocated to high-flying tech stocks. The general superiority of SRI portfolios was quickly reversed in the tech crash of 2000–2002.

USA Mutuals has tried to capitalize on the difference of opinion about performance in SRI and anti-SRI funds by offering a product they now call the Barrier Fund (VICEX). Formed in 2002 after the strong outperformance of tobacco, alcohol, defense, and gaming stocks, the thesis is that these companies enjoy natural barriers to entry and highly priced inelastic demand for their products. Over many parts of the market cycle the fund has been among those with the highest returns, which usually leads to some publicity and a reopening of the debate about performance between SRI and non-SRI approaches.

The fund has been variously named the Vice Fund or The Barrier Fund, depending on what the management company thought had the best marketing impact. After a reasonably solid 18-year track record, the fund had less than $170 million in assets at the end of Q1 2019.[8] Perceptions and reality are priorities for investors.

Meir Statman and Denys Glushkov in a 2009 paper examined returns of portfolios from 1992 to 2007 and found a little bit of everything.[9] They looked at stocks characterized by their social responsibility score. They found that investors that tilted toward highly scoring companies did better than average in their portfolios. But they also found that investors typically shun the type of stocks held by the Barrier Fund, and over that study period, that action more than eliminated the initial advantage. Statman and Glushkov concluded that it was a good idea to tilt toward socially responsible stocks, but only if you didn't also use negative screens. It is highly likely after a decade or so, new finance professors will revisit this thesis and perhaps come to different conclusions as the stock return data go through a new cycle of events.

Much of the research work in this space is executed or commissioned by firms that have a clear commercial axe to grind. It can vary considerably in rigor, but there are thoughtful pieces that add to the dialogue. The Aperio Group is a quantitative-oriented equity manager that works to decompose the performance of any particular benchmark the client may desire. In that way they can examine any impact from eliminating certain stocks from a benchmark portfolio.

They did this exercise in 2014 for carbon stocks.[10] In one exercise they eliminated oil, gas, and coal companies from the S&P 500 Index. This step created a tracking error to the index they sought to eliminate by changing the weights of the remaining stocks. By examining factors like cap size, industry, leverage, and liquidity, they could optimize the allocation to maximize how the new portfolio behaved relative to the benchmark. Their tests yielded index and carbon-free portfolios that were almost indistinguishable in performance over many years, suggesting in this instance, at least, portfolios with negative screens could be effective and not entail a large deterioration in returns.

---

[8]USA Mutuals Barrier Fund (2019). http://www.barrierfund.com, (30 June).

[9]Statman, M. and Glushkov, D. (2009). The Wages of Social Responsibility. *Financial Analysts Journal*. Volume 65, Issue 4. (July–August).

[10]Aperio Group, "Building a Carbon-Free Equity Portfolio," 2014.

Aperio noted, however, that to achieve this result the carbon stocks needed to be replaced with more utilities and materials stocks, which include chemical firms and extraction companies like mines. This raises another set of issues for the SRI discussion. Has the investor really accomplished anything through a carbon negative screen if the portfolio they then own has more companies that are among the biggest consumers of carbon fuels?

This example shows how nuanced SRI investing can be. Some investors will be happy enough to avoid headline holdings in their actively managed funds, regardless of the secondary effects on the portfolio. Others will push further thematically. If one eliminated carbon stocks, utilities, automobile manufactures, and materials stocks in an attempt to distance oneself from most parts of the carbon economy, it would become increasingly difficult to argue that the resulting portfolio could substitute well for the benchmark indexes.

The remaining caution is a special case of warnings made throughout this book. Knowing that there is a potential market for SRI investments of many flavors, managers have responded by offering specialized funds. A small number have been around for decades and are easy to diligence. Many more, however, are relatively new to the scene.

Some managers raising these efforts have experience in mediocre, at best, traditional fund companies. They understand that their track record would not commend them to new investors. They respond by recreating the mandate to reflect SRI themes. There are private equity and debt funds as well as products owning publicly traded stocks and bonds. Many are too young to have a pattern of results that can be analyzed, so they resort to the SRI story to promote fundraising.

When pursuing positive investments such managers have a wonderful set of scenarios. They of course believe their investments will be just as fruitful as traditional portfolios. But if they fall short, the investor is supposedly consoled by the fact that the investments paid off in social welfare what they lacked in private return. Once again the investor is dragged back to the question of how much return is prudent to be sacrificed in pursuit of social goals. Are there better ways to support these missions?

Casual observation suggests that positive screens sometimes push too much money into an apparently desirable area. Very few investors have seen good returns in renewable energy or forestland investments. It is hard to argue that there is no economic purpose behind supporting sustainable industries. But it is possible that over the last many years, such a large number of investors have wanted to do good, that the capacity of these industries to effectively use all of the capital was too small to create attractive returns.

A market-oriented thinker would say low returns signaled that there was already too much capital devoted to an area. The careful SRI investor should not follow the crowd with more positive screen directed investments that are likely to disappoint, but instead invest without such screens and then use the extra earnings to devote to furthering the cause philanthropically.

No investor needs to accept second-rate investment management or returns just to exercise SRI preferences. It may be more challenging to find managers and projects that meet investor standards, but neither ethical nor investment standards should be compromised. With enough effort and care investment portfolios can be constructed that are economically rewarding while being completely consistent with the values of the investor.

CHAPTER 13

Regulation of Investment Activity

This chapter is designed to give the non-professional investor an overview of the regulatory landscape for investment activity in the United States as it exists at the time of publication. It makes no attempt to be technically complete and should not be used as a substitute for current and comprehensive legal advice that is only available from a lawyer or compliance professional. The reason it is included in this discussion at all is because institutional settings matter in how the industry has evolved and what investors should and should not expect from their regulators.

It is a complete myth that regulation can somehow eliminate fraud at the individual level or major market upheavals at the macro level. Attempts over the decades by legislators and regulators to pretend otherwise have only succeeded in making investors less diligent than they should be in watching over their own affairs. It is true, however, that both government and self-regulatory organizations work hard, and mostly effectively, in trying to maintain high standards of professional behavior and market efficiency. The end result is never perfection, but the US capital markets are among the best in the world and are the envy of many.

The Securities and Exchange Commission (SEC) was created in 1934 to formalize the oversight of federal securities law, and it still exists today as the organization most investors think of in this arena. The playing field is, however, much more complicated, with multiple regulators overseeing different parts of an increasingly interknit web of markets. The Commodity Futures Trading Commission (CTFC) and various bank regulators, including the Federal Reserve (FED) and the Office of the Comptroller of the Currency (OCC), round out the major federal government regulators that directly or indirectly touch most investors. Additional oversight comes from independent, non-government regulators like the National Futures Association (NFA) and the Financial Industry Regulatory Authority (FINRA), as well as the operators of the exchanges where securities and derivatives trade.

If this sounds on the surface to be confusing, it is. Most of the regulatory milestones through time were in response to a crisis or a disruption. The OCC was created in 1863 as Abraham Lincoln sought during the Civil War to create a solid and unified national bank system as a complement to the hodgepodge of state banks that had existed exclusively to that point. The Panic of 1907 highlighted that while the OCC might watch individual bank behavior to maintain high standards, there was little oversight of the banking system as a whole. The FED was created in 1913. Post–World War I disruptions and attempted manipulations in the wheat market brought about the Grain Futures Administration in 1922, which eventually became the CFTC in 1974. The market crash of 1929 and subsequent start of the Great Depression induced much of the major securities laws from 1933 through 1940, including the creation of the SEC. Major frauds and corporate scandals at the end of the 1990s bull market led to the *Sarbanes-Oxley Act* in 2002, and the 2007–2009 financial and market crisis prompted the passage of *Dodd-Frank* in 2010. Regulation of the insurance industry, which has major investment elements attached to it, is largely left to the states though federal legislation over the past 40 years has tried to create more uniformity of the state standards.

Each of these individual steps was a massive undertaking, but the end result is something of a crazy quilt of rules and activities that early in the twenty-first century looks like something you might want to avoid if you could start with a blank sheet of paper. As other countries evolve in their capital markets, some have largely copied our framework. Others, like Brazil, have recognized that trading markets have become more integrated through time, and have built their regulatory structures with fewer artificial distinctions. Regardless of whether the regulatory structure is unified or balkanized, there are four broad categories of activity that most regulatory schemes attempt to cover:

- Capital raising: the creation and sale of securities.
- The functioning of the secondary markets.
- Investment companies.
- Behavior of advisors.

This chapter will briefly review the key elements of each of these areas and how they most prominently affect investors.

13.1 CAPITAL RAISING

The *Securities Act of 1933* was the first comprehensive federal statute covering the creation and sales of securities used to raise capital for new or existing public companies. The '33 Act defines financial disclosures that must be made to prospective buyers, prohibiting issuers from providing false or incomplete financial statements that might make the company appear healthier than it is, or using other fraudulent sales practices.

This law can be viewed as a prototype for much of the legislation that followed. There have always been broad, anti-fraud statutes that try to protect people from unscrupulous activity, but the '33 Act made certain activities covering securities explicitly illegal in an attempt to make enforcement easier and hopefully more effective. But narrowly defined rules are a double-edged sword. If someone clearly crosses the line into illegal territory it may be easier to prosecute, but those narrow rules may give less scrupulous people a road map showing how much they can get away with before crossing that line. Legions of securities lawyers are currently employed to give their clients advice on just these boundaries.

The rules affect initial public offerings of stock as well as secondary issues. In both cases the issuing company must register the shares to be sold and create and make public enough financial information about the firm so that potential buyers can make informed decisions. The SEC doesn't guarantee the accuracy of the filing information, but if investors can later show that the data were either materially incomplete or inaccurate, there are well-established paths for seeking compensation.

Not every security is required to be registered. Small companies or those that are only offering securities within one state do not have to follow the federal registration process. Securities issued by municipalities or state and federal governments are also exempt, presumably because public budgets are already a matter of record and further disclosures are not required.

The small company exemption has become useful in the modern Internet age as crowdfunding platforms have appeared and have been sanctioned by the SEC.[1] In the spirit of promoting small businesses, it is now possible to raise meaningful sums of money with almost no disclosure through such sites. Serious investors should be very cautious in these waters as the venues themselves do very little to vet the worthiness of the projects competing for investment dollars.

Private securities transactions are also exempt from the registration process. This makes it possible for Mrs. Smith to sell her company to Mr. Jones without going through the IPO or secondary rules. It has also allowed an interesting market to develop in pre-IPO transactions. Using the broad exemptions that apply to many transactions with qualified investors, investment bankers have arranged early transactions between insiders and eager investors for some of the highest profile IPOs in recent history.

These transactions can be somewhat complicated. An insider can often sell some or all of his holdings in a private transaction before the company becomes publicly traded as long as it does not violate any employment contracts. After the IPO, however, most insiders are prohibited from selling stock for a meaningful period of time. This is not an SEC requirement, but most investment banks sponsoring the IPO insist on some lock-up, often six months, to assure the potential buyers of IPO stock that their purchases won't immediately be met with a wave of insider selling.

Before the IPO there may be interest among potential sellers and buyers for an early, private transaction. Investment banks facilitate these discussions, but cannot broadly advertise selling interest without violating the registration rules. What happens is something of an imprecise dance where the seller and the banker have far superior knowledge about the company and the fair value of the stock relative to the potential buyer.

The crux of the discussion centers on when and at what price the likely IPO will occur. Any such transactions that occur between the time the company files its registration material and the date the SEC declares the registration effective are particularly challenged. This gap is known as the "quiet period." These windows are not formally defined in SEC rules but usually run 40 days during which the company may not release any new information beyond what they had prepared for their registration filing. Related parties are also held to the quiet period. The rules were instituted to prevent investment banks from publishing rosy research reports just before an IPO to pump up interest in the issue.

Some tech-oriented mutual funds have been active in buying pre-IPO shares. The theory is that by getting a toehold in a potentially lucrative name, they will be able to build their ultimate position more efficiently and at better prices. Investors should ask mutual fund managers if they trade in this fashion. If they do, the next

---

[1]Crowdfunding for Investors. (2017). SEC Bulletin. (10 May).

questions should be whether there are any limits on owning these illiquid shares and what is the pricing procedure for non-traded securities. These managers may be trying to enhance long-term returns through the pre-IPO tactic, but they are also taking on different risks and more tracking error to their benchmarks.

Pre-IPO trades are very different from transactions with public securities. What usually happens is that the investment bankers involved in the IPO get indications from potential insider sellers that they might like to dispose of some stock pre-IPO. The bankers then communicate within their network to known institutional and wealthy individual investors who might have an interest. The lure is the chance to acquire stock at pre-IPO prices, presumably lower than where the stock will come out to the public. Transaction data is not publicly recorded since everything is done privately, so whether reality meshes with theory is open to discussion. Anecdotal evidence before the closely followed Facebook IPO suggests trades occurred over a wide price range, both above and below the ultimate IPO price.

Greed can easily overcome fear in these situations, but the investment banker who arranges a private trade wildly different from the ultimate IPO price is going to have only one happy client at the end of the day. Everyone involved should be cautious in analyzing the advantages of an early transaction. The IPO registration rules have been working for a long time and while they do not always insure a smooth or fairly priced issue, buyers and sellers need to think hard whether jumping the gun produces great advantages over having complete and uniform financial data and a more competitive auction process at the IPO.

Another important avenue for raising capital is the corporate bond, and the regulatory process is similar to that for stocks. If the bonds are to be sold to the public there has to be a registration, with appropriate accounting and disclosures provided. There is a much bigger market for private bonds, however, where the ultimate buyer is a sophisticated institution with every expectation that they will hold them to maturity with no intention of trading the bonds. Where this is the case, the buyer signs a letter stating they intend to buy the bonds exclusively for investment services. These *letter bonds* are exempt from many of the public securitization rules.

Rule 144A was introduced in 1990 to improve the potential market for many unregistered securities. For example, an institutional investor may have bought newly issued letter bonds with the expectation of holding them to maturity, only to find that a few years later their circumstances had changed. That institution is allowed to sell those bonds to another qualified purchaser in a 144A transaction without having to go through the registration process. Rule 144A has enhanced the initial market for private securities by opening up eventual options for a subsequent sale.

The final main source of capital for corporations is from commercial banks. Bank loans, even when they are syndicated across many financial institutions, are considered private transactions outside the reach of any SEC rules. There are presumably professionals on both sides of the transaction that can fend for themselves.

13.2 SECONDARY MARKETS

The Securities Exchange Act of 1934 created the SEC, defining the scope of its authority over brokers and exchanges as well as prescribing the reporting that public companies must make to investors. It also prohibited insider trading. One can broadly think of the '33 Act as the bible for initially offering securities and the '34 Act as the rulebook for the trading of those securities in the secondary market.

Prior to the SEC coming onto the scene, regulation of the secondary markets was primarily the domain of the exchanges that policed their member brokers. *Self-regulation* was, and remains, a critical foundation underpinning the fair operation of the securities and derivatives markets. After the trauma of the 1929 crash, however, the general public supported a broader role for government.

While the SEC is the highly visible regulator, most investors do not appreciate how much of the regulatory burden falls upon the markets or *self-regulatory organizations (SROs)*. The Financial Industry Regulatory Authority, or FINRA, grew out of the regulatory arms of NASD, the National Association of Securities Dealers, and the New York Stock Exchange in 2007 when the markets converted into for-profit corporations. Many were concerned that for-profit companies disciplining traders and brokers through the collection of fines was a recipe for trouble and that the exchanges should focus on the business side of trading and leave discipline to FINRA.

At the start of 2015 FINRA oversaw over 4,000 member firms and over 600,000 registered representatives.[2] FINRA is authorized to do its job by the SEC, which in turn reviews FINRA's ongoing efforts, but most people will admit there is much overlap and probably wasted energy between the industry and the government regulators.

The primary function of FINRA is to oversee broker behavior, which primarily consists of transactions in the secondary market, though a meaningful amount of certain brokers' books come from primary issuance. When the exchanges were operated as not-for-profit entities, they almost always had their own compliance departments that monitored the actual transactions as they took place on the exchange. As the exchanges evolved into for-profit entities, they generally decided to outsource this oversight to FINRA to avoid the appearance or reality of a conflict of interests.

The futures industry has evolved somewhat differently. The Chicago Mercantile Exchange (CME) and the Intercontinental Exchange (ICE) are major for-profit businesses and public corporations that grew out of the not-for-profit membership model. Unlike the stock exchanges, they have kept some of their long-standing self-regulatory activities rather than offload them to the NFA. In these activities, the exchanges face the continuing scrutiny of the government regulator, the CFTC, which can sanction them if the rules are not applied in a fair and consistent way.

One of the challenges of modern securities trading regulation is the proliferation of trading venues. There have always been competing exchanges that actively recruited companies to list their shares on their platforms, but today there are also non-exchange trading venues known as *dark pools*. These are privately structured facilities, often sponsored and organized by a large broker dealer, which can act as an intermediary to any trade. They arose out of frustration by large institutional investors who accurately believed that information about their orders was too visible in the traditional exchanges, disadvantaging them from getting good prices for their stock purchases and sales. Large institutional buy or sell orders would come to these dark pools, anonymously except to the organizer. The fact that these venues have increased in number and market share suggests that they have served a valuable purpose, even though they have their critics.

---

[2]FINRA, http://www.finra.org/newsroom/statistics

Most trading rules are designed to protect the prototypical public customer, stating things like orders must be executed observing strict price and time priority. That is, if Customer A is bidding one cent more for a stock than Customer B, Customer A has to get a fill on the order before Customer B gets to buy. If they both bid the same price, the order that was entered into the system first gets the priority on the fill.

All that makes sense at a high level, but it fails to acknowledge that customers are different. An institutional fund manager that is looking to buy a million shares of a stock is in many ways treated identically to the public customer buying ten shares. Many decades ago this was less of a problem because prices were often quoted with a bid/ask spread of $0.25 per share. Many thousands of shares were available at both the bid and the offer, and time priority usually was the deciding factor until enough activity came into the market and moved the price up or down.

That all changed at the end of the 1990s with the introduction of *decimalization*. Prices could be quoted down to the penny and even tiny fractions of a penny. This made a complete hash of time price priority. An institutional investor could be bidding for 100,000 shares of a stock at a price of $30.10 per share. This information would have to be made public in the trading systems to allow possible sellers to know what the depth of the market interest was. Such bids opened the door to opportunistic traders to come in and bid for 1,000 shares at $30.101 per share. The latter trader would buy the stock with confidence that there was little chance of a significant loss given the major bid just below their transaction price.

While trying to be fair to the little guy, the rules inadvertently penalized the large institutional traders that hold most of the equity in America and end up paying most of the bills at the exchanges. The attraction of the dark pools was that trading rules of the type described above did not have to apply. In fact, many dark pools didn't initially disclose what their trading rules were, considering them proprietary.

Since the publication of Michael Lewis's book *Flash Boys*, there has been a lively debate about the state of the US equity market and the fairness of the various trading venues.[3] People on both sides of the topic are largely advocating positions that support their own economic interests. While clearly a gifted storyteller, Lewis is not a great analyst or historian. *Flash Boys* purports to uncover a vast conspiracy among brokers, exchanges, and *high-frequency traders* (HFT) to rig the US stock market in ways that cost innocent investors billions of dollars annually. These revelations spurred the FBI, the New York State Attorney General, and others to begin looking into whether crimes might have been committed.

In Lewis' world there are those who wear white hats and those who wear black hats. A prominent white hat belongs to Brad Katsuyama, once head of equity trading at Royal Bank of Canada and more recently founder of a new private exchange, IEX, which was designed to address the alleged inequities in the current system. Much of the book describes IEX's advertised advantages.

Technology is at the heart of this story. At the early stages of any big change, there is often ignorance and fear of technology. Lewis attempts to play on the fear of the unknown to emphasize negatives resulting from the change and spends little time on the positives. But once technology is fully embraced those positives become well known and we usually find it difficult to imagine going back to the ways before the innovation.

---

[3]Lewis, M. (2014). *Flash Boys*. W.W. Norton and Co

Lewis spends considerable time explaining latency in electronic signals that lies at the heart of the edge high-frequency traders try to extract from other market participants. Latency exists because computers work at different speeds and the distances trade messages must travel vary from market to market. This creates lags between when an order is placed and when it reaches its final destinations. These lags are measured in tiny fractions of a second, too small for human differentiation but large enough for super-fast computers to identify and use.

This difficult subject is boiled down to its essentials very efficiently, which was an absolute must if Lewis was to be persuasive at all. Once that task was completed, he described how the HFT community has spent huge sums of money to connect most efficiently to market data feeds, which allows them to see and react to order flow faster than mortals. He notes that because of their technological edge they can sometimes get in front of public orders before those orders get to all of the ultimate markets. He then broadly concludes that HFT firms are taking profits from other market participants who would have otherwise gotten better executions for their orders.

This last conclusion is the most open to debate because it assumes the existence of bids and offers that might never be present absent the existence of competing HFT firms. Also important is the fact that while these HFT programs produce trade signals that have a high probability of a profit, they still place capital at risk because prospective orders may not materialize.

A more complete examination would have noted that there have always been intermediaries in markets (e.g. *locals* in the commodities pits, *specialists* on the NYSE) who have superior access to information and who translate that into usually profitable trades. The rules of the exchanges and the duty of the regulators should not be to eliminate any advantage these traders have, but to work to assure that there is as level a playing field as possible while still promoting efficient trading.

Before 2001 when the SEC mandated that stock prices be quoted in decimals, the convention was fractions with the smallest available increment being 1/16 of a dollar, or \$0.0625. Much more common for actively traded NYSE stocks, however, was a bid/ask spread of 1/4, or \$0.25 per share. After decimalization and increased competition from new electronic markets the typical bid/ask spread compressed to one or two cents. It is what goes on inside this bid/ask spread and how it moves around that is the subject of the controversy today.

Regulators should examine some of the industry practices Lewis cites, like markets paying brokers for order flow, but his most dramatic conclusions rest on a comparison of what *is* versus an *ideal* that has never been. He also fails to note the fact that the heyday of HFT is probably well past. Best industry estimates are that the total profits of HFT in 2013 were around \$1 billion versus \$5 billion five years earlier. Free entry and competition have a way of largely eliminating any really profitable games. It should also be noted that these annual profit figures are tiny compared to the daily transactions volume.

The book also fails to explain many key steps along the evolutionary trail of trading. We intuitively assume that transparency is a good thing in public markets, but that is not always the case. Dark pools arose in part to allow very large stock traders to transact privately so that their bids and offers do not unduly move the market. These dark pools which are private exchanges (often organized and controlled by big banks or brokers) offer the prospect of anonymity. Lewis points out that these private exchanges have little regulation and sometimes lack written rules governing how transactions occur. The fact that institutional investors sought out these venues says a great deal about their dissatisfaction with the old way public markets were run.

More importantly, long-term retail investors are largely unaffected by most of this. Someone who sees 48.80 bid/48.81 offered for Wells Fargo Bank (WFC) on their Fidelity trading screen can place a market order for 100 shares with confidence that they are going to get the stock faster than they can blink, and probably at a price between the posted bid and offer. If the fill is 48.806 instead of 48.805 that they "should" have had in an ideal world, the difference is 10 cents on a $4,880 transaction. If you plan to hold that stock for several years the HFT edge you paid away is not going be a factor determining the success or failure of the trade. The flip side of this coin is that the presence of competing high-frequency traders is what likely allowed you to trade inside the bid and offer to begin with.

Nobody should ever be casual or dismissive about possible illegalities in our trading markets. If people are breaking the law they should be identified and punished. If there are few illegalities, but perceptions of inequities, the SEC may try to address these issues with modifications to trading rules and better education. But history shows that no matter how comprehensive the rule makers try to be, some market participants will find and act on any remaining advantage. Doing so is not illegal, nor does it mean the markets are rigged.

Wrong-headed attempts to control speculative activity and improve markets through *transactions taxes* have been tried in Europe and the result has been wider bid/ask spreads and more costly trades for the long-term investors the rule makers were trying to protect. Great care should be taken in planning modifications to the market so the cure isn't worse than the disease. It is better to have a slightly uneven playing field and a market that works, rather than a perfectly level one that doesn't.

Real traders understand that they must look out for themselves whether they are working on the floor of an exchange, over the phone, or on an automated transaction network. Markets will continue to change and there will be some who evolve with them faster than others. This won't make everyone happy, but it is not a sign of illegal activity.

Many institutional traders that have no ties to HFT have written publicly since the release of Lewis' book to emphasize the improvements in the markets over the last several years. These individuals may not like everything they see in the markets today, but they believe that on-net technology has produced more competitive and efficient equity markets, not less.

One area that continues to receive a lot of attention from regulators and the press is *insider trading*. Usually the reports focus on personal and somewhat sensational aspects of the topic. Instead of dwelling on the soap opera entertainment value of the events, we should ask why anyone should care about insider trading.

There is a school of thought, more often expressed by academics than market participants, that says insider trading should be encouraged and not criminalized. The theory is that this kind of trading gets important information into the market price of a stock more quickly, improving the efficiency of all stock transactions that follow. But there is more to life than pure price efficiency. What these academics miss is that the chance of there being big winners and losers as a result of insider trading can change investor behavior in ways that ultimately erode the efficiency the purists are trying to promote. Real-world investors should and do care very much about insider trading.

The classic insider trading case involves an individual who has access to material, nonpublic information about a company. That individual, or a family member or friend, buys or sells securities of that company taking advantage of their informational edge versus everyone else in the market. In some cultures such activity is viewed as a benefit of the individual's privileged position. In the United States, insider trading has been a federal criminal act for decades.

Efficiency purists forget an important fact about markets. Trading is a completely voluntary activity and nothing compels anyone to participate if they believe a market is rigged. Scanning the globe, there are many countries today that some investors avoid because of the perception of unfairness. This impacts capital formation and every other dimension of economic life in those countries. One of the truest signs of a developed market is a respect for the individual investor.

Having a fair and efficient market is something of an abstract goal. There are also practical concerns about insider trading of which investors should be aware. It was the Securities Exchange Act of 1934 that made insider trading a federal crime. The Insider Trading Sanctions Act of 1984 toughened the penalties in the 1934 Act by allowing for treble damages. Generally the criminal focus is on the person illegally using the material, nonpublic information, but others can be the targets of sanctions as well.

In recent cases, the government alleged that portfolio managers regularly received material, nonpublic information, which was then used to trade securities for their funds. The direct benefit accrued to the fund investors, with only an indirect benefit going to the portfolio manager through bigger performance fees and the ability to market a strong track record.

In general, most investors want to associate with honest portfolio managers. After all, if a PM is cheating someone else to benefit today's fund investors, what is to suggest those investors won't be on the bad end of a shady deal if circumstances change? That alone is reason enough to avoid such funds. But there may be other tangible risks to these investors.

In previous cases involving fund managers, there seems to have been little attempt to claw back ill-gained profits let alone treble damages from the funds themselves. However, there appears to be nothing keeping the government from pursuing such a course. An investor in a fund where the portfolio manager traded profitably on inside information might find him or herself being asked to return part of their gains.

This risk perhaps helps explain the sizable redemption requests faced by funds where PMs and analysts have been implicated. Investors may believe that by getting their assets out at the first opportunity they minimize the chance of harm should any penalty be ultimately assigned to the fund. This is largely uncharted legal water, and it is certainly understandable if an investor seeks to withdraw.

But even redeeming has its costs. Most managers believe they can meet redemptions without too much market impact, but that belief only holds in normal or moderately disturbed markets. The credit crisis of late 2008 was a vivid example of a time when only the portfolios with the best liquidity could live up to that expectation. Insider trading–driven redemptions potentially pose a similar, but more targeted, risk.

Because of required position disclosures, the world has a good idea of what long stocks need to be sold, or short stocks bought back, by a manager looking to meet redemptions. The resulting market moves are not restricted to the insider trading names, but potentially touch all the positions in the portfolio. The market impact from redemptions hurts all of the fund's investors.

This is clearly a loosely defined area of law. After several well-publicized convictions for insider trading seemed to be making progress against what appeared to be a widespread problem, the Second Circuit Court of Appeals in December 2014 reversed two previous guilty rulings.[4] In doing so the court meaningfully limited the scope of what had previously been considered insider trading. They affirmed the long-held, narrow view that an insider could not disclose nonpublic material information in exchange for personal gain. But they said for the receiver of this information to be criminally liable requires that the *tippee* not only know the information was material and nonpublic, but also know the *tipper* received a benefit for disclosing it.

The two hedge fund managers that had their convictions reversed may have had a strong feeling about the nature of the information they received, but the Second Circuit did not find that they caused or were aware of any compensation to the initial tipper. They had received that information from paid industry consultants, who had in turn gotten the information from the true insider. The ruling opened up many forms of unscrupulous behavior. Leaking insider information to a family member or an old college roommate without explicit payment would not appear to be criminal behavior. Receiving the same information three or four steps down an information chain that cloaks any illegal compensation would also seem to give the tippee a protection from legal liability.

Two years later the Supreme Court picked up the topic in *Salman vs the United States*.[5] In a strongly worded 8–0 decision the highest court foreclosed much of the Second Circuit's arguments. Tips based on insider information, passed on to friends and family, convey many benefits to the tipper beyond direct monetary compensation. If someone trades on information that they reasonably believe to be material, nonpublic information, both they and the tipper are at risk.

There are many successful managers who assert that they have a strong culture of compliance and rigorous internal controls to prevent illegal insider trading. They argue that they have too much to lose in terms of their businesses for them to not be honest and vigilant. Most investors accept the logic of such statements, but they should not equate assertions to proof. Even bad people say the right things.

From the investor's perspective, the best defense is solid due diligence before making an investment. Know as much as possible about how the manager makes money. Associate only with those managers that share your high ethical standards. There is no foolproof way to avoid all the risks of insider trading or any other fraud, but being cautious, informed, and vigilant is a good place to start.

The Second Circuit's ruling in many ways gave unscrupulous traders a road map describing how to avoid legal consequences from acting on material, non-public information. Fortunately, the Supreme Court's decision burned most of that map. Nobody should lose sight of why strong enforcement of these laws is important to us. Public confidence in markets is critical to their ongoing efficiency and to capital formation in the country. Investors already face plenty of natural market risk. They do not need to work in markets where there is little confidence of fairness or the

---

[4]*United States v. Newman, et al.* Nos. 13-1837-cr, 13-1917-cr (2d Cir.) (10 December 2014).
[5]http://www.scotusblog.com/case-files/cases/salman-v-united-states/ (6 December 2016).

additional problem of fund disruptions caused by people trying to rapidly disassociate themselves from bad apples in the market.

13.3 INVESTMENT COMPANIES

In 1940 additional laws were passed governing mutual funds and the behavior of investment advisors (The Investment Company Act of 1940 and The Investment Advisers Act of 1940). The first of these two pieces of legislation is more widely known and is frequently referred to generically as *The '40 Act* and regulated mutual funds are often called *'40 Act Funds*. The mutual fund industry as we know it today stems from this legislation that created a standard set of reporting and disclosures designed to help investors understand what their money was doing inside these organizational structures.

Both 1940 pieces of legislation were as important for what got excluded from the rules as for what was inside the tent. Private partnerships, a broad category of investments that includes most hedge funds, are exempt from the '40 Act rules because they are only sold to qualified or sophisticated investors. What this means is that while the general partners of these funds cannot lie to their limited partners (that's still a no-no under general fraud rules), they do not have to meet all of the disclosure and reporting rules designed to protect less sophisticted investors. The bottom line is *caveat emptor*, which is pretty good advice even for participants in mutual funds. Investors in partnerships need to be forceful, however, in demanding enough information to make educated decisions about risks and attribution. We have cited many examples in this book of partnership investments that went horribly wrong, but were possibly predictable with enough prior due diligence. This can be a particularly difficult discipline to maintain, however, when given the opportunity to invest with a successful but secretive hedge fund manager, and other friends or institutions are enjoying what looks to be a profitable ride.

The SEC requires that all mutual funds provide a complete *prospectus* describing the fund, the investment adviser for the fund and key potential conflicts of interest that may affect potential investors. The fund is also allowed to prepare a less formal version of the above information as a *summary prospectus*, which is often one of the key marketing tools for it.

Advertising is another hot button topic. Any communication that is aimed at retail investors is considered advertising, which can be scrutinized by FINRA and the SEC for completeness, balance, and fairness. It is not allowed, for example, to say the fund was the best performing international equity mutual fund in the Morningstar universe in March of 2009 even if that statement is true. Highlighting a single good data point without describing a longer history is considered deceptive by implying that the superior performance is more repeatable than it likely is.

FINRA has a major division that reviews advertisements before they can be put into first use. They watch new fund companies very closely for a year, but once the firm demonstrates compliance the process becomes fairly mechanical. It is no surprise that all mutual fund advertising has a similar look and feel. Fund companies understand what FINRA will and will not accept and usually try hard to stay compliant. For commodity trading Advisors (CTAs) and commodity pool operators (CPOs) there is a parallel set of rules administered by the NFA and ultimately overseen by the CFTC.

As more and more communications are made on the Internet or by social media, the advertising rules have had to scramble to keep up. To be in compliance, however, fund managers must always remember that *any* communications aimed at retail investors fall under the advertising rules.

There have been many investment innovations since mutual funds came into prominence. Closed-end stock and bond funds and Exchange Traded Funds (ETFs) are just two examples of hybrid instruments that are issued like public equities but are constructed much more like mutual funds. As the industry has evolved, so too have the regulations, in part to ensure that the new entrants are treated approximately the same as traditional mutual funds.

There are many investment features in every mutual fund that need to be disclosed by law. That does not mean they are required to be emphasized in client communications. The vast majority of investors, for example, almost certainly do not know that mutual funds are allowed to use a modest amount of leverage. Even among those that are aware of the theoretical possibility, a minority knows whether their funds use leverage or not. The same is true for derivatives use. The problem with legal disclosures is that they become so detailed and encyclopedic that few investors take the time to go through them carefully.

Some of the biggest and most successful core bond funds on the planet have built their track records around leverage and the selling of options and CDS to generate premium income. These managers would not have enjoyed the success they had unless they were skillful with these tools, but that does not mean simple comparisons between their results and those of more traditional managers are entirely in order. Many investors may think they own a portfolio of high-quality bonds when in fact what they own is a fund that looks more like a low-octane fixed-income hedge fund.

Inquiries on the subject are often met with replies like, "The information is in our prospectus. I'm afraid I can't go into any more detail without violating the SEC Rules." Uniform disclosure rules are designed to prevent one group of investors from getting better information from the fund manager than is available to other investors. They are unfortunately used by less forthright managers to put only that which is necessary in the required disclosures and then say nothing more.

One set of SEC rules mandates semi-annual disclosures of all holdings, cash, securities, and derivatives. These data are available with a lag online at the SEC EDGAR website.[6] This is a treasure trove of information, but it is not easily navigated nor is the data easily extracted or analyzed. Fund companies can submit their reports for all of their funds in a single file. There are no page numbers, nor is the file searchable. Someone, at some time, must have thought this was adequate disclosure, but it is not good communication.

Most mutual fund companies will post their funds' annual reports on their web sites. These sites vary widely in their effectiveness. An investor can go to the PIMCO site, for example, and search for a particular fund, a big improvement over their EDGAR filing. Behind that tab are further tabs for "snapshot," "performance," "portfolio," and "documents." In the documents category there is a tab for holdings, which mirrors the data PIMCO sends to the SEC. In this tab an Excel spreadsheet appears, which gives the impression of a user-friendly format. As of early 2015, it was somewhat user friendly. There are over 3,900 rows listing every bond, loan, futures

---

[6]https://www.sec.gov/edgar/searchedgar/mutualsearch.html

contract, swap, and CDS that the fund entered into. Every entry, even the derived ones, is a number field, which protects PIMCO from anyone improperly manipulating its formulas. If the reader is so inclined, she could modify the spreadsheet to allow subtotals by instrument or to quickly group activities.

For example, PIMCO's Total Return Fund's $117 billion in unaudited holdings contained $872 million in face value of State of California general obligation bonds and notes as of 31 March 2015, which had a market value of $1.278 billion. [7] This may be valuable information to the analyst trying to gain insight into PIMCO's thinking as to how it positions itself against its benchmark, but it doesn't provide any clues as to whether the fund manager bought these bonds profitably or not. PIMCO is exercising its legal right to disclose what nonrequired information it chooses, and in this case it has chosen not to share enough information to allow a detailed performance attribution calculation.

Another fact available from the same holdings report is that the fund owns $76 billion of notional value in US Libor interest rate swaps that appear to have lost $2.7 billion since they were established. None of this is highlighted and PIMCO might have preferred to omit this information covering part of their derivatives activity. But once they produce a report called "holdings" it must be complete and they cannot selectively pick which items to include or omit. The data are, however, almost useless, since they give no information about the duration of the swaps, which makes the $76 billion notional figure impossible to evaluate relative to the fund's $117 billion in net assets. The net profit or loss figure is equally shaky in that it omits any similar swaps activity that happened to have been closed out before the end of the quarter, which might have created profits far in excess of the losses in the schedule.

These examples are not meant to criticize any fund company or practice. They only point out that even the highest-minded regulations can leave meaningful gaps in investors' knowledge and make it more difficult to evaluate funds and managers. Of course, when the conversation shifts to private partnerships in the United States, the landscape deteriorates considerably from even these standards. General partners cannot lie or deceive through omission, but they can be highly selective as to what they say to their current or prospective investors. This makes comparisons across hedge fund managers and private equity partnerships maddening at times.

The US investment world is broken into *sophisticated investors* and everyone else. For more than 70 years it has been assumed that if one is sophisticated (i.e., sufficiently wealthy) one should be able to deal with managers of private placements with minimal protections other than from basic fraud. Hedge funds, exempt commodity trading advisors (CTAs), private equity, venture capital, and real estate partnerships all have operated under this framework for decades. It does not have to be this way.

Before hedge funds became prevalent in Brazil, the Brazilian securities regulator, CVM, created clear definitions of investment fund types, along with reporting and disclosure rules. There are seven categories of funds, ranging from short-term funds (like money market funds in the United States), to stock funds, to a final category called multi-market funds. Most US hedge funds would fall into this latter group. In addition to the categories of marketable funds, there is a broad range of truly illiquid private partnerships identified as well.

---

[7]PIMCO. (2015). https://investments.pimco.com/Products/pages/346.aspx?ShareClassCode=A. Holdings Report (31 March).

The biggest distinction between the two countries' regulations is how hedge funds are treated. Since there is effectively no legal category of private hedge funds in Brazil, these fund managers must follow reporting and disclosure rules that are similar to those observed by long stock, bond, and cash managers. For example, all positions, long and short, are disclosed to the regulator monthly, which then releases the information to the public with a 30-day lag. Additionally, managers must report inflows and outflows on a daily basis, which is also disclosed to the public. These disclosures are more complete and timely than the quarterly filings by US mutual funds.

If one asks most US hedge fund managers their opinion of such disclosure rules, they universally respond that comparable laws would put them at a severe disadvantage in the market. Specifically, they say they sometimes own positions that they don't want "the Street" to know about because if they had to offset the position, dealers and other traders would exploit them.

That seems to be a logical response, as anonymity in a market is usually an advantage. Yet Brazilian managers seemingly have learned to deal with their rules by being very aware of their position sizes and the underlying liquidity of each asset.

Perhaps the biggest disappointments from the crisis of 2008 and early 2009 were hedge fund managers who erected gates and liquidating trusts because of the often esoteric and illiquid nature of substantial parts of their portfolios. Anonymity did not help the managers find bids in the depths of the crisis. These illiquid positions did, however, cause surprise and dismay among many limited partners who discovered that they could not have their money when they asked for and expected it.

If Brazilian-style disclosure had been in place in the United States, would hedge fund managers have been so eager to build their portfolios with odd and illiquid investments? Many of these investments do not fit well in a liquid trading vehicle and more rightly belong in true illiquid partnerships. The hedge funds that put up gates and liquidating trusts in many cases blurred the lines between the two types of funds. They reached for extra returns by adding illiquid securities, while they simultaneously promised periodic fund liquidity. Such an approach works well in a bull market, but the flaws are revealed at times of crisis. Investors in the United States generally lack enough position detail information to assess these risks independently beforehand.

Not all hedge funds behaved this way. Most of the US managers who avoided liquidity problems in 2008 maintained portfolios that were fundamentally highly liquid. They did so not to conform to regulation, but because they believed it consistent with sound business practice and what they had advertised about their funds. Today those managers enjoy higher regard among their investors because of their ability and willingness to perform as promised.

Another feature of the Brazilian regulatory landscape is that the regulator acts as a clearinghouse for marketing material for *all* funds. Every piece of promotional material is filed with the CVM, collected in the regulator's database, and is freely accessible to anyone interested. The regulator not only monitors sales materials, but also attempts to assure their free and accurate distribution.

In all of the current US discussions of financial regulatory reform and customer protection, nothing remotely like the CVM approach is being proposed to address the issue of accurate customer communications. Investors always have the ultimate responsibility for the evaluation and oversight of their investments, but the CVM has proactively provided a wealth of information for investors that the SEC apparently never has considered organizing.

There should be no misunderstanding about what the CVM regulation can and cannot do. It cannot prevent market losses. Many Brazilian hedge funds suffered equally severe losses as their American counterparts in 2008. But examples of unexpected gates and side pockets in Brazil are rare. Portfolio disappointments will always be part of investing. What the CVM has done is minimize the chance of surprises by demanding much more disclosure than the SEC has ever considered for hedge funds or mutual funds. It seems fair and reasonable then for the US investor to ask, "Which is the developing market, and when might we expect to catch up?"

13.4   INVESTMENT ADVISORS

The Investment Advisers Act of 1940 was not created to eliminate conflicts of interest for advisors, but only to ensure that any conflicts are disclosed. This means that it is perfectly legal for an advisor to recommend an investment where he or she receives compensation from the fund or partnership if a placement gets made as long as the advisor tells the client. These disclosures, and other useful information, are contained in Form ADV, filed annually with the SEC. Part 1 of the ADV contains information that the SEC uses to monitor the advisors and guide its own surveillance activities. Part 2 contains information for the public including a plain English description of their business practices, fees, conflicts of interest and disciplinary history. Investors should spend a lot of time with Part 2 of an advisor's ADV, but few do. "Plain English" does not often translate to "interesting reading," and the scope of the required material is so vast that the document is intimidating to most people.

Clients of registered advisors are supposed to receive Part 2 updates annually. Anyone wishing to investigate an advisor can go to www.advisorinfo.sec.gov for the most recent public ADV information.

The other major part of The Advisers Act is an enumeration of who is exempt from these rules. Securities brokers and dealers are the most obvious exclusion, since they are covered by rules governing securities sales. It was believed that double oversight would be inappropriate and possibly conflicting. More interesting, however, is the complete exclusion of lawyers, accountants, engineers, and teachers, as long as they don't hold themselves out to be advisors and that advising is incidental to their main occupation. One might argue that well intentioned, but poorly trained investment amateurs are exactly the people who should not be acting as advisors, but the framers of the Advisers Act obviously thought otherwise.

In the twenty-first century, the most relevant exclusion in the Advisers Act is the one for publishers. Writers in both traditional and electronic media are exempt as long as their investment advice is general in nature, as compared to specific to a client, is objective versus non-promotional, and is routinely produced instead of written in response to episodic market activity. SEC staff has interpreted one-time publications like books on investment management as being excluded from the Act.

What could not have been contemplated in 1940 was the explosion of both general and highly specific social media outlets where all manner of editorial behavior occurs. Some of the more popular sites, like Seeking Alpha, state that the contributing authors must agree to disclose any positions in securities they are writing about, but there is little that the site provider can do to ensure compliance. Other sites are much more free-for-all and submissions regularly test the concept of promotional.

This is not an argument for expanding the Advisers Act, only a warning to readers of these publications that the author may have a highly biased and potentially conflicted position. Successful snake oil salesmen in the old west sounded highly informed as they moved their questionable wares. What is going on around our trading markets is not all that dissimilar.

Securities brokers and bankers may routinely offer advice to their clients but they are not legally considered advisors. The distinction is important. Brokers operate under *suitability rules*. All they need to be sure of is that the recommended investment is appropriate to the client's circumstances. This contrasts to a *fiduciary responsibility* in which the recommended investment has to be in the client's best interest.

An example will show the difference between suitability and fiduciary standards. A broker trying to sell a share in a wildcat natural gas drilling company to an 85-year-old widow with limited assets would likely be viewed as unsuitable. Few would complain about a recommendation for a low duration, high quality bond fund for that client. That would be suitable.

But which bond fund should the broker recommend? Suppose there were two under consideration. One is a fund sponsored by the broker's company that is sold with a legally allowed sales charge, and the other is a no-load index fund. The investment objectives, duration and credit quality of the underlying holdings are similar in both funds. A broker operating under suitability rules could recommend either as long as all of the features, including fees, were disclosed. A true fiduciary could not recommend the fund with the sales load unless it could be convincingly shown that ultimately the more expensive fund would have better net performance.

There have been rumblings for years that brokers should be held to a fiduciary standard. Not surprisingly, that industry has pushed back to preserve greater flexibility in generating higher fees. Investors should always understand whether the person giving them advice is being held to suitability or fiduciary standards. That is the only way to appreciate and be alert to the potential conflicts that might be coming with the advice.

Many of the largest advisors to individuals and institutions establish platforms for recommended managers. Sometimes these arrangements are constructed as exclusives, suggesting the advisor has secured special access and edge because of the exclusivity. Another typical, and less highlighted, feature of such arrangements is the fee splitting that can occur. The manager on the platform may be giving up a meaningful part of their management fee to the advisor as a condition for the listing. In essence the manager has hired the platform advisor to act as a sales agent to help gather assets.

It is difficult to imagine how one might convincingly meet a fiduciary standard to one's advisory clients if the advisor receives compensation from brokers, fund managers, or service providers for recommending their services or products. This is, in fact, however, how a great deal of advisory business regularly gets done in this country, and it is all allowed under the 1940 Advisers Act if it is disclosed.

There are only two defenses to protect you as an investor. The first is to simply refuse to do business with any advisor that earns income from anyone other than advisory clients. The second, less dramatic step is to regularly ask your advisor to disclose specifics of any fee arrangements associated with any fund recommendations. In that way, and in that way only, can an investor make an informed decision as to whether the recommendation is appropriate to their needs and circumstances or merely suitable and of primary benefit to the advisor.

13.5 SUMMARY

Financial market regulation in the United States is something of a crazy quilt of agencies and rules that has evolved over time in response to market crises. Dodd-Frank in 2010 is the most recent major effort, and at no time in its development was there a serious discussion of creating a modern, more efficient form of regulation. It is a useful exercise to ask why.

There were strong distinctions across markets 150 years ago. Banking was different than securities trading and there was almost complete separation from embryonic futures markets dedicated to grain trading. When market events struck (the bank panic of 1907, the wheat market collapse in 1920, the stock market crash of 1929) there were certainly ripples that affected many parts of the domestic economy, but there was the common belief that the response to these events should be specific and not general.

This in turn led to the Banking Committee in the Senate and the Financial Services Committee in the House to oversee the regulators in some of those areas, but not all. The Agriculture Committees have always overseen the CFTC and its predecessor agencies. Even as futures and options on interest rates, currencies, and stock index products have come to dominate that industry, agricultural specialists hold the final say on how derivatives are regulated. It must have come as something of a surprise to swap dealers and participants that when Congress decided to push a great deal of that industry under a regulatory umbrella as part of Dodd-Frank, it was the CFTC and the agriculture committees that would decide their fate.

This balkanization of regulation is difficult to reverse. Agriculture Committee members in both the House and Senate have more power because the CFTC sits on top of major swaps and derivatives players. Of course many of those same firms interact with the Senate Banking Committee and the House Financial Services Committee. It may be obvious that the various committees in Congress are reluctant to give up power, influence, and access to campaign contributions, but a bigger question concerns why the American public and everyone that is regulated doesn't demand a more thoughtful and efficient approach.

George Stigler won the Nobel Prize in economics in 1982 for a wide range of contributions in price theory and industrial organization. Among his most innovative works include major pieces on the economics of regulation.[8] Stigler effectively rebutted the popular belief that regulation is largely created to improve the public welfare. However noble the motivation legislators and regulators have to introduce a new set of rules, the world quickly divides into two camps. On one side there is a broad and diverse population of potential beneficiaries who are occasionally affected by the rules. On the other side is a concentrated and focused group of firms and individuals who operate continuously in the affected industry, and who have extraordinary incentives to shape the rules through time to their benefit.

This theory of regulators being captured by the regulated parties is a much better predictor of actual behavior than any notion of broad welfare maximization to society. This does not mean that the initial regulation was ill-intended or that there were no

---

[8]Stigler, G.J. (1971). The Theory of Economic Regulation. *Bell Journal Economics and Management Science.* Vol. 2 No. 1, pp. 3-21.

deficiencies that needed some kind of attention. It only says that through time the regulated parties have more energy, focus and incentive to influence the regulation to their advantage, and that has been the experience consistently. The Dodd-Frank legislation was filled with directions to the SEC and the CFTC to promulgate rules to achieve a certain outcome. These directions were often open-ended in terms of actual means to achieve those ends. After the passage of Dodd-Frank the lawyers and lobbyists of the regulated firms were most active in helping shape those rules. There was little focused effort coming from the public at large.

Ask any major financial services firm what they think of the current state of financial regulation in this country and most will say it is an expensive, complicated, and cumbersome mess. But nobody really has much of an incentive to change it. The major firms absorb the expenses arising from regulation as just one more cost of service to somehow be passed along to clients. Minor firms and those wanting to enter the industry are often kept off the playing field by formidable regulatory barriers. In the end the largest players spend the most time and energy to promote a regulatory structure that is far from perfect, but works at least somewhat to the advantage of those who are regulated.

Defrauding investors is bad, a fact that has been known for centuries. Sometimes it is helpful to be specific in prohibitions, for example, articulating that Ponzi scheme frauds are specifically illegal. But too many times, detailed rules simply identify safe harbors for what might otherwise be considered iffy behavior.

Investors should have realistic expectations about their regulatory bodies. That is perhaps a sad statement, but history gives us regular reminders that regulators are largely reactive and not always working every day for the ultimate best interests of investors. And then there are more than a few among our elected officials who are generally hostile toward the institutions that create and trade capital in this country. Those legislators who are too cozy with the regulated entities are easy targets for their anti-market colleagues, who regularly rediscover taxes as a cure to all evils. Transactions taxes are seen as a way to curtail "excess speculation" and to help finance the oversight of the markets and many other social programs. All such tariffs have ever done if they are of any meaningful size is chase investors to untaxed markets or to induce innovation to create equivalent exposures that don't carry the same tax burdens. The history of transactions taxes where they have been tried is one of revenues collected falling well short of expectations and a meaningful deterioration of the affected markets.

Ideally regulations would maximize the chance of fair access to the best prices and information in the market. They would set reasonable capital charges and margin requirements for firms entrusted with client money. They would attempt to limit the chance of insider trading and other forms of market manipulation that if left unchecked would ultimately erode our confidence in the capital formation and trading processes.

At a very high level, the existing regulatory structure attempts to do everything in the preceding paragraph, and to a degree succeeds. But WorldCom and Enron lied about their finances, Bernie Madoff went on for years in his Ponzi scheme, Lehman Brothers didn't really have enough capital for all of the leveraged positions they were dealing with, and insider traders now carefully read court rulings for guidance on what they can get away with. If that is not enough of a reminder why investors need to look out for themselves, there will no doubt be new headlines in the future to add to our lesson book.

CHAPTER 14

Looking Ahead

*M*odern *Portfolio Management* was written to bridge a meaningful gap between the promise of modern portfolio theory in its many forms and the actual delivery of investment results. There are some who have been true believers in the power of academic theory. Following this path has created great wealth for some (mostly fund managers selling this vision of the world) but has also led to some spectacular failures like Long Term Capital Management. Most of this book has been devoted to questioning the most extreme attachment to the theory in order to identify its limitations and to suggest ways to navigate around them in the real world.

As history continues in its inexorable march, so too will the academic finance community, sifting through every new data point as it appears on the Bloomberg screen. Just like the medieval quest to turn lead into gold, smart academicians and practitioners will continue to sort data and theory in an attempt to find the one true answer to the puzzle of successful investing.

Such a quest can have two motivations. The first is grounded in hubris; the second comes from practical greed. There are researchers out there who think that they are meaningfully smarter than the market and that their ability to use powerful mathematics guarantees them a leg up on other market participants. The fact that the previous generation of smart researchers using the best data available to them couldn't find the one true path never seems to cause these people to question their quest. This is where the hubris comes in. They are smarter than everyone before them and it is last night's data point that will reveal the true model.

Physicists and chemists operate effectively like this. Improvements in measurements and gathering data really do reveal facts that were not available to Galileo or Einstein. Science progresses because our ability to see and understand improves over time. Finance may be somewhat like this, but only to a small degree.

It has been said many times in this text that markets are not like repeatable experiments in physics. Consider the question of what happens to the stock market if interest rates move up. One may find thousands of examples of interest rates moving up 50 basis points throughout history, but each of those events happened at a unique moment in time and it was certainly true that not all other relevant variables were held constant. Sometimes the stock market fell as future profits were discounted back at a higher rate and investors sold. Other times equities rallied as interest rates rose in anticipation of improved economic conditions and profits.

There are simply too many potentially relevant variables to produce a precise answer to the question, "If interest rates increase 50 basis points next quarter, how will the stock market move?" Accordingly, finance professionals grab as many variables as they can for as long a period as they have data, and then typically look at a regression relationship in order to find out *on average* how history has behaved.

It is a very different statement to say what the average behavior was in the past versus predicting what will happen the very next time the trigger event occurs. Recall that in the first 20 or so years the original league of the winner of the Super Bowl (NFC good, AFC bad) seemed to predict the direction of the US stock market that calendar year. It worked until it stopped and now people look for other equally unrelated variables to predict the market and the Super Bowl.

Modern finance professors are much too sophisticated about probability and statistics to be taken in by obviously spurious relationships between the outcomes of football games and the direction of the stock markets. They are not, however, always as careful when they are looking at a collection of variables that look as if they might logically be connected. This is where hubris does the most damage.

These researchers believe there is a solution out there to be discovered. When one seemingly appears, it is not always looked at with the same critical eye used to discredit football predictions. Instead the scientists, anxious to finally be holding the truth, proclaim their discovery, either through an academic paper or the start of a new fund, and sometimes both.

The potential mistake here is known as a *type I error* in statistics. There are two competing hypotheses. The first is called the *null hypothesis*, which says there is no relationship between the variables in question. The second hypothesis is that there is a meaningful relationship. Researchers work to set up tests so they can reject the null hypothesis with a high degree of confidence. But there is always some small probability that the null hypothesis is rejected even when it is true.

When a researcher says their statistics show a 99% probability that a meaningful investment relationship exists, they also implicitly say there is a 1% chance that the null hypothesis of no relationship is true even though they are rejecting it.

From an investor's perspective, 99% sounds like a pretty reassuring level of confidence. Markets are rarely that highly predictable, but unless we understand all the various tests that have been done by the researcher; we cannot possibly put that figure into the right context. What if the researcher looked at 1,000 different combinations of market variables? If the null hypothesis of no relationship were absolutely true, 10 of these tests (1%) would *appear* to show a meaningful statistical relationship completely by random accident.

The researcher might then have selected the strongest of the tests, or perhaps the one that made the most sense intuitively after the fact, and built the case around that. An academically rigorous researcher would then seek to acquire more data, sometimes called *out-of-sample testing*, and see if the relationship was robust. But such data is not always available so the case is presented and then only checked again years later with new regressions. Or an ongoing check occurs in real time with other people's money.

The activity of sifting through mountains of information looking for statistically significant relationships is known as *data mining*, and it generally is widely criticized. Most researchers would protest that their efforts do not qualify for such a label. It is just that sorting out the best models requires a lot of study. For the potential investor evaluating a fund manager that has less hubris but more greed, the worst kind of data mining is almost always a meaningful risk.

Regulators require some pretty strict disclosures to accompany any presentation of *pro forma* or model-based results. This doesn't stop the manager who is trying to raise funds from placing the "scientific" findings in the best possible light, or backing up the pitch with references to academic papers that may themselves offer spurious results.

Some in the academic finance community are starting to push back against these practices. Harvey, Liu, and Zhu (2015) carefully showed how the standard test statistics are only valid where there is not an environment of multiple models being run on the same data.[1] Given that most researchers "shop" different approaches in their testing of hypotheses, the criteria used to reject the null hypotheses of no effect are usually set too low. The authors conclude boldly by asserting, "most claimed research findings in financial economics are likely false."[2]

Other finance professionals and practitioners are developing new tests to check on the old practices that Harvey et al. question.[3] These are important steps in the practice of financial economics and portfolio management. Many times it takes stronger science to change the world, and not just a child's voice to say that the emperor has no clothes.

While the chance of some breakthrough piece of analysis being able to consistently add extraordinary returns to a portfolio is small, it is still possible. This motivates the searchers. Most investors reading this book rarely get to participate in the earliest stages of a profitable trading program. These rare models are usually applied using insider and proprietary funds first.

This was exactly the pattern followed by the earliest arbitrageurs between cash bonds and their futures markets, options market makers, and those who trade between stock ETFs and their underlying indexes. Market inefficiencies do occur periodically, usually around the introduction of some evolutionary expansion of trading vehicles. When that happens, those most technologically and intellectually gifted gather private capital in order to exploit the opportunity.

Outsized profits can result, at least for a while. Those profits attract other entrants into the market and competition shrinks the returns. When most of the easiest fruit has been picked from the trees, then it is time to advertise the previous track record to attract the outside capital that can generate a new stream of income, but this time from fees. Sadly, the best those outside investors should expect is a normal risk-adjusted rate of return, less the fees they pay the manager.

This pattern of fund evolution also can occur after a major market dislocation. The 2007–2008 market crisis provided many examples where credit spreads blew out to such extremes that there were unusually attractive opportunities for those who had, and were willing to deploy, risk capital. Among the wreckage of failed banks and other financial firms were many skilled and honest traders looking for new homes. Some of these teams were picked up to oversee the trading of proprietary capital.

It was not an unusual story for some of those firms to then launch new funds open to outside investors a year or two after the major scores, using the track record of the proprietary trades as evidence of the team's skill. Every fund that does this is quite careful to state that the environment has changed and that future returns might not replicate the past. However, potential investors are still left with the powerful

[1]Campbell R.H., Liu, Y. and Zhu, H. (2015) and The Cross-Section of Expected Returns. SSRN.
[2]Ibid
[3]Lopez de Prado, M. (2015). Quantitative Meta-Strategies. *Practical Applications*. Spring.

impression that comes from outsized earnings, even if they and other outsiders did not earn them.

Imitation is the greatest form of flattery. If there is some "special sauce" in a public investment fund, other fund managers will quickly see that and attempt to duplicate it. That is the biggest problem with purely quantitative fund management advances. There are no barriers to entry and the more people that follow a model the less likely it is to produce superior returns.

The other great enemy to extraordinary success is size. Massive sovereign wealth funds and public pension plans that are responsible for investing hundreds of billions of dollars in assets face extraordinary challenges. CALPERS at one point had a hedge fund portfolio with more than $4 billion in assets, a large number by any objective standard. But compared with more than $400 billion in total assets, hedge funds barely moved the needle. CALPERS made headlines when it announced it was getting out of the space, and many commentators suggested that this was a sign that the best years for the hedge fund industry in the past. A more realistic explanation is that hedge fund due diligence and oversight consumed a lot of resources at CALPERS that could not be practically justified for a 1% allocation. CALPERS' decision was less likely a reflection of their expectations for risk-adjusted returns and much more an acknowledgment that the costs of the program were high. Building the investment further to a meaningful scale was going to be even more complicated and costly.

The one undeniable global trend is that these institutional asset pools will continue to grow. That is the power of compounding. Just because the funds are larger does not mean that their trustees or professional staff have gotten smarter. If anything they are operating under the added constraints that come with their size.

Logic says it will be increasingly difficult for such massive pools of capital to achieve extraordinary returns. And yet, like the hopeful academic looking for the long-elusive quantitative solution, optimism dominates the process. Performance is heavily benchmarked and many compensation schemes are based on how much alpha the fund generates.

In such an environment, the investment management industry develops products to meet the demand if not always successful in fulfilling the promise. Stay around the industry long enough and an important pattern can be observed:

- A new approach or product is launched with great promise.
- Early adapters may or may not receive a return edge relative to the risks they assume.
- Any effort that shows apparent success will be marketed heavily, gathering impressive amounts of assets.
- The activity gathers enough assets to diminish any edge that once existed, or worse, creates imbalances that can lead to bubble-like situations and outcomes.
- The next new approach appears.

This process is sometimes aided by recommendations from institutional consultants who are always looking for ways to add value to their client portfolios. This is a tricky business in that these institutions are often fairly conservative in their evolutions. If a consultant pushes a highly innovative approach that has a short track record, there is the risk that if it fails, then the entire consultant relationship could be jeopardized.

This is another example of where by waiting a while to see whether the innovation shows promise, the investor increases the chance that they will be sitting down at the table just as the after-dinner mints are being served. But for both the organizations and their consultants, it appears that being wrong with a lot of fellow sufferers is a preferred outcome to taking a lonely, but higher probability, chance for success.

Portfolio insurance was perhaps the best example of this in the 1980s. The 1990s had heavily structured derivatives, major pushes into EM equities, and highly leveraged relative value hedge funds. The first decade of the twenty-first century brought excesses in mortgage-backed securities and other structured products and derivatives that were great enough to create one of the most significant financial crises in the country's history. The list of "investments du jour" is much longer and more varied than this, but the basic pattern is remarkably consistent.

Which of the most popular investment products today will likely fall by the wayside and be replaced by another crop of clever ideas? Chances are good they will share some or all of these characteristics:

- Promise of enhanced returns.
- Promise of reduced risk.
- Reality of fees tilted in favor of the manager.

This is too pessimistic a place to end this book. In many ways the strides in portfolio management over several decades have improved our investment performance in profound ways. The array of efficient investment tools available to us has never been greater. The opportunity to execute a plan cheaply and quickly is impressively large. In most ways managing the modern portfolio is today far superior to what was possible in previous generations.

The challenge is not to fall into the many behavioral traps along the way. Believe in the general principles of portfolio construction and diversification, but don't lean too hard on the analytics setting the framework. We want to believe in the accuracy of all of our beliefs and model assumptions, but the reality is that they are statistical guesses with wide potential for dispersion. Failure to keep that one fact in front of mind over the last 50 years has produced more havoc in markets, portfolios, and occasionally economies than any other single factor.

While you consider all the things that can go right from an investment approach, don't forget to ask what can go wrong. Don't follow the herd into the next investment miracle product before you are confident that it isn't a holding pen to a slaughterhouse. None of these bits of advice come from a solution to a modern portfolio theory model. They all evolve from MPT principles but include careful additions about factors outside the model. Successful investment acknowledges behavioral biases and does not allow them to defeat good decision-making.

If this book has left you with anything, I hope it has convinced you that successful portfolios can be constructed and maintained for generations. But it is not a mechanical process that either you or experts can put on autopilot. Markets and investors change, but sound long-term investment principles do not. By staying true to the basics and not being overwhelmed by the marketing hype from the investment industry, you can plot a sound course. Between growing economies and asset markets and the power of compounding, those who stay true to this course can achieve remarkable results for their families and institutions.

CHAPTER 15

10 Lessons

There are many thoughtful people who believe that investing can be distilled into a science, and all that is really necessary for success is enough knowledge and discipline. Rather than just point to 30 years or more of history where this approach has failed, sometimes spectacularly, this book has tried to explain why investing is not a neat science and any attempt to make it so is flawed. To do so required covering many bases. Foundations were established. Competing approaches were discussed. Shortcomings were identified, and then the difficult part of building an investment portfolio was developed. Investment and operational due diligence form just the first steps. In a dynamic world, the process of evaluating investment themes is ongoing, but understanding a theme is not the same as identifying the best way to exploit it.

If you have made it all the way to this point in the narrative, you have covered a lot of territory. While there are many specific ideas throughout the book, this chapter summarizes the main messages. It would have been possible to start the book with this list. If that had been the organization, hopefully these lessons would have sounded correct coming right out of the blocks. By putting them at the end, however, they should do more than just sound right. They should be firmly supported by everything that has come before and they should *make fundamental sense*. Use them as a guide map along your investment travels.

1. **"Don't run with the crowd" and "Extraordinary results are never accomplished by conventional thinking" are adages about human behavior**

   They are roughly the equivalent of messages like "Eat more fruits and vegetables" and "Try to exercise regularly." While following such advice is probably a good idea, it is not enough. There are countless ways to lose money unconventionally and a diet completely dedicated to fruit and vegetables will not necessarily ensure your health.

   This book was designed to help you set realistic investment goals and identify the best game plan to meet them. Along the way you will be equipped to question both conventional and innovative approaches in productive ways. You don't have to be perfect to be successful. We are all humans with human failings. **By following a careful and skeptical path, most people can become better investors.**

2. There is no simple answer

Investment managers and advisors often try to claim they have discovered the one secret to investing. It doesn't exist. Sifting through historical data for patterns identifies mostly what worked in the past. When too many people try to apply it to the future, whatever relationship might have been present goes away or even reverses. Markets are driven by people's behavior. They are not systems governed by laws of nature. **If there really were a secret, nobody would share it with you.**

3. The risk-free rate is the place where everything begins

The most enduring lesson of all of modern portfolio theory is that risk matters, and that you should expect to be rewarded for assuming greater market risk. This spectrum begins with the risk-free rate of interest, which in most countries is highly influenced if not outright set by the central banking authorities. If the Federal Reserve artificially sets the risk-free rate at zero instead of a more normal positive rate in a growing economy, the expected return for every asset class is lowered. **Managers who build on the risk-free rate, or any other asset class' expected return, need to be evaluated versus the likely environment going forward and not some abstract or historical record.**

4. Historical averages are almost useless

Too much time is spent examining past data. When a central bank fixes the risk-free rate at zero, looking at what historic yield curves did in more normal times conveys little of relevance. If a new 10-year T-note yields 2% today, but the historical average 10-year return for this type of investment is 4.5%, your returns will not miraculously revert to the mean if you buy this note. Unless you think you should put your portfolio on autopilot for 20 years (and you shouldn't) the most relevant information in historical returns data involves how asset classes can move together. The best data in this instance is not revealed in averages, but by observing episodes of extreme movements like market crashes or liquidity crises. Historical month-to-month or annual volatility is not risk. A permanent loss of purchasing power is risk, and once an investment goes to zero, no amount of future asset class compounding will get you out of the hole. A corollary to this lesson involves information provided by managers: no prospective investor being sold a new fund has ever seen a bad back test. **Data collected over 30, 50, or even 100 years are not going to tell you what the next few quarters or years will bring.**

5. In countries with subdued inflation, there seems to be something magical to investors about a 10% return

10% is not a psychological anchor, but instead has a real foundation. If a portfolio grows at 10% in an environment of 2–3% inflation, the investments can provide a meaningful and sustainable contribution to current spending and cover the costs of investing without diminishing the purchasing power of the corpus. Managers know this and it is not surprising that they play upon it in designing products. A fund offering 1% per month may sound attractive until you discover that the underlying investments are risky enough to warrant a 2% per month expected return and the manager is keeping half of the returns through fees and expenses. **It is the investor's responsibility to evaluate the manager's claims going forward to see if they are (1) realistic and (2) provide enough net compensation to the investor for the risks inherent in the structure.**

6. Relative performance is of limited value

If you *know* you are going to place a bet on the Kentucky Derby, then relative performance is all that matters. But the bigger question should be whether you are going to place a bet on that race or not. Investing is exactly the same with study after study showing that allocations across asset classes and not relative performance within those classes explain the lion's share of investment success or failure. Moreover, a manager's relative outperformance in the past has limited predictive ability for future results. Too many managers are added to portfolios after they have outperformed for themselves or other early investors. Too many managers are also terminated for a period of relative underperformance that may have been highly likely given their investment style and risk exposures. **Many managers out there might beat an index over many market cycles, but they are rare and you need to have confidence and patience with them to be successful.**

7. At times of crisis, don't try to be too clever

There have been many episodes in our lifetime of market dislocations somewhere in the world. There will be more of these events in our future. The reasons behind these may vary (see Lesson 9) but the common factor is that they always present a great emotional challenge. Who wants to invest at a time of crisis? But these times offer up a rare "fat pitch" to the investors who can analyze the situation and get the bat off their shoulders. When this happens the best tactic is to execute a simple game plan that might capture 90+% of a potential return quickly and cheaply, perhaps through an index fund or ETF. Too many investors are lured into complex private structures that sound like they could earn 120% of that same potential but by their nature can take so long to execute that a meaningful part of the dislocation may have gone away before the money is fully invested. The credit crisis of 2007–2008 is a prime example of this. If you got basic, low-cost, long-only exposure to credit in the second quarter of 2009 you fared much better than if you went into highly ambitious hedge fund and private equity style partnerships. While these funds had great promise to get every advantage out of the deals in the portfolios, their structures usually meant capital wasn't put to work until the second half of 2009 or even into 2010, long after the fattest pitches had crossed the plate. **In investing, like many aspects of life, the quest for the ideal can be the enemy of achieving excellence.**

8. Liquidity is virtuous – to a degree

After the bull market of the 1990s, many investors were seduced into long lockup investments that offered the promise of slightly better returns. The theory said that thanks to the power of compound interest, even a small edge would ultimately produce a major return advantage. Because more money went into this space than could be profitably absorbed early in the twenty-first century, most of those investors enjoyed neither superior returns nor liquidity. In a reaction to this, some of those investors abandoned private partnerships, even in areas where they offered fine opportunities after adjusting for the illiquidity. Attitudes against illiquid investments were further crystalized when some hedge funds imposed gates and other restrictions on their funds after the credit crisis of 2008. **There are probably liquidity limits below which an investor does not want to fall, but a strict prohibition on illiquid investments likely eliminates many solid opportunities that cannot be properly expressed in liquid vehicles.**

9. At the root of every big investment mess is leverage, fraud, or both

There will always be ups and downs in any market as investors try to allocate capital toward opportunity and away from risk. But there are times when markets come unglued and there is not enough capital in the hands of rational investors to quickly restore a reasonable equilibrium. These are market bubbles and for as long as anyone has analyzed them, there have been two contributing factors: fraud or leverage. Frauds are almost always found eventually, either through a clever discovery or through the deception collapsing under its own weight. Nonfraudulent bubbles can rarely form into something menacing without leverage. The popping of these bubbles can be triggered by increases in supply large enough to swamp leveraged demand, or through the restriction of credit that causes optimistic buyers to no longer be able to support their leveraged purchases. Defense against fraud comes from thorough due diligence to try to avoid those potential situations and then diversification of investments, so that if investors are touched by fraud the impact will be limited. Investors should shun areas operating with great leverage and popularity while being viewed as so different from history that the old leverage rules don't apply. **At the time when the majority of investors are least concerned about a fraud or a market crash is when the successful investor asks the most questions.**

10. Risk is ultimately not volatility but the permanent loss of capital

Much of modern portfolio theory relies on the equation of risk and measured volatility. They are certainly related, but true long-term risk comes from investment blow-ups, frauds, and ill-timed sell decisions after a loss. By having strong due diligence, frauds and blow-ups can be minimized. Low-risk assets as a margin of safety keep market events from forcing bad sales. Self-control over behavioral biases reduces the chance of emotional sales. **Careful portfolio construction and a level head allow compounding to progress over long periods of time, including intervals of heightened volatility. These are the ultimate determinants of investment success.**

There is a final point that is not so much a lesson as a reminder. The themes contained in Fred Schwed, Jr.'s 1940 classic book, *Where Are the Customers' Yachts?* are as true today as they were then and probably 100 years before. Compensation structures are always set up to be generous to the sellers of the product or service. The basic rule of the financial services industry is that the client provides their capital to risk activities in an asymmetric way. If profits are made, they are net of expenses and sometimes performance fees. If there are losses, the client pays them all plus the expenses. The manager sometimes apologizes. Stated this coldly, managers would rarely generate any new business, so instead they emphasize the partnership aspect of what they are selling. Everyone looks like a good partner in a bull market, but the true partners are revealed by the quality of their behavior during times of crisis. Find these people and stick with them. That will give you the best chance to have your own yacht.

This final paragraph is not so much a lesson as it is a few words of advice. Know what you want to achieve with your investments and how much risk you are comfortable taking. Make sure your investment time horizon is consistent with your ability to make careful decisions. Not every person or organization is the same in this regard. If it takes six months for a committee to make an allocation decision, they should not try to time ins and outs from the market. Only investors who are mentally prepared for a large number of losing trades and possess an ability to move past those losses without emotion should do short-term trading. Most of us don't have these traits and our investment horizon should be longer. Never forget that noise is an ever-present element of markets. Not every price change has permanent or profound meaning. If this bothers you, don't watch. By having a well-considered plan and the discipline to stick to it through good times and bad, you will find success. In a growing economy, markets want to go up. Long-term winning portfolios take advantage of this bias and separate themselves from the pack of impatient and emotion-driven investors.

Abbreviations

ABS	Asset-Backed Securities
AIMR	Association for Investment Management and Research
AMEX	American Stock Exchange
AML	Anti-money Laundering
AP	Authorized Participant
BDC	Business Development Company
BIS	Bank for International Settlements
CAPM	Capital Asset Pricing Model
CBOE	Chicago Board Options Exchange
CDO	Collateralized Debt Obligation
CDS	Credit Default Swap
CFTC	Commodity Futures Trading Commission
CLO	Collateralized Loan Obligation
CME	Chicago Mercantile Exchange
CPI	Consumer Price Index
CPO	Commodity Pool Operator
CTA	Commodity Trading Advisor
DB	Defined Benefit Plan
DC	Defined Contribution Plan
ESG	Environmental, Social, and Governance
ETF	Exchange-Traded Fund
ETN	Exchange-Traded Note
ETP	Exchange-Traded Product
FAS 157	Financial Accounting Standards Board Bulletin 157
FDIC	Federal Deposit Insurance Corporation
FINRA	Financial Industry Regulatory Authority
GIPS	Global Investment Performance Standards
GSCI	Goldman Sachs Commodity Index
GSE	Government-Sponsored Enterprise
HFT	High-Frequency Trading
ICE	Intercontinental Exchange
IPO	Initial Public Offering
IRR	Internal Rate of Return
ISDA	International Swaps and Derivatives Association
LOR	Leland O'Brien Rubenstein Associates
LTCM	Long-Term Capital Management
MAR	Minimum Accepted Return
MIV	Microfinance Investment Vehicle

MLP	Master Limited Partnership
MOIC	Multiple of Invested Capital
MPT	Modern Portfolio Theory
NAV	Net Asset Value
NASDAQ	National Association of Securities Dealers Automated Quotations
NFA	National Futures Association
NLY	Ticker Symbol for Annaly Capital Management
NPV	Net Present Value
NYSE	New York Stock Exchange
OCC	Office of the Comptroller of the Currency
REIT	Real Estate Investment Trust
RIA	Registered Investment Advisor
SEC	Securities and Exchange Commission
SRI	Socially Responsible Investing
SRO	Self-Regulatory Organization
TARP	Troubled Assets Relief Program
TINA	There Is No Alternative
UBTI	Unrelated Business Taxable Income

Glossary in Modern Portfolio Management

'40 Act funds   The formal name for mutual funds in the United States, these are investment products organized and distributed according to rules established by the Investment Company Act of 1940 and subsequent amendments.

Ability to pay   The capacity of a borrower to fulfill the interest and capital payment obligations of a loan or bond. Contrasted to Willingness to Pay.

ABS, see Asset-backed securities

Absolute value   The objective of earning a specific rate of return independent of the movement of the stock market or other underlying market.

Active share   The percentage of a fund's returns that is independent of the movement of an underlying benchmark index. Index funds have a zero active share by construction.

Activism   A strategy of fund investing where attempts are made to influence the behavior of a company's management to increase shareholder value. This is usually done through private and public communications and in the extreme through proxy contests for the control of the board.

ADV   Form ADV is the uniform filing used by investment advisors to register with both the Securities and Exchange Commission (SEC) and state securities authorities. It contains information about the investment advisor's business, ownership, clients, employees, business practices, affiliations, and any disciplinary events of the advisor or its employees. The SEC primarily uses it for regulatory purposes, though the information contained therein is available to the public.

ADV, Part II   Part II of Form ADV is a narrative brochure written in plain English that contains information such as the types of advisory services offered, the advisor's fee schedule, disciplinary information, conflicts of interest, and the educational and business background of management and key advisory personnel of the advisor. The brochure is the primary disclosure document that investment advisors provide to their clients.

Advertising   Virtually any communication by a fund manager or advisor, beyond replies to specific client inquiries, is considered advertising by the SEC and other regulators and is subject to rules governing content and disclosure.

Agency mortgage-backed securities   Securities based on pools of mortgages guaranteed by Fannie Mae, Freddie Mac, or Ginnie Mae.

AIMR, see Association for Investment Management and Research

Air pocket   A term describing a sudden change in a securities price, usually down, when a large attempt to sell is met with demand only well below the last price.

Alpha short   A short position established to profit from specific events or news about the company being sold short. This is in contrast to hedge shorts that are established to protect against a general downturn in a sector or the market as a whole.

Alpha, sources of   Alpha is profit that accrues above returns attributable to broader gains in an index. Alpha may arise from having superior information, better judgment or analysis, or lower execution costs. Active managers generally claim to have ability to create sustained alpha, though it is rare in practice.

Alternative investment   A generic labeling of investments that goes beyond traditional cash, stock, bond, and real estate holdings. In the twenty-first century, many investments called alternatives have become increasingly mainstream.

American-style option   An option that may be exercised at any time before expiration.

AML, see Anti-money laundering

Anchoring   The behavioral trait of maintaining an opinion once formed, despite the appearance of contrary evidence.

Angel investor   Among the earliest venture capital providers to a new enterprise, called angels because without their presence the firm might never exist. Typically they have the greatest upside potential if the enterprise is successful, but they also face the greatest chance of a total loss.

Annuity   Investment products designed to provide a steady flow of income over the life of the instrument. Often sold through insurance companies as part of an overall wealth management program.

Anti-money laundering (AML)   Anti-money laundering (AML) refers to a set of procedures, laws, and regulations designed to prevent criminals from disguising illegally obtained funds as legitimate income. Enforcement is by examining the procedures of financial firms that are responsible for determining that transactions through them are not aiding or abetting the illegal transfer of money.

AP, see Authorized Participant

Arbitrage bands   The potential price spread between two related markets determined by the transactional costs of buying and selling in each to execute an arbitrage trade. Prices outside the arbitrage bands should offer an opportunity for a risk-free, profitable trade.

Arbitrage pricing theory   A fundamental tenet of modern finance that says the market price of two equivalent positions should be the same. Violation of this rule would produce greater than the risk-free rate of return for essentially a riskless position.

Articles of incorporation   The articles of incorporation outline the governance of a corporation along with the corporate bylaws and the corporate statutes in the state where articles of incorporation are filed. They typically include the name of the corporation, the type of corporate structure (e.g. profit corporation, nonprofit corporation, or other form), the registered agent, the number of authorized shares, and the effective date of the articles. For a limited liability company (LLC) the parallel document is called the articles of organization.

Asset-backed securities (ABS)   Asset-backed securities, called ABS, are bonds or notes backed by financial assets. Typically these assets consist of receivables other than mortgage loans, such as credit card receivables, auto loans, manufactured-housing contracts, and home-equity loans.

At-the-money   An option that has its exercise price equal to the current underlying price.

Auction rate securities   Auction rate securities are long-dated debt or preferred equity securities that have interest rates that are periodically reset through auctions, typically every 7, 14, 28, or 35 days. The reset provision led many investors to believe they were a substitute for money market funds and other liquid securities. This market largely collapsed in February 2008 when disruptions in the credit market led to insufficient bids to set the next interest rate. Holders of these auction rate securities were then stuck with long-dated, illiquid securities with variable credit quality.

Audit   Audits are typically done for both investment instruments like mutual funds and partnerships and the companies that manage them. Fund audits are essential to confirm the reasonableness of the value of investment holdings and the completeness of cash flowing into or out of the fund. Management company audits only confirm the business financials of the firm.

Authorized participant (AP)   An authorized participant is typically a large institutional investor, such as a broker-dealer, that enters into a contract with an ETF to allow it to create or redeem shares directly with the fund. Many parties can buy or sell ETFs, but only APs are authorized to create or redeem new shares.

Autocorrelation   Autocorrelation measures the degree of similarity between a given time series and a lagged version of itself over successive time intervals. Also called serial correlation.

Background check   Part of the due diligence process in which the work, education, and regulatory history of a firm's principals are reviewed. These can vary from an examination of public records to a deep probing by trained investigators.

Balanced fund   Traditional mutual funds that combine stocks and bonds in a way designed to meet all of an investor's need. Typically a retail product aimed at less sophisticated investors.

Bank deposit   The most basic form of institutional cash in an investor's portfolio, and an immediate source of liquidity.

Bank for International Settlements (BIS)   Owned by central banks and monetary authorities, the Bank for International Settlements (BIS) was established in 1930 in Basel, Switzerland as a result of The Hague Agreements, an international treaty designed to foster international cooperation across central banks and to provide clearing and settlement services among those banks.

Bank loan   The basic asset for commercial banks. Today, bank loans of meaningful size are often securitized or sold to other investors allowing banks to better diversify their asset base.

Barbell   A position in fixed income instruments consisting of short maturities and long maturities, with no exposure to the intermediate part of the yield curve.

Basis risk   Prices between two markets that are differentiated by time, quality, or geography is known as the basis. Change in the basis creates risk for traders buying in one market and selling in the other.

BDC, see Business Development Company

Bear call spread   A combination of long and short call positions that is expected to profit with declining prices of the underlying.

Behavioral finance   An evolving specialty in financial economics that incorporates many elements of psychology to help explain deviations away from totally rational economic behavior.

Belly of the curve   A colloquial term for intermediate maturities along the yield curve.

Beta   The sensitivity of any financial instrument or investment strategy to a relevant benchmark index.

Bid ask spread   The difference between the highest price buyers are bidding (bid) and the lowest price being offered by sellers (ask).

Binomial option pricing model   A guide to valuing options that assumes the next price change of the underlying can only be one of two possible outcomes.

BIS, see Bank for International Settlements

Black box   A trading program with so little communication that it is impossible for the investor to determine the sources of return or risk.

Black-Scholes option pricing model   The pioneering approach developed by Fisher Black and Myron Scholes that used arbitrage pricing theory to estimate the fair value of an option relative to the price of the underlying security and other relevant market factors.

Bond   A form of borrowing that promises to repay capital plus interest over the life of the bond. Superior in the capital structure to equity but subordinate to loans.

Break the buck   The event when a money market mutual fund revalues its NAV below $1.00 because the underlying assets in the fund can no longer support that value.

Break-even inflation rate   The rate of inflation that produces identical total returns for inflation-adjusted and traditional bonds.

Bull call spread   A combination of long and short call positions that is expected to profit with rising prices of the underlying.

Bullet   A fixed income portfolio consisting of bonds of similar maturities.

Bullet bond   Noncallable bonds where the entire principle is paid on the maturity date.

Business Development Company (BDC)   A private or publicly traded specialty direct lender.

Buy-out fund   Private partnership that specializes in acquiring a controlling interest in a company for the purpose of restructuring the firm or altering its business practices with the goal being a profitable sale in the future.

Calendar spread   In futures and forward contracts, any combination of long and short positions with different maturities. In options, a combination of a long and short call, or short and long put, that is based on different option months. The strike prices may be the same or different.

Call option   An option that gives its holder the right to buy the underlying instrument at an agreed upon price for a determined period of time.

Call protected   A bond that may not be called by the issuer for a defined period of time.

Callability   Feature of a security that allows the issuer to redeem the security prior to maturity by calling it in, or forcing the holder to sell it back.

Callable step-up bonds   A bond that is callable by the issuer according to a schedule. If the bond is not called by any given step-up date, the interest paid on that bond is increased according to the same schedule.

Called capital   The amount of a limited partner's committed capital that has been called by the general partner during the investment period to fund specific projects.

Cap rate   The typical measure of a real estate investment's price. It is the rate of return on a real estate investment property based on the income that the property is expected to generate. Low cap rates imply high market prices for any given stream of rental income.

Capital Asset Pricing Model   The capital asset pricing model is a model that describes the relationship between systematic risk and expected return for assets. It is one of the key foundations for modern portfolio theory.

Capital market line   In a mean variance optimization, the line between the risk-free rate of return and the tangent point on the efficient frontier, where the slope is the Sharpe Ratio. When leverage is allowed in the portfolio, the capital market line extends out beyond the frontier to portfolios with higher expected return and volatility.

Capital structure arbitrage   A strategy that evaluates the relative values of different elements of a firm's cap structure and attempts to profit by buying relatively undervalued pieces while selling those that are overvalued.

Capitalization structure   The various sources of a firm's capital from loans at the most senior end to equity at the least.

Carry-forward curve   The situation where forward or futures prices trade at a premium to the cash, or spot price, producing a positive carry for someone holding a long position through time.

Carry trade   A trade that is expected to generate positive income if the price of the underlying instrument remains unchanged.

Cash contract   As opposed to a futures or forward contract, an agreement for prompt delivery.

Cash movements   The transfer of funds arising from the purchase and sale of investments within a fund or portfolio. An area deserving of close scrutiny and regular reconciliation.

Cat Bond   Specialty bonds used to finance the issuance of catastrophic insurance policies. Typically for wind, water, or earthquake damage though other risks can be covered.

Caveat emptor   Latin for "Let the Buyer Beware."

CDO, see Collateralized Debt Obligation

CDS, see credit default swap

CFTC, see Commodity Futures Trading Commission

Churn   The illegal act of a broker buying and selling large numbers of securities in a customer account to generate trading commissions.

Circuit breakers   An intricate schedule of rules to coordinate trading halts across stock, futures, and options markets at times of considerable volatility. Arose after the 1987 stock market crash when communication among closely related markets was found to be substandard, adding to the market stress.

Clearinghouse   An entity organized to match and process trades of buyers and sellers on a cash securities, futures, or options exchange. Usually an independent organization or a division of an exchange.

CLO, see Collateralized Loan Obligation

Closed end mutual fund   A '40 Act mutual fund that has a fixed number of shares and typically trades in real time on an organized exchange. The market price of a closed-end fund can trade at a discount or premium to its underlying NAV depending on market sentiment.

Club Deal   Typically a private equity transaction where two or more GPs act cooperatively to establish a bid for the company, fund the purchase, and oversee the entity until the investment is finally realized.

Co-investments   Funds from LPs on a company-by-company basis to augment GP transactions in those companies. Typically they reduce GP fund risk while providing LPs the opportunity to expand their private partnership investment in a concentrated way while, typically, paying much lower or no fees.

Collared position   A position in a security linked with options to create both upper and lower bounds to its price movements.

Collateral   Capital pledged by a borrower to secure a loan. Collateral is also posted by leveraged investors to secure performance.

Collateralized debt obligation (CDO)   A financial structure that is collateralized by a pool of debt securities like bonds, mortgages, auto loans, or the like. The CDO is divided into tranches that assigns priority of both capital and interest payments ranking from the most senior and safest tranche to the equity tranche responsible for the first losses to the pool.

Collateralized loan obligation (CLO)   A specialized CDO backed by a diversified pool of bank loans.

Collectibles   A broad category of investment assets including art, rare books, autographs, historic artifacts, sports memorabilia, and anything else that strikes a human's fancy.

Collective risk   The chance of a sudden, large price move caused by quickly changing attitudes or preferences by a major share of market participants.

Commercial mortgage REITs   Specialized real estate investment trusts that exclusively own commercial mortgages as their asset base.

Commercial mortgage-backed securities (CMBS)   Securitized pools of mortgages collateralized by commercial properties like office buildings, apartments, malls, warehouses, and hotels.

Commission recapture   The activity where part of a commission for a stock sale or purchase is rebated back to the investment manager initiating the trade.

Committed capital   The amount an investor identifies in private partnership subscription documents as their contractually obligated investment to be called at the discretion of the general partner.

Commodities   A broad category of investment opportunities that includes storable and nonstorable foods, industrial and precious metals, and energy products.

Commodity fund   A specialty fund that invests in commodities, usually through the use of exchange traded futures and options, but sometimes through the physical possession of the underlying assets.

Commodity Futures Trading Commission (CFTC)   The CFTC was created in 1974 as the federal regulator successor to the Grain Futures Administration. It is the counterpart to the SEC responsible for the oversight of futures, options on futures and indexes, and most swaps.

Commodity pool operator (CPO)   An individual or organization that solicits funds for and operates a commodity pool. A commodity pool is an enterprise in which funds contributed by a number of persons are combined for the purpose of trading futures or options on futures, retail off-exchange forex contracts, or swaps, or to invest in another commodity pool.

Commodity trading advisor (CTA)   An individual or organization that, for compensation or profit, advises others, directly or indirectly, as to the value of or the advisability of trading futures contracts, options on futures, retail off-exchange forex contracts or swaps.

Completion fund   A specialty fund that is designed to offset any meaningful divergence between an investor's portfolio and a target benchmark index.

Compliance manual   An internal document that spells out allowed and disallowed procedures and employee behavior at a fund manager or investment advisor.

Compound annualized return   The standard method for displaying returns for an investment of longer than one year. It is the rate, which if continuously compounded, that would reflect the return on invested capital for the holding period.

Compound return   The return from an investment that assumes any distributions of dividends or interest are reinvested at the time they are made.

Consols   Interest-only bonds with no maturity date. Perpetual debt.

Consumer price index (CPI)   A measure of inflation based on a typical basket of consumption goods including housing, food, entertainment, clothing, energy, transportation, and education.

Continuous   The property of price changes that flow from one level to the next with no gaps or jumps. Continuous prices imply that some level of trading can occur at every possible price.

Convertible bond   A hybrid security with properties of both stocks and bonds. Typically pays a coupon and has a fixed maturity, but is convertible into an equity share if the stock price reaches a designated trigger price.

Convexity   The property of nonlinear changes in a bond's price with respect to changes in interest rates.

Core real estate fund Private partnerships with assets consisting of a portfolio of fully developed and leased properties with little or no leverage. Designed more for steady income flows than for capital appreciation potential.

Corner solution In optimization models, the result where one potential investment option is so dominant that it becomes 100% of the portfolio, or is capped at whatever constraint specified by the model builder.

Corporate bond A device for a corporation to raise capital by promising to repay the borrowing with interest after a finite period. Part of a corporation's capital structure junior to loans but senior in priority to equity.

Correlation Correlation is a statistical measure that indicates the extent to which two or more variables fluctuate together. Positive correlations indicate co-movement in the same direction. Negative correlations indicate opposite comovements.

Counterfactual history The act of speculating what subsequent history would have been had a specific event turned out differently. For example, "Would southern states have developed more industry in the last decades of the nineteenth century had the South won the Civil War?" Perhaps useful as a pedagogical exercise, but almost useless as an investment tool.

Coupon The scheduled interest payment from a bond. Named after the physical coupons on bonds that would be regularly clipped and then exchanged for payment by the bondholder.

Coverage The amount of liquid and illiquid assets available to a borrower to meet debt service requirements. Sometimes also used to describe the amount of net revenue a firm generates relative to the current rate of dividend payments.

Covered call A position where the writer of a call also holds a long position in the underlying instrument.

CPI, see Consumer price index

CPO, see Commodity pool operator

Credit default swaps (CDS) A specialized derivative instrument that pays the owner in the event of a default in a bond. CDS has evolved to become one of the more popular tools available for credit traders to express both long and short opinions.

Credit enhancements Supplemental protections offered to lenders. They may consist of extra collateral provided by the borrower or they can come from third parties who offer guarantees for a fee.

Credit hedge funds A type of long-short hedge fund that focuses on different types or credit ratings across fixed income securities.

Credit-oriented partnerships Private partnerships that specialize in debt, potentially varying significantly in terms of priority of payment and fundamental credit worthiness.

Credit quality The fundamental ability to service outstanding debt. Often indicated by a letter or numeric code from a ratings agency, which has historically often been a lagging indicator of true credit quality.

Credit spreads The number of basis points above the similar maturity risk-free rate that a borrower pays to reflect their lower credit quality. Determined by market supply and demand.

Cross elasticity of demand The amount the demand for a good changes when the price of another product changes.

Crowdfunding A collective effort to raise capital for a new product, service, or company. Recognized by the SEC as exempt from registration requirements if below a certain level of activity.

CTA, see Commodity trading advisor

Cumulative preferred   Preferred stock that has the characteristic than any missed dividends are still a liability of the company that accumulate toward future dividend obligations. Unlike common stock dividends that can be suspended at any time without legal consequences.

Custodians   A custodian is a financial institution that holds customers' securities in electronic or physical form for safekeeping to minimize the risk of their theft or loss. They perform many functions including holding, valuing, and transferring securities; receiving interest and dividends; and providing notice of corporate actions.

Custody   The act of holding and safekeeping investment assets.

Cybersecurity   Maintaining the integrity and confidentiality of sensitive financial data in a world increasingly dependent upon computer networks for processing and transmitting information, which is one of the biggest challenges of the twenty-first century.

Dark pool   An alternative to public stock exchanges that matches buyers and sellers of stock anonymously. Participants often do not know the trading algorithm behind a dark pool, and there is limited transparency to the history of transactions.

Data mining   A statistical exercise to fit many, competing models to the same set of data in order to determine the best historical fit.

DB, see Defined benefit plans

DC, see Defined contribution plans

Dealer-speculator   Specialists that make two-sided markets in the commodity or financial instrument in question. They typically try to avoid having directional price risk, but they routinely speculate in basis relationships while trying to capture the bid-ask spread.

Decimalization   The quoting of stock prices in pennies and fractions of a penny. Mandated in 2001, decimalization replaced a fractional system in the United States where the smallest pricing unit was previously 1/4 or 1/8 of a dollar.

Deep in-the-money   A call option that has a strike price well below, or a put with a strike price well above, the current market price of the underlying instrument or index.

Defined benefit plans (DB)   Retirement plans that promise to pay out a future stream of benefits based typically on the earnings history of the employee. Investment risk of DB plans rests with the sponsor.

Defined contribution plans (DC)   Retirement plans that have structured contributions during an employee's working years, but make no promises about future benefits. Investment risk of DC plans rests with the worker.

Delta   The amount an option premium is expected to change given a small change in the underlying instrument's price.

Delta neutral   Positions that have zero instantaneous expected change in value from a small change in the underlying instrument's price.

Derivatives   Synthetic financial instruments that have values determined by market prices of other securities or indexes. May be traded on exchanges or over-the-counter and include futures, options, and swaps among many other structures.

Digital investment advice   Alternative term for robo-advisor, financial advice based on algorithms and current and historical market conditions.

Direct lending funds   Typically private investment partnerships that lend LP investments to borrowers who may lack easy access to traditional sources of capital like bank loans or publicly issued bonds.

Disaster recovery plan   A key element in any business's operation and mandated for regulated investment managers and advisors. Explains in detail how the firm would secure assets, communications, and basic functionality in the event of a natural or man-made disaster.

Distressed debt   The outstanding debt of a borrower that has missed an interest or capital payment.

Downside protection   Negatively correlated securities or derivatives that are expected to protect capital and perhaps make money in the event of a general market decline.

Dry close   The end of a capital-raising period for a private partnership where no cash is called to fund commitments immediately.

Duration   The weighted average maturity of a bond. The duration of a coupon bond gives the effective maturity of the instrument as compared to the stated maturity of the bond.

Duration risk   The price sensitivity of any bond with respect to changes in the risk-free rate. Typically duration risk is measured assuming parallel shifts in the risk-free yield curve, which is a serious and often violated assumption.

Duty of care   One of the two primary obligations of trustees or directors, the duty of care is a requirement that a person act toward others and the public with the watchfulness, attention, caution, and prudence that a reasonable person in the circumstances would use.

Duty of loyalty   One of the two primary obligations of trustees or directors, the duty of loyalty requires decision makers to act at all times in the best interests of the organization they serve, avoiding both the reality and the appearance of any conflicts of interest.

Early stage venture capital   Typically private equity investments made at a point in a company's life cycle before profitability and perhaps before revenue is generated. The first capital after that of friends and family and angel investors, subject to considerable risk of complete loss, but also offering high multiples of invested capital for successful enterprises.

Economies of scale   The condition where increasing the size of an activity increases the cost of operation by a smaller proportion.

Efficient frontier   The collection of portfolios that has the greatest expected return for every given level of expected risk as measured by standard deviation of return.

Efficient Market Hypothesis   The broad belief that information gets incorporated into market prices sufficiently well that extraordinary returns for any given level of risk are not possible.

Endowment effect   A bias in behavioral finance that suggests the simple act of owning an asset increases one's assessment of what it is worth.

Enhanced index strategies   Efforts to systematically add an extra return onto a basic index product.

Environmental, Social, and Governance (ESG)   A broad category of investment strategies designed with either negative or positive screens to avoid investments that do not fit with a person's ethical priorities or to promote activities that do.

Equities   The most junior part of the capitalization structure conveying no special rights to interest or dividends, but offering the greatest potential for gain should the company grow.

Equity REITs   The largest category of real estate investment trusts the assets, of which consist of actual properties. May be specialized by type of property, e.g. offices, apartments, industrial, health care facilities, retirement.

Equity swaps   A form of swap contract where one party agrees to pay the other the total return of an individual security or index in exchange for another payment stream, often a floating rate spread over LIBOR.

Equity tranche   The most junior ownership piece of a securitized pool of assets. Sometimes referred to as the first loss piece, the equity tranche receives the remaining assets in a pool once all of the more senior obligations have been paid.

ESG, see Environmental, Social, and Governance

ETF, see Exchange-traded funds

ETN, see Exchange-traded notes

ETP, see Exchange-traded products

Excess return   The return from an investment beyond that which is earned by its benchmark.

Exchange-traded funds (ETFs)   A group of '40 Act Funds that trade continuously during the business day. As long as supply and demand is roughly in balance around the NAV of the underlying pool of assets, shares are fixed in quantity and are exchanged among participants. If there is an imbalance that creates a spread between the ETF's price and its NAV, an AP creates or retires shares as necessary in real time to restore the balance.

Exchange-traded notes (ETNs)   Related to ETFs, ETNs share the trading characteristics, but are not backed with specific securities. Instead they are promissory agreements where the sponsor of the ETN agrees to pay the buyer a sum based on the performance of a security or index. Very popular with more esoteric underlying securities and commodities where actual ownership of the underlying is more difficult.

Exchange-traded products (ETPs)   A generic term that includes ETFs and ETNs.

Ex-dividend   A stock that is trading after the date of record that identifies all of the recipients of a declared regular or special dividend.

Expected return   The rate of return that one anticipates from a risky investment over any relevant investment horizon.

Fair value   The price of a security that offers no extraordinary return opportunity because it is neither too high nor too low. An integral piece of arbitrage pricing theory.

FAS 157, see Financial Accounting Standards Board Bulletin 157

Fat tails   When compared to a standard normal statistical distribution, the condition where there is a higher chance of observing data points well away from the mean.

FDIC, see Federal Deposit Insurance Corporation

Federal Deposit Insurance Corporation (FDIC)   The Federal Deposit Insurance Corporation (FDIC) is an independent agency created by Congress in 1933 to maintain stability and public confidence in the nation's financial system by insuring deposits, supervising financial institutions, and managing receiverships.

Fiduciary responsibility   The highest standard of care. A legal obligation of one party to act in the best interest of another.

Financial Accounting Standards Board Bulletin 157 (FAS 157)   The U.S. Statement of Financial Accounting Standards that defines fair value, establishes a framework for measuring fair value in generally accepted accounting principles (GAAP), and expands disclosures about fair value measurements.

Financial buyer   A purchaser of a company that does so to make it part of an investment portfolio with an eye toward a future sale. Contrast to a strategic buyer that is motivated to incorporate the company into its existing business practice.

Financial engineering   The act of modifying or combining existing securities or derivatives to create a different risk and return pattern.

Financial Industry Regulatory Authority (FINRA)   FINRA is a not-for-profit self-regulatory organization authorized by Congress to oversee the broker-dealer industry. It writes and enforces rules of behavior, examines firms for compliance with those rules, and educates the public. The SEC oversees its activities.

FINRA, see Financial Industry Regulatory Authority

Firm-specific risk   One of three components that make up any change in a stock price, this is the piece that is caused by events unique to the specific company, as opposed to sector or market-wide events.

First-order autocorrelation   The correlation of elements in a time series with those same elements lagged by one period.

Fixed annuities   Financial contracts typically created by an insurance company that guarantee both the rate of return (the interest rate) and the payout to the investor.

Fixed for floating interest rate swap   The most basic form of a bilateral swap where one party agrees to pay a fixed rate of interest for the life of the contract and the other pays a rate that periodically gets reset according to current market conditions.

Fixed income arbitrageurs   A class of long/short traders that tries to exploit price discrepancies across fixed income securities or derivatives that differ in maturity or credit quality.

Fixed-to-floating preferred shares   A type of preferred stock shares that pays a fixed dividend up to a specific earliest call date. At this time, if the shares are not called by the issuer, the dividend converts to a floating rate structure at a spread that was determined at the original date of issue.

Flash crash   The name given to any sudden change and equally sudden reversal in individual stock or market index prices caused by automated orders in the system being executed faster than other investors are able to respond. 10 May 2010 may be the most well-known example, but disruptive bursts of volatility that can be viewed as flash crashes occur regularly.

Floaters   An alternative name for inflation-linked bonds, which in the United States are called TIPS.

Floating rate loans   Any loan agreement where the interest rate periodically adjusts according to a market-based formula.

Forward contract   Any contract that calls for performance at some time in the future. Usually describes an agreement not made on an organized exchange.

Forward exchange rates   The price of a type of forward contract dealing with one currency in exchange for another.

Free lunch of diversification   The benefit of reducing expected volatility for every given level of expected return by adding assets to a portfolio that are less than perfectly correlated.

Full replication   A style of index fund where every element in the index is represented in the portfolio and held precisely at the index weight.

Full carry   When the difference between the spot price and a forward price completely covers all the cost of storage and financing. Occurs at times of such large inventories that the marginal benefit of adding to the supply is negligible.

Fully collateralized short puts   Written puts combined with cash equal to 100% of the value of the underlying should the put owner exercise the option.

Fund administrator   The outside organization charged with a variety of accounting and regulatory tasks for a mutual fund or a private investment partnership. Includes the calculation of the NAV, reconciling the holdings with custody and broker records, payment of fund expenses, settlement of daily purchases and sales of securities, ensuring collection of dividends and interests, and supervision of the orderly liquidation and dissolution of the fund (if required).

Fund closes   Periodic events in a private partnership where all interested investors make their commitments and are aggregated for the purpose of identifying which LPs will participate in certain fund investments and at what NAV.

Fund of funds   A structure that aggregates multiple funds or private partnerships into a single investment. Used primarily by investors seeking convenience or by those that lack the resources to manage a multimanager portfolio themselves.

Futures contract   A contract to buy or sell a standardized product at some point in the future. In the United States, the only legal futures contracts are those traded on designated exchanges.

Gamma   The sensitivity of the change in an option's delta with respect to a change in the underlying price. The second derivative of an option's price with respect to a change in the underlying.

Gap risk   The risk arising from mismatches of the maturities of assets and liabilities. Funding long-term investments with short-term borrowing is a classic form of gap risk.

Gates   The colloquial term referring to the practice by hedge fund managers that restrict redemption requests to an amount less than the originally advertised terms. Typically used at times of market stress on the theory that large liquidations in that environment would destroy shareholder value.

General obligation bonds   Municipal bonds that are backed by the broadest taxing authority of the issuer. In theory, these are among the most secure types of munis, but in the event of an issuer insolvency, even bonds backed by the full faith and credit of a jurisdiction may be subject to an impairment.

Global Investment Performance Standards (GIPS)   Global investment performance standards (GIPS) are ethical standards to be used by investment managers for creating performance presentations that ensure fair representation and full disclosure of investment performance results.

Global macro hedge funds   A style of hedge fund management that bases long and short positions on macroeconomic themes like movements in interest rates, currencies, and GDPs.

Goldman Sachs Commodity Index (GSCI)   The first broadly followed and traded index of physical commodity futures prices developed by Goldman Sachs in the early 1990s.

Governance   The system of rules, practices, and processes by which any organization is directed and controlled.

Government-Sponsored Enterprise (GSE)   A government-sponsored enterprise (GSE) is a financial services corporation created by the U.S. Congress, typically to facilitate the allocation of credit to a sensitive sector of the economy. The first GSE, the Farm Credit Administration, was created in 1916. The most widely known GSEs are Freddie Mac and Fannie Mae that support residential mortgage creation.

Graham and Dodd   A philosophy of deep value investing based on the works of Benjamin Graham and David Dodd, who first wrote on their theories in the early 1930s. Benjamin Graham was a teacher of Warren Buffet.

Grantor trust   A distinction in tax law, this is any trust where the person who creates the trust is treated as the owner of its property and assets for both income and estate tax purposes. The grantor may change the trust and retains the power to control or direct the trust's income or assets.

Growth equity   A style of stock market investing that emphasizes the growth of future revenues and earnings versus the price of the company relative to its book value.

GSCI, see Goldman Sachs Commodity Index

GSE, see government-sponsored enterprises

Hedge fund mutual funds   '40 Act mutual funds that attempt to mimic the trading exposures of traditional hedge fund partnerships.

Hedge ratio   The number of futures or options contracts that precisely matches the position desired to be offset.

Herding behavior   A behavioral bias that causes individuals to shape their actions and beliefs according to a larger crowd rather than independently from the best available information.

HFT, see High-frequency trading

High-yield bonds   Bonds of firms or municipalities that are of less than investment-grade quality. Also known as junk bonds.

High-frequency trading (HFT)   The application of technology and models to exploit small, ephemeral differences in prices across markets, typically without taking meaningful directional risk.

Hub-and-spoke approach   An approach to portfolio construction that has a core of low-cost, beta-oriented index funds to which are added specialist active managers in an attempt to add alpha.

Idiosyncratic risk   Risk that is not attributable to events in a sector or to the market as a whole. Idiosyncratic risk can be reduced through diversification across equities of different companies.

Illiquid investments   Investments that cannot be converted to cash on the same day or within the settlement period for continuously traded securities.

Immunized portfolio   A portfolio of assets and liabilities that is balanced so that any changes in interest rates leaves no mismatch.

In-the-money   An option that, if exercise were possible, would be profitable. For calls, a strike price below the current price is in-the-money. For puts, it is when the strike is above the current price.

Index funds   A broad category of mutual funds that are based on the total return of broad or narrow indexes.

Indexed annuities   Annuity contracts that have payouts, that adjust to a price index like the CPI.

Industry loss warranties   A type of reinsurance or derivative contract where the purchased protection is based on the total loss arising from an event to the entire insurance industry rather than their own individual losses.

Inelastic supply and demand curves   Relationships where the quantity supplied or demanded in a market is not terribly sensitive to changes in the current market price.

Inertia   A behavioral bias where an action is maintained because it is what has been done in the past rather than because it is the optimal decision based on current information.

Information ratio   The ratio of the active return (return excess to the benchmark) to the standard error of that series. Similar to the Sharpe Ratio except that Sharpe uses return above the risk-free rate in the numerator.

Initial public offering (IPO)   The step of offering the first tradable equity securities to the market. This is the step that converts a private firm into a public company and may only be done after filing a registration statement with the SEC.

Insider trading   The act of knowingly trading on material, nonpublic information.

Interest rate differential   The spread between any two fixed income products that differ by geography, maturity, or credit quality.

Interest rate parity   The arbitrage condition that says there are no extraordinary gains available from buying one currency in the spot market and selling it in the forward market.

Internal rate of return (IRR)   The interest rate at which the net present value of all the cash flows (both positive and negative) from a project or investment equal zero.

International Swaps and Derivatives Association (ISDA)   Originally known as the International Swap Dealers Association, ISDA is a private, nonprofit association established to create standardized terms of exchange and to promote best practice among financial institutions and their counterparties that trade off-exchange derivatives.

Intrinsic value   For options intrinsic value is the degree a call or a put is in-the-money. For other securities the term is less precise and usually refers to the value of the asset if it had to be liquidated.

Inverse ETFs   Exchange-traded funds where the value moves opposite to the underlying security or index.

Inverted forward curve   The condition where the spot price of a commodity or index is higher than the forward prices. Also called backwardation.

Investability   The characteristic that allows an individual or institution to purchase an asset for their portfolio. For example, the shares of companies in some countries may not be purchased by noncitizens making them not investable for those outsiders.

Investment advisor   A broad term covering anyone offering public or private investment advice. May or may not require registration and oversight by a regulatory body depending on the scope of the advice and the target audience.

Investment decision-making   The process by which individuals or organizations decide on portfolio goals, construction, and ongoing oversight.

Investment grade bonds   The general category of bonds that the ratings agencies have deemed as having a low probability of default.

IPO, see Initial public offering

IRR, see Internal rate of return

ISDA, see International Swaps and Derivatives Association

J Curve   The pattern of expected returns in a private equity investment where fund expenses at the start of the investment period exceed returns, producing an early period of losses. As investments are made that generate profits, this pattern reverses into net gains creating a stylized J on a chart of NAV through time.

Junk bonds   Bonds that are either initially issued as, or are subsequently downgraded to, below investment grade status. Also known as high-yield bonds.

K-1 Tax Report   Schedule K-1 is a tax document used to report the incomes, losses, and dividends of a partnership.

Kurtosis   Kurtosis is a measure of whether the data are heavy-tailed or light-tailed relative to a normal distribution.

Laddered portfolio   A bond portfolio that has equal dollars invested in maturities along the yield curve. As bonds mature the proceeds are reinvested in maturities at the longest end of the ladder.

Late-stage venture capital   Private equity investments made in emerging companies but at a point in their life cycle beyond angel investing and the first rounds of venture capital. Along the time spectrum toward growth equity investing when the company has revenue and may have profits.

Leptokurtic   The characteristic of a statistical distribution marked by a high narrow peak of probability around the mean and a large number of extreme observations, or tails, as compared to the normal distribution.

Letter bond   A bond that has not been registered with the Securities and Exchange Commission and cannot be sold to the general public.

Level-one investments   Assets that have readily observable prices, either on public exchanges or active, transparent over-the-counter markets.

Level-three investments   Financial assets and liabilities whose values are based on prices or valuation techniques that require inputs that are both unobservable and significant to the overall fair value measurement.

Level-two investments   Assets that do not have regular market pricing, but whose fair value can be readily determined based on other data values or market prices. Includes most swaps and many individual bonds that may not trade continuously throughout the day.

Leverage   The use of borrowed funds to amplify the profit and loss impact of any change in the market price of an asset.

Leveraged ETFs   Exchange traded funds and notes that pay the investor a multiple of the total return of the underlying security or index underpinning the ETF.

LIBOR   The London Interbank Offered Rate. This is the interest rate for Eurodollar time deposits at major London banks and is used as a reference interest rate for trillions of dollars in swaps, swaptions, and other derivative instruments.

Lifestyle funds   An investment fund featuring an asset mix determined by the level of risk and return that is appropriate for an individual investor.

Limited partner agreement   The legal document setting out the responsibilities and obligations of both the LP and the GP in a private partnership.

Linkers   A common name for bonds that are indexed to the rate of inflation in the issuing country.

Liquid alternatives   A category of mutual funds that attempt to mimic the investment and risk profiles of strategies historically offered in partnership format, while providing daily liquidity.

Liquid real estate   A general label for equity REITs, which allow the investor access to the income and appreciation of real assets while maintaining the ability to get into and out of positions on a daily basis.

Liquidating trusts   A liquidating trust is a means for a fund manager to wind down a fund without having a significant role in the liquidation. Assets of a fund being dissolved are placed into the trust and as they are sold the proceeds are distributed to the beneficiaries who are the remaining investors in the fund and any other claimants to the fund.

Liquidity   A relative concept describing the ease with which investments can be converted into cash.

Liquidity premium   The higher price investors are usually willing to pay to own an asset with a high degree of liquidity.

Litigation funds   A category of hedge funds that supplies capital to fund tort claims in exchange for a percentage of any realized awards or settlements.

Loan origination fees   One-time fees paid by the borrower to the lender to initiate a loan transaction.

Loan servicing charges   Ongoing fees paid by the borrower to the servicer for the collection of periodic payments and the disbursement of those proceeds to the ultimate lenders.

Local currency sovereign debt   Any sovereign debt denominated in the issuer's own currency.

Locals   Traders at an exchange that buy or sell for their own account as opposed to brokers who represent other buyers and sellers.

Long   A position in futures, options, or cash instruments that profits from rising prices.

Long volatility   Positions that are expected to profit when the underlying volatility of a security or index increases.

Long/short equity hedge funds   The most basic form of hedge fund trading consisting of buying and selling short publicly traded securities. Can vary from net short to market neutral to leveraged net long in risk exposure to the overall market.

Loss aversion   The negative utility attached to investment losses. Psychology findings suggest that most people attach more harm to a dollar of losses than they feel good from a dollar of gains, creating an overall aversion to losses.

Managed account   An investment program where all of the assets belong to one party and are legally owned by that party. As distinct from a comingled fund where multiple investors are pooled together in a common vehicle to acquire assets that are legally the property of the fund.

Management fees   The basic fees explicitly charged to investors for the management of a fund, pool, or partnership.

MAR, see Minimum Accepted Return

Mark to market   The process of debiting losses and crediting gains for margin accounts, typically on a daily basis.

Mark to model   The process of estimating the NAV of a little traded investment or portfolio from historical relationships with the market prices of more actively traded securities.

Market bubbles   Extremes of prices versus what fundamental relationships would suggest. Not always easy to identify before the bubble pops.

Market neutral   Portfolio positioning that is not expected to be correlated to the general movement to a market.

Market neutral equity hedge funds   Equity long/short funds that endeavor to minimize net exposure to the stock market by balancing dollar bets, beta equivalent bets, or factor bets in the portfolio.

Market portfolio   All of the equities available to be owned in proportions equal to their capitalization.

Market timing   A strategy to add value via efforts to go long securities or commodities before they increase in price and to go short before prices fall.

Master limited partnership (MLP)   A limited partnership that is publicly traded. Combines the tax benefits of a limited partnership with the liquidity of publicly traded securities.

Matrix pricing   Technique for valuing bonds from a formula capturing common characteristics like maturity, credit quality, sector, and coupon.

Mean   The first moment of a statistical distribution, also called the average.

Mean-variance   The foundation for evaluating the risk and return potential of a security or a portfolio by looking at the average of the return stream and comparing it to the volatility of those returns as measured by standard deviation.

Mean-variance optimizers   A mathematical technique designed to find the best possible combination of investments in terms of the greatest expected return for any given level of risk.

Mezzanine debt funds   Investment pools specializing in owning junior debt securities, which lie just above equity in the capital structure.

Microfinance investment vehicles (MIVs)   Specialized funds that deploy capital by making very small loans to some of the most disadvantaged populations of the world to support small-scale entrepreneurship in the developing world.

Midstream companies   Energy service companies such as gathering stations, pipelines, and storage facilities operating between producers (upstream) and consumers of energy products (downstream).

Minimum acceptable return (MAR)   The minimum rate of return on an investment targeted by the decision maker before adding that item to the portfolio. Used in the calculation of the Sortino Ratio.

MIV, see Microfinance investment vehicle

MLP, see Master limited partnership

Mock audit   An internal control procedure done by some managers and investment advisors where an outside expert goes through all the steps of a regulatory review to identify any deficiencies. Used to improve practice at the firm and minimize the chance of sanctions by a regulator.

Model portfolio   A stylized portfolio designed to target certain risk and return levels while meeting any other relevant constraints on geography, cap size, ESG guidelines, etc. Used by fund managers and consultants to try to gain economies of scale in the management of client funds.

Modern portfolio theory (MPT)   The broad label given to advances in finance stemming from groundbreaking work by Harry Markowitz that stressed the advantages of reducing risk by creating a portfolio of less than perfectly correlated securities.

Modified gross leverage   The sum of long and short positions expressed as a percentage of capital minus 100%.

Modigliani-Miller proposition   The famous finding in finance that a firm's value is not dependent upon the percentage of its capital structure in debt or equity.

MOIC, see Multiple of invested capital

Moments of a distribution   Statistical measures that describe the shape of a distribution. The first two moments of any distribution are the mean and variance.

Momentum   A trading technique that suggests future price movements can be reliably predicted from recent trends.

Money market mutual funds   '40 Act funds that invest within a restrictive set of SEC guidelines with the primary goal being the preservation of capital and the secondary objective of income.

Monte Carlo simulation   A statistical technique relying on assumptions about future returns and correlations, Simulates a large number of potential investment outcomes in order to estimate the range of likely outcomes from any investment or portfolio.

Mortgage REITs   A subclass of real estate investment trusts that invests in mortgage debt, either residential or commercial, as compared to real estate equity.

Mortgages   A label for debt used to buy or improve real estate assets, typically using those assets as collateral.

MPT, see Modern portfolio theory

Multifactor stock price model   A model that attempts to decompose the contribution to a stock's return into several factors like cap size, value versus growth, quality, and momentum.

Multifamily office   A financial organization designed to attend to the financial and investment needs of several families. Used primarily to spread fixed expenses over a broader pool of assets.

Multimaturity bond   Another term for put bond, which allows the holder to force the issuer to redeem at par on a date prior to the scheduled maturity.

Multiple of invested capital (MOIC)   A standard performance metric used in many private partnerships to explain how much the original invested capital has grown during the life of the partnership.

Multistrategy hedge fund   A broad category of hedge funds that employs multiple techniques and exposures to create portfolio benefits within a single hedge fund structure.

Municipal bonds   Long-term debt issued by state and local governments and their agencies.

Mutual funds   Investment vehicles organized, sold, and operated under the rules of the Investment Company Act of 1940.

Naked calls   A short call written by someone with no cash, futures, or options positions that would move in the opposite direction as the short option.

National Futures Association (NFA)   Private, not-for-profit self-regulatory organization that oversees the activities of futures commission merchants, commodity pool operators, and trading advisors, introducing brokers and most swap dealers and trade execution facilities operating in the United States. Authorized by an act of Congress and overseen by the CFTC.

NAV, see Net asset value

Negative convexity   The characteristic of certain bonds where the change in price from a given change in interest rates is less than that predicted by the bond's immediate duration.

Negative roll yield   The condition where selling a front month futures contract and buying a more distant futures contract (the roll) creates losses. Occurs whenever the forward price curve is in a carry.

Negative screen   The act of eliminating potential investments from a portfolio based on criteria like sector, geography, or governance practices. A popular way to shape portfolios to be consistent with ESG criteria.

Negative skew   The characteristic of a nonsymmetric distribution of returns where large losses have a disproportionate probability of happening.

Net asset value (NAV)   The value of a mutual fund or investment partnership that is reached by deducting the fund's liabilities from the market value of all of its assets and then dividing by the number of issued shares.

Net exposure   The difference between the gross long position in a fund and the gross short.

Net present value (NPV)   The discounted value of a stream of payments or receipts through time.

NFA, see National Futures Association

Nominal yield   The basic yield on a stock or bond not accounting for any effects of inflation.

Nonagency mortgage-backed securities   Pools of privately issued mortgages that are not backed by any GSE.

Notional amount   The agreed-upon principle amount on which all payments are calculated in a swap.

NPV, see Net present value

Null hypothesis   In statistics, the hypothesis that there is no significant difference between specified populations. The typical goal is to find enough evidence to reject the null hypothesis with a high degree of confidence.

Omega ratio (Ω)   A performance measurement tool that attempts to measure the likelihood of achieving a given return, such as a minimum acceptable return (MAR). The higher the omega value, the greater the probability that a given return will be met or exceeded.

Open-ended mutual funds   The most popular form of '40 Act mutual funds where transactions occur daily at the end of day NAV and the number of shares fluctuates as capital comes into the fund or is withdrawn.

Opportunistic real estate funds   A characterization of real estate partnerships that strive to buy or develop properties with the goal of capital appreciation versus funds that target the collection of rents and the payment of steady income.

Optimal portfolio   The portfolio on the efficient frontier that is found at the point of tangency with the capital markets line.

Option boxes   Two option spread positions that when combined produce a synthetic long and a synthetic short securities position, netting out to no directional exposure to the underlying.

Option butterfly   A combination of options, either all calls or all puts, that involves a long option at one-strike price, two short options at a higher strike, and another long option at yet a higher price. The difference between the first two strikes should equal the difference between the second and third.

Option condor   A combination of options, either all calls or all puts, covering four strike prices at equal intervals: one long option at each of the first and fourth strike prices and one short option at each of the second and third strikes.

Option straddle   A combination consisting of one put and one call, either both long or both short, at the same strike price and based on the same underlying instrument.

Option strangle   A combination consisting of one put and one call, either both long or both short, with the same underlying instrument but with the put strike below that of the call strike.

Option tender bond   Another term for a put bond, which allows the holder to force the issuer to redeem at par at a date prior to final maturity.

Option writer   The granter of the right to buy (call) or sell (put) an instrument or index at a price and date specified in the option's terms.

Options   A contract conveying the right to buy (call) or sell (put) an instrument or index value at a predetermined price for a fixed period.

Original margin   The collateral initially posted by both the long and the short to secure performance in a futures contract.

Origination fees   An upfront fee charged by a lender for processing a new loan application, used as compensation for putting the loan in place.

OTC, see Over-the-counter

Out trades   Transactions that when submitted for clearing and settlement do not match in some important dimension on the buy and sell sides.

Out-of-sample testing   The process of estimating a statistical model on one set of data and then evaluating its predictive power on data from another time period or from a broader sampling of cross-sectional data.

Out-of-the-money   A call that has a strike price above, or a put with a strike price below, the current market price. Any value an out-of-the-money option has is exclusively time value.

Outsourced CIO   A business model of advisors and consultants where every element of the management of a family's or an institution's investment portfolio is the responsibility of the outside firm.

Over-the-counter (OTC) derivatives   Puts, calls, forwards, and swaps that are privately negotiated versus being traded in standardized forms on an exchange.

Par value   The face value of a bond.

Parallel shift of the yield curve   Interest rate changes that are the same number of basis points at each maturity along the yield curve.

Peer rankings   The comparison of similarly-oriented managers or funds on a relative basis. Often used as a guide to manager selection, peer rankings in many styles have little predictability of future success.

Pop   The moment when a market in a bubble state changes directions.

Portable alpha   The activity of combining alpha returns from one activity and the index returns from another typically through the use of swaps.

Portfolio insurance   A discredited strategy to try to protect against downside equity market moves through the dynamic application of index futures and options.

Positive carry   Any investment that is expected to earn a positive return if the underlying markets don't change.

Positive convexity   The characteristic of certain bonds where the change in price from a given change in interest rates is more than that predicted by the bond's immediate duration.

Positive screen   Actively adding potential investments to a portfolio based on criteria like sector, geography, or governance practices. A popular way to shape portfolios to be consistent with ESG criteria.

Positive skew   The characteristic of a nonsymmetric distribution of returns where large gains have a disproportionate probability of happening.

Preferred return   The threshold return that the limited partners of a private equity fund must receive, prior to the PE firm receiving its carried interest.

Preferred stock   A class of equity senior to common stock, typically with a defined dividend yield. All dividends on preferred shares must be paid before any dividends can be paid on the common.

Pre-IPO trades   Private transactions involving unregistered equities done before the company goes public.

Premium   The term typically used for the price of an option.

Prerefunded bonds   Municipal bonds that the issuing jurisdiction has matched with similar maturity treasury securities. As there is 100% safe collateral backing the bonds, this paper carries very low interest rates relative to less well-secured paper.

Price basis   The difference between the prices of two markets differentiated by geography, time, or quality.

Price improvement   Trades in a market that happen at prices inside the publicly stated bid/ask spread.

Price taker   Any participant in a market that is so small that their transactions do not affect the bid/ask spread.

Prime broker   A specialist broker to hedge funds and other professional traders that combines execution, credit, custody, and sometimes, operational services.

Private equity partnerships   A broad category of partnership investing that includes venture capital, growth equity, and buy-out funds.

Private partnerships   The broadest label of investment funds organized by a general partner and sold to limited partners. Given that they are not publicly traded, private partnerships are exempt from many aspects of '40 Act funds and other widely distributed funds.

Private placement memorandum   The governing document between the general partner and the limited partners for a private partnership.

Pro forma results   Results based on a historical simulation covering a period when a fund was not actually trading client money.

Probability   The likelihood of an event happening.

Prospectus   A disclosure document that describes the relevant features of a security for potential buyers. Must be filed with the SEC before a registration can occur and the fund or security sold to the public.

Provenance   The documented history of ownership of any asset, but particularly relevant for art works and other collectibles.

Put bonds   Bonds that the holder may force the issuer to redeem before the stated maturity date.

Put option   An option that gives its holder the right to sell the underlying instrument at an agreed-upon price for a determined period of time.

Ratio spread   A spread trade with options where the legs are matched on a delta basis rather than on equal dollar values.

Rational expectations   The theory in economics that forecasts are formed using all of the available and relevant information in the market.

Real assets   Tangible assets like property, physical commodities, and artwork as opposed to securities, loans and bonds, or derivatives.

Real estate   The broad category of investment assets that covers residential and commercial properties.

Real estate investment trusts (REITs)   Publicly traded companies that own or finance income-producing real estate in a range of property sectors.

Real yield   The return on a bond after adjusting for the effects of inflation. Equal to the nominal yield less the inflation rate.

Rebalancing   The act of selling investments or assets that have appreciated beyond target weights in a portfolio and using the proceeds to buy under-represented investments.

Rebalancing dates   The dates on which actual portfolio weights are compared to the targets and purchases and sales made to realign the two.

Record date   The day that identifies the legal owner of a stock or bond in order to properly pay dividends and interest.

Registered investment advisor (RIA)   An individual or a firm that receives compensation for giving advice on investing in stocks, bonds, mutual funds, or exchange-traded funds and is registered with the SEC or a state securities regulator.

Registered mutual funds   Any publicly traded open- or closed-end fund that is registered under the terms of the 1940 Investment Company Act.

Regular dividends   Payments to shareholders that are paid on common or preferred stock in the normal course of business.

Regulation T   Federal Reserve Board regulation that sets minimum initial margin requirements for the purchase of stock. Designed originally as a device allowing the Fed to control the flow of credit to securities markets, Reg T margins are a coarse regulatory tool and have not been changed in decades.

Regulatory audits   Audits conducted by regulators to verify that a fund manager or advisor is compliant with regulations and standards.

Rehabilitation real estate funds   A subset of the broad category of real estate investing that focuses on purchasing properties requiring repurposing or other capital improvements and then selling those properties when the improvements have been made and the building is leased out.

Reinsurance   A method of diversifying specific risk of a block of insurance by selling part of the exposure to other insurance companies or independent investors willing to assume some of the risk in exchange for a premium.

Reinvestment period   The window of time in a private partnership where proceeds from realized investments may at the option of the GP be redeployed into new projects.

REITs, see Real Estate Investment Trusts

Relative value   As opposed to absolute value, the evaluation of the attractiveness of an investment in terms of being cheap or dear relative to an alternative investment.

Replication hedge funds   Investment funds that try to mimic the return pattern of different styles of hedge funds by targeting beta and factor exposures rather than buying and selling individual securities.

Resting orders   Transaction instructions that are placed with a broker at prices that cannot be executed immediately, but reside in the order book to be acted upon should the market price change sufficiently. Typically resting orders are either good for the day they are entered or good until cancelled.

Retail structured products   Specialized bonds that incorporate links to an underlying asset or index to modify the return and risk profile, sold typically to wealthy individual investors who lack the resources or sophistication to create that profile through portfolio construction.

Revenue bonds   A class of municipal bonds that are backed by an explicit stream of income from a project or activity. Examples of revenue bonds are paper backed by toll roads, hospitals, and water and sewer systems.

Rho   The amount an option premium is expected to change given a small change in interest rates.

RIA, see Registered investment advisor

Risk arbitrage   A hedge fund investment strategy that speculates on the successful completion of mergers and acquisitions. Also known as merger arbitrage.

Risk-free debt   The paper of the most credit-worthy issuer in any jurisdiction. In the United States, Treasury bills, notes, and bonds define risk-free debt for the relevant maturities.

Risk parity funds   A style of hedge funds that attempts to invest across diversified investments in a ratio such that each investment's contribution to the portfolio's risk is equal.

Risk premium   The difference between the yield or expected return of an investment and the risk-free rate.

Robo-advisors   A twenty-first century business model of advice that relies on profiling clients according to risk and return preferences and then algorithmically suggesting investment portfolios.

Roll yield   The profit or loss that accrues when a position in a nearby futures contract is offset and replaced by the same position but at a later maturity. May be positive or negative.

Rule 144A   A 1990 SEC rule that creates a safe harbor for the resale of privately placed securities that are without SEC registration. Buyers of 144A securities must be qualified institutional investors and may not in turn sell these securities to the public.

Rumortrage   A form of risk arbitrage where long and short trades are based on an analyst's expectation for a merger event rather than on an actually announced deal.

SEC EDGAR filings   Electronic Data Gathering, Analysis, and Retrieval system of the SEC that collects, validates, and indexes submissions by companies and others who are required to file forms with the regulator. It is the primary database of company information freely available to the public over the Internet.

SEC, see Securities and Exchange Commission

Secondary partnerships   A specialty partnership strategy in private equity or real estate where the underlying assets are LP holdings in other partnerships that are usually bought at a discount to NAV from sellers looking for liquidity or a realignment of their portfolios.

Securities Act of 1933   The 1933 Act, passed in part in response to the 1929 stock market crash, was the first major federal legislation to regulate the initial offer and sale of securities, which had previously been the responsibilities of state securities regulators.

Securities Exchange Act of 1934   The follow-up legislation to the Securities Act of 1933, this law created the SEC and specified rules governing the brokerage community and exchanges and focuses on transactions by the public in the secondary market.

Self-insured   The act of assuming the potential financial burden arising from any risks resulting from your activities or investments.

Self-regulation   The process by which an organization sets up and enforces rules of conduct for its members designed to promote best practice and the long-term viability of the organization.

Self-regulatory organization (SRO)   Institutions typically authorized by Congress and overseen by a government regulator to carry out self-regulatory duties for their community. NFA and FINRA are the dominant SROs in the derivatives and securities arenas.

Senior secured debt   Borrowings that have the highest claim on interest and principle repayment backed by collateral that the lender can attach in the event of a default.

Senior unsecured debt   Borrowings that have the highest claim on interest and principle repayment but are not backed by any specific collateral.

Sequence-of-returns risk   Usually important of retirees, the risk of having to make withdrawals at a time after a market loss, locking in those losses and foreclosing any opportunity from a recovery in the market.

Shadow banking   The broad activity of providing lending services by firms outside the regulatory purview of state and federal banking authorities.

Share registry   In the United Kingdom and most Commonwealth countries, the name of the transfer agent that maintains the official list of owners of a public company.

Sharpe Ratio   A measure of an investment's average return above the risk-free rate divided by the standard deviation of that return stream.

Shipping   A specialty area of investments that focuses on the capital value and cargo rates of commercial seagoing vessels. Think of it as floating real estate.

Short   A position that involves the sale of a futures, options, or cash instrument that is expected to profit from a decline in prices. Short can also refer to the individual holding of such positions.

Short out-of-the-money puts   Written put options with strike prices below the current market price. Frequently used as a strategy in bull markets to collect premiums from options that are expected to expire worthless.

Short volatility   Positions that are expected to profit when the variability of prices in a market declines. Typically strategies that result in negative convexity.

Side letter   Any addendum to a partnership agreement that modifies terms for a specific investor. Most often used to change fee or liquidity terms for early investors.

Side pocket investments   A grouping of part of a portfolio that is segregated from the whole in order to address particular liquidity concerns by the GP.

Skew The property of a statistical distribution that describes the degree of asymmetry around the mean. The third moment of any distribution.

Sleep-well-at-night money Assets held in near risk-free form in a quantity sufficient to maintain an investor's lifestyle through any anticipated extreme market event.

Slippage The amount a price moves away from the quoted bid/ask spread as a result of the quantity being bought or sold being larger than that shown in the immediate market.

Socially responsible investing (SRI) The broad activity of tailoring a portfolio to be consistent with environmental, governance, and social principles of the investor.

Soft dollars Implicit rebates paid by brokers on commissions to be used to buy legitimate research products and resources by the broker's client.

Sophisticated investors A loose term to identify those that may participate in private partnerships having less regulatory structure and oversight than funds offered broadly to the public.

Sortino Ratio A measure of an investment's average return above the target rate divided by the downside standard deviation of that return stream.

Sovereign debt Debt issued by a country that is backed by the full faith and credit of that country.

Sovereign state A jurisdiction that has full authority over its governance without outside control.

Special dividends Any distribution to stock owners beyond the stream of ordinary dividends.

Specialists Individuals who make two-sided markets on the floor of a stock exchange and are governed by rules designed to promote liquid, continuous markets. Specialists have been largely replaced by electronic order books and dedicated proprietary traders that have fewer trading rules.

Spending rules Formulas to determine the amount to be taken from endowments in order to support ongoing operations.

Spot delivery Prompt delivery of any security, currency, or commodity.

Spot exchange rates The price at which one currency may be exchanged for another for prompt delivery.

Spot price The price at which a security or commodity can be purchased for prompt delivery.

Spread trading A combination of a long and short positions that typically reduce the risk when compared to outright positions.

Squeeze The act of threatening to take delivery on a quantity of futures contracts larger than the supply immediately available in the market, causing prices to rise.

SRI, see Socially responsible investing and Sustainable, responsible, and impact investing

SRO, see self-regulatory organization

Standard deviation A statistical measure of dispersion. The square root of the variance, the second moment of any statistical distribution.

Standard normal distribution A special case of a normal distribution where the mean is zero and the standard deviation is one. Used as the foundation for most tests of statistical inference.

Staples A colloquial term for the requirement that a potential buyer of LP interests in the secondary market also commits to the GP's next open fund before GP permission to buy those LP interests is granted.

Stop loss orders   Typically sell orders placed below the current market price to be executed as market orders if the price drops to the target. Designed to offset losing long positions before losses grow too large. Can be done with buy orders above the current price to control the risk of short positions.

Strategic buyer   A company buying a firm for the purposes of gaining market share, technical expertise, or cost savings.

Street research   Analysis of stocks and bonds done by sell side brokers, typically given or sold to investors with the hope of encouraging trading and the generation of commissions.

Stressed debt   Bonds of companies that have not yet defaulted but are facing a heightened probability of doing so.

Strike price   The contractual specification in an option that says at what price the put or call may be exercised.

Structured notes   A subcategory of structured products of fixed duration designed to have interest and/or the value of the principle determined by formula based on another security or index price.

Structured products   The broad category of off-exchange instruments created by banks and sold typically to wealthy individuals that vary in value by formula based on other securities or indexes.

Subcustodians   Custodians that typically assume custody responsibility in countries where the master custodian does not maintain a direct presence.

Suboptimal   Any portfolio that could have a higher level of return for each level of risk, or lower risk for any target return. Beneath the efficient frontier.

Subscription document   The legal agreement between a general partner and the limited partners that specifies the size of the commitment and other key features of any investment in a private partnership.

Suitability rules   Criteria that determine whether any given investment can be sold to an investor without violating FINRA or other regulatory bodies' rules of best broker practice.

Summary prospectus   The abbreviated, common English language version of the required prospectus for any security being issued.

Sustainable, responsible, and impact investing   An alternative label for the anagram SRI, reflecting investments that are shaped by environmental, social, or governance principles.

Swap agreement   The legal document between counterparties that specifies the general rights and obligations of both parties for any swaps they may enter into together.

Swaps   An off-exchange, customized derivative contract with a specified term, notional amount and defined payment streams through time between counterparties.

Swaps execution facilities   Any organization where indications of interest in more standardized swaps may be posted, leading potentially to matched and cleared transactions. Typically automated in the modern market.

Swaptions   Swap contracts where the payment streams between counterparties are asymmetric, reflecting imbedded puts or calls.

Synthetic long or short positions   Combinations of options, or options and futures to create the functional equivalent of another position that could be purchased outright in the market. Such positions may be built to create long or short exposures.

Systematic risk   Portfolio risk that arises from general price movement of the market or a sector as opposed to risks that are unique to a company.

TARP, see Troubled Assets Relief Program

Tax anticipation notes   Municipal bonds that are issued as a funding source to bridge the gap between current expenditures and future, highly likely tax collections.

Tax-exempt bonds   Municipal bonds that have the interest they pay exempt from federal income tax. Depending on the jurisdiction, they may be exempt from state and local taxes as well.

The '40 Act   The common name for The Investment Act of 1940.

The rule of 72   A useful heuristic that gives the number of years it will take an investment to double. Divide 72 by the compound rate of return to give the approximate doubling period.

Theta   The sensitivity of an option's price with respect to the passage of time.

Three-card monte   A confidence game where the mark is lured into a game of guessing which of three cards is the money card. Universally rigged against the mark ever winning.

Time decay   The decline of an option's value as time passes and eventual maturity approaches.

Time value   The difference between the price of an option and its intrinsic value.

Tippee   One who receives material, nonpublic information about a security.

Tipper   One who passes along material, nonpublic information.

TIPS   Treasury bonds that adjust principle and interest according to the rate of inflation as measured by the consumer price index. TIPS stands for Treasury Inflation Protected Securities.

Total return swap   A specific type of swap contract where one party agrees to pay the other the equivalent of both price appreciation and dividends for a specified stock index.

Trade allocation   The process by which large block transactions are meted out across all of the relevant portfolios that are to receive that security. Should be designed to be as fair as possible so that differences in price are as small as possible and are likely to offset over time.

Trading frictions   All of the costs that accompany the purchase and sale of securities and derivatives. Will include commissions, regulatory fees and taxes, and any slippage in the market from placing the order.

Transactions taxes   Widely advocated mechanism to tax each trade in a securities or derivatives market to raise revenue and to discourage excessive speculation. Where they have been applied the tax revenues have been less than projected and markets have become less liquid.

Transfer agent   An institution, often a bank, that maintains the official list of owners of a public company.

Troubled Assets Relief Program (TARP)   A series of government programs signed into law in October, 2008, that authorized the government to buy the equity and debt of financial companies in order to stabilize the markets and provide liquidity in the wake of the financial crisis triggered by the collapse of Lehman Brothers.

Type I error   The incorrect rejection of a true null hypothesis, also known as a "false positive."

UBTI, see Unrelated business taxable income

Unrelated business taxable income (UBTI)   Income derived from ongoing, unrelated trade or business activities of an otherwise tax-exempt entity. Characterized in Internal Revenue Code Section 512.

Utility theory   The theory in microeconomics that attempts to identify and scale wellbeing as opposed to measures like income or wealth.

Variable annuities   Annuities that have payouts that can vary through time with the performance of the stock market or some other risk asset.

Variable rate demand obligation　　A floating-rate debt obligation that has a nominal long-term maturity as well as an option allowing the investor to sell the obligation back to the trustee, generally at par plus accrued interest.

Variation margin　　Periodic payments from losing accounts to winning accounts based on changes in market prices. If the value of an account falls below a predefined maintenance margin level, variation margin payments sufficient to restore the original margin will be called for.

Vega　　The amount an option premium is expected to change given a small change in the volatility of the underlying instrument's price.

Venture capital partnerships　　A form of private partnership that specializes in early stage equity investments, often in companies that may not have profits or in some cases revenues.

VIX　　An index of volatility of large cap U.S. stocks. Calculated from index options based on the S&P 500 traded at the Chicago Board Options Exchange.

Volatility　　The degree to which the market prices of a security, commodity, currency, or index vary through time.

Water rights　　Marketable claims to surface or ground water.

Wet close　　A closing of a private partnership where at least some of the committed capital is called immediately.

Willingness to pay　　A factor in the probability of performance on a bond. The resources may be available, but without a willingness to pay there will be a default.

Window dressing　　The act of changing the holdings of a mutual fund, for example, immediately before the date of required disclosures in order to mask unprofitable activity or strategies investors may not believe are consistent with the fund's objectives. Impossible to do with a separately managed account that has full transparency.

Yield　　The effective rate of return on an investment typically expressed as an annual percentage.

Zero-coupon bond　　A bond that makes no explicit interest payments during its life but trades at a discount to its face value.

Index

Notes: Page numbers in *italic* indicate charts, figures, and tables.
Page numbers followed by *n* and a number indicate footnotes.